A+™ Certification

Core Hardware Third Edition - A CompTIA Certification

Judith A Kling
Timothy J Poulsen

A+™ Certification: Core Hardware Third Edition - A CompTIA Certification

Part Number: 085811
Course Edition: 2.1

ACKNOWLEDGMENTS

Project Team

Content Developer: Judith A. Kling and Timothy J. Poulsen • **Development Assistance:** Nancy Curtis, Andrew LaPage, Gail Sandler, Pamela J. Taylor and Jutta VanStean • **Content Manager:** Trina Simpson • **Graphic Designer:** Isolina Salgado Toner • **Project Coordinator:** David Fazio • **Sr. Content Editors:** Angie J. French, Christy D. Johnson and Laura Telford • **Sr. Materials Editor:** Frank Wosnick • **Technical Reviewer:** Richard French • **Project Technical Support:** Mike Toscano

NOTICES

DISCLAIMER: While Element K Content LLC takes care to ensure the accuracy and quality of these materials, we cannot guarantee their accuracy, and all materials are provided without any warranty whatsoever, including, but not limited to, the implied warranties of merchantability or fitness for a particular purpose. The name used in the data files for this course is that of a fictitious company. Any resemblance to current or future companies is purely coincidental. We do not believe we have used anyone's name in creating this course, but if we have, please notify us and we will change the name in the next revision of the course. Element K is an independent provider of integrated training solutions for individuals, businesses, educational institutions, and government agencies. Use of screenshots, photographs of another entity's products, or another entity's product name or service in this book is for editorial purposes only. No such use should be construed to imply sponsorship or endorsement of the book by, nor any affiliation of such entity with Element K. This courseware may contain links to sites on the Internet that are owned and operated by third parties (the "External Sites"). Element K is not responsible for the availability of, or the content located on or through, any External Site. Please contact Element K if you have any concerns regarding such links or External Sites.

TRADEMARK NOTICES Element K and the Element K logo are trademarks of Element K LLC and its affiliates.

A+ Certification is a registered trademark of CompTIA in the U.S. and other countries; the CompTIA products and services discussed or described may be trademarks of CompTIA . All other product names and services used throughout this course may be common law or registered trademarks of their respective proprietors.

Copyright © 2005 Element K Content LLC. All rights reserved. Screenshots used for illustrative purposes are the property of the software proprietor. This publication, or any part thereof, may not be reproduced or transmitted in any form or by any means, electronic or mechanical, including photocopying, recording, storage in an information retrieval system, or otherwise, without express written permission of Element K, 500 Canal View Boulevard, Rochester, NY 14623, (585) 240-7500, (800) 434-3466. Element K Courseware LLC's World Wide Web site is located at **www.elementkcourseware.com**.

This book conveys no rights in the software or other products about which it was written; all use or licensing of such software or other products is the responsibility of the user according to terms and conditions of the owner. Do not make illegal copies of books or software. If you believe that this book, related materials, or any other Element K materials are being reproduced or transmitted without permission, please call 1-800-478-7788.

The logo of the CompTIA Authorized Curriculum Program and the status of this or other training material as "Authorized" under the CompTIA Authorized Curriculum Program signifies that, in CompTIA's opinion, such training material covers the content of the CompTIA's related certification exam. CompTIA has not reviewed or approved the accuracy of the contents of this training material and specifically disclaims any warranties of merchantability or fitness for a particular purpose. CompTIA makes no guarantee concerning the success of persons using any such "Authorized" or other training material in order to prepare for any CompTIA certification exam. The contents of this training material were created for the CompTIA A+ exam covering CompTIA certification exam objectives that were current as of April, 2003.

How to Become CompTIA Certified: This training material can help you prepare for and pass a related CompTIA certification exam or exams. In order to achieve CompTIA certification, you must register for and pass a CompTIA certification exam or exams. In order to become CompTIA certified, you must:

1. Select a certification exam provider. For more information please visit **www.comptia.org/certification/genral_information/test_locations.asp**.

2. Register for and schedule a time to take the CompTIA certification exam(s) at a convenient location.

3. Read and sign the Candidate Agreement, which will be presented at the time of the exam(s). The text of the Candidate Agreement can be found at **www.comptia.org/certification/general_information/candidate_agreement.asp**.

4. Take and pass the CompTIA certification exam(s).

For more information about CompTIA's certifications, such as their industry acceptance, benefits, or program news, please visit **www.comptia.org/certification/default.asp**. CompTIA is a non-profit information technology (IT) trade association. CompTIA's certifications are designed by subject matter experts from across the IT industry. Each CompTIA certification is vendor-neutral, covers multiple technologies, and requires demonstration of skills and knowledge widely sought after by the IT industry. To contact CompTIA with any questions or comments, please call (630) 268-1818 or email questions@comptia.org.

Your comments are important to us. Please contact us at Element K Press LLC, 1-800-478-7788, 500 Canal View Boulevard, Rochester, NY 14623, Attention: Product Planning, or through our Web site at **http://support.elementkcourseware.com**.

KNOWLEDGE²
by Element K Courseware

Knowledge², available exclusively from Element K Courseware, gives you two great ways to learn using our best-in-class content.

This courseware includes a companion online ID. Use your online ID to reinforce what you've learned in the classroom, prepare for certification tests, or as a reference guide. It's easy, and available to you anytime, 24x7, at www.elementk.com.

To use your Knowledge² online ID, follow these five easy steps:

1. Log on to www.elementk.com

2. Click on Student Enrollment

3. Enter the following Enrollment Key

    1523-APLUSOSH-1255

4. Choose a user name and password, complete personal information, and then click Submit.

5. Your profile has been set up successfully. You may now proceed to Login to Element K.

Your Knowledge² online ID is valid for 90-days from initial logon.

A+™ Certification: Core Hardware Third Edition - A CompTIA Certification

Lesson 1: Introduction to Computers

A. A Brief History of Computers 2
    Evolution of Mechanical Computers. 2
    Electronic Computers 4
    Vacuum Tubes 4
    Transistors and Magnetic Memory 5
    Integrated Circuits 5

B. Desktop Computer System Components and Their Functions 9
    External System Components 10
    Internal System Components 10
    System Board 11
    Processor. 13
    Memory. 15
    Interfaces 16
    Adapter Cards 16
    Storage Media 17

C. Software 20
    Software 20
    System Software. 20
    Application Software 21
    Device Drivers. 21
    Firmware. 23

Contents

D. Numbering Systems 24
- The Decimal Number System 24
- The Binary Number System 26
- The Hexadecimal Number System 29

Lesson 2: Tools of the Trade

A. Hardware Tools 36
- Basic Toolkit 36
- ESD Toolkit 38
- Network Toolkit 39
- Circuit Board Toolkit 39

B. Software Tools 41
- Software Utilities 41
- Boot Disk 41
- How to Create a Windows Startup Disk 42
- LAN Connectivity Disk 50

C. Troubleshooting Methodologies 50
- CompTIA Network+ Troubleshooting Model 50
- Novell Troubleshooting Model 53
- Collect, Isolate, and Correct Model 55
- Troubleshooting Tips 58

Lesson 3: Safety

A. Basics of Electricity and Electronics 62
- Electricity 62
- Voltage 62
- Current 63
- Electrical Power and Electrical Energy 63
- Resistance 64
- Measuring Electricity 64

B. Establish an ESD-free Work Area **71**
Static Electricity 71
ESD 72
Preventing ESD 73
Create an ESD-Safe Workstation 74

C. Observe General Safety Precautions **77**
Potential Hazards of Servicing PCs 77
Electrical Hazards 78
Chemical Hazards 80
Lasers 81

D. Potential Hazards of Using PCs **84**
Repetitive Strain Injury 84
Chair 86
Posture 86
Keyboard and Mouse Placement 87
Monitor Placement 88
Work Environment 89
Project Design 90
Vision 90
Other Considerations 91

E. Fire Safety **93**
Fire Prevention Practices 93
Fire Extinguishers 93
Fire Emergency Procedures 94

Contents

Lesson 4: System Components

A. Power Supplies 102

    Power Supply 102

    Power Supply Wire Color Conventions 103

    System Board Power Connectors 103

    Drive Power Connectors 105

    How to Calculate your Power Needs 106

    How to Test your Power Supply 107

    How to Replace a Power Supply 110

    Common Power Problems 113

    How Surge Protectors Protect Computer Equipment 114

    How to Troubleshoot and Correct Power Problems 115

B. ROM BIOS 116

    BIOS 116

    CMOS 116

    BIOS Settings 117

    Methods for Accessing the System BIOS 118

    Configuring the BIOS 119

    The Boot Process 120

    Power-On Self Test 121

    CMOS Error Codes 123

    How to Update the ROM BIOS 123

    How to Troubleshoot Common Boot Problems 125

C. Central Processing Units ... 126

- CPUs ... 126
- How CPUs Interact with System Components ... 128
- Factors that Affect CPU Performance ... 129
- Common Processors ... 131
- CPU Speeds ... 134
- Socket and Slot Types ... 135
- CPU Package Types ... 137
- CPU Cooling Systems ... 139
- Instruction Sets ... 141
- How to Service Processors ... 142
- How to Add a Second CPU ... 145

D. System Boards ... 146

- System Board ... 146
- Clock Speed ... 147
- Form Factors ... 148
- Computer Cases ... 151
- System Board Components ... 151
- How to Upgrade the System Board ... 154
- Symptoms of System Board Problems ... 157
- How to Troubleshoot System Board Problems ... 158

E. Memory ... 158

- Memory ... 158
- ROM ... 159
- RAM ... 161
- Memory Packages ... 166
- How to Add RAM to a System ... 169
- Symptoms of Memory Problems ... 173
- How to Troubleshoot Memory Problems ... 173

Contents

Lesson 5: Bus Architectures

A. What is a Bus? 177
- Bus 177
- Interacting with the Host System 177
- Hardware Resources 177
- Interrupts 178
- Input/Output Addresses 179
- Base Memory Addresses 180
- Direct Memory Access 181
- Device Manager 182
- Configuring System Parameters 183
- Plug and Play 184

B. The 8-bit Bus 186
- The PC Bus 186
- How to Remove and Install Cards 188

C. The ISA Bus 189
- The ISA Bus 189
- Configuration 190

D. The EISA Bus 192
- The EISA Bus 192
- Configuration 193

E. The Micro Channel Architecture Bus 194
- The Micro Channel Architecture Bus 194
- Configuration 196

F. The PCI Bus 196
- The PCI Bus 196
- Configuration 197

G. Video Circuitry Buses 199
- VL-Bus 199
- AGP Bus 199

H. Troubleshooting Adapter Card Problems 203
Common Problems with Adapter Cards. 203
How to Troubleshoot Adapter Card Problems 203

LESSON 6: PORTS, CONNECTORS, AND CABLES

A. Serial Ports 210
Ports 210
Serial Communications 212
Serial Interfaces 212
Serial Port Settings 217

B. Parallel Ports 223
Parallel Communications 223
Parallel Interfaces 223
The Add Printer Wizard 226

C. PS/2 Ports 230
PS/2 Interface. 230
Device Drivers. 232

D. USB Ports 235
USB. 235
USB Power 238
How to Install USB Devices. 238
Common USB Problems. 240

E. FireWire Ports. 241
FireWire 241

F. Wireless Ports. 246
Wireless Connections 246

LESSON 7: EXPANSION BOARDS

A. Drive Controllers 255
Drive Interfaces 255
Drive Controller 260
SCSI 261
Interface Comparison. 262

Contents

B. Video Adapters 267
- Video Adapters 267
- Monochrome Display Adapter (MDA) 268
- Hercules Graphics Card (HGC) 269
- Color Graphics Adapter (CGA) 269
- Enhanced Graphics Adapter (EGA) 269
- Video Graphics Array 270
- Super and Ultimate VGA 271

C. Sound and Game Adapters 273
- Sound Card Interfaces 273
- Sound Devices 274

D. Modem Adapters 279
- Modem 279
- RJ Connectors 281
- Standard Modem IRQs and I/O Addresses 282
- Modem Commands 282
- Installing and Configuring a Modem 283
- Common Problems with Modems 286
- How to Troubleshoot Modems 287

Lesson 8: Fixed Disk Storage Systems

A. Fixed Disk Drives 293
- Drive 293
- Hard Drives 294
- Disk Drive Architecture 294
- Disk Drive Geometry 296
- Reading from and Writing to a Hard Disk 299

B. Installing IDE Drives 302
- Drive Bay 302
- IDE Drives 302
- UltraDMA Drives 305
- Partitioning and Formatting 305

C. Install or Remove Internal SCSI Drives 310
SCSI 310
SCSI Addresses 311
SCSI Signaling Techniques 313
SCSI Termination 313
SCSI Types 314
SCSI Interface 315

D. Correct Hard Drive Problems 321
Common Problems with Hard Drives 321
IDE Drive Troubleshooting Tips 322
SCSI Drive Troubleshooting Tips 322
Slow Drives 323
Hard Drive Maintenance Tools 323

E. RAID 332
RAID 332
How to Create a Striped Volume 335
How to Create a Mirrored Volume 338
How to Create a RAID-5 Volume 343

LESSON 9: REMOVABLE STORAGE SYSTEMS

A. Floppy Disk Drives 349
Floppy Disk Drives 349
How Floppy Disk Drives Work 350
Working with Floppy Disk Drives 351
Replacing a Floppy Disk Drive 352
How to Troubleshoot Floppy Disk Drives 354

B. Optical Disc Drives 358
Optical Disc Drives 358
How to Install Optical Disc Drives 359
Practical Issues 360
Common Problems with Optical Drives 363
How to Troubleshoot Optical Drives 364

Contents

C. Cartridge Disk Drives 370
Cartridge Disk Drives 370
How Removable Cartridge Drives Work 371
Syquest Drives 372
Zip Drives 372
Jaz Drives 373
SuperDisk Drives 373

D. Backup Systems 374
Backup 374
Tape Drives 374
How Tape Drives Work 376
Backup Methods 377
Common Problems with Internal Removable Media Devices 382
How to Troubleshoot and Correct Internal Removable Media Device Problems 382

Lesson 10: Peripheral Devices

A. Primary Input Devices 393
Peripheral Device 393
Keyboard 394
How a Keyboard Works 397
Common Keyboard Problems 399
Pointing Device 400
How Pointing Devices Work 402
Common Pointing Device Problems 404
How to Troubleshoot Keyboard and Pointing Device Problems ... 406

B. Video Output Devices **410**
- Video Output Devices 410
- How CRTs Produce Images 414
- Electron Beam Positioning Technologies used in Monitors 416
- Display Characteristics 417
- Monitor Specifications 418
- Settings 422
- Power Management 424
- How to Connect a Video Output Device 424
- Monitor Safety 430
- Common Monitor Problems 430
- How to Troubleshoot Monitor Problems 432

C. Printers **436**
- Dot Matrix Printers 436
- How Dot Matrix Printers Work 439
- Inkjet Printers 440
- How Inkjet Printers Work 442
- Laser Printers 443
- How Laser Printers Work 445
- Solid Ink Printers 446
- Dye Sublimation Printers 446
- Other Types of Printers 447
- Windows Print Process 447
- Common Printer Problems 448
- Environmental Effects on Printing 451
- How to Troubleshoot Printer Problems 452

D. Other Input/Output Devices **458**
- Scanners 458
- Digital Cameras 459
- Touch Screens 460
- Speakers 462
- Microphones 462

Contents

Lesson 11: Portable Computing

A. Portable Computing Devices 467
    Portable Computing Device 467
    Notebook Computer 470
    Integrated Peripherals 472
    Portable Device Power Sources 475
    DC Controllers 478
    Advanced Power Management 478
    How to Power a Portable Device 479
    Processors 479

B. Docking Solutions 484
    Docking Device 484

C. Portable Computing Device Drives 488
    Portable Computer Drives 488

D. PC Cards 493
    PC Card 493
    Card and Socket Services 494
    PC Card Uses 494

E. Mini-PCI Cards 499
    Mini-PCI Card 499

F. Portable Computing Device Memory 503
    Portable Device Memory Options 503
    Flash Memory 504

G. Replace Internal Components 509
    Internal Components 509
    How to Replace a Hard Disk 511
    How to Replace a Pointing Device 513
    How to Replace a Keyboard 515

H. Personal Digital Assistants 519
    PDA 519

Lesson 12: Networking

A. Network Concepts 529
    Network. 529
    OSI Model 530
    Network Interface Card 531
    Network Cables and Connectors 532
    Twisted Pair Cables 533
    Twisted Pair Cable Connectors 534
    Coaxial Cables. 537
    Coaxial Cable Connectors 538
    Fiber Optic Cables. 539
    Fiber Optic Cable Connectors. 540
    PVC and Plenum Cables. 542
    Physical Network Architectures 544
    Logical Network Architectures. 549
    LANs and WANs 552

B. Network Communications 555
    Server and Network Operating Systems 555
    Workstation and Client Operating Systems 556
    Network Protocols 558
    IP Addresses 560
    Subnet Masking 561
    Public and Private IP Addressing 563
    Subnetting 564
    Auto-IP Configuration 567
    Name Servers 568
    How to Install a Network Adapter 568
    Network Architecture Standards 570

Contents

C. Network Architecture 571
- Ethernet 571
- Token Ring 573
- ARCNet 574
- AppleTalk 574

D. Internet Connections 575
- Internet Connections 575
- LAN Internet Connection 576
- DSL Internet Connection 577
- Cable Internet Connections 578
- ISDN Internet Connection 579
- Dial-up Internet Connection 579
- Satellite Internet Connection 579
- Wireless Internet Connection 581

E. Networking Devices 583
- Networking Device 583
- Hubs 584
- Bridges 585
- Routers 585
- Brouters 586
- Gateways 586
- Channel Service Unit/Digital Service Unit 586
- Firewalls 587
- All-in-one Devices 587

F. Troubleshoot Networks 588
- Common Network Problems 588
- How to Troubleshoot NICs 589
- How to Troubleshoot Networks 589

LESSON 13: PERFORMING PREVENTATIVE MAINTENANCE

A. Maintain the Hard Disk 597
- Fragmentation 597
- Hard Disk Maintenance Tools 597

B. Perform Printer Maintenance **602**
    Cleaning Compounds and Materials 602
C. Use a UPS **610**
    UPS 610
D. Clean Peripheral Components **615**
E. Clean Internal System Components **620**
F. Decide When to Upgrade **623**
    Indications you Need to Upgrade 623
G. Dispose of Computer Equipment **627**
    Material Safety Data Sheets 627
    Hazardous Materials 628

APPENDIX A: CUSTOMER SATISFACTION

A. Importance of Customer Satisfaction **635**
    Professional Manner 635
    Professional Appearance 636
    Professional Behavior 637
    Customer Needs 637
    Better Business 639
    Communication Skills 639
    Active Listening 641
    Conflict Resolution 642
    Service Calls 644
    Customer Interaction 647
    Finishing the Service Call 649

Contents

Appendix B: The OSI Model

Appendix C: A+™ Core Hardware Exam Objectives

Appendix D: A+™ Certification Core Hardware Online Tutorial Components

Lesson Labs 681

Solutions 705

Glossary 735

Index 755

ABOUT THIS COURSE

This course is one of two courses you will need to take if your job responsibilities include entry-level computer service technician support duties. It is also one of two courses of study for the CompTIA A+™ certification program. In this course, you'll build on your end-user background knowledge as you acquire the specific skills required to install, configure, upgrade, troubleshoot, and repair PC hardware components and systems.

This course can benefit you in two ways. Whether you just want to learn how to work with computer hardware or if you want to prepare for the CompTIA A+ Core Hardware Service Technician exam, this course will provide you with the information you need. This course also helps you build up the skills needed to perform hardware technician duties with confidence.

Course Description

Target Student

This course is designed for persons with basic end-user skills with Windows-based personal computers, who wish to begin a career in information technology by becoming personal computer service technicians, or who wish to prepare to take the CompTIA A+ Core Hardware examination.

Course Prerequisites

End-user skills with Windows-based personal computers, including the ability to:
- Start up and shut down the computer.
- Log on to a computer or computer network.
- Run programs.
- Move, copy, delete, and rename files in Windows Explorer.
- Browse and search for information on the Internet.

Basic knowledge of computing concepts, including:
- The difference between hardware and software.
- The functions of software components such as the operating system, applications, and file system.
- The function of a computer network.

You can obtain this level of skills and knowledge by taking any **one** of the following Element K courses:

- *Introduction to Personal Computers Using Windows 95*
- *Introduction to Personal Computers Using Windows 98*
- *Introduction to Personal Computers Using Windows 2000*
- *Introduction to Personal Computers Using Windows XP*
- *Introduction to Networks and the Internet*

How to Use This Book

As a Learning Guide

Each lesson covers one broad topic or set of related topics. Lessons are arranged in order of increasing proficiency with *hardware support*; skills you acquire in one lesson are used and developed in subsequent lessons. For this reason, you should work through the lessons in sequence.

We organized each lesson into results-oriented topics. Topics include all the relevant and supporting information you need to master *hardware support*, and activities allow you to apply this information to practical hands-on examples.

You get to try out each new skill on a specially prepared sample file. This saves you typing time and allows you to concentrate on the skill at hand. Through the use of sample files, hands-on activities, illustrations that give you feedback at crucial steps, and supporting background information, this book provides you with the foundation and structure to learn *hardware support* quickly and easily.

As a Review Tool

Any method of instruction is only as effective as the time and effort you are willing to invest in it. In addition, some of the information that you learn in class may not be important to you immediately, but it may become important later on. For this reason, we encourage you to spend some time reviewing the topics and activities after the course. For additional challenge when reviewing activities, try the "What You Do" column before looking at the "How You Do It" column.

As a Reference

The organization and layout of the book make it easy to use as a learning tool and as an after-class reference. You can use this book as a first source for definitions of terms, background information on given topics, and summaries of procedures.

Course Objectives

In this course, you will install, remove, upgrade, maintain, and troubleshoot computer hardware.

You will:
- explore foundational information about computers.
- describe tools of the trade.
- maintain safe and healthy work habits while servicing computers.
- identify the characteristics of a PC's internal system components.
- identify the features of various bus architectures.
- install or remove devices on standard ports.
- identify the internal expansion capabilities of a PC.
- install fixed disk storage systems.
- identify the technical characteristics of common removable media disk drives.
- identify and troubleshoot input and output peripheral devices.
- install, configure, and work with various portable computing devices.
- describe the basic components of a network.
- perform preventative maintenance procedures.

Course Requirements

Hardware

For each lab station, you will need the following hardware. It is recommended that the documentation and driver disks for each device be included for use by students as needed.

- An ATX-based system with PCI and ISA slots. Whenever possible, have enough components for each lab station to install each device. If the systems you are using have only PCI slots, have at least one other system that contains both ISA and PCI slots. The computer also needs at least one of each of the following ports: parallel, VGA, keyboard and mouse PS/2 ports, serial, USB, FireWire, and sound including Line In, Line Out, Mic, and Game ports. If Windows XP cannot be installed on this additional system, you can install Windows 98 or Windows 2000 on it.
- PCI Cards.
- ISA Cards.
- Internal and external modems.
- USB hub.
- USB devices.
- Extra RAM to install.
- Additional IDE hard drive to install.
- Additional SCSI hard drive or CD/DVD drive to install.
- External SCSI device.
- A serial port device, such as an external modem or serial mouse, to install.

Introduction

- Additional parallel port devices.
- FireWire port.
- FireWire devices.
- FireWire hub.
- Speakers.
- Microphone.
- Joystick or other game controller that connects to the 15-pin game port.
- MIDI device.
- Other quarter-inch mini-jack device (cassette player, musical keyboard, and so on).
- Audio CD.
- AGP video card.
- Wireless devices including mouse and/or keyboard and networking devices.
- At least one system with dual processors.
- Cables for all devices. In addition, you also need the following cables: Null modem, RJ-45, RJ-11, RG 6, RG 8, RG 58, RG 59, STP, fiber optic.
- ESD protection devices such as workbench mats with wrist strap and grounding cord, floor mat with grounding cord and shoe straps.
- Two blank floppy disks for each student to create an MS-DOS startup disk and a Windows XP boot disk.
- Additional IDE floppy disk drive to install. (If you do not have extra floppy drives for all students, they can remove the floppy disk drives already in their computers and then reinstall them.)
- An IDE optical disc drive (CD-ROM, CD-RW, DVD, or DVD-R drive) to install. (If you do not have extra optical drives for all students, they can remove the optical disc drives already in their computers and then reinstall them.)
- An Iomega brand removable cartridge drive and cables. This might be a Zip, Jaz, USB PocketZip (Clik!), HipZip, FotoShow, or Peerless device.
- PDA with serial, USB, and/or Infrared ports and software.
- A 15-pin VGA-style monitor and a computer equipped with a digital video interface, or a digital flat-panel LCD monitor that uses the 29-pin DVI connector.
- Printer with a Parallel port, Serial port, Infrared port, or USB port.
- Portable computer with a Windows operating system installed and a compatible docking station or port replicator. The portable computer should have a single drive bay with a floppy drive in it and a compatible CD/DVD drive; at least one PCI card slot; a mini-PCI card bay; and an empty memory slot.
- Standard desktop peripheral components, including monitor, keyboard, and mouse to connect to the docking station.
- A digital camera.
- An MP3 player.
- At least two PC Cards (Type I, II, or III). One of the PC Cards should be a NIC and the other a modem.
- A wireless Mini-PCI card.
- Memory card for the portable computer.
- A memory module for the MP3 player, the PDA, or the digital camera.

- Network cards for the desktop system, appropriate cables, connectors, and NIC drivers. (You will also need any required networking equipment for students to reach the Internet.)
- UPS.
- PC cleaning supplies such as: a compressed air canister, a printer vacuum, tweezers, lens cloth, lint free cloths, keyboard cleaning wipes, mild household cleaning solution, lint-free cloth, toothpicks, artist's paint brush, cotton swabs, printer cleaning sheets to run through the paper path, CD-ROM cleaning kit, floppy drive cleaning kit, manufacturer-approved removable drive cleaning kit, alcohol, monitor wipes, and replacement parts, ribbons, ink cartridges, toner cartridges, and cleaning supplies that correspond to the manufacturer of the printer you are going to perform maintenance on.
- Digital or analog multimeter, preferably both.
- Spare CPU that is compatible with your lab computers. If you don't have one, students can remove and reinstall the CPU in their lab computers.
- Spare motherboard that is compatible with your lab computers. If you don't have one, students can remove and reinstall the motherboard in their lab computers.

Non-working Devices

For the troubleshooting topics, if you have access to any non-working devices, the devices can be installed for students to troubleshoot.

- A non-working IDE floppy disk drive.
- Non-working memory of a type (SIMM, DIMM, and so on) that is appropriate to the computers in the classroom.
- A non-working keyboard.
- A non-working 15-pin VGA-style monitor or digital flat-panel LCD monitor that uses the 29-pin DVI connector.
- Broken or damaged monitor cables.
- Broken or damaged networking cables.
- Any of the devices students have worked with (from the hardware list for the course) that are not working are suitable for this purpose.
- Damaged CD-ROM.
- Any non-working items that can be broken open to show students the internal workings of devices.

Software

- Windows XP.
- Device drivers for any cards and devices students will install.
- A DHCP server.
- An Internet connection.

INTRODUCTION

Class Setup

1. A working PC for each lab station is configured for the class. The computer has the following ports configured at the start of class:
   - Parallel
   - Serial
   - USB
   - VGA
   - Sound card with line in, line out, mic, and game port
   - FireWire
   - PS/2 keyboard and mouse

   The computers have Internet access and a default DHCP configuration for network access is assumed for the course.

2. Install Windows XP Professional using the entire hard disk as an NTFS partition.
   - When prompted, use Typical Settings. If your network requires different settings, select Custom Settings and configure the network settings accordingly.
   - When prompted to add the system to be a member of the domain, select No, and then continue with the installation.
   - All other settings should be as appropriate to your system and location.

3. Students will need access to drivers for the devices they install and configure. You have several options for providing these drivers.
   - One or more systems connected to the Internet from which students can download the drivers.
   - Download any required drivers and burn them to a CD-ROM for the students to use.
   - Provide the manufacturer's original discs.
   - Download any required drivers and store them on each student station, for example, in a C:\Drivers folder.

4. To test the network components installation, students will need to connect to a network. Internet access via DHCP is assumed. If your location uses static IP addresses, or needs additional TCP/IP settings, assign accordingly.

5. Plug in any UPSs that you will use for lesson 13 so that the batteries will be charged.

6. The class should start with the computers turned off.

List of Additional Files

Printed with each activity is a list of files students open to complete that activity. Many activities also require additional files that students do not open, but are needed to support the file(s) students are working with. These supporting files are included with the student data files on the course CD-ROM or data disk. Do not delete these files.

LESSON 1

Introduction to Computers

Lesson Time
2 hour(s)

Lesson Objectives:

In this lesson, you will explore foundational information about computers.

You will:

- Describe the evolution of today's computers.
- Identify the external and internal components of a personal computer system.
- Describe the characteristics of software.
- Convert numbers from one number system to another.

Lesson 1

Introduction

Before you begin to learn how to install and configure computer hardware, you need the basics of what computers are and where they come from. In this lesson, we'll introduce you to computers by tracing their history and showing you some of what makes them work.

While it might seem like a good idea to jump right into the specifics of computer support and maintenance, it's a better idea to first ground yourself in some basics, such as the history of computers, a description of some of their components, and an explanation of the number systems they use. With the proper foundation, you'll be ready to tackle the more complex subjects in the rest of the course.

The following CompTIA A+ Core Hardware (2003) Examination objectives are covered in this lesson:

- Topic B:
  - 1.1 Identify the names, purposes, and characteristics, of system modules. Recognize these modules by sight or definition: motherboard; processor/CPU; memory; storage devices; and adapter cards.
- Topic C:
  - 1.1 Identify the names, purposes, and characteristics, of system modules. Recognize these modules by sight or definition: firmware.
  - 5.2 Recognize common printer problems and techniques used to resolve them. Content includes the following: printer drivers and firmware updates.

Topic A

A Brief History of Computers

Knowing a little about the history of computers can help you appreciate the current industry situation and prepare you for future developments. And understanding how computers evolved can help you appreciate how they're built and help you better understand why they work the way they do, which makes troubleshooting and repair that much easier.

Evolution of Mechanical Computers

The *abacus* is usually listed as the first mechanical computation device. Created 2,000 or more years ago in India or the Far East, an abacus consists of columns of beads that can slide up and down on rods that are held together in a frame. The position of the beads represents a number. Skilled users could perform calculations more quickly than early electronic computers.

Lesson 1

Figure 1-1: *An abacus.*

The written number for zero appeared around 650 A.D. in India and made written calculations much easier. A Persian scholar wrote the first textbook on algebra in 830 A.D. During the 1100s, Europeans learned the written form of math used by the Arabs and wrote down multiplication tables to help merchants. Five hundred years later, John Napier, a Scotsman, carved a set of multiplication tables on ivory sticks that could slide back and forth to indicate certain results. The use of logarithms on *Napier's Bones* in 1617 led to the development of the slide rule. Today's mature engineers can still remember using slide rules in their college days.

The Frenchman Blaise Pascal is usually given credit for the first calculating machine. In 1642, to help his father—a tax collector—with his work, Pascal invented a machine with eight metal dials that could be turned to add and subtract numbers. Leonardo da Vinci and Wilhelm Schickard, a German, designed calculating machines before Pascal, but Pascal receives the recognition because he produced 50 models of his *Pascaline machine*, not just a prototype or description. In 1673, Gottfried von Leibniz, a German mathematician, improved on Pascal's design to create a *Stepped Reckoner* that could do addition, subtraction, multiplication, and division. Only two prototypes were produced.

A Frenchman, Thomas de Colmar, created an Arithmometer in 1820 that was produced in large numbers over the ensuing 100 years. The Swedish inventor Willgodt T. Odhner improved on the Arithmometer, and his calculating mechanism was used by dozens of companies in the calculating machines they produced.

Punched cards first appeared in 1801. Joseph Marie Jacquard used the holes placed in the card to control the patterns woven into cloth by power looms. In 1832, Charles Babbage was working on a Difference Engine when he realized Jacquard's punched cards could be used in computations. The *Analytical Engine*, the machine Babbage designed but never manufactured, introduced the idea of using memory for storing results and the idea of printed output. His drawings described a general-purpose, fully program-controlled, automatic mechanical digital computer. Lady Ada Augusta Lovelace worked with Babbage on his machine. She became the first computer programmer when she wrote out a series of instructions for the Analytical Engine.

 Charles Babbage's Difference Engine No. 1 was the first successful automatic calculator. Although the 12,000 parts were never assembled into a finished engine, the parts that were completed functioned perfectly.

Punched cards were used in the United States census of 1890, and a data-processing machine created by Herman Hollerith tabulated the census results in only 2.5 years—much shorter than the predicted 10 years. Punched cards provided input, memory, and output on an unlimited scale for business calculating machines for the next 50 years. The company Hollerith founded to manufacture his card-operated data processors, which used electrical contacts to detect the pattern of holes in each card, eventually became IBM.

Electronic Computers

With the beginning of World War II, electronic computers took on national importance. The accurate calculation of projectile trajectories became a life-and-death concern for the military. The calculations needed to develop the atomic bomb also required more calculating power than was available before the war. Between 1939 and 1944, Howard H. Aiken developed the Harvard *Mark I*—also known as the IBM Automatic Sequence-Controlled Calculator (ASCC). The Mark I was made out of mechanical switches, electrical relays, rotating shafts, and clutches totalling 750,000 components weighing 5 tons. Programming instructions were fed to the Mark I on paper tape, and data was fed in on paper punched cards. Grace Hopper worked at Harvard on the Mark I, II, and III, and discovered the first computer "bug" when she removed a moth that had flown into a mechanical relay, causing it to malfunction. Also, during the war, Konrad Zuse was working secretly on his Z3 computer in Germany. Because so little was known about the Z3 for so long, most people describe the Mark I as the first modern (but not electronic) digital computer.

Vacuum Tubes

Dr. John Vincent Atanasoff was an associate professor at Iowa State College when he designed an Electronic Digital Computer (EDC) that would use base two (binary) numbers. In 1939, with his assistant Clifford Berry, he built the world's first electronic digital computer using *vacuum tubes*. After a lecture, Dr. John W. Mauchly asked to see Atanasoff's computer and later used so many of Atanasoff's ideas in the ENIAC that it took a lawsuit to declare that Atanasoff was the first to use vacuum tubes in an electronic digital computer.

Dr. Mauchly and J. Presper Eckert were at the University of Pennsylvania in 1942 when they built the *Electronic Numerical Integrator And Computer (ENIAC)* to aid the United States military during World War II. ENIAC used 18,000 vacuum tubes, had 500,000 hand-soldered connections, was 1,000 times faster than the Mark I, and had to be rewired to change its program. ENIAC was used from 1946 to 1955, and because of its reliability, it is commonly accepted as the first successful high-speed electronic digital computer. Eckert and Mauchly also designed the Electronic Discrete Variable Automatic Computer (EDVAC), which contained 4,000 vacuum tubes and 10,000 crystal *diodes*. After their success with ENIAC, Eckert and Mauchly proposed to build a *Universal Automatic Computer (UNIVAC)* machine to help the Census Bureau handle all its data. After four years of delays and cost overruns, Remington Rand Inc. worked with the Eckert-Mauchly Computer Corporation to develop UNIVAC, the first commercially successful computer. The computer used magnetic tape to store data, a major change from IBM's punched cards, and introduced many other features that are common today. Starting in 1951, 46 UNIVAC I computers were made for the government and businesses, although some experts at the time thought that five computers would be enough to handle all the computational needs of the world.

John von Neumann did not design the electronics in computers, but he is credited with the theoretical work that all modern computers are based on. Von Neumann recommended that a computer program should be able to stop under certain conditions and start again at another point. He also recommended storing both the data and instructions in memory so both could be changed as needed. He realized that physically rewiring a computer to change the program, or feeding in another paper tape to meet different conditions, was not practical for successful high-speed computing. The *Electronic Delay Storage Automatic Computer (EDSAC)* at Cambridge University, England, and Eckert and Mauchly's *Electronic Discrete Variable Automatic Computer (EDVAC)* were among the first to use von Neumann's ideas. Combining von Neumann's stored program concept with a 1,000-word main memory, magnetic tape for secondary memory, printer and typewriter output, and a 2.25 MHz clock rate, UNIVAC set the standard for computers in the 1950s.

Transistors and Magnetic Memory

The progress of electronic computing was limited by technology. Vacuum tubes, which were used to control the flow of electricity in digital computer circuits, were large (several inches high), red-hot to touch, and unreliable. Dr. William Shockley worked at Bell Telephone Laboratories as co-head of a solid-state research group that developed the *transistor*. Transistors performed the same function but were the size of a pencil eraser, generated almost no heat, and were extremely reliable. The replacement of vacuum tubes with transistors opened up new possibilities.

Another important innovation was *magnetic core memory*, which allowed information to be stored in the magnetic orientation of tiny magnetic rings strung together on fine wire. Using magnetic core memory, the huge mainframes increased their memory from 8,000 to 64,000 words. Combining the computational capability made available through transistors with expanded magnetic core memory gave computers so much power that they had to be used in new ways to justify the cost. Some mainframes used batch processing, where a series of programs and data was stored on magnetic drums and fed to the computer one after the other so no computing time was wasted. Other computers used time sharing, where the computing power was shifted among several different programs running at the same time so no power was wasted waiting for an individual program's results to print or for more input to arrive.

At this time, the United States and the former Soviet Union were involved in a race to see who would be first in space. The complex rockets demanded sophisticated computers to control them. The Soviet Union concentrated on designing bigger rockets to carry larger computers into space, while the United States worked on making smaller, more powerful computers that fit into the smaller rockets they had. The millions spent on research to miniaturize computer components used in the space race produced the technology needed for current computers.

Integrated Circuits

Transistors were great, but combining several transistors and the *resistors* needed to connect them on a single semiconductor chip in an *integrated circuit* was even better. In 1958, Jack Kilby at Texas Instruments made several components on a single-piece semiconductor. By 1961, Fairchild and Texas Instruments were mass-producing integrated circuits on a single chip. In 1967, Fairchild introduced the Micromosaic, which contained a few hundred transistors. The transistors could be connected into specific circuits for an application using computer-aided design. The Micromosaic was an Application-Specific Integrated Circuit (ASIC).

 Now usually called just a chip, the first integrated circuit was fabricated in 1958 by Texas Instruments inventor Jack Kilby.

Lesson 1: Introduction to Computers

Lesson 1

Figure 1-2: *Integrated circuit.*

In 1970, Fairchild introduced the first 256-bit static *RAM chip*, while Intel announced the first 1,024-bit dynamic RAM. Computers that could make use of this memory were still monsters to maintain. Hand-held calculators, on the other hand, appealed to everyone from scientists to school kids. Marcian "Ted" Hoff at Intel designed a general-purpose integrated circuit that could be used in calculators, as well as other devices. Using ideas from this circuit, Intel introduced, in 1972, the *8008*, which contained approximately 3,300 transistors and was the first *microprocessor* to be supported by a high-level language compiler called PL/M.

A major breakthrough occurred in 1974 when Intel presented the 8080, the first general-purpose microprocessor. The 8080 microprocessor had a single chip that contained an entire programmable computing device on it. The 8080 was an 8-bit device that contained around 4,500 transistors and could perform 200,000 operations per second. Other companies besides Intel designed and produced microprocessors in the mid-1970s, including Motorola (6800), Rockwell (6502), and Zilog (Z80). As more chips appeared and the prices dropped, personal desktop computers became a possibility.

Personal Computers

About a dozen computers claim to be the first *Personal Computer (PC)*. Credit for the first popular personal computer often goes to Ed Roberts whose company, MITS, designed a computer called the Altair 8800 and marketed a kit for about $400 in 1974. The Altair 8800 used Intel's 8080 microprocessor, contained 256 bytes of RAM, and was programmed by means of a panel of toggle switches. In 1975, Bill Gates and Paul Allen founded Microsoft and wrote a BASIC interpreter for the Altair. More than 2,000 systems were sold in 1975.

LESSON 1

Figure 1-3: *An early PC.*

In 1975, MOS Technology announced its 6502-based KIM-1 desktop computer, and Sphere Corporation introduced its Sphere 1 kit. Both kits were strictly for computer fanatics. In 1976, Steve Wozniak and Steve Jobs formed the Apple Computer Inc. company and modified the Apple I to create the Apple II (with a 6502 microprocessor). In 1977, the Apple II cost $1,300, came with 16 KB of ROM, 4 KB of RAM, a keyboard, and color output. The Apple II is usually listed as the first personal computer that was available for the general public. The Commodore PET (6502) and Radio Shack's TRS-80 (Z80) were also popular. In 1979, VisiCalc, a spreadsheet program for the Apple II, made desktop computers attractive to businesses. As more businesses bought Apples, demand appeared for word-processing applications, and the software development industry took off. In 1981, IBM joined the party with its first PC. Dozens of other models and companies followed IBM's lead, but in 1984, Apple broke from the pack and produced the Macintosh computer with a mouse and graphical user interface that opened the computer world to artists and publishers. Of all the computers designed during this period, only the IBM PC and Apple Macintosh have withstood the test of time.

Today there are several types of personal computers:

- Desktop: A type of computer that's more broad than tall. Designed to sit on top of a desk and support a monitor. Probably the most common type of computer in offices today.

- Minitower: As its name implies, this type of computer is tall and narrow. It can sit on top of the desk or on the floor or shelf beneath the desk. Common in offices and in homes.

- Portable: A small computer that can be transported anywhere. Usually weighs less than ten pounds; in fact, many weigh under five pounds. Used by travelers and those who need to easily carry their work with them to multiple locations.

- Tablet: Designed to look like a writing tablet, these computers are often mostly screen on which users can write or type in data using their fingers or more likely a special pen called a stylus. Some tablet computers have a keyboard that folds out of the way.

Lesson 1

- Handheld/Personal Digital Assistant (PDA): A small computer about the size of a large calculator, these computers can have much of the same functionality that desktops and laptops have, although they're often slower and have less storage space, and there are fewer programs that can be used on them. Highly mobile, PDAs are generally used to manage contacts and calendars, and access email and the Internet through wireless radio connections. Users can input data using a small attachable or attached keyboard or a stylus.

Discovery Activity 1-1

Tracing the Computer's Evolution

Scenario:
During a conversation one day, you are asked to provide information about the evolution of the personal computer.

1. **Match the inventor on the left with his contribution on the right.**

    ___ John Napier   a. Processed census data using punched cards.
    ___ Blaise Pascal   b. Designed a mechanical calculator that could add, subtract, multiply, and divide.
    ___ Gottfried von Leibniz   c. Designed the Difference Engine and the Analytical Engine.
    ___ Herman Hollerith   d. Developed a series of rods that let users do multiplication by adding numbers.
    ___ Charles Babbage   e. Developed the first digital calculating machine that could add and subtract.

2. **Arrange the following devices in the order in which they were invented.**

    Pascaline Machine

    Stepped Reckoner

    Babbage's Difference Engine

    Abacus

    Napier's Bones

    Punch cards

3. Match each technology with its description.

   ___ Vacuum tubes

   ___ Transistors

   ___ Integrated circuits

   ___ Microprocessors

   a. Replaced vacuum tubes to make electronic computers faster, smaller, and more efficient.

   b. Allowed multiple transistors to exist on the same base material and connected transistors without using wires.

   c. Eliminated the need to manually wire a machine and set switches for each different program that was to be executed.

   d. Allowed an entire computing device to reside on a single chip whose function could be controlled by programmed instructions.

4. **Arrange the following technologies in the order they were invented.**

   UNIVAC

   Apple Macintosh

   EDSAC

   IBM PC

   Altair 8800

   Integrated circuits

TOPIC B
Desktop Computer System Components and Their Functions

If you don't understand the main components inside a computer, when you open it up, it will seem like the most elaborate puzzle you've ever seen. Like most puzzles, the inner workings of a computer all have a specific place they need to be, but unlike jigsaw puzzles, for the most part in all kinds of different computers, you'll find that the pieces fit together almost exactly the same way. To help you put the puzzle together, you need to understand what the pieces look like and where they go.

Lesson 1

External System Components

There are several types of devices used to enter data into a computer and receive data back from the computer. They are listed in Table 1-1.

Figure 1-4: *The external components of a typical personal computer system.*

Table 1-1: *External System Components*

Name	Type of Device	Description
Keyboard	Input	A device that looks like a typewriter that plugs into a computer. Allows you to enter commands, create documents, add numbers, and write emails, among other tasks.
Mouse	Input	Another device that you can use to point to, touch, and select items on a computer screen.
Monitor	Output	Displays the output from the computer, the operating system, and any software you use.
Speaker	Output	Allows you to hear warnings and other notifications from the computer, sounds from programs, and plays music.
Printer	Output	Allows you to transfer to paper data you see on the monitor or data stored on the computer.

Internal System Components

Internal system components reside inside the computer system case. Components are composed of integrated circuits and transistors, in addition to specific materials for various device functions. All computers must contain the following internal components:

- Motherboard
- Power supply
- Central Processing Unit (CPU)
- RAM
- ROM BIOS

Other internal components, including adapter cards and disk drives, can be added to the system to increase functionality of the system. Various internal system components are identified in Figure 1-5.

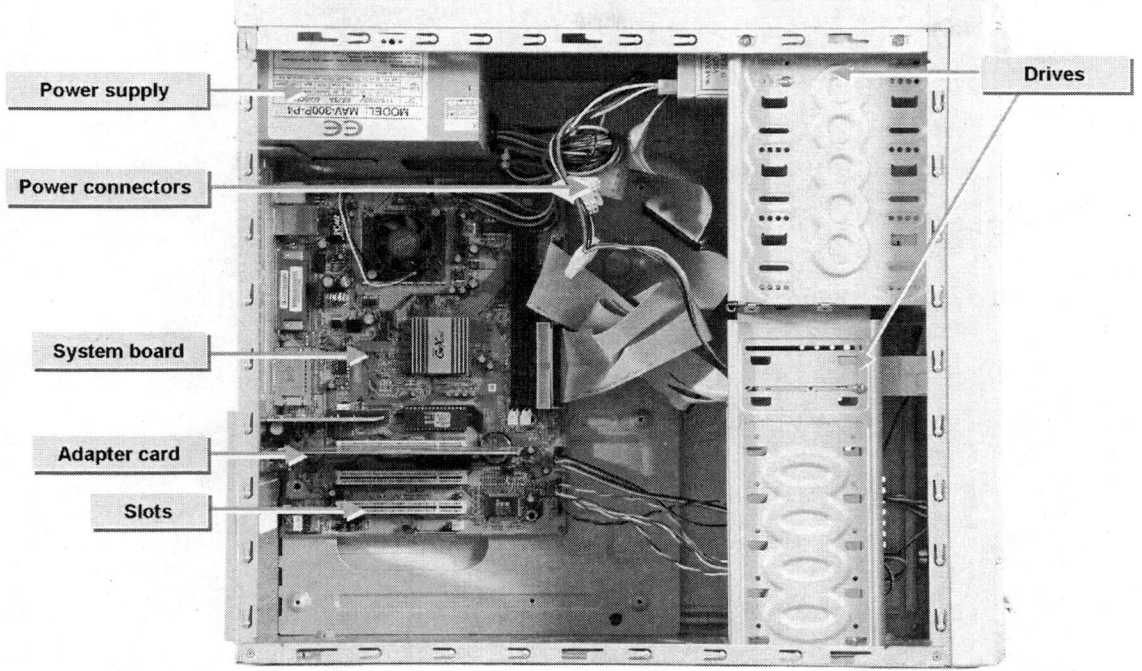

Figure 1-5: *Internal system components.*

System Board

The *system board* is the main circuit board in a computer. It is a very thin plate that has chips and other electrical components on it that make up the Central Processing Unit (CPU), the computer memory, and basic controllers for the system. Sometimes called the *motherboard*, the system board has some electrical components *soldered* directly to it, as well as slots and sockets where other components can be added and removed easily. Figure 1-6 illustrates such a system board.

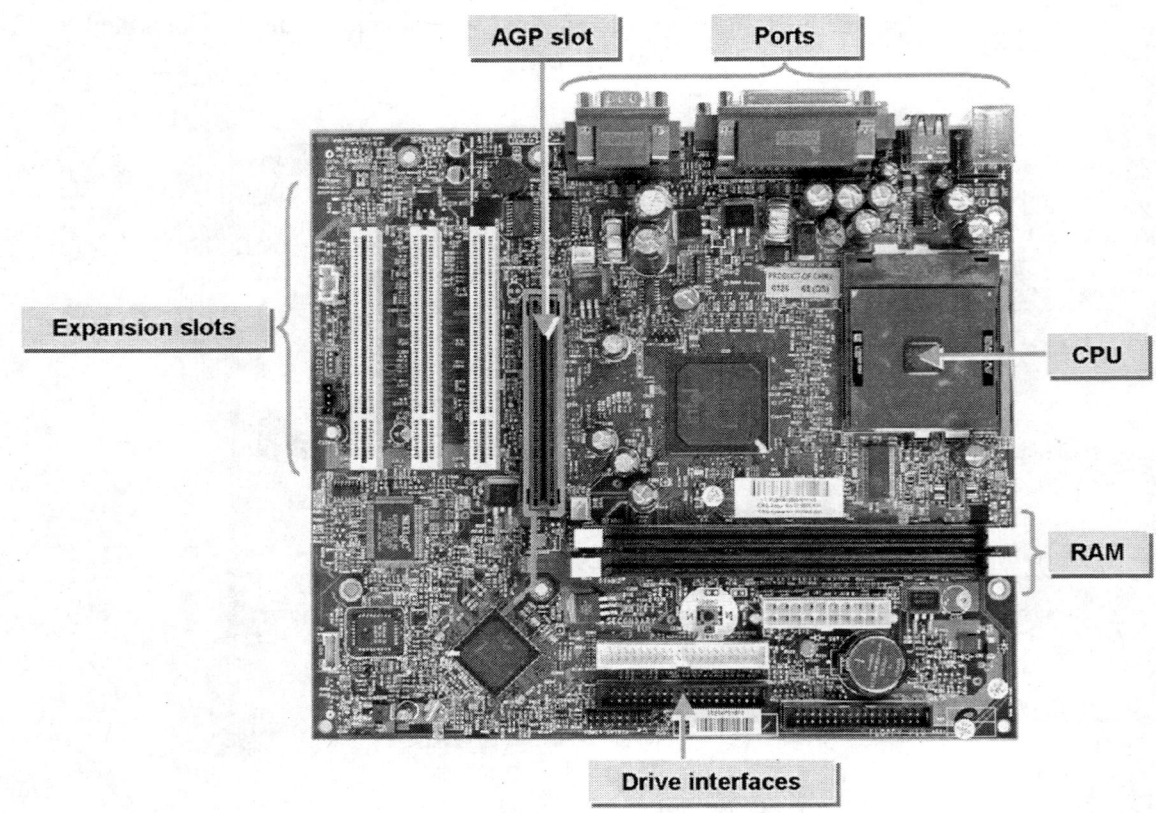

Figure 1-6: *A system board, also known as a motherboard.*

The wires that connect the soldered components, the slots, and the sockets are all permanently built into the system board. Usually the microprocessor, or CPU, is on a large chip that is held in a socket on the system board so you can upgrade the chip when a compatible, newer chip comes out. The chips that control the flow of information to and from the CPU are usually soldered to the system board and are not replaceable. The jacks where you plug in the mouse and keyboard are usually soldered to the system board, but the network and modem connections are usually on interface cards that are easily inserted and removed from slots on the system board.

Because features that are built into the design of the system board cannot be changed without replacing the whole system board, most system boards include only the standard features that most users want—those that will not change much in the near future. Not incorporating features that many users do not use, like SCSI and network connections, helps manufacturers keep the cost of the board low. By allowing users to buy modems with the speed and features they want, and letting the users attach the card to the motherboard, the designers build in flexibility that most users appreciate.

Sometimes computer makers who sell complete systems find it is cheaper to build a system board with the modem, sound card, video, and all other features built-in, rather than add interface cards to a standard system board. The buyers of these complete systems get a low price but give up the freedom of easily upgrading and customizing the computer.

Because system boards must be replaceable, they all come with certain standard features. Unfortunately, the standards for these features change over time. For example, the system board usually has slots that hold cards full of memory chips, rather than having the chips soldered directly to the board. You can increase the memory of your computer by replacing the memory cards with cards with more capacity. Every few years, though, a completely new style of memory card will appear that will not fit into the old-style slots. At that point, you either need to buy a new system board or miss out on the advantages of the new-style memory cards.

 Some of these complete systems include special BIOS settings that you can use to disable the built-in components. Then, you can upgrade or customize these systems by adding expansion cards, just as you would do with a regular system board.

System boards are often described by their general physical characteristics. The original motherboard design was the AT, which was 12 inches wide. A smaller Baby AT board, 9 inches wide by 10 inches long, became popular after 1989 when the demand for small computers increased. New processor chips required a redesigned system board, and in 1996 the ATX design was introduced. This system board was 12 inches wide by 9.6 inches long, while the Baby ATX was about an inch shorter in both width and length. The ATX board design took into account the need to cool the CPU and memory chips, and the need to move high-speed components as close together as possible to reduce errors as the extremely high-speed signals move across the system board.

Another way to classify system boards is by the *chipset* it uses. The chipset is a group of chips on the system board that support the CPU and each of the other subsystems. When buying or working on a computer, you must know the general design of the system board, the make and model of the processor on the board, and the kind of chipset that is on the board.

Processor

The microprocessor, sometimes called just the *processor* or the Central Processing Unit (CPU) is the real brains of the computer where most of the calculations take place. On very large computers, the CPU may consist of many chips mounted on a series of printed circuit boards, but on personal computers, the CPU is housed in a single microprocessor chip. Figure 1-7 illustrates some typical CPUs.

Lesson 1

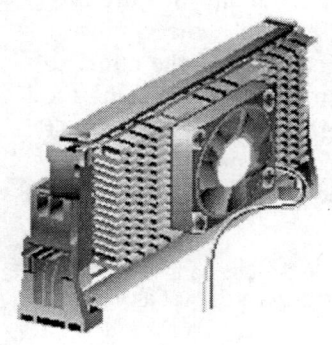

Figure 1-7: *A selection of CPUs.*

The microprocessor is divided into three areas, the first of which retrieves programmed instructions from the computer's memory, decodes, and executes the instructions. The second area is the Arithmetic and Logic Unit (ALU) that does the math operations when needed. The third area sends the results back out to the rest of the computer.

Many companies make microprocessors for IBM-compatible Personal Computers (PCs), but Intel CPUs are the ones against which the other companies' CPUs are compared and rated. The original IBM PCs were based on Intel's 8086 CPU. Other models followed over the years, including 80286 (commonly called the 286), the 386, and the 486. Each of these processors came in a variety of configurations. Because Intel couldn't own the name 486 for a processor, it used a name it could trademark, Pentium, for its 586 processor and Pentium Pro for its 686 equivalent processor.

Today, microprocessors are available in a variety of configurations, including different clock speeds, bus speeds, and cache levels and amounts. Most have backward-compatibility so that they can still run older programs, as well as meet the demands of more current software. Older processors aren't capable of running newer software programs that take advantage of CPU technology advancements that were introduced after their release.

Memory

Memory refers to the internal storage areas in the computer. In common usage, memory refers to actual chips that keep track of computer data and not the information stored on tape or hard drives. Memory chips contain millions of transistors etched on one sliver of a semiconductor. These transistors either conduct electricity and represent the binary number 1, or they don't conduct electricity and represent the binary number 0. Figure 1-8 illustrates a typical memory module for use with a personal computer.

Figure 1-8: *A typical memory module.*

Random Access Memory (RAM) is the main memory. The computer can both read the data stored in RAM memory and write different data into the same RAM memory. Any byte of data can be accessed without disturbing other data, so the computer has random access to the data in RAM memory. RAM memory requires a constant source of electricity to keep track of the data it is storing. If the electricity is cut off, RAM forgets everything. Because of this, RAM memory is described as volatile memory. *Dynamic RAM (DRAM)* is the most common type of RAM. DRAM must be refreshed thousands of times per second. *Static RAM (SRAM)* does not need to be refreshed. SRAM is faster, but more expensive, than DRAM, but both forms of RAM are volatile.

Read-Only Memory (ROM) refers to special permanent memory used to store programs that boot the computer and perform diagnostics. ROM also allows the computer random access to data in its memory. More importantly, the computer cannot change any of the data stored on the ROM, so ROM is read-only memory.

In the early personal computers, you added more memory by filling empty sockets on the motherboard with more memory chips. A *Single In-line Memory Module (SIMM)* made adding memory easier because all the chips were soldered to a single, small, printed circuit board that you inserted into a slot on the system board of your computer. SIMMs transfer information 32 bits at a time, while *Dual In-line Memory Modules (DIMMs)* transfer data 64 bits at a time. Pentium processors require a 64-bit path, so you must add either two SIMMs at a time or one DIMM to a Pentium computer.

Complementary Metal Oxide Semiconductor RAM (CMOS RAM) is special memory that has its own battery to help it keep track of its data even when the power is turned off. CMOS RAM stores information about the computer setup that the computer refers to each time it starts. Because you can write new information to CMOS RAM, you can store information about new disk drives that you add to your system. The computer will remember to look for the drive each time it is turned on.

Lesson 1

Interfaces

An *interface* on a computer is a place where you can connect another device like a disk drive, keyboard, modem, or mouse. Sometimes the interface connection is built into the system board, like the mouse port and keyboard port. Sometimes the actual connector is on a printed circuit card that adapts the signals to and from the attached device so it can communicate with the computer. Modems are generally on an *interface card*.

Interface cards are inserted into a slot on the system board that connects to the microprocessor. The collection of wires that make the connection, and the rules that describe how the data should flow through the wires, is called a *bus*. The Industry Standard Architecture (ISA) bus connects to ISA slots that accept only ISA cards. The ISA slots were used on early IBM computers and became the industry standard. As computers became faster, they needed buses that could transfer more data, more quickly, than the ISA bus could handle. The development of the Peripheral Component Interconnect (PCI) local bus helped to solve this problem. Unfortunately, PCI and ISA cards and slots are **not** interchangeable. PCI cards must go into PCI slots, and ISA cards must go into ISA slots. Most computers have a combination of ISA and PCI slots on the system board.

A slot cover is a thin strip of metal, held in place by a screw or a tab, that protects an opening (in the system case) for an interface card. When you want to add an interface card into a slot on the system board, you need to remove the corresponding slot cover before you can install the card. If you remove a card and don't replace it with another one, you should replace it with a slot cover that's designed to be held in place by a screw. Doing so will help protect the computer from dust and maintain proper airflow currents within the chassis.

Parallel and Serial Interfaces

There are two important types of computer interfaces that are commonly used to connect peripheral devices, including printers and pointing devices, such as a mouse, to a computer.

- Parallel interface, which transmits data across multiple channels at once.
- Serial interface, which transmits data in a single stream.

Adapter Cards

Definition:

An *adapter card* is a printed circuit board that you install into a slot on the computer's system board to expand the functionality of the computer. It is also known as an expansion card, add-in, add-on, or simply a board.

All adapter cards:

- Have a connector that matches the slot they are installed in.
- Contain circuitry to connect a specific device to the computer.
- Increase the capabilities of the computer.

Adapter cards include the following:

- Video cards
- Sound cards
- Network cards
- SCSI host bus adapters
- Internal modems

- USB cards
- IEEE 1394/FireWire cards

Adapter cards can:
- Use a local bus or the main system bus.
- Use different slot types.
- Be built into the system circuitry or be separate physical boards.

Example: A PCI Modem Adapter Card

The example shown in Figure 1-9 is of a PCI modem card. It uses a PCI connector, which fits into the PCI slot in the motherboard. It uses 3.3 volts of electricity powered through the power supply. The circuitry on the adapter card enables this card to be used to connect the computer to a network or another computer through the phone lines.

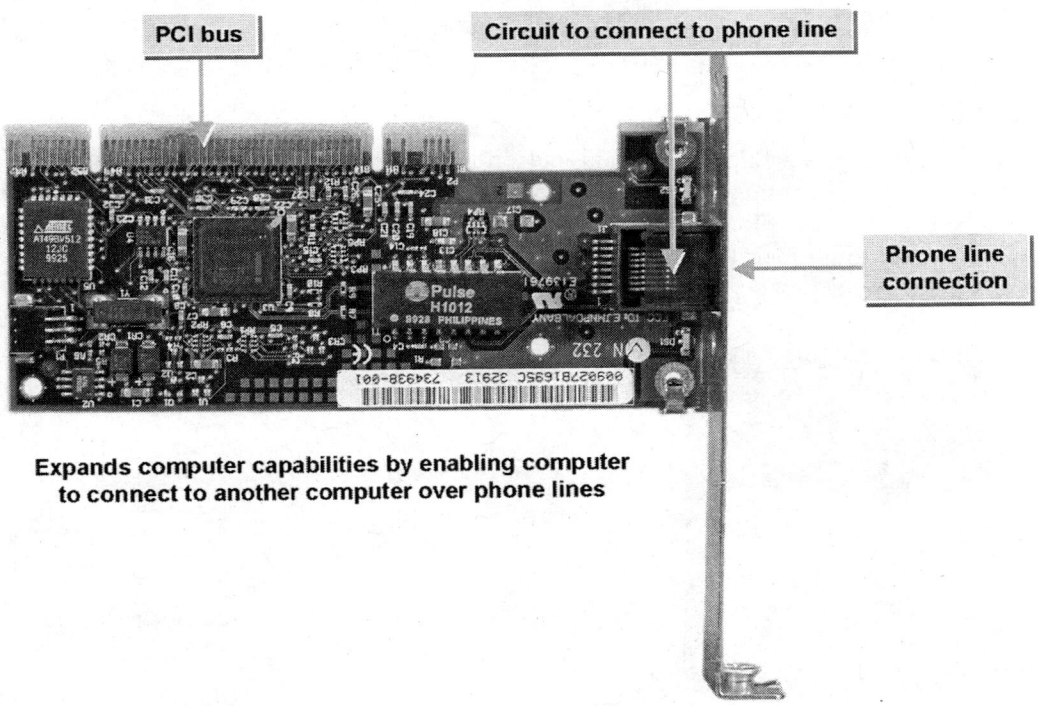

Figure 1-9: *An example of an adapter card.*

Storage Media

In addition to memory, there are other ways to store data on different media.

A hard disk is a fixed unit inside a computer that magnetically stores data on rigid circular platters. The hard disk typically holds all the data on a computer, and usually a computer is run from the hard disk itself. There can be multiple hard disks in a single computer depending on its internal configuration. Figure 1-10 illustrates a typical hard drive.

Lesson 1

Figure 1-10: *A hard disk.*

A floppy disk magnetically stores data, but on a flexible circular medium. Although housed in a rigid case for protection, floppy disks are actually made of a pliable material that you could actually bend or tear. Floppy disks are not fixed inside a computer and can be transported from one computer to another to exchange data. Figure 1-11 illustrates a typical floppy disk and floppy disk drive.

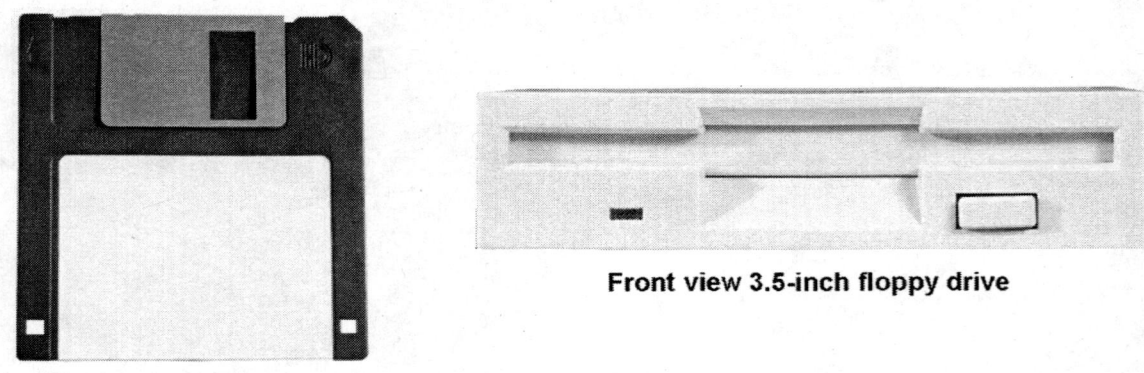

3.5-inch floppy disk

Front view 3.5-inch floppy drive

Figure 1-11: *A floppy disk and drive.*

A Compact Disc-Read Only Memory (CD-ROM or CD-R) drive reads data stored on a rigid, plastic platter on which data is pressed, much like records used to be. Figure 1-12 illustrates a CD-ROM disc.

Lesson 1

A CD-R disc

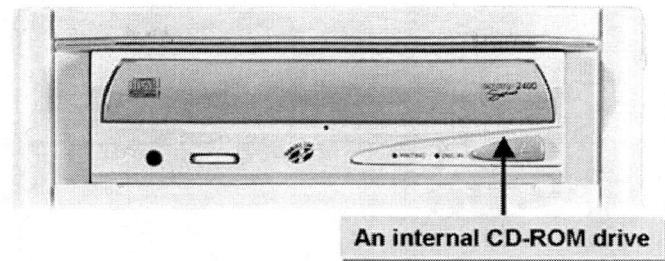
An internal CD-ROM drive

Figure 1-12: *A CD-ROM disc and drive.*

 By convention, optical media are called "discs" (with a C) where magnetic media, such as hard drives and floppies, are called "disks" (with a K).

A Compact Disc-Recordable (CD-R) is a CD on which you can write information. Data is written by a laser beam, which modifies a light-sensitive layer on the CD-ROM. Once the information is "burned" onto the CD-R disc, it can't be modified or deleted.

A Compact Disc-Re-writeable (CD-RW) is another CD on which you can burn data, but unlike a CD-R disc, you can delete and modify (depending on the software and hardware you're using) data on a CD-RW disc.

ACTIVITY 1-2

Identifying System Components

Scenario:
One day you open a computer to swap out a failed processor. Somebody standing next to you has asked you to identify various system components in a computer.

1. **Match the system component to its description.**

_a_	System board	a.	Main circuit board of the computer.
_e_	Processor	b.	The actual chips that keep track of computer data.
_b_	Memory	c.	Means of connecting devices to the system board so that they can communicate with the microprocessor.
_c_	Interfaces	d.	The collection of wires that connect an interface card and the microprocessor, and the rules that describe how data should be transferred through the connection.
_d_	Bus	e.	The real brains of the computer where most of the calculations take place.

Lesson 1: Introduction to Computers

LESSON 1

TOPIC C
Software

Even the most modern and sophisticated computers are just lumps of metal, plastic, and glass if you can't get them to do what you need them to do. This is where software and firmware come into the picture. Software provides the interface between the user and the hardware, as well as among the various hardware components. Knowing about software and how a computer uses it is vital to a computer support technician.

Software

When you buy a program like Microsoft Office, the disks it comes on are considered hardware, but the program code stored on the disk is *software*. Software is written in computer languages like Visual BASIC, C++, Cobol, assembler, and machine language. Unless the program is written in a machine language that the microprocessor can understand, the program must be translated into machine language before it can be used. This translation is also done by software in the machine.

Software can be divided into two categories that sometimes overlap—system software and application software. As usual, experts will disagree on the details, but the following information can give you one way to think about software.

System Software

System software is the low-level program that interacts with the computer at a very basic level. An *Operating System (OS)* is a type of system software found on every personal computer. The operating system is the most important software that runs on the computer, because it is the master control program that determines what the computer will do and how it will do it. Examples of operating systems include Windows XP, Windows 2000 Professional, Windows ME, Windows 98, UNIX, Linux, Macintosh OS, IBM OS/2, and DOS. A computer's OS performs many functions. It recognizes input from the keyboard and mouse, sends output to the display screen, keeps track of files and directories on the disk, and controls peripheral devices such as disk drives, CD-ROM drives, and printers. Some operating systems allow more than one user to use the computer at a time, and more than one application to run on the computer at a time. Multi-user operating systems keep users from interfering with each other and provide security for their work. Multi-user operating systems can also keep track of who uses the computer and determine which programs they can run and which data they can access.

Operating systems are a common base for *application software*. Applications like word processing and graphics programs are written for specific operating systems, not make and model of each computer. The applications communicate with the computer through the operating system. For this reason, Macintosh programs cannot be run on a computer running the straight Windows operating system, and Windows programs will not run on a computer running pure Linux. The operating system does all the hardware communication for the application.

Operating systems have one to two types of interfaces for interacting with users. Operating systems like DOS and UNIX are command-driven interfaces—users type commands in by hand from the keyboard. Operating systems like Windows and the Mac OS are *Graphical User Interfaces (GUIs)*. In a GUI, the user uses a mouse to point, click, and drag graphic elements on the screen. The early Windows programs were DOS programs that translated clicks into DOS commands that were sent to DOS, which actually still had complete control of the computer. Newer versions of Windows are complete operating systems that bypass DOS.

Application Software

Application software is a program designed to help the end-user accomplish a task. An application sits on top of the operating system and uses the operating system to communicate with the computer hardware. The following list shows some of the categories of application software and example applications:

- Database management systems—Microsoft Access, FileMaker Pro, Paradox
- Word processing—Microsoft Word, Corel WordPerfect
- Spreadsheets—Microsoft Excel, Lotus 1-2-3, Quattro Pro
- Presentation graphics—Microsoft PowerPoint
- Communications and email—Microsoft Outlook, Eudora
- Desktop publishing—PageMaker, Quark, Microsoft Publisher
- Project management—Microsoft Project, Milestones, Delegator
- Graphics—Photoshop, CorelDraw, Illustrator
- Contact managers—ACT
- Authoring programs—Macromedia Director, Visual Basic
- Games and education—Flight Simulator, Reader Rabbit
- Web browsers—Netscape Navigator, Internet Explorer, Mozilla, Opera
- Anti-virus software—Norton, McAfee
- Accounting and business management—Peachtree, Quicken, QuickBooks, Microsoft Money
- Flow charts and diagrams—Visio, Corel Flow
- Speech recognition—IBM ViaVoice, Dragon NaturallySpeaking, Voice Xpress, FreeSpeech

Sometimes several programs are bundled together and sold as a suite. Examples of bundled programs are Microsoft Office and Corel WordPerfect Suite. When several applications are combined into a single program, like Microsoft Works or ClarisWorks, the package is called integrated software. Utilities that perform a function for the computer, like disk compression or virus protection, are sometimes listed separately from applications. Computer languages may also be given their own software category. There is really no right or wrong way to categorize software.

Device Drivers

Definition:

> A *device driver* is a piece of software that enables the operating system and a peripheral device to communicate with each other. A device driver:

- Takes generalized commands from the system software or an application and translates them into unique programming commands that the device can understand.
- Provides the code that allows the device to function with the operating system.
- Is installed as part of the installation process for a new piece of hardware.

📌 Some experts consider the device driver to be a type of system software.

A device driver may be:

- Included with the Windows XP operating system or supplied with the device on a CD-ROM or floppy disk when you purchase it. Peripherals that are designed after the operating system comes out must supply their own drivers.

  📌 New operating systems include thousands of drivers that let them work with all current, popular devices.

- Downloaded from the Internet from each manufacturer's Web site.
- Generic for a class of device or specific to a particular device.

📌 A device driver is also known as driver software or just plain driver.

Device Manager

Device Manager is a software tool built in to Windows that enables you to configure settings for hardware devices installed in or connected to your system. Device Manager displays a list of all of the hardware devices installed on your system. You can select a specific device and then set the properties for the device.

Example: Print Driver

A print driver is an example of a device driver. When you install an HP LaserJet 4si printer, Windows XP also installs a driver specific to that printer. Since the printer is being installed on a Windows XP system, the driver must be written for XP (and not some other operating system). Otherwise, the printer driver will not be installed. When a user chooses File→Print in an application, the printer driver translates the instructions to print into code that is specific to the HP LaserJet 4si printer.

Activity 1-3

Identifying Software and Firmware

Scenario:
You have been asked to identify the different types of software and firmware.

1. What role does application software play in the function of a desktop computer?

2. What role does operating system software play in the function of a desktop computer?

3. What role does driver software play in the function of a desktop computer?

Firmware

Definition:
   Firmware is software stored in memory chips that retains data whether or not power to the computer is on. It is most often written on an electronically reprogrammable chip so it can be updated with a special program to fix any errors that might be discovered after you buy the computer.

Example:
   The system BIOS is the most common use of firmware you will encounter. The BIOS contains instructions that permit the computer to boot, communicate with its internal components, and so forth.

Lesson 1

Topic D

Numbering Systems

What would you do one day if you saw the number 3E0H? If you're like most people, you probably don't even recognize that as a number. However, computers do, and that's just one example of a number other than a decimal number you might encounter when working with computers. When you see a number like that, you need to be able to recognize what number system it's from and the value it represents.

The Decimal Number System

Imagine this: You are given a large pail that will hold exactly 1,000 marbles, a can that will hold exactly 100 marbles, and a small cup that holds only 10 marbles. You are asked to report how many pails, cans, and cups of marbles are stored in a large jar as quickly as possible. You could fill the cup over and over until you run out of marbles, but that takes too long. To save time, you put all the marbles in the pail, which is only partly filled. You pour the marbles from the pail into the can, which you can fill up only two times. You pour the remaining marbles into the cup, which you can fill three times. There are seven marbles left in the bottom of the pail. Your report on the number of marbles might be zero pails, two cans, three cups, and seven left over. This report will make little sense to people who do not know the number of marbles that can fit into the pail, can, and cup. A table can make things clearer.

 10^0 equals 1. Why? Division in exponential notation involves subtracting exponents. Follow these examples if you are unsure. 1000/100=10 is the same as $10^3/10^2=10^{3-2}=10^1=10$. Along the same line, 1000/1000=1 is the same as $10^3/10^3=10^{3-3}=10^0=1$. Any number raised to the power of zero is one. This is the same as saying $n^0=1$.

Number in Container	1,000 (10^3)	100 (10^2)	10 (10^1)	1 (10^0)
Times Filled	0	2	3	7

Using the number in a container as a place value, you could say that you counted no thousands, two hundreds, three tens, and seven individual marbles in the jar. This report leaves no room for misunderstanding, but it could be shorter. Stating that 237 marbles were in the jar is just as precise if everyone agrees that the 7 on the right tells how many individual marbles you had, the 3 in the second place from the right tells how many tens of marbles you had, and the 2 in the third place from the right tells how many hundreds of marbles you had. If you only dealt with humans, 237 would be fine, but now you are also working with computers that use other number systems. For a computer, the answer must be 237 Base 10.

A computer would analyze your report this way: Base 10 tells the computer that the place value of each digit in your number is based on some power of 10. The digit in the first place on the right tells how many individuals (ones) you had. Another way of expressing one using exponents is 10^0. The second place from the right tells how many tens (10^1) you had. The third place tells how many hundreds (10^2, or 10*10) you counted, and the fourth place tells how many thousands (10^3, or 10*10*10) you had. Knowing you had 0*1000 plus 2*100 plus 3*10 plus 7 marbles, the computer could then translate the value into its own number system.

Lesson 1

 The asterisk (*) indicates multiplication and is a valid alternative to the times sign (which, because it so closely resembles the letter x, can cause confusion). When you are working with computers, you should always use the asterisk to ensure that the computer correctly interprets the mathematical statement you are making.

Exponential notation is just an extension of this idea. The number 237 could be written as $2*10^2+3*10^1+7*10^0$. Going from right to left, the place value of the digits are 10^0, 10^1, 10^2, 10^3, 10^4, and so on. The following table is a summary of Base 10 information.

Items to Count	Result	Exponential Notation	Decimal Equivalent
	0	$0*10^0$	0=0
I	1	$1*10^0$	1=1
I I	2	$2*10^0$	2=2
I I I	3	$3*10^0$	3=3
I I I I	4	$4*10^0$	4=4
I I I I I	5	$5*10^0$	5=5
I I I I I I	6	$6*10^0$	6=6
I I I I I I I	7	$7*10^0$	7=7
I I I I I I I I	8	$8*10^0$	8=8
I I I I I I I I I	9	$9*10^0$	9=9
I I I I I I I I I I	10	$1*10^1+ 0*10^0$	10+0=10
I I I I I I I I I I + I	11	$1*10^1+ 1*10^0$	10+1=11
I I I I I I I I I I + I I	12	$1*10^1+ 2*10^0$	10+2=12
I I I I I I I I I I + I I I	13	$1*10^1+ 3*10^0$	10+3=13
I I I I I I I I I I + I I I I	14	$1*10^1+ 4*10^0$	10+4=14
I I I I I I I I I I + I I I I I	15	$1*10^1+ 5*10^0$	10+5=15
I I I I I I I I I I + I I I I I I	16	$1*10^1+ 6*10^0$	10+6=16
I I I I I I I I I I + I I I I I I I	17	$1*10^1+ 7*10^0$	10+7=17
I I I I I I I I I I + I I I I I I I I	18	$1*10^1+ 8*10^0$	10+8=18
I I I I I I I I I I + I I I I I I I I I	19	$1*10^1+ 9*10^0$	10+9=19
I I I I I I I I I I + I I I I I I I I I I	20	$2*10^1+ 0*10^0$	20+0=20
I I I I I I I I I I + I I I I I I I I I I + I	21	$2*10^1+ 1*10^0$	20+1=21

Lesson 1

Discovery Activity 1-4

Understanding the Decimal Number System

Scenario:
A user has asked you to convert exponential notation into decimal values.

1. The decimal value for the exponential notation $7*10^0$ is ___ .

2. The decimal value for the exponential notation $4*10^1+3*10^0$ is ___ .

3. The decimal value for the exponential notation $4*10^2+6*10^1+5*10^0$ is ___ .

4. The decimal value for the exponential notation $8*10^3+6*10^2+7*10^1+2*10^0$ is ___ .

The Binary Number System

Computers are electronic devices that use electrical patterns to represent numbers. Modern digital computers recognize only two electrical states—ON and OFF—but their memories contain millions of transistors that can be either on or off. Working with numbers in computers is like making numbers out of a row of lights that can be switched on and off independently. Because there are only two ways to represent a number, computers use the *binary number system* (Base 2). The same concepts that you know work for the decimal system also work for the binary system.

Imagine this: You are given the same jar of 237 marbles to count, but this time you have a series of measuring cups that can hold 256, 128, 64, 32, 16, 8, 4, and 2 marbles. The largest cup holds 256 marbles, so it is not filled. The next cup is filled and takes 128 marbles from the total, leaving 109 marbles. You can't fill the 128 cup a second time, so you move down the row to the cup that holds 64, which you fill, leaving 45. This will not fill the 64 cup again, but it will fill the 32 cup, leaving you 13 marbles. You don't have enough to fill the 32 or the 16 cup, so you fill the 8 cup, leaving you 5 marbles. You fill the 4 cup, cannot fill the 2 cup, and have 1 marble left over. Because there are so many cups, it is easiest to report your results in a table.

Number in Cup	$256\ (2^8)$	$128\ (2^7)$	$64\ (2^6)$	$32\ (2^5)$	$16\ (2^4)$	$8\ (2^3)$	$4\ (2^2)$	$2\ (2^1)$	$1\ (2^0)$
Times Filled	0	1	1	1	0	1	1	0	1

Remember, 2^0 equals 1. This is an important idea, so follow along. 256/32=8 is the same as $2^8 / 2^5 = 2^{8-5} = 2^3 = 8$. Along the same line, 128/128=1 is the same as $2^7 / 2^7 = 2^{7-7} = 2^0 = 1$. Any number raised to the power of 0 is 1.

Lesson 1

A report that you counted 1110 1101 (Base 2) marbles would make little sense to most humans, but would be crystal clear to a computer. A human would have to look at the table and figure you counted 1*128 + 1*64 + 1*32 + 1*8 + 1*4 + 1*1 marbles or 237 (Base 10) marbles. Using exponential notation, the same result would be: $1*2^7 + 1*2^6 + 1*2^5 + 1*2^3 + 1*2^2 + 1*2^0$ marbles or 237 (Base 10) marbles.

Items to Count	Result	Exponential Notation	Decimal Value
	0	$0*2^0$	$0*1=0$
I	1	$1*2^0$	$1*1=1$
I I	10	$1*2^1 + 0*2^0$	$1*2+0*1=2$
I I + I	11	$1*2^1 + 1*2^0$	$1*2+1*1=3$
I I I I	100	$1*2^2 + 0*2^1 + 0*2^0$	$1*4+0*2+0*1=4$
I I I I + I	101	$1*2^2 + 0*2^1 + 1*2^0$	$1*4+0*2+1*1=5$
I I I I + I I	110	$1*2^2 + 1*2^1 + 0*2^0$	$1*4+1*2+0*1=6$
I I I I + I I + I	111	$1*2^2 + 1*2^1 + 1*2^0$	$1*4+1*2+1*1=7$
I I I I I I I I	1000	$1*2^3 + 0*2^2 + 0*2^1 + 0*2^0$	$1*8+0*4+0*2+0*1=8$
I I I I I I I I + I	1001	$1*2^3 + 0*2^2 + 0*2^1 + 1*2^0$	$1*8+0*4+0*2+1*1=9$
I I I I I I I I + I I	1010	$1*2^3 + 0*2^2 + 1*2^1 + 0*2^0$	$1*8+0*4+1*2+0*1=10$
I I I I I I I I + I I + I	1011	$1*2^3 + 0*2^2 + 1*2^1 + 1*2^0$	$1*8+0*4+1*2+1*1=11$
I I I I I I I I + I I I I	1100	$1*2^3 + 1*2^2 + 0*2^1 + 0*2^0$	$1*8+1*4+0*2+0*1=12$
I I I I I I I I + I I I I + I	1101	$1*2^3 + 1*2^2 + 0*2^1 + 1*2^0$	$1*8+1*4+0*2+1*1=13$
I I I I I I I I + I I I I + I I	1110	$1*2^3 + 1*2^2 + 1*2^1 + 0*2^0$	$1*8+1*4+1*2+0*1=14$
I I I I I I I I + I I I I + I I + I	1111	$1*2^3 + 1*2^2 + 1*2^1 + 1*2^0$	$1*8+1*4+1*2+1*1=15$
I I I I I I I I I I I I I I I I	1 0000	$1*2^4 + 0*2^3 + 0*2^2 + 0*2^1 + 0*2^0$	$1*16+0*8+0*4+0*2+0*1=16$
I I I I I I I I I I I I I I I I + I	1 0001	$1*2^4 + 0*2^3 + 0*2^2 + 0*2^1 + 1*2^0$	$1*16+0*8+0*4+0*2+1*1=17$
I I I I I I I I I I I I I I I I + I I	1 0010	$1*2^4 + 0*2^3 + 0*2^2 + 1*2^1 + 0*2^0$	$1*16+0*8+0*4+1*2+0*1=18$
I I I I I I I I I I I I I I I I + I I + I	1 0011	$1*2^4 + 0*2^3 + 0*2^2 + 1*2^1 + 1*2^0$	$1*16+0*8+0*4+1*2+1*1=19$
I I I I I I I I I I I I I I I I + I I I I	1 0100	$1*2^4 + 0*2^3 + 1*2^2 + 0*2^1 + 0*2^0$	$1*16+0*8+1*4+0*2+0*1=20$
I I I I I I I I I I I I I I I I + I I I I + I	1 0101	$1*2^4 + 0*2^3 + 1*2^2 + 0*2^1 + 1*1^0$	$1*16+0*8+1*4+0*2+1*1=21$

The process of converting binary (Base 2) numbers you get from the computer into decimal (Base 10) numbers for yourself is much easier if you make a table. In the top right-most column, put in 2^0 or 1. In the second column from the right, place 2^1 or 2. In the third column, place 2^2 or 4, fourth column 2^3 or 8, and continue until you have a column for every digit in the binary number. Place the binary number in the second row. In the third row, if the binary digit in the column is 1, copy the decimal number (place value) above it into the third row. If the binary number is 0, leave that cell in the third row blank. Add up all the numbers in the third row, and you will have the decimal equivalent of the binary number. For example, to convert 1010 0010 (Base 2) to its decimal value (Base 10), look at the following table where 1010 0010 (Base 2) is equal to 128 + 32 + 2 = 162 (Base 10).

Lesson 1: Introduction to Computers

Place Value	128	64	32	16	8	4	2	1
Binary Number	1	0	1	0	0	0	1	0
Decimal Value	128		32				2	

Converting decimal to binary uses a similar table. In the top row, enter the place values for the binary number system—(1, 2, 4, 8, and so on) going from right to left until you reach a power of 2 that is bigger than the decimal number. In the second row, enter the decimal number in the left-most column. Working from left to right, try to subtract the place value for a column from the decimal number. If the result is positive, put a 1 in the third row of that column and place the remainder of the subtraction in the second row of the next column. If the result is negative, put a 0 in the third row of that column and copy the same number over into the second row of the next column. Keep subtracting binary place values from the decimal number until there is no remainder. For example, to convert 213 (Base 10) into a binary number (Base 2), look at the example in this table, where 213 (Base 10) is equal to 1101 0101 (Base 2).

Place Value	128	64	32	16	8	4	2	1
Decimal Number/ Decimal Remainder	213-128=85	85-64=21	21-32<1	21-16=5	5-8<1	5-4=1	1-2<1	1-1=0
Binary Number	1	1	0	1	0	1	0	1

To check your work, convert the binary number 1101 0101 back to decimal. The values you subtracted from the decimal number until you had nothing left should add up to equal the original decimal number.

Place Value	128	64	32	16	8	4	2	1
Binary Number	1	1	0	1	0	1	0	1
Decimal Value	128	64	0	16	0	4	0	1

The binary number 1101 0101 (Base 2) is equal to 128 + 64 + 16 + 4 + 1 = 213 (Base 10). Your answer checks. Notice that, to convert from binary to decimal, we are adding values, and to convert from decimal to binary, we subtract values. Other techniques for converting numbers work just as well, but this one is the most direct.

Discovery Activity 1-5

Understanding the Binary Number System

Scenario:

You've encountered some numbers that need to be converted from binary to decimal and from decimal to binary. Convert the numbers and provide the appropriate answers.

1. The decimal value of the binary number 1 is ___ .

2. The decimal value of the binary number 10 is ___ .

3. The decimal value of the binary number 101 is ___ .

4. The decimal value of the binary number 1101 is ___ .

5. The binary value of the decimal number 72 is _____ .

6. The binary value of the decimal number 283 is _____ .

7. The binary value of the decimal number 4,096 is _____ .

The Hexadecimal Number System

The *hexadecimal number system* is a compromise by the computer world for humans. Binary numbers tend to be very long and, with only 0s and 1s, tend to all look alike. Humans need a way to communicate with the computer in a number system related to the binary system, but easier to read and understand. The hexadecimal system (Base 16) is the solution.

Imagine this: You are given the same jar of 237 marbles to count, but this time you have a large pail that will hold exactly 256 marbles and a can that will hold exactly 16 marbles. You don't have enough marbles to fill the pail, but you can fill the can 14 times and have 13 marbles left in the bottom of the pail. Your report on the number of marbles might be zero pails, 14 cans, and 13 left over. This report will make little sense to people who do not know the number of marbles that can fit into the pail and can. A table can make things clearer.

Number in Container	256 (16^2)	16 (16^1)	1 (16^0)
Times Filled	0	14	13

Lesson 1

Lesson 1: Introduction to Computers

Lesson 1

Now the trouble starts. Reporting 1413 (Base 16) is too confusing. Did you fill the pail one time, the can 41 times, and have three left over? Computers do not like any doubt in the numbers they are given, so another way of writing hexadecimal values greater than 9 was agreed upon. The letter A (Base 16) is equal to 10 (Base 10), the letter B (Base 16) is equal to 11 (Base 10), C (Base 16) = 12 (Base 10), D (Base 16) = 13 (Base 10), E (Base 16) = 14 (Base 10), and F (Base 16) = 15 (Base 10). Using this notation, you could report you counted ED (Base 16) marbles.

Using exponential notation, the same result would be: $E*16^1 + D*16^0 = 14 * 16 + 13 = 224 + 13$ marbles or 237 (Base 10) marbles.

Items to Count	Result	Exponential Notation	Decimal Value
	0	$0*16^0$	0
I	1	$1*16^0$	1=1
I I	2	$2*16^0$	2=2
I I I	3	$3*16^0$	3=3
I I I I	4	$4*16^0$	4=4
I I I I I	5	$5*16^0$	5=5
I I I I I I	6	$6*16^0$	6=6
I I I I I I I	7	$7*16^0$	7=7
I I I I I I I I	8	$8*16^0$	8=8
I I I I I I I I I	9	$9*16^0$	9=9
I I I I I I I I I I	A	$A*16^0$	A=10
I I I I I I I I I I I	B	$B*16^0$	B=11
I I I I I I I I I I I I	C	$C*16^0$	C=12
I I I I I I I I I I I I I	D	$D*16^0$	D=13
I I I I I I I I I I I I I I	E	$E*16^0$	E=14
I I I I I I I I I I I I I I I	F	$F*16^0$	F=15
I I I I I I I I I I I I I I I I	10	$1*16^1 + 0*16^0$	16+0=16
I I I I I I I I I I I I I I I I + I	11	$1*16^1 + 1*16^0$	16+1=17
I I I I I I I I I I I I I I I I + I I	12	$1*16^1 + 2*16^0$	16+2=18
I I I I I I I I I I I I I I I I + I I I	13	$1*16^1 + 3*16^0$	16+3=19
I I I I I I I I I I I I I I I I + I I I I	14	$1*16^1 + 4*16^0$	16+4=20
I I I I I I I I I I I I I I I I + I I I I I	15	$1*16^1 + 5*16^0$	16+5=21

The process of converting hexadecimal (Base 16) numbers from the computer into decimal (Base 10) numbers for yourself is much easier if you make a table. In the top right-most column, put in 16^0 or 1. In the second column from the right, put 16^1 or 16. In the third column, place 16^2 or 256, fourth column 16^3 or 4,096, and continue until you have a column for every digit in the hexadecimal number. These numbers are the place values for the hexadecimal digits. Place the hexadecimal number in the second row. In the third row, multiply the hexadecimal digit in the second row times the place value of the column in the first row, and write the product in the third row. Add all the numbers in the third row, and you will have the decimal equivalent of the hexadecimal number. For example, to convert A4 B6 (Base 16) to its decimal value (Base 10), take a look at the following table. A4B6 (Base 16) is equal to 40,960 + 1,024 + 176 + 6 = 42,166 (Base 10).

Lesson 1

Place Value	4,096	256	16	1
Hexadecimal Number	A	4	B	6
Decimal Value	10*4,096=40,960	4*256=1,024	11*16=176	6*1=6

Converting decimal to hexadecimal uses a similar table. In the top row, enter the place values for the hexadecimal number system—(1, 16, 256, 4,096, and so on) going from right to left until you reach a power of 16 that is greater than the decimal number. In the second row, enter the decimal number in the left-most column. Working from left to right, try to divide the place value for a column into the decimal number. If the result is greater than 1, put the number of times the place value went into the decimal number in row three of that column, and place the remainder of the division into row two of the next column to the right. If the result is less than 1, put a 0 in row three of the column and copy the same number over into row two of the next column to the right. Keep dividing hexadecimal place values into the remaining decimal number until the remainder is less than 16. Place that remainder into the 1s column. For example, to convert 59,660 (Base 10) into a hexadecimal number (Base 16), look at the example in the following table where 59,660 (Base 10) is equal to E90C (Base 16).

Place Value	4,096	256	16	1
Decimal Number/Decimal Remainder	59,660/4,096=E (14) rem. 2,316	2,316/256=9 rem. 12	12/16<1	12/1=C (12)
Hexadecimal Number	E	9	0	C

To check your work, convert the hexadecimal number E90C back to decimal. This is shown in the following table.

Place Value	4,096	256	16	1
Hexadecimal Number	E	9	0	C
Decimal Value	14*4,096=57,344	9*256=2,304	0*16=0	12*1=12

The hexadecimal number E90C (Base 16) is equal to 57,344 + 2,304 + 0 + 12 = 59,660 (Base 10). Your answer checks. Notice that, to convert from hexadecimal to decimal, you are multiplying values, and to convert from decimal to hexadecimal, you divide values. Other techniques for converting numbers work just as well, but this one is the most direct. Hexadecimal values are often identified by a preceding dollar sign or the letter H (upper or lower case). For instance, $3E0, 3E0h, 3E0H, and 3E0 (Base 16) are all equivalent to the decimal number 992.

Lesson 1

Discovery Activity 1-6

Understanding the Hexadecimal Number System

Scenario:
You've come across more numbers that you need to convert, this time from decimal to hexadecimal. Convert the numbers and provide the appropriate answers.

1. The hexadecimal equivalent of the decimal number 8 is ___ .

2. The hexadecimal equivalent of the decimal number 57 is ___ .

3. The hexadecimal equivalent of the decimal number 166 is ___ .

4. The hexadecimal equivalent of the decimal number 3,416 is ___ .

Computer Values

Many of the values you see on your computer screen are based on numbers converted from the binary number system to decimal or hexadecimal numbers. For example, many addresses, such as memory and network addresses, are often represented in hexadecimal notation. You'll work more with these addresses later in the course. Those numbers may have seemed rather odd before, but with your new knowledge of number theory, you will be able to explain where the numbers came from.

Bits, Bytes, and Nibbles

A *bit* is a single binary digit. A bit may have a value of 0 or 1. In a computer, a switch or transistor that is off represents a 0, and a switch or transistor that is on represents a 1. Most computers work with groups of 8 bits, which is called a *byte*. To make it easier to read, the 8 binary digits in a byte are divided into two groups of four, called *nibbles*, when they are written.

Kilobytes, Megabytes, and Gigabytes

A kilobyte is often referred to as 1,000 bytes, but this is not totally accurate. In computer terms, a *kilobyte* is 1,024 bytes. K is used as shorthand for 2^{10}, which equals 1,024. A file listed as having a size of 67 KB may show a more accurate size of 66.5 KB in the Properties dialog box, or 68,096 bytes. The file hasn't changed size (66.5 KB = 66.5 * 1,024 bytes = 68,096 bytes).

Likewise, a *megabyte* is not exactly 1,000,000 bytes, but 1,024 KB, or 2^{20} bytes, or 1,048,576 bytes. A 200 MB drive can store 204,800 KB or 209,715,200 bytes.

Lesson 1

Following the trend, a *gigabyte* is not 1 billion bytes, but 1,024 MB, or 2^{30} bytes or 1,073,741,824 bytes. Several years ago, a drive manufacturer promoted its new drive as being a better value than other 3 gigabyte drives, because on their drive you had room to store 3 billion bytes, plus room for another 221,225,472 bytes thrown in for free. A quick check of the math shows the drive maker was misleading but numerically accurate. 3 GB is the same as 3,221,225,472 bytes, no matter what type of drive you're using!

Megs and Gigs

Often, you will find hard drives advertised with storage capacity measured in *megs* and *gigs*. These aren't abbreviations for megabytes and gigabytes. Instead, a meg is 1 million bytes and a gig is 1 billion bytes.

By rating a drive in this way, it can appear to have greater storage capacity than it actually has. For example, a 3.22 gig drive actually stores 3.0 gigabytes, or 3,221,225,472 bytes.

DISCOVERY ACTIVITY 1-7

Applying Number Skills

Scenario:

You've been asked to apply your number skills to answer the following questions.

1. You try to save a 1.4 MB file on a disk with 1,400 KB of free space, but the computer states you don't have enough room. What is going on?

2. The value of 4,095 (Base 10) in binary is _____ .

3. The value of 4,095 (Base 10) in hexadecimal is ____ .

4. How many different values can you store in a binary number that is 16 bits long? What is the maximum value you can store?

Lesson 1

Lesson 1 Follow-up

You have learned some basics about computers, including how they evolved and some of their common components. This background is important as you begin to work through this course. The knowledge in this lesson gives you the foundation you need to complete all the remaining lessons.

1. **What experience do you have with the mechanical calculating devices and early computers discussed in this lesson?**

2. **What is the most important component inside a computer?**

3. **Why is it important to know number systems other than decimal?**

LESSON 2
Tools of the Trade

Lesson Time
1 hour(s), 15 minutes

Lesson Objectives:

In this lesson, you will describe tools of the trade.

You will:

- List the tools used to repair hardware problems in personal computers.
- List the software tools used to troubleshoot and repair personal computer problems.
- Describe common troubleshooting methodologies.

Lesson 2

Introduction

As an A+ hardware technician, you'll be asked to install, configure, and correct problems with a variety of PC components. To work with each of these PC components without damaging it, you'll need the appropriate tools—hardware, software, and a plan to get the job done quickly and correctly.

Having the right tool will save you time, trouble, and expense, but you won't usually know what you need until you get to the site. A good collection of software and hardware tools (kept ready to use), as well as a consistent plan to follow to correct the problems you encounter, will make your life much easier. In this lesson, you'll learn what tools you should assemble in toolkits for specific types of jobs and the different troubleshooting methodologies you can follow to diagnose and correct problems.

The following CompTIA A+ Core Hardware (2003) Examination objectives are covered in this lesson:

- Topic A:
  — 3.2 Identify various safety measures and procedures, and when/how to use them. Content includes the following: ESD (Electrostatic Discharge) precautions and procedures—common ESD protection devices.
- Topic C:
  — 2.2 Identify basic troubleshooting procedures and tools, ask how to elicit problem symptoms from customers. Justify asking particular questions in a given scenario. Content includes the following: troubleshooting/isolation/problem determination procedures; determining whether a hardware or software problem; and gathering information from user.

Topic A

Hardware Tools

The hardware tools you need depend on the PC component you are working with. You can install a hard drive using just a screw driver. Installing a network, on the other hand, requires a set of specialized tools. Replacing a chip or broken contact on a circuit board requires yet a different set of tools. No matter what you need to repair, you must make sure you do not inflict damage to the computer during the process. You can ensure this by having the correct hardware tools ready to use. In this topic, you'll learn the hardware tools that are needed to perform specific types of tasks.

Basic Toolkit

Definition:

A technician's toolkit is a set of tools that the technician is likely to need to set up an Electro-static discharge (ESD) free work area, as well as to work on hardware. The tools in the kit should be demagnetized. The tools should be stored in some sort of case to protect and organize them.

All toolkits should include the following tools:

- Phillips screwdrivers (small and large, #0 and #1)

- Flat-blade screwdrivers (small and large, eighth inch and three-sixteenth inch)
- Torx driver (size T15)
- Tweezers
- Container for screws
- Nut driver
- Three-prong retriever

Some toolkits might also contain:
- Chip extractor
- Additional sizes of drivers and screwdrivers
- Ratchets
- Chip inserter
- Allen wrenches
- Cotton swabs
- Batteries
- Multimeter
- Anti-static cleaning wipes
- Canister of compressed air
- Anti-static wrist band
- Flashlight
- Mini vacuum
- Pen knife
- Clamp
- Soldering iron and related supplies
- Spare parts container
- Pen and/or pencil
- Notepaper or sticky notes

Example: A Basic Toolkit

Figure 2-1 shows typical tools in a toolkit.

Lesson 2

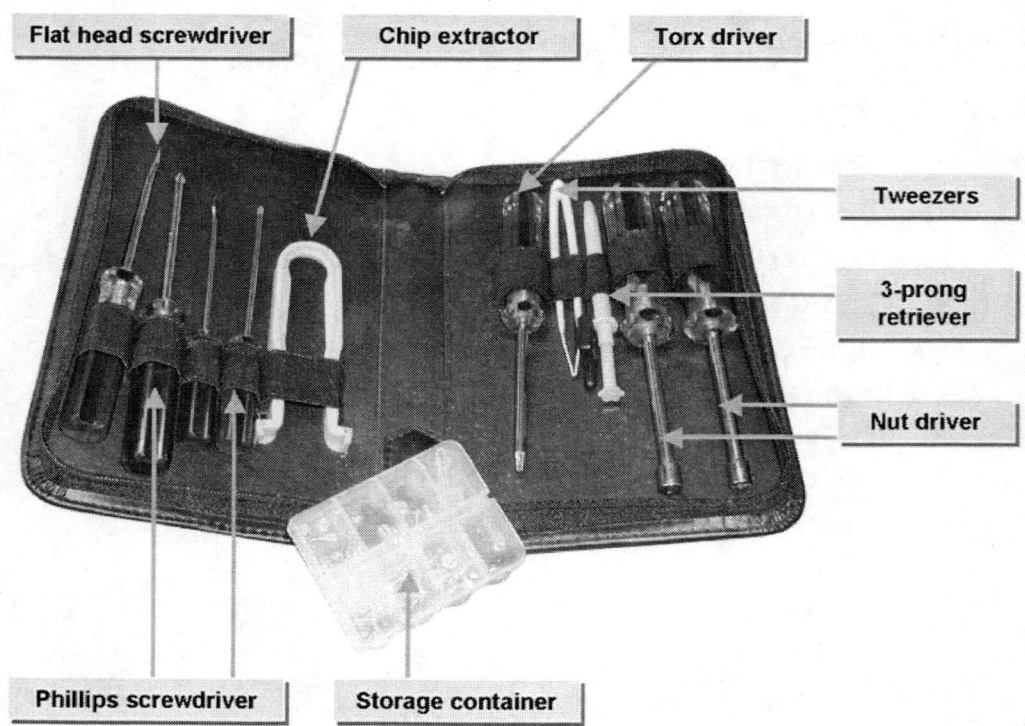

Figure 2-1: *A basic toolkit.*

ESD Toolkit

There are lots of people who work on computer equipment who never use a single piece of ESD safety equipment. They discharge themselves by touching an unpainted metal part of the computer case before touching any components.

In other instances, the company policy might require that you use a properly equipped ESD-free work area. The minimum equipment in this case would be a grounded wrist strap. Other ESD-protection equipment includes grounded mats to cover the work surface, grounded floor mats to stand on, and leg straps. The mats contain a snap that you connect to the wrist or leg strap. If the technician's clothing has the potential to produce static charges, an ESD smock, which covers from the waist up, should be worn. Examples of grounded wrist is shown in Figure 2-2.

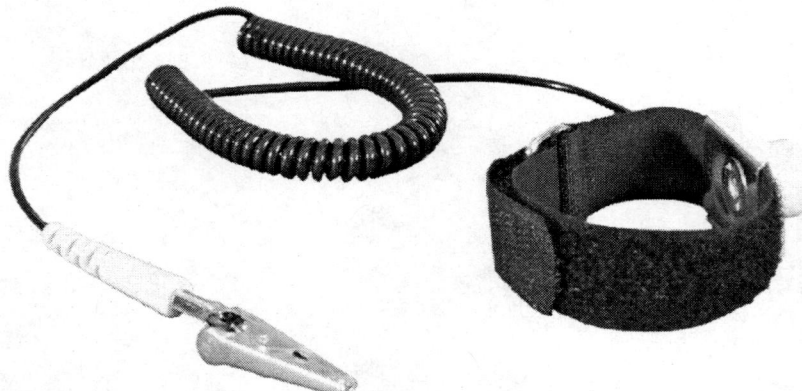

Figure 2-2: *Anti-static wrist strap.*

In addition to the physical ESD safety equipment, there are ways to limit the production of static electricity in the work environment. You might use an air ionizer, which releases negative ions into the air. They attract positively-charged particles and form neutrally-charged particles. If the air is extremely dry, more static is likely, so humidifying the air can help. A humidity rate of 50 to 60 percent is best.

To ensure that the ESD equipment remains effective, you should test it frequently. Even though you may not feel a minor shock, it might be strong enough to compromise the ESD safety equipment.

 The EIA produced a document that covers recommendations for safely handling ESD-sensitive equipment. It is EIA-625 Requirements for Handling Electrostatic Discharge Sensitive Devices. A Web search on EIA-625 using any search engine, should lead you to more information on these recommendations.

Network Toolkit

Specialized tools, in addition to those listed previously, are needed to make and install network cables. Kits containing these tools are available, but the prices vary widely depending on the quality of the tools. A network toolkit will typically include:

- Cable crimper with dies for a variety of cable styles
- Wire stripper for flat and coax cable
- Precision wire cutters
- Curved forceps
- Multi-network LAN cable tester
- Digital multimeter

Circuit Board Toolkit

Usually circuit boards are replaced, not repaired. Sometimes an obviously loose connection can be fixed or a jack with a broken pin can be replaced. Work in this area requires these tools:

- 30w ceramic solder iron
- Desoldering braid
- Desoldering pump
- Solder iron stand with sponge
- Solder
- Miniature pliers and wire cutters
- Heat sink

Before you spend hundreds of dollars on tools or elaborate toolkits, wait until you know the type of work you will be expected to do. Also, check with your employer; sometimes a company will supply some or all of the tools that you might need for servicing computers.

Lesson 2

Activity 2-1

Identifying the Hardware Tools Needed for Servicing PCs

Activity Time:

15 minutes

Scenario:

In each of the scenarios, decide which tools are most appropriate for the assigned task.

1. **You've been asked to repair a system board in a customer's PC. Which set of tools would be best suited for the task?**

    a) Phillips screwdriver (#0); torx driver (size T15); tweezers; and a three-prong retriever.

    b) 30w ceramic solder iron; miniature pliers; wire cutters; and a solder iron stand with sponge.

    c) Wire strippers; precision wire cutters; digital multimeter; and cable crimper with dies.

    d) Chip extractor; chip inserter; rachet; and allen wrench.

    e) Anti-static cleaning wipes; anti-static wrist band; flashlight; and cotton swabs.

2. **You've been asked to correct a network cabling problem at a customer site. Which set of tools would be best suited for the task?**

    a) Phillips screwdriver (#0); torx driver (size T15); tweezers; and a three-prong retriever.

    b) 30w ceramic solder iron; miniature pliers; wire cutters; and a solder iron stand with sponge.

    c) Wire strippers; precision wire cutters; digital multimeter; and cable crimper with dies.

    d) Chip extractor; chip inserter; rachet; and allen wrench.

    e) Anti-static cleaning wipes; anti-static wrist band; flashlight; and cotton swabs.

3. **You suspect that contaminants from the environment have prevented the fan on a PC from working optimally. Which set of tools would be best suited to fix the problem?**

    a) Phillips screwdriver (#0); torx driver (size T15); tweezers; and a three-prong retriever.

    b) 30w ceramic solder iron; miniature pliers; wire cutters; and a solder iron stand with sponge.

    c) Wire strippers; precision wire cutters; digital multimeter; and cable crimper with dies.

    d) Chip extractor; chip inserter; rachet; and allen wrench.

    e) Anti-static cleaning wipes; anti-static wrist band; flashlight; and cotton swabs.

4. Using an Internet search engine, **search the Internet for sources of computer repair tools and kits. Compare prices and quality of the tools you find.**

Topic B
Software Tools

Many companies produce software to diagnose, and, if possible, repair software problems and optimize settings. Most computer stores will have an aisle dedicated to utility software. In this topic, you will learn about different software tools that are available.

Software Utilities

Symantec's Norton SystemWorks and McAfee's Easy Recovery and Easy Recovery Pro include programs that can assist you in detecting, repairing, and preventing hardware and software problems. Other Norton and McAfee programs detect and remove viruses, detect and remove unnecessary programs and files, protect your computer against system crashes and screen freezes, and even back up or clone entire systems. The Windows operating systems come with their own set of diagnostic tools which may help you to detect problems.

Boot Disk

Definition:

A boot disk is a floppy disk that you can use to boot a computer when the operating system installed on the hard disk will not boot. A boot disk contains a minimal set of system files required to boot the computer to a base operating system such as MS-DOS or a Windows product. A boot disk allows you access to the base operating system to make repairs. A boot disk may be created using your operating system or your virus protection software. A boot disk must be created before there is a problem on the computer. A boot disk created by your virus protection software may contain additional files used to scan your computer for malicious code.

Example: Operating System Boot Disks

Operating System	Contains
MS-DOS	The system files: Io.sys, Msdos.sys, Command.com, Config.sys, and Autoexec.bat.
Windows 9x	The system files: Io.sys, Msdos.sys, Config.sys, Autoexec.bat, Win.ini, Win.com, and System.ini.
Windows NT, Windows 2000, or Windows XP	The system files: Boot.ini, Bootsect.dos (if it exists); Ntbootdd.sys (if it exists); Ntdetect.com, and Ntldr.

Lesson 2

Example: AntiVirus Software Boot Disks

Virus Protection Boot Disks	Contains
Norton Rescue Disk Set	The Norton AntiVirus Rescue Disk set contains backup copies of partition information, CMOS information, master boot record information, and system startup files needed to boot your computer into Windows 98. In addition, it contains a virus scanner and virus definition files. It might contain Norton Utilities if it is installed on your computer.
Norton Emergency Disk Set	In addition to containing the system files needed to boot your particular operating system (Windows XP, Windows 2000, Windows 98, or Windows NT), the Norton AntiVirus Emergency Disk set contains a scanning utility that scans your computer and removes viruses.
McAfee Emergency Disk Set	In addition to containing the system files needed to boot your particular operating system, the Norton Emergency Disk set includes BOOTSCAN.EXE, a specialized, small footprint command-line scanner that can scan your hard disk boot sectors and master boot record allowing you to boot into a virus-free environment to make repairs.

How to Create a Windows Startup Disk

Procedure Reference: Create an MS-DOS Boot Disk in Windows 98

You can create a floppy disk to boot a computer using the MS-DOS operating system. To create an MS-DOS boot disk in Windows 98:

1. Start Windows 98.
2. Open Windows Explorer.
3. Format the boot disk using the following steps:
   a. Insert a floppy disk into the floppy disk drive.
   b. In Windows Explorer, right-click 3 1/2 Floppy (A:) and choose Format.
   c. Below Other Options, select Copy System Files.
   d. Click Start.
   e. When the format is complete, click Close to close the Format Results dialog box.
   f. Click Close to close the Format 3 1/2 Floppy (A:) dialog box.
4. Configure Windows Explorer to display file extensions and hidden files for the C:\Windows\Command folder.
   a. Select the C:\Windows\Command folder.
   b. Choose View→Folder Options.
   c. Select the View tab.
   d. Below Hidden Files, select Show All Files.
   e. Uncheck Hide File Extensions For Known File Types.

f. Click OK.

5. If you want to use the boot disk to perform such tasks as creating or deleting partitions, correcting boot problems, changing file attributes, or formatting partitions, copy the following program files from C:\Windows\Command to the boot disk.
    - Attrib.exe
    - Edit.com
    - Edit.hlp
    - Fdisk.exe
    - Format.com
    - Scandisk.exe
    - Scandisk.ini
    - Sys.com

    To copy the files, complete the following steps:
    a. In Windows Explorer, select the C:\Windows\Command folder.
    b. Select the first file you want to copy.
    c. Hold down the Ctrl key and select all other files you want to copy.
    d. Right-click the selected files and choose Send To→3 1/2 Floppy (A).

6. Close Windows Explorer.
7. Test the boot disk to verify that it works.
    a. Restart the computer with the floppy disk in the disk drive to verify that you can boot successfully.
    b. If necessary, run the computer's System Setup utility to configure it to boot from floppy first.
    c. The computer boots successfully if you see an MS-DOS prompt displayed.
8. Remove the MS-DOS boot disk, label it, and store it in a safe location. You might also want to write-protect the disk.

Procedure Reference: Create an MS-DOS Boot Disk in Windows XP

To create an MS-DOS boot disk in Windows XP:

1. Start Windows XP.
2. Log on as a user.
3. Open Windows Explorer.
4. Format the boot disk using the following steps:
    a. Insert a floppy disk into the floppy disk drive.
    b. In Windows Explorer, right-click 3 1/2 Floppy (A:) and choose Format.
    c. Check Create An MS-DOS Startup Disk.
    d. Click Start.
    e. Click OK to confirm that you want to erase all data on the disk.
    f. When the format is complete, click OK.
    g. Click Close to close the Format 3 1/2 Floppy (A:) dialog box.

Lesson 2

5. Close Windows Explorer.
6. Test the boot disk to verify that it works.
    a. Restart the computer with the floppy disk in the disk drive to verify that you can boot successfully.
    b. If necessary, run the computer's System Setup utility to configure it to boot from floppy first.
    c. The computer boots successfully if you see an MS-DOS prompt displayed.
7. Remove the MS-DOS boot disk, label it, and store it in a safe location. You might also want to write-protect the disk.

Procedure Reference: Create a Windows 98 Startup Disk

You can create a startup disk in Windows 98 that enables you to boot the computer to DOS with support for the computer's CD-ROM. You might create such a disk if you want to reinstall Windows 98 on a computer, or if you want to perform diagnostic tests. To create a startup disk for Windows 98:

1. From the Start menu, choose Settings→Control Panel.
2. Double-click Add/Remove Programs.
3. Select the Startup Disk tab.
4. Click Create Disk.
5. When prompted, insert the Windows 98 installation CD-ROM and click OK.
6. Insert a floppy disk into the floppy disk drive.

    You do not have to format the floppy disk before creating the startup disk. Windows 98 automatically formats the disk for you.

7. Click OK.

    It will take several minutes for Windows 98 to create the startup disk.

8. Click OK to close the Add/Remove Programs Properties dialog box.
9. Close Control Panel.
10. Test the startup disk to verify that it works.
    a. Restart the computer with the floppy disk in the disk drive to verify that you can boot successfully.
    b. If necessary, run the computer's System Setup utility to configure it to boot from floppy first.
    c. From the Startup menu, choose from one of the following options:
        - Start Computer With CD-ROM Support.
        - Start Computer Without CD-ROM Support.
        - View The Help File.

        Alternatively, you can press the following key combinations:
        - F5 to start in Safe Mode.
        - Shift+F5 to start in Command Prompt mode.

LESSON 2

- Shift+F8 to start Windows 98 in Step-By-Step Confirmation Mode.

11. Remove the startup disk, label it, and store it in a safe location. You might also want to write-protect the disk.

Procedure Reference: Create a Boot Disk for Windows 2000/XP/NT

To create a boot disk for Windows 2000, Windows XP, and Windows NT:

1. Log on as a user with permissions to the system partition.
2. Open Windows Explorer.

   You must format the disk in the appropriate operating system for the disk to be bootable. Formatting the disk with Windows 2000, Windows XP, or Windows NT instead of DOS modifies the boot sector of the disk so that the system can find and run the Windows 2000, Windows XP, or Windows NT boot files.

3. Format the boot disk using the following steps:
   a. Insert a floppy disk into the floppy disk drive.
   b. In Windows Explorer, right-click 3 1/2 Floppy (A:) and choose Format.
   c. Optionally, check Quick Format to reduce the amount of time required to format the disk.
   d. Click Start.
   e. Click OK to confirm that you want to format the disk.
   f. When the format is complete, click OK.
   g. Click Close to close the Format A:\ dialog box.

4. If necessary, if you're using Windows 2000 or Windows XP, configure Windows Explorer to display system and hidden files on the C drive using the following steps:
   a. Select the C drive.
   b. In Windows Explorer, choose Tools→Folder Options.
   c. Select the View tab.
   d. Below Hidden Files And Folders, select Show Hidden Files And Folders.
   e. Uncheck Hide File Extensions For Known File Types.
   f. Uncheck Hide Protected Operating System Files (Recommended).
   g. Click OK.

   If necessary, if you're using Windows NT, configure Windows Explorer to display system and hidden files on the C drive using the following steps:
   a. Select the C drive.
   b. In Windows Explorer, choose View→Options.
   c. Below Hidden Files, choose Show All Files.
   d. Uncheck Hide File Extensions For Known File Types.
   e. Click OK.

5. Copy the following files to the boot disk:
   - Boot.ini.

Lesson 2: Tools of the Trade

- Bootsect.dos (if it exists). This file will be present only if you dual-boot the computer between Windows 9x and Windows 2000, Windows XP, or Windows NT.
- Ntbootdd.sys (if it exists). This file will be present only if the computer contains BIOS-disabled SCSI disk drives.
- Ntdetect.com.
- Ntldr.

The required files for Windows NT on a RISC-based system are:
- Osloader.exe.
- Hal.dll.
- *.pal for Alpha-based systems.

To copy the files, complete the following steps:

a. Select the boot.ini file.

b. Hold down the Ctrl key and select each additional file.

c. Right-click the selected files and choose Send To→3 1/2 Floppy (A:).

6. Close Windows Explorer.

7. Test the boot disk to verify that it works.

a. Restart the computer with the floppy disk in the disk drive to verify that you can boot successfully.

b. If necessary, run the computer's System Setup utility to configure it to boot from floppy first.

c. If the computer has multiple operating systems, verify that you can start each operating system from the boot disk.

8. Remove the boot disk, label it, and store it in a safe location. You might also want to write-protect the disk.

ACTIVITY 2-2

Creating and Testing a Boot Disk

Setup:

To complete this activity, you will need two blank floppy disks.

Your computer hardware is configured so that the computer can boot from a disk in the floppy-disk drive.

Scenario:

As an A+ technician, you want to be prepared for any emergency, such as computers that won't boot. Your company has standardized their workstations on Windows XP. To be prepared, you need boot disks that you can use to boot to MS-DOS or Windows XP.

What You Do	How You Do It
1. Create the MS-DOS boot disk.	a. Turn on the computer and boot to Windows XP.
	b. **Log on.**
	c. **Open Windows Explorer.**
	d. **Insert a floppy disk into the floppy disk drive.**
	e. In Windows Explorer, **right-click 3 1/2 Floppy (A:) and choose Format.**
	f. **Check Create An MS-DOS Startup Disk.**
	g. **Click Start.**
	h. **Click OK** to confirm that you want to erase all data on the disk.
	i. When the format is complete, **click OK.**
	j. **Click Close** to close the Format 3 1/2 Floppy (A:) dialog box.
	k. **Close Windows Explorer.**

Lesson 2: Tools of the Trade

Lesson 2

2. **Test the boot disk to verify that it works.**

   a. **Verify that you have the boot disk in the floppy drive.**

   b. **From the Start menu, choose Shutdown.**

   c. **Select Restart.**

   d. **Click OK.**

   When the computer restarts, you will see an MS-DOS prompt displayed if the boot disk you created works properly.

   e. **Remove the boot disk from the floppy drive.**

   f. **Label the floppy disk "MS-DOS boot disk."**

   g. **Restart the computer and boot to Windows XP.**

3. **Format a floppy disk for the Windows XP boot disk.**

   a. **Log on to Windows XP**

   b. **Open Windows Explorer.**

   c. **Insert a floppy disk into the floppy disk drive.**

   d. **Right-click 3 1/2 Floppy (A:) and choose Format.**

   e. **Check Quick Format to reduce the amount of time required to format the floppy disk.**

   f. **Click Start.**

   g. **Click OK to confirm that you want to format the disk.**

   h. **When the format is complete, click OK.**

   i. **Click Close to close the Format A:\ dialog box.**

LESSON 2

4. Copy the necessary files to the Windows XP boot disk.

   a. In Windows Explorer, **select the C drive.**

   b. **Choose Tools→Folder Options.**

   c. **Select the View tab.**

   d. Below Hidden Files And Folders, **select Show Hidden Files And Folders.**

   e. **Uncheck Hide File Extensions For Known File Types.**

   f. **Uncheck Hide Protected Operating System Files (Recommended).**

   g. **Click Yes** to confirm.

   h. **Click OK.**

   i. From C:\, **copy the following files to the boot disk:**
      - Boot.ini
      - Bootsect.dos (if it exists)
      - Ntbootdd.sys (if it exists)
      - Ntdetect.com
      - Ntldr

   j. **Close Windows Explorer.**

5. Test the Windows XP boot disk.

   a. **Restart the computer with the floppy disk in the disk drive** to verify that you can boot successfully.

      The computer should check the floppy drive first and use that disk, not the hard disk, to start up. The computer should boot successfully to Windows XP, using the boot information on the floppy disk.

   b. **Log onto Windows XP.**

   c. **Remove the boot disk from the floppy drive.**

   d. **Label the boot disk "Windows XP boot disk."**

Lesson 2

LAN Connectivity Disk

A LAN connectivity disk is a floppy disk that contains the network drivers and network client software needed to connect a computer to your network. The network drivers on the disk will correspond with the network adapter cards you have in the computers in your company. The network client software corresponds with the network operating system on the server you are trying to connect to. For example, if you want to connect to a file server running NetWare, you must have the NetWare client software loaded on the client. Many times a LAN connectivity disk will contain MS-DOS network drivers and software so that you can connect a computer that does not have an operating system loaded on it to the network in order to complete the OS install from a network storage location.

Topic C

Troubleshooting Methodologies

The most elaborate toolkit and expensive diagnostic software can be useless if you don't have a consistent plan of attack for solving problems. Even experienced technicians can sometimes overlook obvious problems or solutions. Troubleshooting is seldom easy, but if you develop or adopt a basic troubleshooting procedure, you will often be able to determine the specific cause of a problem, as well as possible solutions to the problem. Several troubleshooting models have been developed for servicing computers and computer networks.

There are three popular troubleshooting models that can be used to help diagnose and resolve computer problems. Following one of these models can be helpful because it gives you a basis for a systematic approach to troubleshooting. There is no sure-fire method that will work 100 percent of the time, since troubleshooting often requires you to make intuitive guesses based on experience, but using a model can help you identify causes and solutions in areas where you don't have the required type of experience. Ultimately, the troubleshooting process that you follow will be a mix of these models, plus methods that you find useful. If you get stuck on something you've never encountered before, ask your colleagues if they have seen similar problems.

Remember that a logical, methodical approach to troubleshooting usually leads to quicker solutions. Sufficient and proper documentation of setups, configurations, and histories can prove to be invaluable during the troubleshooting process. In this topic, you will review all three common methodologies.

CompTIA Network+ Troubleshooting Model

Procedure Reference: The CompTIA Network+ Troubleshooting Model

Although this troubleshooting model is designed primarily for network troubleshooting, its basic tenets can be used for troubleshooting PCs. It has eight steps. To troubleshoot a computer problem using the CompTIA Network+ troubleshooting model:

1. Identify the exact issue.

    Ask the user a series of open-ended questions to help identify the issue behind the symptoms. For instance, instead of asking if the user can start the computer, try asking what happens when the user tries to start the computer.

2. Re-create the problem.

   If possible, have the user try the procedure again, recording all actions taken and all results received. If you can, watch the user to ensure that he or she is following the correct procedures. If the problem occurs in the same place, the problem will be easier to solve than if it's an intermittent problem. You can also try to re-create the problem by:

   - Trying to perform the task yourself, at the user's computer and at a similarly configured computer.
   - Having another user try the task, at the user's computer and at a similarly configured computer.

3. Isolate the cause.

   After you reproduce the problem, try to determine what's causing it. Use a systematic approach to eliminate possible causes, starting with the most obvious cause and working back through other potential causes. You can also ask the user (and yourself) questions similar to the following, to help isolate the cause:

   - Could you do this task before? If not, maybe the system is simply unable to perform the task without additional hardware or software.
   - If you could do the task before, when did you first notice that you couldn't do it anymore? If the computer suddenly stops doing what it has always done seamlessly, that might not be the only change. Try to discover what happened immediately before the problem arose, since the source of the problem might be related to other changes.
   - What's changed since the last time you were able to do this task? Users might tell you that nothing has changed, so you should follow up with leading questions such as "Did someone add something to the computer?" or "Is the procedure you followed this time different in any way from the way you normally do this?"
   - Were error messages displayed? If you can get the exact text of any error messages displayed, you can try searching the manufacturer's Web site to get an explanation of the message and to see if any problem reports have been logged related to this message.
   - Is the problem always the same, no matter what conditions apply? Determining if the problem is consistent or intermittent can help you narrow down possible causes. For instance, if a user can't open a specific spreadsheet file stored on the hard drive, ask if he or she can open a different spreadsheet stored on the hard drive, or even stored on a network drive, if the computer is connected to a network. If the other files open without any trouble, it's fairly safe to assume that the problem lies with the file and not the application or the hard drive.

4. Formulate a correction.

   Depending on the cause you've isolated, determine at least one way to correct the problem. For instance, if you've isolated the cause as a corrupt spreadsheet file, one possible correction would be to restore the file from a backup. Draw on your own experiences, review support Web sites, and confer with your colleagues to come up with possible corrections, and prioritize them according to their likelihood of success and ease of implementation.

Lesson 2

5. Implement the correction.

   This step is where you actually fix the problem. Before you do so, however, you need to ensure that productivity doesn't suffer and that downtime is minimized. For example, you might need to provide a loaner machine to a user whose PC needs to be rebuilt.

6. Test the solution.

   Make sure that the solution you've implemented actually solved the problem and didn't cause any new ones. Use several options and situations to conduct your tests; for instance, try the task yourself, and then have the user try the task while you observe the process, or test the computer both before and after it's connected to a network, if applicable. Sometimes, you'll need to conduct the testing over a period of time to ensure that the solution you implemented is the right one. Remember to verify that the user agrees that the problem is solved before you proceed.

7. Document the problem and the solution.

   It's a good idea to create detailed descriptions of computer problems and their solutions, and maintain them as part of the overall documentation plan for your company's computers. Not only will this provide you with an ever-growing database of information specific to the computers you're responsible for, it also will be valuable reference material for use in future troubleshooting instances. You might even want to create a troubleshooting template form so that you can ensure that the necessary information is included on all trouble reports, and that all reports are consistent, no matter who completes them. Some of the things you might want to include in a troubleshooting template form include:

   - A general section, listing a description of the trouble call, the date and time the call was received, the person who reported the problem, and the person who has the problem (if the report was made by someone else).
   - A description of the conditions surrounding the problem, such as the type of computer, information about any expansion cards or peripherals connected to the computer, the operating system and version, the name and version of any applications mentioned in the problem report, and, if the computer is part of a network, the network operating system and version, as well as whether or not the user was logged on to the network when the problem occurred.
   - The exact issue you identified in step 1 of this troubleshooting process.
   - Whether or not you could consistently reproduce the problem.
   - The possible cause or causes you identified in step 3 of this troubleshooting process.
   - The correction or corrections you formulated in step 4 of this troubleshooting process.
   - The results of implementing each of the corrections you tried.
   - The results of testing each solution.
   - Any external resources you used, such as vendor documentation, addresses for vendor and other support Web sites, names and phone numbers for support personnel, and names and phone numbers for third-party service providers.

8. Provide feedback.

Don't underestimate the importance of this step. You should never consider a problem to be resolved until the **customer** considers it to be solved. You'll probably also need to inform others of the outcome of the situation, especially in cases where the person reporting the problem is not actually the person experiencing the problem. When you can, provide a brief explanation of the problem and how you fixed it, but make sure that you don't overwhelm the user with information, and never blame the user directly for the problem. Your explanation should always be geared to the knowledge and interest level of the person you're addressing. What you tell the user might differ substantially from what you tell another technician.

Novell Troubleshooting Model

Procedure Reference: The Novell Troubleshooting Model

Similar to the CompTIA Network+ troubleshooting model, this model was also designed primarily for network troubleshooting, although its basic tenets can also be used for troubleshooting PCs. It's has six steps. To troubleshoot computer problems using the Novell troubleshooting model:

1. Try some quick fixes.

   Before getting too deep into the troubleshooting mode, you should check some of the obvious causes of errors or problems. Obvious causes are frequently overlooked, causing you to waste time searching for more complicated reasons for the trouble.

2. Gather basic information.

   This step involves both gathering information before trouble happens, and gathering information about trouble that is occurring. Use the following guidelines to help you complete this step:
   - Determine the symptoms of the problem, what users are affected, and under what conditions the symptoms occur. Environmental issues such as dust, dirt, heat, and humidity should also be checked, as well as the presence of food or drinks near the PC.
   - If the computer is connected to a network, determine the amount of network traffic when the problem occurs to ensure that high traffic volume isn't the problem.
   - Compile baseline data for performance and operating conditions. Compare the current trouble with the baseline data to determine if discrepancies are present.
   - Find out if the computer worked previously, and determine what has changed since it last worked correctly.
   - Check user and usenet groups, as well as online forums, to see if others have encountered similar problems.

3. Develop a plan of attack to isolate the problem.

   In this step, you determine how you'll isolate and correct the problem. Use the following guidelines to help you complete this step:

- Use the basic information that you've gathered and your background knowledge to determine two or three possible causes for the problem. Possible causes might include user error, application error, operating system error, and hardware error.
- Prioritize the likely causes of the problem and your solutions to them. You can use the following factors to help you prioritize: relative ease of solution, time required to implement solution, likelihood of success, and cost of solution.
- Document your strategy for later reference. If your plan works this time, it might work later; if it didn't work, you might want to develop a different plan the next time you have a similar problem.

4. Execute the plan.

   This step begins the actual troubleshooting operation. The goal of this step is to find the cause of the trouble. Use the following guidelines to help you complete this step:

   - Analyze the first possible cause to determine the smallest testable steps.
   - Make one change at a time, and test the change to see if it solves the problem. If the change doesn't solve the problem, undo it. Document all changes as you proceed so that you have a record of what you have tried, in case you need to backtrack.
   - By the end of this step, you should have solved the problem. If the problem still persists, your starting assumptions might have been incorrect. Repeat this step by considering another possible cause of the problem.

5. Verify user satisfaction.

   Remember, you should never consider a problem to be solved until the user considers the problem to be solved. When necessary, train users on how components, peripherals, or software should work. Also, you might need to wait until the solution has been in place for a while before you can consider the problem to be solved.

6. Document the problem and the solution.

   Documentation is the key to solving future problems, getting equipment upgrades, and preventing financial losses from computer troubles. Use the following guidelines to help you complete this step:

   - Record the exact nature of the problem in a log book, along with the solution and the method you followed to reach the solution.
   - Make plans or changes that will prevent future occurrences of this or similar problems. For example, if the failure was due to a faulty network card of a type that you know has been installed in many other computers, you might want to plan to replace the other cards before they fail.
   - Regularly scan the computer for viruses by using up-to-date virus scanning software.
   - Implement a plan to regularly test the system, even when no problems are apparent. Document the tests and the circumstances surrounding them. There are many diagnostic utilities available for you to choose from—use them for preventative maintenance, as well as for problem-solving.

LESSON 2

Collect, Isolate, and Correct Model

Procedure Reference: The Collect, Isolate, and Correct Troubleshooting Model

Another popular troubleshooting model is the Collect, Isolate, and Correct method. This model divides troubleshooting into three large stages, with several steps incorporated into each stage. Ultimately, it achieves the same goal as the other methods, which is to solve computer-related problems. To troubleshoot a computer problem using the Collect, Isolate, and Correct troubleshooting model:

1. Collect.

   In this stage, you gather information, gather user reports, document the process, and keep track of known problems. The key to this stage is to gather a sufficient amount of high-quality information, rather than simply a large amount of information. The experience you gain from troubleshooting your systems will help you determine what data you need to maintain. Steps involved in this stage might include:

   Some of the steps in the Collect stage are done long before trouble is reported. Being prepared is the best way to solve problems quickly and easily when they do arise.

   - Document the troubleshooting process.
   - Gather user reports of the trouble.
   - Gather error messages and view relevant error logs.
   - Make sure that the user is following the proper procedures. You might want to check the order that the user performs certain steps, like loading software, logging on to the computer or network, if any, and so forth.
   - Perform software diagnostics. In some situations, you can do this remotely, before you arrive at the trouble site.
   - Gather the necessary test equipment and tools to take to the trouble site.
   - Gather working replacement parts. Test these parts to ensure that they work. Have them available to use when problems arise.
   - Track known problems and bugs by consulting with other technicians and online resources, and by reading periodicals and trade magazines.
   - Maintain an accurate log of the configurations of all computer equipment.

2. Isolate.

   This stage relies on the proper completion of the Collect stage. The Isolate stage is a balancing act between a methodical series of steps and a best-guess attempt at solving problems. In some cases, an intuitive reaction will lead you quickly to the source of the trouble. In other cases, you'll need to methodically proceed with the troubleshooting process to discover the root of the problem. Steps involved in this stage might include:

   The Isolate stage is often completed nearly simultaneously with the Correct stage.

   - Plan your attack on the trouble, and document your chosen method. Follow the plan you documented.
   - Follow a hierarchical troubleshooting process. Start with the big picture. Check to see how many users are affected with the same problem. If more

than one user is experiencing the problem, start with any items that all of the affected users have in common. Don't waste time checking individual PCs if many users are affected—the trouble probably isn't with the PCs themselves.

- Start with the easiest problem first. Check to see if the power cord is plugged in before you check to see if the internal power supply is burned out. Check for obvious and logical problems before looking for strange or unlikely problems.

- Follow a sequential method to troubleshoot. Complete one testing or isolating procedure before beginning another.

- Document the steps you take to isolate the problem. Keep track of any changes you need or want to make before you implement them.

- Ask isolating questions to narrow the range of possibilities for the cause of the problem.

- Verify that proper versions of software and hardware are being used. Keep a detailed record of versions, upgrades, and known problems. You can then refer to these records as you troubleshoot.

- Swap parts as necessary to determine the cause of the problem. This will help you find faulty hardware components quickly and easily. However, swapping parts won't necessarily help you find problems arising from the interaction between two or more parts that you are swapping.

- Challenge your own assumptions. Better yet, don't make any assumptions when you're troubleshooting. If you find yourself saying, "Well, *that* can't be the problem," you might need to challenge your assumption and try changing that anyway. This is especially true when you seem to have exhausted all other possibilities.

3. Correct.

This stage involves the steps that actually fix the problem, as well as preventative measures. The prioritized list you created in the Isolate stage can help you set a plan for solving the trouble. Follow your plan. Proceed down your list of potential causes, step by step, from top to bottom. Document your progress, and don't skip any steps. Steps involved in this stage might include:

- Document any attempts you make to solve the problem. Note the conditions before and after you've implemented your correction.

- Take one step at a time. Make just one change, and then test to see if the problem has been solved. If so, you've found the problem. Document your solution and take the necessary steps to complete the trouble call. However, if your step didn't fix the problem, undo your changes. Make a change only if you can undo it.

- Test your final solution for full functionality. Ask the user to test the solution, too. The user's perception of fully functional might not match yours. It's better to discover further problems immediately than to get another trouble call.

- Take any steps you can to prevent future troubles. For example, if you noted a potentially faulty network connector or cable, even if that didn't cause the trouble you're there to solve, you would be wise to fix it while you're there at the user's workspace. This will save you the time of returning later to fix a problem that you already knew about.

- Check to see if others are having similar problems. For instance, if the solution was to update a device driver on the user's PC, see if other users also need to have updated drivers installed. Your log will help facilitate this step.
- Document the problem and its solution. This will help you in troubleshooting similar problems in the future.
- Develop standards for preventing problems. For instance, devise a standard naming scheme for networked computers so that when new machines are added to the network, duplicate names aren't accidentally used.

Example:

A user calls the help desk to report that her monitor isn't working. In the collect phase, the help desk technician asks the user questions to gather information about the problem and learns that the user just moved to a new office. In the isolate phase, the technician uses that information to identify the most likely causes for the problem. In this case, because of the recent office move, it's likely that the monitor was disconnected and reconnected. In the correct phase, the technician fixes the problem by asking the user to make sure the monitor power cord is plugged in and that the data cable is firmly seated.

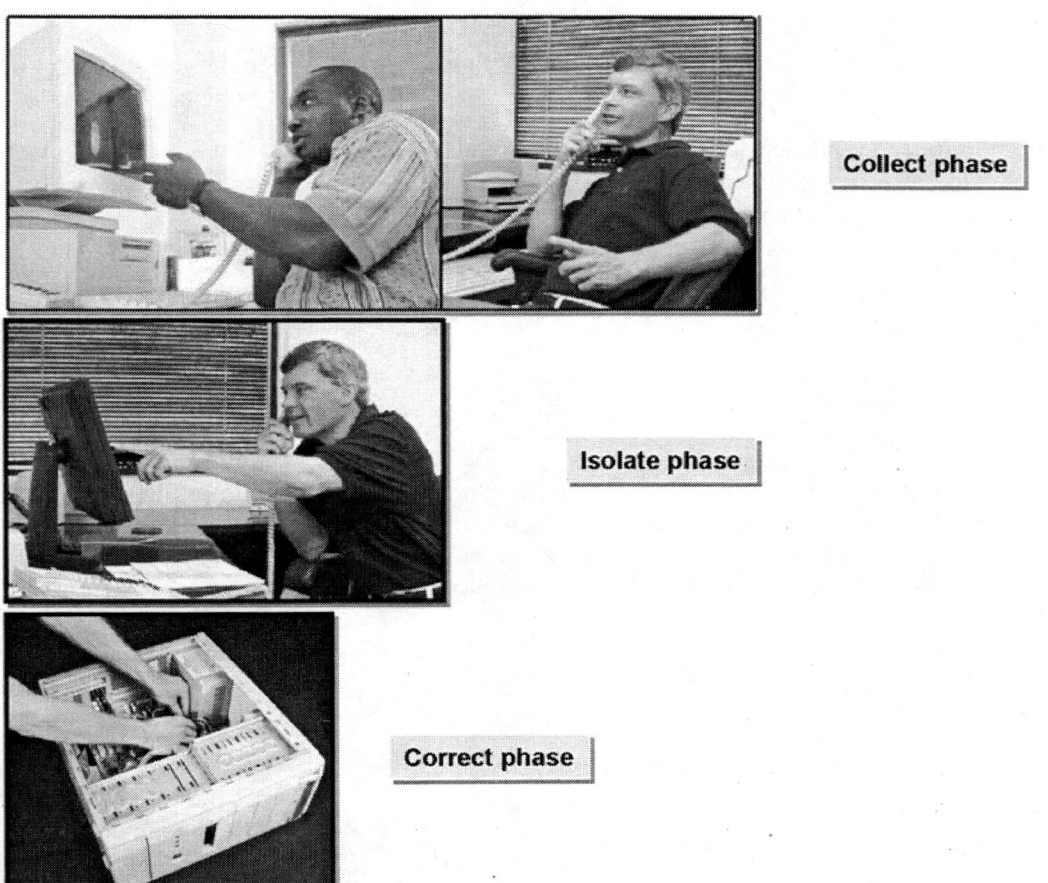

Figure 2-3: *The Collect, Isolate, and Correct troubleshooting process.*

Lesson 2

Troubleshooting Tips

Whenever you are attempting to resolve a problem, you need to keep some general points in mind. The first is to use your common sense. Some solutions are very obvious if you examine the equipment. For example, a cable might be loose or disconnected. Be sure to look for these obvious problems before delving too deeply into troubleshooting mode.

These are the basic troubleshooting steps you will want to take almost every time you face a device problem:

- Check the physical connections. This might involve making sure the device is plugged in and connected to the computer, that it is connected to the right port, that an adapter card is fully seated in the slot, and so forth.

- Check the adapter to which the device is connected. If you are having trouble with a device, it might not be a fault in the device. It might be a problem with the adapter or the adapter card to which it is connected. Be sure to troubleshoot the entire interface including the card, port, cable, and device.

- Check Device Manager. An exclamation point (!) or X in red or yellow over a device indicates there is a problem. The Properties sheet of devices has a Device Status box that indicates whether the device is working properly. This box also contains a Troubleshoot button which accesses topics in the Help And Support Center.

- Use the Help And Support Center utility to have Windows guide you through the things you should check when troubleshooting a particular device problem.

In the procedure references and activities throughout this course, you'll find many of the possible solutions to a given problem. You might not need to perform all of the steps listed in order to resolve the problem.

On the other hand, in some cases, there might be additional causes and solutions that are not listed. You might find these when you access a vendor's Web site. These are often specific to a particular make and model of a device.

Many times when you are troubleshooting a problem, you will find that there is more than one cause for the problem. In this case, you might need to combine several troubleshooting strategies to resolve the problem.

Often you will need to reboot to test whether your attempt to fix the problem has actually worked. If it did, great! If it didn't, just keep trying to work your way through the rest of the list of possible solutions. If none of the solutions work for your problem, ask a colleague for help. Sometimes that second set of eyes sees the solution that you don't.

ACTIVITY 2-3

Discussing Basic Troubleshooting Procedures

Activity Time:

10 minutes

Scenario:

In this activity, you will discuss the three common troubleshooting methodologies.

1. What do the troubleshooting models discussed in this section have in common?

2. When troubleshooting a device problem on a Windows-based computer, what common troubleshooting tips are helpful to try first?

3. When you receive notice that a user is having trouble with their computer, which is the best first step?

    a) Determine how many users are having similar troubles.

    b) Isolate the cause of the problem.

    c) Ask the user leading questions to gather information.

    d) Check for simple solutions.

4. According to the three troubleshooting methodologies, when is a problem considered solved?

    a) When the device is working correctly.

    b) When the problem has been documented.

    c) When the user is satisfied that the problem is solved.

    d) When standards are developed to prevent future occurrences of the problem.

LESSON 2

Lesson 2 Follow-up

In this lesson, you learned what tools you should assemble in toolkits for specific types of jobs and the different troubleshooting methodologies you can follow to diagnose and correct problems. As you will see in this course, as an A+ hardware technician, you'll be asked to install, configure, and correct problems with a variety of PC components. Having a good collection of software and hardware tools (kept ready to use), and a consistent troubleshooting methodology that you follow, will make your life much easier.

1. **What tools do you have assembled and available to you for PC repairs?**

2. **When troubleshooting PC problems, which troubleshooting methodology seems to fit the best with your personal style?**

LESSON 3
Safety

Lesson Time
1 hour(s), 45 minutes

Lesson Objectives:

In this lesson, you will maintain safe and healthy work habits while servicing computers.

You will:

- Define the basic terms used to describe electricity and electronics.
- Establish an ESD-free workspace.
- Observe general safety precautions when servicing PCs.
- Identify the potential hazards involved with using a PC.
- Describe safety equipment and practices to prevent fire when working with PCs.

Lesson 3

Introduction

You have examined the basics of computers and the tools you will use to service them. Before cracking open the case or connecting a single peripheral, you should examine the basic safety precautions that you should follow to keep yourself safe while servicing computers.

Computers depend on electricity to function, but this same electricity can pose a threat to your safety, as well as cause damage to the components in the computer. Learning to handle electricity safely will make your computer work less stressful and more productive.

The following CompTIA A+ Core Hardware (2003) Examination objectives are covered in this lesson:

- Topic A:
    - 3.2 Identify various safety measures and procedures, and when/how to use them. Content includes the following: ESD (Electrostatic Discharge) precautions and procedures; situations that could present a danger or hazard; and potential hazards and proper safety procedures relating to high-voltage equipment.
- Topic B:
    - 3.2 Identify various safety measures and procedures, and when/how to use them. Content includes the following: ESD (Electrostatic Discharge) precautions and procedures; what ESD can do, how it may be apparent, or hidden.

TOPIC A

Basics of Electricity and Electronics

There are a number of different basic electrical terms that you might encounter as an A+ computer technician. Most of these terms have to do with measuring different aspects of electrical charge and flow. Knowing these terms will help you troubleshoot systems and components.

Electricity

Electrons are negatively charged subatomic particles that carry energy with them when they move from one place to another, so the flow of electricity is really the movement of energy. Computer systems use electric energy to turn the cooling fan on and control the microprocessors, memory chips, disk drives, LED lights, video monitors, printers, speakers, and just about everything else. Computer hardware is designed to distribute the correct electricity to exactly the right place at the right time. You must understand electricity to understand how computers work and why they sometimes fail.

Voltage

Voltage, or *potential difference*, is a measurement of the difference in electrical potential energy between two different objects. Voltage describes how many electrons could potentially move from one of the objects to the other, given a circuit over which the electrons can flow, and sufficient time. Voltage is like pressure pushing the electrons along. Voltage is one of the electrical values that is often measured directly. The unit of measure is the volt (V).

Lesson 3

Computers work with voltages in the range of 12 volts (V) and lower. This voltage level is usually harmless for humans. Household electricity is 120 volts, which is enough to kill humans and completely destroy computers. The power supply in the computer acts as a transformer to convert the 120 volts from the electric outlet down to 12 volts or less for the computer. It also acts as a voltage regulator, breaking the voltage down to one of several different standard levels. A standard computer power supply puts out several voltages in this range, including, +12 volts, -12 volts, +5 volts, -5 volts, and zero volts. A negative voltage means the power supply is pushing electrons out, while a positive voltage means the supply is drawing electrons in. Zero volts is referred to as neutral, or ground, and is used as a basis for measuring the other voltages.

Voltage is usually determined by the power supply and is not something under your control. You can detect if a wire is connected to a +12 V or -5 V source, but you cannot easily bring the five volts down to three volts.

Current

Current is a measurement of how many electrons are passing a given point in a circuit over a given period of time. It describes the rate of transfer of electrons. In other words, if voltage measures the pressure or force pushing the electrons, then current measures how fast the electrons go.

The standard unit of measure of current is the ampere, or *amp*, (A), which is the number of electrons transferred per second. The electronics in a computer usually have electric current in the milli-ampere (one one-thousandth of an ampere) or micro-ampere (one one-millionth of an ampere) range. A bright light bulb has a current of one ampere, and an electric room heater might have a current of 10 amperes.

There are two major types of electric current.

- The current used by computers is *direct current (DC)*, which is electrical current that flows in only one direction and at a constant voltage. For example, the voltage output from a power supply remains constant at -12 V, so electrons always flow away from the output, never toward it.

- The current in a wall outlet is *alternating current (AC)*. The voltage in the wall outlet varies from +120 V to -120 V and back to +120 V sixty times a second. Electrons zoom back and forth through the wires, changing direction 120 times a second.

The power supply in a computer not only reduces the voltage of the electricity it receives from the wall outlet, but also switches it from alternating current to direct current.

Electrical Power and Electrical Energy

Electrical power is the energy delivered by a flow of electrons in one second and is defined as voltage times current. Power is measured in *watts* (W). A light bulb connected to a 120 V power source that has 0.5 amps flowing through it uses 60 watts of power. An LED connected to a 2 V source with a current of 10 milli-amperes uses 20 milli-watts of power. A power supply rated at 500 W can deliver twice the electrical power as a 250 W power supply.

The term *electrical energy* is used to describe the total amount of electrical power delivered over any given time period. A high voltage with a high current supplies a great deal of energy. A low voltage with a low current delivers a small amount of energy. The total energy delivered can be spread over a long or short period of time.

Lesson 3: Safety

LESSON 3

Resistance

Resistance is the opposition to the flow of electric current through a material. Insulators like rubber and plastic have a very high resistance. Conductors like copper and silver have very low resistance. Resistance is measured in ohms. Electricians use the Greek letter omega (Ω) as a symbol for *ohms*, the unit of measurement of resistance.

Ohms are named for the German physicist Georg Simon Ohm, who formulated what is now known as Ohm's Law to show the relations between voltage, current, and resistance. Ohm's law states that you can compute resistance (R) in a circuit by dividing the voltage (V) by the current in amperes (I). With Ohm's law, if you know any two of the values, you can calculate the other. Therefore, Ohm's law may be written as an equation in three equivalent ways:

- $R = V/I$
- $V = I*R$
- $I = V/R$

If resistance remains the same in a material, higher voltages will produce higher currents and the power will go up. If the resistance remains the same, lower voltages will produce a lower current and the power goes down.

If the voltage source remains constant, which is the case in most computer circuits, higher resistances decrease current and lower resistances increase current. A volume control on a radio is a variable resistor that decreases in resistance as you turn the volume up so more current carrying more energy can get to the speaker and make more noise. A switch is a variable resistor that has zero resistance in the ON position and infinite resistance in the OFF position.

A transistor can be used as an electronic switch because it can change from acting as a conductor to acting as an insulator. Because of this, it is called a *semiconductor*.

Measuring Electricity

A *multimeter* is an electronic instrument used to measure voltage, current, and resistance. It usually has two wires, one red and one black, that are plugged into two sockets on the meter. Which socket you use will be determined by what you want to measure. Digital meters, as shown in Figure 3-1, have a screen that displays the numeric value of what you are measuring. Analog meters, as shown in Figure 3-2, have a thin needle that swings in an arc and points to a number that indicates the value of what you are measuring.

Lesson 3

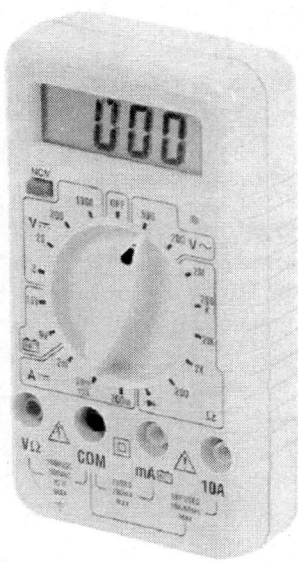

Figure 3-1: *A digital multimeter.*

Figure 3-2: *An analog multimeter.*

Measuring Voltage

Voltage measurement indicates the difference in electrical energy between two sources. Normally, you measure between an electrical source and a *ground*. A ground connection typically creates a circuit with the earth itself. The earth is so massive that, for all practical purposes, it can absorb and neutralize any electrical charge. Electrons on a grounded material have zero voltage because there are no forces trying to push them off or pull them onto the grounded item. The black wire from the multimeter is usually connected to a ground. In a computer, the metal case is an electric ground. A water pipe, or the screw on an electrical outlet cover are also commonly used as ground connections in other situations.

Lesson 3

Before you touch the red probe to the electrical source you want to measure, you need to adjust the meter to the approximate voltage you expect to find. This may be done by turning a large, rotary switch, or by plugging the red probe into a special socket on the meter. If the meter is expecting to measure 2 V, and you touch a 120 V source, the extra voltage can damage the components in the meter. It is better to overestimate the voltage and reduce the settings later, than to underestimate the voltage and destroy the meter. Higher-end digital meters automatically detect the range for you.

If you are measuring direct current voltages, the black wire goes to the source of the electrons in the current, and the red wire goes to the destination for the electrons. If a wire has a +5 V applied to it, you would touch the red probe to the wire, and the black probe to ground (which has 0 V) because a positive voltage means the wire is drawing in electrons from the ground. If a wire has -5 V applied to it, you would touch the black probe to the wire because it is the source of the electrons, and the red wire to the ground because the ground is absorbing the electrons. Some digital multimeters automatically make this adjustment for you.

Measuring Resistance

A multimeter measures resistance by applying a small voltage to a material and seeing how much current flows through the material. A material with high resistance will let very little current flow, while a material with low resistance will let more current flow. The voltage the meter applies is small, but even a small voltage can damage electronic chips. So, you can measure the resistances of cables and wires and connections, but you should not measure the resistances between pins on a chip. If you try to measure the resistance of a component in a live circuit, the voltage in the circuit may be enough to damage the multimeter.

A good conductor will have close to 0 Ω resistance, while a wire with a break in it will have more than 100,000 Ω resistance. Resistance is measured most often to determine if the ends of a cable are making a good connection through the wire, and if a switch is really turning on and off.

Insulators and Conductors

Some materials hold their electrons tightly to the nucleus of the atom. These materials make good *insulators*. Rubber is an example of an insulator. In other materials, the electrons can move very freely. These materials make good *conductors*. Metals are effective conductors. The metals used in computers are used precisely because they are good conductors.

Measuring Current

To measure an electrical current, you have to break the circuit and place a multimeter between the two ends of the break. This step is usually destructive and does not produce useful results, so, in most instances, you probably won't need to measure current.

What to Measure

The most common things to measure during troubleshooting include the output voltage of the power supply. If the computer is not receiving the correct voltages from the power supply, the components will not work correctly. Another place where voltage measurements are important is at the connectors that plug into disk and CD-ROM drives. These drives need the proper voltage to function. Resistance measurements tell if a wire has a break in it, or if a connection between a socket and the system board is good. Many network problems are the result of poorly installed plugs on the ends of network cables, and resistance measurements determine if plugs are properly installed.

You might also measure the wiring of the wall outlet. You would do so to determine if the wires are connected to the outlet correctly and that proper voltage is present.

Figure 3-3: *Wall outlet wiring*

As shown in Figure 3-3, the black wire (load) that connects to the short slit is hot (120 VAC). The white wire (neutral) that connects to the long slit and the bare copper wire (ground) that connects to the round contact go back and join to a common ground in the circuit breaker box. If the outlet is wired properly, the cover screw is in direct electrical contact with the bare copper (ground) wire.

Electrical Terms Summary

Table 3-1 summarizes the terms used to describe electricity and the flow of electricity.

Table 3-1: *Summary of Electrical Terms*

Term	Symbol	Unit	Measures
Voltage	V	Volt	Push behind electrons; indicates the energy of electrons.
Current	A	Ampere (Amp)	The number of electrons per second flowing past a point.
Resistance	Ω	Ohm	Opposition to the flow of electrons.
Electrical power	W	Watt	Energy per second delivered by electric current.

Lesson 3

ACTIVITY 3-1

Measuring Electricity

Scenario:
You have been called to a customer's site to troubleshoot a faulty computer. You suspect that faulty site wiring is the cause.

Lesson 3

What You Do	How You Do It
1. Measure the ground connections in the wall outlet.	a. If necessary, **set the meter to read alternating current voltage (VAC) with a maximum reading above 120 V.**
	b. Being very careful to touch only the insulated handles on the probes, **insert the black probe into the round center contact in the outlet.**
	c. Being very careful to touch only the insulated handles on the probes, **touch the red probe to the cover plate screw on the outlet.**
	d. **Read the meter.** If the reading is not 0, stop and consult your instructor. The outlet is wired incorrectly and could be dangerous to work with further.
	e. **Remove the probes from the outlet.**
	f. **Set the meter to read resistance and set it to zero ohms on the most sensitive scale.**
	g. While holding the insulated handles on the probes, **touch the probes and read the meter.**
	h. If the meter does not read 0 when the probes are in contact with each other, **adjust it so that it reads zero.**
	i. Being very careful to touch only the insulated handles on the probes, **connect the probes to the outlet again: black into the round center contact and red to the cover plate screw.**
	j. **Read the meter.** If the reading is not 0, stop and consult your instructor. The outlet is wired incorrectly and could be dangerous to work with further.

Lesson 3: Safety

Lesson 3

2. **Measure the voltage in the wall outlet.**

    a. If necessary, **set the meter to read alternating current voltage (VAC) with a maximum reading above 120 V.**

    b. Being **very** careful to touch only the insulated handles on the probes, **insert the black probe into the neutral (long) slit of the outlet.**

    c. Being **very** careful to touch only the insulated handles on the probes, **insert the red probe into the hot (short) slit of the outlet.**

    d. **Read the meter.** The expected results is 120 VAC, but local conditions may cause variations.

    e. **Remove the probes from the outlet.**

3. **Measure the resistance of your body.**

    a. **Set the meter to read resistance and set it to zero ohms on the most sensitive scale.**

    b. While holding the insulated handles on the probes, **touch the probes and read the meter.**

    c. If the meter does not read 0 when the probes are in contact with each other, **adjust it so that it reads 0.**

    d. **Moisten your fingers to ensure good contact between you and the probes.**

    e. **Grasp the contact ends of the probes between your forefinger and thumb so that one hand holds the black probe and the other holds the red probe.**

    f. **Read the meter.** The actual meter reading will vary, but you should see a measurable resistance (neither zero nor infinity). The human body is a fairly good conductor of electricity.

Topic B

Establish an ESD-free Work Area

When you work with any electrical system, including the interior of a personal computer, you need to be safety conscious. This is not only so that you avoid damaging delicate system components through electrostatic discharge (ESD), but, more importantly to keep you safe from the dangers of electricity. By establishing an ESD-free work area, you can help prevent electrical damage, and protect yourself as well. You need to make sure your work area is safe for the components and for you. In this topic, you will establish an electrostatic discharge free work area.

To control damage done by an electrostatic discharge (ESD), you need to know what static electricity is, how it is created, how it causes damage, and how to eliminate it from the workplace. Lightening is the most visible form of ESD, but static events on a smaller scale occur constantly. These include static cling in your clothes, dust build-up on TV screens, Styrofoam packing peanuts that stick to objects, and shocks when you touch a doorknob or brush a pet.

Static Electricity

Static electricity is a build up of a stationary electrical charge on an object. It is called static because the charge cannot escape, but remains still. As soon as a circuit is created that permits the electrons to discharge, the static electricity is released with a spark. The spark can be as small as the ones that come off a dry blanket in the wintertime or as massive as a lightening strike, with its millions of volts.

Static electricity is often caused by friction; rubbing one object against another causes a transfer of electrons between the two. Using friction to create a static charge is called *triboelectric generation*. The amount of static that can be built up in this manner depends on various factors, including the types of materials, their surface area and texture, and the ambient humidity. If you have ever rubbed a balloon on your head and stuck it to the wall, you have used triboelectric generation.

Because air has very high resistance, static electric discharge usually requires contact with the statically-charged object. For a static discharge to arc through the air, it requires a very high voltage, and no other path to the ground with lower resistance. You can feel a static discharge starting at around 3,000 V. The drier the air, the greater the resistance, which is why static shocks on dry winter days can fall within the range of 10,000 to 20,000 volts. Keeping a room humidified is one way to reduce the risk of static electricity and ESD.

If 120 V from a household electrical outlet can kill you, why does a static spark of 20,000 V just startle you? Because, while the voltage might be high, the current is very low; very few total electrons are transferred in a static spark. All the energy of all the electrons in a spark added together cannot hurt you, even though it may surprise you. Each electron in a static discharge has extremely high energy, but the human body is just too big for the very small number of electrons involved in the spark to cause widespread damage. A few cells in your fingertip may be damaged, but they easily grow back.

On the other hand, voltages as low as 10 V can damage or destroy sensitive electronic circuits. This is why ESD is such an enemy of integrated circuits. Static charges can build up on both conductors and insulators, as well as in the human body. You can protect against ESD in your work environment by:

- Grounding conductive materials.

Lesson 3

- Ionizing and humidifying the air to speed up static discharge from insulators.
- Grounding yourself before touching electronic equipment. To avoid a static shock, touch a grounded object made of a *dissipative material*. A dissipative material is a conductor, but with high resistance. It loses its electrical charge slowly, so, when you touch it, the electron flow is spread over time and you do not feel a shock.

ESD

Static electricity is the build up of a stationary electrical charge on an object. *Electrostatic discharge (ESD)* occurs when electrons rush from one body with a static electrical charge to another with an unequal charge. The charge follows the path of least resistance between the two objects, so it can also occur between a charged body (for example, you) and an electrical circuit ground (a doorknob or a computer component). ESD can damage sensitive computer equipment. The static electricity process is illustrated in Figure 3-4.

1. Electrons are set in motion when two objects come together, especially if the objects are moved against each other, thus increasing the contact.
2. Electrons are transferred from one object to the other causing one object to have too many electrons and build up a static charge.
3. Another object comes close enough to the charged object to create a circuit. The static charge is released with a spark.

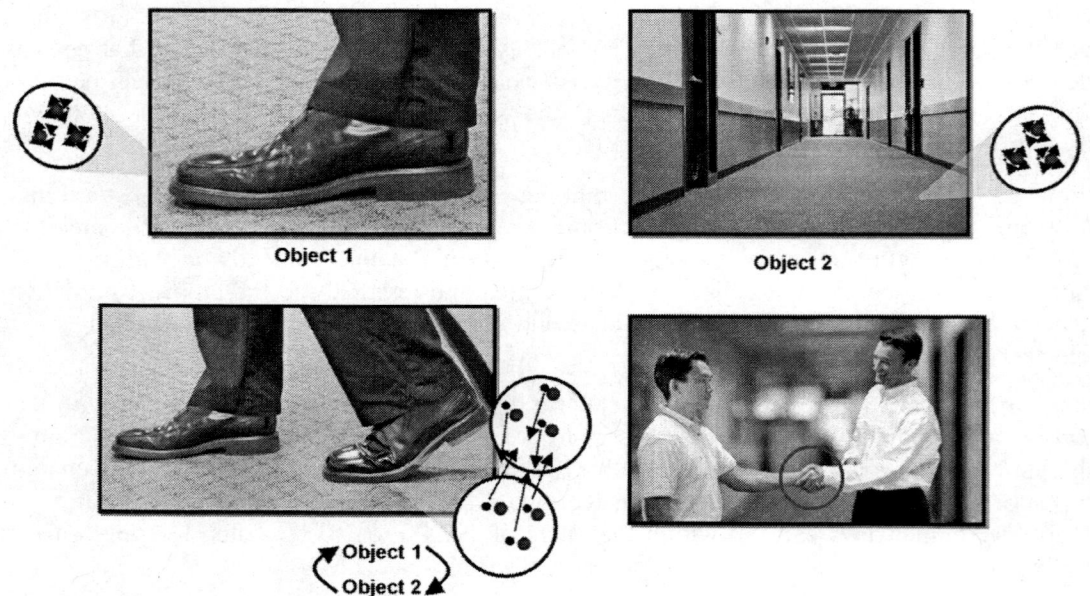

Figure 3-4: *The static electricity process.*

Let's put this all together in an example to see how the ESD process works.

1. You walk across a carpeted area.
2. A large number of electrons are transferred from the carpet to your body.
3. You shake hands with a colleague.
4. You see and/or feel the shock as the excess electrons jump between your hand and your colleague's hand.

EMI

While ESD is the primary electrical danger to computer equipment, *electromagnetic interference* (EMI) can also cause problems with microcomputer circuitry. EMI occurs when a magnetic field builds up around one electrical circuit and interferes with the signal being carried on an adjacent circuit.

Preventing ESD

A conductor can build up an electrostatic charge. If there is no path for the excess electrons to escape from the conductor, they will remain on the conductor. Air will be a path only if the voltage is in the thousands of volts range. If the charged conductor is connected to a ground, the extra electrons can quickly flow off the charged conductor and be absorbed by the ground. The earth can absorb an unlimited number of electrons. If the conductor is connected through an integrated circuit to the ground, all the extra electrons will immediately flow through the circuit. These extra electrons may have enough energy to damage the microscopic electronics on the chip. Often the damage only weakens the chip. The weakened chip will function for a while, but can experience a latent failure after it has passed the initial quality control tests.

Using the same reasoning, an insulator can build up an electrostatic charge. If there is no path for the excess electrons to escape from the insulator, they will remain on the insulator. Air will be a path only if the voltage is in the thousands of volts range. If the charged insulator is connected to a ground, the extra electrons cannot flow off the charged insulator. The electrons cannot move through the insulator to get to the connection that leads to the ground. Electrically charged insulators can lose their extra electrons if they are absorbed by electrically charged ion molecules and atoms that move naturally through the air. To speed up the discharge of insulators, you can use a device that generates extra ions in the air.

A dissipative material falls between a good conductor and a good insulator. A dissipative material allows electrons to flow through it, but has enough resistance to electric current flow to keep the current low. A grounded dissipative object will lose its charge over a period of time, rather than all at once—the way a conductor would. Dissipative materials are better to use near electrostatic-sensitive parts because they get rid of static charge using currents too small to damage chips. For example, walking across a floor and touching a grounded conductor will give you a shock because all the extra electrons flow off your body in a fraction of a second. Touching a grounded dissipative object will discharge the extra electrons from your body slowly so the electron flow is spread over time and you don't feel any shock.

Studies estimate that the cost of ESD damage in the electronics industry is $5 billion a year. This includes the cost of repairing or replacing the ESD-damaged equipment. Many companies have an ESD safety program to cut down on the losses and damage associated with ESD. The programs try to reduce the initial creation of static charges by eliminating unnecessary activities that create static charges, removing unnecessary materials that are known charge generators, using anti-static vacuums for cleaning computer components (like chassis, power supplies, and fans), and using anti-static materials. In spite of efforts to avoid creating static charges, some build-up is unavoidable. The charges on conducting materials can be removed by connecting the conductor to a ground. Humans are conductors, so grounding them will remove their electric charges. Sensitive parts may be stored in bags that conduct electricity safely away from the part and shield it from ESD damage. Insulators will not lose their charge when grounded, so ion generators are set up to flood the air with charged particles that will neutralize the charge on insulators.

Lesson 3

Create an ESD-Safe Workstation

To avoid a damaging static discharge, you should be at the same electrical potential as the device you are servicing. It is not critical, and in fact not desirable, to be at the same electrical potential as the earth's ground. After unplugging a device, you can reach the same potential as the device by touching or connecting an anti-static wrist strap to the device's metal chassis.

Do **not** connect anti-static devices to the electrical system ground or you risk electrocution. You cannot be sure that the electrical system is wired properly or that no devices on the circuit are shorting, sending power through the ground system. If there were ground problems or shorts, your body and your static protection equipment could provide a path from the problem device to ground—the circuit would be completed through your body, causing electrocution.

For the same reason, you **must** unplug devices that you are servicing. Even when turned off, the power supplies in most devices continue to produce voltage if the device is plugged in to an outlet. You and your anti-static devices could provide a better path to ground that the device's wiring leading to your electrocution.

To avoid the build-up of static charges in your service area, you can use an anti-static floor mat made of a conductive material connected to a dedicated ground that will carry any charge safely away from you and sensitive parts. While in the area, you should wear a foot grounder on each foot, so that any electric charge that starts to build up on your body will be conducted through the foot grounder to the grounded floor and carried safely away. You could install a small chain to drag below movable carts so that it connects the cart to the grounded floor even as you roll it around your work area. You should keep wood, plastic, vinyl, and nylon out of your ESD-safe workstation because those materials create static electricity more easily than other materials.

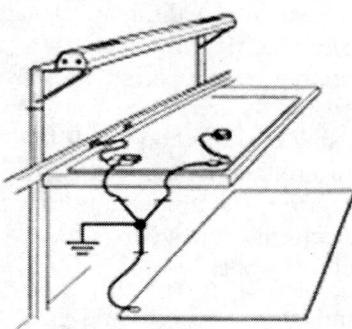

Figure 3-5: *ESD-Safe work area.*

Work surfaces in a workstation should be made of a dissipative material connected to a dedicated ground. Conductors in the workstation area should be covered with a dissipative material to prevent shocks and large currents. Many companies manufacture special mats for this purpose. Keep a supply of dissipative anti-static bags available so you have a safe place to store parts while you are working on the computer. Individual memory chips are usually sold in anti-static tubes that are good to keep around in case you need a safe place to store chips. Also make sure that you use anti-static containers to store any components that you are saving for future use, and store these components in a cool, dry storage area. Compressed air is an ESD-Safe method for clearing dust and small debris from static-sensitive equipment because it avoids rubbing materials together, which can generate static electricity. Another way to clean static-sensitive equipment is to use an anti-static vacuum.

To establish an ESD-free work area:
1. Install or gain access to a dedicated ground connection, not a point in the electrical system.

2. Install an anti-static work surface mat on your table. Connect it to the dedicated ground point.
3. Place an anti-static floor mat at your work area, connecting to the dedicated ground.
4. While servicing or handling equipment, wear a wrist or foot strap that is connected to the dedicated ground in your work area.
5. Have a can of anti-static spray available in case you notice any static electricity in your clothes.
6. Use a multimeter to verify that the resistance of the mat is less than 1 ohm.

Optimal Operating Environment

Keeping the risk of ESD low can be difficult if your equipment has to run in less than optimal operating environments. Factors that you should try to control include:

- Dust
- Ventilation
- Moisture

All systems tend to accumulate dust. The fan that runs to cool the system pulls dust and debris into the interior of the computer. This can lead to shorts and other electrical damage if it is allowed to accumulate. Having the system in a crowded area without enough room around it for adequate air flow can lead to overheating problems. Computers function best in relative humidity of 50 to 60 percent. Computers being run outdoors, such as cash registers at an outdoor plant nursery, could easily run into all of these problems. Computers on a factory floor are also prone to problems from these issues.

When possible, control the humidity with air conditioning or dehumidifiers to keep the moisture level from being too high. Be sure to leave adequate room around the air intake and fan area of the computer to prevent overheating. If possible, keep the computer away from areas that collect excessive dust and dirt.

Lesson 3

ACTIVITY 3-2

Establishing an ESD-free Work Area

Setup:
You have access to an assortment of ESD safety equipment and to a multimeter.

Scenario:
Your company has established ESD-free workstations with grounding wrist straps, anti-static workbench mats, and anti-static floor mats. The hardware technicians carry vinyl notebooks containing pages encased in plastic sheet protectors, because they need to refer to the documents frequently throughout the day. The technicians recently received nylon jackets and plastic styrofoam-covered coffee mugs to celebrate a major project they completed.

There has been a recent increase in ESD damage to systems and components the technicians have been working on. You have been called in to resolve the problem. Also, a new branch office has been set up, and you need to establish an ESD-free work area for repairs that will take place at the new location.

What You Do	How You Do It
1. What recommendations would you make to reduce the ESD damage that has been occurring?	
2. List the objects that need to be purchased to establish an ESD-free work area at the new branch office.	

Lesson 3

3. Using the appropriate ESD safety equipment, **create an ESD-free work area at your lab station.**

   a. **Install an anti-static work surface mat on your lab table.**

   b. **Connect the mat to a dedicated ground point, not the electrical system.**

   c. **Place an anti-static floor mat at your lab area, connecting it to the dedicated ground.**

   d. **Connect a wrist or foot strap to the dedicated ground in your work area. Put it on.**

   e. If necessary, **use a can of anti-static spray in case you notice any static electricity in your clothes.**

4. **Test the resistance on the work surfaces to verify that the ESD damage potential has been neutralized.**

   a. **Clip the black clip from the multimeter to a ground.**

   b. **Clip the other clip to the snap on the mat.**

   c. Using your multimeter, **verify that the maximum resistance of your anti-static mat is less than 1 ohm.**

TOPIC C

Observe General Safety Precautions

Safety first, always safety first. The health and safety of you and those around you are your first priority and your responsibility. You will learn the potential hazards of servicing PCs.

Potential Hazards of Servicing PCs

Your employer is obligated to comply with the Occupational Safety and Health Administration (OSHA) and/or state standards regarding employee safety. Employers must provide:

- A workplace that is free from recognized hazards that could cause serious physical harm.
- Personal protective equipment designed to protect employees from certain hazards.
- Communication—in the form of labeling, Material Safety Data Sheets (MSDS), and training about hazardous materials.

Lesson 3

Your responsibility—to yourself, your employer, your co-workers, and your customers—is to be informed of potential hazards and to always use safe practices.

Electrical Hazards

The previous introduction to electricity and electrostatic discharge (ESD) focused on the damage that electricity can do to the computer. This section deals with the damage that electricity can do to you.

Contact with electrical energy can cause electrical injuries including:
- Electrocution (fatal)
- Electric shock
- Burns
- Collateral injuries

Figure 3-6: *Typical warning signs.*

Electrocution results when the body is exposed to a lethal amount of electrical energy. For death to occur, the body must become part of an active electrical circuit with a current capable of overstimulating the nervous system or damaging internal organs. The extent of injuries received depends on the current's magnitude (measured in Amperes), the pathway through the body, and the duration of flow. The resulting damage to the human body and the emergency medical treatment determine the outcome.

Ohm's Law can help you understand how lethal shocks occur. Electric current flows from a high voltage to a low voltage through the path of least resistance. The lower the resistance, the greater the current will be that flows along the path. The higher the voltage, the greater the current will be that flows along the path. It is the total electric energy carried by the electric current that overwhelms your body's nerves and organs and causes damage (or kills you). To reduce the current, and reduce the possible damage from a shock, you need to decrease the voltage, increase the resistance, or both.

Air is a good resistor, and the more air between you and an electrical contact, the more resistance there is. If you come close to a very high-voltage source, the electrons may form an arc or steady spark though the air and flow into your body. When you touch the source of lower electrical voltage directly, or touch it with a conductor like a metal screwdriver, you have decreased the resistance to a point where low-voltage current can start to flow through you. Water is a better conductor than air or dry skin, so touching an electrical contact with wet hands reduces resistance and increases current flow even more. Electricity will flow through you only if your body completes a path to a ground or lower-voltage point.

Lesson 3

Standing on a totally insulated rubber mat increases the resistance of the path to ground and provides some protection. In some cases, workstations are located in areas with grounded floors and workbenches, so static electricity has a low-resistance, non-destructive path to ground. An anti-static wrist band is specifically designed to provide a low-resistance path for electricity to a ground. All the precautions used to prevent ESD increase your danger when you work near high voltages.

Contact with a source of electrical energy can cause external as well as internal burns. It is possible to have a low-voltage electrocution without visible marks to the body. For example, you are standing in a puddle of water to cool off on a hot summer day and decide now is the time to work with the car battery. A 12 V car battery is generally safe unless the path to ground has such low resistance that a large current can flow. Standing in a puddle and touching the battery with wet hands provides that low-resistance path, and a large electric current will flow through your body. If a tiny pacemaker can control a heartbeat, imagine what the current from a car battery could do to your heartbeat. People around you won't see tremendous sparks and flames during your electrocution, but you will be just as dead. Exposure to higher voltages will normally result in burns at the sites where the electrical current entered and exited the body. High voltage contact burns may display only small superficial injury; however, the danger of these deep burns is destruction of internal tissues.

Electricity can hurt you even if you are careful and avoid becoming part of an electrical ground circuit. The heat generated by an electric arc or electrical equipment can burn your skin or set your clothes on fire. Anyone who has tried to unscrew a hot light bulb has direct experience with electricity-related thermal burns.

Collateral injuries occur when involuntary muscle contractions caused by the shock cause the body to fall or come in contact with sharp edges or electrically live parts. You instinctively pull your hand back from the doorknob when you get a static shock. Electricity flowing through your body can also cause your muscles to twitch uncontrollably. These motions can cause you to hurt yourself on objects around you.

Most of the internal circuitry in a computer is low voltage (12 V or less) and low current, so there is not much of a threat to your personal safety. However, there are exceptions to this, and these exceptions can be very dangerous. The main exceptions that you need to be aware of are power supplies. The computer's power supply has a relatively low voltage, but the current is very high in relation to other components. The power supply in a computer monitor increases the voltage, because monitors contain circuits that require 35,000 V with a high current. In any power supply, current is stored on capacitors that do not discharge when the component is turned off or unplugged. Even after months of inactivity, the capacitors may have enough stored electrical energy to kill you. For this reason, leave the internal workings of the monitor to specialists who have the extra training and special equipment that are required to safely remove a monitor cover and make repairs.

Working on a computer can be safe and enjoyable if you protect yourself from electrical hazards by using some common sense and by taking appropriate precautions:

- Perform only the work for which you have sufficient training.
- Don't attempt repair work when you are tired; you may make careless mistakes, and your primary diagnostic tool, deductive reasoning, will not be operating at full capacity.
- Don't assume anything without checking it out for yourself.
- Don't wear jewelry or other articles that could accidentally contact circuitry and conduct current.
- Suspend work during an electrical storm.
- Don't handle electrical equipment when your hands or feet are wet or when you are standing on a wet surface.

- Perform as many tests as possible with the power off.
- When removing circuit boards, place them on a dissipative ground mat or put them in an anti-static bag.
- Use an anti-static wrist strap when handling static-sensitive components like system boards, sound cards, and memory chips, but remove the strap if you are working on any part of a computer monitor.
- After cleaning the keyboard, be very sure it is dry before powering it up.
- Label wires and connectors as you detach them, and make sure you plug them back into the proper sockets in the proper order.
- When you replace the computer's case, make sure all the wires are inside. The case may have sharp edges that can cut through exposed cables.
- Power supplies have a high voltage in them any time the computer is plugged in, even if the computer power is turned off. Disconnect the power cord before you start work on a power supply and leave it off until you are done.
- Never stick anything into the power supply fan to get it to rotate. This approach doesn't work, and it's dangerous.
- Do not take the case off a monitor. The risk to your life is not worth any repairs you might make.
- Don't bang on the monitor screen with your tools; an implosion will propel shards of glass in every direction.
- To clean the monitor, turn it off and unplug it; do not wear an anti-static wrist strap. Use isopropyl alcohol rather than a general-purpose cleaner; it doesn't create a safety hazard if dripped inside the case. Use an anti-static cleaner to clean the glass on the monitor; never wash the glass with the power on.

Following these precautions will help you avoid accidents and prevent personal injury. If you see others working under potentially hazardous conditions, share your knowledge with them to help prevent accidents and injury in your workplace.

Chemical Hazards

At some point in your career, you might find that you need to work with hazardous chemicals. Your safety—and the safety of those around you—should be a top priority when you are handling and disposing of hazardous chemicals and materials. Your workplace is required by OSHA to make *Material Safety Data Sheet (MSDS)* information available to exposed employees. An MSDS is a technical bulletin designed to give users and emergency personnel information about the proper procedures of storage and handling of a hazardous substance. This applies to any situation in which an employee may be exposed to a chemical under normal use conditions, or in the event of an emergency. For example, MSDS may be kept in a file folder accessible to employees exposed to chemicals, or may be entered into and kept in a computer file.

 You will find a wealth of information at **www.MSDSonline.com/**, as well as at **www.osha.gov**.

Manufacturers supply MSDSs with the first shipment to a new customer and with any shipment after the MSDS is updated with significant and new information about safety hazards. You can get MSDSs online; the Internet has a wide range of free resources. OSHA doesn't require the use of their MSDS (Form 174), but any MSDS must contain the required information.

- Physical data

- Toxicity
- Health effects
- First aid
- Reactivity
- Storage
- Safe-handling and use precautions
- Disposal
- Protective equipment
- Spill/leak procedures

You use liquid cleaning materials to clean or condition the equipment you service, including the computer's case, contacts and connections of adapter cards, and glass surfaces. These compounds may present safety or environmental problems. Be sure to read labels and follow instructions. Follow your company's guidelines for disposing of these materials and their containers. Each municipality has its own regulations that you must learn and practice. You can find out about these ordinances by contacting your local government's environmental office or department for trash disposal and recycling.

Laser printer toner—made of fine particles of iron and plastic—presents its own set of problems due to its reactions with heat. If you spill toner, don't clean it up with a regular vacuum; the particles will get into the motor and melt. Don't use warm water to wash toner off your hands or arms; the toner could fuse to your skin. Instead, brush off as much as you can with a dry paper towel, rinse with cold water, and then wash with cold water and soap. In addition, do not use ammonia-based cleaners on or around laser printers, as the ammonia may react chemically with the toner. Empty cartridges should not be tossed into the trash because of the damage the residual chemicals can do to the environment. Used toner cartridges should be refilled or returned to the manufacturer for recycling and/or disposal. Follow your company's guidelines for disposal procedures.

Laser printers produce ozone gas, usually when the corona wire produces an electrical discharge during printing. Depending on the levels, ozone can be a mild-to-severe irritant. Regulatory agencies have established limits regarding the amount of ozone that employees are exposed to. Be sure the printer operates in a well-ventilated area. The laser printer may have a filter to control ozone emissions; follow the manufacturer's recommendations for replacement and disposal of the filter.

The electrolytes in capacitors are very caustic; treat them as you would any hazardous chemical. Thoroughly wash your hands after handling capacitors.

Batteries are used to maintain the data in CMOS chips and to supply power to remote controls and portable computers. These batteries may contain mercury, cadmium, and lithium, as well as other dangerous chemicals. Used batteries should not be tossed into the trash, but disposed of following your company's guidelines.

Lasers

Lasers are used in printers, CD drives, and DVD drives. You should be aware of the dangers and basic safety precautions.

Lesson 3

Laser is an acronym for Light Amplification by Stimulated Emission of Radiation. It produces an intense, directional beam of light by stimulating electronic or molecular transitions to lower energy levels. This powerful beam can cause damage to the human eye or skin. Lasers have many uses and—like other tools—are capable of causing injury if improperly used. The most likely injury is a thermal burn which will destroy retinal tissue in the eye. Since retinal tissue does not regenerate, the injury is permanent.

To provide a basis for laser safety, standards are established for Maximum Permissible Exposure (MPE). Lasers and laser systems and devices are grouped into classes:

- Class 1 lasers do not emit harmful levels of radiation and are exempt from control measures.
- Class 2 lasers are capable of creating eye damage through chronic, continuous exposure; this class includes barcode readers.
- Class 3 lasers pose severe eye hazards when viewed through optical instruments (for example, microscopes) or with the naked eye.
- Class 4 lasers pose danger to eyes and skin, as well as being fire hazards.

Frequently, lasers are embedded in laser products or systems with a lower hazard rating. For example, laser printers, CD drives, and DVD drives are Class 1 laser products; however, they contain Class 3 or Class 4 lasers. When the printer or drive is used as intended, the controls for the device's class (Class 1) apply. When the system is opened—for example, for service— and the embedded laser beam is accessible, precautions must be based on the classification of the embedded laser (Class 3 or 4).

Learn the precautions associated with computer equipment and peripherals:

- Never point a laser beam in someone's eyes.
- Never look directly at a laser beam.
- Never disable safety mechanisms when servicing a device with an embedded laser.

Activity 3-3

Identify Hazards of Servicing Desktop Computers

Scenario:
Your manager has called you in to ask you some questions about safety and the precautions you should observe on the job.

Lesson 3

1. **Match the computer components with the potential hazards they pose.**

    ___ Enclosure

    ___ Power supply

    ___ Battery

    ___ Capacitor

    ___ Monitor

    ___ Printer

    ___ DVD drive

    a. Chemical; metals used in manufacturing can cause environmental damage if improperly discarded.

    b. Electrical; stored charges might not dissipate for long periods of time. Chemical; contains caustic electrolytes.

    c. Laser; emissions from an embedded laser can burn eyes, skin, and other objects.

    d. Electrical; retains high voltage even when power is off if unit is still plugged in to an outlet.

    e. Chemical; toner can burn or melt when heated and is reactive with ammonia-based cleaners. Laser; emissions from an embedded laser can burn eyes, skin, and other objects.

    f. Electrical; sharp edges can cut through insulation on wires and cables. Physical; sharp edges can cut skin.

    g. Electrical; remains electrocution hazard even after unplugging unit. Physical; glass can shatter and cut skin.

2. **Electrical injuries include electrocution, shock, and collateral injury. Can you be injured if you are not part of the electrical ground current?**

    _____

    _____

Lesson 3: Safety

Lesson 3

3. Consider this scenario: A novice technician arrives at a user's workspace to troubleshoot a sound card. The user assures the technician that the power to the PC is off. As the technician begins working, he finds that the anti-static wrist strap gets in the way, so he removes it. Once the PC cover is off, the technician pulls the sound card out of the expansion slot and places it on a nearby metal filing cabinet, replacing it with a network card that he knows works properly. Finding that the network card doesn't work when installed in that expansion slot, the technician determines that there is a resource conflict, corrects the conflict, and replaces the network card with the user's original sound card. After testing the sound card, the technician and user agree that the problem is resolved. As the user helps the technician clean up by spraying window cleaner on the monitor screen, she mentions a funny ozone smell coming from her laser printer. The technician assures the user that an occasional whiff of ozone is normal, and ends the service call. What would you do differently?

TOPIC D
Potential Hazards of Using PCs

You take responsibility for you own health by practicing safety when you use a computer, as well as when you service one. This information will also be important to communicate when you are working with your customers.

Repetitive Strain Injury

Research shows that repetitive strain injuries account for the largest number of new workers' compensation claims, affecting insurance and health-care costs, as well as productivity and morale. Employers are obligated, by regulation and by economic necessity, to consider the importance of ergonomics in their workplaces.

Ergonomics is the study of people in their working environments, especially of their physical interaction with machines. Studies show that the problems which computer users have developed—including discomfort in the wrist, arm, shoulders, and neck—are ergonomic in nature. While many people have mild and passing symptoms, some individuals develop more severe and chronic symptoms, which may be labeled *Repetitive Strain (or Stress) Injury (RSI)* or Cumulative Trauma Disorder (CTD).

Repetitive strain injuries involve damage to muscles, tendons, and nerves caused by overuse or misuse. Any combination of the following factors can lead to this condition.

Lesson 3

Factor	Description	Example
Repetitive tasks	Small, rapid movements that are repeated over and over	Clicking mouse
Awkward or fixed postures	Working in an awkward position or holding the same position for a long time	Turning head to see monitor placed to one side
Forceful movements	Using force to complete tasks	Excessive pressure when keying
Insufficient rest time	Not taking time to relax	Sitting at computer for two hours

Computer users suffer mostly from repetitive strain injuries to the hand, wrist, and arm. Unlike strains and sprains, which usually result from a single incident—called acute trauma—repetitive strain injuries develop slowly over time. The type of injury depends on whether the muscle, tendon, tendon sheath, or nerve tissue has been irritated or damaged. Symptoms may appear in any order and at any stage in the development of an injury of RSI and can include the following:

- Aching, tenderness, swelling
- Pain, crackling, tingling
- Numbness, loss of strength
- Loss of joint movement, decreased coordination

Symptoms may not appear immediately after the activity that is causing the problem and are not necessarily experienced in the body part where the actual stress is occurring. For instance, if an individual wakes up in the middle of the night with elbow or shoulder pain, that may be a sign of RSI resulting from keying or mousing at a computer. In general, the more intense the symptoms, the more often the symptoms will be experienced, and the longer symptoms last, the more serious the injury is likely to be. A serious injury can develop only weeks after symptoms appear, or it may take years. Older workers may be more at risk because the body's ability to repair from constant wear and tear decreases with age.

If an individual has even mild symptoms, action should be taken. If symptoms are allowed to progress, a person with RSI can develop chronic symptoms. The key to RSI management is to remove an individual from the exposure that causes injury. A period of time away from the keyboard and mouse is followed by a gradual return to keying in an ergonomically correct work setting. Occasionally, a physician will prescribe a medication to help reduce symptomatic inflammation and pain. People with more severe forms of RSI may be referred by their medical provider to an occupational therapist who can do further evaluation and recommend a program of localized treatments, stretches, and exercises. Referral to an orthopedic hand specialist may be needed to determine treatment options. If the individual displays symptoms even at rest, splints may be recommended; while these are useful in the first stages of recovery, they are not the long-term solution.

The best treatment for RSI, of course, is prevention by proper arrangement of computer workstations and reasonable project design. The following sections examine ergonomic points to consider and give suggestions for modifying equipment placement or use.

Lesson 3

Chair

To avoid uncomfortable strains, you should have a good chair that is comfortable and makes you sit with your back straight. The chair should provide good lumbar (lower back) support. If not, a lumbar cushion may help. Sit back in the chair and use the backrest; don't perch. Chair height should be adjusted so that the feet rest flat on the floor with the thighs parallel to the floor. If the work surface is too high, the chair should be raised to an appropriate height and a footrest used. Arm rests must be recessed so that the user can easily pull up to the work surface and work with elbows at approximately right angles. Clearance for the legs should be provided at seated computer workstations.

Figure 3-7: *Proper chair and posture.*

The ergonomic checklist for a chair includes the following:
- Adjustable seat height.
- Correct chair height for user.
- Backrest for firm support to lower back.
- Casters that roll easily on floor.
- Footrest, if needed.
- Padded arm rests (optional).

Posture

To check your posture, raise or lower your computer and/or chair to achieve this position. Sit up straight and verify that your keyboard and mouse are close enough so that you don't have to reach for them.

The ergonomic checklist for posture includes the following:
- Feet resting fully and firmly on floor or footrest.

- Knees bent at approximately right angles.
- Thighs parallel to the floor.
- Upper body straight, with lower back firmly supported by chair backrest.
- Upper arms hanging straight down at sides.
- Elbows against sides and bent at right angles.
- Forearms parallel to the floor.
- Wrists straight, neither bent up or down nor to the left or right.
- Head looking forward with a slight downward tilt.

Some posture and stretching tips are:

- Take regular breaks.
- For the forearms, put palms together with fingers pointing toward the ceiling, and then slowly lower hands toward the floor behind your back until you feel the stretch.
- For the wrists, put arms straight in front of you and move hands up and down so fingers point to the ceiling and then to the floor, and repeat.
- For the hands, make a fist, and then spread out fingers as far as you can, and repeat.
- For the shoulders, shrug, then relax, and roll shoulders forward and back.
- For the back, bend forward in your chair. To stretch the upper back, grasp hands behind head and press elbows back.

Keyboard and Mouse Placement

Elbows should be at sides with shoulders relaxed. Keyboard should be pulled close to the body. Keyboard support surfaces should be wide enough (minimum approximately 30 inches) to accommodate the keyboard and the mouse. An alternative is to use two separate surfaces—for example, a keyboard and a mouse tray which are the same height. Wrists should be flat over the keyboard. Use the wrist rest only when not typing so that you move your hands when reaching for keys; your wrists should not bend or rest on anything as you type. Lowering the back legs on the underside of the keyboard may also help keep wrists neutral while typing. Arms and wrists should not rest against a hard and/or sharp surface. Move the whole hand to reach distant keys; don't stretch the hand.

Studies show that banging on the keyboard increases the risk of developing RSI. Researchers point out that banging the keys does not translate into faster typing speed. Overall, the vast majority of computer users were found to use excessive force—up to five times too much—when striking the keys. Use a light touch; relax and take a break if you find yourself becoming tense.

Repetitive mouse clicking and moving—as well as the double-click, with its rapid motion of the fingers—can be a major source of RSI. Many new and popular options to the standard mouse have appeared on the market, including the trackball, scroll wheel, cordless (using radio waves), ergonomic (to fit hand shape), optical sensor, three to five buttons with various functions, and so on. Left-handed people have more choices than before. Mice may be adaptable for either hand, or software may be able to swap the functions of buttons on a standard mouse. Many RSI sufferers report that they feel less pain when typing than when using a mouse; they prefer to use keyboard shortcuts (for example, Ctrl+S for Save) instead of the mouse.

Lesson 3

Ergonomic keyboards are designed to encourage a more natural hand and wrist position. They feature a split, gently sloped keyboard with a built-in palm rest.

The ergonomic checklist for your keyboard and mouse are as follows:

- Keyboard detached from the monitor.
- Adjustable keyboard height.
- Keyboard at right height so elbows are at sides, forearms parallel to floor, and wrists straight.
- Keyboard thin and level with floor.
- Keyboard on foam pad to soften impact of fingers on keys.
- Keys give feedback to stop from pressing too hard: tactile (feel key pressure decrease when the character is registered) or audible (hear a click when character is registered).
- Fingers reach the Shift key and the function keys without awkward straining.
- Mouse located at same height as the keyboard and as close to it as possible.
- Wrist rests, if used, well padded and proper thickness.

Monitor Placement

The top of the screen should be at eye level or below so the user looks slightly down at the screen without having to tilt back to look at any parts of the screen. People with bifocals have particular trouble with this. Position the monitor directly in front of the user, not to the side, to avoid neck strain. The depth of the computer work surface must be deep enough (minimum 30 inches, depending on the size of the monitor) to allow this setup. The user should keep an arm's length away from the front of the monitor and also from the backs and sides of other monitors.

Glare on the monitor can be a major source of irritation when it obscures the image on a screen, requiring a greater visual effort to see it. Monitor screens are particularly susceptible to two types of glare, reflective and direct. *Reflective glare* is created by a monitor screen's mirror-like surface, which may reflect an operator's bright clothing. *Direct glare* results when a light source is exposed directly to the eye, for example, by brightness from uncovered windows directly behind the terminal. To control screen glare:

- Maintain proper illumination levels.
- Position the monitor screen in relation to light sources to avoid a direct line-of-sight.
- Do not place the monitor back to or directly facing windows.
- Cover windows with drapes or blinds to limit the penetration of direct sunlight.
- Consider attaching a glare screen and/or screen hood.
- Install recessed overhead lighting.

Figure 3-8: *Proper monitor placement.*

The ergonomic checklist for a monitor is as follows:
- Adjustable monitor height.
- If screen is small, top of screen opposite eye level.
- If screen is large, center of screen opposite eye level.
- Monitor at proper viewing distance, usually one and one-half to two feet from eyes.
- Monitor directly in front, rather than off to the side.
- Copy stand or document holder.
- Copy stand and computer screen at the same height and at same distance from eyes.
- Monitor positioned to avoid glare.

Work Environment

Your work environment should provide a physical environment that minimizes ergonomic risks. You should be able to sit comfortably, use the equipment around you without discomfort, and be able to see things clearly.

The ergonomic checklist for your work environment includes the following:
- Desk with lower surface for the keyboard and higher surface for the monitor.
- Enough room for legs under desk.
- Enough space to put the equipment and other materials at the proper distance without crowding.
- Phone can be used without having to squeeze the receiver with shoulder while typing.
- Standing counters available, if appropriate, to alternate sitting and standing while doing computer work.

Lesson 3

- Lighting levels for combined monitor screen and hard-copy reading are 30 to 40 *footcandles*.
- Lighting levels for monitor screen without hard-copy reading are 20 to 40 footcandles.
- Task lighting used if more light is needed at certain work areas.
- Indirect lighting preferred; parabolic lenses with fluorescent fixtures are also good.

Project Design

The Americans with Disabilities Act (ADA) requires employers to make reasonable accommodations to protect the rights of individuals with disabilities. Possible changes may include restructuring jobs, altering the layout of workstations, or modifying equipment.

 You can access the ADA at **www.usdoj.gov/crt/ada/adahom1.htm**.

The Job Accommodation Network (JAN) was founded by the President's Committee on Employment of People with Disabilities. JAN provides free technical support and assistance both to people with disabilities and to businesses on how to fashion job-site accommodations. It can perform individualized searches for workplace accommodations, based on the job's functional requirements and the functional limitations of the individual.

 You can access the JAN at **http://janweb.icdi.wvu.edu**.

The ergonomic checklist for project design as is follows:

- Take short, frequent breaks from computer work; short rests taken often provide better protection than longer breaks after longer periods of work.
- Take a break before feeling any muscle fatigue in upper body.
- Get up and move around whenever any symptoms are felt.
- Pause periodically to do relaxation exercises.
- Adjust workstation furniture.
- Use the same workstation all day so that adjustments are minimized.
- Give input when department is purchasing computer equipment and furniture.

Vision

Many computer tasks are done at a close working distance, requiring the eyes to maintain active focusing. This can cause stress and strain on the eyes and the muscles that control them. A very common health problem reported by users of computer monitors is eye strain—including the following symptoms:

- Blurred vision
- Difficulty focusing
- Double vision
- Tiredness
- Headaches
- Burning, sore, or itchy eyes

Lesson 3

Scientific research offers no evidence that regular use of computer monitors threatens eye health or results in permanent vision damage. However, because of the increased demands on the visual system as a result of monitor use, computer users frequently report visual symptoms. These symptoms may result from a pre-existing condition made worse by monitor use, or they may be a direct result of factors that are unique to the computer workstation.

A vision examination is recommended. A specific eyeglass prescription for computer use may help compensate for the strain involved in looking at a close and fixed point for periods of time.

Dry eyes can be a concern for computer operators. The eye surface becomes dry because computer users tend to blink less and tears evaporate faster during monitor use. Symptoms associated with dry eyes are redness, burning, and excess tearing. Artificial tears—used to supplement the eye's natural tear film and lubricate the dry surface—alleviate symptoms for some computer users.

For visual health:

- Images on the screen should not flicker or appear blurred. A monitor refresh rate of 70 Hz or greater is recommended to reduce screen flicker that can cause eye fatigue.
- Recognize that visual breaks are necessary. Rest the eyes periodically by turning them away from the screen and looking at something 25 to 30 feet away. Change to another task, or close the eyes for a few moments.
- Screen magnifiers reduce the need for near focusing; however, their resolution may be grainy or diffused.
- Enlarge font size.

Other Considerations

Radiation is a broad term used to describe energy in the form of waves or particles. Electromagnetic radiation comes from both natural and manufactured sources, including computer monitors. Circuits within the monitor are responsible for the horizontal and vertical movements of the electron beam. This movement occurs tens of thousands of times each second (Very Low Frequency, or VLF) for the horizontal scan, and 50 to 60 times each second (Extremely Low Frequency, or ELF) for the vertical scan. The VLF and ELF field intensities have been extensively evaluated in many different models of monitors for possible biological effects. Computer monitor users have expressed concerns about the possible health effects—including adverse pregnancy outcomes—from the electromagnetic radiation that monitors produce. While the research continues, current scientific information does not identify a health risk from exposure to these electromagnetic fields.

Noise levels produced by computers and printers are well below those that cause adverse health effects. The equipment has minor noise sources such as the hum of cooling fans and the clicking of keys. Excessive noise from the computer may indicate an internal malfunction. Printers can be noisy and should be located in rooms away from operators, where possible. Noise reduction hoods are recommended.

Lesson 3

Activity 3-4

Identify Safe Computing Practices

Scenario:
Your manager has asked you to review safe computing practices with the other members of the computer support team.

---

1. Match each ergonomic factor with the appropriate description.

   ___ Chair

   ___ Posture

   ___ Keyboard and mouse placement

   ___ Monitor placement

   ___ Work environment

   ___ Project design

   a. Keyboard lower than monitor, room for legs under desk, phone not squeezed with shoulder, standing computer station.

   b. Adjustable seat height, correct height, backrest, footrest, padded armrests.

   c. Short, frequent breaks, move around before feeling fatigued, relaxation exercises, adjust furniture.

   d. Adjustable keyboard height, keyboard on foam pad, elbows at sides, forearms parallel to the floor, wrists straight, mouse at same height as keyboard, mouse close to keyboard.

   e. Feet on floor, knees at right angles, upper body straight, arms straight at sides, wrists straight, head forward with slight downward tilt.

   f. Adjustable monitor height, monitor 1.5 to 2 feet from eyes, directly in front of user, copy stand, glare controlled.

2. Consider this scenario: You are called in to repair a network connection. You notice that the customer's monitor sits on a two-drawer filing cabinet to the right of the desk, the keyboard is on the desk, and paperwork is flat on the desk to the left of the keyboard. In addition, the customer uses an 8-point font and sits in a cafeteria chair. The only light is an overhead incandescent fixture behind your customer. What ergonomic changes could you suggest?

Topic E

Fire Safety

Fire prevention and safety is everyone's responsibility. By practicing sensible and safe practices, and by reacting appropriately in the event of a fire, you can stay out of harm's way while keeping those around you safe.

Fire Prevention Practices

Fire prevention practices include:

- Turn off monitors; they generate high voltage internally and can start an electrical fire or an explosion in a combustible atmosphere.
- Don't operate a computer, monitor, or printer with the protective dust cover in place; this could cause excessive heat build-up and trigger a failure, resulting in an electrical fire.
- Keep beverages and other liquids away from electronic equipment.
- Make sure the equipment is properly grounded and has sufficient power rating to handle the components connected to it.
- Ensure that facilities meet local fire safety codes.

Fire Extinguishers

Fire extinguishers are the first line of defense against unfriendly fires and should be installed in all homes and businesses. Selecting the correct extinguisher is important both to insure suitability for the type of fire and to reduce damage from the extinguishing agents. Using the wrong type of extinguisher can needlessly ruin an expensive computer that gets blasted with spray.

Fire extinguishers are classified according to the type of fire for which they are suitable. There are four classes—A, B, C, and D. Class D is highly specialized and will not be discussed here. Note that Class C fires—which include computer equipment—require extinguishing agents which will not serve as conductors of the electrical current.

Fire Class	Description
A	Ordinary combustibles such as wood, paper, cloth, rags and most plastics.
B	Flammable liquids and gases such as gasoline, oils, paint, greases, and solvents.
C	Electrical fire and energized electrical equipment where non-conductivity of the extinguishing agent is important.

Extinguishers also have numerical ratings which denote the amount of fire the extinguisher will handle. The minimum rating for a Class A extinguisher on light hazards is 2A. For Class B or C hazards, a minimum rating of 10 is recommended. Extinguishers that can handle several types of fires have combined ratings such as 2A:10BC.

Lesson 3

Extinguishing Agents

The extinguishing agent must handle the correct class of fire while keeping damage to a minimum. The common groups of agents and their uses are as shown in the following table.

Extinguishing Agent	Fire Class	Description
Dry chemical, standard type	B and C	Leaves mildly corrosive residue that must be cleaned up immediately to prevent damage to electrical equipment. Best uses are automotive, grease fires, and flammable liquids.
Dry chemical, multi-purpose type	A, B, and C	Versatile and effective on most common types of fires. Highly corrosive and leaves a sticky residue. Not for use around delicate electrical appliances or computers.
Carbon Dioxide	B and C	Very clean, no residue. Short range, must be applied close to fire.
Water-based	A	Inexpensive to refill and maintain.

CAUTION: Halon fire extinguishers work by eliminating oxygen so the fire goes out; unfortunately, they also eliminate oxygen for people in the area. In the past, halon extinguishers were considered excellent for delicate computers and electrical equipment because they were very clean and left no residue. However, halon is the most destructive of all the ozone-depleting gases, so a worldwide phase-out of the production and use of halons has been established. The Environmental Protection Agency has passed strict regulations concerning the use and disposal of equipment containing halon.

Environmentally friendly alternatives to the halon device have been developed for areas that contain sensitive or irreplaceable equipment. These items—which could be damaged or destroyed by water, foam, dry chemical, or carbon dioxide—are found in computer centers, data storage centers, and communications facilities, as well as in control rooms, electronics manufacturing plants, museums, art galleries, and laboratories.

Fire Emergency Procedures

How should you respond if you see a computer smoking or on fire? When a computer or printer burns or electrical components melt, the device will normally give off clouds of foul-smelling black smoke. Your first thought should be safety. Do not take any actions that would put you or anyone else at personal risk. Data can be recovered from seriously damaged equipment; a lost human life can never be recovered.

Each situation will have its own circumstances which you will have to assess quickly. If you have any doubt about your personal safety or whether you can extinguish the fire, leave immediately and close off the area. The following is a mental checklist for a fight-or-flight decision:

- Is the building being evacuated?
- Are toxic gases being produced by the fire?
- Has the fire department been called?
- Is the fire small and contained?
- Can I unplug the computer or the power strip to eliminate the source of ignition?
- Is the exit clear?

- Can I fight the fire with my back to the exit?
- Can I stay low and avoid smoke?
- Is a Class C extinguisher available?
- Do I know how to use it?
- Is someone else available to back me up?

When handling a fire extinguisher, use the memory device of P.A.S.S.:

1. P: Pull the pin from the handle.
2. A: Aim the nozzle at the base of the fire. Hold the nozzle firmly and stand 8 to 10 feet from the fire; movement closer may be necessary for complete coverage.
3. S: Squeeze the handle to activate the extinguisher.
4. S: Sweep the base of the fire from side to side and proceed upward until the fire is out.

Once you exit the building, do not re-enter. Even if you extinguish the fire, call the fire department to make sure the fire is completely out. A small fire that appears to be out may still be burning inside a wall and can turn into a blazing inferno with surprising speed. The firefighters can help remove any damaged equipment from the building. If necessary, they will remove the smoke and toxic gases before people are allowed to re-enter. Recharge any discharged extinguisher immediately after use.

After the fire, do not attempt to restart the computer or restore electrical power to it. This is a job for a specialist. Do not attempt to retrieve data from a damaged computer. Data recovery is a specialized skill requiring specialized tools and techniques to prevent further damage to the drive and/or file system.

Computer equipment can be salvaged from fires, and data can be recovered by specialists. In one structural blaze, the monitor was the source of the fire, which probably started in the high-voltage flyback circuit at the rear of the monitor. When the equipment was inspected, card guides were lying in solidified puddles at the bottom of the case. Circuit boards were charred, wires were melted or burned, and metal parts were warped or twisted. The hard disk's I/O connectors were melted and its circuit board charred. Melted solder had dripped across the surface of the board. The printer was the least recognizable component; it was described as two rods and a dot-matrix print head embedded in a pile of charred plastic. The keyboard's plastic was melted by hot gases. No trace of the mouse was found; however, its serial port connector and several inches of wire verified its existence. No information is available about the damage to the rest of the building. However—as bleak as this situation appeared—by using special techniques, all of the data from this computer was recovered with no losses.

Lesson 3

Activity 3-5

Practice Fire Safety

Scenario:

You are reviewing fire safety practices with the rest of your computer support staff so that you're sure everyone knows how to prevent fires and react in the event of an emergency.

1. List three ways to prevent fires in computer equipment.

2. Match the extinguishing agent with the type of fire it is best suited to extinguish.

   ___ Water   a. Electronics fires.
   ___ Carbon dioxide   b. Wood, paper, or cloth fires.
   ___ Dry chemical, standard type c. Flaming liquids.

3. You encounter a small fire at your office, some papers are on fire. You decide to use the extinguisher that is nearby. Remembering the mnemonic P.A.S.S., what are the steps you take to use the extinguisher?

4. List five considerations in making a fight-or-flight decision in the event of a fire.

5. Consider this scenario: You go on a call to repair a printer. The customer has just put out a small fire in the monitor with a fire extinguisher. The customer assures you that the fire is out and urges you to start work on the printer. What should you do?

Lesson 3 Follow-up

Safety contributes to your well-being as a person and to your productivity as an employee. To be a successful repair technician, you must employ safe practices at all times.

1. **Why is the high voltage in static electricity deadly to electrical components but only annoying to humans.**

2. **What is your first concern in a computer equipment fire? Why?**

3. **Consider the following scenario: You are on a service call to fix a laser printer. As you change the toner, you spill some on the carpet. Your customer asks you to fix the monitor because the display size keeps changing. You hear thunder in the distance. You also notice that your customer's chair is too low for his workstation and that he keeps his coffee cup between the mouse and the keyboard. Which safety issue should you address first? Rank the other issues in terms of safety (most important to least important).**

1. *Cease work during an electrical storm. Work on non-electrical projects, if possible.*
2. *Refer monitor repair to a technician with specialized skills.*
3. *Move coffee cup away from electrical components.*
4. *Clean up the laser toner, but don't use a regular vacuum.*
5. *Offer to help customer raise seat height.*

Lesson 3: Safety

Notes

LESSON 4
System Components

Lesson Time
4 hour(s)

Lesson Objectives:

In this lesson, you will identify the characteristics of a PC's internal system components.

You will:

- Upgrade the power supply in a personal computer.
- Upgrade the System BIOS.
- Upgrade the CPU.
- Upgrade the system board.
- Add memory to a CPU.

Lesson 4

Introduction

In this lesson, you will begin your in-depth examination of personal computers by opening the case and exploring the components that make up a typical PC. You will examine the internal system components before exploring the ways PCs connect to the outside world and external devices in future lessons.

You will examine the major components found inside practically any personal computer, including the power supply, ROM BIOS, central processing unit, system board, and RAM. You will learn how to identify their characteristics, recognize problems associated with them, and how to service them.

The following CompTIA A+ Core Hardware (2003) Examination objectives are covered in this lesson:

- Topic A:
  - 1.1 Identify the names, purposes, and characteristics, of system modules. Recognize these modules by sight or definition: power supply.
  - 1.2 Identify basic procedures for adding and removing field-replaceable modules for desktop systems. Given a replacement scenario choose the appropriate sequences. Desktop components: power supply—AT/ATX.
  - 2.1 Recognize common problems associated with each module and their symptoms, and identify steps to isolate and troubleshoot the problems. Given a problem situation, interpret the symptoms and infer the most likely cause. Content includes: computer case—power supply.
  - 3.2 Identify various safety measures and procedures, and when/how to use them. Content includes the following: potential hazards and proper safety procedures relating to—power supply.
- Topic B:
  - 1.10 Determine the issues that must be considered when upgrading a PC. In a given scenario, determine when and how to upgrade system components. Components include: BIOS.
  - 2.1 Recognize common problems associated with each module and their symptoms, and identify steps to isolate and troubleshoot the problems. Given a problem situation, interpret the symptoms and infer the most likely cause. Content includes: motherboards; CMOS/BIOS settings and POST audible/visual error codes.
  - 4.4 Identify the purpose of CMOS (Complementary Metal-Oxide Semiconductor) memory, what it contains, and how and when to change its parameters. Given a scenario involving CMOS, choose the appropriate course of action. CMOS settings: default settings; CPU settings; printer parallel port; COM/serial port; floppy drive; hard drive; memory; boot sequence; date/time; passwords; Plug & Play BIOS; disabling on-board devices; disabling virus protection; power management; and infrared.
- Topic C:
  - 1.1 Identify the names, purposes, and characteristics, of system modules. Recognize these modules by sight or definition: processor/CPU.
  - 1.2 Identify basic procedures for adding and removing field-replaceable modules for desktop systems. Given a replacement scenario choose the appropriate sequences. Cooling systems—fans, heat sinks, and liquid cooling; and processor/CPU.
  - 1.9 Identify procedures to optimize PC operations in specific scenarios. Predict the effects of specific procedures under given scenarios. Topics include: cooling systems—liquid, air, heat sink, and thermal compound; and additional processors.

Lesson 4

- — 1.10 Determine the issues that must be considered when upgrading a PC. In a given scenario, determine when and how to upgrade system components. Components include: CPU.
- — 2.1 Recognize common problems associated with each module and their symptoms, and identify steps to isolate and troubleshoot the problems. Given a problem situation, interpret the symptoms and infer the most likely cause. Content includes: cooling systems—liquid, air, heat sink, and thermal compound; and processor/CPU.
- — 4.1 Distinquish between the popular CPU chips in terms of their basic characteristics. Content includes the following: popular CPU chips (Pentium class compatible); voltage; speeds (actual vs. advertised); cache level I, II, III; and sockets/slots.
- — 4.3 Identify the most popular types of motherboards, their components, and their architecture (bus structure). Content includes the following: memory—SIMM, DIMM, RIMM, SoDIMM, MicroDIMM; processor sockets—slot 1, slot 2, slot A, socket A, socket 7, socket 8, socket 423, socket 478, socket 370.

- Topic D:
  - — 1.1 Identify the names, purposes, and characteristics, of system modules. Recognize these modules by sight or definition: motherboard; cases; and riser cards.
  - — 1.2 Identify basic procedures for adding and removing field-replaceable modules for desktop systems. Given a replacement scenario choose the appropriate sequences. Desktop components—motherboard.
  - — 1.10 Determine the issues that must be considered when upgrading a PC. In a given scenario, determine when and how to upgrade system components. Components include: motherboard.
  - — 2.1 Recognize common problems associated with each module and their symptoms, and identify steps to isolate and troubleshoot the problems. Given a problem situation, interpret the symptoms and infer the most likely cause. Content includes: computer case—slot covers and front cover alignment.
  - — 4.1 Distinquish between the popular CPU chips in terms of their basic characteristics. Content includes the following: VRM(s).
  - — 4.3 Identify the most popular types of motherboards, their components, and their architecture (bus structures). Content includes: types of motherboards—AT and ATX; components—communication ports, serial, USB, parallel, IEEE 1394/firewire, and infrared; AMR slots; CNR slots; and chipsets.

- Topic E:
  - — 1.1 Identify the names, purposes, and characteristics, of system modules. Recognize these modules by sight or definition: memory.
  - — 1.2 Identify basic procedures for adding and removing field-replaceable modules for desktop systems. Given a replacement scenario choose the appropriate sequences. Desktop components—memory.
  - — 1.9 Identify procedures to optimize PC operations in specific scenarios. Predict the effects of specific procedures under given scenarios. Topics include: memory.
  - — 1.10 Determine the issues that must be considered when upgrading a PC. In a given scenario, determine when and how to upgrade system components. Components include: memory.
  - — 2.1 Recognize common problems associated with each module and their symptoms, and identify steps to isolate and troubleshoot the problems. Given a problem situation, interpret the symptoms and infer the most likely cause. Content includes: memory.

Lesson 4

— 4.1 Distinquish between the popular CPU chips in terms of their basic characteristics. Content includes the following: cache level I, II, and III.

— 4.2 Identify the types of RAM, form factors, and operational characteristics. Determine banking and speed requirements under given scenarios. Content includes: types—EDO RAM, DRAM, SRAM, VRAM, SDRAM, DDR, and RAMBUS; form factors—SIMM, DIMM, SoDIMM, MicroDIMM, and RIMM; and operational characteristics—memory chips (8-bit, 16-bit, and 32-bit), parity chips vs. non-parity chips, ECC vs. non-ECC, and single-sided vs. double-sided.

— 4.3 Identify the most popular types of motherboards, their components, and their architecture (bus structures). Content includes the following: external cache memory (level 2).

Topic A

Power Supplies

Underpowered systems, especially older systems with relatively small power supplies, can experience lockups, random reboots, and other quirky behavior. If you are upgrading components, you might exceed the capacity of the current power supply. Replacing it with an adequate power supply can prevent system power problems and keep the number of support calls down.

Power Supply

Definition:

The *power supply* is an internal system component that converts AC power from an electrical outlet to DC power needed by system components. While not actually a component of the system board, it is required in order for system components to receive power. The power supply is a metal box in the rear of the system that is attached to the computer case and also to the system board. It contains the power cord plug and a fan to cool it, because it generates a lot of heat.

Some power supplies have a voltage switch. This enables you to set the voltage to that used in different countries.

In the past, there was no standard for power supply form factor. They could be whatever size fit the case and met the needs of the system board. Now, manufacturers have settled on an ATX-based power standard that fits an industry-standard ATX case and meets the electrical needs of an ATX system board.

Example:

An example of a power supply is shown in Figure 4-1.

Lesson 4

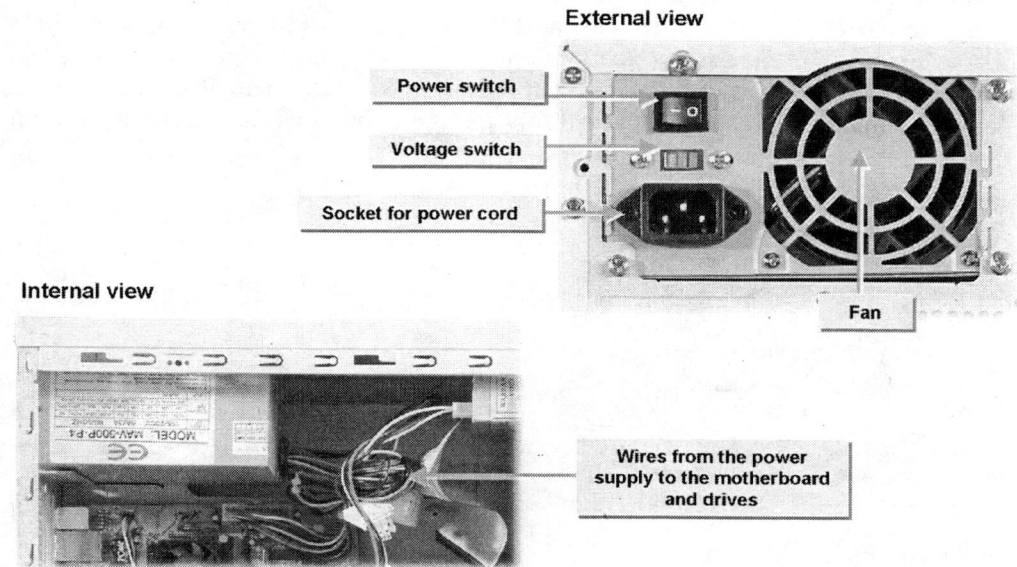

Figure 4-1: *A power supply.*

Power Supply Wattage

Power supply specifications are given in watts. A watt is volts times amps (voltage x amperes). Older systems typically had power supplies under 200 watts and often even under 100 watts.

Power Supply Wire Color Conventions

System components cannot use the 120-volt power coming directly from the electrical outlet. The power supply steps the voltages down to 3.3-, 5-, and 12-volt connections for system components. Wires are color-coded as to their voltages. The following table shows the wire color for each voltage connection.

Color or Component	Voltage
Yellow wire	+12
Blue wire	-12
Red wire	+5
White wire	-5
Motor	+/-12
Circuitry	+/-5

System Board Power Connectors

The power supply connection to the system board is a keyed or unkeyed connection that enables the power supply to supply power to the internal components of the system. Keyed connectors are designed so that the plug and socket have notches which must line up in order for the plug to fit into the socket. Almost all connections are keyed today so that you can't accidentally plug them in backwards.

Lesson 4: System Components

The connection also might use a single connector or two connectors. If there are two connectors, they are labeled P8 and P9, as shown in Figure 4-2. Be sure not to switch them when you plug them in or you could damage the system board. The trend has gone to having a single, keyed connector so that it can be plugged in only one way. This virtually eliminates the damage that can be caused to the system board by plugging the power connections in wrong.

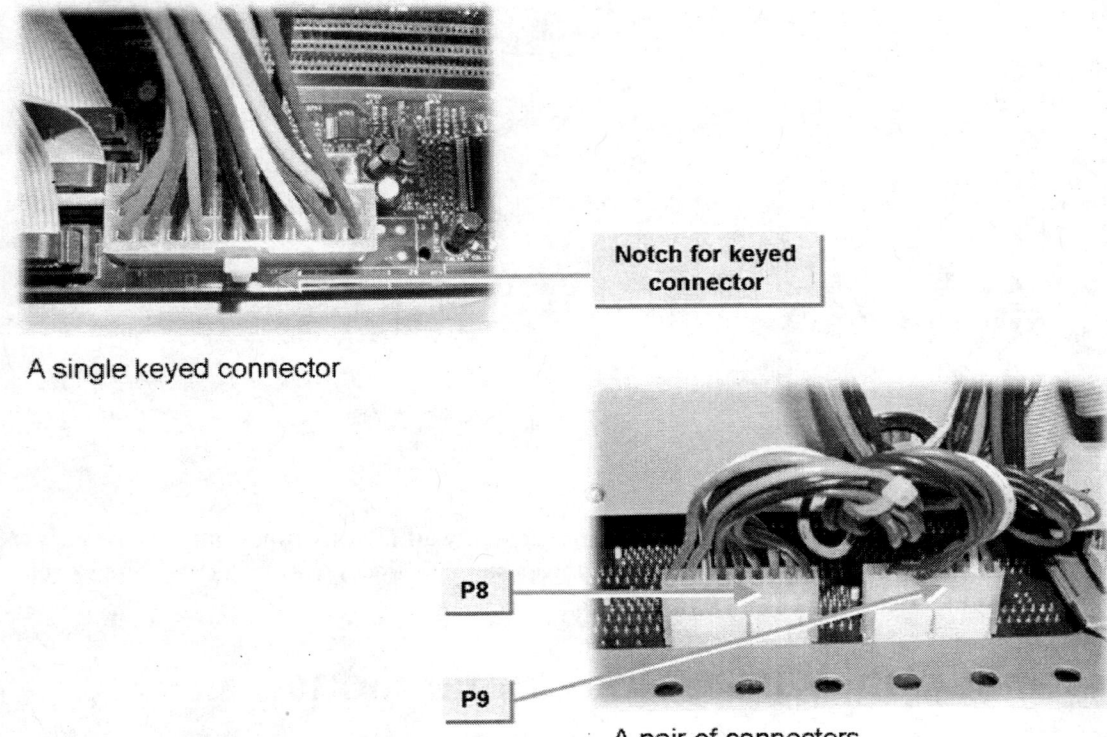

Figure 4-2: *System board power supply connectors.*

Power supplies not only power the components directly connected to the system board through slots, but drives and other internal components as well. The power supply sprouts many connections besides the one to the system board. There are Berg and Molex connections. There is also a connection to the power switch for the system.

Power Supply Pinouts

The pinouts for the system board ATX-based power connector are shown in the following table.

Pin Numbers	Color	DC Output
1, 2, and 11	Orange	+3.3 V
4, 6, 19, and 20	Red	+5 V
3, 5, 7, 13, 15, 16, and 17	Black	Ground
8	Grey	+5 V
9	Purple	+5 V
10	Yellow	+12 V
12	Blue	-12 V
14	Green	PS-ON

Pin Numbers	Color	DC Output
18	White	-5 V

Drive Power Connectors

Definition:

A drive power connector is a connector from the power supply that provides power to the internal drives. There are two types of internal drive power connectors sprouting from the power supply. The *Berg connector* is a small flat connector. This type of connector is typically used for connecting power to floppy drives, Zip drives, or SuperDisk drives. There are usually only one or two of these connectors. The *Molex connector* is the standard peripheral connector for powering internal IDE and SCSI drives. There are usually four or more of these connectors.

Peripheral Device Connector Pinouts

The peripheral device connector pinout is shown in the following table.

Pin Number	Color	Output
1	Yellow	+12 V DC
2	Black	Ground
3	Black	Ground
4	Red	+5 V DC

Example:

Examples of Berg and Molex connectors are shown in Figure 4-3.

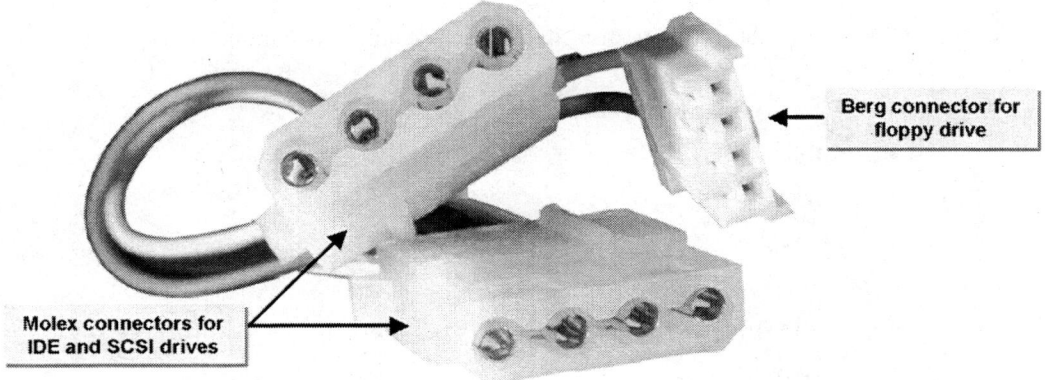

Figure 4-3: *Drive power connectors.*

Lesson 4

How to Calculate your Power Needs

Procedure Reference: Calculate Power Needs

In order to calculate whether your power supply meets your power needs, you will need to add up the maximum power you might use at one time. A range of maximum power consumption for various components has been established. Most components use much less than the maximum. You can check the documentation for the component to determine how much power it actually will use. The following table shows the wattages needed for some of the common components in systems.

Component	Wattage
ISA bus	12.1 watts
PCI bus	56.1 watts
AGP bus	25, 50, or 110 watts
PCI card	5 watts
AGP card	20 to 30 watts
SCSI PCI card	20 to 25 watts
Floppy drive	5 watts
RAM	10 watts per each 128 MB of RAM
7200 RPM hard drive	5 to 15 watts
1 GHz Pentium III CPU	34 watts
1.7 GHz Pentium 4 CPU	65 watts
300 MHz Celeron CPU	18 watts
600 MHz AMD Athlon CPU	45 watts
1.4 GHz AMD Athlon CPU	70 watts

To calculate the amount of power needed for your system:

1. Determine the number of watts used by each component. This should include the following components:
   - System board
   - CPU
   - RAM
   - Hard drives
   - CD drives
   - DVD drives
   - Floppy drives
   - Expansion cards
2. Add up all of the power needed by the system components.
3. Look at the label on the power supply to see what the maximum wattage output is.

4. Compare your computation with the power supply output. If you have not exceeded the power available, you won't need to upgrade. If you have, you will need to obtain a suitable power supply and install it.

How to Test your Power Supply

Procedure Reference: Test Power Supply

To test the power supply in your computer for proper output voltage:

1. Prepare the computer.
   1. Shut down the computer.
   2. Disconnect all cables externally connected to the chassis.
   3. Remove the computer enclosure (cover).
   4. Locate a spare Molex connector, remove it from the bundle if necessary so that you can easily access it without having to reach inside the case to work with the connector.
   5. Reconnect the power cable.
   6. Power on your computer.

   ⚠️ Be sure to not touch the case, internal components, or multimeter probe contacts while measuring the power supply voltage. You could be seriously injured or killed.

2. Measure the 5 volt output from the power supply.
   1. Set your multimeter to measure DC voltage with a scale that will permit readings in the +5 volt range.
   2. Insert the multimeter's black probe into the black (GND) lead of the power connector.
   3. Insert the multimeter's red probe into the red (+5) lead of the power connector.
   4. Examine the voltage measured by the multimeter. It should be approximately +5 volts.

3. Measure the 12 volt output from the power supply.
   1. If necessary, set your multimeter to measure DC voltage with a scale that will permit readings in the +12 volt range.
   2. Insert the multimeter's black probe into the black (GND) lead of the power connector.
   3. Insert the multimeter's red probe into the yellow (+12) lead of the power connector.
   4. Examine the voltage measured by the multimeter. It should be approximately +12 volts.

4. Restore the PC to service.
   1. Shut down the computer.
   2. Disconnect the power cable.
   3. Rebundle wires and return the Molex connector to the location from which you got it.
   4. Replace the computer enclosure (cover).

5. Connect all cables externally connected to the chassis.
6. Power on your computer.

Servicing Power Supplies

When a PC's power supply goes bad, several symptoms can occur, including the computer not booting, constantly rebooting itself, or the fan not working. If the power supply itself isn't working, the system won't turn on. It might be damaged from overheating, lightning, or short circuits.

First, you can try simply cleaning the power supply. The fan and openings around the power supply bring in air to cool system components, but they also allow dirt and dust to gather around the power supply. If this happens, it can short out the power supply, or prevent the fan from working. You can use compressed air to remove this debris from the system. Here are several other things you can try when you suspect a problem with a power supply:

- Make sure that there is power to the outlet. You can do so by plugging in a lamp or other device that you know works. If that doesn't turn on, you know that you have a bad outlet and not necessarily a bad power supply.

- Check that the connections from the power supply to the system board are secure, especially on ATX systems. The power switch at the rear of an ATX system doesn't turn on the power of ATX systems; it just sends a signal to the system board to turn the PC on. Once the rear power switch is turned on, you need to press the power button on the front of the computer.

- If a power connection is incorrectly attached (such as to a drive), it will short-circuit the power supply. The power supply can detect this problem and disable itself. If you fix the short (by putting the power cable onto the drive correctly), the power supply should start working again.

> Other components, especially drives, can also sometimes make a lot of noise. Make sure this isn't where the noise is coming from.

- A whine or squeal from the power supply area is usually from the fan. An accumulation of dust and dirt can lead to fan failure. If this is the problem, clean it with a PC vacuum or compressed air. If the noise isn't from the fan, but from another power supply component, replace the power supply or take it out and send it for service.

ACTIVITY 4-1

Measuring the Output of a Power Supply

Scenario:
You're servicing a customer's computer. You feel that the power supply might be faulty and not putting out the correct voltage.

What You Do	How You Do It
1. **Prepare the computer** so that you can measure the power supply's output.	a. Shut down the computer. b. **Disconnect all cables externally connected to the chassis.** c. **Remove the computer enclosure (cover).** d. **Locate a spare Molex connector, remove it from the bundle** if necessary so that you can easily access it without having to reach inside the case to work with the connector. e. **Reconnect the power cable.** f. **Power on your computer.**
2. Using extreme caution, **measure the 5 volt output from the power supply.**	a. Set your multimeter to measure DC voltage with a scale that will permit readings in the +5 volt range. b. **Insert the multimeter's black probe into the black (GND) lead of the power connector.** c. **Insert the multimeter's red probe into the red (+5) lead of the power connector.** d. **Examine the voltage measured by the multimeter.** It should be approximately +5 volts.

Lesson 4

3. Using extreme caution, **measure the 12 volt output from the power supply.**

    a. Set your multimeter to measure DC voltage with a scale that will permit readings in the +12 volt range.

    b. Insert the multimeter's black probe into the black (GND) lead of the power connector.

    c. Insert the multimeter's red probe into the yellow (+12) lead of the power connector.

    d. Examine the voltage measured by the multimeter. It should be approximately +12 volts.

4. **Restore the PC to service.**

    a. Shut down the computer.

    b. Disconnect the power cable.

    c. Rebundle wires and return the Molex connector to the location from which you got it.

    d. Replace the computer enclosure (cover).

    e. Connect all cables externally connected to the chassis.

    f. Power on your computer.

How to Replace a Power Supply

Procedure Reference: Replace the Power Supply

To replace the power supply:

1. Remove the existing power supply.
    a. Shut down and turn off the system.
    b. Unplug the electrical power cord from the electric outlet and from the power supply.
    c. Remove any components needed to access the power supply and its connection to the system board. Some systems are very cramped inside and components—for instance, drive bay assemblies—might cover the power supply to system board connections, part of the power supply, or both.

d. Unplug all power connections from devices. Be sure to label each connection to make it easier to reconnect them when you are finished installing the new power supply.

   e. Unplug the power supply from the system board.

   f. Unscrew the power supply from the case.

   g. Remove the power supply from the case.

2. Install the replacement power supply.

   a. Insert the power supply into the case.

   b. Secure the power supply to the case.

   c. Plug all power connections to devices.

   d. Plug the power supply into the system board.

   e. Reinstall any components you removed to access the power supply.

   f. Connect the power cord from the power supply to the electrical outlet.

3. Test the new power supply.

   To test it, turn on the system, and then try using the components to verify that they are properly powered. This should include all drives, network connections, and any powered devices. You can also test the output with a multimeter.

Power Management Standards

The power management standards *Advanced Power Management (APM)* and *Advanced Configuration and Power Interface (ACPI)* are standards that were designed to reduce power consumption by enabling system software to manage power consumption. ACPI implements power management through the operating system; APM implements it through the system BIOS.

Two other methods of saving power are Hibernation and Suspend modes. Hibernation shuts down the PC, saving the state it was in. There is a file created on the hard drive that is the same size as the amount of RAM installed on the system. All of the information in RAM is written to this file. Suspend mode turns off the hard drive and CPU, but it does not shut down the system.

AC Power

While internal system components rely on the power supply, other devices such as printers and external modems require their own direct supply of AC power. In such a case, the device must be plugged directly into a source of AC power such as a wall socket or power strip.

Power Supply Fan

Some power supplies enable you to see the RPMs of the power supply fan. You can then adjust the fan speed to run at only the speed needed to cool your system. This can reduce power consumption and save wear and tear on the fan.

Lesson 4

Activity 4-2

Replacing the Power Supply

Setup:

You have a power supply to install into the system. If you don't have another power supply, you can just reinstall the one you take out.

Scenario:

After calculating the power needed for all of the components added to a user's system, you have determined that it exceeds the capacity of the installed power supply.

What You Do	How You Do It
1. Remove the existing power supply.	a. Shut down and turn off the system.
	b. Unplug the power cord from the electrical outlet.
	c. Remove any components necessary in order to access the power supply and its connection to the system board.
	d. Unplug all power connections from devices, marking where each connection went to as you go.
	e. Unplug the power supply from the system board.
	f. Unscrew the power supply from the case.
	g. Remove the power supply from the case.

2. Install the replacement power supply.	a.	Insert the power supply into the case.
	b.	Secure the power supply to the case.
	c.	Plug all power connections into the devices.
	d.	Plug the power supply into the system board.
	e.	Reinstall any components you removed to access the power supply.
	f.	Plug the power cord from the power supply to the electrical outlet.
3. Test the power supply.	a.	Turn on the system.
	b.	Log on as Administrator.
	c.	Test all components.

Common Power Problems

Power problems can result in data loss, erratic behavior, system crashes, and hardware damage. More severe power problems cause more severe computer problems. The following table lists some of the most common power problems and possible causes.

Power Problem	Possible Causes	Can Result In
Line noise.	EMI interference. RFI interference. Lightning.	Erratic behavior, data loss.
Power sag.	Many electrical systems starting up at once. Switching loads at the electric company utility. Electric company equipment failure. Inadequate power source.	Erratic behavior, data loss, system crashes, hardware damage.
Power undervoltage or brownout (may last several minutes to several days). A variation on this is switching transient or instantaneous undervoltage which lasts only a matter of nanoseconds.	Decreased line voltage. Demand exceeds power company supply. Utility company reduced voltage to conserve energy.	Erratic behavior, data loss, system crashes, hardware damage.

Lesson 4

Power Problem	Possible Causes	Can Result In
Frequency variation.	Usually occurs when using a small power generator. As loads increase or decrease, the power frequency varies.	Erratic behavior, data loss, system crashes, hardware damage.
Overvoltage.	Suddenly reduced loads. Equipment with heavy power consumption is turned off. Power company switches loads between equipment.	Erratic behavior, data loss, system crashes, hardware damage.
Power failure.	Lightning strikes. Electrical Power lines down. Overload of electrical power needs.	Data loss, system crashes, hardware damage.

There can also be problems with the power connections to the computer system or with the computer power supply itself. Often, you will need to replace the power supply to correct them. Look for these symptoms that indicate a power problem on the local system.

- At system startup:
  — System does not come on.
  — No fan noise.
  — No power light.
  — No beeps.
  — Continuously repeating beep pattern.
  — POST errors between 020 and 029.
  — Parity error messages.
- While the system is running:
  — No fan noise.
  — Unexpected shutdowns or spontaneous reboots.

How Surge Protectors Protect Computer Equipment

When electrical current varies too much, it can cause lots of problems for computers and for the computer user. If there are sags, surges, or noise on the electrical line, it can lead to damage of hardware. Plugging your equipment into a surge suppressor, UPS, or line conditioner can even out the electrical current.

1. Electrical current flows from the outlet to the line conditioner. This can be a surge protector, a UPS, or a dedicated line conditioner.
2. Electrical current that is within tolerance limits for the circuit flows on through and powers the components plugged into the unit.
3. Extra current from a power surge is diverted to the unit's ground or neutral wire.
4. The unit includes circuitry to work to even out wide fluctuations in the power.
5. If you are using a UPS, it can also deal with undervoltages and sags by providing additional power to the hardware being served.

Figure 4-4 shows a graphical representation of the process used to condition power.

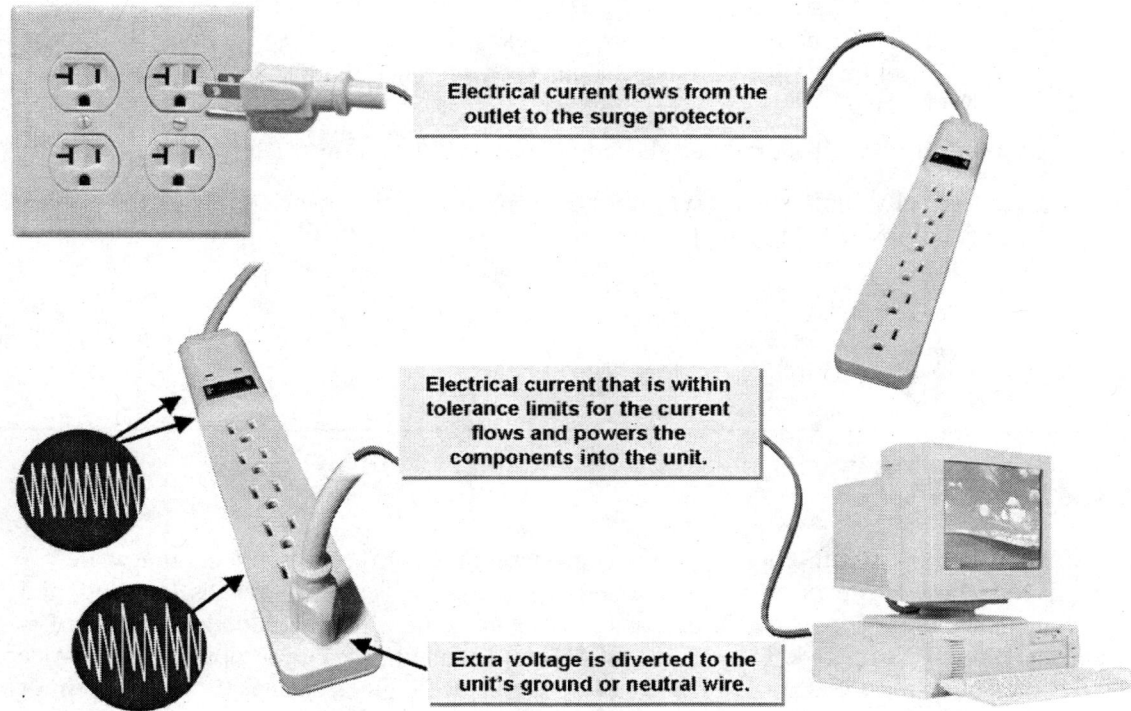

Figure 4-4: *How surge protectors protect computer equipment.*

How to Troubleshoot and Correct Power Problems

Procedure Reference: Troubleshoot Power Problems

To troubleshoot common power problems:

1. The fan does not appear to be working and the system doesn't come on or abruptly shuts itself down.
   - Unplug the system and remove the system cover.
   - Using compressed air, blow out any dust around the fan spindle.
   - Verify that there is no obvious reason that the fan is not spinning.
   - If these suggestions do not fix the problem, replace the power supply. Remember, do not open a power supply as there is a high danger of electrocution.

   This problem should be addressed as soon as possible. Leaving the problem alone would allow heat to build up to dangerous levels, causing serious damage to the system, and possibly fire.

2. There are power-related startup errors, such as the system, fan, and power light not coming on.
   - Verify that the power cord is securely connected to the power supply and to the electrical outlet on the UPS or surge protector (or the wall, but you should always protect it through a UPS or surge protector).
   - Verify that the UPS or surge protector is turned on and plugged in.

Lesson 4

- Verify that the UPS or surge protector is working by plugging in a lamp with a known good light bulb and turning on the light.
- If the lamp did not light, check to see whether any reset buttons need to be reset on the UPS or surge suppressor, or check the electric outlet's circuit breaker.
- If none of these fixed the problem, replace the power supply.

3. If an ATX motherboard will not power up, use a multimeter to check the voltage of the power being supplied.

Topic B

ROM BIOS

The BIOS that shipped with your system was probably fine for the components that were originally installed. However, as you add or replace components, as software is installed, and as enhancements are made available by the BIOS manufacturer, you should check to see if you should install a BIOS upgrade for your users. Sometimes the need will be obvious—the system won't boot. Sometimes, you'll need the upgrade to enhance the performance of the system or to support a particular hardware component. The skills in this topic will help you perform a successful BIOS upgrade no matter what the situation.

BIOS

Definition:

The *Basic Input Output System (BIOS)* is the set of instruction commands stored on a ROM chip that is used to start the most basic services of a system.

The instruction set can be changed by replacing the BIOS chip with one containing the new software or, if it is an EEPROM, by flashing the chip. Early systems required replacement of the BIOS chip. Almost every system you encounter nowadays will support flash updates.

Example:

There are several BIOSes within a computer system. The system BIOS is the one that sets the computer's configuration and environment when the system is powered on. Other expansion cards and components can also contain BIOS chips. The firmware contained on these BIOS chips holds the configuration information for the component and often helps improve the speed of the device. Phoenix, AMI, and Award are popular BIOS manufacturers. PC makers license the BIOS from one of these companies.

CMOS

CMOS is an area of memory with battery backup that is used to store the system configuration settings that the ROM BIOS accesses during the startup sequence. Prior to the use of CMOS, these settings were configured with jumpers and switches. CMOS was introduced with the AT system boards. Newer computers have CMOSs that allow for more configuration options than the switches and jumpers—or even earlier CMOSs—did, primarily because they use an extended CMOS memory area called the *Extended System Configuration Data (ESCD)* to hold information about specific hardware devices. Any time you change a hardware component, you should check the CMOS settings to see if they also need to be changed for the ROM BIOS to recognize the new hardware. Also, you can configure CMOS without needing to open the chassis.

The extent to which you can use CMOS to configure a computer depends heavily on the manufacturer of the particular CMOS; however, in most cases, you should be able to configure **at least** the following—and possibly much more—from the keyboard by using the CMOS Setup program:

- System date and time: You can use the CMOS Setup program to set the PC's real-time clock.

    📌 Using DOS date and time commands won't reset the real-time clock, but setting the clock in Windows will.

- Password: You can specify whether a password is required following the POST.
- Boot sequence: You can specify the order that POST checks drives for the operating system.
- Memory: Some systems require you to specify in CMOS how much RAM is installed on the system. You might also be able to specify whether the system uses parity memory or non-parity memory.
- Hard drive: You can specify the type and size of the hard drives attached to the system.
- Floppy drive: You can adjust the speed and density settings for the floppy drive. You can also disable or enable a floppy drive.
- Display: You can specify the monitor type.
- Parallel ports: You can specify settings such as unidirectional or bidirectional printing, ECP options, and EPP options. You can also disable or enable a parallel port.

    📌 Why might you want to disable a port? If you know that a parallel or serial port will not be used, you can disable the port, thereby freeing up the resources that would otherwise be unusable by other devices. Conversely, if you connect a device to a port and the device won't work at all, you might want to check the CMOS to ensure that the port hasn't been disabled.

- Serial/COM ports: You can specify settings such as what memory addresses and interrupts are used by a port. You can also disable or enable a serial port.
- Power management: In most modern computers, you can specify settings such as powering down components (like the monitor, video card, and hard drives) when the components haven't been used for a specified time period, as well as options and time limits for standby and suspend modes. You can also disable or enable global power management.

BIOS Settings

Definition:

BIOS settings are the low-level hardware configuration settings that are stored in the CMOS on every computer. Exactly what the settings are called, the menus under which they are found, and the settings you can configure vary based on the BIOS manufacturer and the hardware that is installed in the system.

Lesson 4

Example:

The CMOS Setup utility usually has a menu across the top of the screen or down the side of the screen. This will usually have a Main or General menu with settings for things like the system date and time, the language used in the CMOS Setup utility, and so forth. Other menus contain settings for:

- CPUs
- On-board devices (enable/disable)
- Parallel ports (uni- and bi-directional settings, enable/disable, ECP and EPP printer ports)
- COM/serial ports (including base I/O addresses, modes, enable/disable, interrupts, and DMA settings)
- Floppy and hard drives (enable/disable, boot order, speed, density, size, and type)
- Memory (speed, parity, and non-parity)
- Boot (whether the POST messages are displayed, which device to boot from, and in what order the boot devices should be searched)
- Security (passwords)
- Infrared ports
- Plug and Play
- Power (APM, ACPI, and Wake On LAN/PME/Modem Ring)
- Virus protection (enable/disable)
- Event log
- Video configuration settings
- Exiting the utility (with choices to save, discard, set defaults, and load defaults)

Methods for Accessing the System BIOS

Each BIOS manufacturer has their own method to enable users to access system setup menus and configure BIOS settings. A system setup prompt usually appears while the system is booting; for many manufacturers, it is only displayed during a cold boot. The key or key combination you need to press varies between different BIOS manufacturers. You often need to be very quick to catch it and press the appropriate key(s). Also, sometimes while the monitor is warming up, the message can pass, so turn the monitor on first if you need to access the BIOS.

Some of the common methods to access system setup are displayed in the following table.

BIOS Manufacturer	Access System Settings Using
Compaq	F10 or F12
ALR	F2 or Ctrl+Alt+Esc
AMD	F1
AMI	Delete
Phoenix	Ctrl+Alt+Esc, Ctrl+Alt+S, or Ctrl+Alt+Insert

There are many other types of BIOS, each with its own method for accessing system setup. Refer to your screen or your documentation for information on how to access yours.

Lesson 4

Configuring the BIOS

To change CMOS settings, you access the Setup menu, normally by using a key combination during system startup, and make the appropriate configuration changes at the keyboard. If you can't access CMOS for whatever reason, you can remove the CMOS's battery, and it will lose all of its settings and return to factory defaults. You will then need to reconfigure all of the settings that have been changed since the computer left the factory, so it's a good idea to print or make a backup of the current settings each time you change any CMOS settings. Keeping this information backed up can also help you restore valid settings during the troubleshooting process, or when the CMOS battery fails and needs to be replaced. (If a computer seems to keep losing time, or if you get an error message such as "Battery failure—Invalid CMOS settings—Run Setup," you will need to replace the CMOS battery.)

 To print CMOS settings from the Setup program, try using the key combination Shift+Print Scrn.

ACTIVITY 4-3

Examining the System BIOS

Scenario:
You are examining a client's computer to determine whether it is configured correctly.

What You Do	How You Do It
1. If necessary, **shut down your PC**.	a. **Choose Start→Shut Down.** b. **Choose Shut Down.** c. **Click OK.**
2. **Boot your system and enter the BIOS setup utility.**	a. **Boot your computer.** b. As it starts up, **watch for indicators of when to press the BIOS access keys. Press them at the appropriate time.** *Which keys you press to access the BIOS setup utility will depend on the manufacturer of your system's BIOS.* c. If you miss the opportunity to enter the BIOS setup utility, **wait until the computer has fully booted. Then, shut down and try again.**

Lesson 4: System Components

3. Using the keystrokes defined on the setup utility's menus, **determine the system settings for each of these items.**

BIOS Option	Current Setting
Boot Sequence	
Hard Drive Type	
Power Management Support	
CPU Speed	

4. **Exit the setup utility without saving changes and restart your system.**

   a. Use the appropriate keystroke to exit the setup utility without saving changes.

   b. If you're not prompted to restart your PC, reboot your PC.

The Boot Process

When you turn on the computer a whole series of actions are performed by both the computer hardware and software. Figure 4-5 shows the hardware portion of a computer's boot process. The hardware-related steps are:

1. The power supply initializes, and then sends a power good signal to the CPU.
2. Reset process signals the CPU to find the BIOS boot jump address.
3. The Power On Self Test (POST) is run by the BIOS, which results in either:
   - A beep code to indicate an error was encountered.
   - The video BIOS is located, loaded, and run.
4. Any other hardware BIOS are located, loaded, and run.
5. BIOS information is displayed on the screen.
6. BIOS runs system tests including a memory test.
7. Devices identified in CMOS are detected, configured, and tested.
8. PnP devices are detected and configured.
9. BIOS checks CMOS to locate the disk drive from which to boot.
10. The system boots from the specified device or displays an error message if none is found.
    - Master Boot Record (MBR) of the hard drive.
    - First sector of floppy disk.
11. Control passes to the operating system, which completes the boot process.

This only shows the hardware side of the boot process. For information on the remainder of the boot process, refer to the Element K course A+™ Certification: Operating Systems - A CompTIA Certification.

Lesson 4

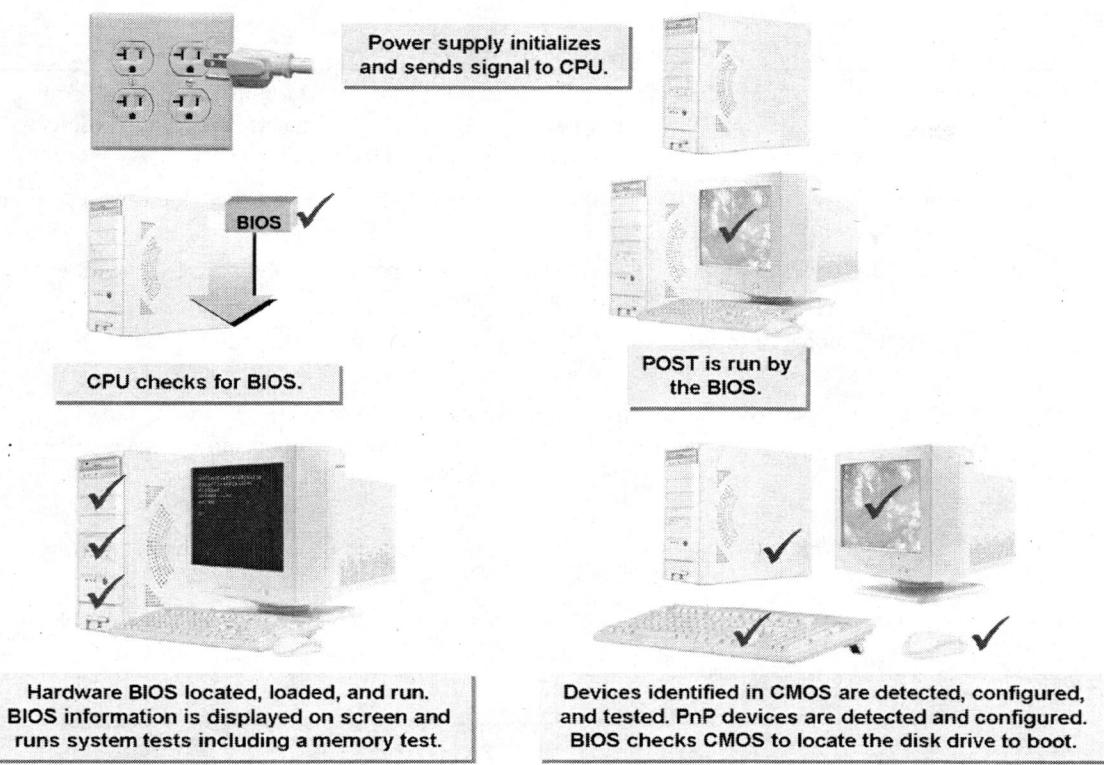

Figure 4-5: *The boot process.*

Power-On Self Test

The Power-On Self Test (POST) routine checks your system for hardware errors, including configuration errors. Either an error code number or a series of beeps will tell you if a problem is detected.

Normally, pressing F1 will enable you to acknowledge the error and continue booting. This might not be possible with the more serious error conditions. The following table lists common audio and video POST error codes and their meanings.

Table 4-1: *POST Audio Error Codes*

Audio Error Code	Video Output	Problem	Solution
One or more short beeps	DOS prompt	None (normal startup beep)	None.
None	None	Power	Check power cords, wall voltage, PC's power supply.
None	Cursor	Power	Check the PC's power supply; check for sufficient wall voltage.
None	DOS prompt	None	May be a defective speaker.
One short, one long beep	None	Display	Check for monitor power; check video cable; check display adapter.
Two short beeps	None or incorrect display (garbage)	Display	Check for monitor power; check video cable; check display adapter.

Lesson 4: System Components

Lesson 4

Audio Error Code	Video Output	Problem	Solution
Two short beeps	None	Memory	Check to see that all RAM chips are seated firmly, swap out RAM chips to determine which is defective, and replace the defective chip.
Two short beeps	Error code number	See the next table for a list of error codes and their interpretations.	
Repeating short beeps	Probably none	Power	Check the PC's power supply; check for sufficient wall voltage.
Continuous tone	Probably none	Power	Check the PC's power supply; check for sufficient wall voltage.
One long, one short beep	Probably none	System board	Check to see that all adapters, memory, and chips are seated firmly; check for proper power connections to the system board; use diagnostics software or hardware to further troubleshoot the system board.
One long, two short beeps	Probably none	Display	Check for monitor power; check video cable; check display adapter.
One long, three short beeps	Probably none	Display	Check for monitor power; check video cable; check display adapter.

The following table lists the error-code numbers and their meanings.

Table 4-2: *POST Numeric Error Codes*

POST Error Code	Problem
02#	Power
01##	System board
0104	Interrupt controller
0106	System board
0151	Real-time clock or CMOS RAM
0162	CMOS checksum error
0163	Time and date (clock not updating)
164 or 0164	System memory configuration incorrect
199 or 0199	User-indicated device list incorrect
02##	Memory
201 or 0201	Memory error (may give memory address)
0202	Memory address error
03##	Keyboard
0301	Stuck key (scan code of the key may be indicated)
0302	Keyboard locked
06##	Floppy disk driver or controller
0601	Floppy disk adapter failure
0602	Disk failure
17##	Hard disk or adapter

Lesson 4

POST Error Code	Problem
1701	Drive not ready or fails tests
1704	Hard drive controller failure
1707	Track 0 failure
1714	Drive not ready
1730-1732	Drive adapter failure

CMOS Error Codes

In addition to the POST error codes, you might also see a CMOS error code. The following are examples of CMOS error codes that you might see displayed after the POST.

- The messages `Bad or missing command interpreter` and `Non-system disk or disk error` are generated when the system can't access the operating system.
- The error `Display Type Mismatch` is displayed if the video settings don't match the monitor attached to the system.
- The error `Memory Size Mismatch` is displayed if the amount of RAM detected and the amount specified in CMOS don't match. This error is usually self-correcting, although you might need to reboot to fix it. Other devices such as hard drives can also generate mismatch errors. This generally happens when the physical device is different than what is specified in CMOS.
- The error `CMOS Checksum Failure` is generated if the CMOS memory is corrupted. This can happen from a bad or dead battery, or a loose connection to the battery. Try replacing the battery to see if it clears up the problem. If it doesn't, the system board might be bad (or getting bad).

How to Update the ROM BIOS

System board manufacturers periodically release BIOS upgrades. In the past, the most common way to upgrade your BIOS was to install a new BIOS chip on your system board. Today, most BIOSs can be flashed; that is, you can reprogram the BIOS with the latest version provided by the manufacturer. You might consider upgrading the BIOS when you are installing new hardware components, to make sure that the system can recognize and communicate with the new devices; when you suspect that the BIOS contains bugs that are preventing you from installing or running the operating system properly; and when you want to enable Plug and Play support or advanced power-management features on an older machine. In most cases, you can download BIOS upgrades from the system board manufacturer's support site on the Internet.

Procedure Reference: Upgrade the System BIOS

To upgrade the system BIOS:

1. Determine the BIOS manufacturer for your system. You can do this by choosing Start→All Programs→Accessories→System Tools→System Information. The BIOS Version/Date and SMBIOS (System Management BIOS) Version fields show information about the currently installed BIOS.

2. Download the BIOS upgrade from the system manufacturer's Web site. You will need to download the exact BIOS for your system. Using the wrong one can make your system unusable.

Lesson 4

3. Following the directions found on the Web site, upgrade the system BIOS. In some cases, this will be to write the appropriate files to a boot or startup floppy disk, and in other cases, it might be to apply the upgrade directly from the Web site. Other options might also be available.

4. Through the System Information window, verify that the new system BIOS is recognized.

Activity 4-4

Upgrading the System BIOS

Scenario:
A new version of the system BIOS for the computers in one of your customer's locations has been released. It should help with one of the problems they have been experiencing.

What You Do	How You Do It
1. Determine the BIOS manufacturer for your system.	a. Choose Start→All Programs→Accessories→System Tools→System Information. 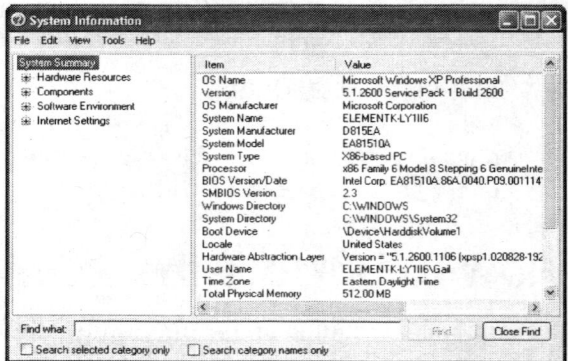 b. Record the BIOS Version/Date: _____. c. Record the SMBIOS Version: _____. d. Close the System Information window.

2.	Upgrade the BIOS.	a.	Access the Web site for your system.
		b.	Locate the upgrade for your particular BIOS.
		c.	Perform the steps indicated on the Web site to upgrade your BIOS.
3.	Verify that the BIOS upgrade was successful.	a.	Reboot the system.
		b.	Open the System Information window and check that the BIOS version/date and SMBIOS version have been updated.

How to Troubleshoot Common Boot Problems

Procedure Reference: Troubleshoot Common Boot Problems

Boot problems typically show up as either POST beep codes or error messages displayed on the screen. These vary based on the BIOS manufacturer. Refer to the documentation for your system BIOS for information on what the codes or messages indicate and how to resolve the problems.

To troubleshoot some common hardware-related boot problems:

1. If the system is slow to boot, refer to the support documents provided by the system board manufacturer. Some system boards have know issues that can cause a slow boot.

2. Beep codes at boot time are specific to the BIOS manufacturer. Refer to the manufacturer's documentation to determine the meaning of the beep codes and the appropriate solution.

3. The error messages Operating System Not Found or Non-System Disk Or Disk Error are usually the result of the user leaving a non-bootable floppy disk in the floppy drive. If that is not the cause, you should follow the directions for troubleshooting hard disk boot problems.

4. Some systems will not boot unless you enter a password. If the power-on password for a system has been lost, you can usually reset it by removing the CMOS battery for a period of time. You will, of course, lose all of the CMOS settings, so hopefully you have them recorded somewhere.

Lesson 4

Topic C

Central Processing Units

Have you ever tried to get a new piece of software or a game to run only to find out that your processor is too slow? If this happens to the users you support, they will want you to fix the problem, which might mean upgrading the CPU. This might seem like a drastic measure, and it can be expensive, but in some cases, it is less expensive to upgrade the CPU than it is to purchase a new system if everything else on your system provides acceptable performance.

CPUs

Definition:

The *Central Processing Unit (CPU)* is the integrated circuit that controls all of the system components. The CPU is composed of the *Control Unit*, the *Arithmetic and Logic Unit (ALU)*, and memory.

 The CPU is the brain of the computer. This is where software instructions are performed and math and logic equations are performed. This little component is the most costly of any system components.

Each processor comes in a variety of speeds. Different CPUs use different connection methods to connect to the motherboard. This includes various sockets, slots, and connection types such as ZIF, LZIF, Single Edge Connector, and others. Different CPUs are packaged differently. This includes the clock frequency, physical size, and voltage. CPUs sold today include onboard cache and an integrated Floating Point Unit, but older CPUs did not include either. Except for the original Pentium and the Pentium Pro, all processors in the Pentium family contain MMX (multimedia extension) capabilities. The voltage, the width of the data bus, and the amount of addressable RAM all vary between different processors. Whether multiple processors are supported varies as well as the number of processors. Some processors run very hot, so they require heat sinks and fans to help cool them.

 If you would like additional information about processor terminology, you can refer to the glossary of terms at **http://processorfinder.intel.com/scripts/help3.asp**.

Physical Characteristics

Physical characteristics of CPUs include the actual size of the processor, the number of transistors, the voltage the processor uses, the number of connection pins, the type of connection used to connect it to the system board, and the packaging.

- The physical size of a CPU ranges from a 1-inch square to 4x6 inches, and is directly related to the number of connecting pins needed to connect the processor to the system board.

- The number of transistors on a CPU usually relates to how powerful the processor is. More transistors mean more processing power.

- A processor's voltage can be attributed to how the processor was manufactured. For instance, early (60 and 66 MHz) Pentiums were manufactured using the 0.8 micron process. This process enables drawing 16,000 lines per inch on the chip. The resulting chips use a fair amount of power, and generate a lot of heat, making the use of a heat sink (explained later in this topic) and fan a necessity. These processors used five volts for operation. With the introduction of the Pentium 75 in 1994, Intel switched to manufacturing processors using the 0.6 micron process, which enables drawing 21,000 lines per inch on the chip. Over time, the manufacturing process evolved to using 0.35, 0.28, 0.25, and 0.18 micron process technology, with processors today most often using the 0.25 and 0.18 micron process technology. Chips manufactured using 0.18 to 0.6 micron processes need less power, and generate less heat, but heat sinks and fans are still necessary. They can run on 3.3 volts, which is the external voltage used by all Pentium processors introduced after the Pentium 66, with the exception of some mobile Pentium processors, which can use 2.5 V external voltage. Newer chips use a design called dual-voltage or split-rail. This design uses a higher external voltage (also called I/O voltage), at 3.3 or 2.5 volts, to provide compatibility with other chips on the system board, and a lower internal, or core, voltage, which runs between 1.35 volts and 2.9 volts, depending on the processor.

- Connection pins, connections, and packaging are all discussed later in this topic. For now, all you need to realize is that they are part of the physical characteristics of the processor.

Example: Mobile Processors

Mobile processors are processors used in portable computers. Common mobile processors include the Intel Pentium M processor, Intel Mobile Pentium 4, Celeron M, and the AMD Mobile AMD Athlon 64 processor.

Non-Example: Math Coprocessors

Math coprocessors are not examples of CPUs. *Math coprocessors,* or floating point units, were designed to be added to a system to help with math calculations. The coprocessor chip must match the CPU. These are 80x87 chips that match up with the 80x86 CPU, including being the same speed. For example, a 33 MHz 80386 CPU chip must be paired with a 33 MHz 80387 math coprocessor chip, if you're going to add a math coprocessor to the system. Math coprocessors were integrated into the main CPU with the advent of the 80486DX and the Pentium.

Lesson 4

CPU Components

Component	Description
Control Unit	Performs the fetch, decode, execute, and store functions. Collectively, these functions are referred to as the machine cycle. Speed is written in reference to the number of cycles that can be performed in a given time period. Each machine cycle performs the following steps: • Fetch—Places the address of the next instruction to be executed on the address bus and reads in the word at that instruction *register* (a high speed memory location within the CPU) location. If an instruction is more than one word long, several fetches will be performed. • Decode—Determines which gates to open between the CPU's functional units and buses, and what the ALU needs to do. This is determined based on the instruction register contents. • Execute—Passes values between function units and buses, and the operation of the ALU. • Store—Writes the results of an instruction either to a register location or a memory location.
Arithmetic and Logic Unit (ALU)	Performs integer math and *boolean* operations. The decode logic from the Control Unit determines which operation should be performed, the *operands* to use, and where the results should be placed in memory.
Memory	Memory locations can be registers, cache, RAM, or ROM.

How CPUs Interact with System Components

To understand some of the defining characteristics of processors, it's essential that you know a little bit about how they work with the other parts of the system. You already know that the CPU is connected to the system board, and it needs to be able to communicate with most every other component in or connected to the computer. These communication pathways are called buses, and some of the bus types that are usually mentioned in relation to the processor are the system bus, internal bus, external bus, data bus, address bus, frontside bus, and backside bus. Because some of these terms describe the same physical pathways, all this talk of buses can become very confusing.

The *internal bus* is the pathway that resides within the CPU itself. When you hear or read about a 32-bit CPU, it's the internal bus width (in this case, 32 bits wide) that's being described.

An external bus is external to the CPU. But each computer contains several buses that are external to the CPU (such as the main system bus, as well as any expansion buses that might be present), so it can be less confusing to use other terminology to differentiate among the various external buses.

The *system bus* is the main communication path between the processor and major system components such as the BIOS and memory. It's also referred to as the frontside bus, or local bus. The system bus runs at a fixed frequency, which, coupled with the width of the system bus, gives you the speed of the system bus. The system bus speed can't come close to the speed of the CPU, because the length of the system bus is many times that of the processor, and because other components such as RAM chips aren't as fast as the processor. So the system bus is a necessary bottleneck, but other components such as cache help offset it.

The system bus, like all other buses, actually contains separate paths for data, address locations, and control signals. The data bus carries data values and program instructions between the CPU and RAM. The address bus carries the memory locations that indicate where the data or instructions are going to or coming from, and the control bus specifies the operations being performed, such as memory read or memory write. As the data bus size increases, more information can be transferred per cycle. As the address bus size increases, larger amounts of RAM can be accessed.

When the CPU executes instructions, it stores the temporary results in registers, which are storage locations found directly within the CPU, for faster access to the results. But the vast majority of instructions and data are stored in RAM, so when the CPU needs more instructions to process, it has to stop and wait for two distinct system-bus operations (request instructions from RAM, and receive instructions from RAM) before it can proceed. To resolve this bottleneck, CPU design engineers developed a special type of RAM, faster and more expensive than traditional RAM, and added it to the CPU itself. This onboard RAM is called the *CPU cache*, primary cache, or L1 (Level 1) cache.

Most programs are comprised of sequential instructions that all need to be loaded from RAM. Traditionally, these instructions were loaded one at a time, in sequence, but now the processor can load several instructions into the cache at once. Accessing the onboard cache is much faster than accessing RAM, and with the ability to load multiple instructions into cache, several calculations can be completed before another set of system-bus operations are needed. When all of the instructions stored in L1 cache have been executed, the CPU sends out a request for more instructions from RAM so that the cache is refilled, and the process begins again.

Other developments that further improve the effectiveness of CPU cache (and therefore the efficiency of the CPU itself) are the inclusion of separate caches for instructions and data and the inclusion of *secondary cache*, which is more commonly known as L2 cache. Like CPU cache, the secondary cache is faster and more expensive than regular RAM, but it's not as fast or expensive as the onboard RAM. When secondary cache is present, the CPU will look there for instructions and data before it sends out a request over the system bus. The communication path between the CPU and the L2 cache is often called the backside bus. L2 cache usually isn't located within the CPU, but between the processor and RAM, and is normally twice the size of the L1 cache.

Factors that Affect CPU Performance

The following table shows factors that affect the performance of a CPU.

Factor	Description
Clock speed	The number of processing cycles that a microprocessor can perform in a given second. Some microprocessors require several cycles to assemble and perform a single instruction, whereas others require fewer cycles.

Lesson 4

Factor	Description
Millions of Instructions Per Second (MIPS)	The number of instructions that a microprocessor can perform in a given second. A microprocessor can have a slower clock speed than another and a higher MIPS rating if the slower processor uses clock cycles more efficiently.
Amount of RAM that a processor can access	Corresponds directly to the width of the address bus. The formula to calculate addressable memory is 2^n, where n equals the address bus width. Most CPUs in use today can address either 4 GB or 64 GB.
Multiprocessing	Using more than one CPU to provide additional processing power.
Cache	Dedicated high-speed memory for storing recently used instructions and data.
Superscalar	Technology that enables the CPU to execute two instructions simultaneously using two different pipelines.
Superpipelining	Ability of the CPU chip to overlap the execution steps (fetch, decode, execute, and write) of four instructions.
Speculative execution	Process of the CPU trying to guess which instruction will be used next, and executing one or more instructions as a result of the guess.
Branch prediction	Process of the CPU trying to anticipate which code will be used next, based on history, and executing that code.
Register renaming	Technology that uses multiple sets of registers in the processor to provide multiple execution paths.
Out-of-order completion	Technology that enables superscalar processors to reassemble the results of instructions that were finished out of order into the correct order, thus assuring correct program execution.
Dual Independent Bus (DIB)	Architecture used in Pentium processors. Uses a bus between the processor and main memory and another bus between the processor and L2 cache. This increases throughput.
Multimedia Extensions (MMX)	A set of additional instructions to support sound, video, and graphics multimedia functions.
Single Instruction Multiple Data (SIMD)	Used in MMX, this processing technique allows a single instruction to work on multiple pieces of data.

Older Processor Performance Characteristics

CPUs are continually being enhanced by their manufacturers. These items are techniques that were used with older processors to improve performance. While these techniques might not be currently used, they have been the basis for the high performance features of modern processors.

- Real and protected modes, which were introduced with the 80286 chip. *Real mode* refers to the CPU addressing the first 1 MB of *conventional memory* by assigning real addresses to real memory locations. In real mode, the 286 CPU acts like it was an 8086/8088 CPU. It can run programs written for the 8086 without modification. Although real mode provides backward-compatibility with the 8086, it prevents the use of the 80286's additional features, which are available in protected mode. When the 80286 is in real mode, it cannot return to protected mode unless you reset the computer. *Protected mode* allows information in RAM to be swapped to disk to make room for other information to go into RAM. It also was designed to allow one program to fail without affecting other programs. (This didn't work too well, though.) In order for protected mode to work, the CPU and the operating system had to work together to swap information in and out of memory. In protected mode, the 80286 can address up to 16 MB of memory, and supports multitasking by protecting memory regions. Problems in one region of memory cannot negatively affect programs running in other regions of memory. If one of the programs in the multitasking computer hangs up, you do not have to reboot the computer. Protected mode also supports virtual memory. Although the microprocessor can address only 16 MB of real memory, it can address up to 1 GB of total memory. Although MS-DOS (through version 6.2) does not directly support protected mode, UNIX and OS/2 do. With the introduction of the 80386, you could switch between protected and real mode without resetting the system, plus it featured a protected mode that worked more consistently than the one introduced with the 80286.

- The concept of *virtual machines*, which was introduced with the 80386. Virtual machines gave users the ability to have several real mode sessions running simultaneously, paving the way for further advancements in multitasking. Each of these virtual machines could address only 1 MB of RAM. By partitioning memory, each partition would run its own copy of DOS acting like each was a separate DOS machine. This idea is very important to all of the Windows-based operating systems.

- The development, marketing, and sale of several variations of a CPU, which was also introduced with the 386. Each of the variations offered different performance and features, enabling you to take advantage of a set of new features in the CPU, while also providing you with the opportunity of saving money by not having all of the new features implemented in some variations. For instance, the 386 was offered in the DX, SX, and SL models, with the DX being the full-featured version, the SX being the cost-conscious version, and the SL being targeted for use in laptop computers.

Common Processors

Intel CPUs include 8086, 8088, 80286, 80386sx, 80386DX, 80486sx, 80486DX, Pentium, Pentium MMX, Pentium Pro, Pentium II, Pentium III, Pentium 4, Celeron, Xeon, and Itanium to name a few of the most popular CPUs. AMD CPUs include the K5, K6, Duron, Athlon, Opteron, and Althon 64 processors. While no longer in business, Cyrix manufactured the MediaGX and M II processor, among others.

The following table summarizes some of the specifications for popular processors.

 For detailed information about Intel Desktop CPUs, you can refer to **http://infohq.com/Computer/intel-cpu.shtml**. Be sure to capitalize the word Computer or else this URL won't work.

Table 4-3: *Characteristics of Popular Processors*

Name	Internal Bus Width (bits)	System Data Bus Width (bits)	System Address Bus Width (bits)	Clock Speed	Addressable RAM
8086	16	16	20	4.77-10	1 MB

Lesson 4

Name	Internal Bus Width (bits)	System Data Bus Width (bits)	System Address Bus Width (bits)	Clock Speed	Addressable RAM
8088	16	8	20	4.77-8	1 MB
80286	16	16	24	6-12	16 MB
80386DX	32	32	32	16-40 [1]	4 GB
80386SX	32	16	24	16-33	16 MB
80486DX	32	32	32	25-50	4 GB
80486SX	32	32	32	16-33	4 GB
80486DX2	32	32	32	50-80 [2]	4 GB
80486DX4	32	32	32	75-120 [3]	4 GB
AMD 5x86	32	32	32	133	4 GB
Cyrix 5x86	32	32	32	100-200	4 GB
Pentium	32	64	32	60-200	4 GB
Pentium MMX	32	64	32	166-233	4 GB
Cyrix 6x86	32	64	32	100-150	4 GB
AMD K5	32	64	32	75-116	4 GB
Pentium Pro	32	64	36	150-200	64 GB
Pentium II	32	64	36	233-333	64 GB
AMD K6	32	64	32	166-266	4 GB
Cyrix 6x86 MX	32	64	32	150-187	4 GB
Celeron	32	64	32, 36	266-1,300 (1.3 GHz)	4 GB, 64 GB
Pentium II Xeon	32	64	36	400-450	64 GB
Pentium III	32	64	36	450-1,400 (1.4 GHz)	64 GB
Pentium III Xeon	32	64	36	600-1,000 (1 GHz)	64 GB
Pentium 4	32	64	32	1,300 (1.3 GHz)-2,400 (2.4 GHz)	4 GB
Itanium	64	64	44	733-800	16 TB
AMD Athlon	32	64	43	500 - 2133 MHz	8 TB

[1,2,3]

[1] Intel versions only to 33 MHz; AMD and Cyrix clones to 40 MHz.
[2] Intel versions only to 66 MHz; AMD and Cyrix clones to 80 MHz.
[3] Intel versions only to 100 MHz; AMD and Cyrix clones to 120 MHz.

The following table lists the number of transistors and internal (core) and external (I/O) voltages.

Table 4-4: *Internal Characteristics of Common CPUs*

Name	Number of Transistors (millions)	Internal Voltages (V)	External Voltages (V)
8086	0.029	5	5
8088	0.029	5	5
80286	0.134	5	5
80386	0.275	5	5
80486	1.2	5, 3.3	5, 3.3
AMD 5x86	1.6	3.45	3.45
Cyrix 5x86	2.0	3.45	3.45
Pentium	3.1-3.3	5, 3.3	5, 3.3
Pentium MMX	4.5	1.8-3.3	2.5, 3.3
Cyrix 6x86	3.0	3.3	3.3
AMD K5	4.3	3.52	3.52
Pentium Pro	5.5 (more for L2 cache)	3.3	3.3
Pentium II	7.5	2, 2.8	3.3
AMD K6	8.8	3.3	2.9-3.3
Cyrix 6x86 MX	6.0	3.3	2.9
Celeron	7.5 (19 for L2 cache)	1.3-2.1	3.3
Pentium II Xeon	7.5	1.3-1.6	3.3
Pentium III	9.5 (28 for L2 cache)	2.8, 1.5-2.05	3.3
Pentium III Xeon	9.5 (28 for L2 cache)	2.8, 5/12	3.3
Pentium 4	42-55	1.75	1.75
Itanium	25.4	Not available	Not available
AMD Athlon	54.3	0.95 - 1.8	3.3

The following table lists the types and amounts of cache and number of processors supported. Earlier CPUs aren't included because they didn't have cache or support multiprocessing.

Table 4-5: *Cache and Multiprocessor Support Among Common CPUs*

Name	L1 Cache	L2 Cache	Multiprocessor Support
80486	8 K-16 K unified	Up to 256 K on system board	No
AMD 5x86	16 K unified	Up to 256 K on system board	No
Cyrix 5x86	16 K unified	Up to 256 K on system board	No
Pentium	8 K-16 K data/8 K-16 K instruction	256 K-512 K on system board	2
Pentium MMX	16 K data/16 K instruction	256 K-512 K on system board	2
Cyrix 6x86	16 K unified	256 K-512 K on system board	No
AMD K5	8 K data/16 K instruction	256 K-512 K on system board	No
Pentium Pro	8 K data/8 K instruction	256 K-1 MB integrated	4

Lesson 4

Name	L1 Cache	L2 Cache	Multiprocessor Support
Pentium II	16 K data/16 K instruction	512 K	2
AMD K6	32 K data/32 K instruction	256 K-1 MB on system board	No
Cyrix 6x86MX	64 K unified, plus 0.25 K instruction	256 K-512 K on system board	No
Celeron	16 K data/16 K instruction	128 K on-die (models 300A and later)	No
Pentium II Xeon	16 K data/16 K instruction	512 K-2 MB on system board	8
Pentium III	16 K data/16 K instruction	256 K on-die, 512 K on system board	2
Pentium III Xeon	16 K data/16 K instruction	256 K-2 MB	8
Pentium 4	12 K data/8 K instruction	256 K on-die	No
Itanium	16 K data/16 K instruction	96 K on-die, plus 2-4 MB L3 cache	32
AMD Athlon	64 K data/64 K instruction	64 - 512 K	14

CPU Speeds

CPU speed is the speed at which instructions are processed. There are two factors that affect the CPU speed. One is the core speed, which is the internal speed at which instructions are processed within the CPU. The other is the bus speed, which is the speed at which instructions are transferred to the motherboard. The following table lists the speeds of some of the popular Intel CPUs.

CPU	Core Speed	Bus Speed
Pentium	75-200 MHz	50-66 MHz
Pentium Pro	150-200 MHz	60-66 MHz
Pentium with MMX	150-266 MHz	66 MHz
Pentium II	233-400 MHz	66-100 MHz
Pentium II Xeon	400-450 MHz	100 MHz
Celeron	266 MHz-2 GHz	66-400 MHz
Pentium III	533 MHz-1.4 GHz	100-133 MHz
Pentium III Xeon	500 MHz-1 GHz	100-133 MHz
Pentium 4	1.32-8 GHz	400-533 MHz
Xeon	1.42-8 GHz	400 MHz

Lesson 4

While chip makers might advertise that a CPU runs at a certain speed, the truth is that the computer won't necessarily run at that speed 100 percent of the time or maybe at any time. The advertised speed is actually the maximum speed at which the chip can run. In fact, the speed your computer will run at is probably less than the advertised speed. Other components, such as memory, frontside bus, and video cards, have an affect on the actual speed of your computer, depending on what you're doing on the computer at any given time.

Socket and Slot Types

Sockets and slots are the connectors that connect a CPU to the motherboard. There are many varieties of sockets and slots that have been developed over the years.

Slot-based processors plug into a system board in much the same way as an expansion board; socketed processors plug into a system board using a grid array of pins. When you replace a processor, you must select a processor that is compatible with the type supported by the system board. Also, you must be careful to line up Pin 1 on the processor with Pin 1 on the socket; otherwise, the processor won't work and might even be damaged. Finally, with socketed processors, you must be careful not to bend the pins when removing or inserting the processor; otherwise, you can ruin the processor, which is costly to replace. You can also purchase adapters that allow you to use a socketed processor in a slot-based system board.

 Information about which processor in which packaging will fit into which socket or slot is available at **www.sandpile.org**.

Socket Types

The following table describes some of the sockets you might encounter.

Socket Type	Pin Layout	Processor Used For
Socket 0	168 pin inline	5v 486DX
Socket 1	169 pin inline	5v 486DX and 486SX
Socket 2	238 pin inline	5v 486DX, 486SX, 486DX2
Socket 3	237 pin inline	3.3v and 5v 486DX, 486SX, 486DX2, 486DX4
Socket 4	273 pin inline arranged in 21 x 21 PGA grid	5v Pentium 60 and 66
Socket 5	320 pin staggered arranged in 37 x 37 SPGA grid	3.3v early Pentium
Socket 6	235 pin inline arranged in 19 x 19 PGA grid	3.3v 486DX4
Socket 7	321 pin staggered arranged in 37 x 37 SPGA grid	Later Pentium, AMD K6, Cyrix 6x86, IDT
Super 7	321 pin staggered arranged in 37 x 37 SPGA grid	AMD K62 and K63
Socket 8	387 pin staggered ZIF arranged in 24 x 26 SPGA grid	3.3v Pentium Pro
Socket 370	Supports PPGA	Original Celeron
Socket 423	SPGA	Pentium 4

Lesson 4: System Components

Lesson 4

Socket Type	Pin Layout	Processor Used For
Socket 478	SPGA	Pentium 4
Socket A	Supports PPGA	AMD Athlon, Duron, Palomino, and Morgan

Figure 4-6: *Examples of CPU sockets.*

Slot Types

The following table describes some of the slots you might encounter.

Slot Type	Description
Slot 1	Contains a 242-pin edge connector. Used for Celeron SEPP, Pentium II SECC and SECC2, and Pentium III processors.

Lesson 4

Slot Type	Description
Slot 2	Contains a 330-pin edge connector. Used for Pentium II Xeon and Pentium III Xeon processors. Designed for multi-processor systems.
Slot A	Contains a 242-pin edge connector. Used for AMD Athlon processors. Pinouts are incompatible with Slot 1.
Slot M	Used for Itanium processors.

Figure 4-7: *Slot 1 (for SECC packaging).*

CPU Package Types

Definition:

A *CPU package* is the physical construction or form factor of a CPU. This includes the size and shape of the CPU, along with the number and layout of the pins or contacts. The package determines how the CPU is attached to the motherboard.

CPU Attachment Methods

The CPU is relatively easy to locate because it is most often the biggest chip on the motherboard. Newer PCs make it even easier to find because it is usually installed in a larger socket, referred to as a Zero Insertion Force or *ZIF socket*. It uses a lever to tighten or loosen the pin connections between the processor chip and the socket, requiring no force to insert or remove a processor chip.

Figure 4-8: *A ZIF socket.*

Lesson 4

Original CPUs were sometimes soldered onto the motherboard. Others used standard 169-pin screw machine sockets. You needed to use a special type of tool called a chip extractor to remove the chip. These look like big tweezers with bent over ends that go under the edge of the chip so you can pull it out. It takes around 100 pounds of force to install a chip in this type of socket. It was easy to damage the socket, the pins, or the chips.

Example: Flip Chip Pin Grid Array (FC-PGA)

This package type is referred to as a flip chip, because the die (the part that makes up the chip) is exposed on the top of the processor to enable better chip cooling. Power and ground signals are uncoupled to improve performance. It uses separate capacitors and resistors on the bottom of the processor and contains 370 pins in a staggered arrangement so that the processor can be inserted into the socket only one way. This type is used in Pentium III and Celeron processors.

Example: FC-PGA2

The Flip Chip Pin Grid Array 2 package contains 370 pins in Pentium III and Celeron versions and 423 pins in the Pentium 4 version. It's different from the FC-PGA in that this version includes an integrated heat sink attached directly to the processor.

Example: OOI

The OLGA On Interposer (Organic Land Grid Array On Interposer) package uses a flip chip design with an integrated heat spreader to assist the heat sink. It's used in Pentium 4 processors and contains 423 pins.

Example: Pin Grid Array (PGA)

With the *PGA* package, pins insert into a socket. It uses a nickel-plated copper heat slug on top of the processor to improve thermal conductivity. It is used with the Intel Xeon processor and contains 603 pins.

Example: Staggered Pin Grid Array (SPGA)

In the *SPGA*, a staggered arrangement of pins around socket's outer edge enables more pins to be placed in the same surface area.

Example: Plastic Pin Grid Array (PPGA)

The PPGA contains 370 pins and was used with early Celeron processors.

Example: Single Edge Contact Cartridge (SECC)

The *SECC* uses gold contacts rather than pins, which plug into a slot. The package is covered in a metal shell and backed with a thermal plate used as a heat sink. This package contains a substrate circuit board to link the processor, L2 cache, and bus termination circuits. SECC versions with 242 contacts are used with the Pentium II Xeon processors. Packages containing 330 contacts are used with Pentium III Xeon processors.

Example: SECC2

The SECC2 version uses less casing material than the original SECC and does not use the thermal plate found on SECC packages. It contains 242 contacts and is used with some versions of the Pentium II and Pentium III processors.

Example: Single Edge Processor (SEP)

Similar to SECC, but without a casing, the SEP package contains a substrate circuit board that is visible from the outside. It contains 242 contacts and was used with early Celeron processors.

> Photos of each of these package types can be found through the links at **http://support.intel.com/support/processors/procid/ptype.htm**.

> Other packaging technologies are used in mobile computing. These include Micro-FCPGA and Micro-FCBGA. The first is a variation on the desktop FCPGA. The second uses balls rather than pins (hence the difference in acronyms). The balls can't be bent like pins can.

CPU Cooling Systems

As processors became more powerful and smaller, they also generated more heat, introducing the possibility of damage to or failure of the chip due to overheating. Damage can cause unpredictable processor behavior such as system lockups, sudden reboots, and the like. Failure obviously means that the chip is no longer usable.

> A whining noise from inside the computer could mean the CPU fan is starting to go bad. It's a good idea to periodically clean any dust from the fan by removing it from the chip (if necessary) and using a computer vacuum to remove accumulated dust.

Starting with the 486 processor, *heat sinks* with fans were added to address the problem of overheating processors. These devices are either glued to the CPU using a *thermal compound* or attached with a clamp. (Thermal compounds are manufactured to provide maximum heat transfer from the CPU to the heat sink.) An example of a heat sink is shown in Figure 4-9. To prevent the CPU from overheating, the fan blows heated air away from the heat sink metal elements, allowing cooler air to be pulled across the heat sink's fins and keeping the air around the processor cool. It is imperative that the connection to the CPU is tight.

Lesson 4

Figure 4-9: *A processor with heat sink and fan.*

CPUs can also be kept cool using a device to circulate a liquid, such as water, around the CPU. The heat from the CPU is absorbed by the cooler liquid, and then the heated liquid is circulated away from the CPU so it can disperse the heat into the air outside the computer. Liquid cooling systems are not as prevalent as heat sinks in most desktop systems or low-end servers.

Temperature Sensors

Modern systems, especially high-end servers, have a temperature sensor to detect a rise in temperature. In some of these systems, an LCD display on the system case shows the current internal temperature. In others, software is used to read the current operating temperature. You can often configure your system to notify you when the temperature is too high or to shut down to protect the components if the temperature reaches a certain level.

ACTIVITY 4-5

Identify Processor Characteristics

Scenario:
You are working on a customer's computer. You suspect problems with the CPU and want to identify its characteristics to determine if you could easily replace it.

What You Do	How You Do It
1. Shut down your computer and open its case.	a. Shut down your computer. b. Unplug its power cord. c. Open the computer case.
2. Determine the packaging type for your processor.	
3. Does your processor use a heat sink, fan, or other cooling method?	
4. What type of processor is in your system?	
5. Close your computer case, reconnect cables, and start your system.	a. Close the computer case. b. Reconnect the power cable and any others you might have disconnected. c. Boot your system.

Instruction Sets

Definition:

An *instruction set* is the collection of commands that is used by a CPU to perform calculations and other computing operations. Instruction sets vary by:

- Whether they require fixed length instructions or not.
- Whether the instructions are carried out by hardware only or hardware and software.
- How many instructions it takes to execute a function.

Lesson 4

Example:
> While every manufacturer has its own instruction set, they can all be generalized into the types described in the following table.

Instruction Set	Description
Complex Instruction Set Computer (CISC)	A design strategy for computer architectures that depends on hardware to perform complicated instructions. Does not require instructions to be of a fixed length. Allows for more complicated functions to be executed in one instruction. Most Intel processors fall into this category.
Reduced Instruction Set Computer (RISC)	A design strategy for computer architecture that depends on a combination of hardware and software to perform complicated instructions. Requires instructions to be of a fixed length. RISC instructions are simpler and fewer than CISC, but more instructions are required to carry out a single function. Macintosh, IBM RS/6000, and Sun Microsystems computers use RISC. IBM, Motorola, and Sun manufacture RISC chips.
Explicitly Parallel Instruction Computing (EPIC)	A design strategy for computer architecture that is meant to simplify and streamline CPU operation by taking advantage of advancements in compiler technology and by combining the best of the CISC and RISC design strategies. EPIC-based processors are 64-bit chips. Intel IA-64 architecture, including Intel Itanium processors, is based on EPIC.

How to Service Processors

Procedure Reference: Service or Replace Processors

Most problems with CPUs can be attributed to overheating, chip creep, and outright failure.

- If you suspect that overheating is causing CPU problems, verify that the CPU fan is installed and functional. If the fan doesn't work, replace it.

- Chip creep occurs over time—vibrations and movements cause components such as CPUs and memory chips to become loosened in their connections. Reseat the CPU if you think that chip creep might be the source of your CPU problems.

- Processors have no serviceable parts. When a processor is defective, you need to install a new one. Thus, CPU failure usually requires you to replace the processor.

1. Shut down the system and remove the existing CPU.
   a. Shut down the system.
   b. Unplug the power cord.
   c. Ground yourself and dissipate any static electricity you might be carrying.

d. Pull up the lever on the side of the ZIF-socket CPU. If you have a different style CPU, refer to the system documentation for how to remove it.
   e. Pick the CPU straight up so that you don't bend any pins.
   f. Place the old CPU in a safe location in an appropriate container to prevent damage to the CPU should you need or want to reinstall it later.
2. Install the new CPU.
   a. Align the pins on the CPU with the holes in the ZIF socket on the system board.
   b. Press the CPU lever back down to lock the CPU in place.
   c. Connect any power connections to the appropriate power connectors.
3. Reboot and verify that the CPU works. If the system boots, then the CPU was installed correctly. To verify that the CPU is reporting the correct information, you can view the System Properties dialog box and verify that the specifications listed match those of your CPU.

ACTIVITY 4-6

Upgrading the CPU

Scenario:

One of your clients has an older system that they need to try to upgrade. The CPU in the system doesn't meet the requirements for the application they need to run on it. They have purchased a CPU upgrade and would like you to install it for them.

Lesson 4

What You Do	How You Do It
1. Remove the existing CPU.	a. **Shut down the system and unplug the power cord.**
	b. **Ground yourself and dissipate any static electricity you might be carrying.**
	c. If necessary, **undo the clip to remove the heat sink and fan from the top of the CPU.**
	d. If necessary, **unplug the power cable from the CPU fan.**
	e. **Pull up the lever on the side of the ZIF-socket CPU.** If you have a different style CPU, refer to the system documentation for how to remove it.
	f. Now that the CPU has been released, **pick the CPU straight up** so as not to bend any pins.
	g. **Place the old CPU in a safe location in an appropriate container** to prevent damage to the CPU should you need or want to reinstall it later.
2. Install the replacement CPU.	a. **Align the pins on the CPU with the holes in the ZIF socket on the system board.**
	b. **Press the CPU lever back down** to lock the CPU in place.
	c. **Lock the heat sink and fan clip.**
	d. **Plug the CPU fan power plug in to the motherboard.**
	e. **Connect any power connections to the appropriate power connectors.**

3. Verify that the CPU is recognized.

   a. Restart the system.

   b. Display the System Properties dialog box.

   c. Verify that the CPU listed on the General page matches what you just installed.

How to Add a Second CPU

Procedure Reference: Add a Second Processor

To add a second processor:

1. Shut down the system, disconnect the power, and ground yourself.
2. Remove the terminator from the second processor socket.
3. Insert a CPU that is identical to the processor in the first processor socket.
4. Restart the system and verify that both processors are recognized in the System Properties window.

Procedure Reference: Remove a Second Processor

To remove a second processor:

1. Shut down the system, disconnect the power, and ground yourself.
2. Following the directions shown in the system board or processor documentation, locate the second processor, and remove it from the socket. The primary socket must contain a processor. So, if you are removing one of the processors, it cannot be the one in the primary socket. Refer to documentation for the system to determine which socket this is.
3. Following the directions shown in the system board or processor documentation, insert the terminator or other device in the second processor socket or set the system board settings for a single processor.
4. Reboot the system and verify that it can boot successfully with the single processor.

Lesson 4

Topic D

System Boards

When it comes time to upgrade the system board, chances are that you also need to upgrade everything else as well, so this is not a very common upgrade that you will be asked to perform. Sometimes, however, you have already spent the money to upgrade everything else, so it makes sense to just upgrade the system board as well.

System Board

Definition:

A *system board* or motherboard is the main circuit board in the computer. It contains the bus, processor, integrated circuits for peripherals, expansion slots, and BIOS chip. System boards come in a variety of shapes and speeds. All system boards are connected to the case and to all components within the system. The form factor varies between system boards. The system board might or might not have a *daughter board* or riser card, which expand the system circuitry, and it might or might not have a *voltage regulator module* (VRM), which is meant to regulate the voltage that's passed to the CPU. The *chipset* is the collection of primary chips used on the motherboard. The functions that a computer supports is determined by the chipset. The chipset usually includes chips for the functions such as the following:

- CPU
- BIOS
- RAM
- Ports, such as parallel, serial, USB, keyboard, and monitor
- Expansion slots
- Drive interfaces

Some system board terms you should be familiar with are:

- *Bus*—A set of physical and logical interconnections between the computer and add-on boards.
- *Datapath*—The width (in bits) of the bus, or the number of channels in the bus.
- CMOS—(Complementary Metal Oxide Semiconductor) A form of memory that stores configuration information. You use software, rather than jumpers or switches, to configure the system settings stored in CMOS.
- RAM—Volatile (non-permanent) memory used by applications to store data.

Daughter Boards

One reason that the system board is called the motherboard is because other boards can be plugged into it. A daughter board is a circuit board that is added to the motherboard to expand its circuitry. Unlike ordinary expansion boards, the daughter board accesses the system memory and CPU directly.

Example: A System Board Without a Daughter Board

The system board shown in Figure 4-10 does not have a daughter board.

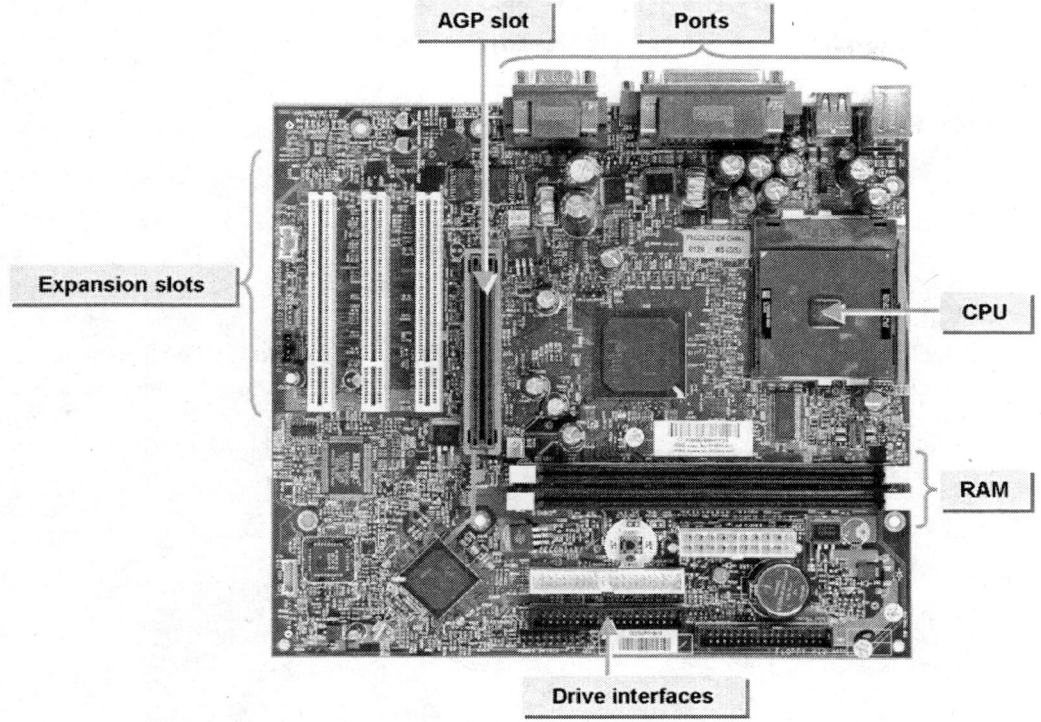

Figure 4-10: *A system board without a daughter board.*

Riser Cards

A *riser card*, like a daughter board, plugs directly into a slot on the motherboard and rises from the motherboard at a 90 degree angle. A riser card contains slots into which you can plug modems, audio cards, or network cards. Riser cards are meant to remove analog I/O processing from the motherboard for modems and audio components to make it easier for motherboard manufacturers to create and gain approval for new motherboard designs.

There are two types of riser cards:

- *Audio/Modem Riser (AMR)*—AMR riser cards are used to connect modems, and they support audio cards for higher-quality audio reproduction.
- *Communication and Networking Riser (CNR)*—CNR riser cards were meant to provide support for local area network (LAN) capabilities, modems, and audio cards.

Clock Speed

People often refer to their systems by the *clock speed*, rather than by the system board type. You will hear someone say they have a 800 MHz (*megahertz*) system or a 2 GHz (*gigahertz*) system. These speed ratings refers to the number of cycles per second or frequency at which the CPU operates. The speed is determined by an oscillator or electronic clock on the system board that is configured for a specific frequency.

Lesson 4

You can configure the clock to run at different clock speeds on most modern system boards. You should configure your system board to run at the highest speed that the CPU is rated to handle. You should not *overclock* your system, that is, configure your system board to run at a speed greater than your CPU is rated to handle. Doing so can cause the CPU to overheat, produce random results, or be damaged or destroyed.

Form Factors

The *form factor* is the size and shape of the motherboard.

Full-size AT

This is usually used in older tower systems. Originally, it was designed from the original XT motherboard. These original full-size systems took up a large amount of desktop space. Vertically-oriented tower systems can stand on the floor and not take up desktop space, and they can still use the full-size system board. The board is 12 inches by 13.8 inches. A transfer bus of 16-bit or better is required. It uses CMOS to retain configuration settings. It has a 5-pin DIN keyboard connection.

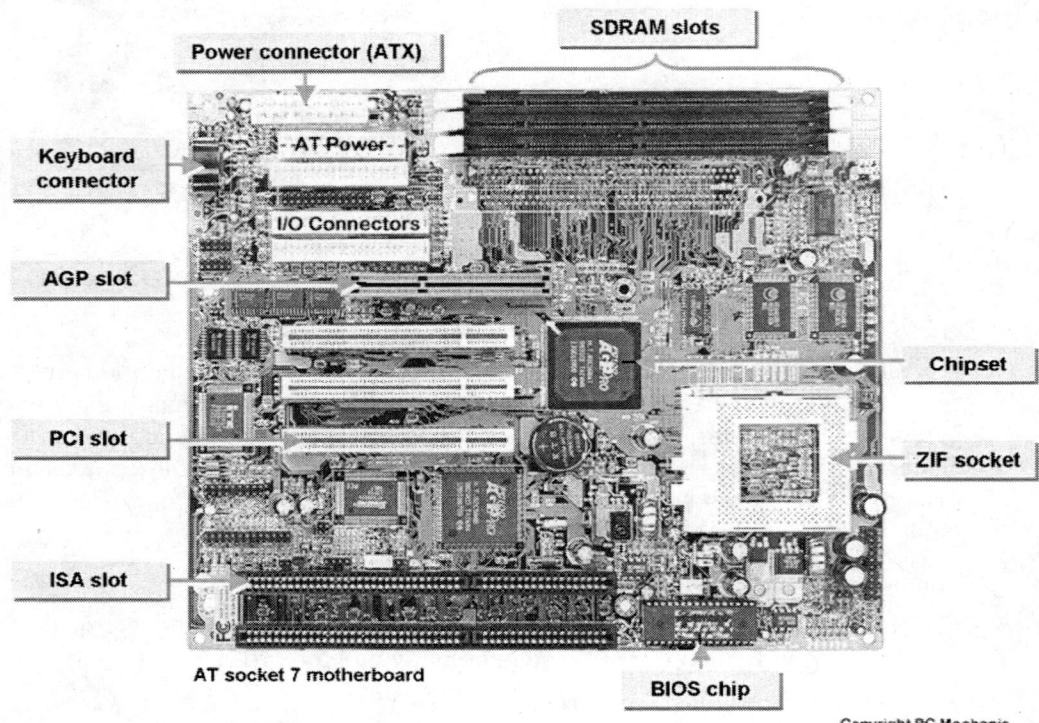

Figure 4-11: *Full-size AT system board.*

Baby AT

This is usually used in older desktop systems. In an effort to free up desk space, manufacturers wanted to build a computer that was smaller than systems with full-size AT motherboards. The popular AT motherboard was scaled down to create the Baby AT motherboard. It fits into a smaller case than the full-size AT board, but it is otherwise the same. It works in any case except for those considered low profile or slimline. This was an extremely popular design. This board is usually 13 inches by 8.5 to 9 inches. It was never developed as a standard, so there are variations on the size of this particular board.

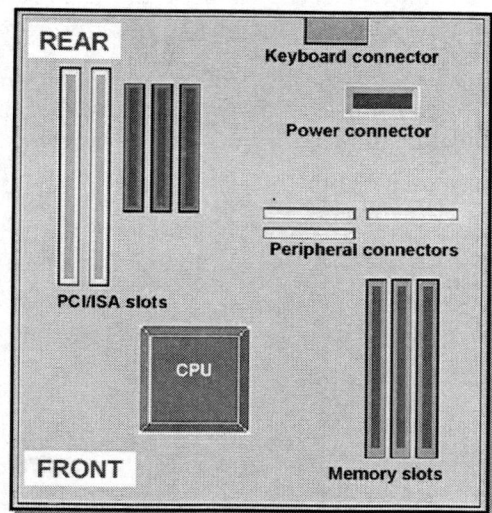

Figure 4-12: *Baby AT system board.*

LPX

Slimline and low-profile cases, which are today's typical desktop cases, were being developed about the same time as the Baby AT motherboard was introduced. However, these smaller cases could not use even the Baby AT board. The LPX and Mini-LPX motherboards were developed for these cases. A riser card is used to plug expansion cards into the motherboard. This riser card enables the expansion cards to lie sideways, in the same orientation as the system board. Thus, the case does not have to be as high as the card. Another difference in this board is that it uses a PS/2-style keyboard connector rather than the 5-pin DIN connector used on the AT boards. Video, parallel, and two serial ports were placed at the rear of the board in standard locations. This board is 9 inches by 11 to 13 inches. A mini-LPX board was also designed, which was 8 to 9 inches by 10 to 11 inches.

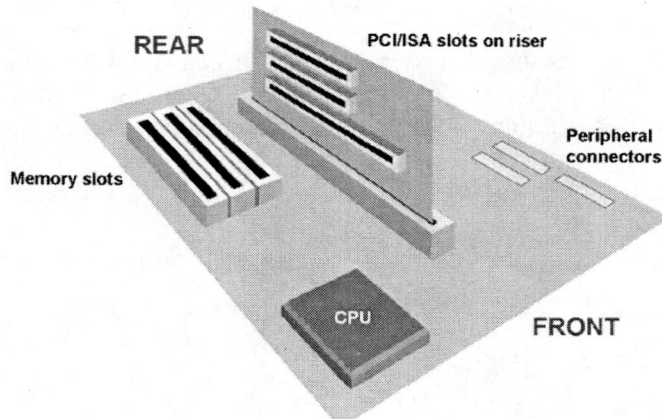

Figure 4-13: *LPX system board.*

ATX

In 1995, Intel introduced the ATX motherboard. It is the standard for new systems. Compared to AT motherboards, the ATX boards provide better I/O support, lower cost, easier use, and better processor support. Some of the features of the ATX board are:

- Power supply with a single, keyed 20-pin connector. Rather than requiring VRMs to reduce voltage down from 5 volts to 3, 3v DC is available directly from the power supply.
- The CPU is closer to the cooling fan on the power supply. Also, the cooling circulation blows air into the case instead of blowing air out of the case.
- I/O ports are integrated into the board along with PS/2 connectors (instead of 5-pin DIN connectors).
- You can access the entire motherboard without reaching around drives. This was accomplished by rotating the board 90 degrees.
- This board cannot be used in Baby AT or LPX cases.
- The board is 12 inches by 9.6 inches.

The ATX Specification standard can be found at **www.formfactors.org/developer/specs/atx/atx2_1.pdf**.

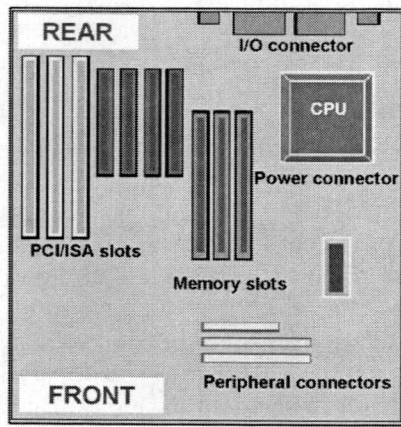

Figure 4-14: *ATX system board.*

NLX

Intel's NLX system board replaces the LPX system board. It is a small form factor designed around the Pentium II processor. It supports DIMM technology and AGP technology. It is used in newer slimline design systems. The board is 8 to 9 inches by 10 to 13.6 inches.

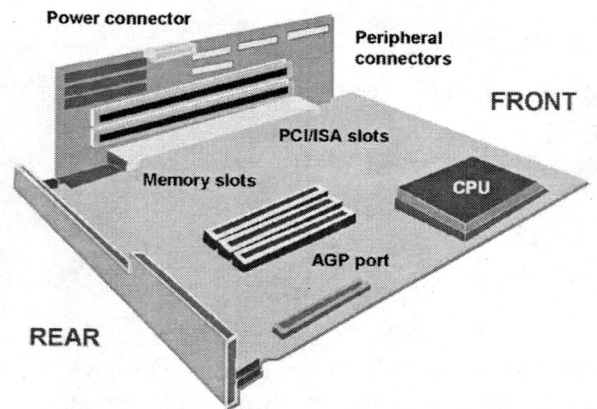

Figure 4-15: *NLX system board.*

Lesson 4

Computer Cases

Definition:

The computer case is the enclosure that holds all of the components of your system. Computer cases come in several formats. Some are designed to hold lots of internal components and have lots of room to work around those components. These cases are usually tower cases and take up a good deal of room. Other cases are designed to use a minimum amount of space. The trade-off is that the interior of the case is often cramped, with little room for adding additional components.

Since the tower proved to be popular, there are now several versions of the tower model. These include:

- Full tower, which is usually used for servers or when you will be installing many drives and other components.
- Mid tower, which is a slightly smaller version of the full-size tower.
- Micro tower, which is the size that replaces the original desktop case in most modern systems.

When you are replacing the system board, you need to make sure you get one that fits your case. This is because the holes in the system board need to line up with the connections in the case. The system board is secured to the case using these connections.

Also, when replacing the cover on the case, you must make sure the cover is properly aligned. If the cover isn't properly aligned, it might affect the cooling system and the operation of the internal drives.

Example: Enclosure Styles

Figure 4-16 shows examples of computer cases.

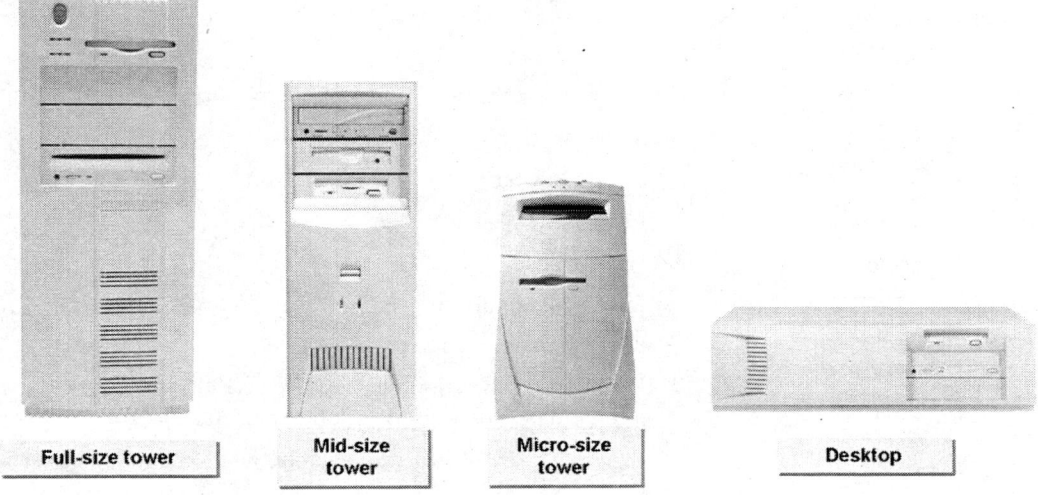

Figure 4-16: *Computer case enclosure styles.*

System Board Components

While every manufacturer's motherboard is slightly different, system boards contain generally the same components. Figure 4-17 illustrates these generic system board components.

Lesson 4: System Components

Lesson 4

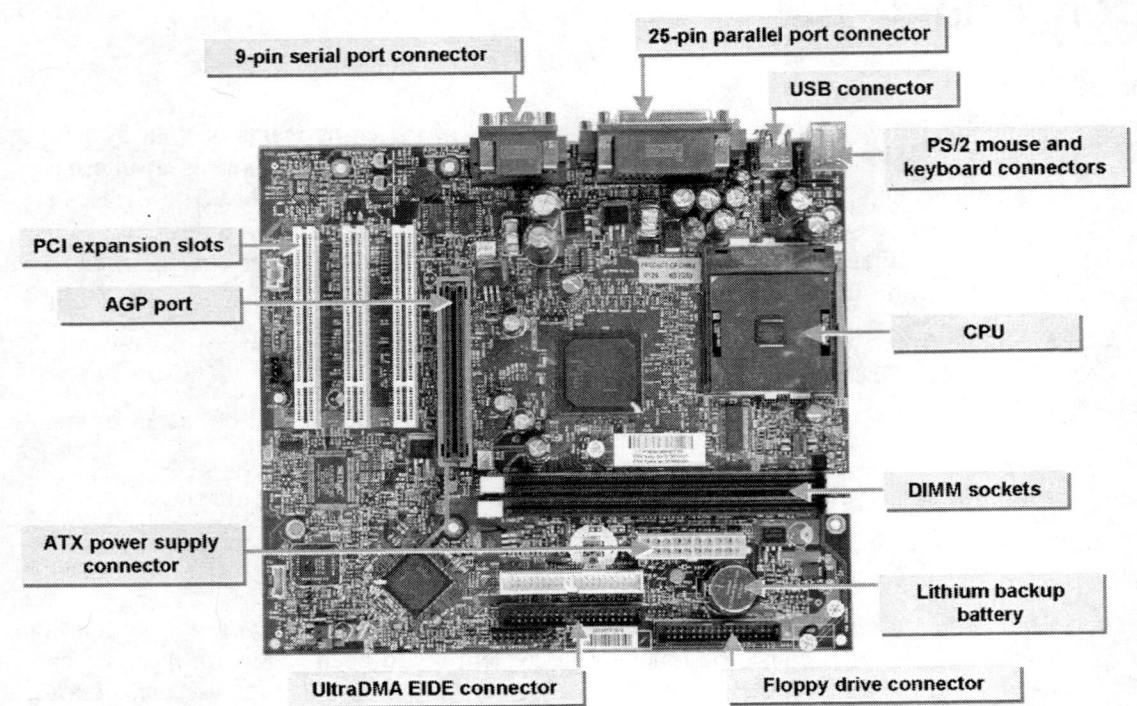

Figure 4-17: *A generic ATX system board.*

The following table describes each of the components.

Component	Description
BIOS	Basic Input Output System; used for configuring system hardware.
Processor slot	Where the CPU is installed.
Memory slots	Where the system RAM is installed.
L2 cache	Where the processor stores frequently used data and instructions.
PCI slots	Slots for 32-bit PCI cards.
ISA slots	Slots for 8-bit and 16-bit ISA cards.
Keyboard connector	PS/2 port.
Mouse connector	PS/2 port.
Serial port	DB9 male connector.
Parallel port	DB25 female connector.
USB port	Peripheral connection designed to be Plug and Play compatible, and to eliminate the need to install expansion cards.
Chipset	Integrated circuit that provides the motherboard's core functionality.
AGP slot	Dedicated video card adapter slot.
Power supply connector	Connects the power supply to the motherboard.
Floppy drive connector	Connects the floppy drive to the system.
IDE connector	Connects fixed and removable IDE drives, such as CD, DVD, and hard drives, to the system.

Other Ports on the System Board

While the following components are not necessarily found on all system boards, you may encounter them on some of the system boards you come across:

- Parallel port
- IEEE 1394/Firewire port
- Infrared port

ACTIVITY 4-7

Identify System Board Characteristics

Scenario:

You are working on a customer's computer. You suspect problems with the motherboard and want to identify its characteristics to determine if you could easily replace it.

What You Do	How You Do It
1. Shut down your computer and open its case.	a. Shut down your computer. b. Unplug its power cord. c. Open the computer case.
2. What form factor motherboard is in this system?	
3. Does this system use a daughter board?	
4. Can you determine the clock speed for this motherboard, or the range it supports, by looking at the motherboard itself?	
5. Close your computer case, reconnect cables, and start your system.	a. Close the computer case. b. Reconnect the power cable and any others you might have disconnected. c. Boot your system.

Lesson 4: System Components

Lesson 4

How to Upgrade the System Board

Procedure Reference: Replace the System Board

To replace the system board:

 If you need to, you can perform these steps in a different order if it makes it easier to physically access components.

1. Remove the original motherboard.
    a. Shut down the system and unplug the power cord.
    b. Disconnect all external devices.
    c. Remove all expansion cards and store them in anti-static bags.
    d. Disconnect cables from the system board, marking each cable as to what it connects to and where it goes.
    e. Unscrew the system board from the case.
    f. Lift the system board out of the case. On some systems, after lifting the system board over the pin(s), you will need to slide it out of the case.

2. Install the replacement motherboard.
    a. Place the new system board into the case and align the mounting holes.
    b. Secure the system board to the case.
    c. Install RAM and processor(s) on the new system board. Some sources recommend installing these components prior to installing the system board. If you do this, be careful not to bend the board or mash any connectors on the bottom side of the system board as you insert the components.
    d. Reinstall cards and cables removed from the old system board.
    e. Test the system.

Repair Versus Replace

Today's system boards are highly integrated and generally not repairable. When you examine a system board, you will find that there are very few components on the board that are actually repairable. For example, if a built-in port fails, you will have to install an expansion card that provides that port's functionality. If an integrated circuit fails, you will have to replace the system board. Even if you are highly skilled in the use of a soldering iron, in most cases, when a system board fails, you will replace it. Other than the battery, there is virtually nothing you can repair.

Configuring the System Board

When you replace a system board, you must ensure that it is properly configured to match the processor that it will host. In essence, you must configure the system board so that the internal and external frequencies of the processor are compatible. You accomplish this by specifying a frequency multiple. Most system boards operate at a specific speed, but some enable you to select the speed via DIP switches, jumpers, or the BIOS setup software.

DIP Switches and Jumpers

To configure older system boards, you used either *DIP switches* or *jumpers*. You might have used these switches to specify the multiplier and the CPU bus frequency. Newer system boards enable you to use software to configure these values (through the BIOS Setup program).

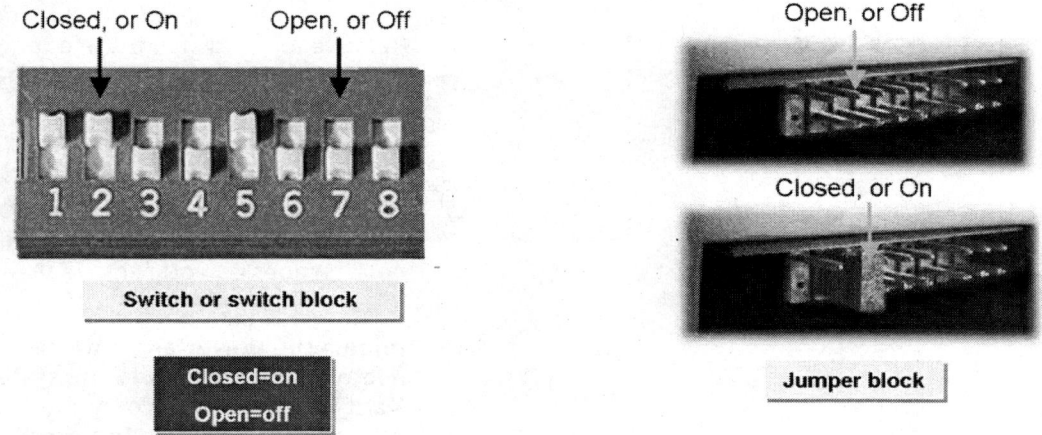

Figure 4-18: *Examples of DIP switches and jumpers.*

ACTIVITY 4-8

Upgrading the System Board

Scenario:

A lightning storm destroyed the system board in one of your customers' systems. You have been assigned the task of replacing the system board. While doing so, the customer would like you to put in an upgraded system board to improve system performance.

Lesson 4

What You Do	How You Do It
1. Remove cards and cables.	a. Shut down the system and unplug the power cord.
	b. Disconnect all external devices.
	c. Remove all cards from the expansion slots and store them in appropriate anti-static containers.
	d. As you disconnect each cable in the system, attach a piece of masking tape to each cable and record where each connection goes as you remove it.
	e. Unplug the power and data cable connectors for all drives in the system. Mark which cable is connected to the primary and which to the secondary IDE connector.
	f. Unplug connectors attached to any front-panel switches or LEDs.
	g. Unplug the power supply from the system board.
	h. If necessary, **remove the drive bay assembly and any other components needed to access all the screws on the system board.**
2. Remove the existing system board.	a. Unscrew the system board from the case. Be sure to set the screws aside to use in mounting the new system board.
	b. **Lift the system board,** and then if necessary, **slide it forward, and then lift it up and out of the case.**
3. Install the new system board. ⚠ Be sure not to screw the system board in too tightly, because this can damage the motherboard.	a. Slide the new motherboard into the case, aligning the mounting holes.
	b. Secure the motherboard to the case using the screws you removed from the old system board.

4.	Install RAM and a processor on the new system board.	a.	Install memory DIMMs beginning with Bank 0.
		b.	Install the CPU according to the manufacturer's directions.
5.	Reinstall the cards and cables.	a.	Reconnect all internal cables and cards, including any LED or front-panel switch connections.
		b.	Reinstall adapter cards.
		c.	If you needed to remove any drive bay assemblies or other components to access the system board, **replace any of those components.**
		d.	Reconnect the power supply to the system board.
		e.	Reconnect all external devices.
6.	Test the system.	a.	Plug in the power cord.
		b.	**Start the system.** If all went well, it should boot. Windows might attempt to reboot several times as it discovers new components.

Symptoms of System Board Problems

System board problems can be among the most difficult to recognize and diagnose. If you have eliminated all of the components, the software, and the operating system as not being the problem, then you should check that the system board is not the problem. Typically, the computer won't boot or the computer is displaying erratic behavior that can't be resolved otherwise.

These are the common sources of system board-related problems.

- Computer viruses infecting the system, including the BIOS.
- Loose connections between system components and the system board.
- Out-of-date BIOS.
- CMOS battery is not holding the BIOS information.
- Damage to the CPU due to overheating or electrical damage. Use a temperature sensor along with cooling systems to combat overheating, and utilize standard ESD prevention methods.
- Electrical shorts on the system board due to improperly-seated components, power surges, or ESD. This is the most common cause of system board problems.
- Physical damage to the system board.

Lesson 4

Preventing System Board Problems

When you have to touch the system board, you can prevent damage by handling it with care. When you install components into the system board, be sure not to bend or break any of the pins. This includes the pins on the cards as well as the system board. Also, the system board could be cracked if you pushed down too hard. When you secure the system board to the case, be sure not to overtighten the screws as this could also crack or damage the system board.

ESD damage, such as that caused by lightning strikes, can fry the system board electronics. Be sure to use proper surge protection to help prevent such problems.

How to Troubleshoot System Board Problems

Procedure Reference: Troubleshoot System Board Problems

To troubleshoot system board problems:

1. Eliminate problems with all other system components.
2. Perform a virus scan.
3. Reseat all components on the system board.
4. Update the system BIOS.
5. Replace the CMOS battery.
6. If you suspect overheating, implement further CPU cooling measures.
7. If you suspect electrical damage to the CPU, replace the CPU.
8. If you suspect electrical or physical damage to the system board, replace the system board.

TOPIC E

Memory

Just as some people say you can never be too rich or too thin, you can never have too much memory. Adding memory is one of the simplest and most cost effective ways to increase performance, whether it's on a brand-new system loaded with high-performance applications, or an older system that performs a few basic tasks. One way or the other, upgrading the memory is a frequent task for any computer service professional.

Memory

Definition:

Memory is a chip or set of chips used to store information. Some memory is volatile. This means the information it contains is lost when the system is powered off. Other memory is non-volatile. This means the information is retained even when the system is powered off. Memory is included on the system board and on some expansion cards.

Lesson 4

Example:

The following table lists some of the types of memory you will encounter. These types of memory hold their data electronically.

Type of Memory	Volatile?	Used For
CMOS	No, because it is maintained by a battery even when the system is off.	Holding the system configuration information.
Read Only Memory (ROM)	No, because the information is permanently stored on the chip.	Holding system or card startup information.
Random Access Memory (RAM)	Yes.	Holding program instructions and data so they can be processed by the CPU while you are using the system.
Sequential Access Memory (SAM)	Yes.	Holding data in a sequential order. When accessing data, each storage cell is checked until the desired information is found. Often used for memory buffers where data is stored in the order it will be used.

Non-Example:

Hard drives and floppy disks are not examples of memory because these devices hold their data magnetically. CD-ROM discs and DVD discs are also not examples of memory because these devices hold their data in pits on the surface of the disc.

ROM

Definition:

ROM is memory that is non-volatile. The original ROM chips could not be altered after the program code was placed on the ROM chip. As time went on, though, users needed the ability to update the information stored on ROM chips. Over the years, various chips have been created that perform the function of ROM, but can be updated one way or another. These are referred to as programmable ROM (PROM).

Example: ROM

A chip that cannot be altered. Technically, this is referred to as a masked ROM chip.

Lesson 4: System Components

Lesson 4

Figure 4-19: *A ROM chip.*

Example: PROM

A blank ROM chip that is burned with a special ROM burner. This chip can be changed only once. After the instructions are burned in, it cannot be updated or changed.

Figure 4-20: *A PROM chip.*

Example: EPROM

Erasable PROM. Like PROM, except that the data can be erased through a quartz crystal on top of the chip. After removing the chip from the system, a UV light is used to change the binary data back to its original state, all 1s.

Figure 4-21: *An EPROM chip.*

Lesson 4

Example: EEPROM

Electronically Erasable PROM. A chip that can be reprogrammed using software from the BIOS or chip manufacturer using a process called flashing. Also known as *Flash ROM*. The chip does not need to be removed in order to be reprogrammed.

Figure 4-22: *An EEPROM chip.*

RAM

Definition:

RAM is memory that is the main memory in the computer. It is used to hold programs and data while you are working on them. It is volatile, meaning that the charge that maintains the contents of memory must constantly be refreshed to avoid data loss. Some RAM is more volatile than other RAM and must be refreshed more often.

RAM is often described as a scratchpad or whiteboard area. This temporary memory area is wiped clean when the system is powered off or rebooted. The following is a list of the characteristics of RAM:

- Data can be accessed in any order.
- When the memory is full, data is purged. It is written to disk.
- Each memory chip is composed of millions of transistors and capacitors, which have been paired to create memory cells.

Example:

Over the years, many different RAM specifications have been developed. Most of these changes have been to improve performance. The following table describes the RAM types you might encounter.

 You can find additional information about Rambus and DDR SDRAM at **http://crucial.com/library/ddr_vs_rdram.asp**.

Lesson 4

RAM Type	Description
FPM	Fast Page Mode memory is used in older 32-pin SIMMs. Faster than previous RAM types because it reads an entire row rather than reading a row and column address at a time.
EDO	Extended Data Output memory is faster than FPM memory because it doesn't require the wait states necessary for FPM. It is often found on SIMMs and in Video RAM.
SRAM	Static RAM is used for cache memory. It does not need to be refreshed to retain information. It does not use assigned memory addresses. It can use synchronous, asynchronous, burst, or pipeline burst technologies.
DRAM	Dynamic RAM is used on single and dual in-line memory modules (SIMMs and DIMMs). It needs to be refreshed every few milliseconds. Uses assigned memory addresses. Can be implemented using FPM, EDO, BEDO, SDRAM, Direct Rambus DRAM, or Double Data Rate SDRAM.
RDRAM	Rambus DRAM is implemented on a RIMM memory module.
SDRAM and *DDR SDRAM*	Synchronous DRAM runs at high clock speeds and is synchronized with the CPU bus. Double Data Rate SDRAM transfers data twice per clock cycle. It is a replacement for SDRAM.
VRAM	Video RAM is a special type of DRAM used on video cards that can be written to and read from at the same time. It also requires less refreshing than normal DRAM.
WRAM	Windows RAM is a special type of video memory that can be simultaneously read from and written to in blocks. The Windows in the title of this RAM type does not indicate Microsoft Windows.

RAM Speed

RAM speed is the time needed to read and recharge a memory cell. It's measured in nanoseconds (ns). A nanosecond is one-billionth of a second. The smaller the number, the faster the RAM. For example, 10 ns RAM is faster than 60 ns RAM.

RAM comes in ever-increasing speeds. The RAM on sale at the local computer store might work just fine in your system, or it might be older, slower RAM they are trying to move out of stock.

 One of the popular memory manufacturers has an article on the speed of SDRAM at **http://crucial.com/library/sfiles4.asp**. They also have another article on the PC100 Standard, including a discussion on the speed of memory, at **http://crucial.com/library/sfiles5.asp**.

Older EDO RAM was often 60- to 70-ns speed RAM. Modern RAM that you are likely to find runs at clock speeds of 100 MHz and 133 MHz. The 100 MHz RAM has a RAM speed of 10 ns. The 133 MHz RAM has a RAM speed of 6 ns.

 The SDRAM used in 168-pin DIMMs has access times in the 6 to 12 nanosecond range.

You need to check what RAM speed is currently installed. All of the RAM in the system runs at the lowest common speed. It is backward-compatible, so it can run at the lower speed if it finds slower RAM. Some systems will not run with mixed RAM speeds, but these are not common. Either way, the RAM will not run any faster than the motherboard's bus speed.

Cache Types

When the CPU executes instructions, it stores the temporary results in *registers*, which are storage locations found directly within the CPU, for faster access to the results. But the vast majority of instructions and data are stored in RAM, so when the CPU needs more instructions to process, it has to stop to wait for two distinct system-bus operations (request instructions from RAM, and receive instructions from RAM) before it can proceed. To resolve this bottleneck, CPU design engineers developed a special type of RAM, faster and more expensive than traditional RAM, and added it to the CPU itself. This onboard RAM, which is a type of memory composed of SRAM, is called the *CPU cache*, *primary cache*, or *L1 cache*. This more expensive RAM does not need to be refreshed constantly, making it faster than the DRAM used for regular system memory.

Modern CPUs include both L1 and L2 cache. *Level 2 (L2) cache*, also known as external or *secondary cache*, is not located on the same microchip as the CPU. Originally, all L2 cache was on the motherboard. Now, at least some of the L2 cache is included in the CPU package. L2 cache is either 256 K or 512 K. A bus or bridge called the *backside bus* connects this L2 cache to the CPU chip. The bridge between regular memory and the CPU is referred to as the frontside bus. L2 cache is located between the processor and RAM and is normally twice the size of the L1 cache. *Level 3 (L3) cache* is memory on the motherboard between the processor and RAM when there's a built-in L2 cache on the processor.

DRAM Banks

You can combine multiple rows of DRAM into a cluster called a *bank*. Each row of DRAM can then be accessed simultaneously. When creating banks, the goal is to match the width of the DRAM to the width of the CPU's external *data bus*, which will generally be 8-bit, 16-bit, 32-bit, or 64-bit. Expressed another way, the number of SIMMs or DIMMs needed to create a bank is the width of the CPU's data bus divided by the width of the SIMM or DIMM. So, for a CPU with a 32-bit data bus, you need 4 SIMMs to create a bank.

Lesson 4

Activity 4-9

Determining the Appropriate Type of RAM

Scenario:
You've been asked to help another A+ technician determine the type and quantity of RAM to be ordered. He has several questions he needs you to answer before he is able to place the order with the vendor.

1. Match the type of RAM with its description.

    ___ VRAM
    ___ DDR SDRAM
    ___ SRAM
    ___ DRAM
    ___ WRAM

    a. A replacement for SDRAM.
    b. A special type of DRAM used on video cards that can be written to and read from at the same time. It also requires less refreshing than normal DRAM.
    c. A special type of video memory, which can be simultaneously read from and written to in blocks.
    d. Used for cache memory. It does not need to be refreshed to retain information. It can use synchronous, asynchronous, burst, or pipeline burst technologies.
    e. Used on SIMMs and DIMMs. It needs to be refreshed every few milliseconds. Uses assigned memory addresses.

2. True or False? RAM will not run any faster than the motherboard's bus speed.
    ___ True
    ___ False

3. True or False? A nanosecond is one-trillionth of a second.
    ___ True
    ___ False

4. In a system that contains RAM modules that run at 6 ns and 10 ns, what speed will the RAM run at?

    a) 4 ns
    b) 10 ns
    c) 6 ns
    d) 16 ns

Lesson 4

5. On a typical system with RAM that runs at a speed of 10 ns, you could add RAM that runs at which speed?

    a) 6 ns

    b) 10 ns

    c) 12 ns

    d) All of the above

6. Match the cache with its description.

    ___ L1   a. Memory on the motherboard between the processor and RAM when there's a built-in L2 cache on the processor.

    ___ L2   b. A type of high-speed RAM that is placed between the processor and conventional RAM to improve computing speed.

    ___ L3   c. A type of high-speed RAM that is added directly to a processor to improve computing speed.

7. The number of SIMMs or DIMMs needed to create a bank is the width of the CPUs data bus divided by the width of the _____ __ _____ .

8. On a system with a CPU with a 64-bit data bus, how many SIMMs would you need to create a bank?

    a) 2

    b) 4

    c) 8

    d) 16

9. On a system with a CPU with a 32-bit data bus, how many SIMMs would you need to create a bank?

    a) 2

    b) 4

    c) 8

    d) 16

Lesson 4

Memory Packages

Definition:

A *memory package* is a circuit board that holds several memory chips so that they can be plugged, as a group, into the memory expansion slots on the motherboard. The memory expansion slots in a computer are collectively known as the *memory bank*. These small, printed circuit boards are either one-sided or two-sided—that is, they contain RAM chips on one or both sides of the board. The circuit board has edge connector pins to connect it to the motherboard. Memory packages might or might not use parity for error-checking. Memory packages come in 8-bit, 16-bit, 32-bit, and 64-bit modules.

Originally, RAM chips were installed individually directly onto the motherboard. This made it difficult to upgrade the amount of RAM in a system or to pinpoint which chip was bad if there was a problem. Memory packages make it much easier to upgrade the RAM in a system. If there is a problem with a chip, the memory package module can be easily removed and replaced, eliminating the need to determine exactly which chip is bad.

 Additional information about how to visually identify memory can be found at **http://dewassoc.com/performance/memory/how_to_ID_memory.htm**.

Example: SIMM

SIMMs are groups of DRAM chips on a printed circuit board which fits in a socket on the system board. The chips are placed in a line, hence the name. The modules have opposing pins on either side of the board connecting to form a single electrical contact.

Older 486 systems used 30-pin SIMMs. Later 486 systems had slots for both 30-pin and 72-pin SIMMs. Because of this, they were known as transition boards; however, you couldn't mix 30-pin and 72-pin SIMMs on these boards—you had to use one type or the other exclusively. With the development of system boards that supported the Pentium, SIMMs were standardized to have 72 pins.

Figure 4-23: *A SIMM.*

All types of SIMMs must be installed in pairs, and can hold up to 32 MB of RAM. To install a SIMM, insert the stick into the slot at a 45-degree angle and then rotate it up until it clicks into place.

Don't mix different types of SIMMs within a memory bank. This prevents the CPU from determining how much memory it has, resulting in either a boot failure or not using some memory.

If you use SIMMs with different speeds within a memory bank, you need to use the same or faster speed of module than what you are replacing or adding to. All of the memory banks together run at the speed of the slowest SIMM.

Example: DIMM

DIMMs are Dual In-line Memory Modules. These have opposing pins on either side of the board that are electronically isolated to form two separate contacts with the system board. DIMMs are often used in systems with 64-bit or wider memory buses. Older Pentium systems used 72-pin DIMMs that could send 32 bits of data to the system bus at a time. Newer system boards support 168-pin DIMMs, which can send 64 bits to the system bus at a time. DIMMs can be installed individually as opposed to pairs, and can hold from 32 MB to 512 MB of RAM.

Figure 4-24: *A DIMM.*

Example: RIMM

A Rambus In-line Memory Module (*RIMM*) is a 184-pin, 2.5 volt, 600 or 800 MHz, 16-bit and 18-bit memory module for Direct Rambus Dynamic Random Access Memory (Direct RDRAM). A RIMM memory module can support from one to 16 direct RDRAM devices in a Rambus channel. A Direct Rambus channel provides support for up to three RIMMs. RIMM's primary use is as main memory installed on system boards.

Figure 4-25: *A RIMM.*

Rather than using a single data channel, RIMM uses multiple high-speed channels, enabling each channel to supply dedicated bandwidth to multiple devices simultaneously. It is composed of RDRAM chips. The chips are used in series on parallel channels, as compared to DIMM, which uses DRAM chips in parallel.

Example: Other Memory Packages

The following table describes other types of memory packages you might encounter.

Memory Package	Description
SODIMM	Small Outline Dual Inline Memory Module. Used in some notebook systems and Apple iMac systems. Measures about 2 inches by 1 inch and has 144 pins. Capacity ranges from 16 to 256 MB per module.
MicroDIMM	Micro Dual Inline Memory Module. Used in small, sub-compact notebooks. Measures about 1.5 inches long and has 144 pins.

Memory Package	Description
Proprietary	Many notebook manufacturers use proprietary formats for their memory modules. So, when you want to upgrade or replace the memory in those systems, you will need to purchase the memory from the notebook manufacturer in most cases.

Parity

Parity is an error correction method that is used on some memory modules for error-checking. Eight bits are for data, and the ninth bit is the parity bit.

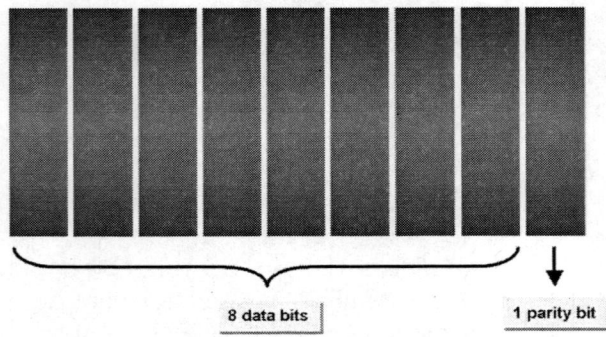

Figure 4-26: *Parity.*

Parity can be odd or even, meaning that the total number of 1s is an odd or an even number. The parity bit (the ninth bit) is set to 0 or 1, as needed, to create the correct total number of 1s.

For example, for even parity, if there are three 1s in 8 bits of data to send, the parity bit is set to 1 so that the total number of 1s is an even number. If there are four 1s, the total is already an even number, so the parity bit is set to 0. When the data is read, the 1s in the data bits are totalled again and the total is compared to the value of the parity bit. If the sum is an odd number like 3, and the parity bit is set to 1, the data is sent to the CPU with the assumption that the data was valid. If the sum is odd and the parity bit was set to 0, the data is not sent to the CPU, because this result indicates there is an error somewhere within the 8 bits of data. If an error is detected, nothing is done to fix it. The system simply tries again after discarding the data.

Parity is rarely used; other system components are relied on to verify that the data contained in memory is accurate when non-parity memory is used. Some chips use fake parity. In this case, the values are always 1s and it is assumed that there are never any memory problems. Other pieces of hardware and/or software take over in verifying that the information contained in the memory is correct.

ECC

Another error-checking method is *Error Correction Code (ECC)*. This method uses several bits for error-checking. A special algorithm is used to detect and then correct any errors it finds. ECC is used only in upper-end systems such as high-end workstations and servers; other desktop systems use non-ECC memory.

How to Add RAM to a System

Procedure Reference: Add Additional RAM to a System

To add RAM to a system:

1. Determine how much RAM is currently installed so that you can determine afterwards if the new RAM you installed is recognized. You can check the CMOS settings or use the System Properties dialog box to verify the amount of RAM.

    To check the RAM through System Properties:
    a. From the Start menu, choose My Computer.
    b. In the System Tasks box on the left side of the window, click View System Information.

2. Shut down your computer and disconnect the power cord.

3. Discharge any static electricity from yourself or your clothes. While this is always important to do, it is especially important to do when working with memory cards. These components are more delicate and more easily damaged by static charges than other system components.

4. Locate an empty memory expansion socket on the system board, or, if there are no empty slots, remove a smaller memory module to make room for one containing more memory.

    To remove an existing memory module:
    a. Press down on the ejection tabs.
    b. Firmly grasp the memory module and pull it out of the slot.

5. Align the notches in the connector edge of the memory module with the notches in the memory expansion socket, and then firmly press the memory module down into the socket.

6. If the ejection tabs did not lock into the notches on the ends of the memory module, push them up until they lock.

7. Restart the system.

8. Follow any on-screen prompts or perform any steps described in your system's documentation for getting the system to recognize additional memory. This is not required on all systems.

Lesson 4

9. Verify that the additional memory was recognized by the system.

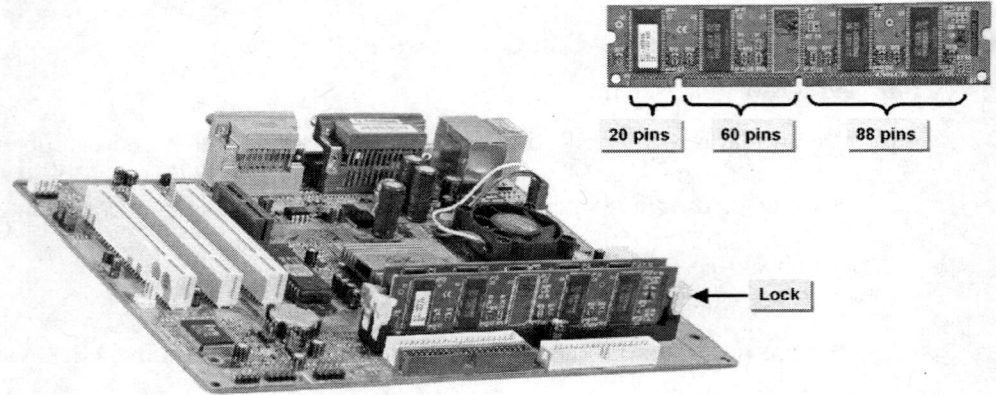

Figure 4-27: *Adding RAM to a system.*

ACTIVITY 4-10

Adding RAM to a System

Scenario:
The systems your customer purchased have been performing sluggishly. Additional RAM has been purchased for these systems.

Lesson 4

What You Do	How You Do It
1. Determine how much RAM is currently installed.	a. From the Start menu, **choose My Computer**. b. **Click View System Information.** 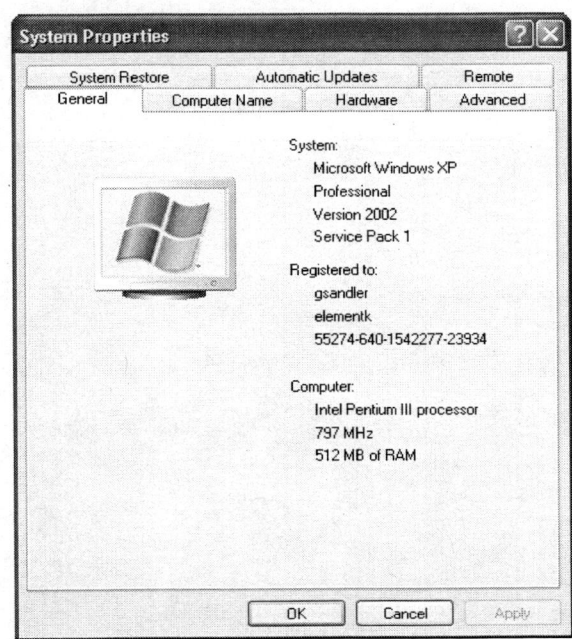
2. How much memory is currently installed?	

Lesson 4: System Components

3. Install more memory in the system.
   a. Shut down your computer.
   b. Disconnect the power cord.
   c. Discharge any static electricity from yourself and your clothes.
   d. Locate the memory expansion sockets in your system.
   e. If there are no empty memory expansion sockets, **push the ejector tabs on each end of the memory module out** to release the memory module, **and then remove the memory module.**
   f. Align the notched edge of the memory module with the memory expansion slot, and then firmly press the module down into the socket.
   g. If the ejector tabs did not automatically lock into each end of the memory module, **push both ejector tabs up until they lock into the notches on each end of the memory module.**

4. Verify that the additional memory is recognized by the system.
   a. Plug in the power cord and restart the system.
   b. If prompted at startup, **follow any on-screen prompts** to make the system recognize the memory.
   c. **Display the System Properties dialog box and record the amount of memory shown.** If the additional memory isn't recognized, you can check documentation to see if any steps need to be performed. Also, verify that the memory was correctly seated in the slots and was the correct type of memory for the system.

Symptoms of Memory Problems

Memory problems typically show themselves as memory-specific errors, erratic behavior of the system, or frequent crashes. The following table lists some of the common symptoms and possible causes of the problems.

Symptom	Possible Causes
Computer crashes or reboots itself periodically. Application data is corrupted.	ESD, overheating, or other power-related problems that then affect memory. Registry writing to bad memory, General Protection Faults (GPFs), and exception errors caused by software and operating system.
Memory errors are displayed on the screen.	Memory address errors at boot time. Memory mismatch errors in which you are prompted to specify how much RAM is installed to clear the message. Applications that require large amounts of memory or that don't properly release memory.
Computer appears to boot, but the screen remains blank.	Memory is not correct for the system. For instance, the computer is expecting memory that uses error checking and you installed non-parity memory. Memory module is not fully inserted into the slot.
Computer does not boot. POST beep codes are heard.	CPU cannot communicate with memory due to the memory being improperly installed or the BIOS not recognizing the memory. Beep codes are specific to the BIOS manufacturer and the ones for memory can be found in the manufacturers' beep codes list.
Newly installed memory is not recognized.	You exceeded the maximum amount of RAM that can be addressed by the system. Even though the slots can accept SIMMS containing more memory, the system can only recognize a certain amount of memory on most systems. The wrong memory type was installed.

How to Troubleshoot Memory Problems

Procedure Reference: Troubleshoot Memory Problems

To troubleshoot memory problems:

1. Perform a virus scan. Viruses can cause symptoms that mimic those of a memory problem.
2. Verify that the correct memory modules were installed in the system. You can check the part numbers against the memory or PC manufacturer's Web site. For example, be sure that you aren't trying to use DDR RAM in an EDO RAM system.

Lesson 4

3. Verify that the memory was installed and configured properly. Older systems required that memory be installed in pairs. In all cases, verify that the memory modules are fully seated. Always start with memory in the first bank. Check your documentation for other requirements specific to your system.

4. Try swapping the memory between slots. For example, if you only experience problems when many applications are open, the chance is that one of the memory modules in the higher banks is the problem. If the system won't boot, try one of the other modules in the first bank to see if it then boots. Try putting a known good module in the first slot and removing all of the other memory modules.

5. Check for BIOS upgrades. If there are known problems, then a fix has probably been issued. This usually applies to older systems.

Lesson 4 Follow-up

In this lesson, you examined the major components found inside practically any personal computer, including the power supply, ROM BIOS, central processing unit, system board, and RAM. You determined their characteristics, explored common problems associated with them, and looked at how to service them.

1. **Describe the primary function of a power supply.**

2. **Describe the observable, physical characteristic that distinguishes Pentium and earlier processors from many Pentium II and later processors.**

3. **Describe the characteristics of a standard ATX system board.**

4. **Describe the difference between a SIMM, DIMM, and RIMM.**

LESSON 5
Bus Architectures

Lesson Time
2 hour(s), 15 minutes

Lesson Objectives:

In this lesson, you will identify the features of various bus architectures.

You will:

- Define the purpose of a bus and how it works.
- Identify the characteristics of the 8-bit expansion bus.
- Identify the characteristics of the ISA expansion bus.
- Identify the characteristics of the EISA expansion bus.
- Identify the characteristics of the Micro Channel Architecture bus.
- Identify the characteristics of the PCI expansion bus.
- Identify the characteristics of video circuitry buses.
- Troubleshoot adapter cards.

Lesson 5

Introduction

In this lesson, you will examine expansion buses and the adapter cards they enable. You will look at the different types of buses that have been commonly used with PCs of the past decade or so. You will also examine how to troubleshoot adapter card problems.

Because it would be so cost-prohibitive to create systems containing every available option in a PC, designers developed various standards for the interfaces between the computers and the components to be installed later. This architecture is referred to as the bus, or expansion bus.

The following CompTIA A+ Core Hardware (2003) Examination objectives are covered in this lesson:

- Topic A:
  - 1.4 Identify typical IRQs, DMAs, and I/O addresses, and procedures for altering these settings when installing and configuring devices. Choose the appropriate installation or configuration steps in a given scenario. Content includes the following: specialized devices; and floppy drive controllers.
- Topic C:
  - 1.1 Identify typical IRQs, DMAs, and I/O addresses, and procedures for altering these settings when installing and configuring devices. Choose the appropriate installation or configuration steps in a given scenario. Content includes the following: legacy devices.
  - 4.3 Identify the most popular types of motherboards, their components, and their architecture (bus structures). Content includes the following: ISA.
- Topic F:
  - 4.3 Distinguish between the most popular types of motherboards, their basic components, and their architecture (bus structures). Content includes the following: PCI—PCI 32-bit, PCI 64-bit.
- Topic G:
  - 4.3 Identify the most popular types of motherboards, their components, and their architecture (bus structures). Content includes the following: AGP—2X, 4X, and 8X (Pro).
- Topic H:
  - 2.1 Recognize common problems associated with each module and their symptoms, and identify steps to isolate and troubleshoot the problems. Given a problem situation, interpret the symptoms and infer the most likely cause. Content includes: adapter—sound card and video card.

TOPIC A

What is a Bus?

Computer designers can't foresee every desired feature in a single computer. If such a computer were manufactured, it would be so expensive that few people would be able to afford it. For this reason, computers are designed in a modular fashion. You can customize or upgrade a computer by adding adapter cards that offer the special functions you need.

Bus

Computer designers develop standard interfaces between their generic computers and the specific adapters that you install later. This interface is called a bus. Specifically, an adapter bus is a set of physical and logical interconnections between the computer and add-on boards.

Bus designs usually specify the placement of connections, the electrical signals that are allowable on each connector, and what those signals mean. Most bus interface designs even specify the size of the adapter card that can be inserted and the power that the card can consume.

Different computer systems use different bus designs. Computers based on the Intel chips generally use one or more of the ISA, EISA, VESA Local Bus, PCI, PCMCIA, AGP, or Micro Channel buses.

Interacting with the Host System

Adapters, as well as other hardware and applications, must communicate with the host system in an orderly and established way. Communication must be orderly to avoid setting conflicts when configuring adapters to gain the attention of the host processor. Conflicts are a main cause of problems in communication between adapter and host systems. It's important to keep this in mind for any changes you may make to your system.

In general, a device gains the attention of the host processor, and then transfers data. A number of techniques can be used to gain the exclusive attention of the processor, such as periodic polling of adapters. Each technique relies on a set of hardware resources that constrain the communications between the host processor and adapter.

Hardware Resources

Hardware resources are uniquely-assigned communications paths that enable a device to exchange information with the CPU and operating system. The hardware resources, which include Direct Memory Access (DMA) channels, Input/Output (I/O) ports, Interrupt Request (IRQ) lines, and memory addresses, can be assigned manually (for a non-PnP device) or by the operating system (for a PnP device), at the time it is installed. No two devices can operate simultaneously with the same hardware resources. You can use Device Manager to see the hardware resources assigned to a particular device.

Most resources cannot be shared. If more than one device is configured to use a resource, a *device conflict* occurs. When this happens, neither device can function properly. For resources to be shared, the hardware, operating system, and device drivers must all be able to support shared resources.

Lesson 5

If the device you install is not PnP (Plug and Play) compatible, you will need to set the resources yourself, either through Device Manager, using software included with the device, or manually at the device itself. You set resources manually either by moving DIP switches, which are usually implemented as rocker switches, or configuring jumpers, which are caps placed over pins to complete a circuit. The resources set on the hardware must match those specified in the operating system or device driver in order for the device to function properly.

Interrupts

An interrupt request line (*IRQ*) is a hardware line connected to a controller chip and assigned to a device. When the device needs to request the attention of the computer processor, it sends a signal, called an *interrupt*, over the IRQ line, and the controller chip signals the CPU. A unique IRQ is required for each device.

When signaled, the processor puts its current task on hold and responds, or services, the interrupt. The Intel family of computer chips and compatible chips supports hardware, exception, and software interrupts.

- *Hardware interrupts* are those that come from the system hardware, such as the keyboard or the system clock, and from adapter cards. For example, under DOS or Windows 9x, one such signal, interrupt 25, causes the processor to reset and the system to reboot. This is what happens when you press Ctrl+Alt+Delete under those operating systems.
- *Exception interrupts* are used mainly by the processor itself to handle error conditions. An exception interrupt will be issued, for example, when a process requests the processor to divide a number by zero.
- *Software interrupts* are interrupts sent by an application that is running on the computer. Software interrupts generally trigger one of the built-in ROM BIOS routines. These built-in routines can be replaced by routines available from third-party vendors. The substituted routines would be called in the case of a software interrupt.

Should two or more adapters share an IRQ number, the processor will be unable to determine which adapter actually sent an interrupt. In such a situation, the processor might attempt to service either or neither of the adapters, usually resulting in erratic behavior.

IRQ Assignments

This table shows the default IRQ assignments for the early 8-bit ISA bus and for the current 16-bit systems. Note that some IRQs are shared between two components.

IRQ	8-bit Defaults	16-bit Defaults
0	System timer	System timer
1	Keyboard	Keyboard
2	Available	Cascade to IRQ9
3	COM2	COM2 & COM4
4	COM1	COM1 & COM3
5	Hard disk controller	LPT2
6	Floppy drive controller	Floppy drive controller
7	LPT1	LPT1
8		Real Time Clock (RTC)
9		Cascade to IRQ2

IRQ	8-bit Defaults	16-bit Defaults
10		Available
11		Available
12		Bus mouse port
13		Math coprocessor
14		Hard disk controller
15		Available

An IRQ controller chip manages the first eight IRQs. The CPU answers the interrupts in numerical priority order, starting with IRQ 0 (the system clock) and cycling through IRQ 7. On a 16-bit system, the eight additional IRQs reside on a second IRQ controller chip, which itself uses interrupt 2 on the first controller chip. Thus, the IRQ priority order becomes 0, 1, (8, 9, 10, 11, 12, 13, 14, 15), 3, 4, 5, 6, 7.

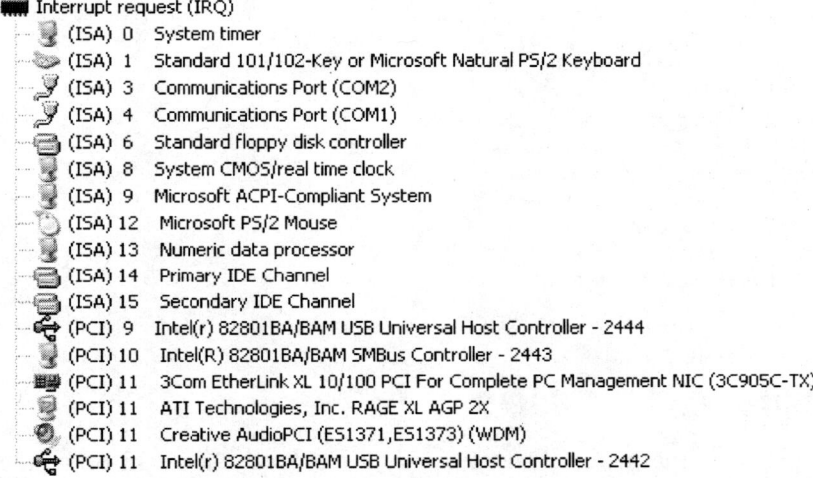

Figure 5-1: *Example of IRQ settings.*

Input/Output Addresses

Once the adapter has used an interrupt to signal the processor that it needs attention, it then needs a way to communicate with the host system. This is accomplished with an *I/O address*. Several terms are used to describe this feature, such as I/O address, Base I/O address, and I/O port.

An I/O address marks the beginning of a range of memory, usually in the lowest portions of memory (conventional memory), that is used for communications between the processor and the adapter. Each adapter must have its own unique, non-overlapping I/O address space.

I/O addresses are generally ranges of memory on the order of 4 to 32 bits of contiguous memory space. These addresses usually fall between 0x200 and 0x3FF (hexadecimal).

Lesson 5

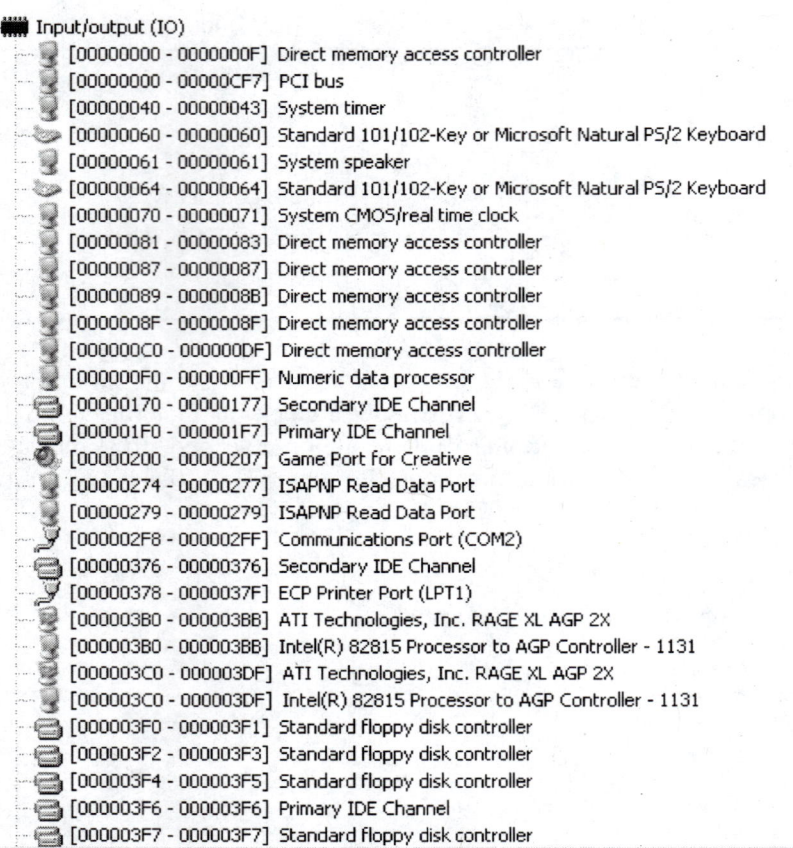

Figure 5-2: *Example of I/O address settings.*

Base Memory Addresses

The *Base Memory address* is the memory address of any memory that might be on the adapter card. This feature is often used to provide a buffer space, or a control program execution space, on the adapter. This configurable area is usually associated with adapters that contain their own BIOS chips or memory. Memory addresses for these on-board memories are most often mapped to the range between 640 kilobytes (KB) and 1 megabyte (MB), which is the Upper Memory Block (*UMB*) region of the host computer. Each adapter in a system must have a unique Base Memory address.

DOS memory managers, such as HIMEM.SYS, EMM386.SYS, or QEMM, load *TSRs*, drivers, and other programs into the UMB region. Most of these, especially the commercial ones, are fully capable of managing access to this memory region by adapter cards, drivers, and TSRs.

Memory Address Assignments

The following table shows the standard base memory address assignments for various system components.

Port	Base Memory Address
LPT1	378h
LPT2	278h
COM1	3F8h

Lesson 5

Port	Base Memory Address
COM2	2F8h
COM3	3E8h
COM4	2E8h
Primary IDE	1F0
Secondary IDE	170
Floppy disk drive	3F0
Network adapter	300–310

Memory
- [00000000 - 0009FFFF] System board
- [000A0000 - 000BFFFF] ATI Technologies, Inc. RAGE XL AGP 2X
- [000A0000 - 000BFFFF] Intel(R) 82815 Processor to AGP Controller - 1131
- [000E0000 - 000FFFFF] System board
- [00100000 - 1FFFFFFF] System board
- [20000000 - FFEFFFFF] PCI bus
- [F4700000 - F47FFFFF] Intel(R) 82815 Processor to AGP Controller - 1131
- [F8000000 - FBFFFFFF] Intel(R) 82815 Processor to AGP Controller - 1131
- [FC9FEC00 - FC9FEC7F] 3Com EtherLink XL 10/100 PCI For Complete PC Management NIC (3C905C-TX)
- [FCA00000 - FEAFFFFF] Intel(R) 82815 Processor to AGP Controller - 1131
- [FD000000 - FDFFFFFF] ATI Technologies, Inc. RAGE XL AGP 2X
- [FEAFF000 - FEAFFFFF] ATI Technologies, Inc. RAGE XL AGP 2X
- [FFB00000 - FFBFFFFF] Intel(r) 82802 Firmware Hub Device
- [FFF00000 - FFFFFFFF] Intel(r) 82802 Firmware Hub Device

Figure 5-3: *Example of Base Memory settings.*

Direct Memory Access

Direct Memory Access (DMA) is a technique for speeding data transfers within the computer. In a non-DMA situation, the system processor is involved with transferring every single byte of data between adapters and system memory. While dealing with these data transfers, the processor can't perform other tasks.

In a DMA situation, the DMA controller works with the processor and other components in the system to speed data transfer by relieving the processor from this duty and handling all of the related issues. The DMA controller also communicates with the adapters to facilitate transferring data from them directly to system memory.

Adapters must each use a unique DMA channel to communicate with the DMA controller. Failure to do so will prevent proper operation of the conflicting adapters.

DMA Assignments

The following table shows the standard DMA assignments for various system components.

DMA Channel	Default DMA Assignments on an 8-bit Bus	Default DMA Assignments on a 16-bit Bus
0	Dynamic RAM refresh	Available
1	Hard disk controller (XT)	Available

Lesson 5: Bus Architectures

Lesson 5

DMA Channel	Default DMA Assignments on an 8-bit Bus	Default DMA Assignments on a 16-bit Bus
2	Floppy drive controller	Floppy drive controller
3	Available	Available
4	n/a	2nd DMA controller
5	n/a	Available
6	n/a	Available
7	n/a	Available

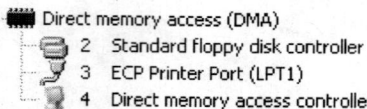

Figure 5-4: *Example of DMA settings.*

Device Manager

Device Manager is a software tool built into windows that enables you to configure settings for hardware devices installed in or connected to your computer. Device Manager displays a list of all the hardware devices installed on your system. You can select a specific device and then view or set the properties for the device.

ACTIVITY 5-1

Identifying System Parameters

Scenario:
In preparation for adding a new device to your system, you want to check the current communication parameter assignments.

What You Do	How You Do It
1. **Open Device Manager.**	a. From the Start Menu, **right-click My Computer and choose Properties.**
	b. **Select the Hardware tab.**
	c. **Click Device Manager.**

2. View the current DMA, IRQ, I/O address, and base memory assignments.	a.	Choose View→Resources By Type.
	b.	**Expand Direct Memory Access (DMA)** to examine the current DMA assignments on your computer.
	c.	**Expand Interrupt Request (IRQ)** to examine the current IRQ assignments on your computer.
	d.	**Expand Input/Output (IO)** to examine the current I/O address assignments on your computer.
	e.	**Expand Memory** to examine the current base memory assignments on your computer.
3. Close Device Manager and System Properties.	a.	**Close Device Manager.**
	b.	**Click Cancel** to close the System Properties dialog box.

Configuring System Parameters

Older adapter cards, such as ISA adapters, were most often configured with switches (also known as DIP switches, where DIP stands for DIPolar or Dual In-line Package) or jumpers. With these, you physically alter circuitry paths on the card by selectively opening or closing switches. This configuration process adds difficulty and labor requirements to the use of ISA cards.

The settings needed for a particular card that will be used in a particular system are specific to that installation. Each manufacturer will list the valid settings for its cards. Check the manuals that come with your system to determine the valid settings for your computer as well, because they can differ among computer makes and models:

- You configure cards with jumper pins by using the jumpers, which are plastic-coated metal clips, to close a circuit represented by a bank or group of jumper pins. If a jumper goes bad, the circuit will not be completed until the jumper is replaced. One way to save jumpers so that they are available for replacement (or reconfiguration of the board) is to place them over only one of the jumper pins in a pair.

- Switches are usually found in even-numbered banks or groups. You configure cards with switches by using a small object such as a mini-screwdriver, pen point, or bent paper clip to set the switches to ON or OFF. Do not use a pencil to set switches—the graphite can get into and foul the switch mechanism.

Lesson 5

Plug and Play

Plug and Play (PnP) is a standard that enables a PnP-compatible computer and a PnP-compatible operating system to work together to automatically configure settings when PnP-compatible hardware is connected to the system. After you install a component into a Plug and Play computer, the system detects the new component and configures the settings.

 Plug and Play, in its early days, was often also called Plug and Pray. This is because, especially in older systems, both PnP and legacy (non-PnP) components were often found in the same system, opening up the potential for conflicts and improper configuration. Systems on the market today are all PnP-compliant. as are the current operating systems. Problems are much less likely in such systems. In general, the fewer legacy devices you have installed in your system, the less likely you will be to encounter problems.

When you install hardware, this is a very high-level overview of what happens:

1. You connect a piece of hardware to a PnP-compatible system running a PnP-aware operating system.
2. All PnP cards enter Configuration mode by enabling PnP code built into the card.
3. One at a time, PnP cards are isolated and a handle is assigned to the card. The handle is used to identify that card.
4. Resources are allocated to each card that don't conflict with resources allocated to any other card.
5. All PnP cards are activated and exit Configuration mode.

For PnP to work, the following components must support Plug and Play:

- The device/adapter you want to install.
- The BIOS.
- The operating system.

The Add New Hardware Wizard

If you install a new device and Windows doesn't automatically detect it, you can also use the Add New Hardware Wizard to install and configure PnP devices. You will find the Add New Hardware Wizard in the Control Panel. When using the wizard, you should initially let Windows try to scan for new hardware (this is the default selection). If Windows can find the new device, it will identify and install the driver for the device. If Windows can't find the device, you can then either choose the device from a list of devices offered by Windows and Windows will install the appropriate driver, or you can click Have Disk to point to a driver from the manufacturer on floppy disk, CD-ROM, or from the manufacturer's Web site.

Plug and Play Devices

Most new devices you buy will be PnP-compliant. Such devices might include modems, network cards, CD-ROM drives, and even specialized devices, such as CAD/CAM input or output devices, touch screens, or biometric devices. You can run into problems when using legacy devices. PCI devices are always PnP devices. ISA devices should state whether they're PnP or not on the packaging, and in the documentation.

Plug and Play BIOS

Today's BIOSs all support PnP. If you have a Pentium computer, you can pretty much count on the BIOS supporting PnP. To verify whether the BIOS supports PnP, watch the screens during the boot process. If it does, you will see a screen that will make reference to the Plug and Play BIOS extension. If your BIOS doesn't support PnP, you should look into upgrading the BIOS, if possible. Alternatively, you can install a new system board with a BIOS that supports PnP.

Here's how a PnP BIOS handles resource assignment for both PnP devices and legacy devices: during boot-up, after the POST routine finishes, the BIOS takes over, and first looks to see if there are legacy devices in the system. If there are, the BIOS determines what resources they need (as assigned by you or the operating system) by checking a list of resources that are already assigned. Then, it queries PnP devices and identifies the resources required by those devices. Typically, a PnP device can only use certain resources, and thus the BIOS can choose from only those resources. Thus, even though resource assignment is automatic, it can become complicated if other devices are already using all of the resources a new PnP device can use. The symptom you will likely see is that the device just won't be recognized. In this scenario, you might need to re-allocate resources for legacy devices or let the BIOS reconfigure all devices. You can do this through PnP's Reset Configuration Data option in the system BIOS, which means that, like so many other parts of the PC, PnP can be configured through the CMOS Setup program.

Plug and Play Operating System

The operating system you're running must support Plug and Play for Plug and Play devices to be recognized and configured automatically. Windows 95, 98, Me, NT, 2000, and XP all support Plug and Play. When you install a PnP device in the system and restart the operating system, Windows will display a message that a new device was detected and will try to locate and install the correct driver for the device. If it's successful, you don't have to do anything; the device driver will be installed automatically, and the proper resources will be allocated and resource information saved. If Windows can't find a driver, you will be able to either choose the correct driver from a list or specify that you have the driver on a disk (as supplied by the hardware manufacturer).

You can use the Device Manager in Windows to see current resource assignments and the driver that is used for any device installed in your system. Select a device in Device Manager, and click Properties. You will find driver information on the Driver tab, and resource information on the Resources tab. On the Resources tab, you will see a check box called Use Automatic Settings. If checked, PnP is used to allocate resources. If unchecked, you can manually assign resources (even to PnP devices) by clicking Change Setting and making the necessary assignments. Note, however, that if you manually assign resources, those resources are no longer available for possible future PnP reconfiguration or assignment, but are instead permanently assigned to the device for which you made the manual assignment.

 Note that if you manually assign a resource in Device Manager, that resource is no longer available for future PnP reconfiguration or assignment. It is permanently assigned to the device for which you made the manual assignment.

Lesson 5

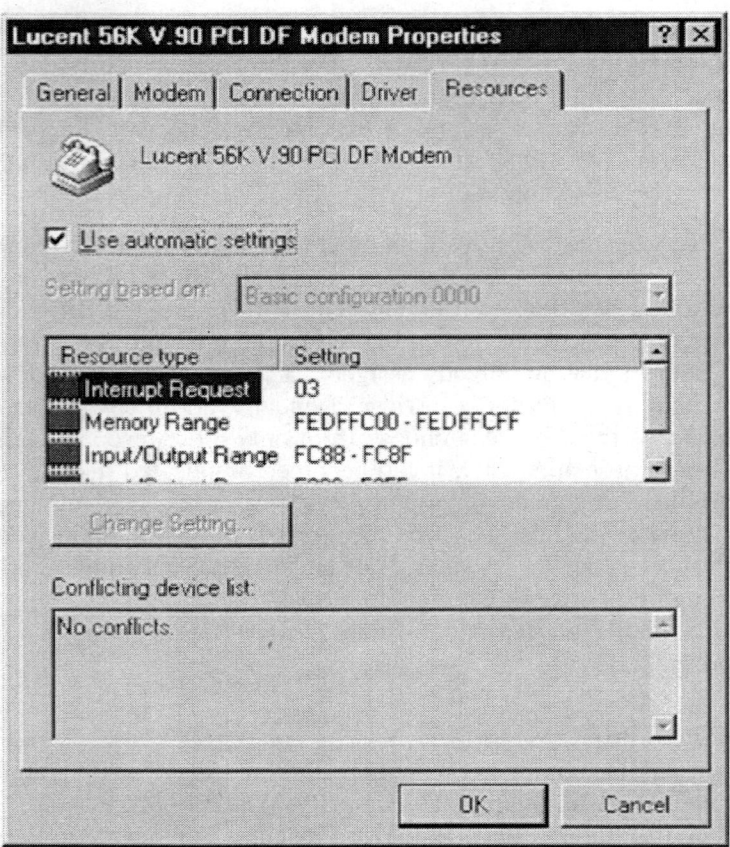

Figure 5-5: *The Resources tab of a device indicating that Plug and Play is used for resource assignments.*

Topic B

The 8-bit Bus

The original IBM PC and its successor, the PC/XT, used simple expansion buses. Its architecture provided an 8-bit data bus, with minimal support circuitry. In this topic, you will examine the characteristics of the 8-bit expansion bus. You will learn how to recognize an 8-bit expansion card and how to install an 8-bit card into a 16-bit ISA slot.

The PC Bus

The original IBM PC and its successor, the PC/XT, used simple expansion buses. Its architecture provided an 8-bit data bus, with minimal support circuitry.

Lesson 5

Figure 5-6: *An 8-bit expansion card.*

This bus has a clock speed of 4.77 MHz. It supports eight interrupts and four DMA channels; however, except for IRQ 2 and DMA 3, all resources were already assigned, so you didn't have many choices when you installed additional cards.

The cards for an 8-bit slot have only one edge connector. It also has many resistors and larger components because *Very Large-Scale Integration (VLSI)* hadn't come out yet, so the circuitry had to be included on the card.

Be sure you're able to identify each card type based on its edge connector.

PC Bus cards were configured with jumpers and DIP switches to operate with the computer. Drivers were then loaded on the computer to support the card.

Lesson 5

How to Remove and Install Cards

Procedure Reference: Remove a PC Bus Adapter

To remove a card:

1. Shut off the computer, unplug it, and open the case.

2. Disconnect all cables, making a note of where they were installed and the orientation (such as white wire on left pin).

3. Unscrew the card from the chassis.

4. Gently rock the card front to back (not side-to-side) to remove it from the slot.

5. Place the card in an anti-static bag to prevent electrostatic damage to the card. Always store the card with its documentation and driver disks.

6. Replace the cover, plug in the computer, and turn it on.

Procedure Reference: Install an Internal Adapter Card

To install an internal adapter card:

1. Determine unused IRQ, DMA, and I/O Addresses that can be assigned to the card if needed. You can use the Device Manager in Control Panel to print a list of the resources by choosing View→Resources By Type.

2. Shut down the computer. Then, referring to your system documentation for the procedure, remove the system cover and access the slots on the system board.

3. Remove the slot cover from an empty slot. Traditionally, slot covers are secured by a screw to the chassis, but some newer ones slide out or are punched out of the metal case. Save the slot cover so that if you decide to remove the adapter card later, you can replace the slot cover. This will help keep dust and dirt out of the computer and help with regulation of the operating temperature.

4. If card resources are set with DIP switches or jumpers, configure the card prior to installing it into the system.

5. Holding the card where there are no metal contacts (by the upper edge), firmly press the card into the slot.

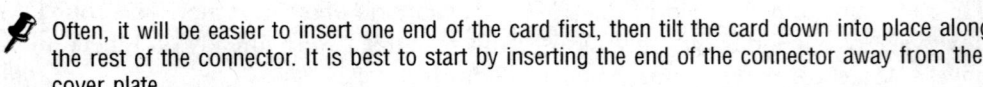
Often, it will be easier to insert one end of the card first, then tilt the card down into place along the rest of the connector. It is best to start by inserting the end of the connector away from the cover plate.

6. Connect any necessary internal cables.

7. Secure the card to the chassis with the screw from the slot cover (or another screw if the slot cover was not screwed to the case). Secure the cover back on to the system when you are through working.

8. Configure the card for the system by installing any drivers required for operation. If the card resources are configured through software, configure DMA, I/O Addresses, or interrupts as required.

9. Verify that the card is functioning properly. You can use Device Manager to view the properties for the port or device. You can also check for IRQ, I/O Addresses, or DMA conflicts as well.

TOPIC C
The ISA Bus

The Industry Standard Architecture (ISA) bus was developed by IBM for the IBM AT. At that time, it was not called the ISA bus, but was simply called the expansion bus. In this topic, you will examine the characteristics of the ISA expansion bus. You will learn how to recognize a 16-bit expansion card and how to install one.

The ISA Bus

The ISA (Industry Standard Architecture) bus was originally developed for the IBM PC/XT and PC/AT. Many systems still have some ISA slots along with the newer types of buses. The following table describes the *ISA bus*. Devices using this legacy bus sometimes need to be manually configured through either jumpers or proprietary software. Newer ISA cards support Plug and Play.

Table 5-1: *Characteristics of ISA Adapters*

ISA	Description
Physical characteristics of cards	Card size varies, but must have ISA edge connectors. Slot on the motherboard is black. Can be an 8-bit (short) or 16-bit (long) slot.
Configuration	Configured through jumpers, dip switches, or software. PnP ISA cards are automatically configured by the operating system.
Used for	8-bit or 16-bit ISA adapters. Most 8-bit adapters fit in 16-bit slots. Can access up to 16 MB of RAM.
Number of data lines	8-bit or 16-bit. 16 or 24 data address lines.
Communication method	Boards signal that they are ready to transfer data, send one byte, and repeat this process until all data has been sent.
Pronounced	EYE-sah or I-S-A.

Figure 5-7 shows an example of ISA.

Lesson 5

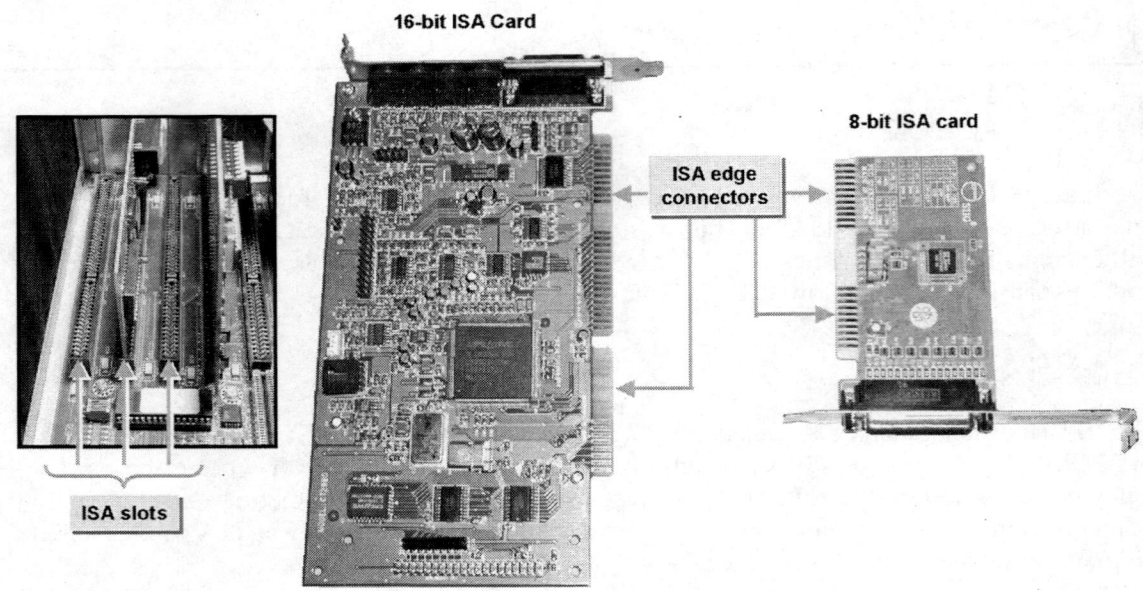

Figure 5-7: *ISA.*

Configuration

Although you will probably see switches and jumpers on older equipment that you service, software-configurable and Plug and Play adapters are becoming more and more prevalent.

Some older ISA cards require proprietary setup software. That setup software communicates with special circuitry on the adapter. This circuitry sets the appropriate communications parameters, such as the IRQ or DMA channel. During normal operation, the host computer uses these settings to communicate with the card.

To communicate with the card before the communication parameters have been established, the software uses a pulsed signal on the ISA bus. Electronic pulses send out a code, analogous to Morse code, across certain lines on the bus. The circuitry of the card is designed to detect such pulses. The configuration software uses this pulse-coding to inform the card of the proper settings. Those settings are configured and stored in on-board, non-volatile memory. Settings are saved on the board itself by the use of an EEPROM chip. (Remember, EEPROM stands for Electrically Erasable Programmable Read-Only Memory.)

Activity 5-2

Installing ISA Cards

Setup:
You have at least one open ISA slot on the system board. You have an ISA card and any drivers needed for the ISA card.

Scenario:
You have been asked to install several expansion cards in a user's system. You determine that the first card is an ISA card. The appropriate drivers for the card are also available to you should you need them.

What You Do	How You Do It
1. Open the system cover and access the slots.	a. Turn off the system power.
	b. Unplug the computer from the electrical outlet.
	c. Unplug peripherals from the system.
	d. Remove the cover.
	e. Determine if any components need to be moved or removed in order to access the slots.
2. Insert the ISA card in an available slot. ⚠ Do not rock the card side-to-side when installing or removing it.	a. Locate an open ISA slot.
	b. Remove the slot cover.
	c. Firmly press the card into the slot.
	d. **Secure the card to the chassis with the screw from the slot cover.** Normally, you would now secure the cover back on to the system, but since you will be doing more work inside the system, you will leave it off.

Lesson 5: Bus Architectures

Lesson 5

3. Configure the card for the system.
   a. Reconnect the peripherals you disconnected in step 2.
   b. Power on the system.
   c. Install any required drivers.
   d. Configure DMA, I/O addresses, and/or interrupts as required for the device.

4. Verify that the card is functioning properly.
   a. Connect any devices to the card that are required for testing the card functionality.
   b. Access or use the device connected to the card.

Topic D

The EISA Bus

During 1988 and 1989, the "Gang of Nine," a group of vendors including Compaq, Hewlett-Packard, and others, formed a consortium to extend the features and capabilities of the ISA bus. They jointly developed the Extended Industry Standard Architecture (EISA) bus, and named the ISA bus in the process. In this topic, you will examine the characteristics of the EISA expansion bus. You will also learn how to recognize an EISA expansion card.

The EISA Bus

The EISA (Extended Industry Standard Architecture) bus was a higher-speed bus designed for PCs starting with the Intel 80386 processor. EISA has never been widely adopted. The following table describes the *EISA bus*.

EISA	Description
Physical characteristics of cards	Most cards are 5 inches high. Compared to ISA cards, they contain an additional row of connectors and additional guide notches. They run at 8 or 10 MHz.
Configuration	Software configurable through an EISA configuration disk. Configuration is saved in *CMOS*, in System Configuration Information (SCI) files, and in onboard non-volatile memory.
Used for	EISA and ISA cards. Can access up to 4 GB RAM.

EISA	Description
Number of data lines	32 bit. 32 address lines and 32 data lines. If it is really just a ported ISA card, it uses 24 address lines instead so it can access only 16 MB of RAM.
Communication method	Cards use the same signaling techniques as ISA. In addition, EISA can use bus mastering, which enables one adapter to occasionally take control of the bus during a data transfer.
Pronounced	EEE-sah.

An example of an EISA card is shown in Figure 5-8. Notice that the EISA card has a double row of pins on the connector edge. This card is not frequently encountered and usually only in older server class machines.

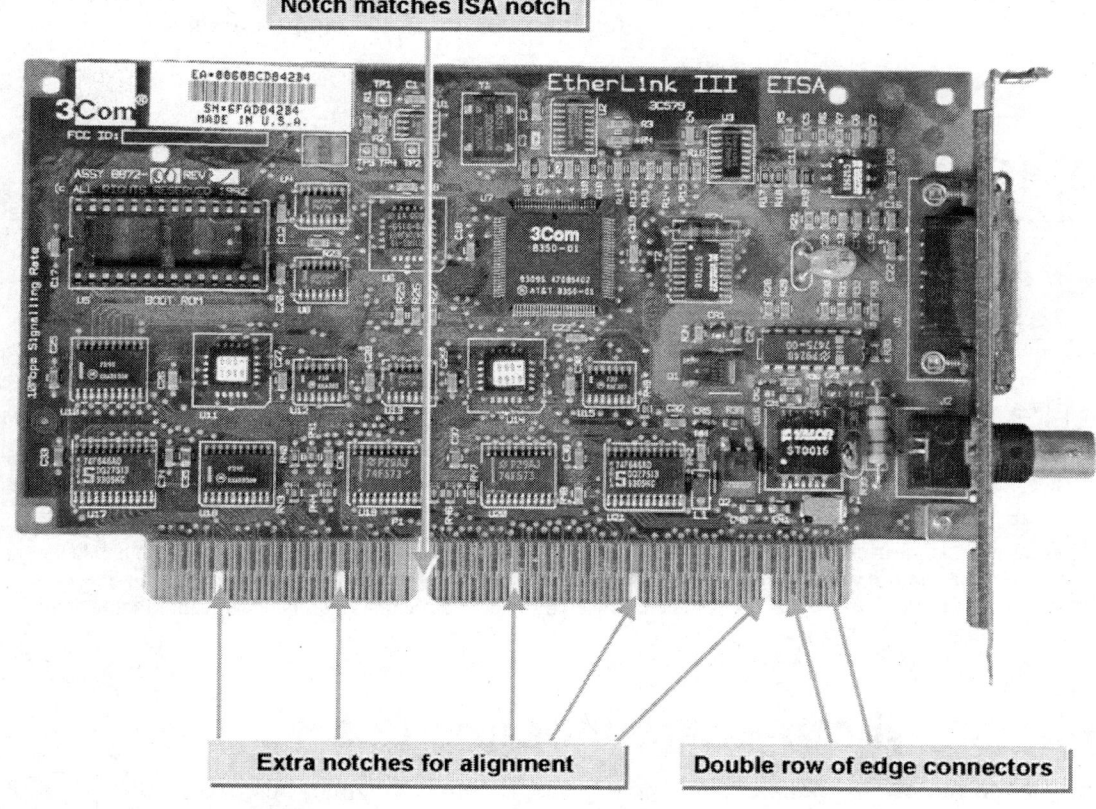

Figure 5-8: *An EISA card.*

Configuration

One of the most important new features of the EISA bus was the way in which EISA adapters were configured. Jumpers and switches were not necessary with EISA adapters; configuration was accomplished with software. System configurations were saved in non-volatile CMOS memory and a System Configuration Information (SCI) file. EISA adapters also stored their configurations in on-board, non-volatile memory.

When an EISA system is booted, it checks the configuration of the currently installed adapters and options. It compares the current configuration to that stored in CMOS memory. If differences are found, the configuration program is run.

Lesson 5

The configuration program is supplied on a set of floppy disks, but you can copy the program to the hard disk for convenience. These floppy disks, after they have been used to configure a system, are specific to that system. The steps required for the configuration program are specific to the system's manufacturer.

Because the configuration is also stored in an SCI file, if the CMOS memory becomes corrupted or gets lost, you can restore the settings from that file. You might want to back up your current CMOS configuration information to a floppy disk. The configuration utility for your system should offer that option. Printing the CMOS information is another good backup strategy.

EISA systems support existing ISA adapters, but cannot configure those adapters through software. To install an ISA card in your EISA system, run the configuration program (by booting with the floppy disk in the drive, for example) to look for available interrupt, memory I/O settings, or other needed settings. Then set the jumpers or switches on the ISA adapter based on that information. Once your system is turned off, you can install the adapter in your system. The configuration utility can include an option to inform the system that an ISA adapter is located in a particular slot. If so, set such information by using the configuration utility.

Topic E

The Micro Channel Architecture Bus

In 1987, IBM developed the Micro Channel Architecture bus, or Micro Channel bus, for its PS/2 line of computers. This bus can accept 16-bit and 32-bit adapter cars. However, cards for ISA or EISA systems cannot be used in Micro Channel systems. In this topic, you will examine the technical specifications for the Micro Channel Architecture bus. You will learn how to recognize a Micro Channel expansion card and how to configure it.

 When first released, it became common usage to call the Micro Channel Architecture bus the MCA bus. However, Universal Studios, who owned the MCA entertainment companies and the trademark on "MCA" at the time, legally challenged IBM's use of that abbreviation. While you might still find some references using that terminology, it is incorrect to do so.

The Micro Channel Architecture Bus

IBM developed the *Micro Channel Architecture bus*, or Micro Channel bus, for its PS/2 line of computers. This bus operates at 10 MHz and can accept 16- and 32-bit adapter cards. However, cards for ISA or EISA systems cannot be used in Micro Channel systems, and IBM required the payment of royalties for implementations of the architecture—both cards and system boards. Because few vendors were willing to pay such royalties, this bus was never widely adopted.

Micro Channel cards and slots are either 16- or 32-bit. The 32-bit versions use an extra edge connector in line with the first, 16-bit, connector. One slot in a system will have an additional connector that provides direct access to video circuitry on the motherboard. These connections allow designers of video boards to use some of the built-in video circuitry and to avoid duplicating engineering effort.

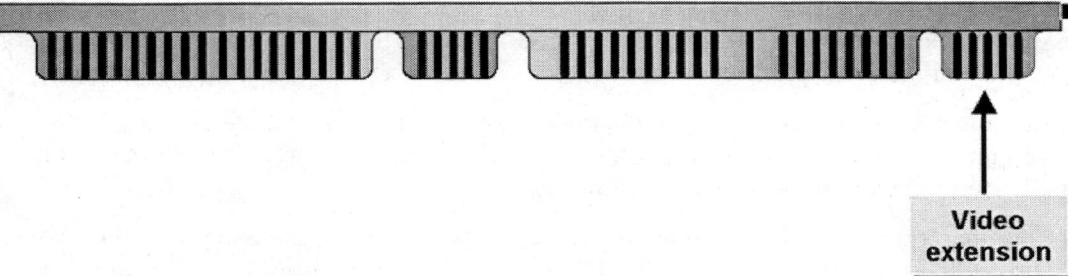

Figure 5-9: *A representation of the 32-bit Micro Channel bus connection with a video extension.*

Like the EISA bus, the Micro Channel bus calls for 32 data lines and 32 address lines. The Micro Channel bus can also address up to 4 GB (4,096 MB) of system RAM. Like many EISA cards, many Micro Channel cards are simple ports of ISA cards and use only 24 address lines. Such cards (for example, the Novell DCB-2) work properly only in systems with 16 MB of memory.

IBM developed the Micro Channel architecture to overcome many of the limitations of the ISA bus architecture. The Micro Channel bus offers many performance improvements that make it ideally suited for server applications. However, due to the compatibility limitations and royalty issues, it didn't gain as wide a following as EISA and was eventually replaced by the PCI bus architecture.

ISA and EISA cards communicate with the host system in a two-step process: they signal that they are about to transfer some data, and then they transfer one byte. This process is repeated until all of the data is transferred. Micro Channel offers three additional modes of data transfer: burst mode, streaming mode, and multiplexed streaming mode.

- Micro Channel burst mode uses one signal for the transfer of more than one byte of data.
- Streaming mode is used when the data to be transferred exists as a large block, such as data in a disk drive's read buffer. The streaming mode operation offers the ability to transfer data at up to 40 MBps.
- To further improve data-transfer performance, Micro Channel offers the multiplexed streaming mode. In this mode, the data is transferred across the 32 data lines and across the 32 lines usually reserved for address information. In this special mode, data is transferred at 64 bits per cycle, offering higher performance than the streaming mode.

Micro Channel is an asynchronous bus; it does not depend on the timing of the system for its interaction with that system. Micro Channel cards can actually slow the bus, if necessary, in order to work properly. Thus, slow or inadequately engineered boards will work properly in a Micro Channel system.

The Micro Channel Architecture bus allows up to 15 adapters in a system to occasionally act as bus masters during a data transfer. The Micro Channel specification calls for smaller board dimensions and lower power levels. Thus, Micro Channel boards are harder to design and are more expensive than either ISA or EISA adapters.

Lesson 5

Configuration

Micro Channel introduced the software configuration concept that was later adopted by the EISA design committee. IBM calls this feature Programmable Option Select (POS). The POS feature operates in a manner similar to the EISA configuration process.

At boot time, the system checks for installed options and compares this information with the configuration information stored in CMOS. If a discrepancy is discovered, the system attempts to load the configuration program.

Micro Channel systems can access the configuration program from a Reference Disk. Systems that are purchased from IBM and are configured with a hard drive have the configuration programs loaded on a special 3 MB partition of the hard disk.

To access the programs from the Reference Disk, simply boot the computer with the disk in the A drive. To access the programs stored on the configuration partition on the hard drive, you must first perform a warm boot by pressing Ctrl+Alt+Delete. At a certain point as the system starts, the cursor will jump to the upper-right corner of the screen. When it does, press Ctrl+Alt+Insert. The system will then load the configuration programs from the hard-disk partition.

During the configuration process, you need to provide Adapter Definition Files (ADFs). These are provided by the manufacturer of the board you are configuring. They hold similar information to the EISA SCI files. The configuration program compares the valid settings in all of the ADF files and chooses appropriate settings for each board. The finished configuration information is stored in non-volatile CMOS memory. In addition, Plug and Play specifications exist for Micro Channel systems.

Topic F

The PCI Bus

The Peripheral Component Interconnect (PCI) bus is a local bus standard. This standard was introduced in 1992 by Intel and has become a popular standard for high-end systems. In this topic, you will examine the technical specifications of the PCI expansion bus. You will also learn how to recognize a PCI expansion card and how to install a PCI expansion card.

The PCI Bus

The PCI (Peripheral Component Interconnect) bus is the most common system bus found in today's PCs. The following table describes the *PCI bus*.

PCI	Description
Physical characteristics of cards	33 or 66 MHz. 133 MBps throughput at 33 MHz. Up to eight functions can be integrated on one board. Card size varies, but must have a PCI edge connector. Slot on the motherboard is white.
Configuration	Supports up to 5 cards per bus and a system can have two PCI buses for a total of 10 devices per system. Can share IRQs. Uses PnP.

PCI	Description
Used for	All current adapters in client and server systems.
Number of data lines	64-bit bus often implemented as a 32-bit bus.
Communication method	Local bus standard. 32-bit bus mastering. Each bus uses 10 *loads*. A load refers to the amount of power consumed by a device. PCI chipset uses three loads. Integrated PCI controllers use one load. Controllers installed in a slot use 1.5 loads.
Pronounced	Pea-Sea-EYE.

A PCI slot and a PCI card are shown in Figure 5-10. Notice that the connector pins on the PCI card are very close together. The connector and slot are much shorter than previous buses even though there are more pins and faster communication rates.

 The PCI slots in Figure 5-10 are shared PCI/ISA slots. They share a single opening on the back of the case, so if an ISA card is in one of the slots, the PCI slot cannot be used unless the ISA card is removed.

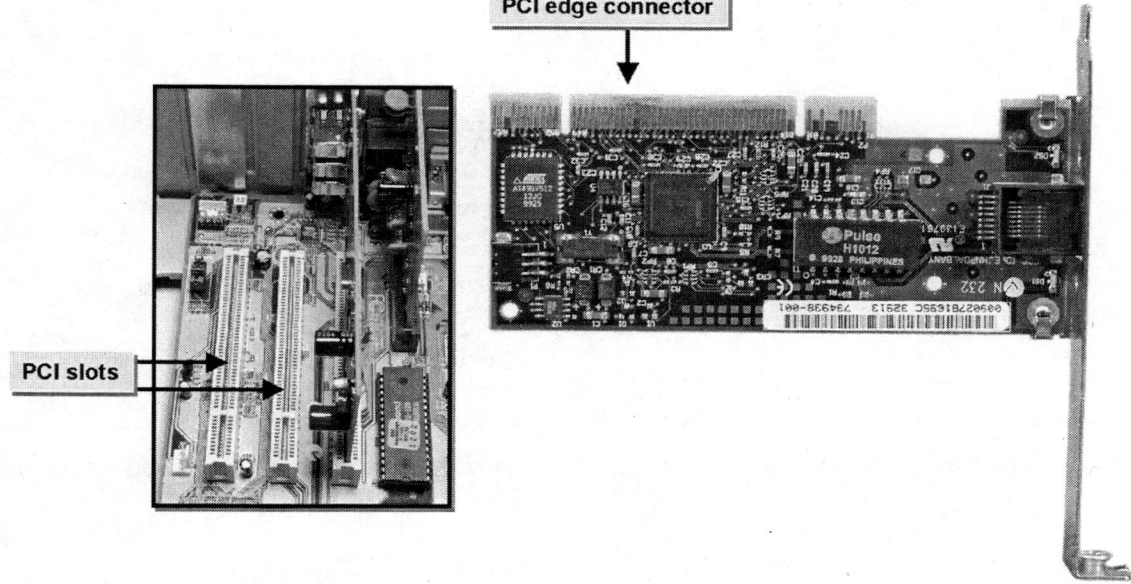

Figure 5-10: *PCI.*

Configuration

You don't need to configure jumpers or switches on PCI cards. Most times, you don't need to use proprietary software to configure them either. Most PCI cards fully support Plug and Play. With these cards, configuring a PCI card is something the computer does for you. You simply install the card, boot the system, install the necessary drivers and you're done.

Lesson 5

Activity 5-3

Installing PCI Cards

Setup:
The cover has been removed from the system. You have a PCI card and any drivers needed for the PCI card you install are available to you. There is an open PCI slot on the system board.

Scenario:
Now that you have installed an ISA card in the system from the stash of cards the customer discovered, the next card you decide to install is a PCI card. The appropriate drivers for this card are also available if you are prompted for them.

What You Do	How You Do It
1. Insert a PCI card in an open PCI slot.	a. Turn off the system power and unplug the computer.
	b. Unplug peripherals from the system.
	c. Locate an open PCI slot.
	d. Remove the slot cover.
	e. Firmly press the card into the slot.
	f. Secure the card to the chassis with the screw from the slot cover.
2. Configure the card for the system.	a. Reconnect the peripherals you disconnected in the previous step.
	b. Power on the system.
	c. Install any required drivers.
	d. If a SCSI card was installed, **reboot when prompted**.
	e. In Device Manager, **verify that the device's properties show that the device is working properly and that there are no IRQ, I/O address, or DMA conflicts, and then click Cancel**.

3. Verify that the card is functioning properly.

   a. Connect any devices to the card that are required for testing the card functionality.

   b. Access or use the device connected to the card.

Topic G

Video Circuitry Buses

Specialized video circuitry buses enable video adapters that offer better performance and additional features. For example, such advanced cards can support multiple monitors on a single system so that users can see more information at once. Other specialized video cards include those with the ability to connect to television or other consumer video sources. In this topic, you will you will examine the technical specifications of video circuit buses. You will also learn how to recognize and install a video card.

VL-Bus

In 1992, the Video Electronics Standards Association (VESA) introduced the *VESA Local-Bus (VL-Bus)* standard. A motherboard can contain up to three VL-Bus slots. Bus mastering is supported by the VL-Bus standard. A 32-bit or 64-bit slot is located next to an ISA, EISA, or Micro Channel Architecture slot and enables vendors to design adapters that use the local bus or both buses simultaneously.

VL-Bus boards are generally software-configurable. Like some ISA systems, configuration information is stored in on-board, non-volatile memory and EEPROMs.

Although the VL-Bus standard provides for theoretical speeds up to 66 MHz, the maximum practical speed is 33 MHz. Even so, the increased speed (over ISA and EISA) enhances performance on systems that run graphics and other applications requiring intensive I/O operations.

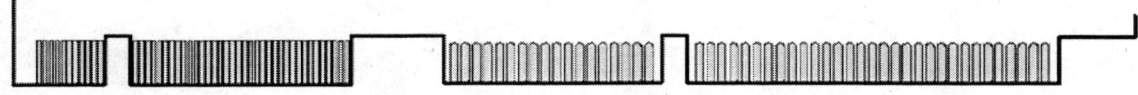

Figure 5-11: *A representation of the VL-Bus connection on an adapter.*

AGP Bus

The AGP (Accelerated Graphics Port) bus was developed by Intel specifically to support high-performance video requirements, especially fast 3D graphics. The following table describes the *AGP bus*.

Visit **www.intel.com/technology/agp** for complete information about the AGP bus.

AGP	Description
Physical characteristics of cards	Brown slot on the motherboard. AGP 1.0 is a 1x/2x slot. This is the shortest of the AGP slots with a small separator that divides it into two sections. AGP 2.0 is a 2x/4x slot that has extra pins at one end. There is also an AGP Pro Slot. See **www.tomshardware.com/graphic/20000922/agppro-01.html** for a complete description of the AGP Pro slot.
Used for	Video cards in systems that support the AGP chipset. The system board needs an AGP bus slot or an integrated AGP chip.
Number of data lines	32 bits wide with a throughput of 266 MBps for AGP 1.0. Faster modes with throughput of 533 MBps are available on AGP 2.0 and 1.07 GBps for AGP Pro.
Communication method	Directly accesses RAM rather than needing to transfer data-to-video RAM first.
Pronounced	A-G-P.

AGP comes in several versions, with 3.0 being the most recent. Each version runs in several modes, as described in the following table.

AGP Version	Mode	Speed	Bytes/Clock Cycle(s)
1.0, 2.0, Pro, 3.0	1x	266 Mbps	8 bytes per 2 clock cycles
1.0, 2.0, Pro, 3.0	2x	533 Mbps	8 bytes per clock cycle
2.0, Pro, 3.0	4x	1.07 Gbps	16 bytes per clock cycle
3.0	8x	2.1 Gbps	32 bits per clock cycle using isochronous communications

An example of an AGP slot and an AGP video card are shown in Figure 5-12.

Lesson 5

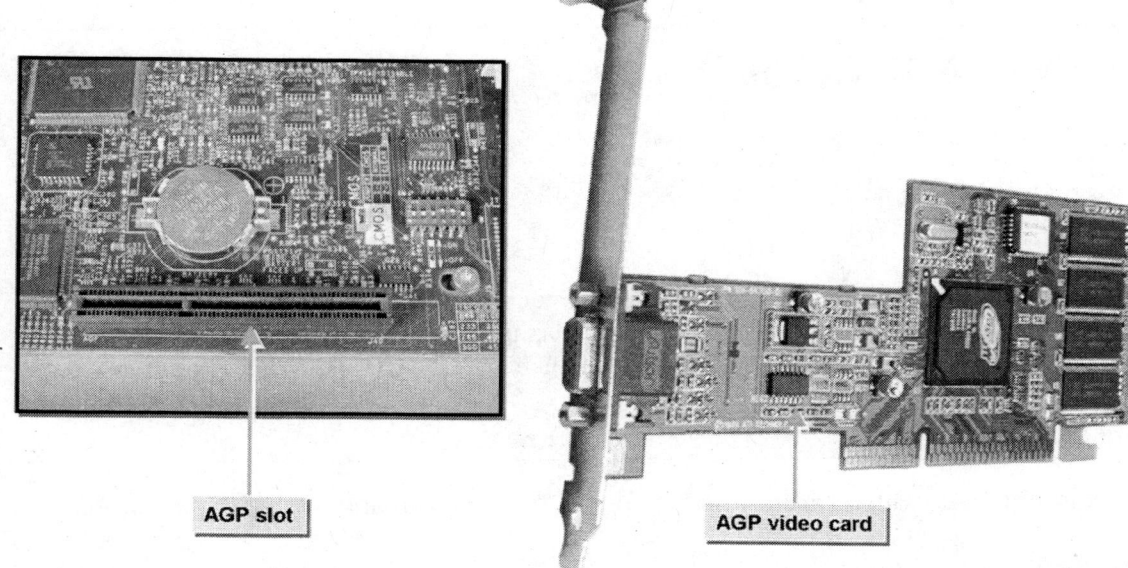

Figure 5-12: *An AGP slot and card.*

Specialized Video Cards

More and more users are using dual monitors so that they can see more information at once. Some AGP cards have a dual head—one card has two monitor ports so that you can connect dual monitors to a system. In other cases, you can use two PCI video cards to implement dual monitors. It works best if the cards are the same model.

Other specialized video cards include those with the ability to connect to television or other consumer video sources. This enables you to transfer data from the television or video device to store on the computer. You can also send data out to be displayed on the television screen.

Lesson 5

Activity 5-4

Installing AGP Cards

Setup:
You can complete this activity if you have an AGP video card to install in your system.

Scenario:
One of your customers wants to run a game that requires a 3D video card. He is currently using the built-in video on the system board. He has purchased an AGP 3D card that was listed on the game box as being supported by the game.

What You Do	How You Do It
1. Install the AGP video card.	a. Shut down and unplug the computer.
	b. Locate the AGP slot.
	c. Insert the video card in the AGP slot.
	d. Close the system case.
	e. Reconnect peripherals.
2. Test the video card.	a. Restart the system.
	b. If prompted, **install drivers for the video card.**
	c. Verify that the image on the screen is satisfactory.

Lesson 5

Topic H

Troubleshooting Adapter Card Problems

Your mechanic often knows just what component in your car is acting up based on your description of the way your vehicle is acting. Knowing the common problems associated with adapter cards will enable you to quickly correct the problems your users encounter. Being able to quickly resolve problems for your users will make them more productive.

Common Problems with Adapter Cards

The most common problem you will encounter with adapter cards is hardware or system resource conflicts. The following table lists some additional symptoms of adapter card symptoms and possible problems that cause those symptoms.

Symptom	Possible Problem	Solution
Adapter seems to work fine until you replace the system case.	Adapter card is grounded against the case.	Visually inspect card and case for bent or damaged areas. If the card is in contact with the case, it can cause electrical shorts or other faults.
Card works fine in another slot, but when any card is inserted in this particular slot, it doesn't work.	Bus slot damaged.	Visually inspect the bus slot. Test the bus slot with a multimeter; voltages should be within prescribed ranges for the slot and adapter card.
Card tests fine and slot tests fine, but services are unavailable.	Cables not connected, loose, or damaged.	Visually inspect cards and cables and reconnect if necessary.
Services provided by the adapter or a device connected to the adapter work intermittently.	Adapter card (or cards) not seated properly. Hardware resource conflict. Adapter card physically damaged. Adapter card electronically damaged.	Reseat adapter card (or cards). Resolves any hardware resource conflicts. Replace any adapter card that is physically damaged. Replace any adapter card that is electronically damaged.

How to Troubleshoot Adapter Card Problems

Procedure Reference: Troubleshoot PC Adapter Card Problems

To troubleshoot some of the most common problems with adapter cards:

1. If you are having adapter card problems:
   - Locate the adapter card and make sure that it is fully seated into the slot, and then see if this fixed the problem.

Lesson 5: Bus Architectures

LESSON 5

- If a video card is having troubles, determine if it is in a PCI, ISA, or AGP slot. If it is not in the AGP slot, try moving the card to another slot. Because there is only one AGP slot on the system board, you cannot move an AGP card to a different slot.
- Remove the card and press down on all four corners of socketed chips to verify that they are fully seated, and then reinstall the card.
- If another hardware device has recently been added to the system, check Device Manager and verify that there is not a resource conflict between the device and the video card.
- Verify that the drivers are properly installed. You could use the Add/Remove Hardware Control Panel utility to remove all the drivers for the card, then restart the system. It should detect the "new" hardware and install the drivers again. You can also remove the card, restart to remove the drivers. Then, reinstall the cards. When you restart, the drivers should be installed.

    If you're servicing a legacy system that doesn't support PnP configuration, consult your adapter card's documentation to determine how to verify, remove, or install the necessary drivers.

2. If you suspect a resource conflict between devices:
    - Open Device Manager and display the Resources By Connection view.
    - Determine if there is a conflict between any devices. ISA cards cannot use the same IRQ as another card. IRQs have been set aside for PCI cards to share with each other. However, the PCI cards cannot share that IRQ with ISA cards.
    - Change the conflicting resource to an unused setting. This might be the IRQ, DMA, or I/O Address.
    - Verify that both devices now work properly.

3. If you suspect a card was damaged due to electrostatic discharge (from improper handling, power surges, or a lightning storm):
    - Check whether the card in question is listed in Device Manager.
    - Display Properties for the card and verify whether the Device Status indicates that it is working properly.
    - If the device is not working properly, click Troubleshoot and follow the Troubleshoot Wizard steps.
    - If the problem is not resolved, replace the card and verify that the problem has been resolved.

4. If you have a problem with a device, and replacing the device, device cable, and device power cord doesn't fix it, then you should suspect the adapter card. This applies to any adapter card, including ISA, PCI, AGP, and others. To test if this is the problem:
    - Remove the problem device from the port.
    - Connect a replacement device to the port.
    - If necessary, install drivers for the new device.
    - If it works, then the adapter card is okay.
    - If it doesn't work, then try replacing the cable between the device and the port.

- If it works, then the adapter card is okay.
- If it doesn't work, then try disconnecting the cables from the port, unscrewing the adapter card from the case, and pulling it straight out to remove the adapter card. Then insert a replacement card.
- If it works, then the adapter card replacement solved your problem.

Lesson 5 Follow-up

In this lesson, you examined buses and the adapter cards they enable. You looked at the different types of buses that have been commonly used with PCs of the past decade or so. You also examined how to troubleshoot adapter card problems. With this knowledge in hand, you will be able to help your clients customize their PCs in cost-effective ways that provide the most performance and capability.

1. **What types of expansion buses have you encountered most frequently in the PCs you have used or serviced?**

2. **If you were buying a new PC, what buses would you need it to support?**

Notes

Lesson 6
Ports, Connectors, and Cables

Lesson Time
2 hour(s), 30 minutes

Lesson Objectives:

In this lesson, you will install or remove devices on standard ports.

You will:

- Connect a serial device to a serial port.
- Connect parallel devices to the parallel port on a computer.
- Install PS/2 devices.
- Describe USB ports and the devices you connect to them.
- Install FireWire devices.
- Establish a wireless connection between a wireless device and a computer.

Lesson 6

Introduction

One of the most common and basic tasks for a computer technician is to assemble computer components into a working computer system. So, in this lesson, you will connect ports and connectors for basic system components and configure them for use.

Your users are excited—they just received brand new PCs. You have been asked to unpack and set them up. Putting together a PC is similar to putting together a puzzle—if you put the pieces in the right place, everything will work perfectly. The skills in this lesson will show you how to put the PC puzzle together quickly and correctly.

The following CompTIA A+ Core Hardware (2003) Examination objectives are covered in this lesson:

- Topic A:
    - 1.1 Identify typical IRQs, DMAs, and I/O addresses, and procedures for altering these settings when installing and configuring devices. Choose the appropriate installation or configuration steps in a given scenario. Content includes the following: ports.
    - 1.4 Identify typical IRQs, DMAs, and I/O addresses, and procedures for altering these settings when installing and configuring devices. Choose the appropriate installation or configuration steps in a given scenario. Content includes the following: I/O ports—serial.
    - 1.5 Identify the names, purposes, and performance characteristics, of standardized/common peripheral ports, associated cabling, and their connectors. Recognize ports, cabling, and connectors, by sights. Content includes the following: port types—serial; cable types—serial; connector types—serial (DB-9 and DB-25).
    - 2.1 Recognize common problems associated with each module and their symptoms, and identify steps to isolate and troubleshoot the problems. Given a problem situation, interpret the symptoms and infer the most likely cause. Content includes: I/O ports and cables—serial.
- Topic B:
    - 1.4 Identify typical IRQs, DMAs, and I/O addresses, and procedures for altering these settings when installing and configuring devices. Choose the appropriate installation or configuration steps in a given scenario. Content includes the following: I/O ports—parallel.
    - 1.5 Identify the names, purposes, and performance characteristics, of standardized/common peripheral ports, associated cabling, and their connectors. Recognize ports, cabling, and connectors, by sights. Content includes the following: port types—parallel; cable types—parallel; connector types—parallel (DB-25 and centronics).
    - 2.1 Recognize common problems associated with each module and their symptoms, and identify steps to isolate and troubleshoot the problems. Given a problem situation, interpret the symptoms and infer the most likely cause. Content includes: I/O ports and cables—parallel.
- Topic C:
    - 1.5 Identify the names, purposes, and performance characteristics, of standardized/common peripheral ports, associated cabling, and their connectors. Recognize ports, cabling, and connectors, by sights. Content includes the following: PS2/MINI-DIN.
- Topic D:

- 1.2 Identify basic procedures for adding and removing field-replaceable modules for desktop systems. Given a replacement scenario choose the appropriate sequences. Content includes: adapters—USB.
- 1.4 Identify typical IRQs, DMAs, and I/O addresses, and procedures for altering these settings when installing and configuring devices. Choose the appropriate installation or configuration steps in a given scenario. Content includes the following: I/O ports—USB ports.
- 1.5 Identify the names, purposes, and performance characteristics, of standardized/common peripheral ports, associated cabling, and their connectors. Recognize ports, cabling, and connectors, by sights. Content includes the following: port types—USB ports; cable types—USB; and USB.
- 2.1 Recognize common problems associated with each module and their symptoms, and identify steps to isolate and troubleshoot the problems. Given a problem situation, interpret the symptoms and infer the most likely cause. Content includes: I/O ports and cables—USB ports; adapters—USB.
- 4.3 Identify the most popular types of motherboards, their components, and their architecture (bus structures). Content includes the following: USB (Universal Serial Bus).

- Topic E:
  - 1.2 Identify basic procedures for adding and removing field-replaceable modules for desktop systems. Given a replacement scenario choose the appropriate sequences. Content includes: adapters—IEEE 1394/Firewire.
  - 1.4 Identify typical IRQs, DMAs, and I/O addresses, and procedures for altering these settings when installing and configuring devices. Choose the appropriate installation or configuration steps in a given scenario. Content includes the following: I/O ports—IEEE 1394/Firewire.
  - 1.5 Identify the names, purposes, and performance characteristics, of standardized/common peripheral ports, associated cabling, and their connectors. Recognize ports, cabling, and connectors, by sights. Content includes the following: port types—IEEE 1394/Firewire; and IEEE 1394/Firewire.
  - 2.1 Recognize common problems associated with each module and their symptoms, and identify steps to isolate and troubleshoot the problems. Given a problem situation, interpret the symptoms and infer the most likely cause. Content includes: I/O ports and cables—IEEE 1394/Firewire; adapters—IEEE 1394/Firewire.

- Topic F:
  - 1.2 Identify basic procedures for adding and removing field-replaceable modules for desktop systems. Given a replacement scenario choose the appropriate sequences. Content includes: adapters—wireless.
  - 1.4 Identify typical IRQs, DMAs, and I/O addresses, and procedures for altering these settings when installing and configuring devices. Choose the appropriate installation or configuration steps in a given scenario. Content includes the following: I/O ports—infrared.
  - 1.5 Identify the names, purposes, and performance characteristics, of standardized/common peripheral ports, associated cabling, and their connectors. Recognize ports, cabling, and connectors, by sights. Content includes the following: port types—infrared.

Lesson 6

— 1.8 Identify proper procedures for installing and configuring common peripheral devices. Choose the appropriate installation or configuration sequence in given scenarios. Content includes the following: infrared devices.

— 2.1 Recognize common problems associated with each module and their symptoms, and identify steps to isolate and troubleshoot the problems. Given a problem situation, interpret the symptoms and infer the most likely cause. Content includes: I/O ports and cables—infrared.

Topic A

Serial Ports

Most users require more than the basic monitor, keyboard, and mouse peripherals connected to their system. As the computer support technician for the company, users will be asking you to add equipment to their systems to increase functionality. Some of these will be serial devices. You will need to be able to quickly and efficiently install the devices so users can complete their work.

Ports

Definition:

A *port* is a hardware connection interface on a computer system that enables devices to be connected to the system. All ports:

- Connect a device that uses a cable that matches the configuration of the port.
- Carry the signals from a device to the computer system.
- Carry the signals from the computer system to a device.
- Are composed of wires, plugs, and sockets that enable two devices to be connected. The plugs will be either on the port or the cable and the sockets will be on the other.

Ports vary by:

- The number of pins or connectors they contain.
- The layout of the pins.
- The signals they carry.
- The devices that can be connected to the port.
- The location. Some connect internal devices and others connect external devices.

Example:

A monitor port is a 15-pin female connector. The monitor cable ends in a matching 15-pin male connector, which plugs into the port on the system. An example of a monitor port and cable is shown in Figure 6-1.

Lesson 6

📌 Some systems contain specialized video cards that contain a second 15-pin port so that you can connect two monitors to one system. Other video cards might contain additional ports for connecting a TV to the computer.

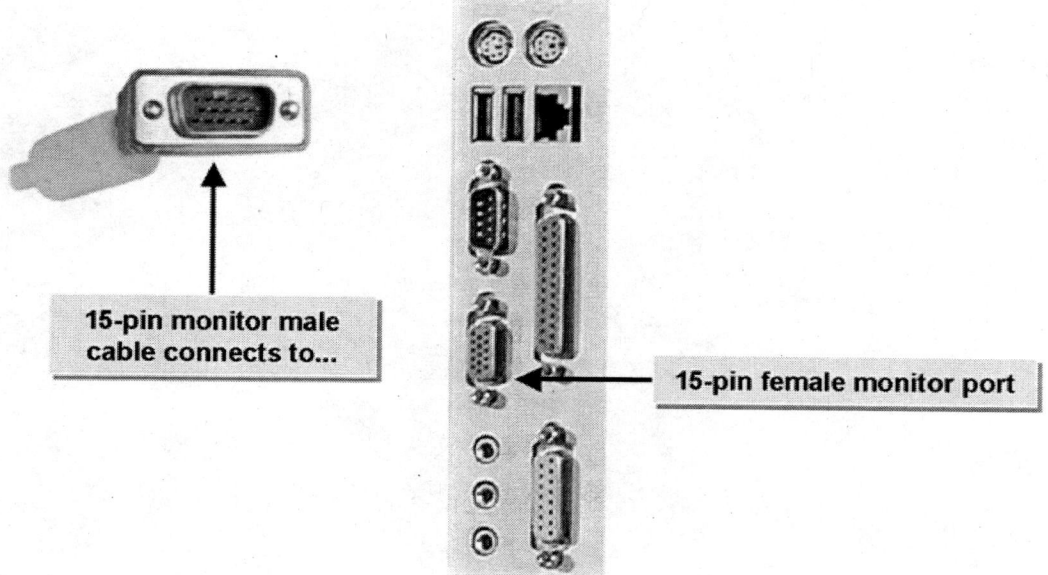

Figure 6-1: *A monitor port and cable.*

Gender

Cables and ports have genders. For example, if a computer port has plugs, the matching cable connection will have sockets. The port in this case would be the male connector and the cable would be the female connector. An example of male and female connectors is shown in Figure 6-2.

Lesson 6: Ports, Connectors, and Cables

Lesson 6

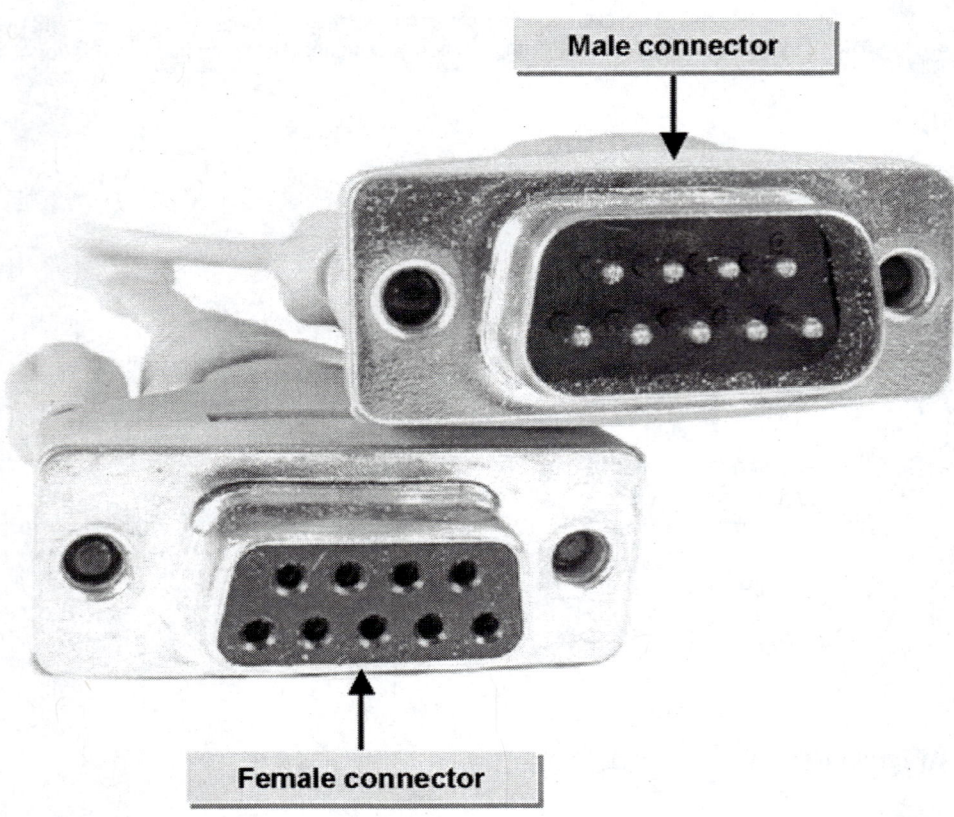

Figure 6-2: *Male and female connections.*

Serial Communications

In a serial transmission, data is sent and received one bit at a time over a single wire. This process is shown in Figure 6-3. To accomplish this, the serial communication process:

1. Disassembles bytes into bits on the sending end of the communication.
2. Sends the bits across the communication wires.
3. Reassembles the bits into bytes at the receiving end.

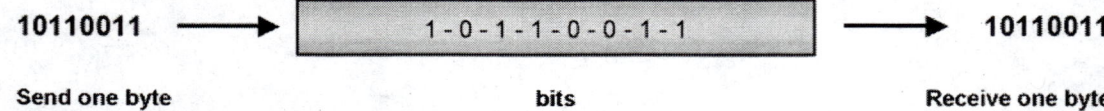

Figure 6-3: *Serial transmission sends one bit at a time.*

Serial Interfaces

Definition:

A serial interface is a computer hardware interface that enables a serial device to connect to a computer. It is composed of a serial port, serial cable, and a device with a serial connection.

All serial connections have these characteristics:

- They support two-way communication.

- There can be up to four serial ports on a system, but only two of them can be in use simultaneously. The ports are called COM1, COM2, COM3, or COM4. COM is short for communications port.
- A serial cable ends with a female connector to plug in to the male connector on the system.
- If serial ports are color-coded, they will be teal colored.

Serial connections vary in that:

- Serial ports can be DB-9 or DB-25 male ports. The serial cable usually does not have all of the wires connected, so that made it possible to reduce serial ports from 25 pins down to nine pins.
- Most systems today only include one or two 9-pin serial ports.
- The cable will have the wires connected that are needed for a particular purpose. Pinouts vary based on the purpose of the connection. If a cable other than a standard serial cable is needed, it is usually shipped with the device.
- Wires in the cable can be connected straight through, jumpered, or mirrored.
  — A straight through cable has the same color wire connected to the same pin number on each end of the cable.
  — A jumpered cable combines the output of one or more wires to a single wire on the other end or it can take the output of one pin and send it to multiple pins on the other end.
  — A mirrored or roll-over cable reverses the order of the wires. This is used on flat cables that use a phone-type clip connector.

Serial connections are typically used for external modems. They can also be used for direct PC-to-PC connections and to connect some mice, printers, and Personal Digital Assistant (PDA) devices.

 Typically only one or two serial ports will be installed on a system. This port is being phased out in favor of other standards, so you might find some systems with no serial ports at all.

Example:

Figure 6-4 shows an example of a serial interface.

Lesson 6

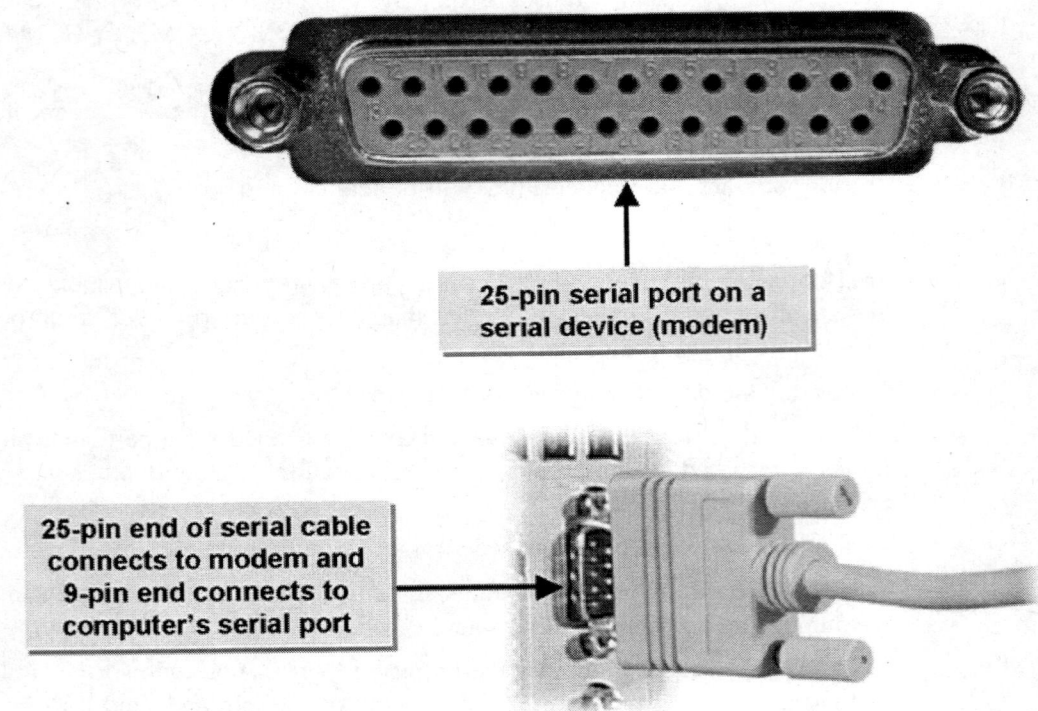

Figure 6-4: *A serial interface.*

Serial Port Pinouts

The pinouts for a standard 25-pin serial cable are shown in Figure 6-5.

Lesson 6

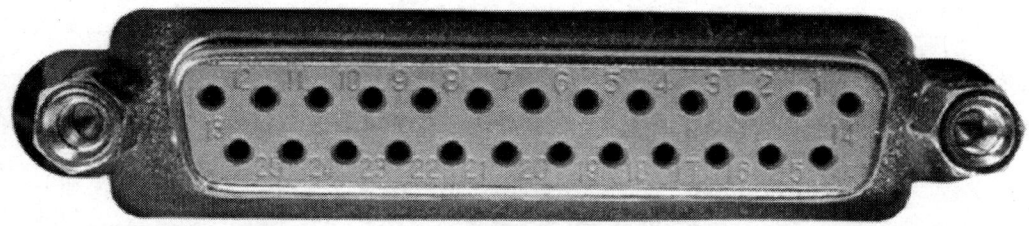

Pin	Signal	Pin	Signal
1	Protected ground	14	Secondary transmitted data
2	Transmitted data	15	Transmit timing signal
3	Received data	16	Secondary received data
4	Request to send	17	Receive timing signal
5	Clear to send	18	Unassigned
6	Data set ready	19	Secondary request to send
7	Signal ground	20	Data terminal ready
8	Data carrier detector	21	Signal quality detector
9	Reserved for data set testing	22	Ring indicator
10	Reserved for data set testing	23	Data rate selector
11	Unassigned	24	External timing signal
12	Secondary carrier detector	25	Unassigned
13	Secondary clear to send		

Figure 6-5: *Serial DB-25 connector pins.*

Most implementations do not use all of the pins shown in Figure 6-5. In fact, it is possible to use nine or fewer pins to provide a functional two-way serial connection. For this reason, many computers provide a 9-pin rather than a 25-pin connector for their serial ports. The pinouts for a 9-pin connector are shown in Figure 6-6. This is the male end of a serial cable that would connect to the female serial port on the PC.

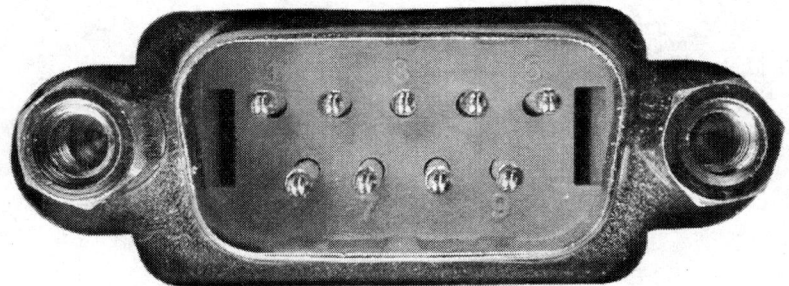

Figure 6-6: *Serial port pinouts for a 9-pin connector.*

Table 6-1: *Serial Port Pinouts for a 9-pin Connector*

Pin	Signal
1	Received line signal detector
2	Received data

Lesson 6: Ports, Connectors, and Cables

Pin	Signal
3	Transmitted data
4	Data terminal ready
5	Signal ground
6	Data set ready
7	Request to send
8	Clear to send
9	Ring indicator

Example: Null-modem Cables

Another type of serial cable you might encounter is a null modem cable. This cable crosses the wires so that the receiving pin on one end is connected to a transmitting pin on the other end. If two devices need to connect and are within tens of meters of each other, a cable wired in a null-modem or "dumb" configuration can be used in place of a true modem or of a physical network connection.

Figure 6-7 shows an example of the pinouts for a 9-pin null-modem cable. In some cases, such as from Pin 4 on the left to Pins 6 and 1 on the right, a single pin will be jumpered to two or more pins on the other end. If you require a null-modem cable with a different configuration, you will need to refer to the documentation for establishing the connection to figure out which wires need to be jumpered or crossed. This cable has female connectors on both ends to connect to the male serial ports on the PC.

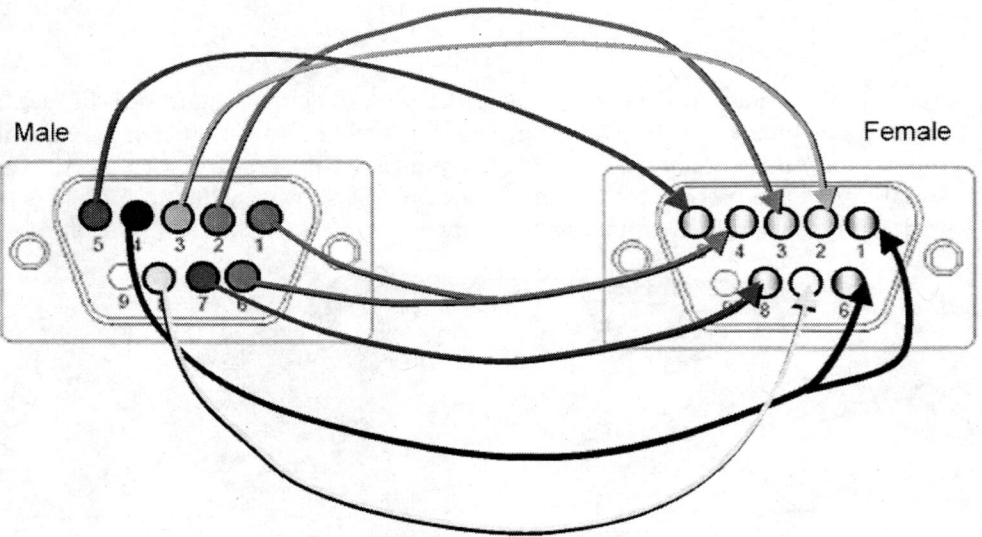

NOTE: Line colors are not intended to represent wire colors.

Figure 6-7: *Null-modem pinouts.*

Serial Port Settings

Definition:

Serial port settings are the property settings needed for two serial devices to communicate. The settings need to match on the systems that are communicating with each other. You can configure these settings in Device Manager on the Port Settings page of the serial port's property sheet.

The following table shows the various serial port settings.

Setting	Specifies
Bits per second	The maximum communication speed at which data will pass through the port. The default is 9600. For best performance, you will want to set it to the maximum speed at which the sending and receiving devices can communicate.
Data bits	How many data bits are used for each character that is exchanged. This value is usually 8 for PC-based systems and 7 for Macintosh-based systems.
Parity	The error-checking method. Your choices are: • None—This disables error-checking and is the default value. No parity bit is added to the data bits when transmitting data. • Even—This error-checking method is when a parity bit is added to the data bits when transmitting data, if needed, to have an even number of data bits. • Odd—This error-checking method is when a parity bit is added to the data bits when transmitting data, if needed, to have an odd number of data bits. • Mark—This error-checking method always adds a parity bit that is set to 0. • Space—This error-checking method always adds a parity bit that is set to 1.
Stop bits	The time (in bits per second) between the transmission of each character that is sent. The default is 1.

Lesson 6

Setting	Specifies
Flow control	How the flow of data is controlled and acknowledged. Just as when two people are talking, electronic devices need to know when one device has finished talking so that the other device can talk. Devices also need a way to confirm that they have received data that was sent to them. The choices are: • None—This is default value. • Hardware handshaking—This uses a separate wire for flow control. The receiving device sends a signal over this wire to inform the sending device that it is ready to receive data. • Xon/Xoff (transmit on/transmit off)—This protocol is a type of software handshaking, which reserves special characters for the receiving device to send control signals to the sending device. With Xon/Xoff, the receiving device sends a Control-S character (ASCII value 19) to request that the sending device stop sending data. The receiving device sends a Control-Q character (ASCII value 17) to request that the sending device resume sending data.

Example:

Figure 6-8 shows the default settings for COM1.

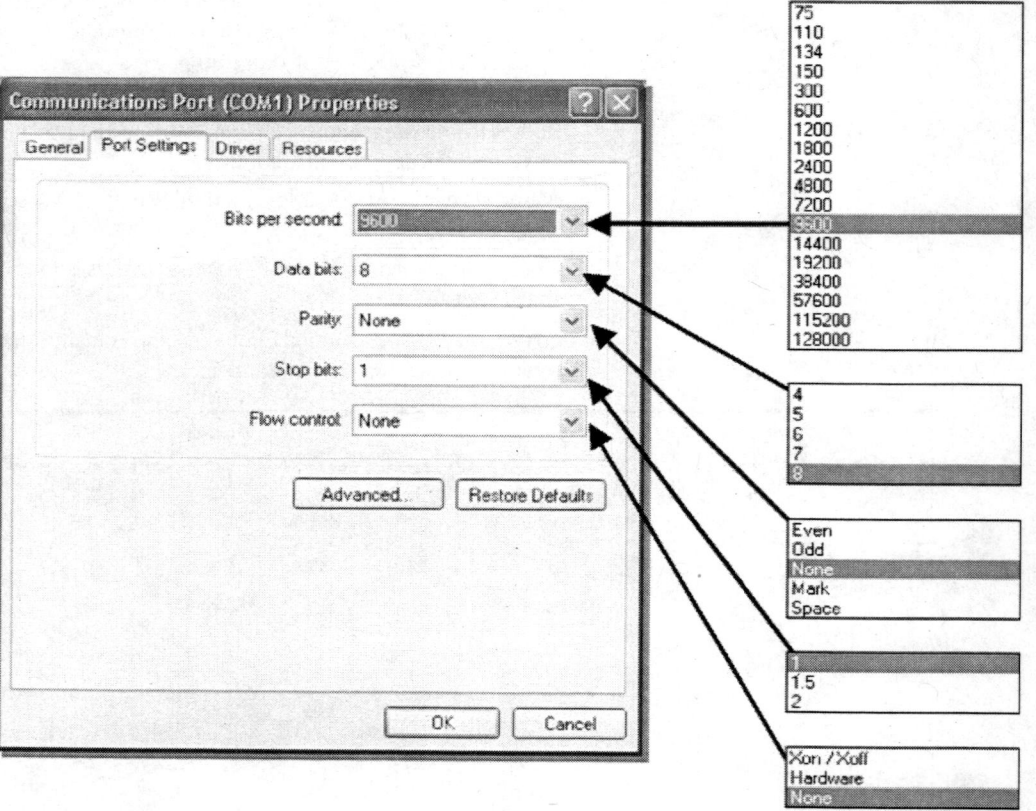

Figure 6-8: *Default settings for COM1.*

218   *A+™ Certification: Core Hardware Third Edition - A CompTIA Certification*

LESSON 6

How to Connect a Serial Device

Procedure Reference: Install Serial Devices

To install a serial device:

1. Turn off the computer power.
2. Locate an available serial port, and determine if it is a 9-pin or 25-pin connection.
3. If necessary, locate an appropriate serial cable to connect the device to the computer. Some devices (such as mice) come with the cable already attached, so you don't need to locate an appropriate serial cable.
4. If necessary, connect the male end of the cable to the device.
5. Connect the female end of the cable to the system serial port, carefully aligning the pins.
6. If necessary, connect the AC adapter to the device and plug it into an electrical outlet.
7. Boot the computer.
8. Install the device driver as described in the device documentation.
9. Verify that the device works correctly.

Procedure Reference: Configure a Serial Port

To configure serial port settings:

1. From the Start menu, choose Control Panel→System.
2. Click the Hardware tab, and then click Device Manager.
3. Expand Ports (COM & LPT).
4. Right-click the COM port and choose Properties.
5. Display the Port Settings page.
6. Configure the settings as required for the device to function properly. Consult the device documentation if necessary.
7. Click OK.
8. Close Device Manager.
9. In the System Properties dialog box, click OK.

Lesson 6: Ports, Connectors, and Cables

Lesson 6

ACTIVITY 6-1

Installing a Serial Device

Setup:
You have been given a serial device. If a separate serial cable is required, it has been provided to you. Any drivers needed have also been provided.

Scenario:
A user bought two pieces of equipment and doesn't know how to connect them to her system. After you install the two serial devices on the computer, you need to confirm that the configuration of the serial ports meets the company standard. You have been given a document with the settings the company uses for modems and serial printers as shown in the following table.

Device	Settings
Modem	8 Data Bits, 1 Stop Bit, No Parity, Bits Per Second to match the modem.
Mouse	Defaults.
Printer	9600 Bits Per Second, 8 data bits, No parity, 1 Stop Bit, Xon/Xoff protocol.
Other serial devices	Defaults.

Lesson 6

What You Do	How You Do It
1. Connect the serial device to the serial port on the computer.	a. Turn off the power at the computer. b. Identify an available serial port and determine if it is a 9-pin or 25-pin port. c. Locate the connector on the device and determine if it requires a 9-pin or 25-pin cable, and whether the cable needs to have a male or female connection on the device end. d. Locate a serial cable that meets the requirements as determined. e. If necessary, **plug the serial cable into the device.** f. Plug the other end of the serial cable into the serial port on the computer. g. Secure the cable at both ends by turning the screws on each side of the cable's connector. h. Boot the computer. i. If prompted, **install drivers.**
2. Display the Port Settings list in Device Manager.	a. From the Start menu, **choose Control Panel→System.** b. Click the Hardware tab, and then click Device Manager. c. Expand Ports (COM & LPT).

Lesson 6

3. **Configure the settings for the serial device you installed.**

   a. **Right-click the COM port to which the serial device is connected and choose Properties.**

   b. **Select the Port Settings tab.**

   c. On the Port Settings page, **configure the settings for the device as given in the scenario for this activity.**

   d. **Click OK** to save the changes.

   e. **Close Device Manager.**

   f. **Click OK** to close the System Properties dialog box.

4. **Test the device.**

   a. If you installed a modem, on the Diagnostics page of the modem's Properties sheet, **click Query Modem.**

   b. If you installed a serial printer, on the Properties page for the printer, **click Print Test Page.**

   c. If you installed a serial mouse or other pointing device, **move the mouse or pointing device around on the screen, and then click an icon** to select it.

Topic B
Parallel Ports

With a keyboard, mouse, and monitor, users can work on their computer system, but what happens when they want to send information to another device? At the very least, your users are likely to want to print hard copies of documents, and they will turn to you to set up and configure print devices to the appropriate port on their computer.

Parallel Communications

In a parallel transmission, eight wires are used to send an entire byte at a time. No disassembly or reassembly of bytes is necessary. Figure 6-9 illustrates how the bits in a byte are transmitted over separate wires in a parallel transmission.

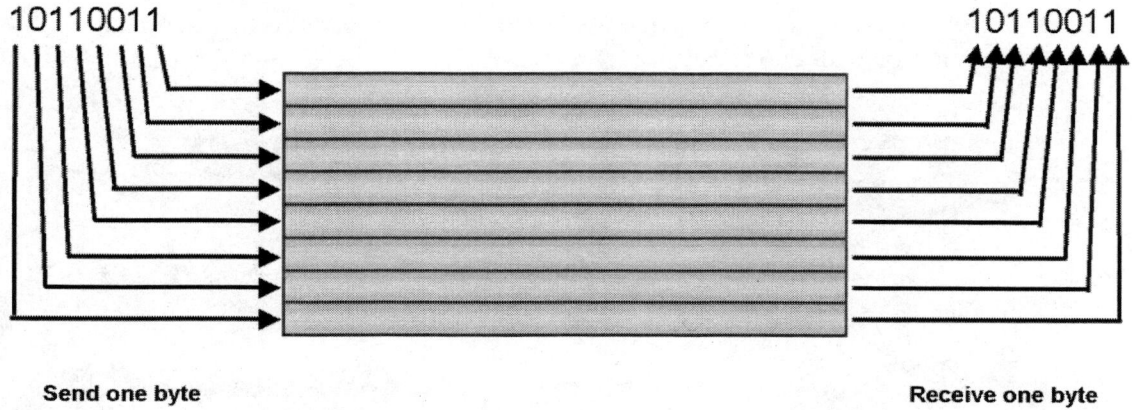

Send one byte   **Receive one byte**

Figure 6-9: *Parallel transmission sends a whole byte at a time over eight conductors.*

Parallel Interfaces

Definition:

A parallel interface is the hardware interface that enables a parallel device, typically a printer, to be connected to the computer. It is composed of the parallel port on the computer, a cable with parallel connectors on it, and a device with a parallel connection. A PC can have up to three parallel ports, referred to as LPT1, LPT2, and LPT3. LPT is short for *line printer*. Other devices, such as scanners, some network adapters, CD-ROM drives, and other types of external drives, can also be connected through parallel ports. Some devices have piggy-back connections, enabling you to install a second parallel device on a port with the first device.

The original parallel ports were unidirectional—they could send but not receive data. As parallel devices increased in their capabilities, designers needed a way to make the port faster and to allow communication back and forth between the parallel device and the computer. Now, the parallel port is bidirectional by default. The computer's standard parallel port (SPP) is a DB-25 female port. The parallel cable has a 25-pin male DB-25 connector that connects to the 25-pin female port. The device end of the parallel cable ends either in a 25-pin connector or in a 36-pin Centronics connector. If it is color-coded, the parallel port is burgundy or dark pink.

Centronics

The Centronics standard describes a type of parallel port used to connect printers. It is named after the company that designed the original interface. The Centronics standard uses a 36-pin Centronics connector to connect to the printer and a DB-25 (25-pin) connector to connect to the PC.

IEEE 1284

The *IEEE (Institute of Electrical and Electronic Engineers)* 1284 standard describes the bidirectional communication between the computer and peripherals over a parallel port connection. IEEE 1284 supports parallel cable runs up to 33 feet long without performance degradation. The IEEE 1284 standard also identifies three different types of connectors. Examples of the connectors are shown in Figure 6-10. These include the:

- 1284 Type A connector, which uses a 25-pin DB-25 connector.
- 1284 Type B connector, which uses a 36-conductor, 0.085 centerline Champ connector with bale locks.
- 1284 Type C connector, which uses a 36-conductor, 0.050 centerline mini-connector with clip latches.

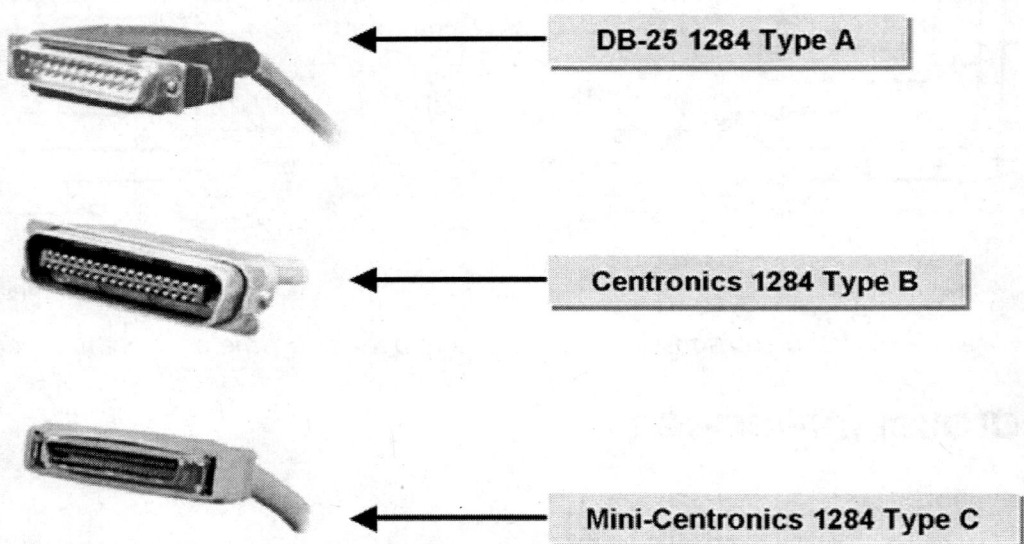

Figure 6-10: *IEEE 1284 Types A, B, and C cable ends.*

The IEEE 1284 standard also describes two bidirectional ports: Enhanced Parallel Port (EPP) and Extended Capability Port (ECP).

- *EPP* is used primarily by non-printer parallel port peripherals.
- *ECP* is used by newer-generation printers and scanners.

Both ECP and EPP provide *throughput,* the amount of data processed in a given time, that is many times faster than the Centronics standard provides. Beginning with Windows 95, all Windows operating systems have built-in support for IEEE 1284. Both the parallel port and the device must support IEEE 1284 to achieve the higher speeds.

Parallel Port Pinouts

The pinouts for the parallel port are shown in the following table. Figure 6-11 shows the pins referred to in the table.

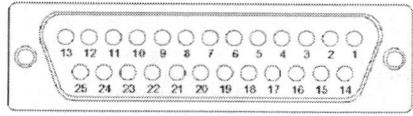

Figure 6-11: *DB-25 parallel port pinouts.*

Pin	Signal	Pin	Signal
1	- Strobe	14	- Auto feed
2	+ Data bit 0	15	- Error
3	+ Data bit 1	16	- Initialize printer
4	+ Data bit 2	17	- Select input
5	+ Data bit 3	18	Ground
6	+ Data bit 4	19	Ground
7	+ Data bit 5	20	Ground
8	+ Data bit 6	21	Ground
9	+ Data bit 7	22	Ground
10	- Acknowledge	23	Ground
11	+ Busy	24	Ground
12	+ P.End (out of paper)	25	Ground
13	+ Select		

Example: Parallel Connections

Figure 6-12 shows an example of the cable that would be used for a parallel connection between the parallel port on the computer and a parallel port Zip drive.

Lesson 6

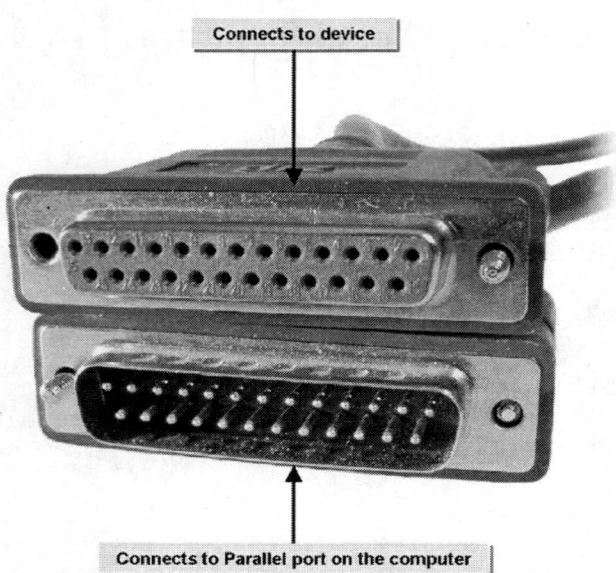

Figure 6-12: *A parallel cable for connecting a non-printer parallel port device.*

The Add Printer Wizard

You can use the Add Printer Wizard to add a printer to a Windows computer. This wizard guides you through the steps of specifying the type of printer you want to use and assigning a printer name and port. You can also specify whether you want to use the printer as the default printer. After you've installed the printer, you can configure it through the printer's properties.

How to Connect Parallel Devices

Procedure Reference: Connect a Device to a Parallel Port

To install a device on a parallel port:

1. With the computer and device turned off, connect the parallel cable between the device and the system.
2. If necessary, connect the AC adapter to the device and plug it into an electrical outlet.
3. Turn on the device and computer.
4. Install appropriate drivers for the device.
5. Verify that the device functions properly.

ACTIVITY 6-2

Installing a Parallel Printer

Setup:
The drivers for the parallel printer that you install will be provided to you by your instructor. They will be in one of the following locations: in a directory on your local drive, on a network drive, on floppy disks, or on CD-ROM.

Scenario:
As you continue to unpack equipment for the marketing department manager, you next take out a printer and a parallel port cable. You will install it so the manager can use it.

What You Do	How You Do It
1. Connect the cable between the parallel printer and the system.	a. Turn off the power at the computer. b. Locate an available parallel port. c. Connect the Centronics end of the cable to the printer, securing the clips on either side of the connector. d. Connect the 25-pin male end of the cable to the parallel port on the system. e. Plug in the printer's power cord.
2. Install the driver.	a. Turn on the power to the device and the computer. b. If prompted, **follow the New Hardware Wizard prompts.** c. If you are not prompted with the New Hardware Wizard, **note the System Notification bubble pop-up in the System Tray stating that the device was installed.**

Lesson 6

3. Verify that the correct printer driver was installed.

   a. From the Start menu, **choose Printers And Faxes.**

   b. **Verify that the correct printer make and model is listed.**

   c. If it is not listed, **click Add Printer**, and then follow the prompts in the Add Printer Wizard.

4. Test the connection by printing a test page.

   a. Right-click the printer and choose Properties.

   b. **Click Print Test Page.**

   c. **Click OK twice.**

   d. **Close all open windows.**

5. The manager would like the printer on the far side of the office so that it is out of his way. You measure the distance the cable would need to reach (down the desk leg, across the floor next to the file cabinet, and then around the edge of the room to the far corner) and find that the cable would need to be 25 feet long. Explain to the manager whether moving the printer to this location is possible. Also, explain any issues or problems that might arise from the longer cable.

OPTIONAL ACTIVITY 6-3

Connecting Additional Parallel Devices

Setup:
You have been given a parallel port device (such as a portable drive, scanner, or other device), a parallel cable, documentation, and any drivers needed for the device. The device has a piggy-back port through which you can connect another parallel port device including a printer.

Scenario:
Some of the employees you provide hardware support for have other devices that connect through the parallel port in addition to their parallel port printers. They need your help in connecting both the second parallel port device and the printer so that both can be used without the need to disconnect one and then use the other.

What You Do	How You Do It
1. Connect the parallel device with the piggy-back port.	a. Turn off the printer and the computer.
	b. Disconnect the printer from LPT1.
	c. Connect the parallel cable between the non-printer parallel device and the computer.
	d. Plug in the power cord for the device you just connected.
2. Install the device driver for the new device.	a. Turn on the device and the computer.
	b. If prompted, **install the device driver software.**
	c. If you are not prompted to install the device drivers, **verify that the System Notification message indicates that the drivers were installed.**
	d. If no System Notification message is displayed, **manually install the drivers for the device following the installation instructions in the documentation for the device.**

Lesson 6: Ports, Connectors, and Cables

3. Connect the printer through the piggy-back parallel port connection on the first device.	a. Turn off the device and the computer.
	b. Connect the printer cable to the parallel port on the parallel device.
	c. Turn on the parallel port device, the printer, and the computer.
4. Test that both devices function properly.	a. Read from, write to, or use other functions of the device connected directly to LPT1.
	b. Print a test page from the printer's Properties dialog box.

TOPIC C

PS/2 Ports

A computer system with no keyboard would be like a car with no steering wheel—you might be able to see where you were going, but you wouldn't be able to do anything about it. And a system with no mouse would be like a car with no dashboard controls for the radio or lights; you could drive the car, but there would be no easy way to adjust common settings or issue commands. So, as a computer technician, you'll need to know how to install and configure these common devices on the proper computer port.

PS/2 Interface

Definition:

A *PS/2 interface* is how *PS/2* devices are connected to the computer. PS/2 is an abbreviation of Personal System/2, an early IBM personal computer. The connections used for keyboards and mice on that computer became the standard connector type for keyboards and mice on most present-day personal computer systems. The PS/2 interface is composed of a PS/2 port on the computer, a PS/2 device, and a cable to connect the two together. An example of the PS/2 interface is shown in Figure 6-13. PS/2 ports are typically used to connect the keyboard and mouse to the computer. PS/2 ports, also called mini-DIN ports, are 6-pin round ports that are built in to the system. The keyboard and mouse ports look identical, but plugging the mouse in to the keyboard port and vice versa does not work.

To avoid confusion between the identical-looking ports, most systems somehow indicate which port is the keyboard and which is the mouse. The port is often color-coded to match the end of the cable on the device: purple for the keyboard and green for the mouse. Or, there will be a sticker with a picture of a mouse and keyboard near the connectors. On some systems, the sticker is under the connectors and perpendicular to the actual ports. The picture on the left goes with the upper port.

Lesson 6

📌 Color-coded ports were defined in 1999 by Microsoft, Intel, and Toshiba, to help users connect devices to the computer. Their standard has slowly been adopted by most manufacturers. Some older systems used other color codes that might not match the colors defined by this group. A list of the colors can be found at **www.microlanduk.com/support/external%20connections.htm#colours**.

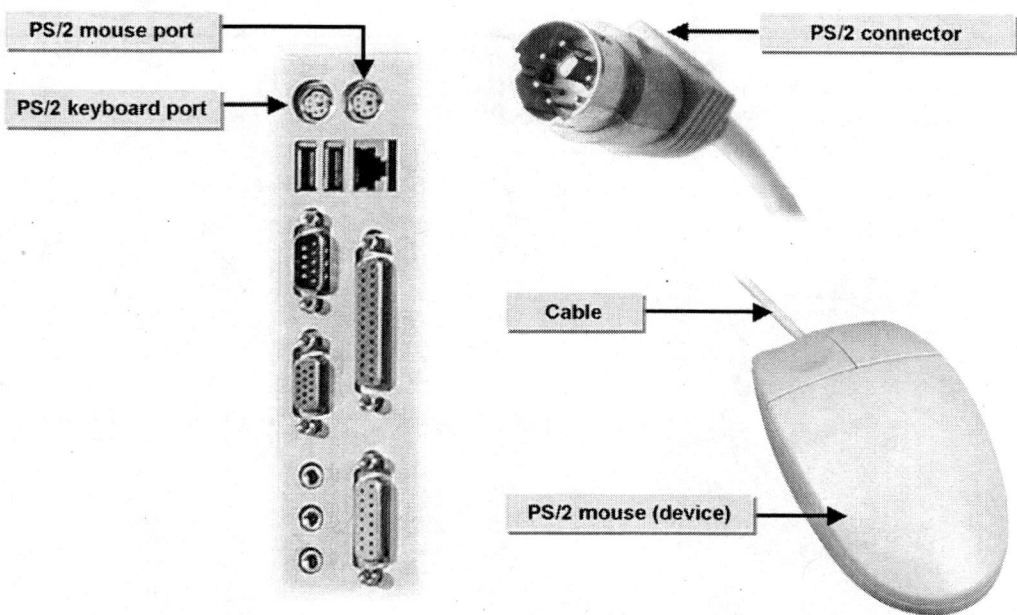

Figure 6-13: *A PS/2 interface.*

PS/2 Pinouts

The *pinouts* for a port specify the signal carried on each pin and connection for a port. The signal is carried from the device to the computer through the cable. Each of the pins is connected to a wire in the cable that performs a specific purpose.

Older keyboards use a large 5-pin DIN connector. The pinouts for that style of connector are shown in Table 6-2. The pinouts for the PS/2 connector are shown in Table 6-3.

Table 6-2: *5-pin DIN Connector Pinout*

Pin	Name	Purpose
1	CLK	Carries clock timing signals
2	DATA	Transmits key data
3		Nothing; not connected
4	GND	Ground connection
5	+5 V DC	Carries +5 volts of direct current

Table 6-3: *6-pin Mini-DIN Connector Pinout*

Pin	Name	Purpose
1	DATA	Transmits key data
2		Nothing; not connected
3	GND	Ground connection

Lesson 6: Ports, Connectors, and Cables

Pin	Name	Purpose
4	+5 V DC	Carries +5 volts of direct current
5	CLK	Carries clock timing signals
6		Nothing; not connected

Example: PS/2 Keyboard and Mouse Ports

Figure 6-14 shows an example of the keyboard and mouse ports found on the back of a computer system. They are usually one above the other as shown here, but could be side-by-side.

Figure 6-14: *PS/2 mouse (shown on top) and keyboard (bottom) ports.*

Device Drivers

Definition:

A *device driver* is a piece of software that enables the operating system and a peripheral device to communicate with each other. A device driver:

- Takes generalized commands from the system software or an application and translates them into unique programming commands that the device can understand.
- Provides the code that allows the device to function with the operating system.
- Is installed as part of the installation process for a new piece of hardware.

📌 Some experts consider the device driver to be a type of system software.

A device driver may be:

- Included with the Windows XP operating system or supplied with the device on a CD-ROM or floppy disk when you purchase it. Peripherals that are designed after the operating system comes out must supply their own drivers.

📌 New operating systems include thousands of drivers that let them work with all current, popular devices.

- Downloaded from the Internet from each manufacturer's Web site.
- Generic for a class of device or specific to a particular device.

📌 A device driver is also known as driver software or just plain driver.

Example: PS/2 Drivers

The software that enables your keyboard and mouse to communicate over the PS/2 port are examples of device drivers. PS/2 port drivers are typically installed when you install the operating system; you don't typically need to worry about installing them unless you install a new or non-standard device.

How to Install PS/2 Devices

Procedure Reference: Install a PS/2 Device

To install a PS/2 device:

1. Verify that the computer is turned off.
2. Locate the PS/2 keyboard and PS/2 mouse ports on the computer.
3. Align the pins on the cable with the openings in the PS/2 port on the computer and plug the device into the port, being sure to plug the keyboard in to the keyboard port and the mouse in to the mouse port. The rectangular plastic piece at the end of the cable helps you align the pins.
4. Verify that the PS/2 devices are working correctly.
    a. Boot the computer.
    b. Check for error messages when the system boots. If you see a keyboard error message, the cables are probably switched. Power down the system and switch the cables, and then try powering on again.
    c. Enter text from the keyboard.
    d. Move the mouse to different parts of the screen and click an icon or text to verify that the mouse pointer moves where you point it and that the buttons work properly.

LESSON 6

ACTIVITY 6-4

Installing PS/2 Devices

Setup:

Your computer is shut down. You have a keyboard and mouse that have been unplugged from your working computer.

Scenario:

You're setting up a new computer. You need to connect the standard input devices before employees can begin using their systems.

What You Do	How You Do It
1. **Plug in the keyboard.** ⚠ You should have the power turned off when adding or removing keyboard and mouse peripherals.	a. **Verify that the power is off at the computer.** b. **Identify the keyboard port.** c. **Locate the keyboard and examine the connector.** d. **Insert the keyboard connector in to the keyboard PS/2 port on the computer, being sure to align the pins with the holes.**
2. **Plug in the mouse.**	a. **Identify the PS/2 mouse port.** b. **Locate the mouse and examine the connector.** c. **Insert the PS/2 mouse connector in to the PS/2 mouse port on the computer, being sure to align the pins with the holes.**

3. Verify that the keyboard and mouse are fully functional.

    a. Turn on the computer power switch.

    b. Watch the monitor for error messages.

    c. If an error message indicating "no keyboard found" is displayed, **turn off the computer, and then switch the connections and reboot again.**

    d. **Log on as Administrator.**

    e. **Click Start→All Programs→Accessories→Notepad** to start an application and verify that the mouse works.

    f. In Notepad, **type *Does this keyboard work?*** to verify that the keyboard works.

    g. **Choose File→Exit** to close Notepad.

    h. When prompted to save changes, **click Yes.**

    i. In the File Name text box, **type *test.txt* and click Save.**

TOPIC D
USB Ports

USB is an extremely popular new standard for general-purpose computer ports, and you'll find at least one USB port on every modern computer system. Because USB supports so many devices and device types, it won't be long before you have users coming to you with collections of USB cables, devices, and hubs, asking you to connect and configure everything to work smoothly together. If you can do that, you'll be able to help your users take full advantage of this new technology.

USB

Definition:

The *Universal Serial Bus (USB)* standard is a hardware interface that enables you to connect multiple peripherals to a single port with high performance and little device configuration. Compaq, Digital, IBM, Intel, Microsoft, NEC, and Northern Telecom worked together to develop the USB standard.

Lesson 6

PCs typically come with one to four USB ports installed. You can add more devices by connecting a USB hub, which usually contains between four and seven USB ports. You can daisy-chain up to five hubs. Some devices, including monitors and keyboards, have their own USB ports, enabling you to daisy-chain even more USB devices. In all, you can connect up to 127 USB devices, including the hubs, to a single USB port.

Many devices receive power through the USB connection, rather than requiring an external power transformer or power cord.

 For more information on the USB standard, visit **http://usb.org/**.

USB Classes

The USB standard defines three classes:

- USB devices. These are further divided into:
  — Functions: Devices that can send, receive, or control data sent over a USB connection. This would include any peripherals that are connected to the computer through a USB interface.
  — Hubs: Devices that provide the ability to attach USB functions to the USB bus.
- USB host. There is only one host per system. It is also known as the USB interface, and it can be implemented as hardware, software, or firmware. The host is responsible for managing:
  — The attachment or removal of devices.
  — Power to devices.
  — The flow control of data between the host and devices.
  — The gathering of statistics about device activity.
- USB interconnect. This defines how devices communicate with and connect to the host.

USB devices themselves belong to classes. Examples are shown in Table 6-4.

Table 6-4: *USB Device Classes*

Class	Typical Devices in the Class
Human Interface	Mouse, keyboard, tablet, game controller
Imaging	Scanner, printer, digital camera
Mass Storage	CD-ROM, DVD, and floppy disk drives

USB Cables and Connectors

A USB cable usually has two different connectors. The upstream end of the cable, the one that is heading towards the computer, ends in a Type A connector. The downstream end of the cable, the one that is heading away from the computer towards the device, ends in a Type B connector. The cable can be up to 3 meters long for low-speed devices and up to 5 meters long for full- or high-speed devices.

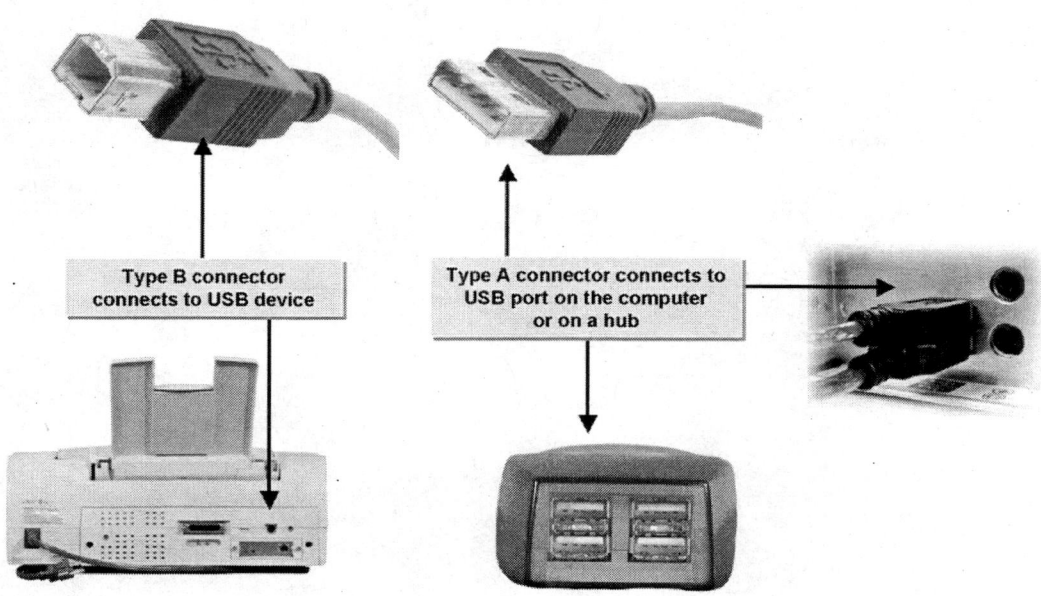

Figure 6-15: *USB connectors.*

USB Standards

USB 2.0 is the current standard. It can communicate at up to 480 Mbps. The original USB 1.1 standard is still commonly found in devices and systems. It can communicate at up to 12 Mbps. A USB 2.0 device connected to a USB 1.1 hub or port will only communicate at USB 1.1 speeds, even though it might be capable of faster speeds.

USB 2.0 defines three data rates. Table 6-5 lists the maximum speeds and typical devices for each.

Table 6-5: *USB 2.0 Data Rates*

Speed	Maximum Data Rate	Typical Devices
Low speed	1.5 Mbps	Keyboard, mouse, stylus, game peripherals, virtual reality peripherals
Full speed	12 Mbps	Telephone service, broadband service, audio, microphone
High speed	480 Mbps	Video, storage, imaging, broadband

Example:

You can connect modems, digital cameras, printers, scanners, network adapters, CD/RW drives, touch screens, external hard drives, external floppy drives, keyboards, mice, and many other devices to USB ports. A typical USB interface is shown in Figure 6-16.

Lesson 6

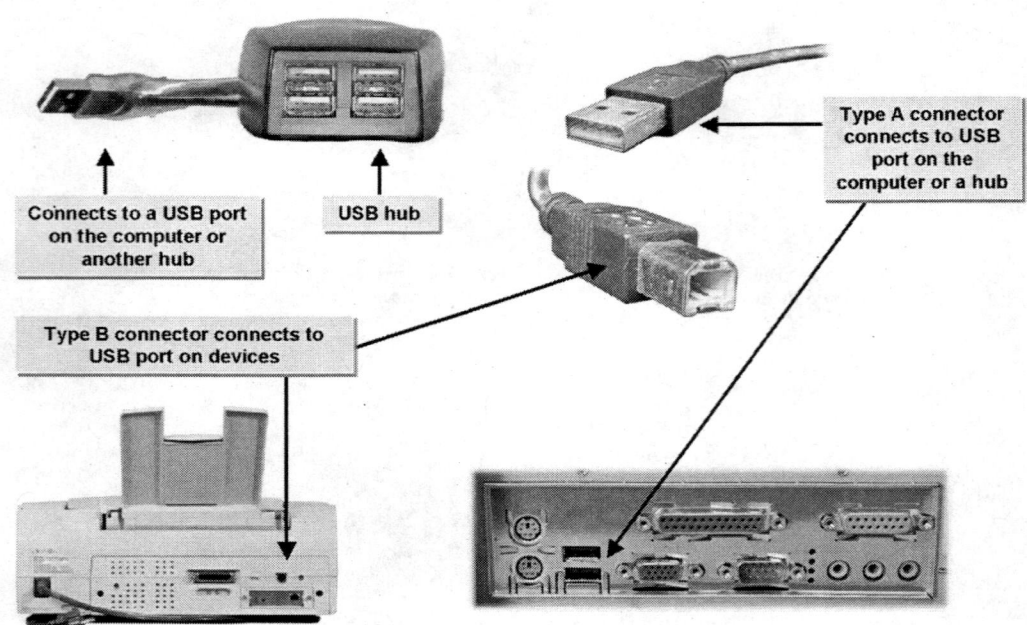

Figure 6-16: *USB ports, cables, and connectors.*

USB Power

A 5-volt power supply is carried along with the USB signal. This allows small devices, such as hand-held scanners or speakers, to use power from the PC, rather than requiring their own power cables. Devices are plugged directly into 4-pin sockets on PCs or hubs using a rectangular Type A socket.

The USB bus distributes power through each port. This allows low-power devices that normally need their own power adapters to be powered through the cable. Through USB, the PC automatically senses the power that is required and delivers it to the device. Hubs may get all of their power from the USB bus (bus-powered), or they may be powered from their own AC adapter. Powered hubs provide the most flexibility for other downstream devices.

How to Install USB Devices

Procedure Reference: Connect USB Devices to a System

To connect a USB device to your system:

1. Connect the USB Type B end of the USB cable into the device.

2. Connect the USB Type A end of the USB cable into the computer or the USB hub.

3. If necessary, connect the AC adapter to the device and to an electrical outlet.

4. If required, install any device drivers. You might be presented with a wizard that prompts you to install the driver or you might not be prompted. If you are installing an unsigned device (a device that Microsoft has not given its approval for and provided a signed signature for), you might be prompted several times to install the same device.

5. Test that the device connected through the USB port works properly.

ACTIVITY 6-5

Installing a USB Device

Setup:
You have a USB device, any cables needed, and any drivers required for the device.

Scenario:
You are a technician who has been assigned to install and support new peripherals for users when they purchase them at your store. A customer has purchased a device that contains a USB interface. The customer's computer has two USB ports. The device was packaged with the appropriate USB cable, drivers, and manuals.

What You Do	How You Do It
Your instructor will provide you with one of a variety of USB devices and the supporting cables and documentation to be able to install it.	
1. Connect the USB device to your computer.	a. Turn off your computer.
	b. Locate the USB port on your system.
	c. Locate the USB cable.
	d. Locate the USB connection port on the USB device.
	e. Connect the Type B end of the cable to the USB device.
	f. Connect the Type A end of the cable from the USB device to the USB port on your computer.
	g. Restart your computer.
2. Install the USB device driver.	a. When prompted that new hardware was detected, **insert the disk containing the driver**.
	b. **Follow the wizard's steps to install the device driver.**

Lesson 6: Ports, Connectors, and Cables

LESSON 6

239

3. Verify that the device works.

    a. Turn on the USB device.

    b. Access the device through the software available on your computer.

Common USB Problems

Generally speaking, you should run into few problems with USB ports, hubs, and devices. Due to their true Plug and Play nature, things should go smoothly whenever you install a new USB device. However, here are some of the problems you might run into when working with USB.

Symptom	Possible Problem	Solution
USB devices don't work	USB support not enabled in the BIOS.	USB BIOS support must be enabled to assign an IRQ to the PCI USB host bus controller. USB may be enabled by default; if it isn't, enter the BIOS during the POST and enable it. If your BIOS supports USB, you will likely find USB support under the Input/Output Ports menu, under Peripheral Setup, or under Advanced Options. If your BIOS doesn't have USB support, upgrade it, or install a PCI to USB adapter card.
Can't connect USB devices	No USB port on the system.	Install a PCI to USB adapter card in the computer.
Devices don't function or aren't detected	USB 1.0 system with cable over 5 meters.	Reduce cable length to 5 meters. The USB 1.0 specification specifically states that cable extensions are not allowed and might lead to signal loss. Later USB specifications allow for cables with internal repeaters, but signal loss can still occur.
Device cannot be seen in Device Manager	Operating system does not support USB. USB device failure.	Windows 95 provides limited USB support, and requires version B (OSR2) and supplemental USB support. To check if the USB supplement has been installed, open Add/Remove Programs from Control Panel, and look for USB Supplement to OSR2. If the supplement is not present, install USBSUPP.EXE from the Windows 95 OEM Service Release 2.1 and 2.5 CDs. You cannot download this supplement from Microsoft's Web site. Upgrade to Windows 98, Windows 2000, or Windows XP, which natively support USB. If the system supports USB, this is probably a hardware problem.

Symptom	Possible Problem	Solution
USB device displays an unknown device icon in Device Manager	If the USB host controller but not the Root Hub appears, there could be a possible problem with the USB.INF file.	Remove the USB host controller from Device Manager, and then click Refresh. Windows will then redetect hardware, and should see and install both the USB host controller and the Root Hub. Then, browse to \Windows\Inf, right-click the USB.INF file, and choose Install. Windows should then detect your USB device, and you should be able to find it in Device Manager.

TOPIC E

FireWire Ports

Suppose the marketing department of your company is starting to incorporate streaming video multimedia components into the presentations they design for trade shows. They're excited to be able to get state-of-the-art multimedia computer systems, complete with high-performance digital video cameras and other multimedia hardware. But standard PC connections might not be able to handle the performance needs of this leading-edge equipment; they need FireWire, and they need you to get it connected.

FireWire

Definition:

A *FireWire* interface is a high-speed hardware interface that enables up to 63 FireWire devices to be connected to the computer at the same time. FireWire is the name given by Apple to the IEEE 1394 standard, and the two terms are used interchangeably. Another name coined by Sony for this standard is iLink. FireWire was pioneered by Apple Computer, which was later joined by Microsoft, Philips, National Semiconductor, and Texas Instruments in the 1394 Trade Association. FireWire connectors are 6-pin bullet-shaped or 4-pin square connectors. You might need to upgrade your operating system in order to use FireWire. It works with Windows 98 SE and above. It doesn't work with Windows 95 or the original Windows 98.

FireWire is a hot-swappable serial interface. *Hotswap* means that you can change out a device without needing to power down the PC during installation or removal of the device.

FireWire can transmit data at up to 400 Mbps, which makes it a good solution for connecting digital cameras, digital video cameras, printers, TVs, network cards, and mass-storage devices to PCs.

The IEEE 1394 specification calls for two data-transfer methods. If data can be interrupted (such as when the buffer is full), it uses asynchronous transfer methods. If the data needs to flow at a specific rate so that there are no interruptions, then isochronous transfer methods are used. This is often used for multimedia presentations where buffering and pauses would interrupt the presentation to the user.

Two Levels of Interface

There are two levels of interface in IEEE 1394, one for the backplane bus within the computer and another for the point-to-point interface between device and computer on the serial cable. A simple bridge connects the two environments.

The backplane bus supports data-transfer speeds of 12.5, 25, or 50 Mbps. The cable standard supports speeds of 100, 200, and 400 Megabits per second. This is about four times as fast as a 100BaseT Ethernet connection and much faster than the 12 Mbps provided by USB 1.1. Future speeds will include 800 Mbps, and 1,200 Mbps.

The 1394b specification plans to use a different coding and data-transfer scheme that will provide 800 Mbps per second, 1.6 Gbits per second, and even higher speeds. This high speed makes IEEE 1394 a viable solution for connecting digital cameras, video cameras, printers, TVs, network cards, and mass-storage devices to PCs.

FireWire Cables and Connectors

Electrical contacts are inside the structure of the connector of an IEEE 1394-compliant cable. This helps prevent shock to the user or contamination of the contacts by the user's hands. These connectors are derived from the Nintendo GameBoy connector. Field-tested by children of all ages, this small and flexible connector is very durable and easy to use, even when the user must blindly insert it into the back of a machine.

IEEE 1394 uses a 6-conductor cable which contains two pairs of wires for data transport, and one pair for device power. In most cases, the cable can be up to 4.5 meters long. In some cases the cable can be up to 14 meters long, but if there are powered devices the voltage could drop too low at these longer lengths. There is also a small square 4-wire cable connector that connects to the device. Some systems also include a port for this connection on the system. Examples of the FireWire connectors are shown in Figure 6-17.

Figure 6-17: *FireWire connectors.*

The design is similar to a standard 10BaseT Ethernet cable; each signal pair is shielded and the entire cable is shielded. Cable power is specified to be from 8 V DC to 40 V DC at up to 1.5 amps. It is used to maintain a device's physical layer continuity when the device is powered down or a malfunction occurs. This is a unique and very important feature for a serial topology. It also provides power for devices connected to the bus. As the standard evolves, new cable designs are expected to allow longer distances without repeaters and with more bandwidth.

FireWire Chips

Every IEEE 1394 connection contains two chips per device: a physical layer and a link layer semiconductor chip. The physical interface (PHY) is a mixed-signal device that connects to the other device's PHY. All PHY chips use the same technology, whereas the link is device-specific allowing IEEE 1394 to act as a peer-to-peer system as opposed to USB's client-server design. Therefore, an IEEE 1394 system doesn't need a serving host or a PC.

FireWire supports both asynchronous and isochronous transport. Asynchronous transport is the traditional method of transmitting data between computers and peripherals, data being sent in one direction followed by acknowledgement to the requester. Asynchronous data transfers place emphasis on delivery rather than timing. The data transmission is guaranteed, and retries are supported. Isochronous data transfer ensures that data flows at a preset rate so that an application can handle it in a timed way. Isochronous data transfers operate in a broadcast manner, where one or many 1394 devices can listen to the data being transmitted.

Up to 63 channels of isochronous data can be transferred simultaneously on the 1394 bus. Because isochronous transfers can only take up a maximum of 80 percent of the 1394 bus bandwidth, there is enough bandwidth left over for additional asynchronous transfers.

IEEE 1394's scalable architecture and flexible peer-to-peer topology make it ideal for connecting high-speed devices: everything from computers and hard drives, to digital audio and video hardware. Devices can be connected in either a daisy-chain or tree topology.

The 1394 bus bridge isolates data traffic within each work area. IEEE 1394 bus bridges allow selected data to be passed from one bus segment to another.

Because the 1394 cable is powered, the PHY signalling interface is always powered, and data is transported even if a PC in the chain is powered off. Over 1,000 bus segments may be connected by bridges, thus providing a large growth potential. An additional feature is the ability of transactions at different speeds to occur on a single-device medium. For example, some devices can communicate at 100 Mbps while others communicate at 200 and 400 Mbps.

IEEE 1394 devices can be added to or removed from the bus while the bus is in full operation. Upon altering the bus configuration, topology changes are automatically recognized. This Plug and Play feature eliminates the need for address switches or other user intervention to reconfigure the bus.

FireWire uses memory-based addressing, rather than channel addressing, which views resources as registers or memory that can be accessed with processor-to-memory transactions. This makes for easy networking. A digital camera can easily send pictures directly to a digital printer without a computer in between. Using IEEE 1394, the PC might become just a very intelligent peer device.

IEEE 1394 peripherals will be more expensive than SCSI, IDE, or USB devices. This is because two pieces of silicon instead of one are needed. This will make it too expensive for low-speed peripherals. However, it will probably catch on in higher-end applications like digital video editing. So far it is mainly used in digital camcorders, where it is known as iLink.

Device Bay

Compaq, Intel, and Microsoft proposed an industry standard called Device Bay. It combines the fast interface of IEEE 1394 with the USB interface. It offers a bay slot to slide in peripherals such as hard disks or DVD-ROM players. Other devices that use IEEE 1394 include ZIP drives, scanners, and CD-RW drives.

Example:

Figure 6-18 shows a FireWire interface.

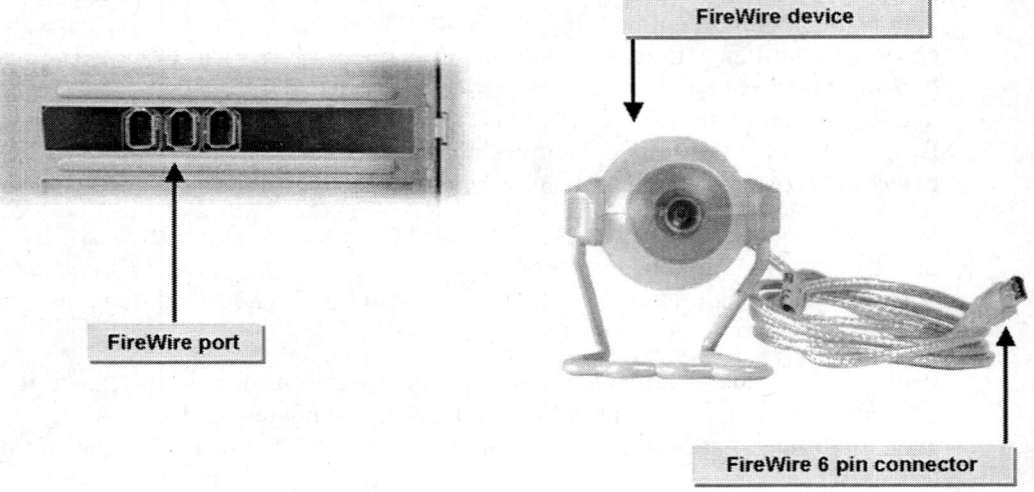

Figure 6-18: *FireWire connections.*

How to Install FireWire Devices

Procedure Reference: Connect FireWire Devices

To connect a FireWire device to your system:

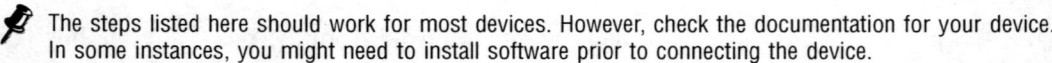 The steps listed here should work for most devices. However, check the documentation for your device. In some instances, you might need to install software prior to connecting the device.

1. Connect the FireWire cable to the device.
2. Connect the FireWire cable to the FireWire port on your computer.
3. If necessary, connect the AC adapter to the device and to an electrical outlet.
4. If necessary, install any required FireWire device drivers.
5. Verify that the device works properly.

ACTIVITY 6-6

Installing a FireWire Device

Scenario:
You are a technician who has been assigned to install and support new peripherals for users when they purchase them at your store. A customer has purchased a device that contains a FireWire interface. The customer's computer has a FireWire port. The device was packaged with the appropriate FireWire cable, drivers, and manuals.

What You Do	How You Do It
1. Connect the FireWire device to your computer.	a. Locate the FireWire port on your computer.
	b. Locate the FireWire cable.
	c. Locate the FireWire connection port on your FireWire device.
	d. Connect the cable to the FireWire device.
	e. Connect the cable from the FireWire device to the FireWire port on the computer.
	f. If necessary, **connect an AC adapter to the FireWire device.**
	g. If necessary, **install any required drivers.**
2. Verify that the FireWire device works properly.	a. Access the FireWire device.
	b. Transfer the data from the FireWire device to your system.

Lesson 6: Ports, Connectors, and Cables

LESSON 6

TOPIC F

Wireless Ports

Wireless functionality is a great tool for users who need to move about or to interact with their PCs from a distance. For example, a sales rep giving a presentation might want to run a slide show off her PC while she moves about the room to interact with the audience. Or, a medical professional might use a portable computer to take notes during examinations, but he doesn't have the time to plug the computer into the wall each time he goes to a different exam room. If you have users who need this kind of functionality, you'll need to set up their wireless connections so that they work reliably.

Wireless Connections

Definition:

A wireless connection is a method for a device to communicate with the computer without a physical connection between the device and the computer. Some wireless devices must have a direct line of sight to the wireless port on the computer. Others can communicate around corners and over piles of paper and other equipment. There are several wireless communications standards, including infrared, digital radio, and Bluetooth profiles.

Infrared devices use infrared transceivers that are compliant with the Infrared Data Association's (IrDA) standards. With infrared communications, there is no physical connection between the devices that communicate over the infrared link. Instead, data is sent over a beam of light. Most commonly, infrared technology is used to connect printers to computers (typically portable computers, such as laptops or palmtops), but it can also be used to connect workstations in a network. Figure 6-19 shows how data is transferred over an infrared connection.

Lesson 6

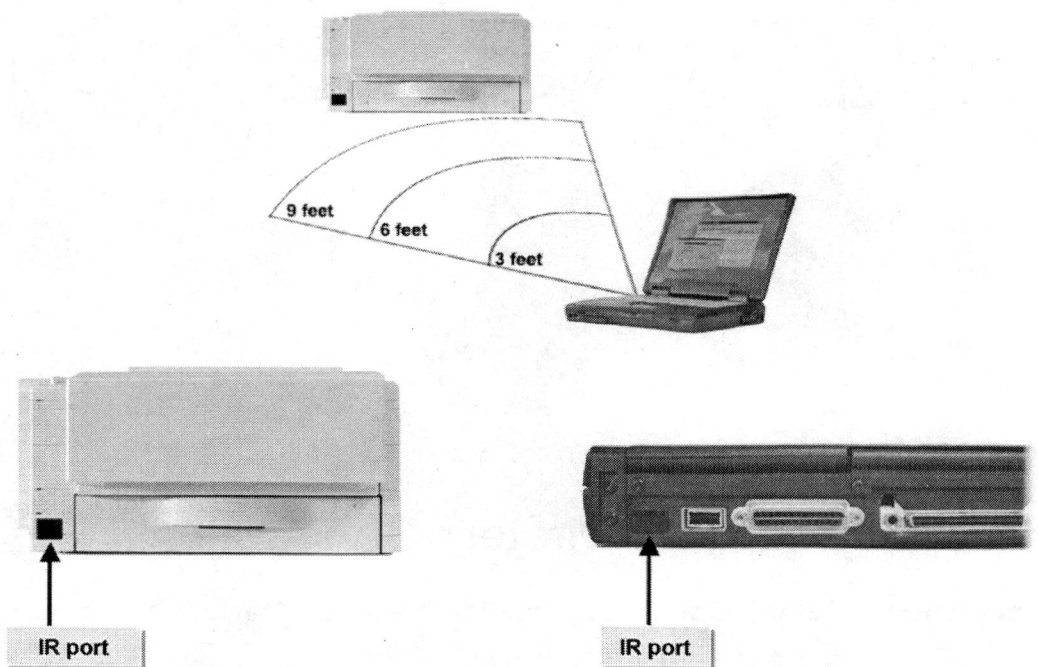

Figure 6-19: *Transferring information over an infrared connection.*

Data transfer speed ranges from 9.6 Kbps (*slow IrDA*) to 4 Mbps on newer devices (*fast IrDA*). Infrared communication uses line-of-sight technology, and the distance between the devices must be minimal (no more than approximately 3 to 9 feet). For example, if you have an infrared printer, the computer's infrared port must be in the line of sight of the printer's infrared port and the two must be positioned relatively close to each other. Having the devices' infrared ports facing each other head-on is best, but most devices will still connect when placed at a slight angle to each other. An angle of less than 45 degrees is usually required.

Digital radio connections enable you to connect devices to your computer without wires. It does not require a direct line of sight between the device and the computer. Cordless keyboards and mice typically use digital radio frequency technologies.

The Bluetooth wireless communications standard uses short-range radio technology for communications between computers and personal digital devices such as cell phones and Personal Digital Assistants (PDAs).

Example:

An example of a digital radio frequency mouse is shown in Figure 6-20. The receiver plugs into a USB or PS/2 port on the computer and receives radio signals from the mouse, which acts as a transmitter.

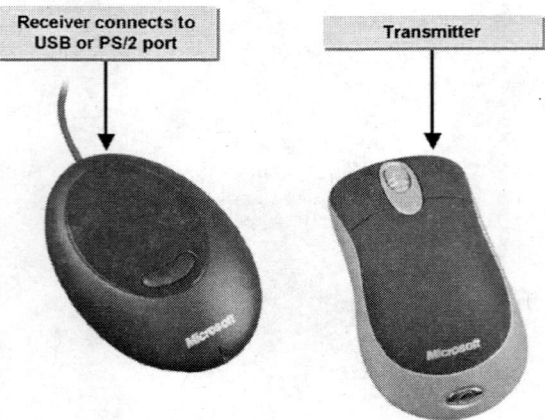

Figure 6-20: *A digital radio frequency mouse.*

How to Establish a Wireless Connection

Procedure Reference: Connect Digital Radio Wireless Devices

To connect a device that uses digital radio wireless connections:

1. If necessary, install the wireless device software.
2. Connect the receiver device. Depending on the device, there might be power connections you need to plug in. Other devices can be powered directly from the PC.
3. If necessary, install batteries in the remote transmitter devices.
4. Connect and test the transmitter devices.
5. If desired, disconnect the equivalent hardwired devices.

   In some cases, you might choose to leave the hardwired devices connected. For example, if you have a child-sized mouse and a normal-sized mouse, you could leave both connected and use whichever one is more comfortable for the user.

Procedure Reference: Connect Infrared Devices

To connect a device containing an infrared port to a system that has an infrared port:

1. Establish a clear line of sight between the infrared peripheral port on the device and the infrared port on the computer.
2. If necessary, connect the AC adapter for the device and connect it to an electrical outlet.
3. If necessary, configure the device.

   If the device is connected through USB, PCMCIA, or any device that is Plug and Play compatible, the appropriate driver should be installed automatically. However, if you are installing the device through a serial port, some USB devices, or any device which was not automatically detected and installed, you will need to configure the device for your system. This might include installing drivers, enabling the IR port on your system or on the device, or other such steps as documented in the device manual.

4. With the infrared ports aimed at each other, transfer data between the peripheral and the system. For example, if you have a printer, send a file to print.

ACTIVITY 6-7

Connecting Digital Radio Devices

Scenario:
Several of the employees in your company have purchased wireless keyboards and mice. You have been assigned to install them so users can begin using them.

What You Do	How You Do It
1. If device documentation requires software installation prior to installing wireless devices, **install the wireless device software.**	a. If necessary, **insert the CD-ROM containing the wireless device software into the CD-ROM drive.** b. If the CD-ROM doesn't auto-run, **choose Start→Run, and then browse for the file on the CD-ROM to start the installation. Click Open, and then click OK.** c. **Install the software by following the on-screen prompts.**
2. **Connect the receiver device.**	a. If necessary, **plug the receiver into an electrical outlet.** b. If necessary, **power the receiver on.** c. **Connect the receiver to the port matching the cable.** 📌 This is usually connected to the USB, PS/2, or serial port. d. If the New Hardware Wizard runs, **follow the prompts to install the device.**
3. **Connect the transmitter devices.**	a. **Insert batteries in each device.** b. **Click the Connect button on the receiver and/or each transmitter.** Check the manufacturer's documentation. c. If the New Hardware Wizard runs, **follow the prompts to install each device.** d. **Test each device.**

4. Disconnect any hardwired connection devices you are replacing with the newly installed wireless devices.

   a. Turn off the system.

   b. Disconnect the devices to be removed.

   c. Reboot the system.

   d. If necessary, uninstall any software for the devices you removed.

OPTIONAL DISCOVERY ACTIVITY 6-8

Connecting Infrared Devices

Setup:
You can complete this activity only if you have an infrared device and computer with an infrared port or to which you can add an infrared port.

Scenario:
The head of the marketing department uses wireless devices in order to keep her desk clear from cables. She has a wireless mouse, keyboard, PDA, and printer. She has asked you to set up her equipment.

1. Position each device and the computer so that you can make the connection between the wireless device and the computer.

2. Configure the device as appropriate to the system.

3. Transfer data between the devices.

Lesson 6 Follow-up

In this lesson, you installed and removed devices connected to standard ports. You connected keyboard and pointing devices to the PS/2 ports, connected parallel and serial devices to the relevant ports, connected USB and FireWire devices, and established wireless connections. In the same way that the jigsaw pieces made a complete picture, the peripherals connected to your computer have created a complete computer system.

1. Which peripherals will you need to install most often?

LESSON 6

2. Which peripherals do you feel you will need to practice installing before you are comfortable with quickly and easily installing them to work right the first time?

Notes

Lesson 7
Expansion Boards

Lesson Time
2 hour(s), 30 minutes

Lesson Objectives:

In this lesson, you will identify the internal expansion capabilities of a PC.

You will:

- Install a drive controller.
- Install a video adapter.
- Connect game and sound devices to the appropriate ports.
- Install a modem.

Lesson 7

Introduction

You have examined the internal system components of the typical PC. You also looked at expansion buses, which are designed to enable you to expand the functionality of your PC. In this lesson, you will examine the expansion boards that you plug into those buses.

This lesson will focus on internal expansion boards that you can install or replace in any PC. These boards enable you to expand the functionality of your computer.

The following CompTIA A+ Core Hardware (2003) Examination objectives are covered in this lesson:

- Topic A:
  - 1.2 Identify basic procedures for adding and removing field-replaceable modules for desktop systems. Given a replacement scenario choose the appropriate sequences. Content includes: adapters—SCSI.
  - 1.4 Identify typical IRQs, DMAs, and I/O addresses, and procedures for altering these settings when installing and configuring devices. Choose the appropriate installation or configuration steps in a given scenario. Content includes the following: hard drive controllers.
  - 1.6 Identify proper procedures for installing and configuring common IDE devices. Choose the appropriate installation or configuration sequences in given scenarios. Recognize the associated cables. Content includes the following: IDE interface types—EIDE, ATA/ATAPI, serial ATA, and PIO.
  - 1.9 Identify procedures to optimize PC operations in specific scenarios. Predict the effects of specific procedures under given scenarios. Topics include: disk subsystem enhancements—controller cards.
  - 1.10 Determine the issues that must be considered when upgrading a PC. In a given scenario, determine when and how to upgrade system components. Components include: adapter cards.
  - 4.3 Identify the most popular types of motherboards, their components, and their architecture (bus structures). Content includes the following: IDE—ATA, ATAPI, ULTRA-DMA, and EIDE.
- Topic B:
  - 1.2 Identify basic procedures for adding and removing field-replaceable modules for desktop systems. Given a replacement scenario choose the appropriate sequences. Content includes: adapters—video card.
  - 1.9 Identify procedures to optimize PC operations in specific scenarios. Predict the effects of specific procedures under given scenarios. Topics include: disk subsystem enhancements—specialized video cards.
- Topic C:
  - 1.2 Identify basic procedures for adding and removing field-replaceable modules for desktop systems. Given a replacement scenario choose the appropriate sequences. Content includes: adapters—sound card.
  - 1.4 Identify typical IRQs, DMAs, and I/O addresses, and procedures for altering these settings when installing and configuring devices. Choose the appropriate installation or configuration steps in a given scenario. Content includes the following: multimedia devices.
- Topic D:

Lesson 7

- 1.2 Identify basic procedures for adding and removing field-replaceable modules for desktop systems. Given a replacement scenario choose the appropriate sequences. Content includes: adapters—modem.
- 1.4 Identify typical IRQs, DMAs, and I/O addresses, and procedures for altering these settings when installing and configuring devices. Choose the appropriate installation or configuration steps in a given scenario. Content includes the following: internal modems.
- 1.5 Identify the names, purposes, and performance characteristics, of standardized/common peripheral ports, associated cabling, and their connectors. Recognize ports, cabling, and connectors, by sights. Content includes the following: connector types—serial (RJ-11).
- 1.8 Identify proper procedures for installing and configuring common peripheral devices. Choose the appropriate installation or configuration sequence in given scenarios. Content includes the following: modems and transceivers—dial-up.
- 2.1 Recognize common problems associated with each module and their symptoms, and identify steps to isolate and troubleshoot the problems. Given a problem situation, interpret the symptoms and infer the most likely cause. Content includes: adapters—modem.

TOPIC A

Drive Controllers

Without a drive controller, your computer will not be able to access disk drives, whether they be floppy drives, hard drives, or other sorts of drives. Many motherboards come with drive controllers built in. However, some don't and sometimes you will require features that the built-in component doesn't provide. In this topic, you will install a drive controller.

Drive Interfaces

Definition:

A *drive interface* is the connection between a drive and the computer system. There are two types of interfaces, but each has many variations. They are *IDE* and *SCSI*. The following table lists the features of each.

Lesson 7

Interface	Features
Integrated Drive Electronics (IDE), also known as Advanced Technology Attachment (ATA)	Controller is built into the drive. Limited to two channels, each with up to two devices. Supports single-drive only configuration, (for one drive on a channel), and master/slave configurations (for two drives). The master device is the boot disk; it is first on the chain and controls the second device, which is the slave. If the drive type is not automatically detected, it must be set in system BIOS. Less expensive than SCSI. Many updates with improvements in speed and reliability. ATA is the formal name chosen by the American National Standards Institute (ANSI) group X3T10. It specifies the interface specifications for the power and data signals between the motherboard, the drive controller, and the drive. The manufacturer can use any physical interface, but must have an embedded controller that uses the ATA interface controller to connect the drive directly to the ISA bus. The original IDE specification does not support CD-ROMs or hard drives larger than 528 or 504 MB. The size limitation is stated as either 528 MB, or as 504 MB. The size of 504 MB is derived by dividing 528,000,000 bytes by 1,048,576 (the exact number of bytes per MB), and it is realistically the more accurate number.
Small Computer System Interface (SCSI)	No controller, but is actually a separate bus within the computer system. Supports up to seven devices (15 devices in more recent versions). Must configure separate ID settings for each device. More expensive than IDE. May need to set system BIOS to no drive, and then configure SCSI software to recognize drive to boot from. Several variations on the interface.

Extending IDE Drive Capacities

The original IDE specification limits hard drive size to 504 MB. Three ways were developed to overcome this limitation.

- You can extend the drive size limit to 8.4 GB through the use of *Logical Block Addressing (LBA)* or *Extended CHS (ECHS)*. With LBA or ECHS, hard drives can be up to 8.4 GB in size. LBA and ECHS are methods of sector translation (translating a hard drive's logical geometry into physical geometry) that essentially give the BIOS incorrect information about the geometry of the drive so that larger hard-drive capacities can be supported, while staying within BIOS limitations. The cylinder value after translation never exceeds 1,024. LBA was developed by Western Digital. ECHS was developed by Seagate. They differ only in the sector

Lesson 7

translation results they produce. If you want to move a hard drive from one computer to another, however, the other computer must support the same sector translation method as the computer out of which you're taking the hard drive. Otherwise, you will lose the data on the disk if you move the drive. This is a problem mostly if one computer is significantly older than another. But you do want to check, and always back up your data before moving a drive. Today's hard disks and BIOSs all support LBA and ECHS to accommodate the need for large disk capacity.

- To address the need for even larger hard drive capacities, Phoenix Technologies developed *Interrupt 13h (INT13h) extensions.* Developed in 1994, INT13h extensions are a newer set of BIOS commands that enable support for hard drives larger than 8.4 GB. This support is made possible by using 64 bits for addressing, instead of 24 bits, and by using 1,024 cylinders. This expands hard drive support for drives up to 137 GB. INT 13h extensions are supported by modern hard drives and Windows 95 and newer OSs, but must also be supported by the system BIOS or the hard-disk controller.

- Another recent development is *Large LBA.* This translation mode enables support for hard disks greater than 137 GB. It uses 48 bits for addressing, instead of 24 bits.

Example: IDE or ATA

Figure 7-1 shows the IDE interface. The controller is built into the drive. The jumpers determine whether it is a master or slave drive.

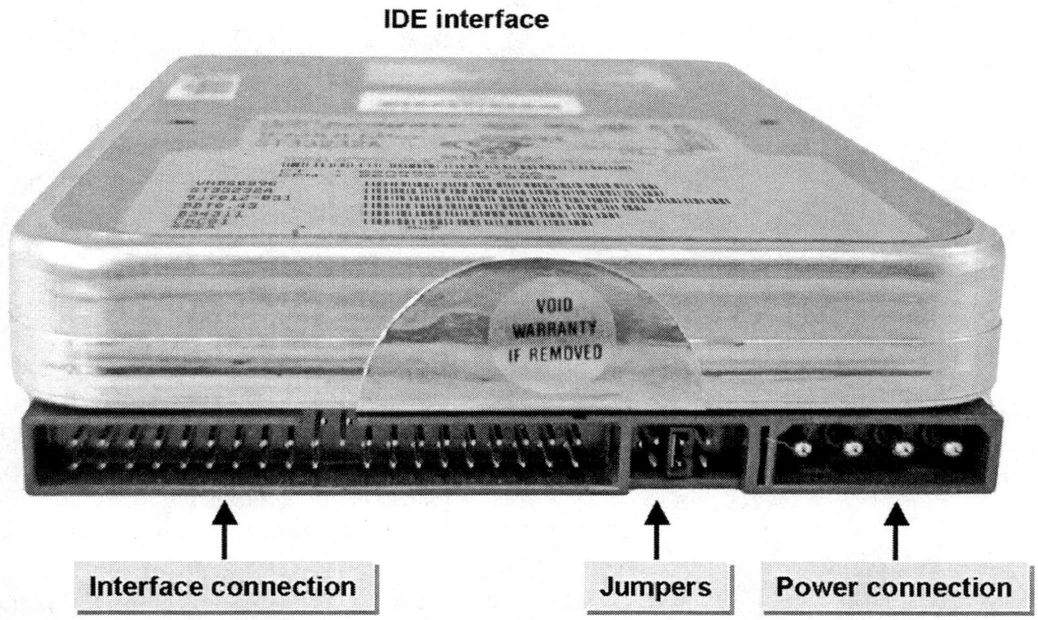

IDE interface

[Interface connection] [Jumpers] [Power connection]

Figure 7-1: *Drive interface.*

PIO Modes

The ATA and ATA-2 standards use the *Programmed Input/Output Mode (PIO Mode)* to indicate the speed of data transfer between two devices that use the computer's processor as a part of the datapath. See the following table for the different PIO Modes and transfer rates. The PIO Mode is set in the BIOS. It is originally set when you install an IDE or EIDE drive. You will learn more about installing IDE and EIDE drives in the Storage Systems lesson.

Standard	PIO Mode	Transfer Rate
ATA	0	3.3 MBps
ATA	1	5.2 MBps
ATA	2	8.3 MBps
ATA-2	3	11.1 MBps
ATA-2	4	16.6 MBps

ATA Standards

IDE was the original name for what became ATA when ANSI standardized the specification. The following table describes the variations on the ATA standard.

IDE or ATA Standard Variations	Description
ATA	The original ATA specification supported one channel, with two drives configured in a master/slave arrangement. PIO modes 0, 1, and 2 were supported, as well as single-word DMA modes 0, 1, and 2 and multi-word DMA mode 0. No support for non-hard disk devices was included, nor were block mode transfers, logical block addressing, and other advanced features.
ATA-2	Also known as the Advanced Technology Interface with Extensions. Western Digital's implementation was called Enhanced IDE (EIDE). Seagate's implementation was called Fast ATA or Fast ATA-2. Supports PIO modes 3 and 4 and two multi-word modes, 1 and 2, all of which are faster than the modes supported by the original ATA specification. Support for 32-bit transactions. Some drives supported DMA. Could implement power-saving mode features if desired. Specification also covered removable drives.
ATA-3	Minor enhancement to ATA-2. Improved reliability for high-speed data transfer modes. Self Monitoring Analysis And Reporting Technology (SMART) was introduced. This is logic in the drives that warns of impending drive problems. Password protection available as a security feature of the drives.
ATAPI	AT Attachment Packet Interface is an EIDE interface component that includes commands used to control tape and CD-ROM drives.
ATA-4	Also known as Ultra-DMA, UDMA, Ultra-ATA, and Ultra DMA/33. Doubled data transfer rates. Supported ATAPI specification.

IDE or ATA Standard Variations	Description
ATA-5	The ATA-5 specification introduced Ultra DMA modes 3 and 4, as well as mandatory use of the 80-pin, high-performance IDE cable. Additional changes to the command set were also part of this specification. Supports drives up to 137 GB.
ATA-6	Supports Ultra DMA/100 for data transfers at up to 100 MB/second. Supports drives as large as 144 PB (petabytes), 144 million MB or 144 quadrillion bytes.
PIO	Programmed Input/Output is a data transfer method that includes the CPU in the data path. It has been replaced by DMA and Ultra DMA.
DMA	Direct Memory Access is a data transfer method that moves data directly from the drive to main memory.
Ultra DMA	Transfers data in burst mode at a rate of 33.3 MB per second. The speed is two times faster than DMA.
Ultra DMA 100	Also known as ATA-100, this standard supports data transfers in burst mode at a rate of 100 MB per second.
Serial ATA	An emerging storage-interface standard that uses serial instead of parallel signaling technology for internal ATA and ATAPI devices. Serial ATA employs serial connectors and serial cables, which are smaller, thinner, and more flexible than traditional parallel ATA cables. Data transfer rates are 150 MB per second or greater.

Older Interface Technologies

The *ST-506* interface, later upgraded and renamed the ST-412 interface, is one of the oldest drive interfaces still in use. Due to its low speed, it has not been a popular choice for some time; however, it was popular enough that the PC architecture is built around the ST-506 design. When you are installing drives, the PC's BIOS will require you to set a drive type. These types are based on the ST-506 interface and operational parameters. For compatibility reasons, newer drive and interface types use this same method.

ESDI, or Enhanced Small Device Interface, is similar to the ST-506 interface. However, it offers at least double the performance of the ST-506 interface. ESDI is still occasionally used, but is being supplanted by the newer interfaces. (The ESDI acronym is often pronounced as "ez-dee.")

ESDI controllers can generally support up to two drives each. Drives are connected by two cables: a 34-pin control cable and a 20-pin data cable. ESDI drives must have jumpers set to designate their drive numbers (first or second on the chain). This setting is described as the drive select; the jumper that sets the drive select is the drive select jumper. ESDI drives must also be properly *terminated*. The drive that occupies the end position on the ESDI chain must have a terminating resistor pack installed. Other ESDI drives and the controller are not terminated. Figure 7-2 illustrates an ESDI drive chain of two drives.

Lesson 7

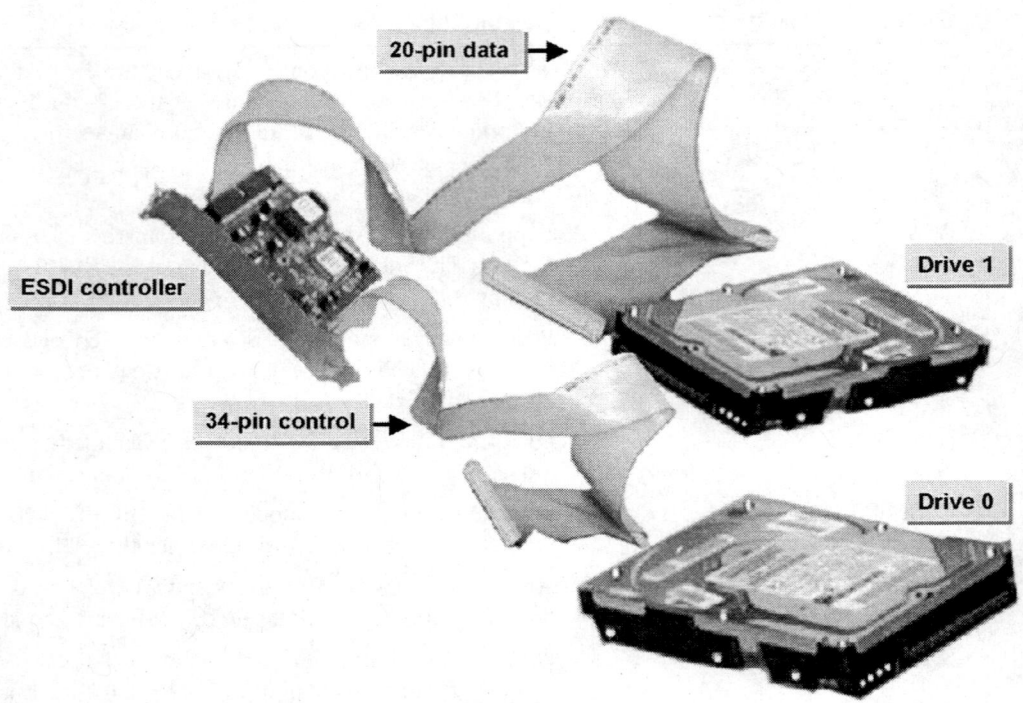

Figure 7-2: *An ESDI installation of two drives.*

Other ESDI settings can include drive speed, interface transfer rate, or spindle synchronization. ESDI drives require that you set the BIOS drive type in the same way that you would for an ST-506 drive, unless your controller contains its own BIOS chip.

Manufacturers of ESDI drives and controllers have worked hard to get maximum performance from the ESDI interface. Often, ESDI controllers will include large amounts of RAM-based cache and an intelligent cache controller. Reads and writes to this cache are faster than reads and writes to the actual disk, so the performance enhancement can be significant.

Drive Controller

Definition:

The *drive controller* is the circuitry that enables the drive and CPU to communicate with each other. The controller circuitry is built onto the drive, and other drives are controlled by the *host bus adapter (HBA)*, a dedicated adapter that manages data transfer between the devices on a channel.

Example:

An IDE drive includes the circuitry to control the drive. Figure 7-3 shows the controller circuitry on an IDE drive.

Figure 7-3: *IDE drive controller circuitry.*

SCSI

Definition:

SCSI is a parallel bus standard that connects internal and external peripherals. SCSI is commonly used to connect internal drives. In addition, it is also used to connect external devices including drives, scanners, network adapters, and monitors, and has been used as a network topology. The following characteristics apply to all SCSI devices.

- It is a hardware interface, as well as a logical interface.
- It moves data in parallel mode a chunk at a time rather than a bit at a time.
- SCSI is technically not a controller, but is an adapter. It converts messages between the system bus and the SCSI bus. The Host Bus Adapter (HBA) is the card or component in the system that connects the SCSI bus to the system bus. This is usually on a separate card, but could be built into the chipset of the computer.
- All SCSI devices have a device ID.
- All devices are connected to the SCSI bus as a device on the daisy chain.
- Both ends of the SCSI chain must be terminated.

SCSI devices vary, with some devices not being compatible with other SCSI devices. Some of the ways they vary include:

- The SCSI type.
- The length of the SCSI chain's cabling.
- The connectors on the devices and the cabling.
- The signal type used to put data on the cable.
- The number of devices that can be on the chain. This depends on the SCSI type and the available device IDs on the devices.
- The bus width. Narrow SCSI has an 8-bit bus; wide SCSI has a 16-bit bus.

Lesson 7

Example:

Figure 7-4 shows an example of a SCSI chain. This SCSI chain has two external devices connected to the HBA and one internal drive. It is a 16-bit SCSI 2 HBA with a 68-pin internal connection.

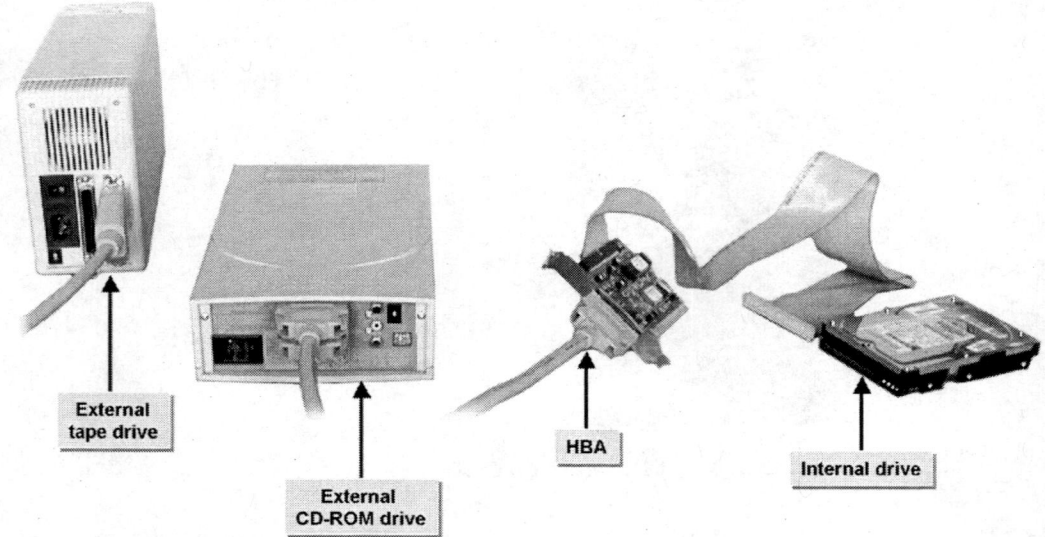

Figure 7-4: *A SCSI chain.*

Interface Comparison

You can use the information in the following tables to determine the type of drive that is best suited to your needs.

Type	Characteristic	Description
ST-506/ST-412	Speed	52.5 KBps.
	Cables required	Power; 20-pin data; 34-pin control.
	Cable length	24 inches maximum.
	Devices per controller	Two.
	Required settings	BIOS type; termination on the last drive; set drive select (indicate drive 1 or 2 on controller).
	Other considerations	The ST-506 and the ST-412 interfaces are limited to drives with fewer than 1,024 cylinders.
ESDI	Speed	Up to 3 MBps.
	Cables required	Power; 20-pin data; 34-pin control.
	Cable length	3 meters maximum.
	Devices per controller	Two (specification allows seven, but few manufacturers have implemented the full specifications).

LESSON 7

Type	Characteristic	Description
	Required settings	BIOS type; termination on the last drive; set drive select (indicate drive 1 or 2 on controller).
	Other considerations	ESDI implementations are usually heavily cached for maximum performance.
SCSI-I	Speed	Up to 5 MBps.
	Cables required	Power; 50-pin cable (shielded if external).
	Cable length	Maximum of 6 meters.
	Devices per controller	Seven (actually, eight devices are allowed, but one is the host bus adapter; the specification also allows seven logical devices per device through the use of LUNs, for a total of 49).
	Required settings	Set computer BIOS to indicate that no drive is installed; set SCSI ID (0-7); install termination on first and last devices on SCSI bus; may need to configure the adapter BIOS.
	Other considerations	The SCSI bus can be used for devices other than hard drives, such as monitors, printers, networks, and so forth.
SCSI-II	Speed	Up to 20 MBps.
	Cables required	Power; 50- or 68-pin cable.
	Cable length	1.5 meters for up to three devices; 3 meters for more than three devices; 25 meters for High Voltage Differential (HVD) SCSI; 12 meters for Low Voltage Differential (LVD) SCSI.
	Devices per controller	Seven (actually, eight devices are allowed, but one is the host bus adapter; the specification also allows seven logical devices per device through the use of LUNs, for a total of 49).
	Required settings	Set computer BIOS to indicate that no drive is installed; set SCSI ID (0-7); install termination on first and last devices on SCSI bus; may need to configure the adapter BIOS.

Lesson 7

Type	Characteristic	Description
	Other considerations	SCSI-II Fast increases the clock rate of SCSI-I; SCSI-II Wide uses a double-wide datapath; maximum data-transfer rates are realized with SCSI-II Fast/Wide implementations.
SCSI-III	Speed	Up to 160 MBps.
	Cables required	Power; 50-pin, 68-pin, or 80-pin cable.
	Cable length	Maximum of 12 meters; 25 meters for High Voltage Differential (HVD) SCSI, 12 meters for Low Voltage Differential (LVD) SCSI.
	Devices per controller	15 (actually, 16 devices are allowed, but one is the host bus adapter).
	Required settings	Set computer BIOS to indicate that no drive is installed; set SCSI ID (0-15); install termination on first and last devices on SCSI bus; may need to configure the adapter BIOS.
	Other considerations	SCSI-III Fast increases the clock rate of SCSI-I; SCSI-III Wide uses a double-wide datapath; maximum data-transfer rates are realized with SCSI-III Fast/Wide implementations.
IDE	Speed	3-4 MBps.
	Cables required	Power; 40-pin ribbon cable (IBM sometimes uses 44- or 72-pin cables).
	Cable length	Maximum of 24 inches.
	Devices per controller	Two.
	Required settings	Set BIOS type based on emulation; set drives to be master or slave, set drive type (often auto-detected).
	Other considerations	The IDE interface is a popular PC drive interface; it is often built into the motherboard.
EIDE	Speed	Up to 16.6 MBps.
	Cables required	Power; 40-pin ribbon cable (IBM sometimes uses 44- or 72-pin cables).
	Cable length	Maximum of 24 inches.
	Devices per controller	Two.

Lesson 7

Type	Characteristic	Description
	Required settings	Set BIOS type based on emulation; set drives to be master or slave.
	Other considerations	The EIDE interface is a popular PC drive interface; it is often built into the motherboard.
Ultra DMA	Speed	33, 66, or 100 MBps.
	Cables required	Power; special 40-pin IDE ribbon cable with one blue connector on one end and one black connector on the other end; 80-wire, 40-pin cable for Ultra DMA/66 and Ultra DMA/100.
	Cable length	Maximum of 24 inches.
	Devices per controller	Two.
	Required settings	Enable in BIOS (can be automatic); set drives to be master or slave, enable DMA support in operating system.
	Other considerations	Ultra DMA drives are quickly becoming very popular due to the faster transfer speeds they offer; backward-compatible with EIDE motherboards or controllers, but the drive will run at EIDE's speeds.

How to Install Drive Controllers

Procedure Reference: Install a Drive Controller

To install a drive controller:

1. If you are installing a drive controller that is not Plug and Play compatible, determine unused IRQ, DMA, and I/O Addresses that can be assigned to the card. You can use the Device Manager (right-click My Computer, choose Properties, select the Hardware tab, and then click Device Manager) to print a list of the resources by choosing View→Resources By Type.

    After printing out this report, you can use it when you need to configure system components so that you can avoid conflicts with other components already in the system.

2. Shut down and unplug your computer.
3. Referring to your system documentation for the procedure, while observing proper ESD prevention techniques, remove the system cover and access the slots on the system board.

Lesson 7: Expansion Boards

Lesson 7

4. Remove the slot cover from an empty slot. Traditionally, slot covers are secured by a screw to the chassis, but some newer ones slide out or are punched out of the metal case. Save the slot cover so that if you decide to remove the adapter card later, you can replace the slot cover. This will help keep dust and dirt out of the computer and help with regulation of the operating temperature.

5. If card resources are set with DIP switches or jumpers, configure the card prior to installing it into the system.

6. Holding the card where there are no metal contacts (by the upper edge), firmly press the card into the slot. ISA slots are black with two areas of gold contacts, about 5.5 inches long. PCI slots are white and about 3.5 inches long. In some instances, it might help to align the bottom tab of the card before inserting the card into the slot.

7. Secure the card to the chassis with the screw from the slot cover (or another screw if the slot cover was not screwed to the case). Secure the cover back on to the system when you are through working.

8. Boot your computer.

9. Configure the card for the system by installing any drivers required for operation. If the card resources are configured through software, configure DMA, I/O Addresses, or interrupts as required.

10. Verify that the card is functioning properly. You can use Device Manager to view the properties for the port or device. You can also check for IRQ, I/O Addresses, or DMA conflicts as well.

ACTIVITY 7-1

Installing a Drive Controller

Setup:
To complete this activity, you will need a computer, Plug and Play compatible drive controller card, and associated drivers. You will also need a technician's toolkit.

Scenario:
You are preparing a new computer for one of your clients. The computer requires a drive controller card, as the system's motherboard does not include such functionality.

What You Do	How You Do It
1. **Shut down your computer and open its case.**	a. **Choose Start→Shutdown** to shut down your computer.
	b. Referring to your system documentation, **remove the system cover.**

2. Install the controller to an available slot.	a.	Locate an available slot that is conveniently accessible to where the drives are installed in your computer.
	b.	Remove the slot cover.
	c.	Insert the controller into the bus slot connector.
	d.	Secure the card using the screw from the slot cover.
3. Configure the card.	a.	Boot your computer.
	b.	Install any drivers you are prompted to install.
	c.	Use Device Manager to confirm that there are no resource conflicts caused by this new drive controller.

TOPIC B

Video Adapters

Without a video adapter, your computer will not be able to display output on a monitor. Many motherboards come with display adapters built in. However, some don't and sometimes you will require features in the built-in component doesn't provide. In this topic, you will install a display adapter.

Video Adapters

Video displays for IBM and IBM-compatible computers typically consist of two components: a *display adapter* that goes in an expansion bus slot, and a video *monitor* that is compatible with that adapter. These items determine the video capabilities of the computer, including (but not limited to):

- Display modes, such as text only or graphics.
- The number of characters that can be displayed.
- Resolution, the number of horizontal and vertical graphics dots (pixels) that the screen displays. The greater the resolution, the higher the quality of the display image.
- The number of different colors that can be displayed at one time. A display might be monochrome (black and white, for example) or it might be able to display millions of different colors. More colors might seem more important than high resolution when you want to display a realistic graphic image.

- Scan rate, or how frequently the display image is refreshed. A low scan rate is detected by the eye as a flicker.

Figure 7-5 illustrates a typical video adapter card.

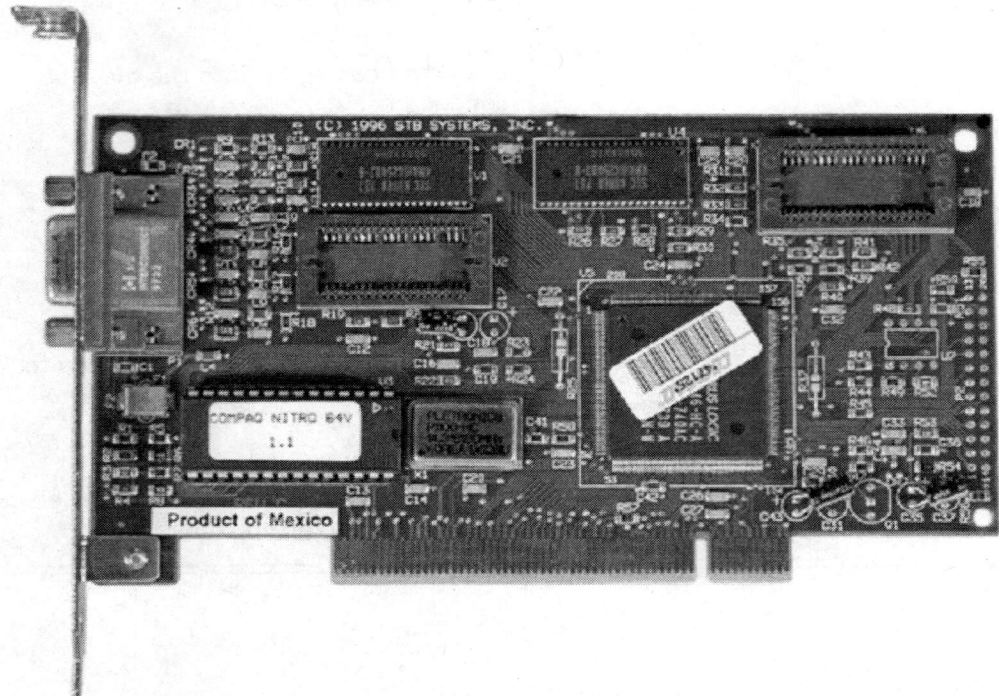

Figure 7-5: *A video card.*

Monochrome Display Adapter (MDA)

MDA, developed in 1981, provides the minimum display configuration for IBM and IBM-compatible computers. This standard provides a text-only display. Although the hardware is considered to be monochrome, it can display characters of various intensity, characters in reverse video, and underlined characters. For computers using a non-graphical operating system and applications, MDA is inexpensive and it produces a legible image.

MDA connects to a *TTL monitor*. The TTL monitor uses transistor-transistor logic signals, which are the same types of signals used in the computer.

Mode	Resolution	Colors/Grays	Number of Characters	Character Box
Text	720 x 350	4	80 x 25	9 x 14

Lesson 7

Hercules Graphics Card (HGC)

In 1982, Van Suwannukul, who founded Hercules Computer Technology, developed a PC graphics display system, the *Hercules Graphics Card (HGC)*. It is also referred to as the Hercules Graphics Adapter (HGA). It was able to produce high-resolution graphics (720 x 348), as well as text on monochrome monitors. It was extremely popular because it could display graphs and charts in that all-popular 1980s program, Lotus 1-2-3. The reason he developed this technology was so he could use his native Thai language alphabet on the PC when he wrote his doctoral thesis.

 Even though color cards eventually replaced the HGC, the company went on to produce graphics accelerators, which are popular with gamers. The company went out of business when it was acquired by Guillemot Corporation.

Color Graphics Adapter (CGA)

CGA, also developed in 1981, was the first color graphics display configuration for IBM and IBM-compatible computers. This standard displays 16 colors in text and graphics modes. CGA is compatible with software that supports MDA. However, CGA's low resolution can make it difficult to view text.

Typically, the IBM RGB monitor was used with this adapter. RGB stands for red, green, and blue—the three basic colors that this monitor combines to make a total of 16 colors. The RGB monitor uses TTL signals, similar to the monochrome monitor.

CGA can also drive a composite monitor, which connects to the display adapter with a single phono-type plug. This type of monitor is not widely accepted because it has a low resolution. However, a television can be used as a composite monitor by adding a device called a Radio Frequency (RF) modulator.

Mode	Resolution	Colors/Grays	Number of Characters	Character Box
Text	320 x 200	16	40 x 25	8 x 8
Text	640 x 200	16	80 x 25	8 x 8
Graphics	160 x 200	16	-	-
Graphics	320 x 200	4	40 x 25	8 x 8
Graphics	640 x 200	2	80 x 25	8 x 8

Enhanced Graphics Adapter (EGA)

EGA, developed in 1984, enables you to upgrade an adapter from MDA or CGA and use your old monochrome or RGB monitor. With the old monitors, EGA emulates CGA and MDA adapters, and provides a higher resolution.

The EGA adapter can also be used with the IBM Enhanced Color Display monitor. With this monitor, the EGA adapter can display 16 colors in a 640 x 350 resolution. Text, with an 8 x 14 character box, is easier to read than CGA text. EGA has been made obsolete by the new VGA standards.

Lesson 7: Expansion Boards

Lesson 7

Mode	Resolution	Colors/Grays	Number of Characters	Character Box
Text	320 x 350	16	40 x 25	8 x 8
Text	640 x 350	16	80 x 25	8 x 14
Text	720 x 350	4	80 x 25	9 x 14
Graphics	320 x 200	16	40 x 25	8 x 8
Graphics	640 x 200	16	80 x 25	8 x 8
Graphics	640 x 350	4	80 x 25	8 x 14
Graphics	640 x 350	16	80 x 25	8 x 14

Video Graphics Array

VGA, developed in 1987, uses an analog signal rather than a digital signal to control the display monitor. MDA, CGA, and EGA transmit digital signals to indicate the color or intensity to be displayed. Analog circuits lend themselves to large numbers of variations, which make them ideal for color displays. VGA can display up to 256 colors at 320 x 200 resolution. (An enhanced version of the VGA standard, called Super VGA, can display 256 colors at a resolution of 800 x 600.) VGA can emulate MDA, CGA, and EGA.

VGA monitors must use the same scan rate as the video adapter that drives them. For this reason, you need to purchase a monitor that is compatible with the display adapter that will drive it. Some monitor manufacturers have manufactured multiscan monitors that support multiple scan rates and automatically match themselves to the scan rate of the display adapter.

Mode	Resolution	Colors/Grays	Number of Characters	Character Box
Text	360 x 400	16	40 x 25	9 x 16
Text	720 x 400	16	80 x 25	9 x 16
Text	720 x 400	16	80 x 25	9 x 16
Graphics	320 x 200	4	80 x 25	8 x 8
Graphics	640 x 200	2	80 x 25	8 x 8
Graphics	320 x 200	16	80 x 25	8 x 8
Graphics	640 x 200	16	80 x 25	8 x 8
Graphics	640 x 350	4	80 x 25	8 x 14
Graphics	640 x 350	16	80 x 25	8 x 14
Graphics	640 x 480	2	80 x 25	8 x 16
Graphics	640 x 480	16	80 x 25	8 x 16
Graphics	320 x 200	256	80 x 25	8 x 8

LESSON 7

Super and Ultimate VGA

SVGA and UVGA are higher-resolution versions of the VGA standard. There is no SVGA or UVGA standard. SVGA cards are produced by various companies who each have different commands and ways of configuring the cards and monitors.

How to Install Video Adapters

Procedure Reference: Install a Video Adapter

To install a video adapter:

1. If you are installing a video adapter that is not Plug and Play compatible, determine unused IRQ, DMA, and I/O Addresses that can be assigned to the card. You can use the Device Manager in Control Panel to print a list of the resources by choosing View→Resources By Type.

   After printing out this report, you can use it when you need to configure system components so that you can avoid conflicts with other components already in the system.

2. Shut down and unplug your computer.

3. Referring to your system documentation for the procedure, while observing proper ESD prevention techniques, remove the system cover and access the slots on the system board.

4. Remove the slot cover from an empty slot. Traditionally, slot covers are secured by a screw to the chassis, but some newer ones slide out or are punched out of the metal case. Save the slot cover so that if you decide to remove the adapter card later, you can replace the slot cover. This will help keep dust and dirt out of the computer and help with regulation of the operating temperature.

5. If card resources are set with DIP switches or jumpers, configure the card prior to installing it into the system.

6. Holding the card where there are no metal contacts (by the upper edge), firmly press the card into the slot. ISA slots are black with two areas of gold contacts, about 5.5 inches long. PCI slots are white and about 3.5 inches long. In some instances, it might help to align the bottom tab of the card before inserting the card into the slot.

7. Secure the card to the chassis with the screw from the slot cover (or another screw if the slot cover was not screwed to the case). Secure the cover back on to the system when you are through working.

8. Boot your computer.

9. Configure the card for the system by installing any drivers required for operation. If the card resources are configured through software, configure DMA, I/O Addresses, or interrupts as required.

10. Verify that the card is functioning properly. You can use Device Manager to view the properties for the port or device. You can also check for IRQ, I/O Addresses, or DMA conflicts as well.

Lesson 7

Activity 7-2

Installing a Video Adapter

Setup:

To complete this activity, you will need a computer, Plug and Play compatible video adapter card, and associated drivers. You will also need a technician's toolkit.

Scenario:

You are preparing a new computer for one of your clients. The computer requires a video adapter card, as the system's motherboard does not include such functionality.

What You Do	How You Do It
1. Shut down your computer and open its case.	a. Choose Start→Shutdown to shut down your computer. b. Referring to your system documentation, remove the system cover.
2. Install the video adapter to an available slot.	a. Locate an available slot. b. Remove the slot cover. c. Insert the video adapter into the bus slot connector. d. Secure the card using the screw from the slot cover.
3. Configure the card.	a. Boot your computer. b. Install any drivers you are prompted to install. c. Use Device Manager to confirm that there are no resource conflicts caused by this new video adapter.

Topic C

Sound and Game Adapters

As a computer technician, you might support corporate users, such as marketing or sales reps, who will need to use game and sound devices to create multimedia business presentations. Or, you might work for a retail computer outlet, supporting home users who like to play music and games on their PCs. In either case, the users will need a lot of different devices, connected to a number of different computer ports that are often poorly marked. In either case, the users will rely on you to connect and configure their sound and game devices, such as speakers and microphones, to the proper PC ports.

Sound Card Interfaces

Definition:

Sound card interfaces are ports on a *sound card* that enable you to connect sound devices to a computer. The circuitry on a sound card converts digital signals to sound waves. SoundBlaster from Creative Labs is the default standard other sound cards are usually designed to meet. All sound cards have at least a Line In and Line Out port along with a microphone port. Most also have a 15-pin female game port. Some also have additional ports specifically for headphones and speakers in addition to the Line Out port.

The following table describes typical sound card connections.

Port or Interface	Description
Mic In	Receives signals from an external microphone.
Speaker Out or Line Out	Sends signals to a speaker set or headphones. Sends signals from the sound card to an external sound source that can be connected through an eighth-inch jack.
Line In	Receives signals from the output of an external sound source that can be connected through an eighth-inch stereo jack.
Game Port	Enables you to attach a joystick or similar game controller to the sound card. MIDI devices are also often connected to the computer through the game port. Some sound cards do not include the game port.

There are also internal connections on the sound card. One is a CD audio connection that enables you to play audio CDs on the computer and output the sound through the sound card. Some cards also include an interface to connect CD-ROM drives or hard drives.

Today's sound cards are configured through software, but some of the older cards you might encounter might use jumpers. On some systems, the functions of a sound card are built into the system, rather than on a separate expansion card.

Lesson 7

Example:

The typical sound card interface is shown in Figure 7-6.

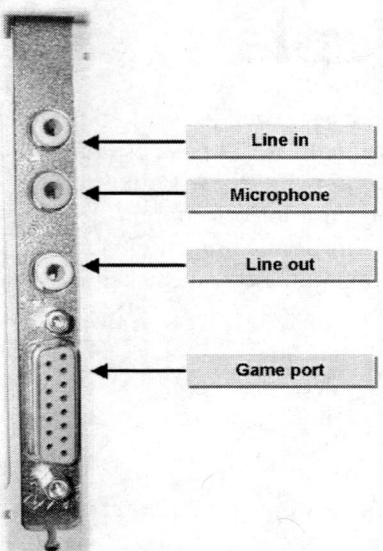

Figure 7-6: *Sound card interfaces.*

Sound Devices

The devices you can connect to the sound card are shown in Figure 7-7. The following table describes typical sound card devices.

Lesson 7

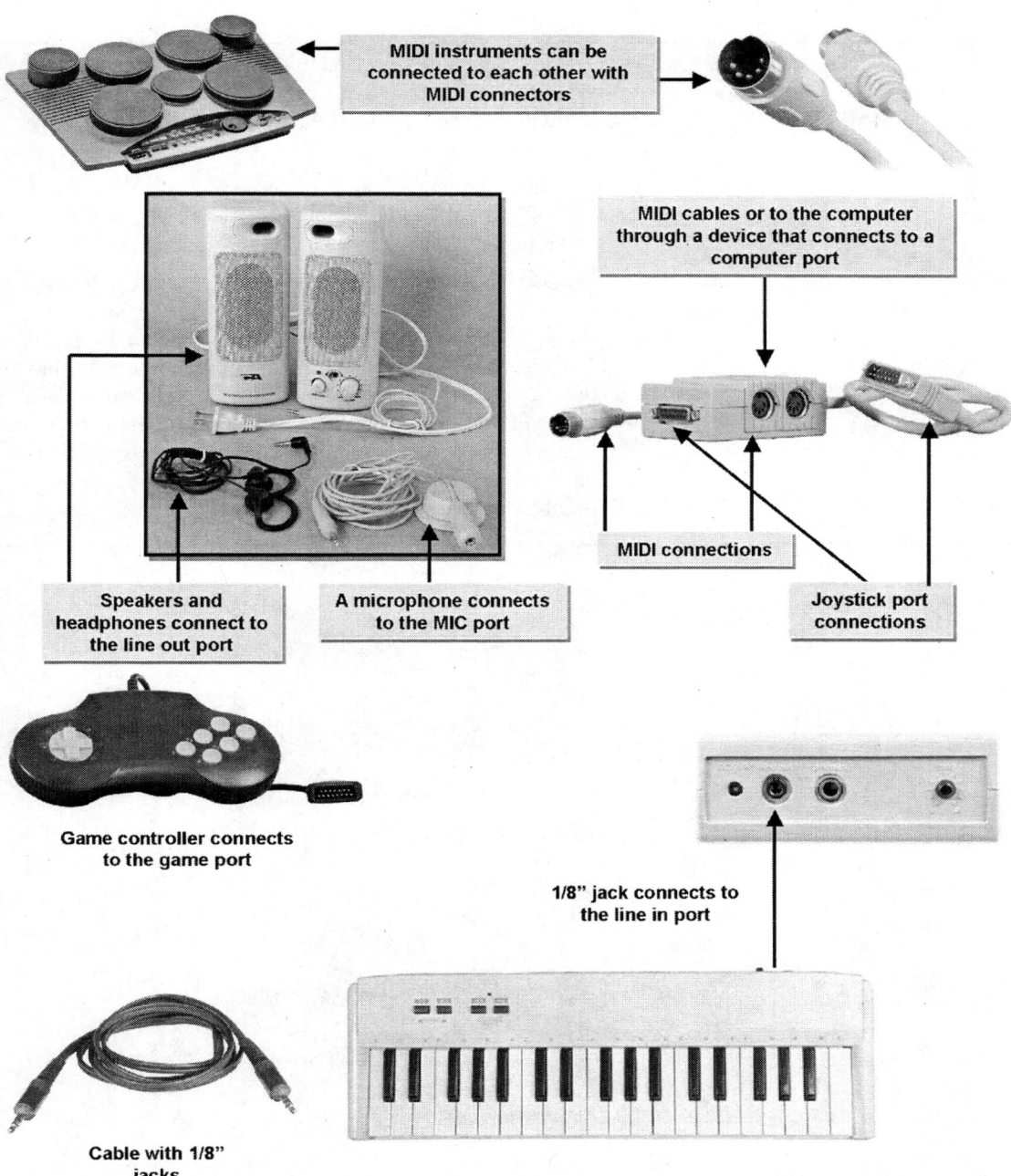

Figure 7-7: *Devices to connect to a sound card.*

Device	Description
Speakers	Speakers are connected to the Line Out port on the sound card. Some speaker sets are permanently connected to each other. Other speaker sets are connected by the user to each other. A cable runs from one of the speakers to the Line Out port to connect both speakers to the computer. If it is color-coded, it will be green or lime. The port might be marked with Line Out, Spkr, Speaker, or have a marking indicating the direction of the audio (out).

Lesson 7

Device	Description
Non-MIDI electronic instruments, tape players/recorders, or radios	Any device that can use an eighth-inch jack can be connected to the Line In port. It is often light blue if color-coded. Otherwise, it will be marked Line In or have a marking indicating the direction of the audio (in).
Microphone	A computer microphone can be connected to the MIC port. If color-coded, it will be pink. Otherwise, it will be marked MIC or have a picture of a microphone.
Game devices including controller pads, joysticks, steering wheels, and flight controllers; MIDI devices	Game controllers can be connected to the game port. If it is color-coded, it will be goldenrod. It is a 15-pin female port composed of one row of eight pins and one row of seven pins. It is usually found on the sound card, but it can be built into the system board or found on a separate adapter card in some systems. Musical Instrument Digital Interface (MIDI) cables are also sometimes connected to this port. Devices that can be connected to the Game port are shown in Figure 7-8. Examples of MIDI cables are shown in Figure 7-9.

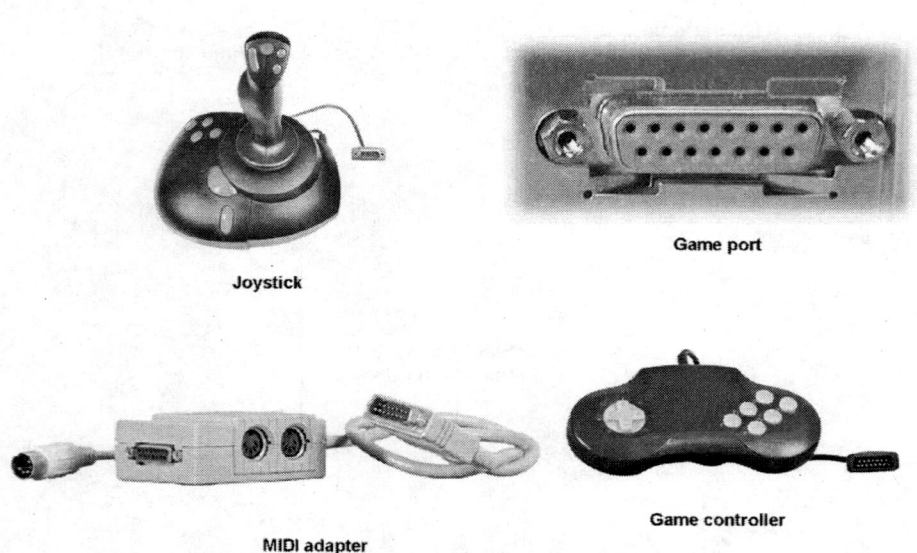

Figure 7-8: *Devices that connect to the game port.*

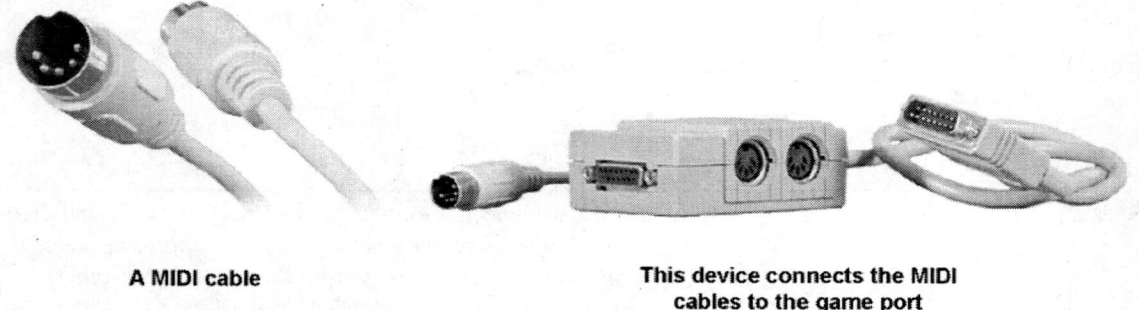

Figure 7-9: *MIDI cables.*

Lesson 7

MIDI

The Musical Instrument Digital Interface or *MIDI* connection allows you to connect and control musical devices such as electric keyboards (also known as electric pianos), synthesizers, guitars, and drum kits. Sound cards usually include built-in synthesizers as well, to produce MIDI sounds. If the MIDI connection is made through the game port, then the MIDI cable usually includes an additional port so that a game controller can still be added to the system. MIDI connections can also be made via other ports other than the game port. MIDI devices can be connected to each other and then to the computer. Examples of MIDI devices are shown in Figure 7-10.

The MIDI connectors are also known as AT DIN5 connectors. AT DIN5 connectors were originally used on older AT style computers as the keyboard connector; now, MIDI devices use them.

Figure 7-10: *MIDI instruments.*

How to Connect Game and Sound Devices

Procedure Reference: Connect Sound Devices to a Sound Card

To connect sound devices to a sound card:

1. Connect the speakers to the jack on the sound card marked for speakers. Some speakers use an external AC adapter for power, some are powered by the computer, some use batteries, and some contain a standard electrical plug. If necessary, connect the speakers to their power source.

2. Connect any external devices to the Line In jack.

3. Connect a microphone to the MIC jack.

4. Connect MIDI devices or game controllers through the game port. If necessary, connect the AC adapter to the device and to an electrical outlet.

5. If necessary, use Device Manager to configure MIDI device or game controller settings.

6. Test the components by powering on the system and using each device. Verify that Mute is not checked in the Volume Controls. If Microphone is not listed, choose Options→Properties. Select Recording, check Microphone, and then click OK. You can then adjust the sound levels for it.

Lesson 7

ACTIVITY 7-3

Connecting Sound Devices

Scenario:
A group in the marketing department is responsible for creating and presenting audio visual presentations. These users have sound cards installed in their systems. They all have speakers and microphones connected to their sound cards. Some of them also have MIDI instruments and instruments that connect through an eighth-inch stereo jack. The users have just received these sound devices and want to begin using them.

What You Do	How You Do It
1. Connect the speakers to the sound card.	a. Determine if you need to connect the speakers to each other, and if so, connect them to each other. b. Locate the speaker jack on the sound card. c. Plug the speaker into the jack.
2. Connect an external device to the Line In jack.	a. Locate the Line In jack. b. Connect an eighth-inch stereo jack from the device to the computer.
3. Connect a microphone to the MIC jack.	a. Locate the MIC jack on the sound card. b. Connect the microphone to the MIC jack.
4. If you have a MIDI device, **connect the MIDI device through the game port.**	a. Locate the game port. b. Connect the MIDI adapter to the game port. c. If necessary, **connect MIDI cables to the MIDI adapter.** d. Connect the MIDI cable to the MIDI instrument. e. If necessary, **install drivers for the MIDI instrument.**

A+™ Certification: Core Hardware Third Edition - A CompTIA Certification

5. Test the sound components.

   a. Choose **Start→All Programs→Accessories→Entertainment→Sound Recorder** to test the microphone.

   b. With the Sound Recorder window open, **click the Record button** ⬤.

   c. **Speak into the microphone and say a few words.**

   d. **Click the Stop button** ■.

   e. **Click the Play button** to test the speakers. The words you just recorded should be played back.

   f. If you installed a MIDI device, **play a few notes** to verify that it works correctly.

   g. **Close the Sound Recorder without saving changes.**

TOPIC D

Modem Adapters

Sharing information between computers is one of the most powerful ways to use a PC. Thanks to the Internet, it is also one of the most popular. In this topic, you will examine modems to see how you can use them to connect to other computers.

Modem

A *modem* is a serial communications device that enables computers to communicate with one another over standard telephone lines. Modem is short for *mo*dulate/*dem*odulate. A modem modulates a digital signal to analog so that it can go across the phone line. When the analog reaches the other system, another modem demodulates it into a digital signal.

Most PCs have modems these days. These can be internal or external devices. External modems have LEDs that can be useful in seeing whether the modem is transmitting and receiving data. Internal modems don't have this feature, although it is often simulated in software.

Figure 7-12 illustrates the ways you can connect a modem to a phone line.

Modems can also be hardware-based or software-based (often referred to as controller-less modems or Win-modems). Software modems are slower than hardware modems because of the overhead in translating code. They leave the processing to the PC's CPU, rather than incorporating a controller chip on the card as the hardware modems do. The main advantage of doing so is that they can be sold very inexpensively. A disadvantage is that these modems are designed for Plug and Play operating systems only, but not other operating systems.

Modern modems include fax and voice capabilities. This allows you to use your PC to send documents as faxes and to use your PC as a phone and answering machine.

Asynchronous and Synchronous Modems

Asynchronous (or async for short) modems are the most common type of modem. Serial data transmission includes start and stop bits in the data stream to indicate the beginning and end of each character.

The data flow is controlled by the slower of the two systems. This slower system interrupts the transmission whenever the buffers are full and it needs time to catch up. Since this method has great potential for errors, a parity bit is used for control. This is why many PCs are configured with eight data bits, none for parity, and one stop bit (often referred to as 8-none-and-one).

Synchronous modems are less prone to errors. They use a timing mechanism to regulate transmissions between systems. Data is sent in frames that contain synch characters before each frame. The frame only needs to be re-sent if the synch character doesn't arrive at the prescribed point.

Several synchronous protocols have been defined. They are listed in the following table.

Protocol	Description
Binary Synchronous Communications (BSC)	Also known as bi-sync. Replaced by SDLC. Developed for use in connecting IBM 360 mainframes and IBM 3270 terminals. Frames include header and trailer synch characters.
Synchronous Data Link Control (SDLC)	Designates one system to be the controlling system and the other to be controlled. Replaced by HDLC.
High-level Data Link Control (HDLC)	Bit-oriented protocol that supports variable length frames.

ITU Modem Standards

Modem standards, or V dot modem standards, are defined by the International Telecommunications Union (ITU). Some standards have *bis* or *terbo* version suffixes; these are French for second and third.

The most recent standard is V.90. This includes technology that enables receiving data faster than 56 Kbps by bypassing modulation of the data. When sending data, it must be modulated, resulting in a slower 33.6 Kbps data rate.

The following table describes some of the most popular ITU standards. These include V.32, V.32 bis, V.34, V.34 bis, V.42, V.42 bis, V.90, and V.92.

ITU Standard	bps	Notes
V.32	9,600	Synchronous to 9600; Asynchronous is 4800.
V.32 bis	14,400 (14.4 K)	Synchronous and Asynchronous.
V.34	28,800 (28.8 K)	
V.34 bis	33,600 (33.6 K)	
V.42	57,600	Specifies standards for error checking.
V.42 bis		Specifies standards for compression.
V.90	56,000 (56 K)	Incorporated 3COM 56 K Flex technology and US Robotics 56 K X2 technology.
V.92		Reduces connection time by using previously negotiated handshaking settings. Supports call waiting (data session is put on hold while a voice call is taken).

MNP Modem Standards

The *Microcom Networking Protocol (MNP)* defines classes 1 to 5 for modem standards. Each class offers different levels of error correction and detection. Most modems use the MNP Class 5 protocol, which includes data compression. This basically provides a data-transmission rate of twice the speed you would normally achieve.

RJ Connectors

Definition:

An RJ (registered jack) connector is a flat connector that connects a computer to a computer network or the telephone public data network. RJ connections are a type of serial connection. RJ cables can be 4, 6, or 8 wires; the wires can be connected straight through or be mirrored on each end. The RJ types are defined by the FCC (Federal Communications Commission).

Example: RJ-11

RJ-11 cables are used to connect phones to the public telephone network. They are also used to connect between a computer's modem and the phone outlet. An RJ-11 cable contains six wires that are connected straight through. An example of an RJ-11 connector is shown in Figure 7-11.

Lesson 7

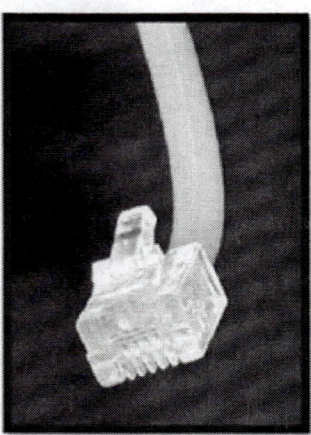

Figure 7-11: *An RJ-11 jack.*

Standard Modem IRQs and I/O Addresses

Let's quickly review the default IRQs and I/O addresses associated with the COM ports. Remember that those devices with the same IRQ can't be used at the same time, even though you can configure multiple devices with the same IRQ. In fact, if Plug and Play is enabled, you can't configure devices to share an IRQ at all. So, you couldn't have COM1 and COM3 or COM2 and COM4 in use at once.

Port	IRQ	I/O Address
COM1	04	03F8 - 03FF
COM2	03	02F8 - 02FF
COM3	04	03E8 - 03EF
COM4	03	02E8 - 02EF

The two Control Panel utilities on Windows systems used to configure the modem are Device Manager and Modem Configuration. Many modems also include custom configuration utilities.

Modem Commands

The *AT*, or Attention, commands are the modem commands set used on most modems. Hayes originally developed it for its line of modems. Since other companies wanted to be Hayes-compatible, they developed their modems to use this command set. The AT command set is used by almost all PC modems.

The most basic command is AT, which alerts the modem that you want to communicate with your modem. The following table lists some of the most common commands.

 For more information on the extended AT command sets, visit **www.modems.com/general/extendat.html**.

Command	Description
AT	Attention used at the start of modem command lines.
DT	Dial using touchtone.
H	Hang up or disconnect.
A	Answer.
DP	Dial using pulse (rotary dial).
,	Pause (each comma is roughly 3 seconds by default). Often used when you need to dial an access code for an outside line so that you wait for the dial tone. For example, 9,,,7165557300.
*70	Disable call-waiting.
Z	Reset.
A/	Repeat. Repeats the last command. Often used to redial.
+++	Escape character sequence. Returns you to the command mode. You can then adjust modem configuration, or hang up. The modem responds with OK to indicate that you are in command mode.
O	Online. Often used after the escape character sequence to continue communication.

Installing and Configuring a Modem

Before you start with the configuration, make sure your modem is connected to the computer and turned on. It is not necessary to have a phone cable plugged into a telephone line for configuration purposes. Typically, you install and configure a modem using the New Hardware Wizard, which is launched automatically after you install your modem into the computer.

LESSON 7

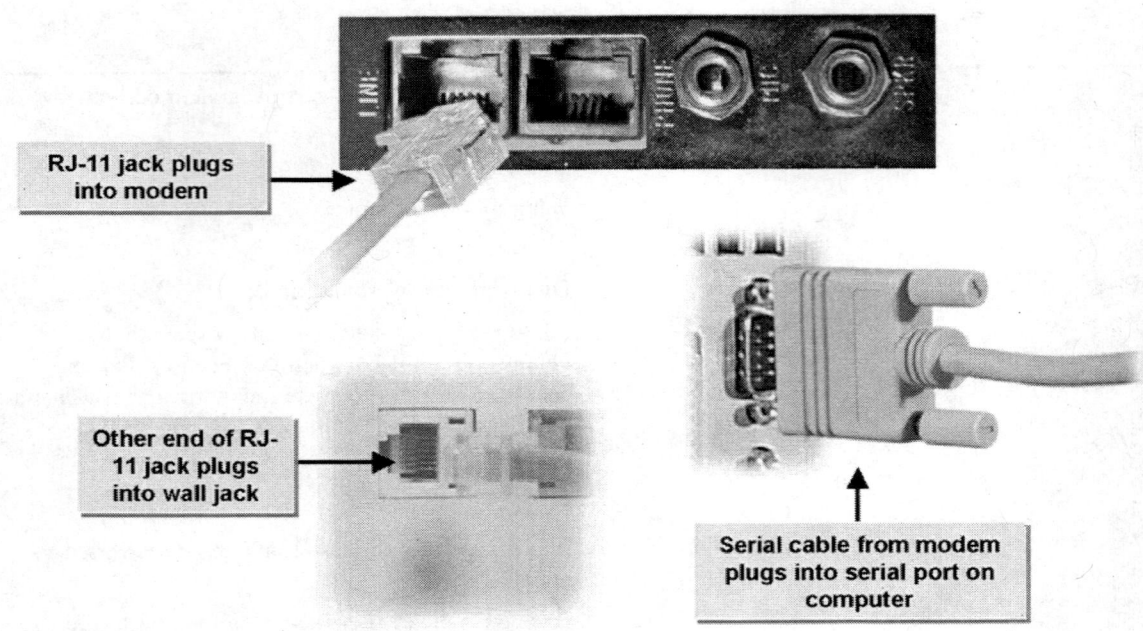

Figure 7-12: *Connecting a modem.*

To configure the modem, use the Phone and Modem Options Control Panel utility. Select the Modem tab, if necessary, select the modem, and then click Properties. The options that can be configured are listed in the following table.

 Enabling the FIFO buffers in your modem configuration enables the UART on the modem. This increases the speed of transmissions.

Property to Configure	Tab on Which it's Located	Description
Port	Advanced, then click Advanced Port Settings	Specifies the port on which the modem is installed.
Speaker Volume	Modem	Specifies the volume of phone tones including the dial tone and dialing sounds.
Maximum Speed	Modem	Specifies the highest speed at which the modem will communicate across the COM port.
Connection Preferences	Advanced, then click Change Default Preferences	Used to configure the data, parity, and stop bits.
Driver	Driver	Used to update, change, or rollback the driver used by the modem.

Activity 7-4

Installing and Configuring a Modem

Setup:
You will need an internal modem and associated drivers to complete this lab.

Scenario:
Your customer needs to use a modem to connect to a dial-up service. They've purchased an internal modem and asked you to install it into their PC.

What You Do	How You Do It
1. Shut down your computer and open its case.	a. Choose Start→Shutdown to shut down your computer.
	b. Referring to your system documentation, remove the system cover.
2. Install the modem into an available slot.	a. Locate an available slot.
	b. Remove the slot cover.
	c. Insert the modem adapter into the bus slot connector.
	d. Secure the card using the screw from the slot cover.

3. Configure the card.
   a. Boot your computer.
   b. Install any drivers you are prompted to install.
   c. Use Device Manager to confirm that there are no resource conflicts caused by this new modem adapter.
   d. If prompted, enter your area code, and if required, any access number required to access outside lines.
   e. Use the Phone and Modem Options Control Panel utility to verify the modem settings.
   f. Close the Phone and Modem Options utility and the Control Panel.

Common Problems with Modems

There are many problems you might encounter with modem connections. The problem could be with the settings on your end or the other end, with the hardware on either end, or with the phone company or phone lines in between. The following table lists some of the problems you are likely to encounter and possible causes of those problems.

Problem	Possible Causes
Modem doesn't work. Message "Modem Not Responding" is displayed.	Modem is not on the hardware compatibility list (HCL) for the operating system. Modem is not properly connected and powered on.
Cannot connect to the ISP.	Using the wrong phone number. Entering the user name and/or password incorrectly. Phone line is damaged, is not an analog line (is digital), or phones are down.
ISP server not responding.	ISP server is down. Modem speed is set too high for the phone line conditions or for compatibility between the modem and the ISP modems.
Connection is dropped.	Call waiting was not configured and a call was received through call waiting. Some ISPs disconnect a connection after a certain period of inactivity. The modem cable or phone line got physically disconnected. Modem drivers need to be updated. The ISP made changes and the user needs to make changes to their settings to match.

Problem	Possible Causes
Error messages when you attempt to make the connection.	No Dialtone. This could be due to the phone line not being connected, there being a phone company problem with the line, or with settings on your modem. Also, EMI and RFI (Radio Frequency Interference) can cause such problems. Dial-Up Networking Could Not Negotiate a Compatible Set of Network Protocols. This could be due to modem settings or to incompatibilities between you and the host into which you are attempting to dial.
Busy signal.	Make sure that the cables are not tangled, that the user is dialing properly, and that you can manually dial the number through a utility such as HyperTerminal. Also, check that the phone company is not experiencing problems.

How to Troubleshoot Modems

Procedure Reference: Troubleshoot Modem Problems

To troubleshoot some of the common problems with modems:

1. The message No Dialtone appears when the user tries to place a call through the modem.
   - Verify that there really is a dial tone by picking up a phone connected to the same phone line and listening for the dial tone. If there is no dial tone, determine whether the problem is with the phone lines in the neighborhood or within your home or office.
   - Verify that the telephone line is connected to the correct port on the modem. This might be marked as line-in, Line, or Telco.
   - Verify that the other end of the telephone line is plugged into the wall phone jack.
   - Unplug any other devices attached to the telephone line such as an answering machine or fax machine.
   - Verify that your telephone receiver is not off the hook.
   - Untangle the phone line, especially from power cords.
   - Add X3 to the modem init string to ignore the message and continue trying to dial into the server.

2. The error message Modem Not Responding appears.
   - If you are using an external modem, verify that it is plugged in, turned on, and properly connected to the system.
   - Run diagnostic scans on the modem under Windows XP.
     1. From the Start menu, choose Control Panel→Phone And Modem Options.
     2. On the Modems page, verify that the correct modem make and model is listed.
     3. Select the modem and click Properties.
     4. Display the Diagnostics page.

Lesson 7: Expansion Boards

5. Click Query Modem, and then review the results of the query.
6. Click View Log. After reviewing the log file, close Notepad. Close the Modem Properties dialog box.
- If it is still not working, remove the modem and reinstall it or replace it.

3. The error message Dial-Up Networking Could Not Negotiate A Compatible Set Of Network Protocols appears.
   - Verify that the correct driver for your make and model of modem is installed.
   - Check the modem configuration.
     1. Display the Modem Properties dialog box.
     2. On the Advanced page, click Change Default Preferences.
     3. On the General page of the Default Preferences dialog box, verify that Port Speed, Data Protocol, Compression, and Flow Control match the settings needed to connect to the network.
     4. On the Advanced page of the Default Preferences dialog box, verify that the Hardware Settings for Data Bits, Parity, Stop Bits, and Modulation are the appropriate settings for your network connection. Click OK.
     5. On the Advanced page, click Advanced Port Settings.
     6. Verify that Use FIFO Buffers UART settings are the appropriate settings for your modem.
     7. On the Modem page, use the Maximum Port Speed drop-down list to lower the speed.
   - Try the connection again.

4. The remote system always appears to be busy.
   - Determine whether the user is trying to dial internationally. Additional setup might be required.
   - Open HyperTerminal and enter the command ATX0. Then enter the phone number. This manually sets the modem and dials the number.
   - Straighten any kinks or tangled phone lines. The line might be getting feedback if the lines are kinked or tangled.
   - Verify the phone number. Some companies required that you dial a prefix for an outside line.
   - Contact the other party to see if there are problems with the phone system on the other end of the connection.

5. A newly installed modem does not respond.
   - Verify that the phone line is correctly connected to the modem.
   - Verify that external modems are securely connected to the system. The power supply needs to be connected to the modem and plugged in to a power outlet as well.
   - Close any other open applications and attempt dialing again.
   - Verify that the modem settings in Control Panel match the physical modem COM and IRQ settings.
   - Change the external modem cable.
   - Reset the modem through HyperTerminal with the command ATXF.
   - Try dialing again.

6. The connection acts like it is connected, but the user can't log in
   - Disconnect and reconnect with the correct user name and password.
   - Verify that the settings for the connection are correctly configured.

Lesson 7 Follow-up

In this lesson, you examined internal expansion boards that you can install or replace in any PC. These boards enable you to expand the functionality of your computer. You're ready now to expand the capabilities of your PC to suit your needs.

1. **Compare and contrast IDE and SCSI.**

2. **Describe the differences between VGA and SVGA display technologies.**

3. **What is the purpose of the line in port on a sound card?**

4. **Describe the operation of a modem**

Notes

Lesson 8
Fixed Disk Storage Systems

Lesson Time
4 hour(s)

Lesson Objectives:

In this lesson, you will install fixed disk storage systems.

You will:

- Install fixed disk drives.
- Install and remove an IDE drive.
- Install a SCSI drive.
- Troubleshoot and correct hard drive problems.
- Identify RAID levels.

Lesson 8

Introduction

You have examined many of the components inside the computer case that provide for its basic operation and expansion. In this lesson, you will examine fixed disk storage systems. You will examine the technical characteristics and functional operation of hard disk drives. You will also investigate hard disk installation and troubleshooting procedures.

You would probably find computers rather useless devices if you could not save information from one working session to the next. Fixed disk storage systems provide that necessary function, saving information so that it's available the next time you power up your PC.

The following CompTIA A+ Core Hardware (2003) Examination objectives are covered in this lesson:

- Topic A:
  - 1.9 Identify procedures to optimize PC operations in specific scenarios. Predict the effects of specific procedures under given scenarios. Topics include: disk subsystem enhancements—hard drives.
  - 1.10 Determine the issues that must be considered when upgrading a PC. In a given scenario, determine when and how to upgrade system components. Components include: hard drives.

- Topic B:
  - 1.2 Identify basic procedures for adding and removing field-replaceable modules for desktop systems. Given a replacement scenario choose the appropriate sequences. Content includes: storage device—HDD.
  - 1.6 Identify proper procedures for installing and configuring common IDE devices. Choose the appropriate installation or configuration sequences in given scenarios. Recognize the associated cables. Content includes the following: master/slave/cable select; devices per channel; primary/secondary; and cable orientation/requirements.

- Topic C:
  - 1.7 Identify proper procedures for installing and configuring common SCSI devices. Choose the appropriate installation or configuration sequences in given scenarios. Recognize the associated cables. Content includes the following: SCSI interface types—narrow, fast, wide, ultra-wide, LVD, and HVD; internal versus external; SCSI IDs—jumper block/DIP switch settings (binary equivalents); cabling—length, type, and termination requirements (active, passive, auto).
  - 1.8 Identify proper procedures for installing and configuring common peripheral devices. Choose the appropriate installation or configuration sequence in given scenarios. Content includes the following: external storage.
  - 1.9 Identify procedures to optimize PC operations in specific scenarios. Predict the effects of specific procedures under given scenarios. Topics include: disk subsystem enhancements—cables.
  - 4.3 Identify the most popular types of motherboards, their components, and their architecture (bus structures). Content includes the following: SCSI—narrow, wide, fast, ultra, HVD, and LVD.

- Topic D:
  - 1.7 Identify proper procedures for installing and configuring common SCSI devices. Choose the appropriate installation or configuration sequences in given scenarios. Recognize the associated cables. Content includes the following: SCSI IDs—resolving ID conflicts.

— 2.1 Recognize common problems associated with each module and their symptoms, and identify steps to isolate and troubleshoot the problems. Given a problem situation, interpret the symptoms and infer the most likely cause. Content includes: I/O ports and cables—SCSI; storage devices and cables—HDD; adapters—SCSI.

- Topic E:
  — 1.6 Identify proper procedures for installing and configuring common IDE devices. Choose the appropriate installation or configuration sequences in given scenarios. Recognize the associated cables. Content includes the following: RAID (0, 1, and 5).

  — 1.7 Identify proper procedures for installing and configuring common SCSI devices. Choose the appropriate installation or configuration sequences in given scenarios. Recognize the associated cables. Content includes the following: RAID (0, 1, and 5).

  — 1.9 Identify procedures to optimize PC operations in specific scenarios. Predict the effects of specific procedures under given scenarios. Topics include: disk subsystem enhancements—controller cards.

Topic A

Fixed Disk Drives

Disks are the most commonly used type of storage. There is a wide variety of different disk types, including many sizes and formats of disks. In general, all sorts of disk storage share certain common elements. In this topic, you'll examine the common elements that define fixed disk drives.

Drive

A *drive* is a computer component that stores data for the long term. Data on the drive is retained even if the power is turned off. All drives read data; some can both read and write data. All disk drives rotate very fast. All drives store data on some type of media. The drive media can be fixed or removable. There could be one or more surfaces that data can be stored on and one or more read/write heads. The drive can be internal or external. The data can be stored magnetically or optically. Drives can be connected through different interfaces. Most devices enable you to randomly access a specific location, but others require sequential access to reach a specific location. The size (or form factor) of the drive is typically either 3.5 inches or 5.25 inches. The capacity of a drive is measured as shown in the following table.

 Drives are also referred to as mass storage devices since they can store large amounts of data.

Measurement	Contains	Usually Used for Measuring Size Of
KB (kilobytes)	1,024 bytes	Floppy drives
MB (megabytes)	1,024 KB	CDs, small hard drives, cartridge drives, small tape drives
GB (gigabytes)	1,024 MB	Hard drives, large-capacity cartridge drives, some tape drives, and DVDs

Lesson 8: Fixed Disk Storage Systems

Measurement	Contains	Usually Used for Measuring Size Of
TB (terabytes)	1,024 GB	Very large hard drives and some tape drives

Hard Drives

Hard disk drives, sometimes called fixed disk drives (FDD), are read/write drives that use fixed media, which means that the disk is built into the drive and the drives are not removed from the computer unless you are performing an upgrade or a repair. The hard disk itself consists of several hard plastic platters with a magnetic surface coating. Hard drives connect to the motherboard through either an IDE or SCSI interface. Data is stored magnetically and can be accessed directly. Most hard drives are internal, but you might encounter some that are external as well. These drives are usually 3.5 inches wide, but you might encounter some older 5.25-inch drives. An example of a hard drive is shown in Figure 8-1.

Figure 8-1: *A hard drive.*

Disk Drive Architecture

The architecture of a hard drive is hidden from view behind the case of the drive. All of the components inside a hard drive together are called the Head Disk Assembly (HDA). On the outside of the drive is the logic board that controls movement of internal components as well as controlling the flow of data to and from the drive. You should never open a drive, because any contamination from the air or dust would render the drive useless. Figure 8-2 shows the internal components of a hard drive.

Lesson 8

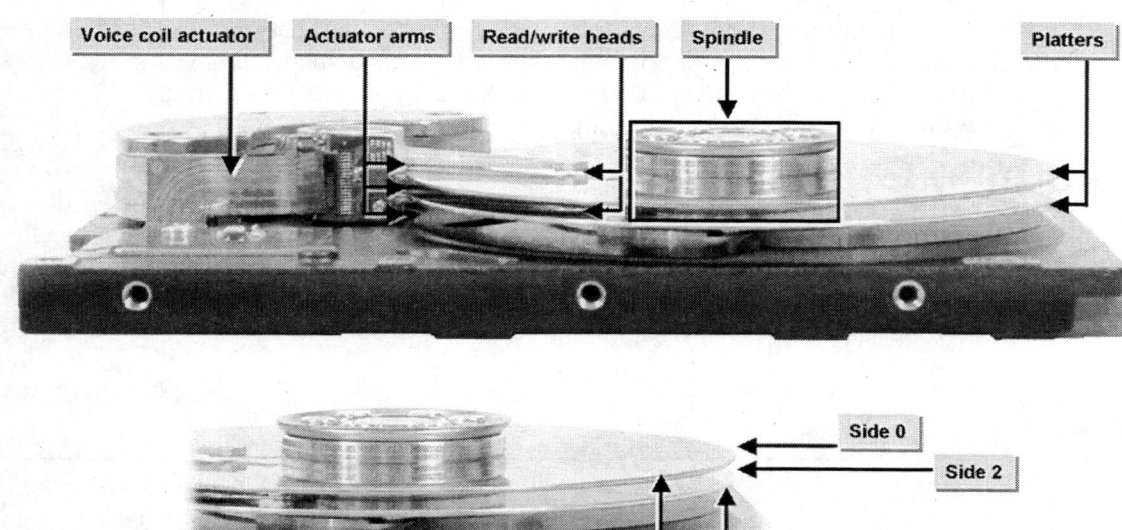

Figure 8-2: *Hard drive architecture.*

 Side 0 is the top side of the top platter. Side 1 is the underside of that platter. Side 2 is the top side of the second platter. Side 3 is the underside of it.

The architecture of the drive includes the components shown in the following table.

Component	Description
Platter	The disks on a spindle in the drive.
Read/write heads	The magnetic heads on the actuator arms that float just above and just below the platter.
Actuator arms	Arms from the drive motor that hold the read/write heads. The entire arm assembly moves together so all read/write heads move together.
Voice coil actuator	A voice coil motor that moves the actuator arms that hold the read/write heads.
Spindle	Holds the platters.
Spindle motor	Spins the platters.

Avoiding Head Crash

You should never transport or jar a hard disk that is spinning, because you can easily cause a *head crash*. If the read/write heads bang against the surface of the disk, you might damage that part of the disk, and possibly the read/write heads as well. Most hard-disk drives automatically *park* over an unused section of the disk when the computer is switched off.

Lesson 8: Fixed Disk Storage Systems

Lesson 8

Hard-disk drives are tightly sealed to prevent dust and other particles from entering the drive. A single dust particle is likely to be larger than the gap between the head and the disk platter. With the platter spinning, dust acts like sandpaper on the surface of the disk. For this reason, you should never break the seal on a hard-disk drive.

Disk Drive Geometry

The disk in a disk drive is divided up into sections so that data can be read and written as efficiently as possible. A drive with the geometry labeled is shown in Figure 8-3. This division is called the disk geometry. The components that make up the disk geometry as this is referred to are shown in the following table.

Disk Drive Geometry Term	Description
Track	Concentric circles on a platter. Tracks are numbered from the outer edge in, beginning with Track 0.
Cylinder	The tracks that can be accessed on all platters without moving the read/write head. The tracks that make up a cylinder are all the same distance from the spindle.
Sector	A division of a track. A sector is the smallest unit that can be written to. Traditionally these were pie-shaped units with the outer tracks able to hold more data per sector since they were bigger. This is shown in Figure 8-4. Zoned-bit recording is used on modern drives and divides the outer tracks into smaller segments so that they contain more sectors than inner tracks contain. This is shown in Figure 8-5.

Lesson 8

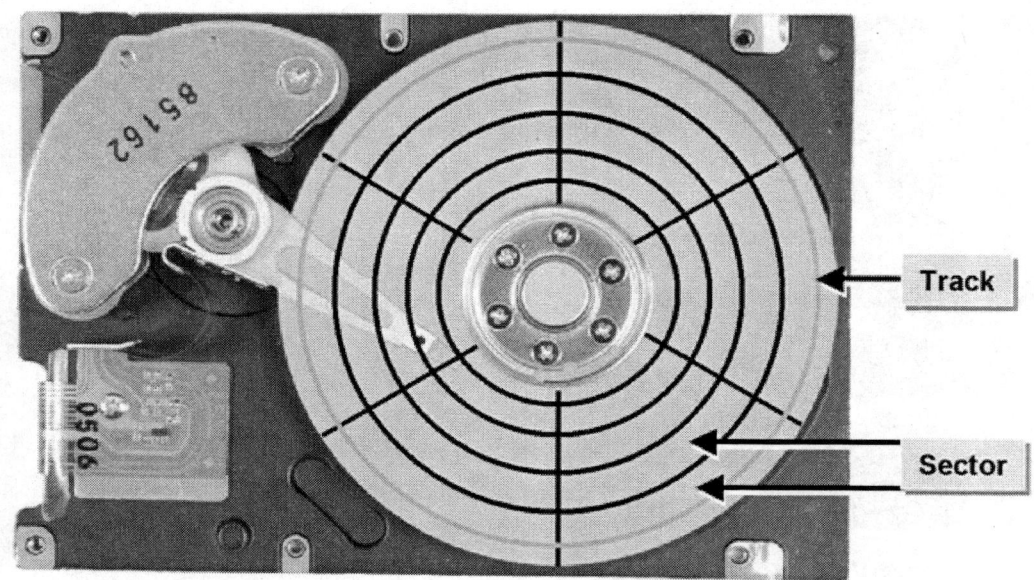

Figure 8-3: *Disk drive geometry.*

Figure 8-4: *Traditional sectors.*

Lesson 8: Fixed Disk Storage Systems

Lesson 8

Figure 8-5: *Zoned-bit recording sectors.*

Sector Interleave

The disk format assigns logical sector numbers to the physical sectors on the disk. The logical sectors can be placed sequentially around a track, mapping one-to-one with the physical sectors. Or, the logical sector assignments can be staggered and assigned to non-sequential physical sectors. The mapping of logical sectors to physical sectors is called the *sector interleave*. For example, in a two-to-one interleave, the logical sectors might appear around the disk in the order 0, 5, 1, 6, 2, 7, 3, 8, 4. Sector interleave can improve disk performance. When the sectors appear sequentially, by the time the system processes data from sector 1, there is no time to read from sector 2, because the disk has already spun away from the disk read/write head. The disk has to complete a full revolution before it can access sector 2. With sector interleave, the sector placement is optimized to match the disk rotation time, so that the read/write head encounters sector 2 as soon as it is ready to process the data from that sector.

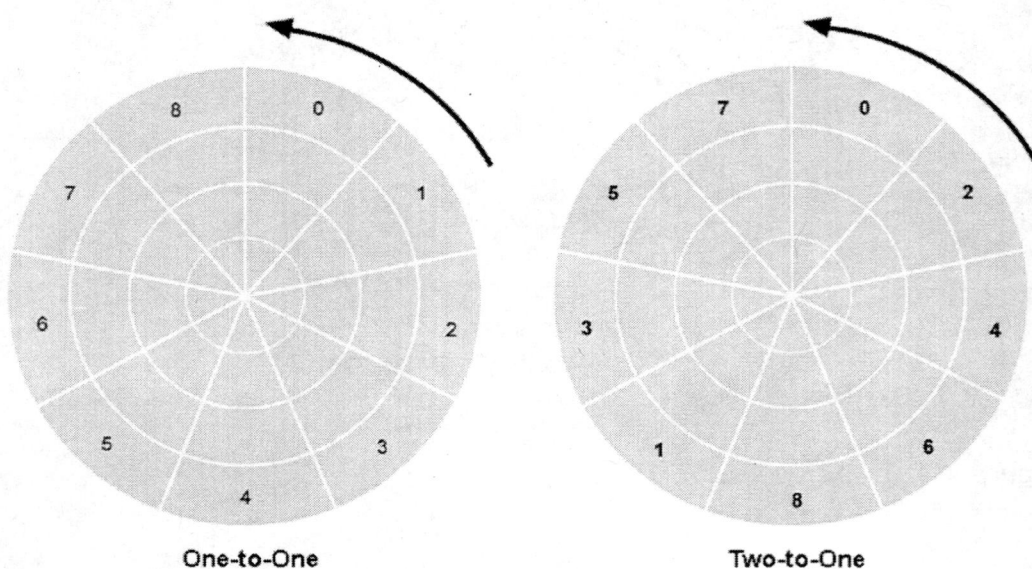

Figure 8-6: *Sector interleave.*

BIOS Drive Types

Most systems automatically recognize the geometry of a new hard disk and save those settings in the CMOS. With older systems, you might have to specify the disk geometry manually by selecting a drive type in the computer's BIOS setup utility.

Drive types are numbered according to the characteristics of the hard disk, such as number of cylinders and heads, capacity (in MB), and sectors per track. Check the hardware documentation for the IDE disk for these values so that you can determine which disk type to assign to the new hard disk.

For some disks, you also need to determine write pre-compensation, which deals with the timing problems associated with the disparity of track sizes. (Cylinders near the center of the disk have shorter tracks than those near the edge of the disk.) Newer disks do not usually need to have write pre-compensation defined; when you do need to determine this value, divide the maximum number of cylinders by 2.

Setting the CMOS Drive type is usually accomplished by one of the following methods:

- Selecting a type from the list provided in the CMOS setup program. Avoid selecting a disk type that has more cylinders, heads, or RAM capacity than are present on the new disk, but select the highest number of cylinders possible to derive maximum use of the medium.

- Defining a new type. If this option is available, you will see a type designation called User Defined. (This is often designated as Type 47, but the actual number designation depends on the system's BIOS.) Choose the User Defined designation and supply the specific parameters for the new hard disk. Make sure that you label the hard disk with these parameters, in case the CMOS battery fails and you need to restore the CMOS.

- Using auto-detection. On many systems, the BIOS will detect the hard disk's type and supply the parameters to CMOS.

Reading from and Writing to a Hard Disk

To write to a hard drive:

1. The computer positions the head in a particular track. Read/write heads hover over the platters approximately 2/1,000,000th of an inch above the platter.
2. When the appropriate sector passes by, pulses of electricity are sent through a coil of wire in the head. This creates an electromagnetic field that aligns magnetic particles on the disk surface.
3. By alternating the flow of the current to the head, ones and zeroes can be encoded magnetically.
4. The data is encoded, or written, in circular tracks as the head floats over the rotating platter. The platters spin at a rate of between 5,200 and 10,000 RPMs.

To read data from a hard drive:

1. The computer positions the head over the appropriate track.
2. When the sector passes by, the magnetic particles on the disk create an electrical current in the head through a phenomenon known as *inductance*. Inductance is a circuit or device in which a change in the current generates an electromotive force.

Lesson 8: Fixed Disk Storage Systems

Lesson 8

3. In the head, the alternating patterns of magnetism on the disk translate into alternating flows of electrical current, which can be converted into ones and zeroes.

Figure 8-7: *How hard drives work.*

Activity 8-1

Examining Fixed Disk Drive Characteristics

Scenario:

You visit a client's site to examine their computer for possible upgrades. You need to examine the characteristics of their current hard drive to determine whether their current hard drive is sufficient or needs to be upgraded.

Lesson 8

What You Do	How You Do It
1. Restart your computer and enter the BIOS setup utility.	a. From within Windows, **choose Start→Shut Down. Confirm that Shut Down is selected and click OK.**
	b. After your computer has shut down, **press the power button to turn on your computer.**
	c. As it boots, **press the appropriate key to enter the BIOS setup utility.** (Typically, you press F10, Delete, or Esc when the flashing cursor is displayed in the upper-right corner of your screen.)
2. Locate the settings for the hard drive.	a. **Use the arrow keys, other keys, or mouse, as appropriate to your system's BIOS utility to navigate to the hard drive settings screen.**

Each manufacturer's BIOS is different. Your BIOS setup utility may not display all of these parameters or may provide information beyond what is listed here.

3. **Examine the settings for your system's hard drive and record them in the following table.**

Hard Drive Setting	Your System's Value
Cylinders	
Heads	
Sectors	
CHS Capacity	
Maximum LBA Capacity	
PIO Mode	
UltraDMA Mode	

4. Exit the BIOS setup utility without saving changes.	a. **Press the appropriate key or use the mouse to select the appropriate menu item to leave the setup utility without saving changes.**

Lesson 8: Fixed Disk Storage Systems

Lesson 8

Topic B

Installing IDE Drives

Most systems today come with fairly large hard disks, but given the size of applications and the amount of data many users need to store, they might need additional disk space. Adding a drive or replacing a drive can greatly increase the local storage space on a system, but it's a procedure few end users are likely to want to attempt. As a professional computer technician, you'll need to install drives so that you can meet your users' local storage needs.

Drive Bay

The location inside a system where drives are placed is referred to as a drive bay. These are either 3.5-inch or 5.25-inch wide openings that are tall enough to hold a drive. If you have a 3.5-inch drive and only have a 5.25-inch drive bay open, you can add rails to the drive to adapt it to fit the larger drive bay. Rails are usually included with the drive, but you might need to buy them separately in some instances. The drive slides into the bay and is secured to the chassis with screws. Align the holes in the side of the drive with one or more of the holes in the rail of the drive bay to secure the drive to the chassis.

Drives can have a 3.5-inch or 5.25-inch form factor. The top drive in Figure 8-8 is a 3.5-inch drive and the bottom drive is a 5.25-inch drive.

Figure 8-8: *Form factor.*

IDE Drives

Definition:

An IDE drive is an internal mass storage device that connects to the motherboard through an IDE interface. On a typical motherboard, there are usually two IDE connections. Each IDE channel can support two drives. You will need to configure the first drive on each IDE channel as a master, and the other drive as a slave unless you use cable select. If you have a combination of IDE hard drives and other types of IDE drives, the hard drives should be on the first or primary channel and the other, slower devices on the secondary channel.

The IDE hard drive uses jumpers to set the drive to be the master, the slave, or to use cable select. *Cable select* uses a data cable with special connectors to designate the master and slave devices. You might also need to set the drive type in CMOS. The IDE interface cable connects to the drive on one end and to the IDE controller on the motherboard on the other end. Pin 1 of the data cable is marked with a colored stripe and is usually located closest to the power connection. The Molex power connector connects to the drive to power the drive. An example of an IDE hard drive is shown in Figure 8-9.

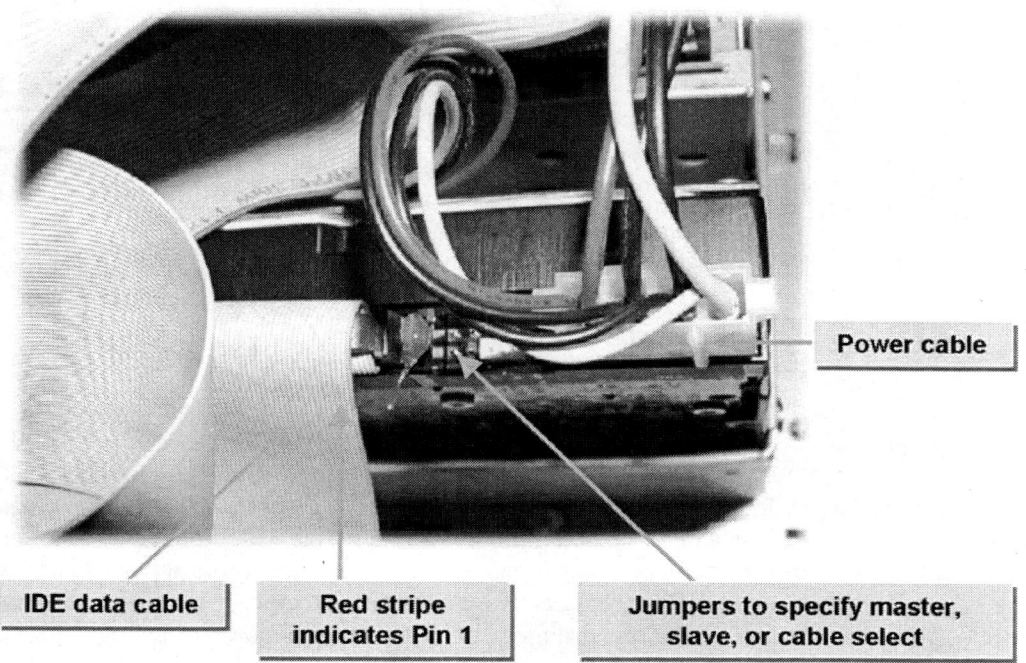

Figure 8-9: *An IDE hard drive installed in a computer.*

Example:

The hard drive is connected to the primary IDE controller on the motherboard. A second hard drive installed in the computer is connected as the second device on the primary channel. The first drive, HD0, is set as the master device and the second drive, HD1, is set as the slave device. HD0 is the drive from which the computer boots.

The secondary IDE controller on the motherboard has slower optical drives connected to it. The first device on the secondary channel is the CD-RW drive, which is set to be the master. The second device on the secondary channel is the DVD drive, which is set to be the slave. Primary and secondary IDE drives are shown in Figure 8-10.

Lesson 8

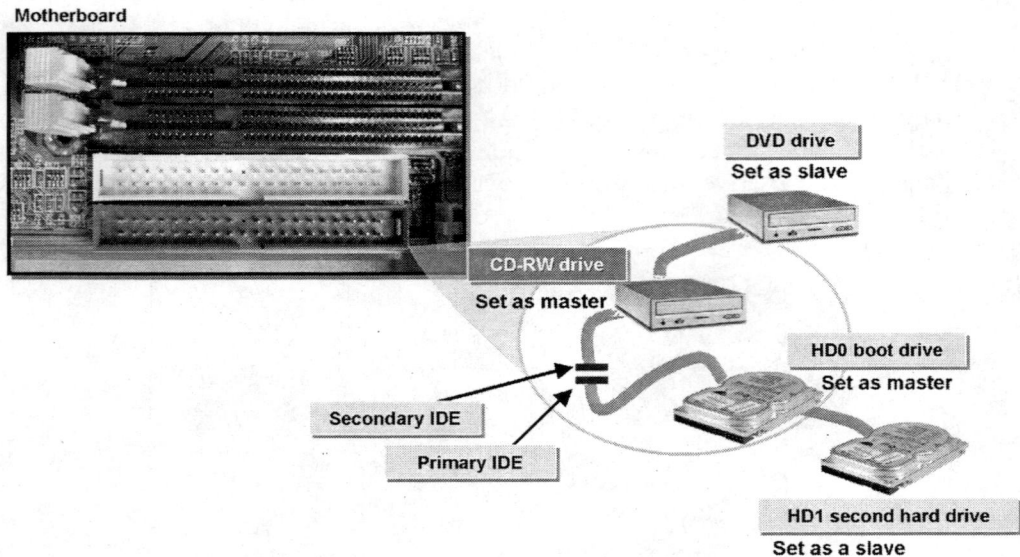

Figure 8-10: *Primary and secondary IDE drives.*

Cable Select

To use cable select, you need to set the jumpers on both drives to cable select. You also need a special cable select cable rather than the normal IDE cable. It has pin 28 configured differently to determine whether the drive should be treated as master or slave. The master and slave determination is made by which connector on the cable the drive is connected to. The connector in the center of the cable is the master, and the end connector is the slave. If only one drive is connected, it is recommended that you use the end connector. This arrangement is shown in Figure 8-11.

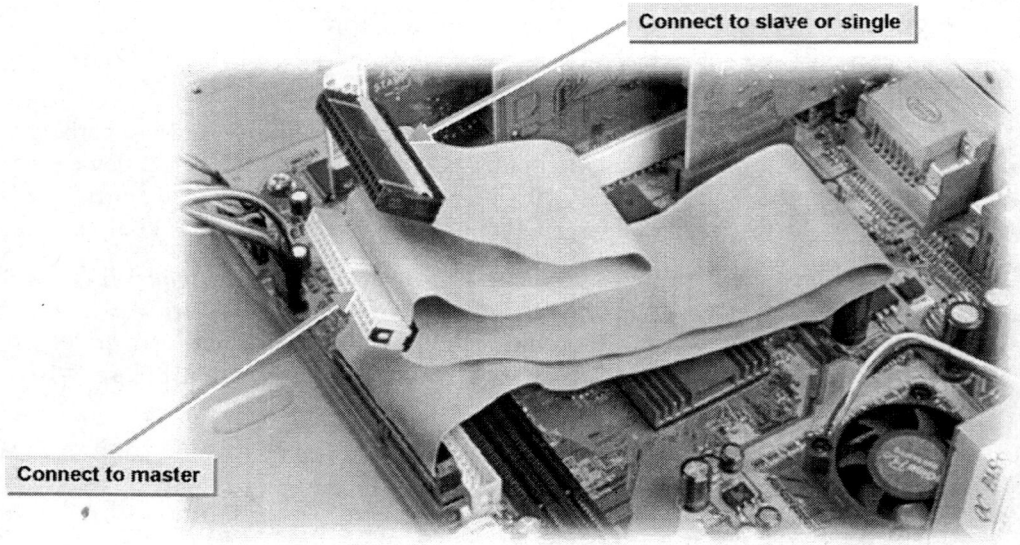

Figure 8-11: *Where to connect IDE drives to the cable.*

LESSON 8

UltraDMA Drives

In the context of IDE and EIDE drives, we will also have to look at Ultra DMA drives. Ultra DMA is an extension to the ATA disk interface. Ultra DMA drives provide transfer rates of 33, 66, or 100 MBps, a great improvement over traditional IDE or EIDE drives. Note that Ultra DMA drives are backward-compatible with EIDE system boards and controllers; however, if you use an Ultra DMA drive on an EIDE system board or controller, the data-transfer rate will be limited to 16.6 MBps. You can also run EIDE drives from an Ultra DMA system board or controller, but you won't get any improvement in speed. If you run an EIDE drive and an Ultra DMA drive off of the same channel on an Ultra DMA controller, the speed will also be limited to 16.6 MBps. To avoid losing the speed advantage of the Ultra DMA drive, place it on a different channel.

To upgrade to Ultra DMA, if a system doesn't currently support it, you will have to upgrade the system board. You can't get Ultra DMA support by simply upgrading the BIOS and drivers. Alternatively, you can purchase and install a separate controller.

Ultra DMA also requires appropriate operating system device drivers, and you have to enable DMA support. Microsoft's QFE513 driver for Windows 95 (not supplied with the retail package of Windows 95 or Windows 95 Release 2), Windows 98, Windows 2000, and Windows XP drivers all support Ultra DMA. For the retail package of Windows 95 or Windows 95 Release 2, and for Windows NT, you will have to get and install Intel's latest bus master DMA driver. The retail package of Windows 95 Release 2 actually does come with a driver for UDMA support, but it has known problems. For Windows NT with Service Pack 2 or 3, the correct driver is installed automatically during installation of the Service Pack, but you have to enable Ultra DMA support by running DMACHECK.EXE. Note that this utility is included only with the CD-ROM version of the service pack, not the downloadable version.

After you've enabled DMA support in the operating system, you may also have to enable it in the BIOS. You have to do this only if it's not automatically detected and configured. If so, after enabling DMA support in the OS, restart the computer and enter the CMOS setup. Locate the channel to which the Ultra DMA hard drive is connected, and set the value to Auto. This enables DMA support.

Partitioning and Formatting

A *partition* is an isolated section of a disk that functions like a separate physical drive. Partitions enable you to create a logical disk structure to organize hard drives. You can have from one to four primary partitions on a disk, and you can also have free space that is not included in any partition. Unpartitioned free space is not available to store data. You can partition a drive through the operating system software.

Formatting is a system function that prepares a mass storage medium to hold data. Each partition on a drive is formatted separately. There are two types of formatting for hard disks:

- *Low-level formatting* is the process of writing track and sector markings on a hard disk. This level of formatting is performed when the hard disk is manufactured.
- *High-level formatting* is an operating system function that builds file systems on drives and partitions. It tests disk sectors to verify that they can be reliably used to hold data. It marks any unreliable sectors as bad sectors which cannot be used.

When you format a floppy disk in Windows or by using the `format` command at a command prompt, you perform both a low-level and a high-level format.

Lesson 8

How to Install IDE Drives

Procedure Reference: Install an IDE Drive

To install an IDE drive:

1. Locate an available drive bay, IDE data connection on the IDE data cable, and a power connector.

2. Set the jumpers for cable select, master, or slave, as appropriate to your needs. There is usually a sticker on the top of the drive that specifies the jumper settings for each of these settings. If there is not a sticker, then the documentation for the drive will include this information.
   - If the drive is the first drive on the channel, it should be configured as cable select or the master.
   - If the drive is the second drive on the channel, it should be configured as cable select or the slave.
   - If cable select is not available on your system, you should use the slave setting.

3. If necessary, attach rails to the drive to fit in the drive bay.

4. Slide the drive into the bay, and then connect the data and power cables.

5. Restart the system, and if necessary, access CMOS setup to specify the drive type. You might need to know the number of cylinders, heads (tracks), and sectors on the disk as part of the CMOS setup procedure. You can usually find this information printed on a label on the drive or in the documentation that came with the drive.

Procedure Reference: Remove an IDE Drive

To remove an IDE drive:

1. Shut down the system.

2. Disconnect the data and power cables from the drive.

3. Unscrew the drive from the bay and slide it out of the bay.

4. If you are removing the master drive, reset the jumpers on other drives if necessary.

Procedure Reference: Format a Hard Drive

To partition and format a hard drive using Windows XP:

1. In the Computer Management utility, click Disk Management.

2. Right-click the newly installed disk, and choose New Partition.

3. Follow the New Partition Wizard prompts to partition and format the new drive.

ACTIVITY 8-2

Installing an IDE Drive

Setup:
There is an available power cable in your system. The IDE data cable has an available connection. There is an empty drive bay. You have been provided with an IDE hard drive and documentation. All cables and documentation have been provided with the drive.

Scenario:
One of your customers needs an IDE drive added to his system.

What You Do	How You Do It
1. Locate available bay, power, and data connection resources for the drive.	a. Power off the system. b. Locate an available drive bay and determine if the bay is the same form factor as the drive. If you are using a 5.25-inch drive bay and a 3.5-inch drive, you will need to install the drive using rails to adapt the drive to the larger bay. c. Locate an available IDE data connection on an IDE data cable. If necessary, connect an IDE data cable to the IDE controller connection on the system board. d. Locate an available power connector. If necessary, connect a power splitter to an existing power connection.
2. Prepare the drive for installation.	a. Set the jumpers or switches to Cable Select or Slave. b. If necessary, attach rails to the drive to fit in the bay.
3. Install the IDE drive into the system.	a. Slide the drive into the bay. b. Connect the data cable to the drive. c. Connect the power cable to the drive. d. Secure the drive to the bay chassis with screws.

Lesson 8: Fixed Disk Storage Systems

Lesson 8

4. Verify that the drive is accessible.	a. Plug all peripherals back into the system.
	b. Restart the system.
	c. If prompted, **access CMOS and set the disk type according to the drive documentation.**
	d. If you accessed CMOS, **exit CMOS and save your settings.**

OPTIONAL ACTIVITY 8-3

Partitioning and Formatting the New Drive

Scenario:
You just installed the new hard drive. Before the user can use the drive, you need to prepare it for use. The company standard is NTFS.

What You Do	How You Do It
1. Open the Disk Management utility.	a. On the Start menu, **right-click My Computer.**
	b. **Choose Manage.**
	c. **Click Disk Management.**
	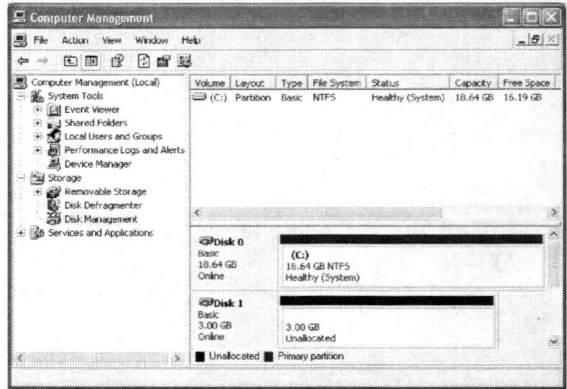

308 *A+™ Certification: Core Hardware Third Edition - A CompTIA Certification*

Lesson 8

2. **Partition and format the new drive.**

   a. **Right-click the unallocated space for Disk 1.** The new disk is all unallocated.

   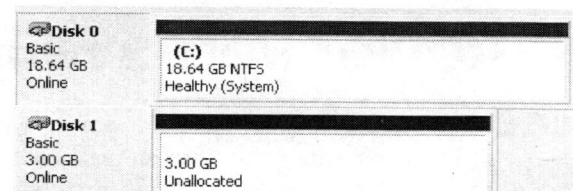

   b. **Choose New Partition.** The New Partition Wizard starts.

   c. **Click Next.**

   d. With Primary Partition selected, **click Next.**

   e. **Accept the defaults for partition size and click Next.**

   f. **Accept the default drive letter and click Next.**

   g. **Format the partition as NTFS using Default as the Allocation Unit Size and New Volume as the Volume Label. Click Next.**

   h. **Click Finish.**

   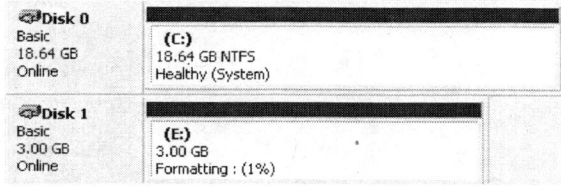

Lesson 8: Fixed Disk Storage Systems

LESSON 8

TOPIC C

Install or Remove Internal SCSI Drives

Just as you saw earlier that there are different connection standards for adapter cards, such as ISA and PCI, there are also different standards for drives. Installing a SCSI device is different than installing IDE. So, if your company standard is SCSI, knowing how to install and configure a SCSI internal drive will be an essential skill for you to have.

SCSI

Definition:

SCSI is a parallel bus standard that connects internal and external peripherals. SCSI is commonly used to connect internal drives. In addition, it is also used to connect external devices including drives, scanners, network adapters, and monitors, and has been used as a network topology. The following characteristics apply to all SCSI devices.

- It is a hardware interface, as well as a logical interface.
- It moves data in parallel mode a chunk at a time rather than a bit at a time.
- SCSI is technically not a controller, but is an adapter. It converts messages between the system bus and the SCSI bus. The Host Bus Adapter (HBA) is the card or component in the system that connects the SCSI bus to the system bus. This is usually on a separate card, but could be built into the chipset of the computer.
- All SCSI devices have a device ID.
- All devices are connected to the SCSI bus as a device on the daisy chain.
- Both ends of the SCSI chain must be terminated.

SCSI devices vary, with some devices not being compatible with other SCSI devices. Some of the ways they vary include:

- The SCSI type.
- The length of the SCSI chain's cabling.
- The connectors on the devices and the cabling.
- The signal type used to put data on the cable.
- The number of devices that can be on the chain. This depends on the SCSI type and the available device IDs on the devices.
- The bus width. Narrow SCSI has an 8-bit bus; wide SCSI has a 16-bit bus.

Example:

Figure 8-12 shows an example of a SCSI chain. This SCSI chain has two external devices connected to the HBA and one internal drive. It is a 16-bit SCSI 2 HBA with a 68-pin internal connection.

Lesson 8

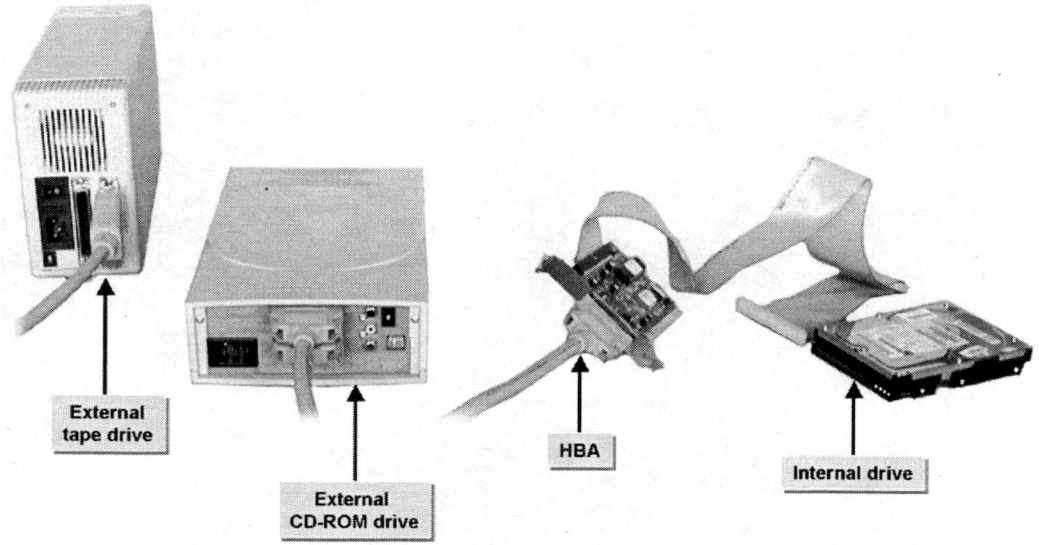

Figure 8-12: *A SCSI chain.*

SCSI Addresses

Each SCSI device has a SCSI ID number, also called a SCSI address. The ID uniquely identifies the device on the SCSI bus. IDs are 0 to 7 for narrow SCSI or 0 to 15 for wide SCSI. Priority is given based on the drive ID, with 7 being the highest priority. For this reason, the HBA is usually assigned ID 7. Slower devices should have higher priority IDs so that faster devices don't monopolize the bus. So, the primary hard drive should be assigned a lower number and a slow device such as a tape drive would be assigned a higher ID number. Priority for narrow SCSI is 7, 6, 5, 4, 3, 2, 1, 0 and for wide SCSI it is 7, 6, 5, 4, 3, 2, 1, 0, 15, 14, 13, 12, 11, 10, 9, 8. SCSI IDs are set using jumpers or DIP switches on the SCSI device.

Some versions of UNIX require specific SCSI IDs be set for specific devices.

SCSI device IDs are shown in Figure 8-13. The devices shown here use two different methods for selecting the device ID. One shows using jumpers and the other two examples use a switch. One switch has two choices, so the manufacturer chose to use a slide switch. The other device has choices from 0 to 6, so the switch is pressed to move from one device ID to the next unused device ID in the SCSI chain.

Lesson 8: Fixed Disk Storage Systems

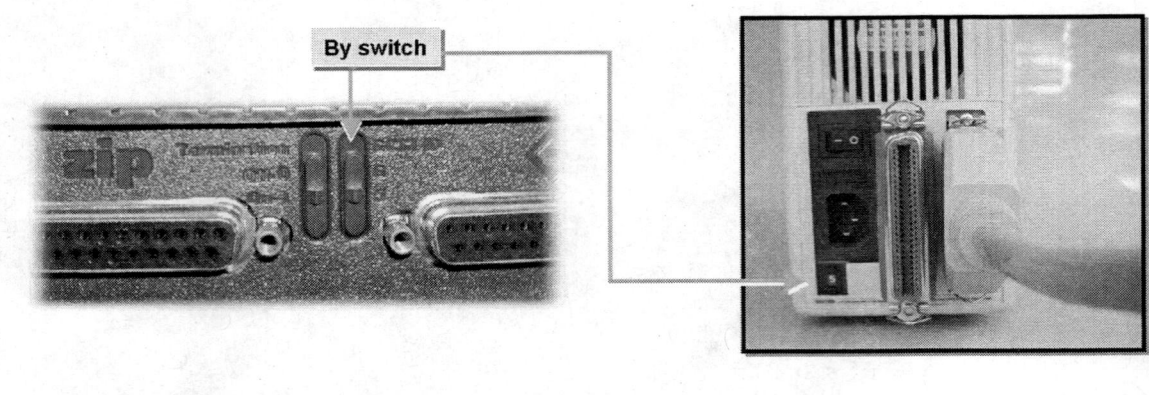

Figure 8-13: *SCSI device IDs.*

SCSI Jumper Settings

The jumpers used to set SCSI IDs each have a binary value assigned to them. Narrow SCSI has three pin pairs with values of 1, 2, and 4. Wide SCSI has four pin pairs with values of 1, 2, 4, and 8. The assignment of the values to specific pin pairs varies by manufacturer. Adding up the value of the jumpered pins gives you the SCSI ID. If no pin pairs are jumpered, the binary value is 0 and the SCSI ID is zero. If the first pin pair is jumpered, the binary value is 1 and the SCSI ID is 1. If the pin pairs with the values 4 and 2 are jumpered, then the SCSI ID will be 6. If all the pin pairs are jumpered, the SCSI ID is 15 (8 + 4 + 2 + 1 = 15).

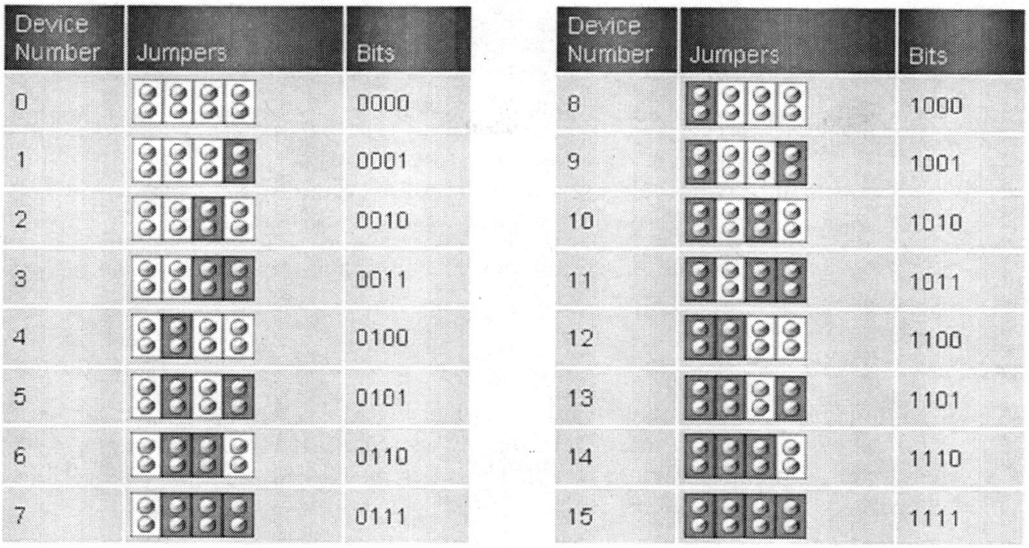

Device Number	Jumpers	Bits		Device Number	Jumpers	Bits
0		0000		8		1000
1		0001		9		1001
2		0010		10		1010
3		0011		11		1011
4		0100		12		1100
5		0101		13		1101
6		0110		14		1110
7		0111		15		1111

Figure 8-14: *SCSI binary jumper settings.*

SCSI Signaling Techniques

SCSI signaling techniques are the methods used by the SCSI interface to place signals on the SCSI cable. SCSI devices use one of the following techniques.

- *Single-Ended (SE)*—Uses a single wire for each bit of data. Cable length is limited to 6 meters due to noise.

- *High Voltage Differential (HVD) Signaling*—Also known as differential signaling. Uses two wires for each data bit—one for the actual data and one for the inverse of the data. By comparing the data and its inverse, noise can be identified and rejected. Cable length can be up to 25 meters. Connecting an HVD device in an SE chain damages SE devices and sometimes also the HVD devices.

- *Low Voltage Differential (LVD) Signaling*—Uses less power than HVD devices and can be chained with SE devices without damaging any devices. An LVD device on an SE chain will function like an SE device, so you lose the advantages of differential signaling. LVD cabling is limited to 12 meters.

 SCSI cable length is the total of all cabling in the SCSI chain.

SCSI Termination

Definition:

SCSI termination prevents errors that can be caused by reflections, which occur when electrical signals bounce back from the end of the SCSI chain. Both ends must be terminated. This prevents signal reflection and makes the cable appear to be of infinite length. The host bus adapter (HBA) is terminated at one end of the bus by default. The last device on the SCSI chain must also be terminated. No other devices in the chain can be terminated. Termination can be accomplished by:

- Setting switches on the device if the device uses switches.
- Setting jumpers on the device if the device uses jumpers.

Lesson 8

- Connecting a terminating resistor or terminating connector to the SCSI port on the device.

Termination varies in that it can be active, passive, or automatic.

- Active termination uses a voltage regulator so that the proper termination voltage is used.
- Passive termination uses resistors to terminate the SCSI chain. It can only be used for low performance SCSI devices on short SCSI chains.
- Automatic termination sets the correct voltage automatically if the device is at the end of the SCSI chain.

Example:

Examples of SCSI termination are shown in Figure 8-15. Each of the devices shown here has a different method of terminating the chain. If the device is not at the end of the chain, termination should be off. If it is at the end of the chain, termination should be enabled.

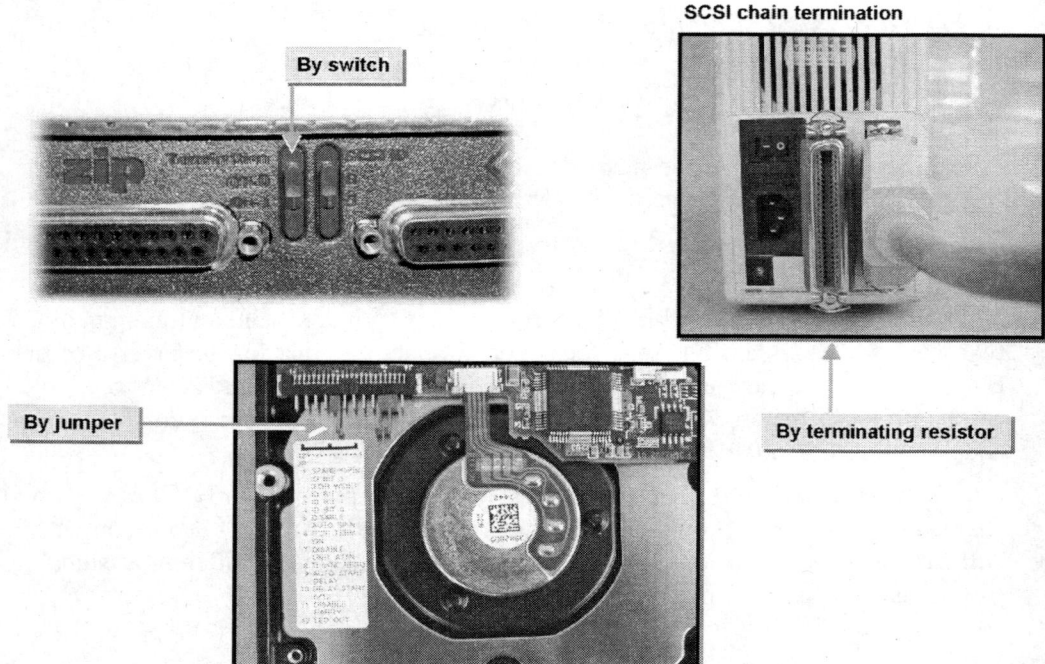

Figure 8-15: *SCSI termination.*

SCSI Types

Over the years, the speed of SCSI has increased greatly. There have been many SCSI types, each with their own specifications. The table shows key characteristics of the most popular SCSI types.

SCSI Type	Description
SCSI-1 (narrow SCSI or regular SCSI)	8 bits wide. Supports up to 8 devices (7 plus the HBA). Uses a 50-pin connector; transfers data at up to 5 MB per second.

Lesson 8

SCSI Type	Description
Wide SCSI	16 bits wide. Supports up to 16 devices (15 plus the HBA). Transfers data at up to 20 MB per second.
Ultra Wide SCSI	16 bits wide. The 50-pin (or lower) connections carry one byte at a time. Ultra Wide connections carry two bytes at a time. Transfers data at up to 40 MB per second.
Fast SCSI	8 bits wide. Transfers data at up to 10 MB per second.
Fast Wide SCSI	16 bits wide. Transfers data at up to 20 MB per second.
Ultra SCSI	16 bits wide. Transfers data at up to 40 MB per second. If implemented on an 8-bit bus, data is transferred at up to 20 MB per second.
Ultra2 SCSI	16 bits wide. Transfers data at up to 80 MB per second. If implemented on an 8-bit bus, data is transferred at up to 40 MB per second.
Ultra3 SCSI	16 bits wide. Transfers data at up to 160 MB per second. If implemented on an 8-bit bus, data is transferred at up to 80 MB per second.
Ultra 320 SCSI	16 bits wide. Transfers data at up to 320 MB per second. If implemented on an 8-bit bus, data is transferred at up to 160 MB per second.

 For a complete list of the SCSI types, refer to the SCSI Trade Association Web site at **www.scsita.org**, and then follow the links About SCSI and Terms & Terminology. This site has a chart listing the terms, bus speeds, bus widths, cable lengths, and number of supported devices.

SCSI Interface

Definition:

The SCSI interface is a hardware interface that is used to connect internal and external peripherals to the SCSI bus. It is composed of the HBA, one or more SCSI devices, and cables to connect devices to the SCSI bus. Cables vary based on the connection type on the devices. They also vary based on whether it is an 8-bit or 16-bit SCSI bus.

SCSI cables vary, as shown in the following table.

SCSI Cable	Description
SCSI 1 Internal	Internal 50-pin flat cable, standard cable, used for 8-bit SCSI chain.
SCSI 3 Internal	Internal 68-pin flat cable, high-density cable, used for 16-bit SCSI chain.
SCSI 1 External A	Centronics external 50-pin connector.
SCSI 2 External A	50-pin high-density connector, 36 mm across.

Lesson 8: Fixed Disk Storage Systems

Lesson 8

SCSI Cable	Description
SCSI 3 External P	68-pin high-density connector, 47 mm across.
DB25 SCSI	25-pin DB 25 connector, commonly used for scanners and SCSI Zip drives.
VHDCI	Used for connecting RAID drives.

 Visit **www.ramelectronics.net/html/scsi_connecters.html** for pictures and descriptions of these and other SCSI connectors.

Example:

Examples of SCSI connectors are shown in Figure 8-16 and Figure 8-17.

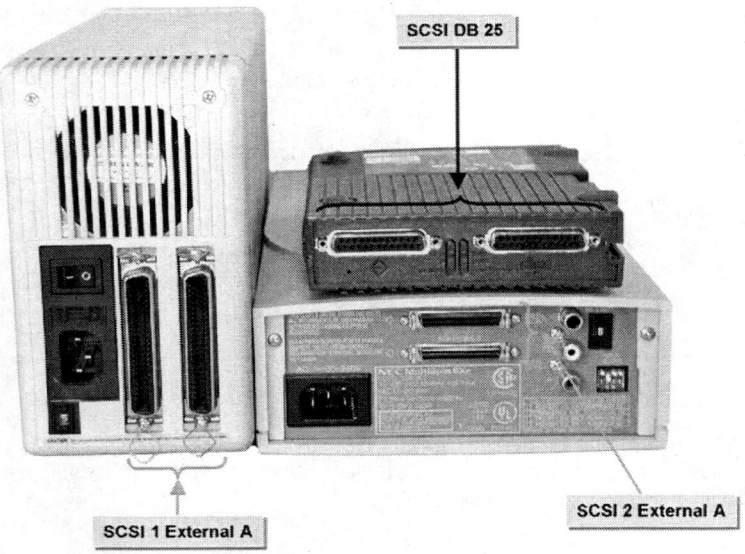

Figure 8-16: *External SCSI connectors.*

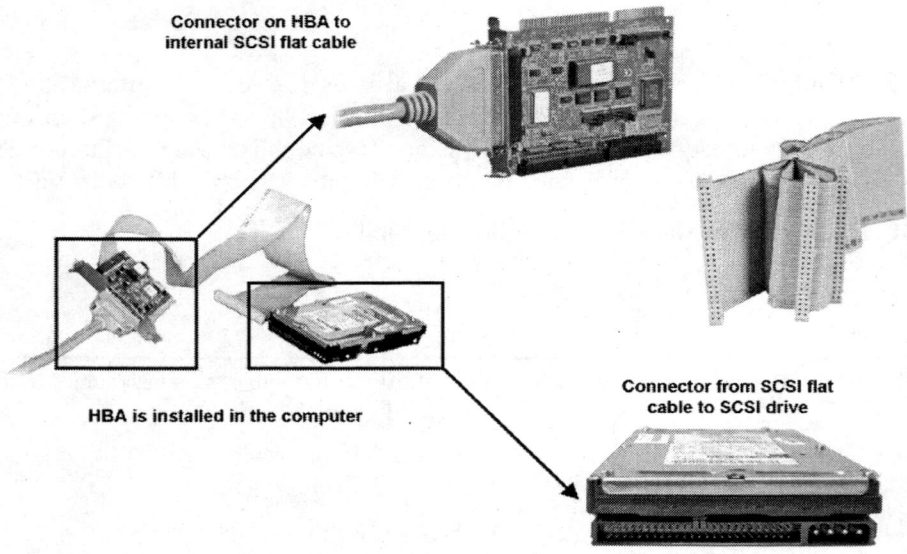

Figure 8-17: *Internal SCSI connectors.*

How to Install a SCSI Drive

Procedure Reference: Install an Internal SCSI Drive

To install an internal SCSI drive:

1. Set the drive ID on the drive. A sticker on the drive or the drive documentation will show how to set the ID and any other settings required to successfully install the drive.

2. Determine which device is at the end of the chain and terminate each end of the chain. Remove termination from any other devices in the SCSI chain. Termination is accomplished by changing jumper settings, switches, or by physically inserting a termination plug into the port. Refer to the documentation for the device to determine how termination is accomplished on the particular device you are working with.

3. Insert the drive in an available drive bay. If you are using a 5.25-inch drive bay and a 3.5-inch drive, you will need to install the drive using rails to adapt the drive to the larger bay.

4. Connect the SCSI cable from the host bus adapter to the drive.

5. Connect the power cable to the drive. Most modern systems have plenty of power connectors for all of the internal devices you might install. Some systems might run out of connectors, though. If this happens, you can purchase splitters to enable two (or more) devices to be connected to one existing power connection to the power supply.

6. Restart the system. If prompted, access CMOS setup and set the disk type, and then exit CMOS and save the settings.

Procedure Reference: Connect an External SCSI Device

To connect an external SCSI device to your system:

1. Connect the SCSI cable to the device and the other end of the cable to the SCSI port on the computer, being sure not to confuse the SCSI port with the parallel port.

2. If the SCSI device is the last device in the SCSI chain, terminate the device; if it is not the last device in the chain, remove termination from the device.

3. If you are adding additional SCSI devices to the chain, repeat steps 1 and 2, being sure to only terminate the last device in the chain.

4. Test that all devices in the chain function properly.

ACTIVITY 8-4

Installing an Internal SCSI Drive

Scenario:
You have been given an internal SCSI drive to install in a customer's system. There is no SCSI HBA in the system.

What You Do	How You Do It
1. Install a SCSI HBA in the system.	a. Power down the system.
	b. Locate an available slot that matches the bus type of the SCSI HBA card.
	c. Install the SCSI HBA card in the slot.
	d. Restart the system, and if prompted, configure the HBA.
2. Locate available bay, power, and data connection resources for the drive.	a. Power off the system.
	b. Locate an available drive bay and determine if the bay is the same form factor as the drive.
	c. Connect the internal SCSI data cable to the SCSI host bus adapter.
	d. Locate an available power connector. If necessary, **connect a power splitter to an existing power connection.**
3. Prepare the drive for installation.	a. Set the SCSI ID to an unused ID number.
	b. If necessary, **attach rails to the drive** to fit in the bay.
	c. If the drive is at the end of the SCSI chain, **terminate the device** and, if necessary, remove termination from the previously terminated device.

4.	Install the SCSI drive into the system.	a. Slide the drive into the bay.
		b. Connect the data cable to the drive.
		c. Connect the power cable to the drive.
		d. Secure the drive to the bay chassis with screws.
5.	Verify that the drive is accessible.	a. Plug all peripherals back into the system.
		b. Restart the system.
		c. If prompted, **access SCSI BIOS and set the disk type according to the drive documentation.**
		d. If you accessed CMOS, **exit CMOS and save your settings.**

OPTIONAL PRACTICE ACTIVITY 8-5

Formatting an Internal SCSI Hard Drive

Setup:
Perform this activity only if the internal SCSI drive you installed is a hard drive.

Scenario:
You just installed an internal SCSI hard drive. Now you need to prepare it for use by the customer. The business uses NTFS as the standard file system.

1. In the Computer Management utility, **open Disk Management.**

2. **Partition and format the new drive.**

Lesson 8

Optional Activity 8-6

Connecting an External SCSI Device

Setup:
A self-terminated SCSI adapter or built-in SCSI port is available on the system.

Scenario:
The artist in the Marketing department often needs to access files from multiple computers and would like to be able to carry an external hard drive with her as she moves from computer to computer. She also has a SCSI scanner to connect to the system.

What You Do	How You Do It
1. **Install the first SCSI device.** ⚠ Be sure that you do not install it into the parallel port, which looks identical to the SCSI ports on some systems.	a. With the computer powered off, **connect the SCSI cable from the scanner to the SCSI port on the computer.** b. If necessary, **remove termination from the device** in preparation for adding the second SCSI device.
2. **Install the second SCSI device.**	a. **Connect the SCSI cable from the scanner to the external SCSI drive.** b. **Terminate the second device.**
3. **Verify that both SCSI devices work.**	a. **Boot the computer.** b. **Install any required device drivers.** c. **Access a file on the external hard drive.** You can list the files through Explorer or from the command line. d. **Place your manual on the scanner bed, and then scan the page into the system.**

Topic D

Correct Hard Drive Problems

Hard drives, because they are one of the few system components that contain moving parts, are particularly susceptible to wear and damage. There is a saying that there are two types of hard drives: the ones that have failed and the ones that are failing. Because the drive supports so many system functions, it is not always obvious that the hard drive is the culprit, yet hard drive problems can have a truly devastating effect on a system and on a user's productivity. So, being able to spot, identify, and correct hard drive problems early, before they cause data loss, will be an important skill for you as a support technician.

Common Problems with Hard Drives

There are many problems you might encounter when troubleshooting hard drives. Some problems that appear to be hard drive problems are actually virus infections. These can cause physical hard drive damage as well, but usually just damage the files on the disk and not the disk itself. The following table lists the most common symptoms of hard drive problems and possible problems that cause those symptoms.

Symptom	Possible Problem	Solution
Error message at boot Drive Not Ready—System Halted	Drive is damaged. Drive is not configured for Master or Cable Select as appropriate to the system. Data cable is not connected or incorrectly connected to the drive.	Visually inspect the drive and its connections, correct as needed.
POST error codes in the 17xx range	1701: Drive not found. 1702: Hard drive adapter not found. 1703: Hard drive failure. 1704: Hard drive or adapter failure. 1780, 1790: Hard drive 0 failed. 1781, 1791: Hard drive 1 failed. 1782: Hard drive controller failed.	Visually inspect connections and reconnect drive. Replace failed component.
Can't read from or write to the drive	Bad sectors on the drive. IRQ conflicts. Drive failure. Virus attack.	Run Scandisk to try to recover information from bad sectors and to mark those sectors as unusable. Check Device Manager for hardware resource conflicts and for indications of drive failure. Run virus check software and remove any viruses found.
System will not boot	Drive disconnected, damaged, not recognized by the BIOS.	Visually inspect and reconnect drive. Enable drive in CMOS setup utility.

Symptom	Possible Problem	Solution
Drive is making grinding noises that keep repeating in a regular pattern	Physically damaged drive, most likely due to a head crash.	Replace the hard drive. Remind users and technicians not to move a machine while it is in use since that is the most common cause of head crashes.
Data is frequently being corrupted or utilities are not running properly	System not being shut down properly, drive is in the process of failing, virus.	Educate users on how to properly shut down the system. Run virus protection software. Back up the data, replace failed or failing drive.

IDE Drive Troubleshooting Tips

Keep these points in mind as you troubleshoot IDE drive problems:

- If you have one drive on a channel, it must be configured as single—not master or slave. Alternatively, set it to cable select and plug it in to the IDE cable connector furthest from the motherboard.
- With two drives on a channel, set both to cable select or configure them both manually, setting one to master and the other slave. Don't mix these settings by setting one to be cable select and the other as either master or slave. Make sure both aren't set to master or slave.
- If you remove the second IDE hard disk from a computer with two IDE drives installed, verify that the disk that remains in the computer is set as single. The Master/Slave setting should be used only when there is more than one hard disk in a system; otherwise, a disk-controller error will occur when you restart the computer.
- If you need to move an IDE drive from one computer to another, you likely won't run into problems. However, especially if there is a great difference in age between the computers, you might run into problems. The BIOS of another computer might not support LBA or Large (ECHS), or the computer might not be set up for it. In that case, data on the hard drive would be lost if you install it in that system. You can change the mode for a hard drive (from LBA to Large, or vice versa), but this poses a risk of data loss. Typically, you should only set the mode when you first install the disk. If you do need to change it, make sure you have a working backup of all of the data on the disk before doing so.

SCSI Drive Troubleshooting Tips

Keep the following points in mind as you troubleshoot SCSI drive problems:

- The vast majority (up to 95 percent) of problems with SCSI disks are due to incorrect ID settings and improper termination.
- When a SCSI system is booted or reset, SCSI controllers generally need to renew all SCSI device connections before activating the devices, causing a delay during POST.
- SCSI cables should be handled carefully to minimize problems. For instance, rolling SCSI cable onto itself can cause crosstalk and impede the signal. Running long lengths of it next to metal or past power supplies can also cause errors due to signal impedance.
- If you intend for a SCSI disk to be bootable after you install it, you must enable the SCSI BIOS by using jumper settings or software configuration.

- Verify that all SCSI devices have unique SCSI ID numbers.
- If you are installing an additional SCSI hard drive into a computer where only one connector is available on the SCSI cable and the cable itself is terminated, remove and replace the cable with one that has multiple connectors.

Slow Drives

Some hard drives are just inherently slow. The drive simply revolves at a slower speed than other drives. In other cases, though, a drive that was quite fast might, either suddenly or over time, start to retrieve files slowly. Some of the possible reasons for slow drives include:

- Drive is too full—Windows needs free drive space to write temporary and swap files. It needs at least 100 to 200 MB, but 1 to 2 GB is highly recommended.
- Fragmentation—Pointers link all the parts of a fragmented file together, but this takes time to reassemble the next time you read the file. Run a disk defragmenter program monthly to clean up defragmentation and put files in contiguous blocks.
- Controller too slow—If you have a fast drive connected to a slower controller, the drive will transfer data at the slower rate.
- The wrong cable is used—IDE drive cables all look about the same. However, if you use a cable for a slower drive, it can result in decreased performance.

Hard Drive Maintenance Tools

Just as you can perform physical maintenance on devices, you can perform software maintenance on some devices as well. The following table lists some of the software tools you can use to maintain hard drives.

Utility	Description	Syntax
chkdsk	Enables you to check the hard disk for errors. If any errors are reported, you can then use other tools such as ScanDisk to repair those errors.	At a Command Prompt, enter `chkdsk drive letter`. For example, to check the C drive, enter `chkdsk C:`.
Disk Defragmenter (Defrag.exe)	Rearranges the files on your computer's hard disk to make them contiguous. Use Disk Defragmenter when a hard disk's performance has slowed down.	Choose Start→All Programs→Accessories→System Tools→Disk Defragmenter, or choose Start→Run and enter `defrag` in the Open text box.
Disk Management	Windows XP's graphical tool for managing drives and partitions.	From the Start menu, right-click My Computer and click Manage. Select Disk Management in the Computer Management window.
Fdisk.exe and Format.exe	DOS-based disk and file-management tools; Fdisk is for disk partitioning and Format is for formatting.	Boot with a bootable DOS floppy disk containing the utilities and run them at the command prompt.

Lesson 8

Utility	Description	Syntax
Scandisk (Scandisk.exe)	Scans and repairs problems with your computer's hard disk.	Choose Start→All Programs→Accessories→System Tools→ScanDisk, or choose Start→Run and enter `scandisk` in the Open text box.

How to Troubleshoot and Correct Hard Drive Problems

Procedure Reference: Troubleshoot Hard Drive Boot Problems

To troubleshoot some of the most common issues with a hard drive that won't boot:

1. Examine the POST codes and other messages displayed at boot time.
   - The numbers in the 17xx range indicate that the hard drive or controller were not found. Check that both devices are connected and functional.
   - The message No Boot Device Available indicates that the BIOS could not find an installed operating system on the hard drive or a bootable floppy disk. Verify that the operating system was installed. If it was, try to boot from floppy disk and access the hard drive, then check the boot partition for errors.
   - The messages No Operating System Found or Ntldr Can't Load are often caused by a non-bootable floppy disk being left in the drive.
   - Configuration or CMOS error indicates that the information reported by CMOS is different than the hard drive found by the POST. Check CMOS settings. If the settings won't stick, check the battery on the system board.
   - The message Hard Drive Not Found or Fixed Disk Error indicates that the hard drive was not found during the POST. Check all hard drive and hard drive controller connections. The hard drive or controller might be dead.
   - The message Reboot And Select Proper Boot Device Or Insert Boot Media In Selected Boot Device indicates that the BIOS found no bootable device in the system. It could also indicate that a removable media drive does not contain media if no hard disk was found and it found a removable media drive (such as a floppy disk drive, Zip drive, SuperDrive, or the like).

2. If the drive is newly installed, verify that it has an operating system by booting with a DOS boot floppy disk and entering the drive letter at the command prompt.
   - If the drive letter is recognized, it might need an operating system installed.
   - If the drive letter is not recognized, the drive might need to be partitioned and formatted, and then have an operating system installed. If the `fdisk` and `format` utilities are on the DOS boot floppy, you can use them to partition and format the drive.

3. Otherwise, diagnose and correct the boot problem.
   - Perform a cold boot.

- Verify that CMOS lists the correct device settings for the hard drive. This includes the correct drive type, whether LBA is enabled, and the CHS (cylinders, heads, and sectors) settings.
- Verify that CMOS is set to boot from the hard drive.
- Listen to the drive or touch the drive to determine if it is spinning during POST. It should be spinning up to full speed during this time. It usually makes noise during this time and you can feel the vibrations of the drive while it is spinning.
- Use your multimeter to verify that the power connection readings are correct. They should be +12v for Pin 1 and +5v for Pin 4. Pins 2 and 3 should be grounded.
- Verify that the data cable is correctly oriented. Pin 1 is almost always on the side nearest the power connection. Pin 1 on the cable is on the side with the stripe.
- Check drive settings. For an IDE drive, verify that it is set to master, slave, or cable select as appropriate to the drive and its location in the drive chain within the system. For a SCSI drive, verify that the termination is correct for its location in the chain and that it has a unique device ID.
- Look for data recovery options. There are some built-in recovery capabilities in some operating systems. You can also purchase software to assist you in recovering data. In many cases though, you will need to resort to sending the drive out to a company that specializes in recovering data from damaged drives.
- If none of these fix the problem, replace the drive.

4. Verify that the drive now works.
   - Boot the system.
   - Verify that you can read from and write to the drive you repaired.

Lesson 8

ACTIVITY 8-7

Troubleshooting Why a Hard Drive Won't Boot

Scenario:
Georgetta Larsen cannot boot her system. She got an error message at POST, but did not write it down.

What You Do	How You Do It
1. List at least two POST messages that would indicate a problem with the hard drive. What does the message mean? How would you fix it?	

2. Diagnose and correct the problem.	a.	Perform a cold boot.
	b.	Verify that CMOS lists the correct drive settings.
	c.	Listen to the drive or touch the drive to determine if it is spinning during POST.
	d.	Using your multimeter, verify that power connection readings are +12v for Pin 1, and +5v for Pin 4. Pins 2 and 3 should be ground.
	e.	Verify that data cable is correctly oriented.
	f.	Check drive settings: • IDE: Master, slave, or cable select • SCSI: Termination and device ID
	g.	If nothing else corrects the problem, replace the drive.
3. Test that the drive now works.	a.	Boot the system.
	b.	Verify that you can read and write to the drive you repaired.

Procedure Reference: Troubleshoot Why a Newly Installed Second Hard Drive Isn't Recognized

To troubleshoot some of the most common problems with a newly-installed second hard drive:

1. Verify that the CMOS settings are correct.
2. Verify that the drive was installed correctly.
3. Access the drive by drive letter in My Computer or at a command prompt to verify that the drive was partitioned and formatted. You can use DOS utilities from a bootable DOS floppy disk or Windows XP's disk management utilities.

Lesson 8

Discovery Activity 8-8

Troubleshooting why a Newly Installed Second Hard Drive Isn't Recognized

Scenario:

You just finished installing a new hard drive as the second drive in the system, but it is not being recognized by the system.

1. One of the things you need to check when a newly installed drive isn't recognized is the CMOS settings for the drive. What in particular do you need to check in CMOS for this problem?

2. Another thing you should check when you encounter this problem is that the drive was installed correctly. What exactly would you be checking?

3. The drive was properly installed but you can't access it by its drive letter. What should your next step be?

Procedure Reference: Troubleshoot Hard Drive Data Access Problems

To troubleshoot some of the most common hard drive data access problems:

1. Document the symptoms.
   - If the system boots and the drive is recognized, but you can't access data and the message Can't Access This Drive is displayed, this could be a problem with the letter assigned to the drive or an indication of drive damage.
   - If the user attempts to access a drive or files on a drive, which causes the system to lock up, and you hear a clicking sound, this indicates drive damage.
   - If the user reports that some folders have disappeared and folder and file names are scrambled with strange characters in their names, this indicates either a computer virus or drive damage.

2. If you suspect a drive letter problem, verify that the drive letter assigned to the drive matches the letter the user is entering, and copy a file to and from the drive to verify that it is working.

Lesson 8

3. If you suspect a computer virus, run virus-scanning software.
4. If you suspect drive damage, repair or replace the disk.
   - Run the Windows XP Error-checking option on the Tools pane of the Local Disk Properties dialog box.
   - Use an older version of Scandisk from floppy disk to try to identify and repair the errors it encounters.
   - Open My Computer, right-click the drive letter in question, and then display the Hardware pane. Use the Troubleshooting Wizard to attempt to locate the problem.
   - Back up the data from the drive if possible, and then reformat the drive. Remember, reformatting will destroy any data on the drive.
   - If you cannot repair the errors using these methods, back up the data if possible, and replace the drive.

DISCOVERY ACTIVITY 8-9

Troubleshooting Hard Drive Data Access Problems

Scenario:

- Ticket: 112001

  Location: Main building, 25L17

  User: Reanna Kerwin

  System boots fine and everything works until the user tries to access data on the second hard drive, the D drive. The message Can't Access This Drive is displayed when she tries to access the D drive. The user would also like an explanation about what the error message means.

- Ticket: 112002

  Location: Elmwood Place, cube 58

  User: Leland Wolter

  When the user tries to access the hard drive containing his data, the system locks up and makes a clicking sound. From the DOS prompt, he can change to drive D, but when he tries to access a file or list the files on the drive, it locks up and begins clicking again.

- Ticket: 112003

  Location: Training center, main office

  User: Kamron Langley

  User reports that some of his folders have begun disappearing and some folder and file names are scrambled with strange characters in their names.

Lesson 8

1. List some of the steps you might take to resolve trouble ticket 112001.

2. What steps might you take to attempt to resolve trouble ticket 112002? What is the most likely cause of the problem?

3. What steps might you take to attempt to resolve trouble ticket 112003? What is the most likely cause of the problem?

Procedure Reference: Troubleshoot the Wrong Drive Size Being Reported

To troubleshoot some of the most common reasons why a system reports the wrong hard drive size:

1. If the system contains an older BIOS that does not recognize large drives, it will report that there is only about a 500 MB drive in the system. To resolve this problem, update the BIOS so that the entire drive can be recognized. If the BIOS cannot be upgraded, a Dynamic Disk Overlay driver can be installed to enable the older BIOS and the large drive to work together.

2. A system running Windows 98 SE might report that the drive can store less than 64 GB even though you know the drive is much larger. This is a known problem that can be resolved with a fix from the Microsoft Web site at **http://support.microsoft.com/default.aspx?scid=KB;EN-US;Q263044&**.

3. Users are often misled about the exact size of a drive. When talking in general terms, most people round 1024 bytes to 1000 since it is easier to talk in round numbers. By the time you get up to billions of bytes as you will with the newer drives, those 24 bytes for each 1000 bytes starts to add up to significant amounts.

 For more information about binary multiples as used in denoting drive sizes, see **http://physics.nist.gov/cuu/Units/binary.html**.

DISCOVERY ACTIVITY 8-10

Troubleshooting Wrong Drive Size

Scenario:
Several older systems have been put back in service following a big hiring phase. These systems are being upgraded with larger hard drives and additional RAM. However, some systems are not reporting the correct drive size.

1. A 30 GB hard drive was installed, but the system reports that the drive is about 500 MB. What can be done to resolve this problem?

2. The system is running Windows 98 SE. After installing and partitioning a 70 GB drive with FDISK, FDISK reports that the drive is less than 64 GB. Why is this happening? How can you resolve the problem?

3. A user is questioning the difference between the sizes in GB and bytes. Why is there such a big difference? The disk reports in some places as 9.33 GB and in other as 10,025,000,960 bytes. Why isn't it 10GB?

Lesson 8: Fixed Disk Storage Systems

Lesson 8

Topic E

RAID

What if a drive failed and you never knew the difference because another drive just took over? What if you could replace that failed drive without needing to power down the system? Both of these things can be a reality if you implement RAID on the computer system.

RAID

Definition:

A *Redundant Array of Independent Disks (RAID)* array is an arrangement of multiple disk drives and a sophisticated controller that provides higher performance or reliability, or both, than a single disk drive. In general, RAID is more expensive to implement than standard disk configurations. Some versions of RAID implementation are more expensive than others. RAID comes in several levels, each with specific goals and requirements. All implementations of RAID require:

- Multiple disk drives.
- An operating system that supports RAID.

> Originally, the RAID acronym was defined as Redundant Array of Inexpensive Disks.

RAID varies by:

- Level. Different levels have been defined that have specific hardware and operating system requirements to meet specific needs.
- The number of drives required for the RAID level.
- Whether additional drive controllers are required.
- Whether specific RAID controllers are required, or whether regular drive controllers can be used.
- Whether it improves reliability or performance or both.
- How data is written to the disks.
- Whether it is implemented using IDE or SCSI drives and controllers.

Example: RAID Level 0

RAID level 0 is also referred to as striping. In this RAID implementation, data is spread in small chunks across multiple drives. This is illustrated in Figure 8-18. Features of RAID level 0 include:

- It requires Windows NT or Windows 2000 to implement through software.
- It requires at least two physical drives and can use up to 32 physical drives.
- Improved read and write performance. Since there are multiple heads and read/write heads, data can be read and written more quickly.
- It includes no provisions for recovering or rebuilding data. Because data is spread across multiple drives, if any drive fails, the risk of losing data is increased. This level provides no fault tolerance.

- It uses a single controller, which can be a regular drive controller or a special RAID controller.

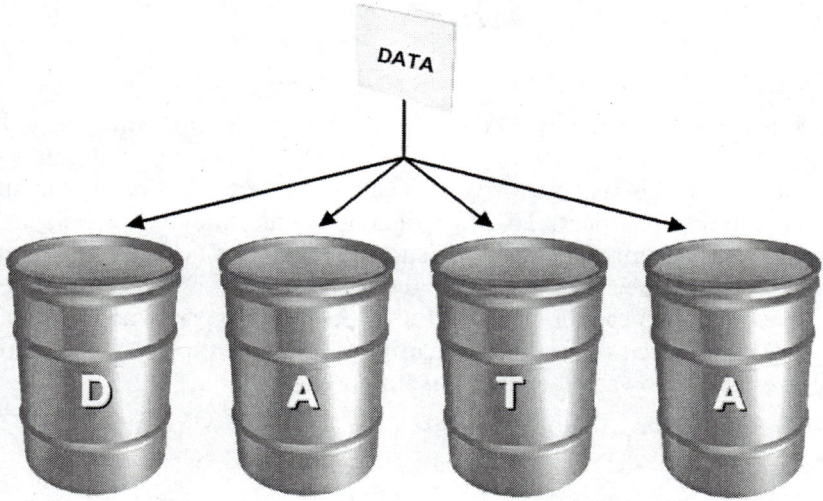

Data is divided across all drives.

Figure 8-18: *Striping with RAID level 0.*

Example: RAID Level 1

RAID level 1 duplicates an entire partition on another partition. All data and drive information is duplicated on the second partition. Drive information that can be duplicated includes the system and boot partitions. It can be implemented in two ways. Both are shown in Figure 8-19.

- Mirroring uses two physical disks and one disk drive controller for both disks.
- Duplexing uses two physical disks and two disk drive controllers, each drive connected to a separate controller.

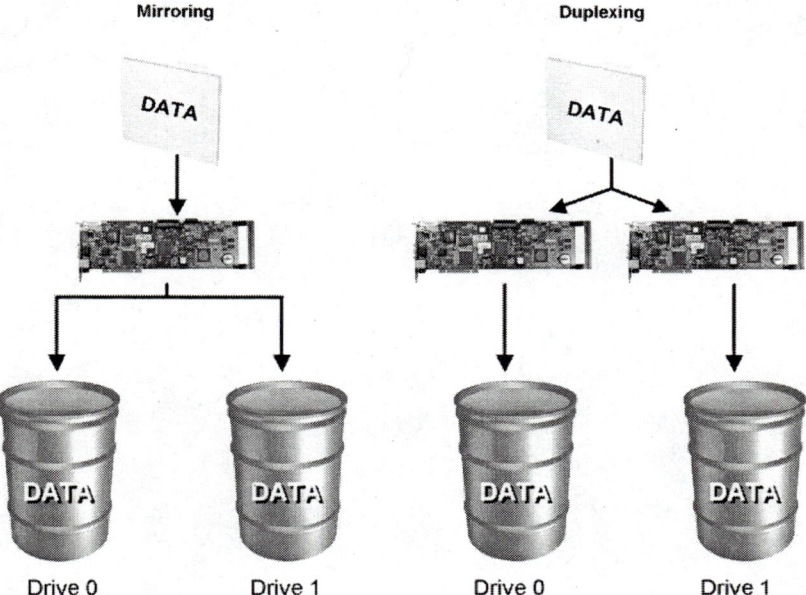

Figure 8-19: *RAID level 1.*

RAID level 1 can be implemented through software on Windows NT or 2000 operating systems. Even though it is the most expensive RAID level, since all equipment is duplicated without any gain in productivity or capacity, it is the only method that can protect the boot disk.

Example: RAID Level 5

RAID level 5, as shown in Figure 8-20, is also known as striping with parity. It is implemented using 3 to 32 separate physical disk drives over which the data is written. Parity data is also spread across the drives. Because both data and parity are spread across the drives, more than one read and write can occur simultaneously. Hardware-based RAID Level 5 systems offer features such as continuous operation, the ability to schedule failed-drive replacement, and even the ability to hot-swap failed drives. The system and boot partitions cannot be part of a stripe set with parity across multiple drives. They must be stored on a separate partition. Implementing RAID 5 through software requires a Windows NT or 2000 operating system.

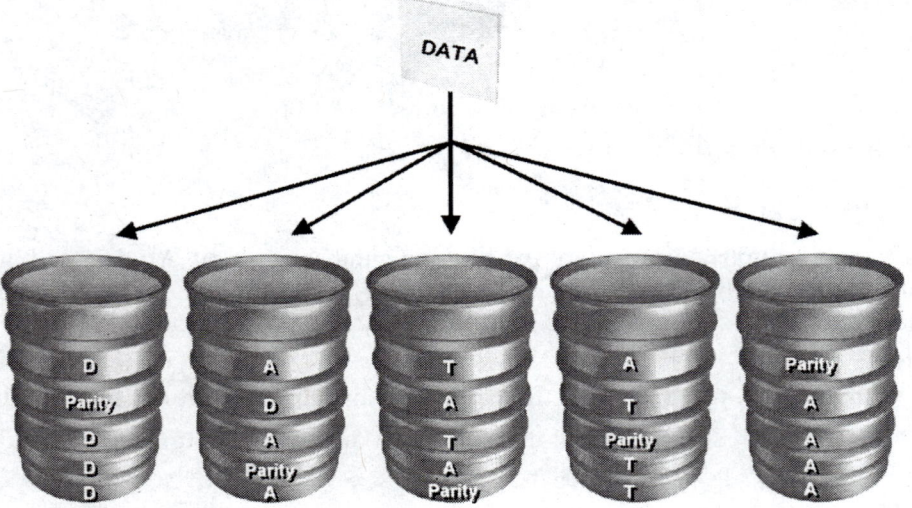

Figure 8-20: *RAID level 5.*

ACTIVITY 8-11

Choosing an Appropriate RAID Level

Scenario:
Evaluate the needs of each customer to determine which level of RAID should be implemented.

1. Your customer can afford to install only one additional disk to the system, yet they want the benefits of RAID technology. Which RAID level should they implement?

2. Your customer needs to improve fault tolerance and performance, and they also need to hot swap failed drives. Which RAID level should they implement?

3. If the customer would like to protect the boot partition and can afford duplicate disks and duplicate controller cards, they should implement ___ ___ ___ ___ ___ ___ ___ ___ .

How to Create a Striped Volume

RAID levels 0, 1, and 5 can be accomplished using Microsoft's Server operating system products—Windows NT Server; Windows 2000 Server, Advanced Server, and Datacenter; and Windows Server 2003 both Standard and Enterprise Editions.

Procedure Reference: Create a Striped Volume

To create striped volume (RAID level 0) on multiple dynamic disks in any Windows 2000 Server product:

1. Open Disk Management.

2. Right-click an area of unallocated space on the first dynamic disk that will be part of the striped volume, and choose Create Volume to launch the Create Volume Wizard.

3. Follow the prompts in the wizard to create a striped volume that contains all the dynamic disks you want to include. The volume size number you enter will be the amount of space you'll use on each disk. The total size of the volume will be the volume size times the number of disks.

4. Finish the wizard. It will create and format the new volume.

ACTIVITY 8-12

Creating a Striped Volume

Data Files:

- Striped.exe

Setup:

Your three dynamic disks are Disk 1, Disk 2, and Disk 3.

You will be setting aside 60 MB on each disk for the stripe set.

Scenario:

Your Windows 2000 Server has three dynamic disks. You would like to enhance the disk performance by creating a striped set that will enable simultaneous reads and writes across the multiple drives.

Lesson 8

What You Do	How You Do It
1. Create a striped volume.	a. From the C:\085811data\Simulations folder, **run Striped.exe** to launch a simulation of Computer Management. You're looking at a Windows 2000 Server system with multiple dynamic disks.
	b. **Right-click the unallocated space on Disk 1.**
	c. **Choose Create Volume and click Next** to launch the Create Volume Wizard.
	d. Under Volume Type, **select Striped Volume. Click Next.**
	e. In the Selected Dynamic Disks list, **make sure that Disk 1 is already selected.**
	f. In the All Available Dynamic Disks list, **select Disk 2 and Disk 3.** (Use Shift+click.)
	g. **Click Add** to add them to the volume.
	h. In the Size For All Selected Disks box, **type *60*** We're using a small number so that the formatting process will be quick.
	i. **Look at the Total Volume Size value.** It reads 180 MB; each of the three disks you selected will hold 60 MB. **Click Next.**
	j. **Assign drive letter S. Click Next.**
	k. **Change the volume label to Striped.**
	l. **Check Perform a Quick Format. Click Next.**
	m. **Click Finish** to create and format the new volume.
	n. **Look in the lists pane** to make sure the volume was created, and **scroll down in the disks pane** to verify that all the disks have been added to the striped volume.

Lesson 8: Fixed Disk Storage Systems

o. **Click Exit** at the bottom of the simulation window to close the simulation.

How to Create a Mirrored Volume

Procedure Reference: Create a Mirrored Volume

To create a mirrored volume (RAID level 1), the member disks in a mirrored volume can be different sizes and types, but they both have to be dynamic. They also have to have an equal amount of free space available. To create a new mirrored volume (RAID level 1) on multiple dynamic disks in any Windows 2000 Server product:

1. Open Disk Management.
2. Right-click an area of unallocated space on the first disk in the volume, and choose Create Volume to launch the Create Volume Wizard.
3. Follow the prompts in the wizard to create a mirrored volume from the two dynamic disks you want. The volume size number you specify will be the total amount of space available for storage; the total amount of space used by the volume will be twice this amount.
4. Finish the wizard. It will create and format the new volume.

ACTIVITY 8-13

Creating a Mirrored Volume

Data Files:

- Mirror.exe

Setup:

You will mirror the dynamic disks with the volume labels Disk 1 and Disk 2.

Your mirror will be 20 MB in size.

Scenario:

You have an empty disk on your Windows 2000 Server computer that you would like to begin using. You want to create fault-tolerance for the data that will reside on the disk by setting it up as a mirrored volume with a second disk.

Lesson 8

What You Do	How You Do It
1. Create a new mirrored volume.	a. From the C:\085811data\Simulations folder, **run Mirror.exe** to open another simulation of Computer Management.
	b. In the disks pane, **right-click the unallocated space on Disk 1.**
	c. **Choose Create Volume and click Next** to run the Create Volume Wizard.
	d. Under Volume Type, **select Mirrored Volume. Click Next.**
	e. **Make sure that Disk 1 shows up in the Selected Dynamic Disks box.**
	f. Under All Available Dynamic Disks, **select Disk 2. Click Add** to add this disk to the mirrored volume.
	g. In the Size For All Selected Disks box, **type 20** This means that you're going to use 20 MB on each of the selected disks.
	h. **Take a look at the Total Volume Size value.** Even though you're using 20 MB on each disk, you only have a total of 20 MB available for storage because the data is completely duplicated between the two disks. **Click Next.**
	i. **Assign drive letter M. Click Next.**
	j. **Change the volume label to Mirrored.**
	k. **Check Perform A Quick Format. Click Next.**
	l. **Click Finish** to create and format the new volume. It should show up in the list of volumes in Computer Management.
	m. **Click Exit** to close the simulation.

Lesson 8: Fixed Disk Storage Systems

Lesson 8

Procedure Reference: Mirror an Existing Volume

You can add a mirror to a simple volume that already exists on a Windows 2000 Server computer. To add a mirror to an existing simple volume:

1. In Disk Management, right-click the volume you want to mirror.
2. Choose Add Mirror.
3. Select the disk you want to mirror onto. This disk has to have enough free space to hold the contents of the original volume.
4. Click Add Mirror. The data from the original volume is mirrored onto the second disk.

ACTIVITY 8-14

Mirroring an Existing Volume

Data Files:

- Add.exe

Setup:

You will mirror the existing disk, Disk 1, onto Disk 2.

Your mirror will be 20 MB in size.

Scenario:

You have a disk on your Windows 2000 Server computer with critical data. You've added a second disk to the computer and you would like to create a mirror of the existing volume to fault-tolerance purposes.

Lesson 8

What You Do	How You Do It
1. Mirror the existing volume onto Disk 2.	a. From the C:\085811data\Simulations folder, **run Add.exe**.
	b. In the simulation window, **look at the configuration of Disk 1.** It has a 100 MB simple volume labeled Databases.
	c. **Right-click the Databases volume and choose Properties.**
	d. **Look at the amount of disk space being used.** Out of the 100 MB on the volume, about 2.5 MB are actually in use. **Click Cancel.**
	e. **Right-click the Databases volume and choose Open.** You can see in the Databases window that this volume contains a single database file.
	f. **Close the Databases window.**
	g. **Right-click the Databases volume and choose Add Mirror.**
	h. From the Disk list, **select Disk 2.** The disk you add to the mirror has to have at least as much free space as the total size of the volume you're mirroring.
	i. **Click Add Mirror.** The mirrored volume is generated, and the data is copied to the new member of the volume.
	j. In Disk Management, **look at the new mirrored volume.** The Databases volume has been extended onto Disk 2, and the disk status is Healthy. The disk takes up 100 MB on each of the member disks.
	k. **Click Exit** to close the simulation.

Lesson 8: Fixed Disk Storage Systems

Lesson 8

Procedure Reference: Recover from a Drive Failure

The whole point of creating a fault-tolerant configuration like a mirrored volume is that you can lose a drive without losing data. So if a member disk in a mirrored volume fails, Windows 2000 will direct all reads and writes to the remaining member. In Disk Administrator, you'll see the volume's status change to Failed Redundancy, which means the volume is working but isn't fault-tolerant any more. You should fix or replace the failed drive as soon as possible to regain fault tolerance. Or you can remove the fault-tolerant volume and just operate with a single drive in place of the set.

To repair a failed mirrored volume:

1. Shut down the system, replace or repair the failed disk, and restart the system.
2. In Disk Management, verify that the new drive is recognized. If need be, import it as a foreign disk.
3. If the disk's status isn't Online, right-click the disk and choose Reactivate Disk.
4. At this point, the volume status should return to Healthy. If not, you'll have to remove the failed part of the mirror and re-create it. Removing a mirror removes one copy of the data; you might do this with a healthy mirror if you wanted to reclaim the disk space for other uses.
   a. Right-click either part of the failed mirror and choose Remove Mirror to open the Remove Mirror dialog box.
   b. In the dialog box, select the failed drive and choose Remove Mirror. This exposes the working member of the set as a simple volume.
   c. Mirror the simple volume onto free space on a working disk.
5. You can break a mirror to expose both copies of the data as simple volumes. Right-click the volume and choose Break Mirror.

ACTIVITY 8-15

Removing and Replacing a Mirrored Volume

Data Files:
- Regen.exe

Scenario:

You have a mirrored volume between Disk 1 and Disk 2 on your Windows 2000 Server system. The power to Disk 1 was temporarily interrupted and then restored. Now you have to repair the mirror.

Lesson 8

What You Do	How You Do It
1. Remove and replace the mirrored volume.	a. From the C:\085811data\Simulations folder, **run Regen.exe**.
	b. **Look at the status of the volumes on Disk 1.** The mirrored Databases volume shows up with a Failed Redundancy status. This is what you might see if you repair a failed disk but the mirrored volume can't automatically regenerate.
	c. **Right-click the Databases volume on Disk 1 and choose Remove Mirror.**
	d. In the Remove Mirror dialog box, **make sure that Disk 1 is selected. Click Remove Mirror.**
	e. **Click Yes to confirm.** The mirrored volume is removed, and the Databases volume on Disk 2 is exposed as a simple volume.
	f. **Right-click the Databases volume on Disk 2. Choose Add Mirror.**
	g. In the Add Mirror dialog box, **select Disk 1. Click Add Mirror.** The mirror set regenerates, and the status returns to Healthy.
	h. **Click Exit** to end the simulation.

How to Create a RAID-5 Volume

Procedure Reference: Create a RAID-5 Volume

A RAID-5 volume in Windows 2000 Server is the equivalent of a stripe set with parity in Windows NT. You'll need at least three dynamic disks to make a RAID-5 volume. Keep in mind that you can't extend or mirror RAID-5 volumes. To create a RAID-5 volume in any Windows 2000 Server product:

1. Open Disk Management.

2. Right-click an area of unallocated space on the first dynamic disk that will be part of the striped volume with parity, and choose Create Volume to launch the Create Volume Wizard.

Lesson 8

3. Follow the prompts in the wizard to create a striped volume with parity that contains all the dynamic disks you want to include. The volume size number you enter will be the amount of space you'll use on each disk. The total size of the volume will be the volume size times the number of disks minus one. You must subtract the amount of one disk for overhead for your parity. The parity overhead will be 1/N the total amount of space, where N is the number of disks in the volume.

   You need at least three disks—at least two for the stripe set and one for the parity.

4. Finish the wizard. It will create and format the new volume.

ACTIVITY 8-16

Creating a RAID-5 Volume

Data Files:

- RAID.exe

Setup:

Your Windows 2000 Server system has three disks—Disk 1, Disk 2, and Disk 3.

The size of the stripe set you will be creating is 20 MB on each disk.

Scenario:

You have three dynamic disks on your Windows 2000 Server computer that you would like to create fault-tolerance and enhance data read-write performance on. You've decided to create a stripe set with parity across the three disks.

Lesson 8

What You Do	How You Do It
1. Create a RAID-5 volume across the three disks.	a. From the C:\085811data\Simulations folder, **run RAID.exe**.
	b. **Scroll down twice and then up once in the disks pane** to see the disk configuration. Disks 1 through 3 contain nothing but unallocated free space.
	c. **Right-click the unallocated space on Disk 1.**
	d. **Choose Create Volume and click Next** to launch the Create Volume Wizard.
	e. Under Volume Type, **select RAID-5 volume. Click Next.**
	f. Under All Available Dynamic Disks, **select Disk 2 and then click Add** to add Disk 2 to the RAID-5 volume.
	g. **Add Disk 3 to the volume.** You need at least 3 disks for a RAID-5 volume.
	h. In the Size For All Selected Disks box, **type *20***
	i. **Look at the Total Volume Size value.** The total is only 40 MB even though you're using 20 MB on each of 3 disks because of the overhead needed to store the parity information. The amount of disk overhead will be 1/N the total amount of space, where N is the number of disks in the volume.
	j. **Click Next.**
	k. **Assign drive letter R. Click Next.**
	l. **Change the volume label to RAID.**
	m. **Check Perform A Quick Format and click Next.**
	n. **Click Finish** to create and format the RAID-5 volume.
	o. **Scroll in the disks pane** to see the new

Lesson 8

volume. It includes space on Disks 1 through 3.

p. **Click Exit** to end the simulation.

Lesson 8 Follow-up

In this lesson, you identified and described the technical characteristics of fixed disk drives. You installed IDE and SCSI drives and troubleshot faulty storage systems.

1. **Contrast IDE and SCSI fixed disks.**

2. **Describe the master/slave relationship for IDE drives.**

Lesson 9
Removable Storage Systems

Lesson Time
2 hour(s)

Lesson Objectives:

In this lesson, you will identify the technical characteristics of common removable media disk drives.

You will:

- Install and maintain floppy disk drives.
- Install an optical disc drive.
- Identify the characteristics and function of cartridge disk drives.
- Identify system backup policies and procedures.

Lesson 9

Introduction

It is often necessary to share files with other people. One way to do this is to use removable disks. Another use for removable disks is to provide a second copy or backup of important files. In this lesson, you will examine the characteristics that define various kinds of removable disk drives, learn how to replace removable disk drives, and to identify which device is most appropriate for a particular application. You will also examine backup strategies for safeguarding your data using removable storage disks.

The following CompTIA A+ Core Hardware (2003) Examination objectives are covered in this lesson:

- Topic A:
  - 1.2 Identify basic procedures for adding and removing field-replaceable modules for desktop systems. Given a replacement scenario choose the appropriate sequences. Content includes: storage device—FDD; and removable storage.
  - 2.1 Recognize common problems associated with each module and their symptoms, and identify steps to isolate and troubleshoot the problems. Given a problem situation, interpret the symptoms and infer the most likely cause. Content includes: storage devices and cables—FDD.

- Topic B:
  - 1.2 Identify basic procedures for adding and removing field-replaceable modules for desktop systems. Given a replacement scenario choose the appropriate sequences. Content includes: storage device—CD/CDRW; DVD/DVDRW; removable storage.
  - 2.1 Recognize common problems associated with each module and their symptoms, and identify steps to isolate and troubleshoot the problems. Given a problem situation, interpret the symptoms and infer the most likely cause. Content includes: storage devices and cables—CD/CDRW; and DVD/DVDRW.

- Topic C:
  - 1.2 Identify basic procedures for adding and removing field-replaceable modules for desktop systems. Given a replacement scenario choose the appropriate sequences. Content includes: removable storage.

- Topic D:
  - 1.2 Identify basic procedures for adding and removing field-replaceable modules for desktop systems. Given a replacement scenario choose the appropriate sequences. Content includes: storage device—tape drive; and removable storage.
  - 2.1 Recognize common problems associated with each module and their symptoms, and identify steps to isolate and troubleshoot the problems. Given a problem situation, interpret the symptoms and infer the most likely cause. Content includes: storage devices and cables—tape drive; and removable storage.

Lesson 9

Topic A

Floppy Disk Drives

In the first personal computers, data storage was done exclusively on floppy disks. When hard disks were added to PCs as the primary storage area, floppy disks moved to the role of enabling data transfer and software installation. Today, the increasingly large size of software files and the proliferation of networked personal computers has pushed even these two roles off to newer technologies such as the CD-ROM, file servers, and Internet. However, the floppy disk still exists in many personal computers today because of its universality—the 3.5 inch 1.44 MB floppy drive is present on virtually every PC made in the last two decades, which makes a very useful tool for transferring files from one PC to another.

With the use of compression utilities, even moderate-sized files can be transferred to a floppy disk. Once you've transferred the file to the floppy disk and given it to another user, you can be confident that other user's PC will be able to read it. The PC 3.5-inch floppy is such a standard that many Macintosh, and even UNIX, computers can read them, thus making these disks useful for small, cross-platform file transfers.

For individual users, the floppy disk is still a useful method of storing and backing up small files. You will also find that the floppy disk is still used by hardware manufacturers for distributing driver software, although most software manufacturers have moved to CD-ROMs to distribute their software. In this topic, you will learn how floppy disk drives work and how to support them as an A+ technician.

Floppy Disk Drives

A floppy drive is a read/write drive that uses removable disks made of flexible Mylar plastic covered with a magnetic coating. The floppy Mylar disk itself is enclosed in a stiff, protective, plastic case. The vast majority of floppy drives are internal and connect to the motherboard through a floppy disk controller. The drive can access data on the disk directly. The form factor of floppy drives is usually 3.5 inches. Depending on the number of sectors per track on the disk, 3.5 inch floppy disks can usually hold 1.44 MB of data; the floppy drive can accommodate either disk capacity. 5.25-inch floppy disks and drives were once standard, but now are only seen on the very oldest computers still in use. Examples of a floppy drive and media are shown in Figure 9-1.

Lesson 9

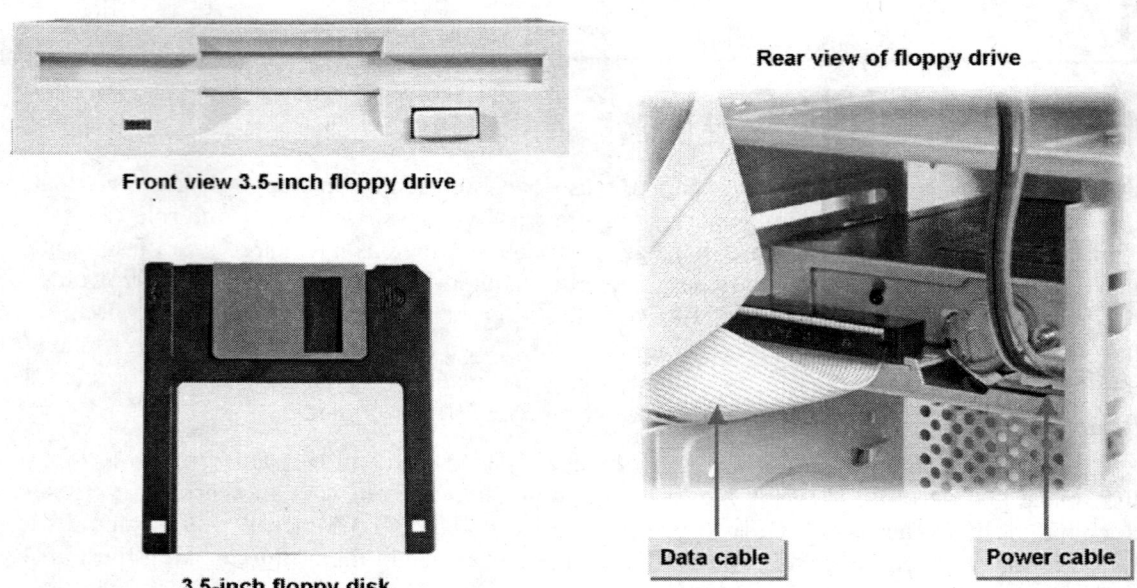

Figure 9-1: *Floppy disk drive.*

How Floppy Disk Drives Work

When you insert a floppy disk into a floppy disk drive:

1. The metal door slides open revealing the mylar disk surface. This disk is also referred to as a cookie.
2. The controller motor spins the floppy disk at about 360 RPMs.
3. A worm gear operated by a stepper motor moves the read/write heads (one on each side of the disk) to the desired track.

LESSON 9

Figure 9-2: *How floppy disk drives work.*

Write Protection

Floppy disks can be protected so that you cannot write over data on the disk. On the back side of the floppy disk, you will see a slider in the upper left corner. If the slider is pushed down, it blocks the write protect hole and allows you to write to the floppy disk. If the slider is pushed up and the write protect hold is visible, you will not be able to write to the disk.

Working with Floppy Disk Drives

Here are some things to keep in mind when you are installing or replacing a floppy drive:

- When you look at the back of the drive, the data connection is on the right and the power connection is on the left (or above the data connection). This configuration is the opposite of hard drives.
- For floppy drive data connectors, Pin 1 is on the left side. To connect the data cable, place the red strip on the cable nearest to the red wire on the power connection cable.

Lesson 9

- Data cables for floppy drives have a twist in them, so that the computer can recognize and distinguish between multiple floppy drives (drives A and B, usually) in a system. When you are connecting only one drive, connect it *after* the cable twist. When you are connecting more than one drive, connect drive A **after** the twist and drive B **before** the twist.

Figure 9-3: *Connectors for a typical 3.5-inch floppy disk drive.*

Replacing a Floppy Disk Drive

Procedure Reference: Replace a Floppy Disk Drive

To replace a floppy disk drive:

1. Remove the original floppy disk drive.
    a. Disconnect the power connector from the rear of the disk drive.
    b. Disconnect the controller cable from the rear of the disk drive.
    c. Remove the screws that mount the disk drive in the chassis bay.
    d. Slide the disk drive out of its bay.
2. Install the replacement floppy disk drive.
    a. Insert the disk drive into its bay.
    b. Mount the disk drive to the chassis using the appropriate screws.
    c. Connect the controller cable to the rear of the disk drive.
    d. Connect the power connector to the rear of the disk drive.
    e. Start the system and verify that the disk drive works properly.

ACTIVITY 9-1

Replacing a Floppy Disk Drive

Setup:
To complete this activity, you will need a computer and a compatible floppy disk drive.

Scenario:
John got a floppy disk stuck in his floppy disk drive. In his attempts to pry the disk out, he broke the drive. The purchasing department ordered a replacement and it has arrived. You've been assigned to remove John's broken drive and replace it with the new one.

What You Do	How You Do It
1. Remove the floppy-disk drive from the computer.	a. If necessary, **shut down the computer and unplug the power cord from the power supply.**
	b. **Disconnect the power connector from the rear of the disk drive.**
	c. **Disconnect the controller cable from the rear of the disk drive.**
	d. **Remove the screws that mount the disk drive in the chassis bay.**
	e. **Slide the disk drive out of its bay.**
	f. **Examine the controller cable connectors and power cable connector on the rear of the drive.** Notice that this data cable and power cable are different than those used on the hard drives.

Lesson 9: Removable Storage Systems

Lesson 9

2. **Connect the new floppy drive to the system.**

   a. Insert the disk drive into its bay.

   b. Mount the disk drive to the chassis using the appropriate screws.

   c. Connect the controller cable to the rear of the disk drive.

   d. Connect the power connector to the rear of the disk drive.

   e. Start the system and verify that the disk drive was properly installed.

How to Troubleshoot Floppy Disk Drives

Procedure Reference: Troubleshoot Floppy Drive Problems

To troubleshoot some of the most common problems with floppy drives:

1. If, when attempting to read data from the floppy disk, the user receives the error message This Disk Is Not Formatted. Do You Want To Format It Now Or Insert Disk Now?, you should:

   - Check that the disk is readable. You can do this by trying to read it in another floppy disk drive.
   - Try reinserting the floppy disk in the drive.
   - If you received the floppy disk from another user with data on it, determine if it was formatted on another operating system such as Macintosh or Linux. If it was, you will not want to format it as this would erase all of the data on the disk.
   - Verify that the floppy disk functions properly. The shuttle window should open and shut easily. There should be no foreign matter on the mylar disk surface. The mylar disk should spin easily within the plastic case.
   - Check the floppy disk for viruses.
   - Check the floppy disk for bad sectors.
   - Check whether or not other floppy disks can be read in the drive.

2. If the user cannot write to a floppy disk in the drive, you should:

   - Check that the floppy disk is not write-protected. If it is, move the switch to unprotect the floppy disk. Looking at the back side of the floppy disk, the slider on the upper left corner should be down, blocking the write-protect hole, in order to write to the floppy disk.
   - Verify that the floppy disk has been properly formatted. A floppy disk formatted using the native format on a Macintosh or Linux system for example cannot be read on a Windows system.
   - Verify that the floppy drive is working properly. Open the system and verify that the floppy drive cable and power connections are properly connected and

that the floppy drive mechanisms (you can often see some of them through the holes in the floppy drive case) are functioning properly when you insert a floppy disk in the drive.

- Clean the floppy drive read/write heads. You can purchase a special cleaning disk with a cleaning solution to insert in the drive. With the cleaning disk in the drive, you attempt to access the drive, causing the disk to spin and thus cleaning the drive.

3. The error message The System Cannot Find The Drive Specified indicates that the operating system cannot locate the floppy disk drive. You should check the CMOS settings to verify that the system knows there is a floppy drive, and then clean the drive, check the alignment of the drive, and check all connections (power and data cables) for the drive.

4. If you attempt to read a floppy disk and receive a message that the disk is not formatted, it was most likely formatted using a different operating system such as Macintosh or Linux. If so, then the original owner of the disk will need to provide the information to you on a medium that Windows can read. This might be over the network, or, on a Windows formatted floppy disk (both Macintosh and Linux can read and write to Windows formatted floppy disks).

5. If you can read and write to floppy disks on this system, but they cannot be read on another system, you should suspect that the drive is out of alignment. In a drive that is out of alignment, the read/write head is not properly aligned with the tracks on the disk and covers parts of tracks rather than a single track. While there are tools for adjusting the drive alignment, it is often cheaper to simply replace the drive. More information about the types of misalignment, causes, and methods for repairing the damage can be found at **www.accurite.com/FloppyPrimer.html**.

6. If none of the previous solutions fixed the problem, you might need to replace the floppy drive.

Lesson 9

Activity 9-2

Troubleshooting Floppy Drive Problems

Activity Time:

20 minutes

Scenario:

Users have opened trouble calls with the help center for the following problems which are related to the floppy drive on their systems.

- Ticket: 235001

    Location: Main building, 23D41

    User: Angharad Phatek

    When the user attempts to access the floppy drive, he sees the message This Disk Is Not Formatted. Do You Want To Format It Now Or Insert Disk Now?

- Ticket 235002

    Location: Main building, 32G37

    User: Gary Toomey

    The user cannot write to a disk in the floppy drive.

- Ticket: 235003

    Location: Elmwood Place, cube 37

    User: Zoe Isaacs

    When trying to access the floppy drive from the command prompt, she sees the message The System Cannot Find The Drive Specified.

- Ticket: 235004

    Location: Elmwood Place, cube 42

    User: Etta Romero

    User received a floppy disk containing important information from another user. When Etta tries to access the disk through Windows Explorer, she receives a message that the disk is not formatted.

Lesson 9

1. Identify some issues you should check in resolving trouble ticket 235001.

2. List the issues to check in resolving trouble ticket 235002.

3. What might cause the user to receive the error message shown in trouble ticket 235003?

4. What would you recommend to the user to resolve trouble ticket 235004?

Lesson 9

Topic B

Optical Disc Drives

Optical CD and DVD drives have become common in both home and business computers, so it's likely that you'll be supporting these types of drives. Problems with the drives can prevent users from accessing data or installing software they need to do their jobs. As a support technician, it's your responsibility to correct the problem to get the user back to work as quickly as possible. In this topic, you'll learn how to install, support, and troubleshoot problems with, optical disk drives.

Optical Disc Drives

Optical drives include CD-ROM (Compact Disc-Read Only Memory), CD-R (CD-Recordable), CD-RW (CD-Rewritable), DVD-ROM (Digital Video Disc-ROM or Digital Versatile Disc-ROM), DVD-R, and DVD-RW. They can be connected via IDE, SCSI, USB, FireWire, or parallel interfaces. Data is stored optically, rather than magnetically, and can be accessed directly. Optical drives use removable plastic discs with a reflective coating; data is written, by either pressing or burning with a laser to create pits (recessed areas) or lands (raised areas) in the reflective surface of the disc. Each pit represents a 0 and each land represents a 1. A laser in the disc drive then reads the data off the disc. CD-ROM and DVD-ROM discs are read-only; data is permanently burned on during manufacture. CD-R and DVD-R discs can be written to once; CD-RW and DVD-RW discs can be written to multiple times. Optical drives can be internal or external, and they have a 5.25-inch form factor. Examples of optical drives and media are shown in Figure 9-4.

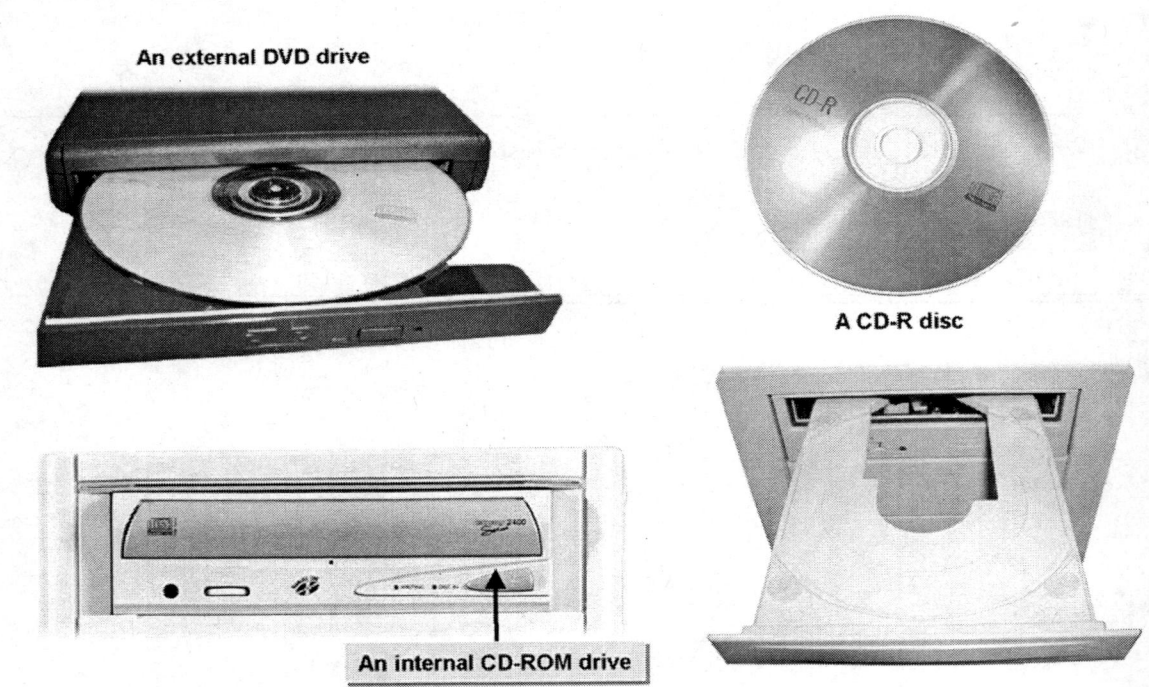

Figure 9-4: *Optical drives.*

Optical Disk Types

The two major types of optical discs are CD-ROM discs and DVD-ROM discs.

- CD-ROM discs store data on one side of the disc and most hold up to 700 MB of data, although older discs may only hold up to 650 MB of data. (Some CD-ROMs can hold up to 1GB). CD-ROM discs are widely used to store music as well as data. To meet the audio CD standard, the CD-ROM drive on a computer must transfer data at a rate of at least 150 kilobytes per second (150 KB/sec). Most CD-ROM drives deliver higher speeds: at least twice (2X, or double speed) or four times (4X, or quad speed) the audio transfer rate. There are also drives with much higher transfer rates. CD-ROM drives use one of two special file systems: CDFS (Compact Disc File System) or UDF (Universal Disc Format).
- DVD-ROM discs can typically hold 4.7 GB on one side of the disc; it is possible to write to both surfaces of the disc, in which case the disc can hold up to 9.4 GB. DVD drives access data at speeds from 600 KB/sec to 1.3 MB/sec. Because of the huge storage capacity and fast data access, DVD-ROM discs are widely used to store full-length movies and other multimedia content. DVD-ROM drives use UDF as the file system.

ATAPI

AT Attachment Packet Interface (ATAPI) is an extension to EIDE that enables support for CD-ROM drives (including CD-R and CD-RW drives), as well as tape drives on an IDE controller. You can install an ATAPI drive as if it were just another EIDE drive. With ATAPI drives, it's not necessary to perform CMOS configuration. All configuration is handled automatically. ATAPI drives can be set up as master or slave drives (through jumpers) and can run off the primary or secondary controller.

How to Install Optical Disc Drives

Procedure Reference: Install Optical Disc Drives

To install an optical drive:

1. Determine whether the optical disc device is installed internally within the PC by IDE or SCSI connection, or externally by USB, FireWire, or Parallel interface.
2. If an IDE or SCSI device, remove the computer case cover.
3. If an IDE drive:
   a. Locate an available drive bay, IDE data connection on the IDE controller cable, audio cable, and a power connector.
   b. Set the jumpers for cable select, master, or slave, as appropriate to your needs. There is usually a sticker on the top of the drive that specifies the jumper settings for each of these settings. If there is not a sticker, then the documentation for the drive will include this information.
   c. If necessary, attach rails to the drive to fit in the drive bay.
   d. Slide the drive into the bay, and then connect the controller, audio, and power cables.
   e. Restart the system, and if necessary, access CMOS setup to specify the drive type. You might need to know the number of cylinders, heads (tracks), and sectors on the disk as part of the CMOS setup procedure. You can usually find this information printed on a label on the drive or in the documentation that came with the drive.
   f. Verify that you can read data from the optical drive.

Lesson 9

4. If a SCSI drive:
   a. Set the drive ID on the drive. A sticker on the drive or the drive documentation will show how to set the ID and any other settings required to successfully install the drive.
   b. Determine which device is at the end of the chain and terminate each end of the chain. Remove termination from any other devices in the SCSI chain.
   c. Insert the drive in an available drive bay. If you are using a 5.25-inch drive bay and a 3.5-inch drive, you will need to install the drive using rails to adapt the drive to the larger bay.
   d. Connect the SCSI cable from the host bus adapter to the drive.
   e. Connect the power cable to the drive.
   f. Restart the system. If prompted, access CMOS setup and set the disk type, and then exit CMOS and save the settings.
   g. Verify that you can read data from the optical drive.
5. If an external USB, FireWire, or Parallel device:

   ⚠ Some devices require that you install the drivers before connecting the device to the system. Read the documentation that came with your device before completing these steps.

   a. With the computer and device turned off, connect the appropriate cable between the device and the system.
   b. If necessary, connect the AC adapter to the device and plug it into an electrical outlet.
   c. Turn on the device and the computer.
   d. Install appropriate drivers for the device.
   e. Verify that you can read data from the optical drive.

Practical Issues

Keep the following in mind when you are using optical drive resources:

- Some older optical drives require that the disc be placed in a disc caddy, or protective plastic container, before they can be inserted into the drive. You may want to consider purchasing additional caddies for storage purposes.
- Internal optical drives are connected to a host computer by using a SCSI bus or an IDE bus.
- If you put a SCSI optical drive on the same controller as a hard disk, you might see a performance loss. Check with the hardware vendors for known incompatibilities.
- When you connect the data cable and power to the drive, the configuration is similar to that of a hard drive—data cable to the left, power cable to the right, and red stripe closest to the red power wire.
- Make sure that the jumpers are set properly and that the audio cable is attached. Audio cables carry only analog sound; digital sounds are carried on the data cable.

Lesson 9

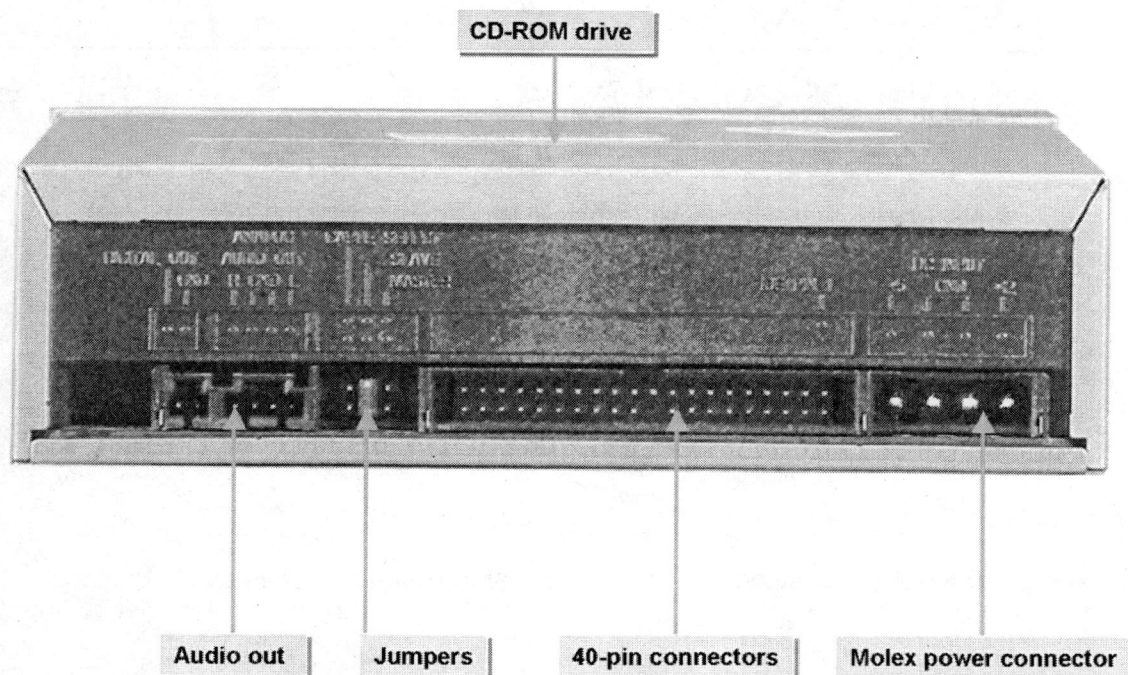

Figure 9-5: *Connectors for a typical CD-ROM drive.*

Using CD-ROMs

Some operating systems—such as UNIX, OS/2 2.x, Windows versions not requiring MS-DOS, and others—inherently support CD-ROM drives. Other operating systems, such as DOS, DOS/Windows, and some versions of NetWare, require additional software in order to use CD-ROM drives. CD-ROM drives often provide driver software for the operating systems that need them. Third-party driver software is also available.

Many CD-ROM drives use the SCSI interface to connect to the host system. A common interface for SCSI CD-ROM drives and other devices, called the Advanced SCSI Programming Interface, or ASPI, has been developed. This enables use of a single ASPI device driver for multiple SCSI devices. An example of such a driver is Adaptec's ASPIDSK.SYS.

Lesson 9

Activity 9-3

Replacing an IDE Optical Drive

Setup:

To complete this activity, you will need a computer and a compatible IDE optical drive.

You will also need a CD-ROM containing data to test the CD-ROM drive.

Scenario:

While the tray to Jane's optical drive was open, a large book fell from her shelf and broke off the tray. A new IDE was ordered and has arrived. You've been assigned to remove Jane's broken drive and replace it with the new one.

What You Do	How You Do It
1. Remove the old IDE CD-ROM drive from the computer.	a. Shut down the computer, and unplug the power cord from the power supply.
	b. Disconnect the power connector from the rear of the CD-ROM drive.
	c. Disconnect the controller cable from the rear of the CD-ROM drive.
	d. Disconnect the audio cable from the rear of the CD-ROM drive.
	e. Remove the screws that mount the CD-ROM drive in the chassis bay.
	f. Slide the CD-ROM drive out of its bay.

Lesson 9

2. Install the new IDE CD-ROM drive in the computer.

   a. Examine the controller cable connectors and the jumper block for master/slave configuration on the rear of the drive. Verify that the CD-ROM drive is set as master/single.

   b. Insert the CD-ROM drive into its bay.

   c. Mount the CD-ROM drive to the chassis using the appropriate screws.

   d. Mount the CD-ROM drive to the chassis using the appropriate screws.

   e. Connect the controller cable to the rear of the CD-ROM drive. Make sure the colored stripe on the controller cable lines up with Pin 1 on the drive.

   f. Connect the audio cable to the audio out connector at the rear of the CD-ROM drive.

   g. Connect the power connector to the rear of the CD-ROM drive.

   h. Verify you can read data from the CD-ROM drive.

Common Problems with Optical Drives

CD-ROM, CD-RW, CD-R, DVD-ROM, DVD-R, and DVD-RW drives are often referred to simply as CD and DVD drives. The following list of problems applies to any variation on CD and DVD drives.

- Misaligned case—Prevents drive door from opening and the tray from moving in and out properly.
- Tray out of balance—Inexpensive trays in drives or stickers that don't cover the entire surface of the disc can cause it to wobble because it throws the balance of the drive off. Data can be hard or impossible to read because of the wobble.
- Drive mechanism won't pull disc or tray in—The gears may be stripped, especially if the user pushed on the tray directly rather than using the buttons to manipulate the drive.
- CD drive won't release the CD—Sometimes it is because the software is still accessing the disc, or the tray can simply be stuck. You can use a straightened paper clip to insert in the hole in the front of the drive to release the catch on the drive so that you can remove the disc.

LESSON 9

- Disconnected wires—If you can't hear the sounds or music when you attempt to play an audio CD, then chances are that the wires from the CD drive to the sound card are disconnected. Other possibilities are that the speakers are turned off or down or that the sounds were muted through the Windows settings.
- Driver problems—If the drive is acting strangely and nothing seems to fix it, check the drivers. You might need to uninstall and reinstall the drivers to fix the problem.
- Overheating—If a CD-R or CD-RW drive overheats, there is a good chance that the CD you burn will not be readable. If you have an overheating problem, try fans, or try burning a single CD at a time rather than one right after the other.
- Software—If you want to view DVD movies on a DVD or DVD-R drive, you will need software to play the movie.
- The default audio device may not be set to the system's audio drive.

How to Troubleshoot Optical Drives

Procedure Reference: Troubleshoot Optical Drive Problems

To troubleshoot some of the most common optical drive problems:

1. If the optical drive door won't open:
   - Verify that there is power to the drive.
   - Press the Eject button on the drive.
   - Verify that no applications are attempting to read from the drive.
   - Open My Computer and right-click the drive icon, then choose Eject.
   - If all else fails, use a straightened paper clip to insert in the hole on the drive to manually push the gears that drive the drawer open. You may need to press firmly.

2. If the optical drive reads data and program disks, but the user can't hear audio CDs:
   - Verify that you can read a data CD.
   - Verify that speakers are connected properly to the sound card.
   - Verify that the speakers are powered and turned on.
   - Verify that the volume is turned up on the physical speakers.
   - Right-click the Volume icon in the System Tray and choose Open Volume Controls. Verify that Volume Control is not all the way down and that Mute is not checked. You can also adjust the volume through Control Panel.
   - Play a system sound:
     a. Open the Control Panel.
     b. Click Sounds, Search And Audio.
     c. Click Adjust The System Volume.
     d. Display the Sounds panel.
     e. Select an event, and then click the Play button next to Sounds to see if the associated sound for the event is played.
   - Verify that the audio cable inside the system case that connects the CD-ROM drive to the sound card is properly installed and that there are no broken wires.

- Verify that the correct sound drivers are installed.
    a. In Control Panel, display the Sounds, Speech, And Audio Devices dialog box, and then display the Hardware page.
    b. Verify that the Devices list includes the proper driver and that Audio Codes is listed.
    c. If not, use the Add/Remove Hardware program to add the appropriate drivers.
- Use the Troubleshooting Wizard for the Sounds, Speech, And Audio Devices.
- Attempt to play the default song in the Windows Media Player.
    a. From the Start menu, choose All Programs→Accessories→Entertainment→Windows Media Player.
    b. Choose Tools→Options.
    c. Display the File Types panel and verify that all File Types are checked.
    d. Click OK.
    e. Click the Play button to attempt to play the default song.
- Verify the default audio is set to the system audio drive.
    a. In Control Panel, open Sounds And Audio Devices.
    b. Select the Audio tab.
    c. Under Sound Playback, verify the audio drive is listed under Default Device.
    d. Click OK.
- Verify that the user can now play the audio CD.

3. If, after upgrading to Windows XP, a user can no longer access their CD/DVD drive:
    - Verify that the drive is on the Windows XP hardware compatibility list.
    - Verify that the drive is properly installed.
    - Verify that Windows Explorer lists a drive letter for the CD/DVD drive.
    - Verify that the appropriate driver is installed.
        a. Open My Computer.
        b. Right-click the drive icon and choose Properties.
        c. Display the Hardware panel.
        d. Verify that the appropriate driver is listed.
    - Use the Troubleshooting Wizard.
        a. Open My Computer.
        b. Right-click the drive icon and choose Properties.
        c. Display the Hardware panel.
        d. Click the Troubleshoot button and follow the prompts to troubleshoot the problem.

4. If there is a drive letter conflict, specify a free drive letter for the drive.
    a. On the taskbar, click Start, right-click My Computer, and then choose Manage.
    b. Under Computer Management, click Disk Management.

c. In the list of drives in the right pane, right-click the Removable Device and then click Change Drive Letter And Paths.

d. Click Change, and in the drop-down list, specify a drive letter for the Removable Device, choosing one that is not assigned to the mapped network drives.

e. Click OK twice.

5. If the user inserts a blank CD in the CD-RW drive, and the drive ejects it before the user can write to it:

- Confirm that the user has a CD-R or CD-RW drive and not just a CD-ROM drive in their system.
- Make sure the media is rated for the speed at which you are trying to write.
- Make sure the user is not trying to write more than the disc can hold. A CD can only hold approximately 700 MB of data.
- Check for software error messages that indicate what the problem might be.
- There might be debris inside the drive. Dust and other foreign matter can cause a drive to constantly eject the disc.
- Check whether the operating system or the hardware is causing the problem by unplugging the data cable from the drive before inserting the disc. If there is a pause before the disc is ejected or if the drive light blinks steadily, it might be because the media is defective or not high enough quality for the drive to use. Try a different brand of discs.
- If the hardware appears to be fine, the operating system might be causing the problem. Try disabling auto insert for all CD devices.

    a. In Device Manager, display properties for the CD-RW drive.

    b. Display the Settings page.

    c. Under Options, uncheck Auto Insert Notification. Be sure to leave Disconnect checked.

    d. Reboot for the changes to take effect.

- See if the CD-RW drive will write after the system has been off for awhile. Some systems overheat and have trouble writing when the drive gets too hot.

6. DVD drives can read and play CD-ROM and audio CDs as well as read DVD-ROMs. If you can't get video from a DVD disc, you might need to install decoder software to emulate the hardware decoder in stand-alone DVD players.

ACTIVITY 9-4

Troubleshooting Optical Drive Problems

Scenario:

The following are the trouble tickets related to CD-ROM, CD-R/RW, DVD, and DVD-R drives that have been assigned to you for resolution.

- Ticket: 232001

    Location: Main building, 31A57

    User: Nichole Lombard

    The door will not open on the CD-ROM drive. The user needs the CD that is in the drive.

- Ticket: 232002

    Location: Main building, 41A23

    User: Ruth Dalton

    User needs to be able to listen to audio CDs. System reads data and program CDs just fine.

- Ticket: 232003

    Location: Main building, 11A10

    User: Richard Alston

    The user's CD-RW drive was listed as D. A new drive was added to the system and now, the D drive does not point to the CD-ROM drive. Some applications cannot find the CD-ROM when he attempts to run the application even though the CD is in the drive.

- Ticket: 232004

    Location: Main building, 12D52

    User: Mark Glick

    User needs to burn a CD and the drive keeps ejecting the CD media before he can write the disc.

- Ticket: 232005

    Location: Elmwood Place, cube 7

    User: Jennifer Kulp

    The user needs to be able to watch DVDs on her system. She can read CDs, play audio CDs, and read data DVDs in the drive.

Lesson 9

What You Do	How You Do It
1. Resolve trouble ticket 232001.	a. Verify that there is power to the drive.
	b. Press the Eject button on the drive.
	c. Verify that no applications are attempting to read from the CD-ROM.
	d. Open My Computer. Right-click the CD-ROM drive icon and choose Eject.
	e. Straighten out a small paper clip, and then insert the end into the hole on the front of the CD-ROM drive.

2. Resolve trouble ticket 232002.

   a. Verify that you can read a data CD.

   b. Verify that speakers are connected properly to the sound card.

   c. Verify that speakers are properly powered and turned on.

   d. Verify that volume is turned up on the physical speakers.

   e. In the System Tray, **right-click the Volume icon and choose Open Volume Controls.**

   Verify that Volume Control is not all the way down and that Mute is not checked.

   f. Play a system sound such as the Asterisk.

   g. Verify that the proper sound device drivers are installed.

   h. Verify the audio drive is the default sound playback device.

   i. In the Sounds And Audio Devices window, select the Hardware tab and click Troubleshoot. Follow the prompts in the Troubleshooting Wizard to attempt to resolve the problem.

   j. Open the Windows Media Player and attempt to play the default song.

   k. Verify that the audio cable inside the case that connects the CD-ROM to the sound card is properly installed and that there are no broken wires.

   l. Verify that the user can now play the audio CD.

3. Regarding trouble ticket 232003, explain to the user what the reason for their problem is and what needs to be done to correct it.

Lesson 9: Removable Storage Systems

Lesson 9

4. What would you suggest that the user try in resolving trouble ticket 232004?

5. After checking over the hardware for the DVD drive on the system, you find no problems. What else might the problem be in trouble ticket 232005?

Topic C
Cartridge Disk Drives

Removable cartridge drives have been available for a long time, but back in the 1980s, there were few options to choose from. Those that were available (such as the Bernoulli boxes), were prone to many problems and were quite expensive. As storage prices came down and storage needs rose, a new generation of removable drives came onto the scene. The first popular version of these was the Zip drive. Syquest and SuperDisk soon followed with their own versions of removable disk drives. In this topic, you will examine the characteristics of the various cartridge disk drives that were available.

Cartridge Disk Drives

Cartridge drives are internal or external, read/write drives that store data magnetically on a removable cartridge. They can be connected via IDE, SCSI, USB, FireWire, or parallel interfaces. Data can be accessed directly. The size of these drives varies, but they usually have a 5.25-inch form factor. Examples of cartridge drives and media are shown in Figure 9-6.

Lesson 9

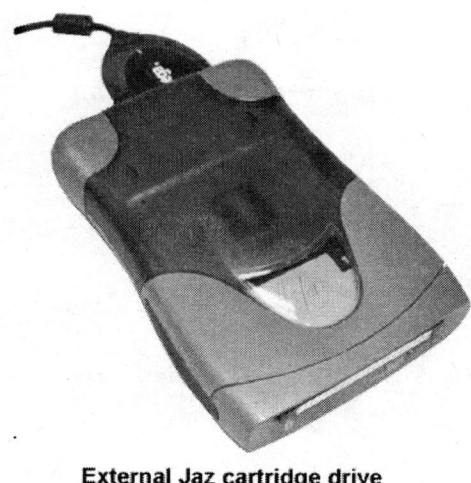

External Jaz cartridge drive with cartridge inserted

Rear view of SCSI external Zip drive

Zip cartridge

Figure 9-6: *Cartridge drives.*

How Removable Cartridge Drives Work

When you insert a cartridge in a removable cartridge drive:

1. The metal door slides open revealing the mylar disk surface. This disk is also referred to as a cookie.

2. A hub in the drive engages with the center hole of the disk. The hub enables the disk to spin at roughly 3,000 RPMs. This is faster than a floppy disk spins but not as fast as a hard drive spins.

3. Read/write heads move into the opening on the case. There is one for each side of the disk. The heads lightly touch the disk surface. The heads are smaller than those for floppy drives by a factor of about 10.

 The disk is coated with high energy level particles that enable more bits to be packed into a smaller area. It also uses zoned sectors to increase the capacity of the disk.

Lesson 9: Removable Storage Systems

Lesson 9

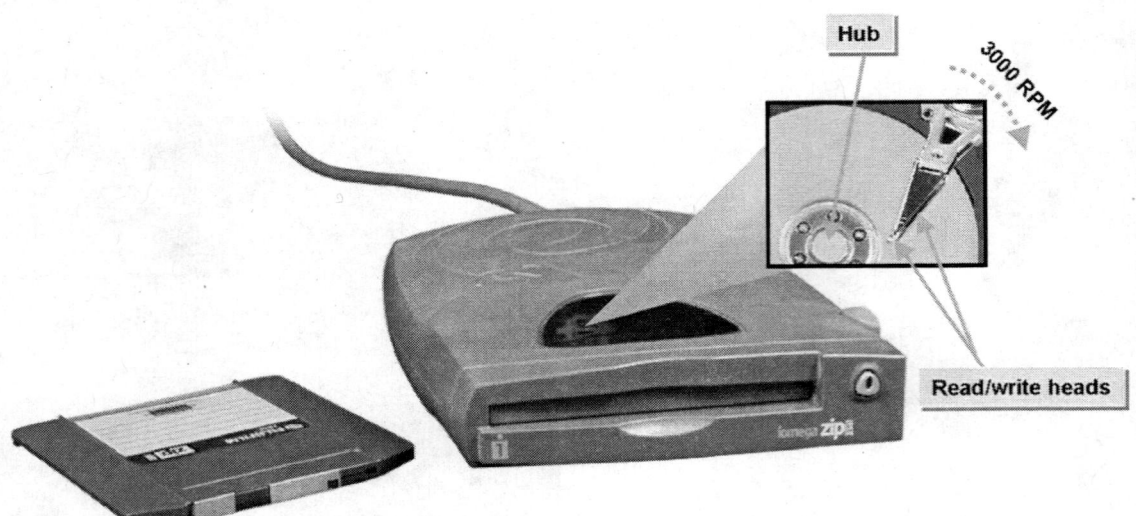

Figure 9-7: *How removable cartridge drives work.*

Syquest Drives

SYQT, Inc. (formerly known as SyQuest Technology, Inc.) came up with the idea of removable hard disk cartridges back in 1982. Their current offerings include the removable cartridge drives shown in Table 9-1.

Table 9-1: *Syquest Drives*

Name	Description
SparQ	A 1 GB cartridge for PCs with a parallel port or EIDE interface. The speeds are equivalent to most hard disks.
SyJet	A 1.5 GB cartridge for PCs and Macs. Interface choices include parallel port, and internal and external EIDE and SCSI. Macs can only use the SCSI version. Seek time is 12 ms and average transfer rate is 6.9 MB per second.

Zip Drives

Iomega's Zip disks are slightly larger and twice as thick as regular 3.5-inch disks. The Zip drive can only read Zip disks. The original Zip disk was 100 MB and connected through the parallel port. Currently, there are also 250 MB and 750 MB versions. Larger zip drives are backward-compatible and can read the lower storage size cartridges. Iomega's Zip drives can be used in both PCs and Macs. Connection options now include external USB, FireWire, parallel, and SCSI; as well as internal ATAPI.

Lesson 9

Jaz Drives

Another Iomega product, the Jaz drive comes in 1 GB and 2 GB versions. The 2 GB drive can also read 1 GB cartridges. The Iomega Jaz drive is considered a legacy device as it is no longer manufactured. When it was being manufactured, it was available in Ultra SCSI PCI, SCSI ISA, SCSI-to-parallel, and SCSI-to-PCMCIA connections. Currently, the Iomega Corporation only supports the 2 GB internal SCSI and external Ultra SCSI models. The average access time is 10 ms. The transfer rate is about the same as for a hard drive. Iomega's Jaz drives can be used in both PCs and Macs.

SuperDisk Drives

Imation Corporation's SuperDisk uses super-high-density 3.5-inch disks. They are formatted at the factory in a servo pattern with 2,490 tracks. This means that you can store 120 MB of data per disk. The SuperDisk Drive can also read regular 3.5-inch 1.44 MB disks (which have only 135 tracks). SuperDisk is available with parallel port, SCSI, USB, internal, and PCMCIA connections. Imation has discontinued the manufacture of Imation SuperDisk diskettes and drives.

ACTIVITY 9-5

Discussing Cartridge Disk Drives

Activity Time:

5 minutes

Scenario:

In this activity, you will discuss cartridge disk drives.

1. Cartridge drives are available in which connection types?

    a) IDE

    b) SCSI

    c) USB

    d) FireWire

    e) Serial

2. True or False? The disk in a cartridge drive is referred to as a cookie.

    __ True

    __ False

3. The hub in a cartridge disk drive enables the disk to spin at roughly 3,000 RPMs. True or False? This is faster than both floppy and hard disks spin.

    __ True

    __ False

Lesson 9: Removable Storage Systems

4. Which cartridge disks are no longer manufactured and considered legacy devices?

   a) Syquest drives

   b) Zip drives

   c) Jaz drives

   d) SuperDisk drives

Topic D

Backup Systems

Consider the value of the data stored on your PC. A week's worth of changes and additions to files or to a database have greater value than the entire system on which it is stored.

As companies use PCs for more and more of their business communications and data storage, the value of the information kept on these systems increases dramatically. The loss of any of this information can be devastating to a company. Therefore, it is essential that companies back up this information. In this topic, you will learn how to back up your data on PC systems and then troubleshoot problems with the removable tape drive systems you use for backup.

Backup

You can use the backup utilities included with the operating system, or you can purchase third-party backup products. Many organizations have developed backup software to address this need. When you plan the implementation of a backup system, you should consider the following questions:

- What backup media will you use?
- Does the system give you the performance and reliability you need?
- Is the system flexible and easy to use?
- In the event of a disaster, will the recovery be complete?
- How fast can the system be up and running again?

Tape Drives

In order to back up your systems, you will need a tape drive or other device. Tape drives are internal or external, read/write drives that store data magnetically on a removable tape. They can be connected via IDE, SCSI, USB, FireWire, or parallel interfaces, although they are most often connected to your system through a SCSI adapter due to its higher access speeds over other connection types. Data on the tape must be read sequentially. The size of these drives varies, but they often have a 5.25-inch form factor. An example of a tape drive is shown in Figure 9-8. The tape drive you use will determine the type of media you use to back up to.

Lesson 9

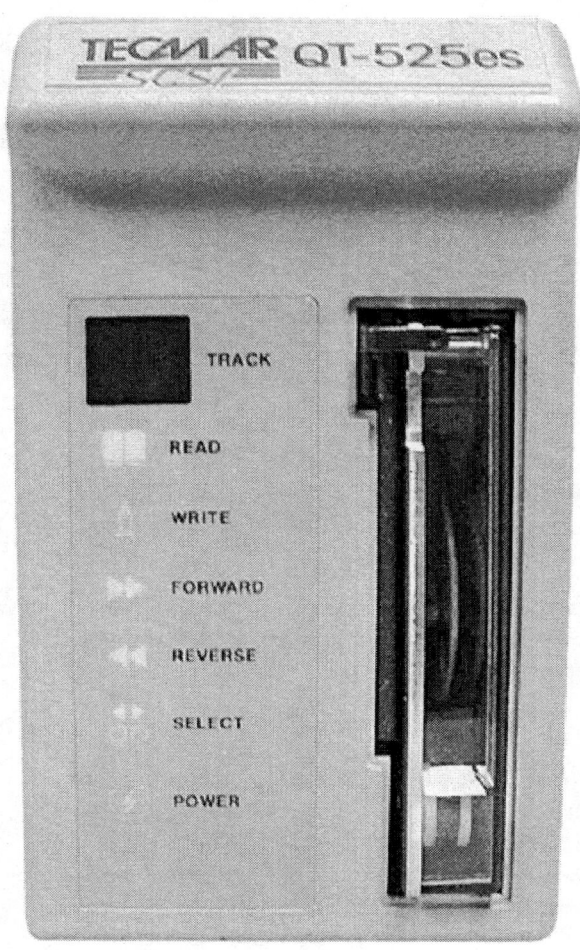

Figure 9-8: *Tape drive.*

Quarter-Inch Cartridge

Quarter-Inch Cartridge (QIC) technology is among the oldest, most standardized, and most reliable of the tape technologies. QIC drives are available for most computer platforms.

QIC cartridges are available in 60 MB, 150 MB, 250 MB, 525 MB, and larger sizes. Most of the drives designed to read the higher-capacity cartridges can also read the lower-capacity cartridges.

Two of the biggest detractions to QIC technology are cost and speed. QIC drives are inexpensive; however, the cartridges are expensive when dollars per megabyte is considered. Quarter-inch cartridge drives are slow, having about the slowest transfer rates of any of the tape technologies.

4 mm DAT

Originally adapted from the audio market, the 4 mm *DAT* tape format offers higher storage capacities at a lower cost than does QIC technology. The term DAT, or Digital Audio Tape, is often used to describe 4 mm tape technology.

DAT cartridges are quite small compared with QIC cartridges, and therefore, are much easier to store and use. Capacities for 4 mm tapes range from 1 GB to 12 GB and more.

Lesson 9

DAT tapes are considered to be less reliable than QIC tapes. They are especially vulnerable to heat and moisture. Because the tape is pulled out of the cartridge during operation, to be wrapped around the spinning read/write head, the tapes wear more quickly than do QIC tapes.

Due to lack of strict standards, 4 mm tape drives are not always compatible: tapes from one drive might not be readable in another drive. This will probably only be a problem for larger installations with a large variety of computing equipment.

8 mm (Exabyte)

The 8 mm tape format was originally developed by Exabyte, which continues to be the only manufacturer of 8 mm drives. Many other manufacturers purchase raw drives from Exabyte and integrate them into internal or external 8 mm tape drives. This arrangement ensures compatibility between 8 mm drives.

These 8 mm tape drives offer storage capabilities between 2.2 GB and 10 GB per cartridge. The tape cartridges are only slightly larger than DAT tapes. They are often considered more reliable than 4 mm drives; however, the drives and tapes are more expensive than 4 mm units.

The 8 mm tape drives are popular in the UNIX and workstation industry. These drives have only recently become popular with network administrators as the amount of data on LANs has grown.

DLT

Digital Linear Tape (DLT) was developed by DEC who sold this technology to Quantum. The tape is a half-inch cartridge with a single hub. There are 128 or 208 linear tracks, holding 10 to 35 GB of data. Another DLT format, Super DLT, holds up to 50 GB. Currently, DLT transfer rates are in the 1.25 MB to 5 MB per second range. The forecast is for DLT to soon hold up to 500 GB with up to 40 MB per second transfer rates.

Table 9-2: *Popular Backup Media*

Media	Maximum Storage Sizes	Description
Digital Audio Tape (DAT)	At least 1 GB, up to 12 GB	Used in many different size networks; 4 mm tape, about the size of an audio tape.
Digital Linear Tape (DLT)	At least 10 GB, up to 50 GB	Used mainly in mid- to large-size networks; 0.5-inch cartridges.
Quarter-Inch Cartridge (QIC)	At least 40 MB, up to 525 MB	Original width was 0.25-inch; available in 3.5-inch (Traven) or 5.25-inch cartridges; usually used in smaller networks and stand-alone PCs.
8 mm (Exabyte)	At least 2.2 GB, up to 10 GB	Popular in the UNIX and workstation industry. Exabyte is the only manufacturer of the drives.

How Tape Drives Work

Whereas hard drives, floppy drives, and removable cartridge drives are direct access devices, tape drives are sequential access devices. Rather than being able to go to a specific file directly, with a tape, you have to read past every file on the tape until you get to the one you want. For this reason, tape drives are typically used to store backup copies of information, not for live data access.

When you insert a tape cartridge in a tape drive and perform a backup of files from your hard drive:

1. The computer reads the file system table on the hard drive, locates the files that you want to back up, and begins reading file data into RAM.
2. Data is then dumped from RAM to the tape drive controller buffer as memory fills.
3. The controller sends commands to the drive to start spooling the tape.
4. The capstan in the center of the supply reel turns the rollers in the cartridge. The belt around the tape and the rollers provide resistance and keeps the tape taught and tight to the drive heads.
5. Data is sent from the controller to the read/write heads.
6. The tape is composed of parallel tracks. Data is written from the center out towards the edge on each pass. Holes in the end of the tape signal when the direction of the tape needs to be reversed. When it gets to the end, it reverses and moves out one track.

Backup Methods

When you plan your backup methods, it is important to establish a policy and to set up procedures to be followed. Some considerations include:

- *Hardware*—Choosing the appropriate hardware for your environment.
- *Assignment of backup administration*—Who is responsible for performing the backup?
- *Backup frequency*—Evaluating the cost of potential data losses and establishing an acceptable minimum backup frequency.
- *Backup types*—Choosing the appropriate backup method for your organization.
- *Backup set*—The number of tapes (or other media) required to complete a backup.
- *When the backup is performed*—Evaluating the best time to run the backup, depending on your needs.
- *Data identification*—Labeling backup media and storing it in the safest possible location.
- *Data testing*—Occasional testing of backup data.
- *Maintenance schedule*—Hardware and media maintenance (or replacement).
- *Recovery operation plan*—Laying out a specific plan for the complete recovery of lost data.
- *Backup methods*—The structure of how backup media are rotated in and out of the backup schedule.

Rotation Method and Backup Types

Everybody's backup schedule varies; however, it is a good idea to maintain a minimum daily backup to update new and changed data. Different criteria help to determine the best strategy for backing up data.

 In a network environment, backups are usually taken care of for you by your system administrator. However, if they don't back up often enough for your needs, you might need to perform your own backups in between their backups.

Lesson 9

Rotation Methods

A common, secure backup rotation method is the Grandfather method. One backup set is designated for Mondays, one for Tuesdays, one for Wednesdays, and one for Thursdays. These backup sets are reused on the same day the following week. Every Friday during the month, you use a new backup set. The next month, these Friday backup sets are reused in the same order. At the end of each month, a new backup set is used. Depending on your needs, these monthly backup sets can be reused the following year or kept as a permanent record and replaced with new backup sets.

Label each of the daily backup sets with the name of the day of the week; label the weekly tapes with numbers 1 through 4 for each Friday; and label the monthly tapes with the name of the month.

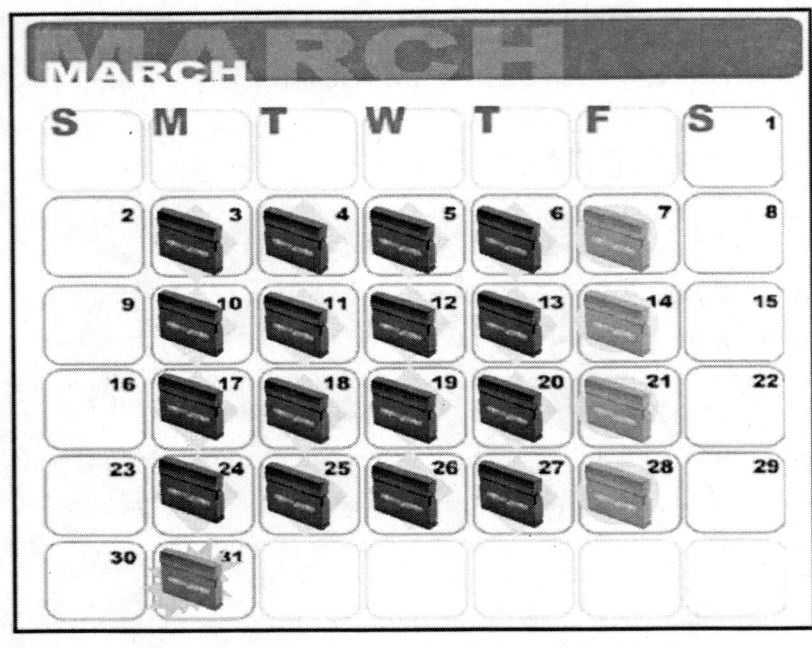

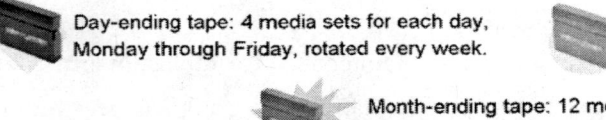

Figure 9-9: *The Grandfather backup method.*

Another backup rotation method in use at some companies is the Tower of Hanoi method. In this method, five media sets are used. Media set A is used every other day (two days apart). Media set B is used every fourth day. Media set C is used every eighth day. Media set D is used every sixteenth day. Media set E is alternated with Media set D. This doubles the backup history with each media set used (two, four, eight, or 16 days until the media set is overwritten). This enables you to have media sets with the most recent versions of files (those media sets used most frequently, such as sets A and B).

Label each of the media sets with a letter or number (Media set 1 or A). You can apply this rotation method to a daily or weekly rotation schedule. Five media sets is the minimum required when performing a daily rotation, and eight media sets are required for a weekly rotation.

You should archive media sets as needed. For example, you might save the E set each month for a permanent archive. The tape sets you pull for archive will be based on your company needs.

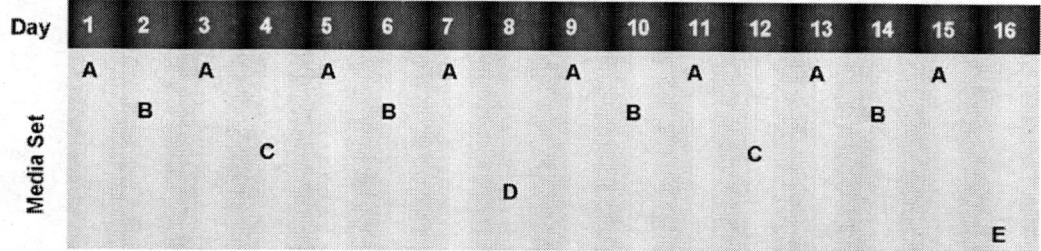

Media Set	Used Every
A	2 days
B	4 days
C	8 days
D & E	16 days alternating between set D and E

Figure 9-10: *The Tower of Hanoi backup method.*

Backup Types

Table 9-3 describes the different backup types supported by some backup utilities.

Table 9-3: *Backup Types*

Backup Type	Description
Full	All information is backed up, regardless of whether it has been backed up before.
Incremental	New files and files that were created or modified since the last **full** or **incremental** backup are backed up.
Differential	All files that were created or modified since the last **full** backup are backed up.

Lesson 9

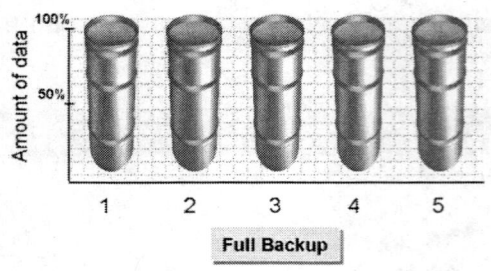
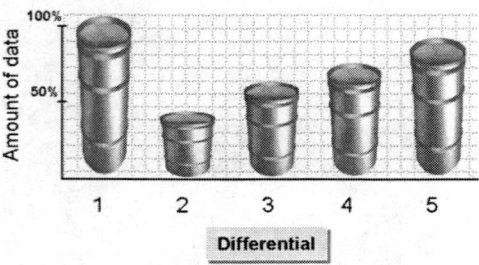
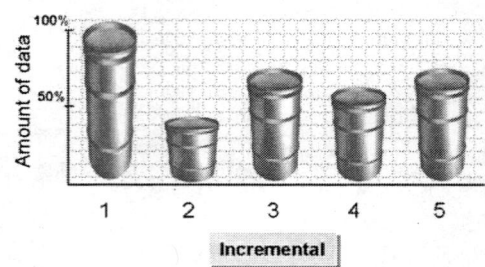

Figure 9-11: *Relative time to back up data.*

Although an incremental backup combined with a regularly scheduled full backup is usually the fastest type of backup to perform, any time that you need to perform a full restore, you must restore the last full backup plus every incremental backup since the last full backup (in the same order they were backed up). This process can be become very time-consuming.

In the long run, it might be more advantageous to perform differential backups, combined with a regularly scheduled full backup, because all new or modified files since the last full backup are included, and you would need only two media sets to perform a full restore. Each differential backup following the last full backup will take an increasing amount of time. Because differential backups are based on the last backup that cleared the archive bit, you should not mix incremental and differential backups. Differential backups count on the archive bit **not** being cleared. Any differential backups following an incremental backup would not back up all of the modified files since the last full backup because the archive bit was cleared with the incremental backup.

If you choose to perform full backups every time you back up your data, be aware that a full backup takes the longest amount of time. On the other hand, it is also the method that allows the fastest full restores, because you will need only one media set to restore data.

Backup Types and Their Backup and Restore Time Requirements

Table 9-4 summarizes each of the three backup schemes and describes how long a full backup and full restore will take for each scheme, measured in relative time.

Table 9-4: *Backup Scheme Time Comparisons*

Backup Type	Relative Time Necessary to Perform a Full Backup	Relative Time Necessary to Perform a Full Restore
Full backup only	Longest	Shortest
Incremental backup with full backup	Shortest	Longest

Backup Type	Relative Time Necessary to Perform a Full Backup	Relative Time Necessary to Perform a Full Restore
Differential backup with full backup	Time increases each day; shorter than full backup, overall, but longer than an incremental backup	Shorter than an incremental backup, but longer than full backup

Using Figure 9-11, Table 9-5 compares the number of tapes required to restore data. The necessary tapes and amount of time for restoring data depends on what is being restored and the type of backup that was used.

Table 9-5: *Tape and Time Data for Backups*

When Restoring	Full	Incremental	Differential
Full week	One tape from Day 5	All five tapes	Tapes 1 and 5
All data up to Day 3	One tape from Day 3	Tapes 1, 2, and 3	Tapes 1 and 3

Storage

It is advisable to keep backup media in a safe location, preferably in a locked, fire-safe room. In addition, you should consider moving at least one full backup per week to an offsite location. Many companies offer this service and store your tapes in a locked and fire-safe area. Consider how critical your data is when you decide how often to move backups offsite. A disadvantage of offsite storage is that, when you need to restore data, you will have to involve a third party in delivering the media back to your location. This process can be time-consuming.

ACTIVITY 9-6

Discussing Backup Strategies

Activity Time:
5 minutes

Scenario:
In this activity, you will discuss backup strategies.

1. How many tape sets are required when using the Grandfather rotation method?

Lesson 9

2. How many tape sets are required when using the Tower of Hanoi rotation method?
   a) One
   b) Three
   c) Five
   d) Seven

3. Match the backup type with its description.

   ___ Full   a. New files and files created or modified since the last full or incremental backup are backed up and the archive bit is cleared.

   ___ Incremental   b. All information is backed up.

   ___ Differential c. All files created or modified since the last full backup are backed up and the archive bit isn't cleared.

4. List some of the backup media choices available today.

Common Problems with Internal Removable Media Devices

The following concerns might arise when dealing with internal removable media devices:

- If the computer case is not properly aligned with the chassis, the opening for the internal drive might be difficult to access.
- Because there are large openings in the case for these devices, it is common for them to gather large amounts of dust, so be sure to keep them clean.
- Be sure to properly store the media so it is not dirty or damaged. Using dirty or damaged media can damage the drive.

How to Troubleshoot and Correct Internal Removable Media Device Problems

Procedure Reference: Install and Use IomegaWare Utilities

To install and use IomegaWare utilities for Iomega drives:

1. Download the IomegaWare software if you do not have a current version available on CD-ROM.
2. Following the instructions that came with the CD-ROM or the downloaded file, install the software.
3. When you access the Iomega drive through Windows Explorer or other such utilities, you should now see several additional menu options with the Iomega symbol preceding them.

ACTIVITY 9-7

Installing and Using IomegaWare Utilities

Setup:
To complete this activity, you need to connect an Iomega brand removable cartridge drive to your system. This might be a Zip, Jaz, USB PocketZip (Clik!), HipZip, FotoShow, or Peerless device.

Scenario:
You installed an Iomega removable cartridge storage drive. You would like to install the IomegaWare utilities that shipped with the device, but the cartridge has been reformatted and used to store data files.

What You Do	How You Do It
1. What options are listed when you right-click the Iomega removable disk drive in My Computer?	
2. Download the IomegaWare software.	a. Access *www.iomega.com/software/ioware402pc.html*.
	b. Click the Download Now link.
	c. Fill out the Software Registration page, and then click Submit.
	d. Click Save.
	e. In the Save As dialog box, **verify that Save In is set to the Desktop.**
	f. Click Save.

LESSON 9

Lesson 9

3. **Install the IomegaWare software.**
    a. On the Desktop, **double-click the ioware-w32x86402.exe file.**

    b. **Click Next.**

    c. **Click Yes.**

    d. **Click Next.**

    e. **Click Close.**

    f. With Shut Down Now selected, **click OK.**

Lesson 9

4. Verify that the installation was successful and that you can use the tools that were installed.

   a. **Restart your computer and log on to Windows XP.**

   b. **Open My Computer.**

   c. **Right-click the removable cartridge drive.**

   d. **Verify that some of the menu options have the Iomega symbol in front of them.**

   e. **Choose Properties.**

   f. **Click the Iomega tab.**

   g. In the Disk box, **click More Information.**

   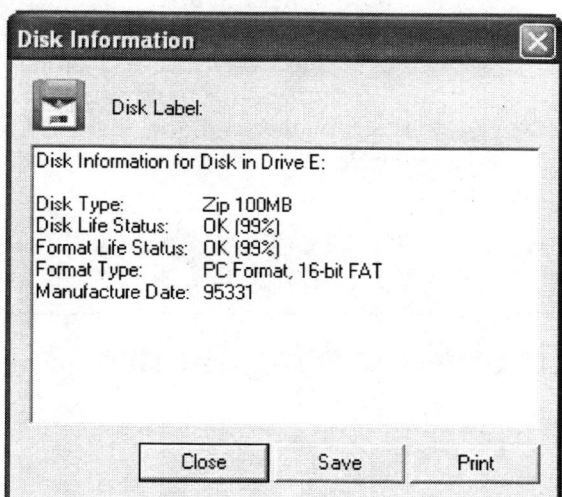

   h. **Click Close.**

   i. **Click Cancel.**

Procedure Reference: Troubleshoot Removable Cartridge Drive Problems

To troubleshoot some of the most common problems with removable cartridge drives:

1. If no drive letter is displayed in Windows Explorer for a removable cartridge drive, verify that the drivers for the drive have been installed on the system. If that is not the problem, verify that the drive is connected to the proper port with the proper cable. After fixing either of these problems, you should restart the system.

2. If the user cannot write to the removable media:

- Check that it has not been write protected. This might be a software enabled write protection or a physical write protection on the disk depending on the media you are using.
- If the disk still cannot be written to, try another disk in the drive.
- If the disk still cannot be written to, verify that the drive is properly connected to the system and that the power supply is plugged in for external models.
- If the disk still cannot be accessed, try moving the drive as far from the monitor, speakers, power supplies, or other electronic devices as possible. There might be interference from the devices.

3. If the media was formatted under an operating system other than Windows, you might have problems reading or writing to it. You can sometimes view the properties of the drive to determine the format of the disk.

4. If the disk will not come out of the drive, you can try using a straightened paper clip. Most drives have a hole that you can insert the paper clip wire into then press it to manually release and eject the disk from the drive mechanism.

5. The original Zip drive used the parallel port. The parallel cable that it came with is not always compatible with the default settings on current parallel ports. You might need to change the settings so that the port is not using unidirectional or ECP settings. It should use bidirectional settings. After making the change, restart the computer and now that ECP has been disabled, you should be able to access the drive.

ACTIVITY 9-8

Troubleshooting Removable Cartridge Drive Problems

Setup:

Prior to resolving each scenario in this activity, you will need to connect the drive if you don't have the specific drive indicated connected to your system. You can then have the instructor simulate the problem you are troubleshooting. The IomegaWare software has been installed.

Scenario:

Some of your users have high capacity removable cartridge drive systems including Zip, Jaz, LS120, and LS240 drives. The following are the trouble tickets that have been assigned to you related to those devices.

- Ticket: 234001

    Location: Main building, 42E51

    User: Daniel Price

    User cannot access the Zip drive because no drive letter is being displayed for the device.

- Ticket: 234002

    Location: Main building, 24A61

    User: Naomi Lincoln

User cannot write to Jaz drive. She can see the drive letter, but when she tries to write to the disk, she gets an error message.

- Ticket: 234003

  Location: Elmwood Place, cube 18

  User: Yolande Vaughan

  The user is having problems accessing data on a Zip disk. She is not sure whether it was formatted for a Macintosh system or Windows system. She needs to access the information on a PC.

- Ticket: 234004

  Location: Training center, main office

  User: Sara Jenks

  User has a SuperDisk drive and the cartridge won't come out of the drive.

What You Do	How You Do It
1. **Resolve trouble ticket 234001.**	a. If necessary, **connect a Zip drive to your system.**
	b. **Open My Computer.**
	c. **Determine whether there is an icon for the Zip drive.**
	d. If not, **verify that the driver is loaded for the drive and load it if it has not been loaded.**
	e. **Verify that the drive is connected to the proper port with the proper cable.**
	f. **Restart the system.**
	g. If the problem is still not resolved, **access the troubleshooting guide at *www.iomega.com/support/documents/11076.html*, following links as needed until the problem is resolved.**

Lesson 9

2. **Resolve trouble ticket 234002.**

    a. If necessary, **connect a Jaz drive to your system.**

    b. **Right-click the Jaz drive icon and choose Protect.**

    c. **Select Not Protected, and then click OK.**

    d. If the disk still cannot be read, **try to use another disk in the drive.**

    e. If the disk still cannot be read, **verify that all cables are correctly connected.**

    f. If the disk still cannot be read, **move the drive as far from the monitor, speakers, power supplies, or other electronic devices as the cables will enable you to place the drive.**

3. **Resolve trouble ticket 234003.**

    a. If necessary, **connect a Zip drive to your system.**

    b. **Right-click the Zip drive letter and choose Properties.**

    c. **Display the Iomega panel, and then in the Disk Box, click More Information.**

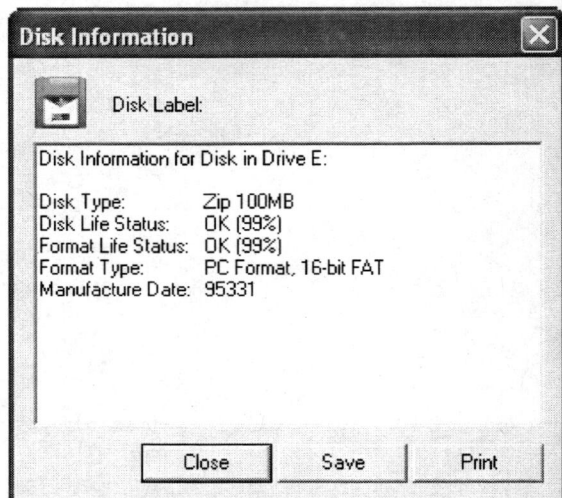

    d. **Verify that the disk is formatted for PC use.**

    e. **Click Cancel.**

388   *A+™ Certification: Core Hardware Third Edition - A CompTIA Certification*

4. Resolve trouble ticket 234004.

   a. If necessary, **connect a SuperDisk drive to your system.**

   b. **Right-click the drive letter and choose Eject.**

   c. If this does not work, **straighten a small paper clip.**

   d. **Insert the end of the paper clip in the hole to release the catch and eject the cartridge.**

Lesson 9 Follow-up

In this lesson, you examined the characteristics that define various kinds of removable disk drives. You learned how to replace removable disk drives and to identify which device is most appropriate for a particular application. Removable disks enable users to share files with other users. They also provide a second copy or backup of important files. You examined backup strategies for safeguarding your data using removable storage disks.

1. **In your company, what removable storage systems are in use? Of the removable storage systems your company uses, which are currently manufactured and which are legacy devices?**

2. **What backup strategy does your company employ?**

Notes

LESSON 10
Peripheral Devices

Lesson Time
3 hour(s), 15 minutes

Lesson Objectives:

In this lesson, you will identify and troubleshoot input and output peripheral devices.

You will:

- Describe the function of primary input devices.
- Connect and troubleshoot a video output device.
- Connect and troubleshoot printers.
- Connect and troubleshoot other input/output devices.

LESSON 10

Introduction

A computer and its internal system components are not much good to a user if they cannot get data in or out of the computer. Peripheral devices allow the user to interact with the computer's operating system. Input devices allow the user to send data to the computer. Output devices allow the user to see the results of their interaction. In this lesson, you will identify the different peripheral devices that can be connected to the computer to input or output data, and you'll learn how to troubleshoot these devices.

The following CompTIA A+ Core Hardware (2003) Examination objectives are covered in this lesson:

- Topic A:
  - 1.2 Identify basic procedures for adding and removing field-replaceable modules for desktop systems. Given a replacement scenario choose the appropriate sequences. Content includes: input devices—keyboard; and mouse/pointing devices.
  - 2.1 Recognize common problems associated with each module and their symptoms, and identify steps to isolate and troubleshoot the problems. Given a problem situation, interpret the symptoms and infer the most likely cause. Content includes: peripherals; input devices—keyboard; and mouse/pointing devices.

- Topic B:
  - 1.1 Identify typical IRQs, DMAs, and I/O addresses, and procedures for altering these settings when installing and configuring devices. Choose the appropriate installation or configuration steps in a given scenario. Content includes the following: display devices.
  - 1.2 Identify basic procedures for adding and removing field-replaceable modules for desktop systems. Given a replacement scenario choose the appropriate sequences. Content includes: display devices.
  - 1.9 Identify procedures to optimize PC operations in specific scenarios. Predict the effects of specific procedures under given scenarios. Topics include: monitors.
  - 2.1 Recognize common problems associated with each module and their symptoms, and identify steps to isolate and troubleshoot the problems. Given a problem situation, interpret the symptoms and infer the most likely cause. Content includes: display device.
  - 3.2 Identify various safety measures and procedures, and when/how to use them. Content includes the following: potential hazards and proper safety procedures relating to—CRTs.

- Topic C:
  - 1.9 Identify procedures to optimize PC operations in specific scenarios. Predict the effects of specific procedures under given scenarios. Topics include: printers.
  - 5.1 Identify printer technologies, interfaces, and options/upgrades. Technologies include—laser, ink dispersion, dot matrix, solid ink, thermal, and dye sublimation; interfaces include—parallel, network, SCSI, USB, Infrared, Serial, IEEE 1394/ Firewire, and wireless; options/upgrades include—memory, hard drives, NICs, trays and feeders, and finishers.
  - 5.2 Recognize common printer problems and techniques used to resolve them. Content includes the following: printer drivers; firmware updates; paper feed and output; calibrations; printing test pages; errors (printed or displayed); memory; configuration; network connections; connections; paper jam; print quality; safety precautions; consumables; and environment.

Lesson 10

- Topic D:
  - 1.2 Identify basic procedures for adding and removing field-replaceable modules for desktop systems. Given a replacement scenario choose the appropriate sequences. Content includes: input devices—touch screen.
  - 1.3 Identify basic procedures for adding and removing field-replaceable modules for portable systems. Given a replacement scenario, choose the appropriate sequence. Content includes: input devices—touch screen.
  - 1.8 Identify proper procedures for installing and configuring common peripheral devices. Choose the appropriate installation or configuration sequence in given scenarios. Content includes the following: external storage.
  - 1.9 Identify procedures to optimize PC operations in specific scenarios. Predict the effects of specific procedures under given scenarios. Topics include: digital cameras.
  - 2.1 Recognize common problems associated with each module and their symptoms, and identify steps to isolate and troubleshoot the problems. Given a problem situation, interpret the symptoms and infer the most likely cause. Content includes: input devices—touch screen.
  - 5.1 Identify printer technologies, interfaces, and options/upgrades. Options/upgrades include—scanners/fax/copier.

Topic A

Primary Input Devices

Computers need your input before they can do anything useful. In the early days of computing, user input involved physically rewiring the computers. Later computers could accept input on cards and paper tape. Keyboards and pointing devices are now the standard input devices for personal computers. In this topic, you will learn what each of these primary input devices are, how you work with them, and how to troubleshoot problems with the devices.

Peripheral Device

Definition:

A *peripheral* is any computing device besides the CPU and memory. Peripherals expand what you can do with a computer. They all have connectors of some sort to connect to the computer. Peripherals can be internal or external to the computer system case. Internal peripherals are also called integrated peripherals. Most peripherals have a cable to connect them to the computer, but others are able to use various wireless connection methods. Some peripherals are powered by the computer, but others need their own power supply.

 This is just one definition that is commonly used for peripheral devices. Other definitions for this word (including something on the edge, something of less importance, or an accessory) define peripherals as any device connected externally to the system case. Still others define it as anything other than the CPU, memory, monitor, and keyboard. For this course, we will use the first definition.

Lesson 10

Example:

Peripheral devices include monitors, keyboards, pointing devices, printers, scanners, or any other devices you can connect to one of the system ports. Even consumer electronic devices, such as mobile phone or televisions, can now be used as peripheral computer devices. Figure 10-1 shows an example of a computer with several external peripherals attached.

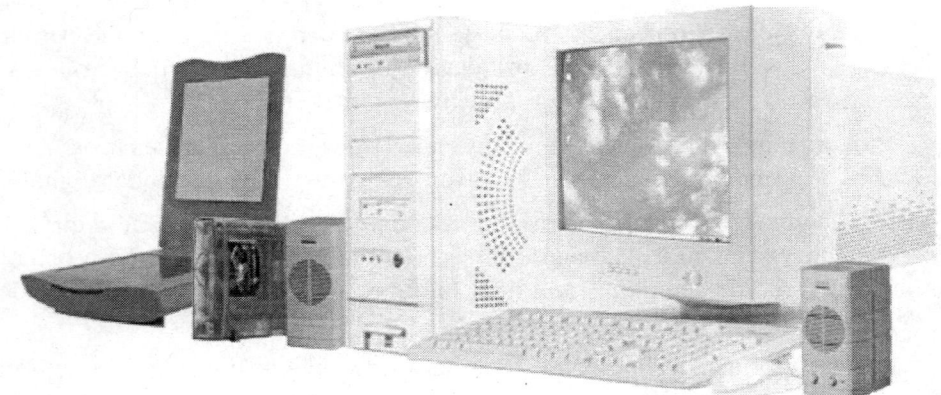

Figure 10-1: *A computer with peripherals attached.*

Keyboard

Definition:

A keyboard is one of two standard input devices for personal computers. It is made up of a set of typewriter-like keys that enable you to enter data into the computer. A keyboard will have a set of alphanumeric keys for entering letters and numbers; a set of punctuation keys for entering grammatical punctuation marks; and a set of special keys, such as the function keys, arrows, and control keys, for entering other commands into the computer. The number of keys on a PC keyboard is typically 84 or 101. Sometimes you will find more if special operating system keys such as the Windows key or Internet function keys are integrated into the keyboard. The standard layout of the keys on a computer keyboard is QWERTY. (It is called QWERTY because the top six keys spell QWERTY.)

 The QWERTY keyboard layout was designed in the 1800s in an effort to slow typists down so that they did not jam the keys on the mechnical typewriters of the time.

Keyboards have historically been a straight rectangle shape containing keys, but can now include a wrist rest or an integrating pointing devices such as a track ball or touchpad.

Example:

There are three different PC keyboards:

- The original PC keyboard which has 84 keys. A numeric pad is integrated to the right of the alphabetical keys. Function keys are along the left side of the keyboard.
- The AT keyboard which also has 84 keys. The AT keyboard is very similar to the original PC keyboard. On the AT keyboard, the numeric pad is separate from the alphabetical keys.

- The enhanced keyboard has 101 keys. The function keys are integrated across the top. Arrow keys have been added, as well as a set of six keys—insert, delete, home, end, page up, and page down. There are also additional command keys such as Esc and Ctrl.

XT Keyboard

AT (Standard)

AT (Enhanced)

Figure 10-2: *A comparison of the three different PC keyboard types.*

Alternative Keyboards

A huge variety of keyboards are available. Here are just a few of them:

- Natural or ergonomic keyboards, shown in Figure 10-3 usually split the keyboard in half so each hand can comfortably use its own set of keys.
- Keyboards for children or users with special needs may have enlarged or specially constructed keys.

Lesson 10

- Wireless keyboards may use radio or infrared light to communicate with the computer.
- USB boards require a USB port, rather than the standard PS/2 port.
- Computer programs can simulate a keyboard on the screen, which may be activated by touch or a special light source.
- Foreign language keyboards have a variety of different keys.
- Dvorak keyboards rearrange the keys into a more natural arrangement that makes faster typing possible.

Figure 10-3: *A natural (ergonomic) keyboard.*

Dvorak Layout

Figure 10-4: *A Dvorak keyboard.*

Standard DIN Keyboard Connectors

For keyboards that are not wireless or USB, there are two standard DIN connectors that are used to connect the keyboard to the system board: a larger 5-pin DIN connector and a smaller 6-pin mini-DIN connector, also called a PS/2 style connector. Each of the pins in these connectors is numbered and has a specific purpose as shown in Figure 10-5 and described in Table 10-2 and Table 10-1.

Lesson 10

Figure 10-5: *Standard keyboard connectors: 6-pin mini-DIN, 5-pin DIN.*

Table 10-1: *6-pin DIN Connector Pin Descriptions*

Pin Number	Name	Description
1	DATA	Line for serial data transmission.
2	No connection	
3	GND	Electrical ground.
4	+5 V	Power source.
5	CLK	Clock signal for timing.
6	No connection	

Table 10-2: *5-pin DIN Connector Pin Descriptions*

Pin Number	Name	Description
1	CLK	Clock signal for timing.
2	DATA	Line for serial data transmission.
3	No connection	
4	GND	Electrical ground.
5	+5 V	Power source.

How a Keyboard Works

When you press and release a key on your keyboard, this is what happens:

1. The microprocessor built into the keyboard continuously scans for changes from the key circuits. This comes in as a change in the current for the key. Each key has a scan code for its down state and one for its release state.

2. The scan code for the key being pressed is stored in the keyboard buffer. The scan codes for the shift key and toggle keys such as Ctrl, Alt, Caps Lock, Scroll Lock, and Insert are stored in a separate buffer.

3. An interrupt is sent to the CPU over IRQ 1 to alert it to the fact that the keyboard needs attention.

4. The keyboard BIOS reads the contents of the special shift and toggle key buffers along with the scan codes for other keys and sends the appropriate key state to the CPU. For example, a letter could be sent as upper or lowercase, or a key can be pressed in combination with another key such as Shift, Ctrl, or Alt.

5. The scan code is deleted from the keyboard's buffer after it has been transferred. The shift and toggle key scan codes are not deleted after they have been sent, but are retained in the special buffer until the key is pressed a second time and the key state changes.

6. When the key is released, a separate scan code is sent.

The Typematic Repeat Rate determines how many times per second the scan code is sent to the BIOS when a key is held down for an extended period of time.

Figure 10-6 shows an example of what happens when you press a key on a keyboard.

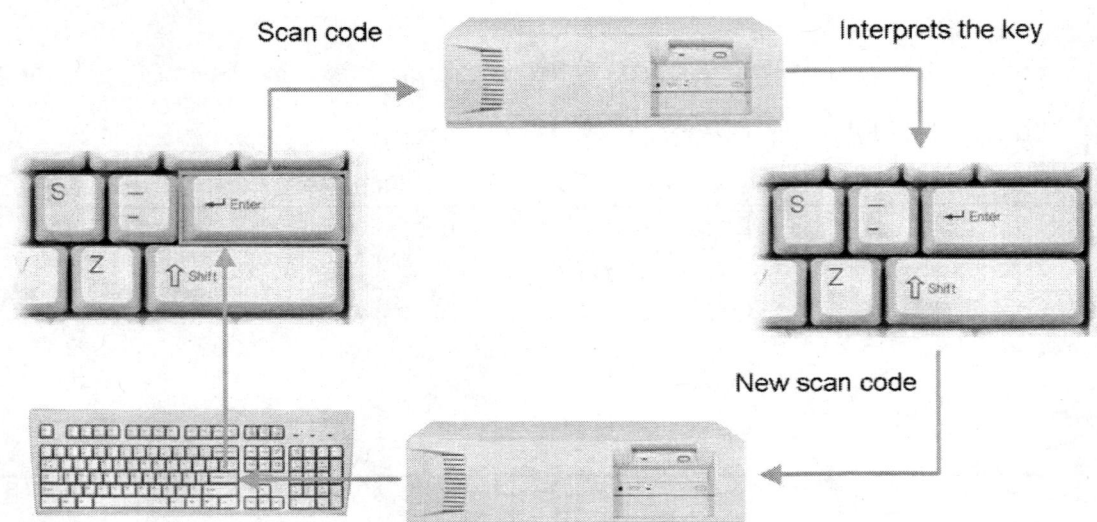

Figure 10-6: *How a keyboard works.*

Keyboard Scan Codes

ASCII (American Standard Code for Information Interchange) and *ANSI (American National Standards Institute)* have produced well-known number codes for each character in the English language, as well as some special and foreign characters. For example, A is 65, B is 66 and C is 67 in both ASCII and ANSI. Character maps, symbol selection options, and special character codes refer to ASCII numbers. Programming language looks at text as a series of ASCII codes, with one number representing each letter.

Keyboard Manufacture Techniques

Keyboards are manufactured using two different techniques:

- The first method uses coiled metal springs to push the key up after the user has depressed it and made the electrical contact that tells the computer which key has been pressed.

- The second method uses rubber or plastic membranes. When a key is pressed, a bump in the rubber membrane is pressed down, and a conductive material on the membrane completes a circuit that lets the keyboard know which key was pressed. The compressed rubber bump then bounces back into its original shape and pushes the key up into its starting position.

Keyboards need a force of about 100 grams to press the key down. Most keyboards require electric current that has a maximum load of 300mA (milliAmps). This power comes to the keyboard through the cable from the main computer power supply.

Common Keyboard Problems

Keyboards are so inexpensive that there is usually not much troubleshooting that is done on them. Sometimes the problem is with the keyboard port on the computer, so replacing the keyboard will not correct the problem. Troubleshooting keyboard problems usually involves physically examining the connection, examining the keyboard for foreign materials under the keys, and verifying that the keyboard is connected to the correct port. Table 10-3 describes some common keyboard symptoms and problems and how to troubleshoot them.

Table 10-3: *Common Keyboard Problems*

Symptom	Possible Problem	Solution
Keys stick.	Foreign matter under the keys causes contact to be made with the wrong key or not at all.	Physically shake the keyboard upside down or use compressed air to blow out debris.
User with physical limitations is currently unable to use the standard keyboard.	Accessibility features for the keyboard have not been enabled.	In Control Panel, enable the Accessibility options such as StickyKeys, FilterKeys and/or ToggleKeys to enable handicapped users to more easily use the keyboard.
No input is sent when keys are pressed.	Keyboard unplugged. Keyboard plugged into mouse port. Keyboard interface contains bent or broken pins. User attempted to connect the keyboard using a PS/2-to-USB adapter on a keyboard that doesn't support this translation. Keyboard port on the computer is damaged.	Physically check the connections.
Keyboard-related message or beep codes given during computer boot.	Keyboard might be disconnected or plugged into the mouse port. Keyboard might be damaged.	
Wrong characters are displayed on the screen when user inputs information.	The language was changed in the Keyboard Properties within Windows. Short or incorrect contacts being made due to beverage spilled into the keyboard or another foreign matter in the keyboard. Keyboard interface on the computer is damaged.	Check the Keyboard Properties settings, then physically check the keyboard for foreign matter under the keys.
Multimedia buttons not working properly.	Device driver needs updating. File related to the button has been moved, renamed, or modified in some way.	Download updated drivers from the manufacturer's Web site. Verify that the file associated with a given button is correctly named, and if any options are needed, that they are correctly formatted.

Lesson 10

Symptom	Possible Problem	Solution
New keyboard won't plug into the same port as the old keyboard.	Older keyboards use large 5-pin DIN connector, while new keyboards use a smaller 6-pin mini-DIN connector, also called a PS/2 style connector. See Figure 10-5.	Because the keyboards are the same except for the connector, you can buy an adapter to allow you to plug the new keyboard into the old port on the system board. Often a new keyboard with the correct adapter can be purchased for about the same price of an adapter.

Pointing Device

Definition:

A pointing device sends electronic signals to the computer to control the movements of a pointer drawn on screen in the Graphical User Interface (GUI). The pointer on the screen is then used to select commands and options in the GUI. A pointing device may have buttons that you click to make selections in the GUI. Peripheral pointing devices can connect to the computer through PS/2, serial, USB, or wireless connections.

Example: Mouse

A mouse is a small object that contains a ball on the underside that is run across a flat surface and at least one, but typically three, buttons that send electronic signals to the GUI. Its name is derived from its appearance—a small rounded rectangle shape with a single cord attached at one end. There are three types of mice:

- Mechanical—Mechanical sensors detect the direction the ball is rolling and move the screen pointer accordingly.
- Opticalmechanical—Optical sensors detect motion of the ball and move the screen pointer accordingly.
- Optical—A laser detects the mouse's movement as you move it along a special mat with a grid. The special mat provides the optical mechanism a frame of reference. Optical mice have no mechanical moving parts, but they respond more quickly and precisely than other types of mice.

LESSON 10

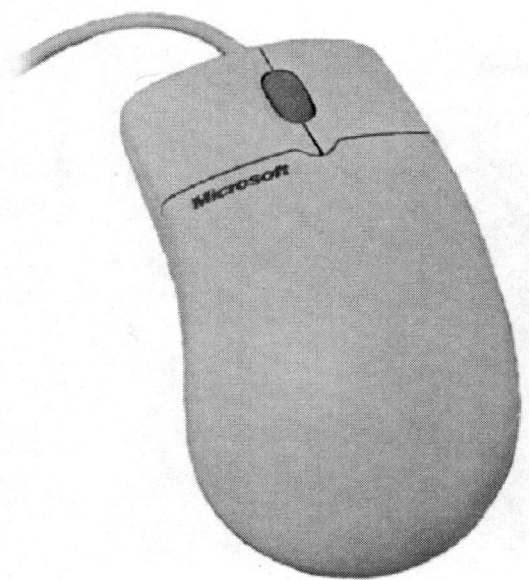

Figure 10-7: *A mouse.*

 The mouse was invented by Douglas Engelbart of Stanford Research Center in 1963 and pioneered by Xerox in the 1970s. It frees the user from strict keyboard input and makes computers accessible to a much wider audience.

Example: Trackball

A trackball is basically an upside down mouse. The ball is mounted on the top of the case instead of the bottom and signals are sent to the computer by moving the ball with your fingers or palm instead of by rolling the ball across a flat surface. Like a mouse, a trackball has at least one button that is used to send electronic signals to the computer.

Lesson 10

Figure 10-8: *A trackball.*

Example: Touchpad

A touchpad is a small, touch-sensitive pad where you run your finger across the surface to send electronic signals to the computer to control the pointer drawn on the screen. Touchpads can have buttons like a mouse or trackball, or the touchpad can be configured to detect finger taps on its surface and process those signals like a button click.

Figure 10-9: *A touchpad.*

How Pointing Devices Work

When the user moves the mouse, the computer detects the direction and amount of motion by electrical signals sent through the mouse cord and redraws a pointer that mimics that motion on the screen. The computer knows the position of the pointer relative to other objects drawn on the screen.

To summarize how a mechanical mouse works:

1. The user moves the mouse over a flat surface.

Lesson 10

2. The ball inside the mouse turns in the direction the mouse is moved. This ball is usually a rubber-coated steel ball.
3. The ball rests against two rollers which send X- and Y-axis information to the computer. All mice report their location several times per second. The more reports per second, the smoother the mouse pointer movement on the screen. A third roller holds the ball in place against the other two rollers.
4. The rollers are connected to encoder wheels. These encoders contain metal contacts around the edge. Two bars are connected to the mouse shell which make contact with the metal contacts on the encoder wheels and create an electrical signal. The computer counts the number of signals sent to know how far and how fast you are moving the mouse.
5. The mouse buttons are simple switches. Signals are sent each time the mouse button or buttons are pressed. The computer translates the mouse clicks or presses and the software program interprets them to mean whatever the programmers programmed the mouse signals to mean.
6. When the user clicks one of the buttons on the mouse, the computer determines what icon or graphic the user was pointing at, if anything, and then performs the action that the icon has associated with a mouse click. An icon may have specific actions programmed to run if the mouse moves the pointer into its area, out of its area, or pauses over its area. If a mouse button is pressed while the pointer is in its area, it may have specific actions programmed to run if a mouse button is:
   - Down
   - Up
   - Clicked (pressed and released)
   - Double-clicked (clicked two times with a short time span between clicks)
   - Ctrl-clicked (clicked while the Ctrl key on the keyboard is held down)
   - Shift-clicked (clicked while the Shift key on the keyboard is held down)
   - Alt-clicked (clicked while the Alt key on the keyboard is held down)
7. The user can drag an icon by pointing at it, holding the mouse button down, and while holding the button down moving the mouse (press and drag). The icon can be programmed to respond differently if the button used is the left, right, or center (if available or both buttons together) mouse button.

Lesson 10

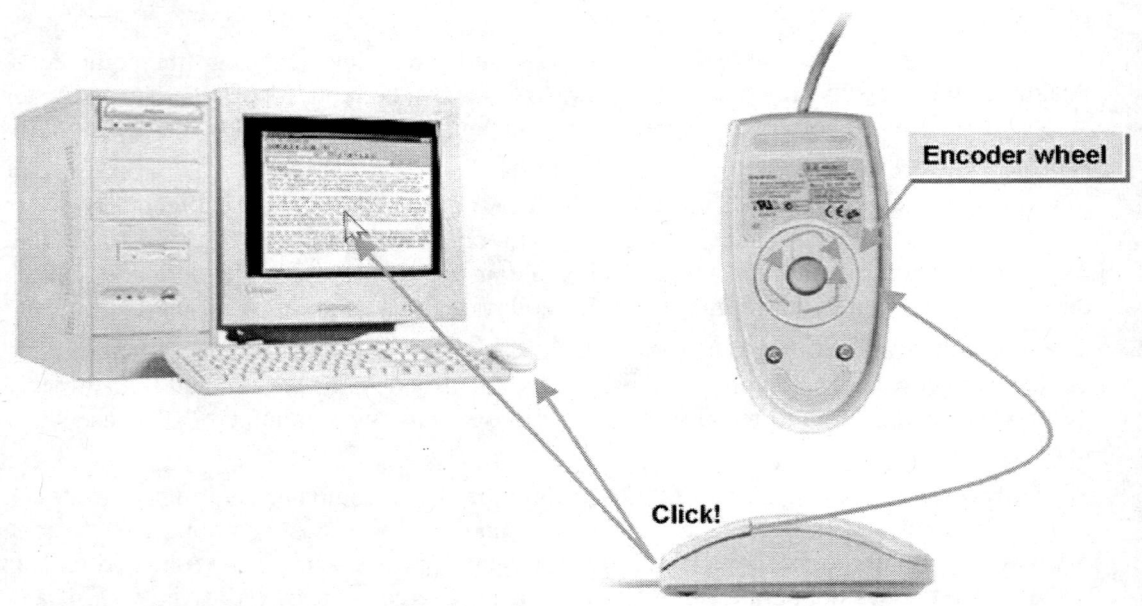

Figure 10-10: *How a mechanical mouse works.*

Common Pointing Device Problems

There are many problems you might encounter when troubleshooting pointing devices. Table 10-4 lists some of the most common symptoms of pointing device problems that cause those symptoms.

Table 10-4: *Common Pointing Device Problems*

Symptom	Possible Problem	Solution
Mouse pointer jumps around on the screen.	Mouse ball or rollers are dirty. Mouse has reached the end of its useful life. Mouse is not being rolled over a flat surface. Mouse is being rolled over a dirty mouse pad. Mouse settings are incorrect.	Visually inspect the mouse, the mouse pad, and the area around the mouse. Clean the mouse, replace the mouse pad. Use the Device Manager and Help And Support Center utilities to check the status of the pointing device. With an older mouse, regular maintenance might reduce this problem, but not eliminate it. From Control Panel, open Printers And Other Hardware. Click Mouse. Check the pointer speed, click speed, and other settings that might affect performance.

Symptom	Possible Problem	Solution
Cordless mouse is in use and mouse pointer is jumping around or not moving.	Batteries low. Obstruction between the mouse and the receiver. Connection lost.	Check the batteries and replace if necessary. Verify that there is no obstruction between the transmitter and the receiver. Press the Reset or Connect buttons on each device to try to re-establish the connection. Replace the batteries in the mouse. Press the Reset or Connect buttons on each device again. Verify that the receiver device is connected to the port. Try a corded mouse connected to the port. If this works, replace the cordless mouse with either a corded mouse or another cordless mouse.
Mouse works sometimes, but not others.	IRQ conflict between the mouse and the modem (or another device).	Use Device Manager to check for hardware conflicts; change the mouse to an open IRQ such as IRQ 12.
Mouse is not working.	Mouse is not plugged in. Mouse is plugged in to the keyboard port. Mouse was connected after the computer was started. Some pointing devices require special drivers and possibly additional software to function properly. Pointing device is not on the Windows Hardware Compatibility List (HCL). Driver for the pointing device was corrupted or outdated.	Physically check the pointing device connection. Use Device Manager to verify that the correct driver is installed. Check the pointing device's documentation to see if any additional software is required for it to function properly. Check the Web site of the device manufacturer to see if newer drivers or software should be installed.
USB mouse is not working properly.	A problem with the root hub or USB host controller. Mouse is plugged into an unpowered USB hub and is not getting enough power to operate properly.	Check the status of the root hub or USB host controller in Device Manager. Plug the mouse directly into a USB port on the computer; if this works, and the hub is working properly, the mouse is probably not getting enough power. Physically remove some of the devices on the same hub as the mouse to another port or hub or use a powered USB hub.

Lesson 10

How to Troubleshoot Keyboard and Pointing Device Problems

Procedure Reference: Troubleshoot Keyboard and Pointing Device Problems

To troubleshoot some of the most common problems with keyboards and pointing devices:

1. If the keyboard is not working at all:
   - Verify that the keyboard is plugged in to the keyboard port.
   - Verify that the keyboard cable is securely connected. Some keyboard cables need to be plugged in to the keyboard as well as to the system's keyboard port.
   - If the keyboard still does not work, switch it with a known good keyboard. Pull the connector straight out of the port so as not to bend any of the pins.
   - If the keyboard still does not work, verify that CMOS is configured to recognize the keyboard.
   - If the keyboard still does not work, test the keyboard port with a multimeter. Pin 4 should have a reading of +5 V and pin 3 is ground. If the port is damaged, you will need to replace the system board.

2. If the keyboard is producing the wrong characters when the user types:
   - Verify that no Function key, Scroll Lock, or other key, is enabled or stuck down.
   - Verify that the correct drivers are in use.
   - If that is not the problem, replace with a known good keyboard. Unplug the keyboard and plug in the replacement keyboard.

3. If liquids are spilled on the keyboard, it is most likely permanently damaged. However, you can try:
   - Remind users that all drinks must be covered when used near computer equipment.
   - Unplug the keyboard and turn it upside down over a wastebasket.
   - Move the keyboard around to remove as much liquid as possible.
   - Rinse keyboard in running water if the liquid was sticky (soda pop or sweetened drinks).
   - Set on end to dry for several days.
   - Replace the keyboard with another keyboard so that the user can get back to work until their keyboard is ready to use again.

4. If the mouse pointer is jumping around on the screen:
   - Clean the rollers inside the mouse.
   - Replace the mouse. Unplug the mouse and plug in the new mouse.

5. If a cordless mouse is in use and the mouse pointer is not moving on the screen:
   - Verify that there is no obstruction between the transmitter and the receiver.
   - Press the Reset or Connect buttons on each device to try to re-establish the connection.

- Replace the batteries in the mouse. Press the Reset or Connect buttons on each device again.
- Verify that the receiver device is connected to the port.
- Try a corded mouse connected to the port. If this works, replace the cordless mouse with either a corded mouse or another cordless mouse.

📌 Keyboards and pointing devices are so inexpensive, that unless the device is a special one designed for a specific need, it is more cost effective to simply replace the device.

ACTIVITY 10-1

Troubleshooting Keyboard and Pointing Device Problems

Scenario:

Several users have opened trouble tickets with the support center about problems with their keyboards and pointing devices. All of the users need their systems fixed before they can continue with their work. You need to resolve the problems and get the users back to work. The following is a list of the trouble tickets you are responding to:

- Ticket 299001:

    Location: Elmwood Place, cube 24

    User: Al Mikels

    The user's keyboard is not working at all.

- Ticket 299002:

    Location: Training center, room 1

    User: Andy Potarnia

    User's keyboard is producing the wrong characters when he types.

- Ticket 299003:

    Location: Main building, 42B31

    User: Toma Wright

    User's mouse jumping around on the screen.

- Ticket 299004:

    Location: Main building, 31C93

    User: Jason Zeh

    User has a cordless mouse, and the mouse pointer is not moving on the screen.

- Ticket 299005:

    Location: Main building, 26B15

    User: Daniel Bidlack

    Root beer has been spilled on user's keyboard.

Lesson 10

What You Do	How You Do It
1. If you have been assigned trouble ticket 299001, **resolve trouble ticket 299001.**	a. **Verify that the keyboard is plugged in to the keyboard port.** b. **Verify that the keyboard cable is securely connected.** c. If the keyboard still does not work, **switch with a known good keyboard.** d. If the keyboard still does not work, **verify that the keyboard is recognized by the CMOS.** e. If the keyboard still does not work, **replace the system board.**
2. If you have been assigned trouble ticket 299002, **resolve trouble ticket 299002.**	a. **Verify that no Function key, Scroll Lock, or other key is enabled or stuck down.** b. If that is not the problem, **replace keyboard with a known good keyboard.**
3. If you have been assigned trouble ticket 299003, **resolve trouble ticket 299003.**	a. **Make sure the surface the mouse is being rolled on is clean and smooth.** b. **Clean the rollers inside the mouse.** c. **Clean the mouse ball by blowing on it or by using warm water and mild detergent.** d. From the Start menu, **choose Control Panel. Click Printers And Other Hardware. Click Mouse. Check the pointer speed, click speed, and other settings that might affect performance.** e. If the problem is not resolved, **replace the mouse.**

Lesson 10

4. If you have been assigned trouble ticket 299004, **resolve trouble ticket 299004.**

   a. Verify that there is no obstruction between the transmitter and receiver devices.

   b. Press the Reset or Connect buttons on each device to try to re-establish the connection.

   c. Replace the batteries in the mouse.

   d. Press the Reset or Connect buttons on each device.

   e. Verify that the receiver device is connected to the port.

   f. Try reinstalling the latest software or driver for the cordless mouse.

   g. If it still has not been resolved, **try a corded mouse connected to the port.**

   h. If the previous step worked, **replace the cordless mouse with either a corded or another cordless mouse.**

5. If you have been assigned trouble ticket 299005, **resolve trouble ticket 299005.**

   a. Remind users that all drinks must be covered when used near computer equipment.

   b. Unplug the keyboard and turn it upside down over the wastebasket.

   c. Move the keyboard around to remove as much liquid as possible.

   d. Rinse the keyboard in running water.

   e. Set on end to dry for several days.

   f. Replace the keyboard so user can get back to work until their keyboard is ready to use again.

Lesson 10: Peripheral Devices

Lesson 10

Topic B

Video Output Devices

The display device is a user's window into the computer system. Without the display device, you can't see the computer interface to issue commands, and you can't see the results of your work. Correctly installing and configuring the display system enables you to meet these basic user needs. In this topic, you will learn how to install, configure, and troubleshoot a video output device.

Video Output Devices

Definition:

A video output device is a computer peripheral that enables users to view information on a computer system. Similarities between video output devices include:

- All video output devices display an image of some type.
- They all have controls to change the settings for the device.
- They connect to the computer system using a cable.

Differences between video output devices include:

- The size and shape of the display. Monitors are measured like television sets—diagonally across the glass screen.
- The location and type of controls. These could be separate control buttons for each function, or the controls could be grouped together into an on-screen menu that is superimposed over the Windows display when a single button is pressed.
- Some have a curved screen and others have a flat screen.
- Some use analog signals and some use digital signals. Analog signals are carried on 15-pin VGA cables to the video port on the computer. Digital signals are carried on digital-only or digital-analog cables to a digital or analog port on the computer. These digital cables vary in the number of pins and types of connections used.
- Some use *Cathode Ray Tube (CRT)* technology and others use *Liquid Crystal Display (LCD)* technology. CRTs are at least as deep as the screen size to enable the image to be created. LCD screens are very thin—often only 2 or 3 inches thick.
- The way they produce the image varies:
  — CRTs use a phosphorous coating inside a glass screen.
  — LCD monitors use different colored crystals sandwiched between two sheets of plastic.
  — Projection systems display the image on a wall or movie screen, rather than showing the image on the video output device itself.

Example: Cathode Ray Tube (CRT)-based Monitors

The original personal computers were designed to use television as video displays, but televisions at that time were limited to about 40 characters per line. The first computer monitors could display up to 80 characters per line and 25 lines of text in bright green or white on a black background.

As demand for color graphics increased, the monochrome standard of the Monochrome Display Adapter (MDA) was replaced by the Color Graphics Adapter (CGA), which could show from two to 16 colors at resolutions from 160 x 200 to 640 x 200 pixels (picture elements or unique dots on the screen.) The Enhanced Graphics Adapter (EGA) could show up to 640 x 350 pixels. Monitors of this vintage used digital video signals—TTL for transistor-to-transistor logic—and are completely incompatible with today's computers.

Starting with IBM's Video Graphics Array (VGA) standard, the switch was made to analog color, which uses three consecutive signals—one each for red, green, and blue. Super VGA (SVGA) is the current standard and is still evolving.

Today's CRT monitors can have curved or flat screens. However, they should not be confused with flat-panel monitors. An example of a CRT monitor is shown in Figure 10-11.

Figure 10-11: *A CRT monitor.*

Example: Liquid Crystal Display (LCD) Flat Panel Monitors

Liquid Crystal Display (LCD) flat-panel displays are a compact, lightweight alternative to traditional CRT monitors. LCD displays are more expensive than CRT monitors, but the price is dropping rapidly as they become more popular. LCDs now come in large-screen sizes of 17 inches and more, with high screen resolution and high color capacity. Older LCDs have two disadvantages: they are not as bright as CRT monitors, and the user must sit directly in front of the LCD screen to see the display properly. LCDs consume much less energy than CRTs and do not emit electromagnetic radiations as CRTs do. An example of an LCD flat panel monitor is shown in Figure 10-12.

Lesson 10

Figure 10-12: *An LCD flat-panel monitor.*

Example: Personal Display Devices

Virtual reality games and special-purpose imaging needs led to the development of glasses that substitute for a monitor. Figure 10-13 shows an example of glasses that can be used in lieu of a monitor.

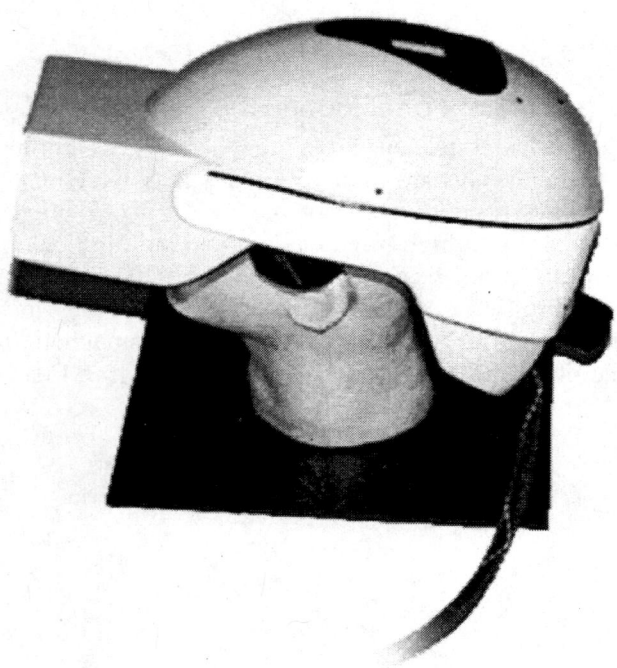

Figure 10-13: *Virtual reality glasses.*

Example: Video Projectors

Video projectors are often used to display the contents of a monitor onto a white board or other surface so that an audience can see the output on a computer screen. An example of an image being displayed on a white board using a video projector is shown in Figure 10-14.

Figure 10-14: *An image on the monitor is also displayed on the white board using a video projector.*

Example: Touchscreen Monitors

Touchscreen monitors enable input by touching images on the screen. This technology is used in bank ATM machines, some point-of-sale terminals at fast food restaurants, and other situations where a separate keyboard for input is not appropriate. An example of a touchscreen monitor is shown in Figure 10-15.

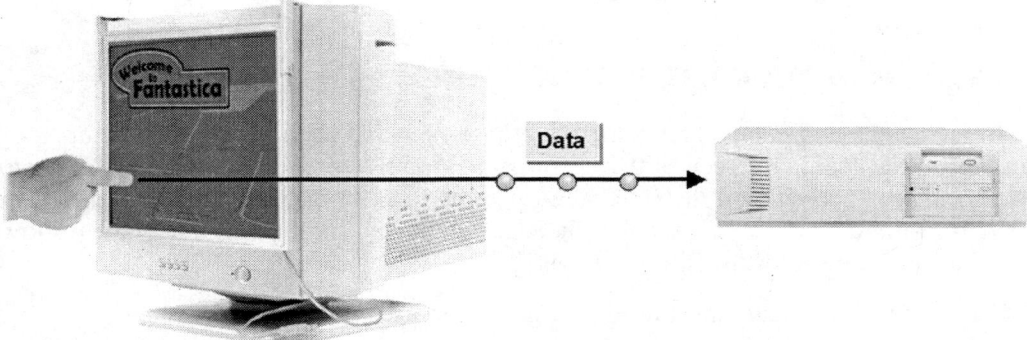

Figure 10-15: *A touchscreen monitor.*

Example: Video Display Systems

Video display systems can be used to display one image to several monitors (often used in training situations) or display an image covering a huge screen (often used at trade shows).

Lesson 10: Peripheral Devices 413

Lesson 10

Digital and Analog Signals

There are two methods for representing data electronically: digital and analog. Digital signal data is composed of discrete values: for example, a string of 0s and 1s, or a set of switches that can be set on or off. Analog signal data is composed of a signal that varies in frequency. A clock with a numeric readout is a digital clock. It gives a precise value for the current time. A clock with hands that move around the clock face is an analog clock. It gives an approximate value for the current time.

Internally, the computer uses digital values for everything it does. Some display devices, such as digital flat panel monitors, can use this digital data directly. However, common video display devices such as CRT monitors use analog signals to produce an image. So, to support these devices, the computer has to convert the digital data to an analog signal that the monitor can display.

Digital Video Interface (DVI) is a cable and connector standard that does the signal conversion from video card to accommodate both analog and digital monitors. There are three types of DVI connections: DVI-A, DVI-D, and DVI-I. DVI-A (the A stands for Analog) is used to convert the digital signal from the video card to analog signals an analog monitor can display. DVI-A is analog only and uses one row of 5 pins, one row of 3 pins, and one row of 4 pins, along with 2 contacts above and below a flat blade. DVI-D (the D stands for Digital) can be used to directly send the digital signal from the video card to a digital monitor without the conversion to analog that typically occurs to send the signal along the cable and then reconversion back to digital for the monitor. DVI-D is digital only and uses three rows of 8 pins each with no contacts above or below a flat blade. DVI-I (the I stands for Integrated Analog/Digital) is an analog and digital connection that uses three rows of 8-pins each and 2 contacts above and below a flat blade. DVI-I can be used to transmit digital signals from the video card to a digital monitor, or analog signals from a video card to an analog monitor, but it cannot convert digital signals to analog or vice versa. DVI-D and DVI-I cables can be single or dual-link. Dual-link cables double the transmission power of a single-link cable, thus increasing the transmission speed and signal quality.

How CRTs Produce Images

Most televisions and computer monitors are based on CRT technology. The computer output you see on the monitor screen is the result of a carefully controlled stream of electrons hitting the phosphorous coating on the screen and making parts of it glow. Because the phosphorous glows for only a fraction of a second, the electron stream must return and start it glowing again so the image remains on the screen.

The process for producing an image on a non-interlaced monitor is:

1. Information from main memory is received by the video adapter in digital form. The color information for each visible pixel on the screen, which may be composed of several of the physical phosphorous dots on the screen, is stored in the video memory.

2. The Random Access Memory Digital-Analog Converter (*RAMDAC*) circuit converts the digital information from analog information. A separate digital to analog converter (DAC) is used for red, blue, and green signals.

3. A table containing information about the voltage levels needed to produce a specific color for a pixel is read from the video card.

4. The video adapter sends signals through the monitor cable to electron guns in the monitor. There are three separate guns—one for each color. The guns are in the back of the monitor.

5. The inside of a CRT is a vacuum. The electron guns shoot streams of electrons through this vacuum. Electron stream intensity is specified by the information sent from the video adapter.
6. A magnetic deflection yoke inside the monitor bends the electron streams using electromagnetism. The path is aimed by additional information sent by the video adapter. This information includes what the resolution and refresh rate are.
7. Electron streams are aligned by the shadow mask, aperture grill, or slotted mask that they pass through. The dot pitch is determined by how close the holes in the mask are to each other.
8. The electron stream hits the phosphorous coating inside the screen, causing the phosphorous to glow. Each of the three colors uses a different phosphorescent substance.
9. The electron stream passes across the screen and is then turned off. The yoke refocuses the electrons on the left of the screen again, this time just below the previous scan line. This is repeated, with the yoke adjusting the angle of the electrons so that all lines on the entire screen are illuminated. One pass over the entire screen is referred to as a frame.
10. Since the phosphorous glows for only a fraction of a second after being hit by the electrons, they need to be hit repeatedly. The usual rate is at least 60 frames per second. So, that means that this entire process is repeated at least 60 times per second.

A graphical representation of how a non-interlaced monitor produces an image is shown in Figure 10-16.

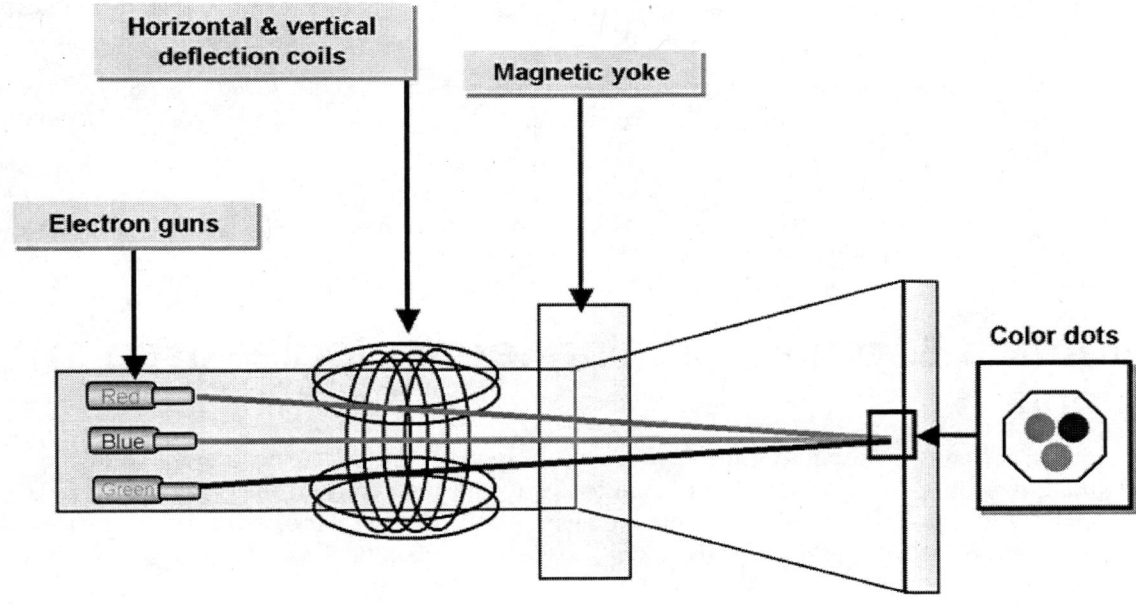

Figure 10-16: *How color CRT monitors work.*

Dot Pitch

Dot pitch is the distance between the same color dots on the screen. The closer the dots are together, the smoother the image will be and the finer the detail that can be shown. Monitors are manufactured with their dot pitch setting configured.

Interlaced Monitors

If you have an interlaced display adapter, every other line is scanned during each pass until the entire screen has been covered. This method improves resolution, but produces a noticeable flicker as the phosphors lose luminescence before they are hit again.

Lesson 10

Aspect Ratio

The *aspect ratio* is the ratio of width to height of a display. Most software expects a 4:3 ratio, and the display will appear to be distorted if other ratios are used. The aspect ratio is found by determining the proportion of the number of pixels across the screen to the number of pixels down the screen. For example, a resolution of 640 x 480 has a 4:3 aspect ratio. Table 10-5 lists some common resolutions and their aspect ratios.

Table 10-5: *Common Aspect Ratios*

Resolution	Number of Pixels	Aspect Ratio
320 x 200	64,000	8:5
640 x 480	307,200	4:3
800 x 600	480,000	4:3
1,024 x 768	786,432	4:3
1,280 x 1,024	1,310,720	5:4
1600 x 1200	1,920,000	4:3

Degaussing

Monitors aim electrons onto the display screen through a device called a shadow mask. Magnetic forces outside of the monitor, such as powerful speakers, can magnetize the monitor's shadow mask, pulling it out of alignment. This can result in distorted images and colors.

Degaussing a monitor demagnetizes the monitor. Many monitors degauss automatically when they are turned on. Some also include a degauss button so that you can manually degauss the monitor.

 Some degaussers are so strong, that when you degauss your monitor, other monitors sitting nearby are also degaussed!

Electron Beam Positioning Technologies used in Monitors

Monitor electron beams require precise positioning. Because the red, green, and blue dots are so small, it is difficult for the electron beam to always hit the center of the right dot. In CRT monitors, you will find one of three technologies used to position the electron beams produced by the electron guns at the back of the monitor. These are shadow mask, aperture grill, or slotted mask.

Technology	Description
Shadow mask	One way to keep the beam from hitting the wrong dot is to use a metal sheet with a tiny hole for each trio of adjacent red, green, and blue dots. This grill is a shadow mask; it keeps stray electrons from bleeding over into other colored dots.

Technology	Description
Aperture grill	Other monitors use very thin vertical strips of metal to block the stray electrons from hitting the wrong dots on the tube. These strips form an aperture grill. Monitors using the aperture grill may have a brighter display with a sharper image, but wires used to stabilize the strips form very thin horizontal lines on the screen image.
Slotted mask	This is a combination of shadow mask and aperture grill technologies. It uses vertical slots with horizontal masks to produce a stable image that is brighter than shadow mask.

Display Characteristics

You can configure a number of display characteristics for each video output device. You control some of the display characteristics through a dialog box in Windows, and you adjust others through controls on the physical monitor. Table 10-6 describes the settings you can control through Windows.

Table 10-6: *Windows Display Settings*

Characteristic	Description
Resolution	The maximum number of *pixels* on a monitor. A pixel is the smallest discrete element on a video display. A single pixel is composed of a red, a blue, and a green dot. The resolution value is given as horizontal pixels by vertical pixels, usually in the ratio 4:3. Common resolutions are 640 x 480, 800 x 600, 1024 x 768, and 1600 x 1200. The higher the resolution, the more objects or information you can fit on the screen at once.
Refresh rate	The number of times per second that the entire monitor is scanned to illuminate the pixels. Each scan is referred to as a frame. The rate is expressed in Hertz (Hz). Typical refresh rates are 60-70 Hz or 60-70 times per second. Any setting lower than 60 Hz usually produces noticeable flickering.
Color depth (also known as color quality)	The number of bits used to store the color of a pixel: the more bits per pixel, the more colors can be displayed. The following are the color depths you will likely encounter: • 4-bit color depth requires 0.5 bytes per pixel and can display 16 colors. This is standard VGA mode. At 640 x 480 resolution, this requires 0.5 MB of memory. • 8-bit color depth requires 1 byte per pixel and can display 256 colors. This is 256-color mode. At 800 x 600 resolution, this requires 2 MB of memory. • 16-bit color depth requires 2 bytes per pixel and can display 65,536 colors. This is High Color mode. At 1024 x 768 resolution, this requires 4 MB of memory. • 24-bit color depth requires 3 bytes per pixel and can display 16,777,216 colors. This is True Color mode. At 1600 x 1200 resolution, this requires 8 MB of memory.

Lesson 10

Characteristic	Description
Font	A size and style of typeface. Computers use fonts to display text on the screen. To use a different set of screen fonts, you will have to install the fonts and restart the system.

Physical monitor adjustments are usually located on the front of the monitor just below the screen. There might be separate buttons for each control and function, or there might be one or more buttons that display on-screen menus for each adjustable parameter. For example, to adjust brightness and contrast, you might turn a knob or press a button, or you might need to access the settings through a menu that is superimposed on the screen over your Windows images. Physical monitor adjustments you can make might include those shown in Table 10-7.

 The location of buttons or how to access menus varies from monitor to monitor. Refer to your physical monitor or to the monitor documentation for instructions on how to adjust the settings for the particular monitor you are working with.

Table 10-7: *Physical Monitor Adjustments*

Setting	Description
Brightness	The amount of white in a display image. If the brightness is set too high, you might get an "aura" effect displayed on the screen. If it is set too low, you might not see anything on the screen.
Contrast	The difference in intensity between adjacent colors in an image. If the contrast is not set correctly for the monitor and the lighting conditions in the room (for example, a really bright or really dark room), you might not be able to see anything on the screen, or you might get strange results.
Image position	The location or size of the display in relation to the physical monitor. Sometimes the image is not centered on the monitor. Other times the image doesn't fill the screen, leaving a black band around the edge. Or, part of the image can scroll off the screen. There are usually separate buttons or menu options to adjust each of these issues.
Distortions	Curves or waves in the video image. If lines don't appear straight on the monitor, you might need to adjust settings. Refer to the monitor documentation for how to resolve such issues.

Monitor Specifications

The DB 15 high-density VGA connector is the most common connector for PC monitors. Figure 10-17 shows the pin numbering for the connector at the video card, while Table 10-8 provides a description for each of the pins. Pins 4, 11, 12, and 15 receive information from the monitor, while pins 1, 2, 3, 13, and 14 send information to the monitor.

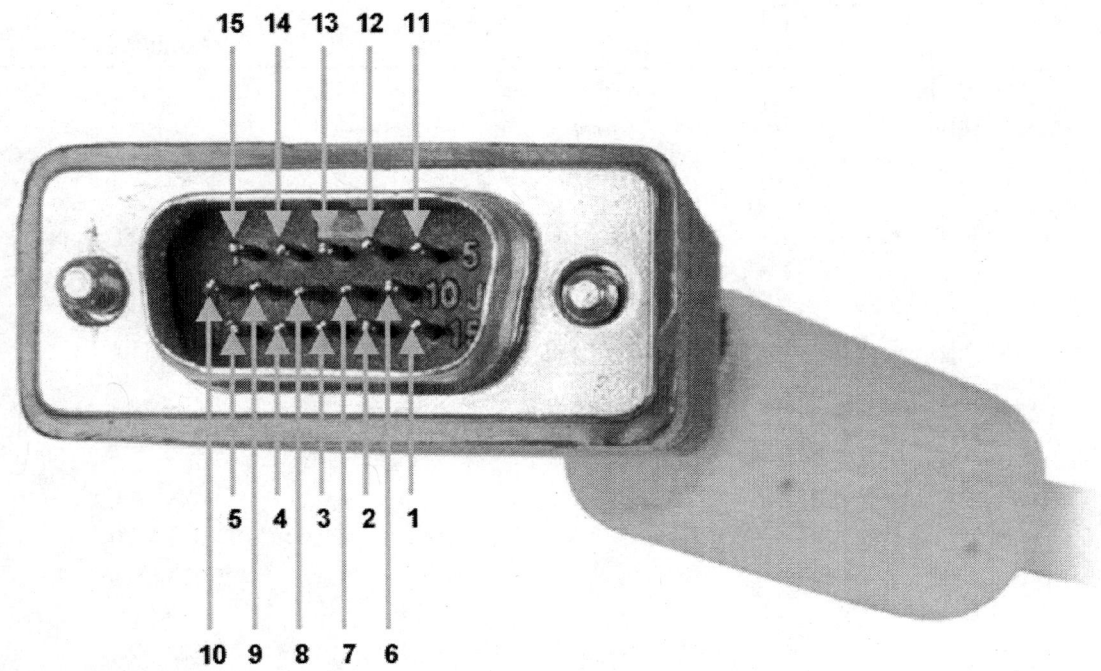

Figure 10-17: *DB 15-pin high-density VGA connector.*

Table 10-8: *Monitor Pin Specifications*

Pin Number	Name	Description
1	RED	Red Video
2	GREEN	Green Video
3	BLUE	Blue Video
4	ID2	Monitor ID Bit 2
5	GND	Ground
6	RGND	Red Ground
7	GGND	Green Ground
8	BGND	Blue Ground
9	KEY	Key (No pin)
10	SGND	Sync Ground
11	ID0	Monitor ID Bit 0
12	ID1 or SDA	Monitor ID Bit 1
13	HSYNC or CSYNC	Horizontal Sync (or Composite Sync)
14	VSYNC	Vertical Sync
15	ID3 or SCL	Monitor ID Bit 3

Table 10-9 summarize the numerical data that is used to describe monitors and their displays and Figure 10-18 shows a visual comparison of some of these standards.

Lesson 10

Table 10-9: *Video Standards*

Video	Year	Colors	Type	Resolution
Monochrome Display Adapter (MDA)	1970s	Mono—no graphics	Digital (TTL)	720 x 350
Hercules Graphics Card (HGC)	1982	Mono—with graphics	Digital (TTL)	720 x 350
Color Graphics Adapter (CGA)	1981	2	Digital (TTL)	640 x 200
CGA		16		160 x 200
Enhanced Graphics Adapter (EGA)	1984	16	Digital (TTL)	640 x 350
Video Graphics Array (VGA)	1987	16	Analog	640 x 480
VGA		256		320 x 200
8514/A	1987	256	Analog Interlaced	1,024 x 768
Extended Graphics Array (XGA)	1990	256		1,024 x 768
XGA		65,536	Analog	800 x 600
TI 34010		256	Analog	1,024 x 768
Super VGA (SVGA)		16 million	Analog	800 x 600
		16 million		1,024 x 768
		16 million		1,280 x 1,024
		16 million		1,600 x 1,200

Lesson 10

The aspect ratio of most computer monitors is 4:3

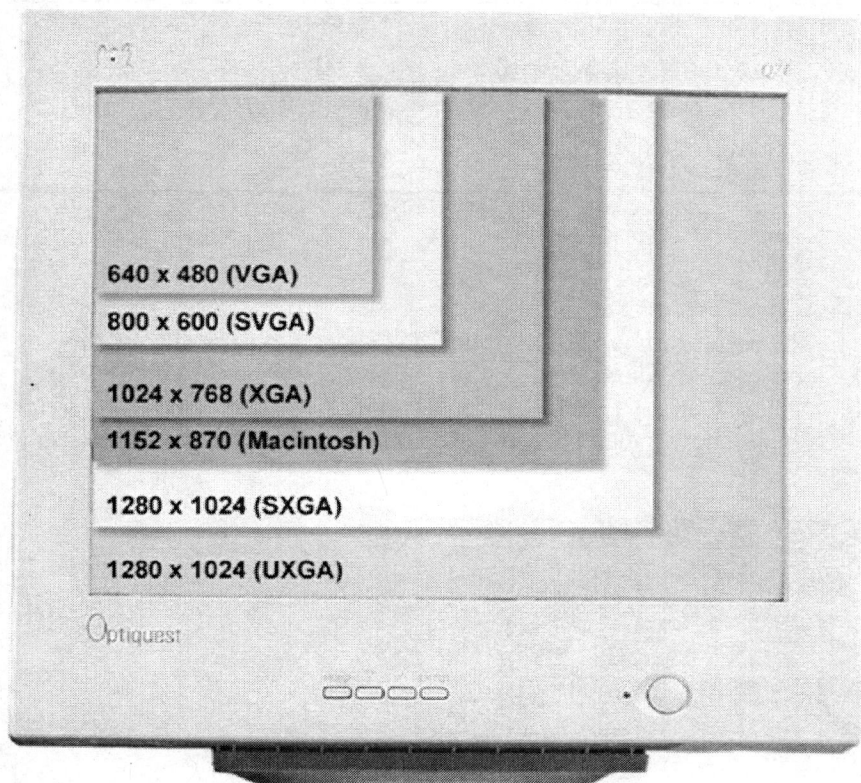

Figure 10-18: *Relative screen sizes.*

The color depth, or the number of bits used to store the color of a pixel, determines how many different colors can be displayed. For example, 8 bits may store decimal values from 0 to 255, so 8 bits or 1 byte can represent, at most, 256 different colors. Table 10-10 describes the different color depths.

Table 10-10: *Color Depth*

Color Depth	Number of Displayed Colors	Bytes of Storage per Pixel	Common Name for Color Depth
4-bit	16	0.5	Standard VGA
8-bit	256	1.0	256-color Mode
16-bit	65,536	2.0	High Color
24-bit	16,777,216	3.0	True Color

The colors that a video card can display depends on the resolution and the color depth, as well as its memory. Table 10-11 summarizes the video memory required to display some of the common resolutions and color depths. The memory is calculated by multiplying the number of pixels displayed by the number of bytes used to represent the color of each pixel. For example, 800 x 600 True Color requires a minimum of 800*600*3 = 1,440,000 bytes. Because video memory generally comes in 0.5, 1, 2, 4, and 8 MB configurations, and more than the minimum memory is used, this resolution and color requires 2 MB of video memory. For a given card, the higher the resolution, the smaller number of colors that the card can handle.

Table 10-11: *Video Memory Requirements*

Resolution	Number of Colors	Memory
640 x 480	256 (1 byte/pixel)	0.5 MB
800 x 600	High Color (2 bytes/pixel)	2 MB
1,024 x 768	True Color (3 bytes/pixel)	4 MB
1,600 x 1,200	True Color	8 MB

Settings

Many monitor problems are the result of unwanted settings. Problems with the size of the icons, color of the fonts, aggravating screen savers, and obnoxious wallpaper are all settings that can be changed in the Display Control Panel. Windows supplies color schemes that coordinate the appearance of all the window's elements. Any scheme may then be modified to suit the user's needs.

Figure 10-19: *Display control panel.*

Depending on the price range and quality of the monitor, there may be a series of controls on a front panel or knobs on the back of the case to adjust some of the distortion problems, shown in Figure 10-20. No monitor is perfect, and often fixing one type of distortion will increase other problems.

Lesson 10

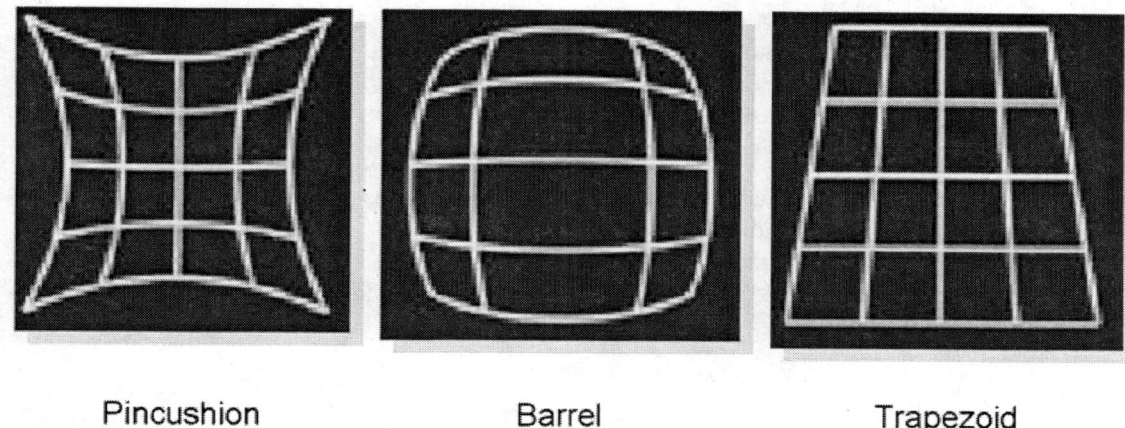

Figure 10-20: *Monitor distortions.*

Many companies make test patterns that are designed to help make the fine adjustments needed to get a perfect display. Patterns tend to reveal flaws in the monitor that were not noticed before, but would probably bother the user every time he or she looks at the screen. The Nokia Monitor test is shown in Figure 10-21.

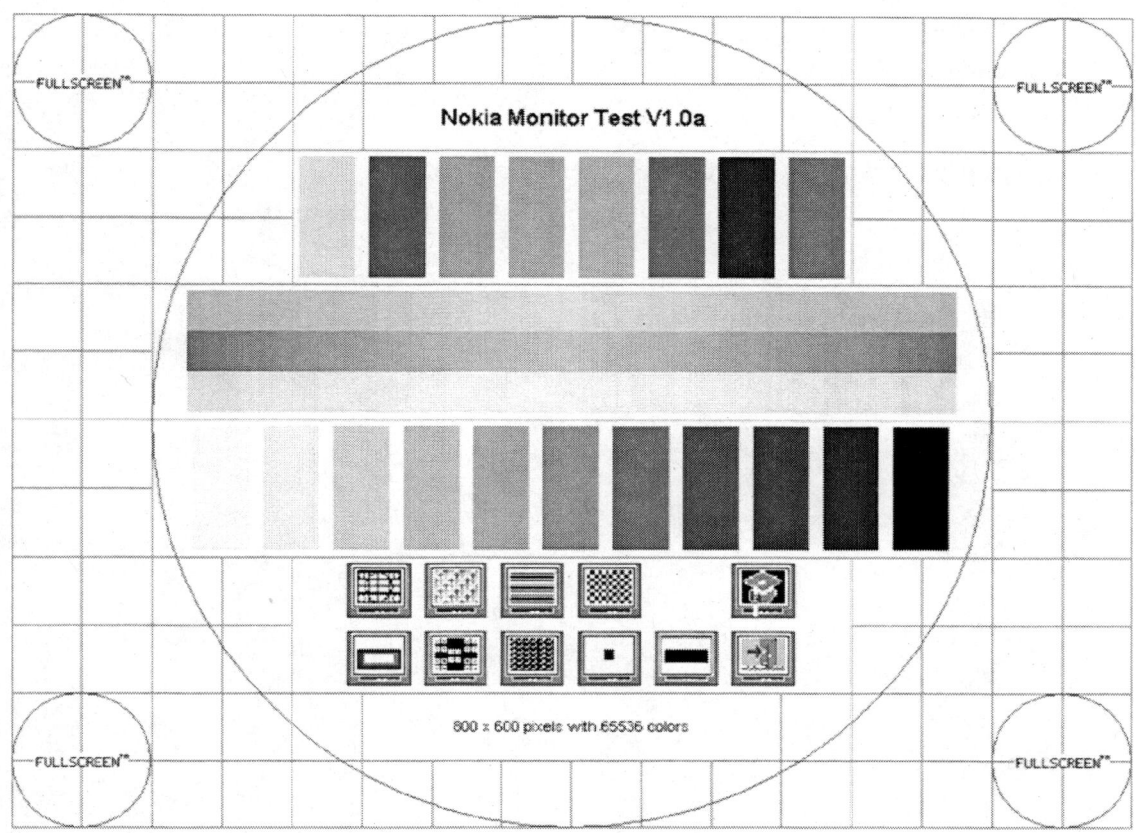

Figure 10-21: *Monitor test patterns.*

The Nokia Monitor test is a free utility that you can download from www.majorgeeks.com/download960.html.

Lesson 10: Peripheral Devices

Lesson 10

Power Management

Power management settings can affect the performance of monitors and other peripherals. Power management is configured in CMOS. It can be configured to specify when power conservation settings take effect. You can specify which components are automatically powered down and under what conditions.

With the power management enabled in CMOS, you can then use Windows XP Power Schemes to reduce power consumption of specific devices or the computer as a whole. Windows XP comes with several preconfigured power options you can choose from, or you can create your own settings. These features must be supported by the hardware in order for Windows XP to implement them. After a specific interval, you can:

- Turn off components such as the monitor or hard drive.
- Go into Standby Mode. This puts devices in a low power state and turns off some devices.
- Go into Hibernate Mode. This saves the contents of RAM to disk, and then turns off the monitor, drives, and, finally, the computer itself.

How to Connect a Video Output Device

Procedure Reference: Install a Monitor

To install a monitor:

1. Turn off the computer.
2. Locate the monitor port on the computer:
   - 15-pin VGA adapter. An example is shown in Figure 10-22.

- 29-pin DVI adapter. An example is shown in Figure 10-23.

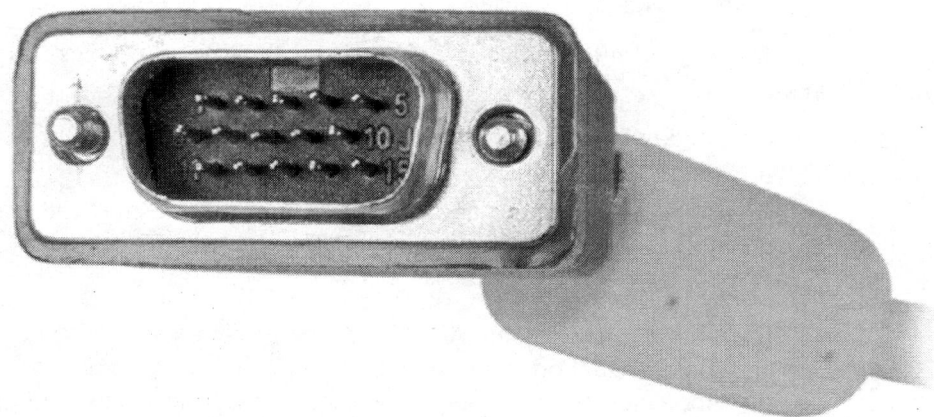

Figure 10-22: *DB 15-pin high-density VGA connector.*

DVI-I receptacle connector

Figure 10-23: *A DVI-I receptacle connector.*

3. Align the pins on the monitor cable with the holes in the adapter port and plug in the monitor.
4. Secure the monitor to the port by tightening the screws on each side of the port.
5. Plug in the monitor power cord.
6. Turn on the computer.
7. Turn on the monitor.
8. Verify that the monitor works.
   - Check that the power light is on, that it is green, and that it is not blinking.
   - Make sure the colors display correctly (they are not washed out or the wrong colors).
   - Make sure there are no lines or distortion in the image displayed on the monitor, and no waviness in the display.

Procedure Reference: Adjust Video Settings

To adjust the video settings for a monitor:

1. Use the control buttons located on the physical monitor to adjust the display size and location. Through these buttons you can change the:
   - Vertical display position.
   - Horizontal display position.

Lesson 10

- Display height.
- Display width.

2. Use the control buttons located on the physical monitor to adjust brightness and contrast.

3. Use the Windows Display Properties dialog box to adjust user preference for screen resolution.

   a. Right-click the Desktop and choose Properties to display the Display Properties dialog box.

   b. Click Settings.

   c. Drag the Screen Resolution slider to the desired setting. If your video card and monitor support only one resolution, you won't be able to change it. If the video card supports only two resolutions, instead of dragging the indicator, click above the desired resolution to change it.

   d. Click Apply.

   e. Click OK.

   f. If prompted to retain the settings, click Yes. If you don't click within the allotted time, the setting reverts to the previous setting.

4. Use the Windows Display Properties dialog box to adjust user preference for font size.

   - To select a standard font size:

     a. Right-click the Desktop and choose Properties.

     b. From the Display Properties dialog box, display the Appearance page.

     c. Display the Font Size drop-down list.

     d. Choose the desired font size. Choices include Normal, Large, and Extra Large.

     e. Click OK.

   - To select a custom font size by adjusting the dpi setting for the monitor:

     a. From the Display Properties dialog box, on the Settings tab, click Advanced.

     b. From the drop-down list, select the desired DPI Setting size: Normal (96 DPI), Large, (120 DPI), or Custom Setting.

     c. If you selected Custom Setting, either select a percentage of normal font size from the drop-down list or drag the ruler to the desired scale. Click OK, and then click OK again to acknowledge that you will need to install the fonts and restart.

     d. Click OK.

     e. If prompted to use existing files, click Yes.

     f. Click Close, and then click Yes to restart the computer.

ACTIVITY 10-2

Installing a Monitor

Setup:
You have a working computer with either a 15-pin VGA-style monitor port and a computer equipped with a digital video interface, or you have a digital flat-panel LCD monitor that uses the 29-pin DVI connector. The computer is turned off and the monitor is unplugged.

Scenario:
It is your first day on the job as a hardware support technician. The marketing department of your company is moving to new offices, and you've been assigned the task of setting up the computers in their new offices. The computers and standard VGA CRT monitors or LCD monitors with 29-pin DVI connector have been delivered to each office. Employees want to begin using their computers as soon as possible.

What You Do	How You Do It
1. **Plug in the monitor.** ⚠ It's easy to bend the pins, so align them carefully. Bent pins can result in poor video display or no video display.	a. **Verify that the power is off at the computer.** b. If you have a standard VGA CRT monitor, **locate the VGA adapter port.** If you have an LCD monitor with 29-pin DVI connector, **locate the DVI port on the computer.** c. If you have a standard VGA CRT monitor, **locate the monitor cable and examine the connector.** If you have an LCD monitor with 29-pin DVI connector, **locate the LCD monitor cable and examine the connector.** d. If you have a standard VGA CRT monitor, **insert the monitor cable into the VGA adapter, being sure to align the pins carefully.** If you have an LCD monitor with 29-pin DVI connector, **insert the LCD monitor connector into the DVI port, being sure to align the pins with the holes.** e. **Tighten the screws.**

Lesson 10

2. **Verify that the monitor is functional.**

   a. **Turn on the monitor power.**

   b. **Turn on the computer power.**

   c. **After the system has started to boot, verify that the power light on the monitor is green and is not flashing.**

   d. **Watch the monitor and verify that the display is clear.**

ACTIVITY 10-3

Adjusting Video Settings

Setup:
The computer is turned on and the Windows Login dialog box is displayed on the screen.

Your instructor has altered the brightness, contrast, vertical and horizontal display position, height and width of the display image, the screen area size, and enabled large icons for your monitor's display.

Scenario:
A monitor was recently moved from the old location to the new location. The employee reports that the display does not appear in the center of the monitor. The images are too dark, making it difficult to see, and he can't see as much on the screen as he would like. The icons on the screen are too small and the font is too big. The employee needs you to resolve these issues so that he can get back to work.

What You Do	How You Do It
1. **Adjust the monitor display.**	a. **Log in as Administrator.**
	b. Referring to documentation as necessary, **locate the control to adjust the brightness of the display image.**
	c. **Adjust the brightness** so that the monitor is comfortable to view.
	d. **Adjust the contrast** so that you can view all screen elements easily.

Lesson 10

2. **Adjust the horizontal and vertical position of the image.**

   a. **Referring to documentation as necessary, locate the controls to adjust the size and centering of the display image.**

   b. **Adjust the vertical display position** so that the display is centered top-to-bottom on the screen.

   c. **Adjust the horizontal display position** so that the display is centered side-to-side on the screen.

   d. **Adjust the height and width of the image** so that there is either no border or the smallest border allowed.

3. **Change the resolution.**

   a. **Right-click the Desktop, and then choose Properties.** The Display Properties dialog box is displayed.

   b. **Click the Settings tab** to display this page of the dialog box.

   c. In the Screen Resolution box, **drag the slider to the right or click to select a screen area that is less than the one currently set.**

   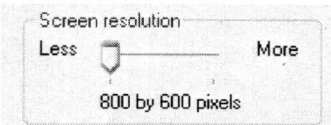

   d. **Click Apply.**

   e. If prompted, **click OK** to acknowledge the informational message.

   f. In the Monitor Settings dialog box, **click Yes** to confirm the changes.

Lesson 10: Peripheral Devices

Lesson 10

4. Reduce the font size.

   a. Click the Appearance tab.

   b. Display the Font Size drop-down list.

   c. Select Normal.

   d. Click OK.

Monitor Safety

The monitor poses the single greatest set of electrical safety hazards of any computer component. Monitors store high-voltage electricity on large capacitors for long periods of time after the monitor is turned off and unplugged. The 20,000 volts are combined with enough current to kill you. The CRT tube can implode and spray you with shards of glass. The 120 volts of power from the wall outlet are present in parts of the monitor even when it is turned off. Always use extreme care when handling a monitor. Never open a monitor. For repairs inside the monitor, hire a specially-certified monitor technician or monitor repair facility.

 All the monitor repairs in this course can be performed without taking the cover off the monitor or inserting anything inside the cover.

Common Monitor Problems

There are many problems you might encounter when troubleshooting monitors. The following table lists the most common symptoms of monitor problems and possible problems that cause those symptoms.

Symptom	Possible Problem	Solution
No image displayed on the monitor.	Power is not turned on. Power button is turned on, but monitor is plugged into a power strip, surge protector, or UPS that is not turned on. Data cable to the VGA port on the PC is disconnected. Brightness control is adjusted improperly. Contrast control is adjusted improperly. The monitor is in power saving mode.	Physically manipulating the monitor: turn on the power, connect the cables, adjust the settings, or press a key or move the mouse to wake up the monitor.

LESSON 10

Symptom	Possible Problem	Solution
Monitor flickers.	Monitor cable is not securely connected to the video port or there are bent or broken pins. Incorrect display adapter and monitor device drivers are in use. Display adapter and/or monitor settings are corrupted. Refresh rate is too low. Monitor is interlaced.	Verify that the monitor cable is securely connected to the video port and that there are no bent or broken pins. Through Device Manager, verify that the correct display adapter and monitor device drivers are in use. Through Device Manager, check the Device Status box for the display adapter and monitor. Set the refresh rate higher if supported by the monitor and adapter card. Replace with a non-interlaced monitor.
Monitor is dark or power indicator light is not lit.	No power.	Check whether the power cord is securely connected on the monitor and to the electrical outlet. Check whether the fuse in the monitor is blown. Check whether the monitor is plugged in to a power strip, surge protector, or UPS that is not turned on. Check whether the monitor is plugged in to an outlet that has tripped its circuit breaker. Check if the monitor power button is stuck. Might be able to unstick it by wiggling it.
Monitor turns itself off.	Power management is enabled.	In CMOS, if the ACPI power settings are enabled, you can use the Display Properties Screen Saver and Monitor Power settings to control when the power is lowered or turned off to the monitor. In Display Properties, on the Screen Saver page, adjust the Wait Time to meet the user's needs. Click the Power button to access the Power Schemes and settings for the Power Options Properties dialog box and set those as appropriate to the user's needs as well.
Screen is fine until a specific application is started, then the screen goes blank, flickers, or acts bizarrely.	Application requires different color quality (also known as color depth) or screen resolution.	Adjust settings on the Settings page of the Display Properties dialog box.

Lesson 10: Peripheral Devices

Symptom	Possible Problem	Solution
Monitor is on, but rather than displaying an image or being black, it is white.	This is usually because the monitor is not connected to the video port on the computer. If it is not due to being disconnected, disconnect it and check for bent or broken pins.	Connect the monitor cable; straighten bent cable pins.

How to Troubleshoot Monitor Problems

Procedure Reference: Troubleshoot Monitor Problems

To troubleshoot monitor problems.

1. If the monitor will not come on and the power light is not lighting up either, verify that the monitor power cord is plugged in. Some steps to take in resolving this problem might include:
   - Plugging in a lamp or other device to the electrical outlet to verify that the outlet is working. If it is not, contact the electrician to fix the outlet and plug the monitor in to another outlet.
   - If the monitor is plugged in to a UPS, power strip, or surge protector, verify that the unit is turned on and has power.
   - Verify that the connections of the power cord and monitor cable are secure on the monitor as well as on the PC and electrical outlet.
   - If there is a fuse on the back of the monitor, remove the fuse and check for a broken wire. Replace the fuse with a good fuse or put the fuse back in if it isn't blown.
   - If the monitor still is not working, replace it with a known good monitor. Unplug the video cable from the monitor port on the computer and unplug the monitor electrical cord from the electrical outlet.

2. If the monitor is flickering and the display is distorted, you might try:
   - Verifying that the monitor cable is firmly plugged in to the monitor and to the computer.
   - If the monitor has one, press the degauss button. A monitor with a degauss button lets you demagnetize the monitor in an attempt to resolve color blotching problems or distortions. Most monitors automatically degauss when they are turned on.
   - Check the monitor cable for any bent pins and straighten them if necessary.
   - Move the monitor away from florescent lights, speakers, other monitors, or other electronic devices with powerful motors.

3. If the monitor power light is on, but nothing is displayed on the screen, you might:
   - Determine if the power light is glowing green or orange. If the power light is orange, the monitor is in energy-saving mode or is getting no data from the computer. A green power light indicates that the monitor is on and is receiving data.
   - Verify that the cable is connected to the monitor and to the PC.

- Adjust the contrast using the buttons on the monitor.
- Adjust the brightness using the buttons on the monitor.
- If it is still not working, swap the monitor with a known good monitor.

4. If the monitor comes on, but then goes blank after a few moments, you should:
   - Determine if the monitor power light is glowing green or orange.
   - If the light is orange, press a key to arouse the system from energy-saving mode. Some monitors only seem to wake up when the Windows key is pressed on the keyboard.
   - Change the Power Management settings in CMOS to disable sleep or doze mode. The exact steps for this vary based on your system BIOS, so the setting might not be called Power Management and could be under a variety of different options.
   - Change the power scheme settings within Windows.
     a. Right-click the Windows Desktop and choose Properties.
     b. Display the Screen Saver page and click Power.
     c. From the Power Schemes drop-down list, select Always On.
     d. Change all settings in the Always On power scheme to Never.

   After you have determined that the monitor is not shutting down due to electrical malfunctions, the user can adjust these settings to meet their needs.

5. If the monitor is making noises, determine whether it is making a crackling or whining noise.
   - If it is a crackling noise, clean the monitor and try to vacuum or blow dust out of monitor vents. Remember, **do not open the monitor!** If necessary, send it to a monitor repair facility for more in-depth cleaning.
   - If it is a whining noise, try moving the monitor. You might also try changing the refresh rate. If it is still whining, send it out to a monitor repair facility for adjustment and replace it with a quieter monitor.

6. If none of your attempts to correct the problem are successful, it might be because the monitor has failed and needs to be replaced. It is usually less expensive to replace the monitor than to send it out for repairs. To replace the monitor:
   a. Remove the existing monitor.
      1. Shut down the computer.
      2. Turn off the power on the computer and the monitor.
      3. Unplug the monitor from the electrical outlet.
      4. Unplug the monitor data cable from the monitor port.
   b. Install the new monitor.
      1. Connect the data cable from the monitor to the computer's monitor port.
      2. Plug the monitor power cable into an electrical outlet.
      3. Turn on the monitor and computer power.
      4. Start the computer and verify that the new hardware was detected.

Lesson 10

Activity 10-4

Troubleshooting Monitor Problems

Scenario:

Several users have opened trouble tickets with the support center about problems with their monitors. All of the users need their systems fixed before they can continue with their work. You need to resolve the problems. The following is a list of the trouble tickets you are responding to:

- Ticket 296001:

    Location: Main building, 31H21

    User: Robert Allen

    The user's monitor is not coming on. The power light is not lighted up. The user has checked that the monitor is plugged in and the monitor is connected to the system.

- Ticket 296002:

    Location: Main building, 13B19

    User: Althea Gavin

    User's monitor is flickering and the display is distorted.

- Ticket 296003:

    Location: Elmwood Place, cube 32

    User: Chris Parker

    The monitor power light is on, but there is no display.

- Ticket 296005:

    Location: Main building, 62B35

    User: Joan Paris

    The monitor is making noises.

What You Do	How You Do It
1. Resolve trouble ticket 296001.	a. **Unplug the monitor from the electrical outlet and plug in a lamp or other device** to verify that the monitor is plugged into a working outlet. If the device works, **plug the monitor back into the outlet.** If the device does not work, **contact the electrician to fix the outlet and plug the monitor in to another outlet.** b. If the outlet is on a UPS, surge protector, or power strip, **verify that the unit is turned on.** c. **Verify that the connections of the power cord and monitor cable are secure on the monitor as well as on the PC and electrical outlet.** d. **Try to turn on the monitor again.** e. If the monitor still doesn't come on, **replace the monitor with a known good monitor.**
2. Resolve trouble ticket 296002.	a. **Verify that the monitor cable is firmly plugged in to the monitor and to the computer.** b. If available, **press the Degauss button.** c. **Check the monitor cable for any bent pins and straighten if necessary.** d. **Move the monitor away from florescent light, speakers, other monitors, or other electronic devices with powerful motors.**

Lesson 10

3. Resolve trouble ticket 296003.

   a. **Verify that the monitor cable is connected to the monitor and to the PC.**

   b. **Adjust the contrast using the buttons on the monitor.**

   c. **Adjust the brightness using the buttons on the monitor.**

   d. If it still is not working, **swap the monitor with one that you know works** to determine if the problem is with the monitor or the video card.

4. Resolve trouble ticket 296005.

   a. **Determine whether noise is crackling or whining noise.**

   b. If it is a crackling noise, **clean the monitor and try to vacuum or blow dust out of monitor vents. Do not open the monitor!** If necessary, send it out for more in-depth cleaning.

   c. If it is a whining noise, try the following to fix it: **move the monitor or change the refresh rate.** If it won't stop whining, send it out for adjustment and **replace the monitor with a quieter one.**

TOPIC C
Printers

Often it is necessary to have a hard copy of your data. This is where printers come in. Printers allow you to transfer your data from the computer to paper. How the different types of printers accomplish this transfer varies. In this topic, you'll learn about the different types of printers available and how to troubleshoot and correct common printer problems.

Dot Matrix Printers

Definition:

A *dot-matrix printer* is a printer that forms images using a set of pins that strike an inked ribbon. All dot-matrix printers:

- Create letters and images from dots.
- Can print on continuous roll paper.

- Can print on multi-part forms that use carbon or on No Carbon Required (NCR) paper.
- Have printheads that contain a vertical column of small pins that are controlled by an electromagnet.
- Use ribbons coated with ink to create images.

Dot-matrix printers vary by:

- The number of pins in the printhead.
- The ribbon used in the printer.
- Whether they can produce black-and-white or color output.
- Whether they can print on cut-sheet paper, continuous form paper, or both.
- Whether they can adjust how close the ribbon is to the paper. If it is too close, you might get smear or drag marks. If it is too far away, the output might be too light.
- The speed of printing.
- The paper path.
- The hardware interface used to connect the printer to the computer.
- Size and weight of paper that can be used.
- The tractor feed mechanisms; the number and location of wheels with pins varies. There might also be additional guides that latch over the holes in the paper to guide it through the paper path.
- The menus or buttons to configure settings, including default fonts, print quality, and character pitch.
- The number of slots for different fonts (if any).
- The ability to upgrade their memory.

Example: OkiData Microline 390

Figure 10-24 shows an example of a dot-matrix printer. This is a 24-pin printer. It is currently set up to use individual sheets of paper using the cut-sheet feeder rather than the continuous form paper and tractor feed. It has a slot to add more fonts to its memory. Using the buttons on the front of the printer, you can set the default font, print quality, and character pitch.

Lesson 10

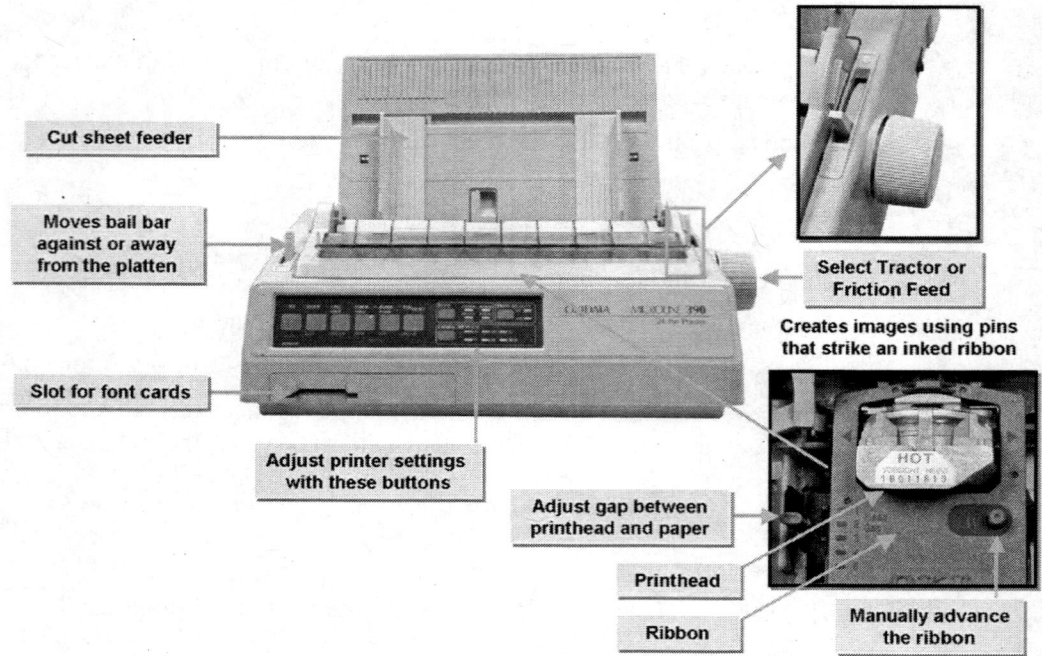

Figure 10-24: *A dot-matrix printer.*

Tractor Feed

Tractor feed uses pairs of wheels with pins evenly spaced around the circumference at a set spacing. Paper with matching holes in the edges fits over the pins. As the wheels turn, the paper is pulled through the printer. Usually just two wheels are used, but there might be additional wheels or pin guides that the paper is latched to. There is usually a lever or other setting on the printer that needs to be engaged in order to use the tractor feed. Figure 10-25 shows a printer set up to use tractor feed.

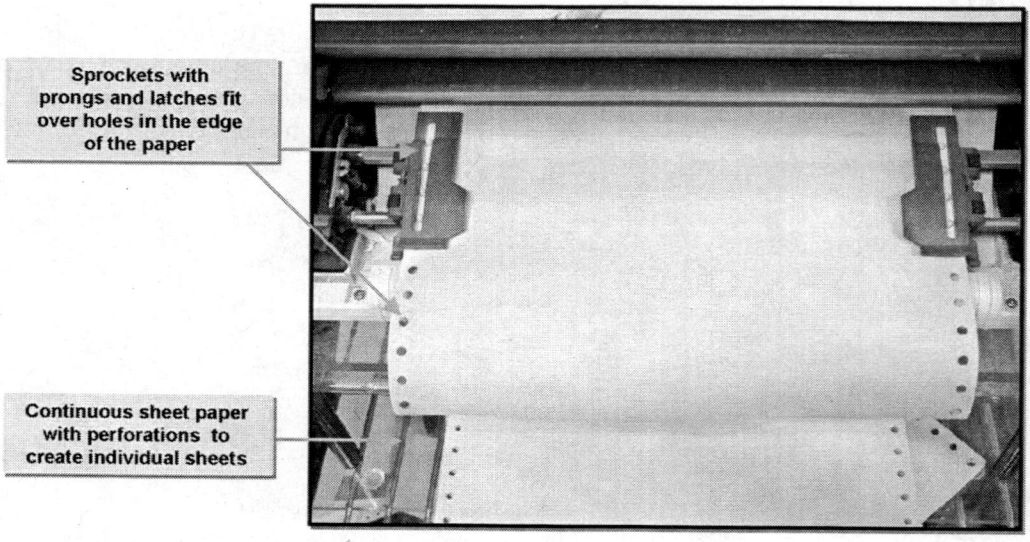

Figure 10-25: *Tractor feed.*

Friction Feed

Friction feed uses two rollers placed one on top of the other. As the rollers turn, the paper is forced through the paper path. This is used to print on individual sheets of paper (cut-sheet paper) and envelopes. Be sure to set the printer lever or other setting to the cut-sheet mode when printing using friction feed. Figure 10-26 shows a printer set up to use friction feed.

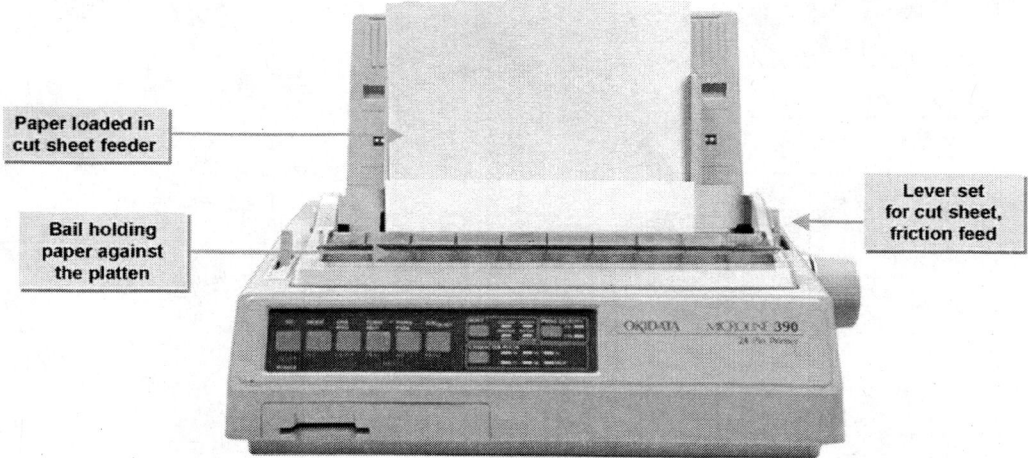

Figure 10-26: *Friction feed.*

How Dot Matrix Printers Work

Dot-matrix printers are still used today, in spite of their high noise level and low quality, because they can print on a continuous roll of paper, as well as on multi-part forms that use carbon or no-carbon-required (NCR) paper. The process for creating output using a dot-matrix printer is described here. Figure 10-27 shows a graphical representation of the process.

1. The dot-matrix print head has a vertical column of small pins that are controlled by an electromagnet. The pins shoot out of the print head and strike an ink-coated ribbon.

2. The impact of the pin transfers ink from the ribbon to the printed page. This physical impact is responsible for the printer's ability to print multiple-layer forms.

3. After a set of pins has fired, an electromagnet pulls them back in, the print head moves a fraction of an inch across the page, and another set of pins is fired.

4. The dots created on the page become the printed text or graphics. More, smaller pins create better quality images. Printers come in 9-pin and 24-pin varieties.

5. Near Letter Quality (NLQ) printers usually use two or more passes over a line of text to increase the number of dots used per letter. This connects the dots to form sharper and clearer letters.

Lesson 10

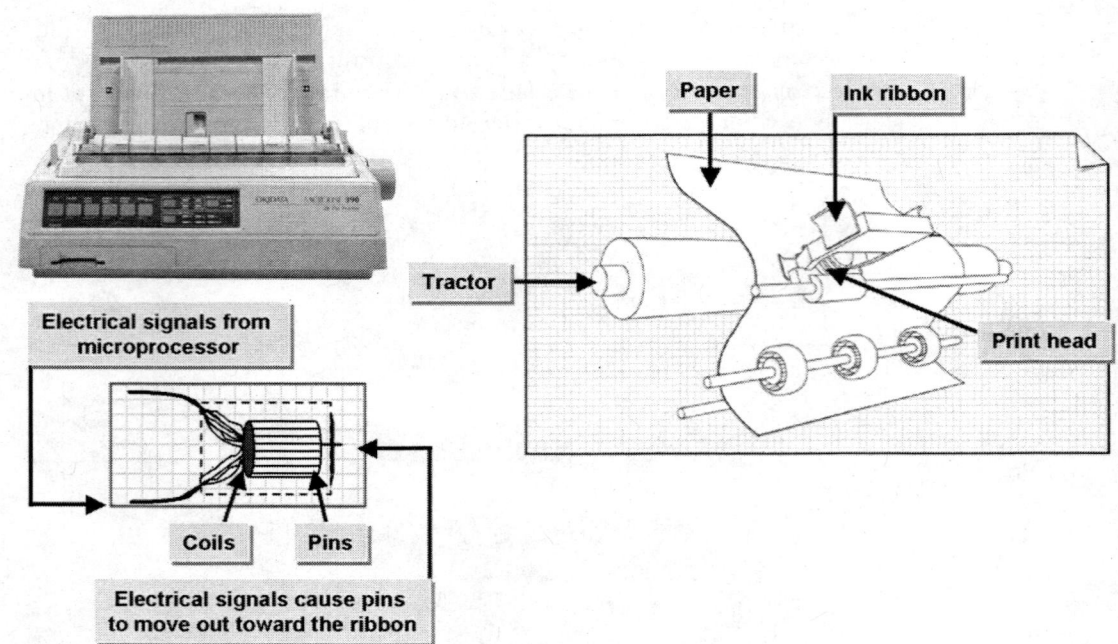

Figure 10-27: *How a dot-matrix printer works.*

Inkjet Printers

Definition:

An *inkjet printer* is a printer that forms images by spraying ink on the paper. Inkjet printers are sometimes referred to as *ink dispersion printers*. All inkjet printers:

- Force liquid ink out of nozzles aimed carefully at the paper.
- Use ink cartridges.
- Have a stepper motor to move the printhead across the paper.
- Use rollers to advance the paper.
- Have a cleaning cycle.
- Park the printhead.
- Contain memory buffers.

Inkjet printers vary by:

- The hardware interfaces that can be used to connect the printer to the computer. These might include the following:
    — Parallel
    — USB
    — Serial
    — AppleTalk
    — SCSI
- The media they can print on. This includes the following:
    — Inexpensive copier paper
    — Bright paper made specifically for inkjet printers

- Photo paper
- Transparencies
- Labels
- Card stock
- Envelopes
- Whether they produce black and white or color output.
- Whether black is produced using a separate cartridge or by combining the cyan, yellow, and magenta color output.
- Whether there are separate tanks for each color or if they are all in one unit. The black cartridge is separate on almost all printers, except for some very low-end printers. If the colors are in one unit and one color runs out, the entire cartridge needs to be replaced.
- The size of cartridges and how much ink each cartridge contains.
- The cost of cartridges.
- The speed at which they print.
- Whether the printhead is part of the printer or part of the print cartridge.
- The paper path. Some printers have a straight-through paper path and others turn the paper over as it passes through the printer.
- The resolution or dots per inch (dpi).
- How the ink is released. It could be by:
  - Piezoelectric, used in Epson printers. This uses a vibration to release a droplet of ink from the cartridge.
  - Thermal, used in most other printers. This method releases a droplet of ink by heating up the ink.

 Many printers are multi-function devices that include scanner, fax, and copier functions.

Example: Epson Stylus Color 500

Figure 10-28 shows an example of an inkjet printer. This printer uses a separate black cartridge, and the color cartridge contains all three colors. The head is parked to the right of the roller. When the printer is turned on, it goes through its cleaning cycle. It has a straight-through paper path in which the paper feeds from the top of the printer and comes out in the output tray the same side up. It uses Piezoelectric technology to release ink onto the paper.

Lesson 10

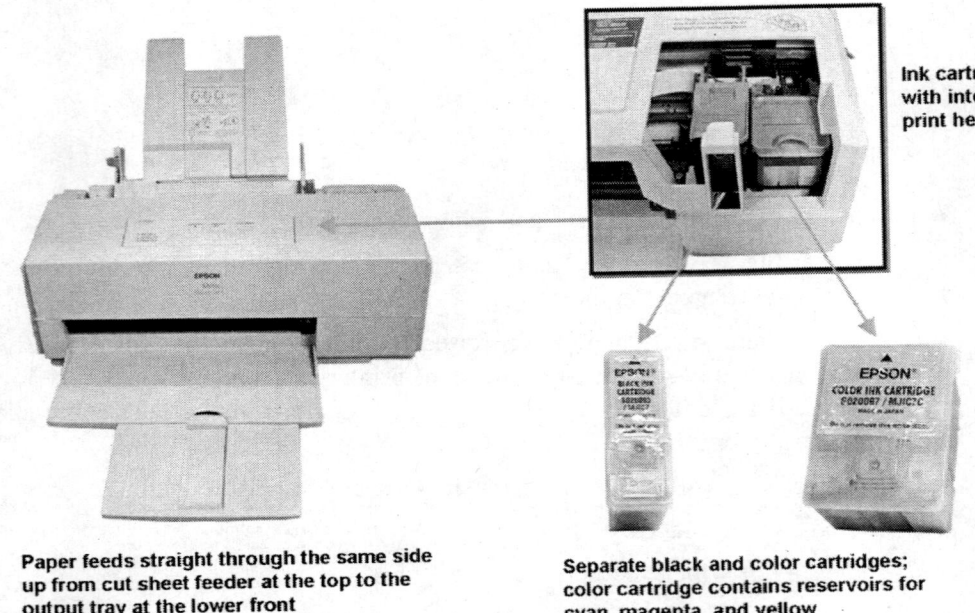

Figure 10-28: *An inkjet printer.*

How Inkjet Printers Work

Inkjet technology has been developing since the late 1970s. This has become an inexpensive printing technology. The process used to create inkjet printouts is outlined here. Figure 10-29 shows a graphical representation of the process.

1. Liquid ink is forced out of carefully aimed nozzles onto the paper.
2. The print head moves back and forth across the paper, printing one row of the image at a time. Each row is several dots wide. The print head typically produces at least 300 distinct dots per inch (300 dpi). Some printers can print at up to 1200 dpi.
3. The paper advances after every row until the page is covered.
4. The amount of ink shot onto the a page is determined by the driver software that controls where and when each nozzle deposits ink.

Lesson 10

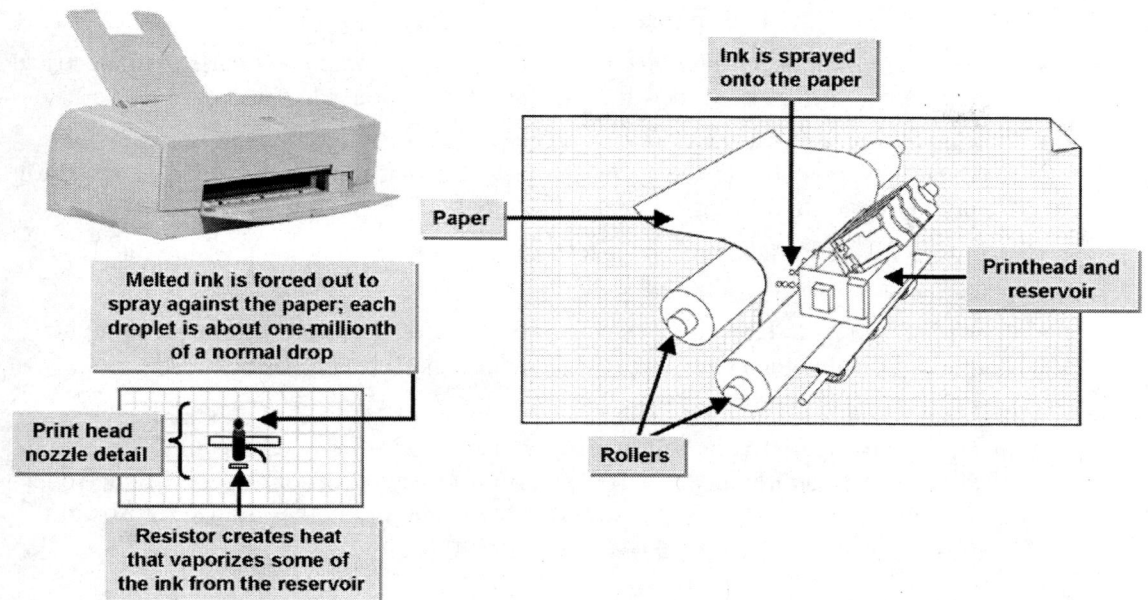

Figure 10-29: *How an inkjet printer works.*

Thermal Inkjet Technology

Some inkjet printers use thermal inkjet technology. Thermal technology uses heat to release the ink from the nozzle. Ink is heated to create a bubble that bursts and shoots ink onto the paper. The heat is turned off, the element cools, and more ink is sucked into the nozzle when the bubble collapses. Each thermal print head has about 300 to 600 nozzles that shoot blobs of ink that can create dots about 60 microns in diameter.

Piezoelectric Inkjet Technology

Some inkjet printers use piezoelectric technology. Piezoelectric technology uses a piezo crystal that flexes when current flows through it. When current flows to the crystal, it changes shape just enough to force a drop of ink out of the nozzle and onto the paper.

Laser Printers

Definition:

A *laser printer* is a printer that forms images on paper by using a laser beam and an electrophotographic drum. All laser printers:

- Produce high-quality images.
- Output one page at a time.
- Produce images using a combination of electrostatic charges, toner, and laser light.

Components of a laser printer include the following:

- *Toner* cartridge. This is a single, replaceable unit that contains the fine powder used to create images as well as additional components used in image production.
- Laser scanning assembly. This is a unit that contains the laser.
- High-voltage power supply.
- DC power supply.

Lesson 10

- Paper transport assembly. This unit contains the rollers and motors that move the paper through the laser printer.
- *Electrostatic Photographic drum (EP drum)*. This component carries an electrical charge that attracts the toner. It then transfers the toner to the paper.
- Transfer *corona* assembly. This is a component that contains the corona wires, which is responsible for charging the paper so that it pulls the toner off the drum and charging the drum itself.
- *Fusing assembly*. This unit, also known as the fuser, applies pressure and heat to the paper to seal the toner particles to the paper.
- Formatter board. This unit processes all of the data received from the computer and coordinates the steps needed to produce the finished page.

All laser printers work by first giving the EP drum a high overall electrical charge (typically of about -600 volts), then using a laser beam to reduce this uniform charge (typically down to approximately -100 volts) on selected portions of the drum. Toner is attracted to the less highly-charged areas of the drum and is then transferred from the drum to the paper as the paper passes over the drum.

Laser printers vary by:

- The hardware interface used to connect the printer to the computer.
- Whether they produce black and white or color output.
- The number of paper trays and the amount of paper each tray can hold.
- How adjustable paper trays are.
- Output locations. Usually this is an output bin on top of the printer, but there might be an additional or alternate straight paper path through a drop-down door on the rear of the printer.
- The printer language used.
- Print resolution or Dots Per Inch (dpi).
- The speed at which they print.
- Whether they use a single laser or a strip of LEDs.
- Whether consumable components are separate components or built together into a single unit.
- Status lights and their location.
- Paper sizes and weights that can be accommodated by the printer.
- The energy-saving features.
- The toner-saving features.
- The operating systems supported.
- The amount of memory installed, whether the memory is upgradeable, and the type of memory.

Example: HP LaserJet 6P

Figure 10-30 shows an example of a laser printer. Features of this printer include:

- It can be connected to the computer using:
  — A LocalTalk connection for Macintosh computers or LocalTalk networks.
  — A 1284 B Centronics parallel port.
  — A 1284 C parallel port.

— An infrared port.
- It has two input trays and two output trays.
- It can use either Printer Control Language (PCL) or PostScript commands, and it can automatically switch between them as needed.
- It outputs images at 600 dpi at eight pages per minute.
- It has 2 MB of memory.

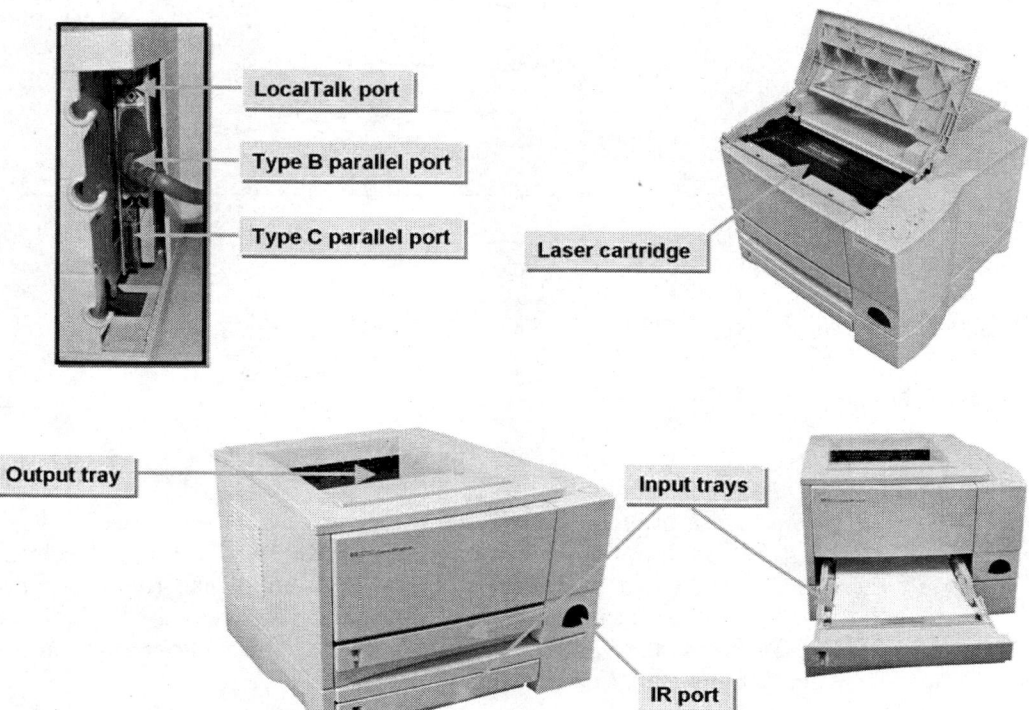

Figure 10-30: *A laser printer.*

How Laser Printers Work

Laser printers print a page at a time using a combination of electrostatic charges, toner, and laser light. The following steps describe the process the laser printer uses to produce the finished printed page.

1. Cleaning—The Electrostatic Photographic (EP) drum is cleaned with a rubber blade.
2. Erasing—Charges are removed from the EP drum in preparation for the next image.
3. Charging or conditioning—The EP drum is given a strong negative charge of about -600 volts by the primary corona wire.
4. Writing—A laser beam writes to the EP drum giving portions of the drum a weaker negative charge.
5. Developing—Toner is attracted to the areas of the drum that were hit by the laser light.
6. Transferring—The transfer corona wire charges the paper with a positive charge. The paper runs beneath the EP drum as the drum turns and loses its toner to the paper.
7. Fusing—The paper runs through the fusing assembly, which is heated to 350 degrees Fahrenheit. The fuser's high temperature and pressure fuse or melt the toner into the paper.

A graphical representation of the process is shown in Figure 10-31.

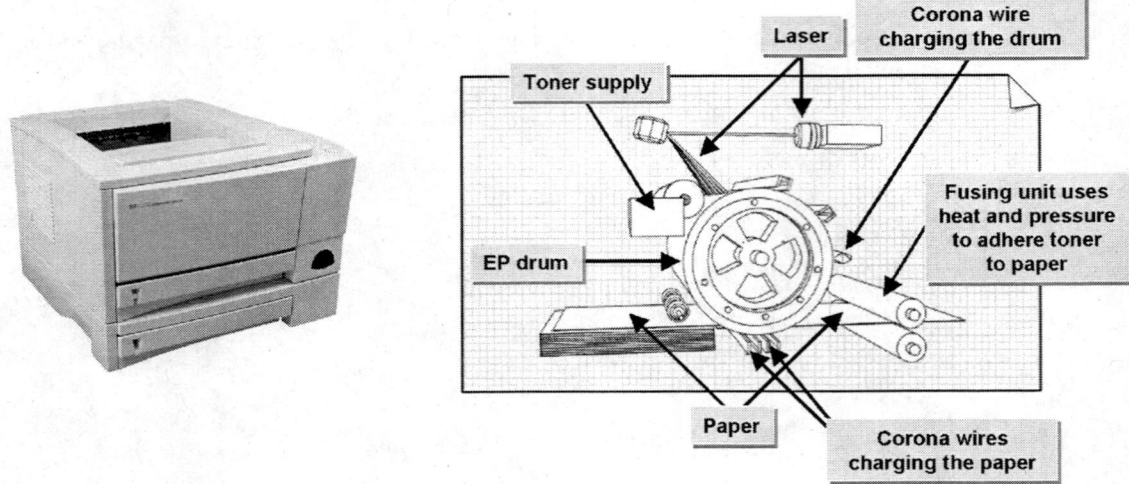

Figure 10-31: *How a laser printer works.*

Solid Ink Printers

Definition:

Solid ink printers are printers that use ink from melted solid-ink sticks. The ink is melted and forced into a printhead, where it's transferred to a drum, which then transfers the image to the paper as it rolls over the drum. Solid ink printers can print on standard paper. Some solid ink printers can produce better results than laser printers or inkjet printers because they produce an image with a clearer, finer edge on a wide variety of media, such as paper or transparency.

 Because of the danger from melted wax, solid ink printers are usually kept in isolated areas and shared over the network.

Example: Xerox Phaser 8200B

The Xerox Phaser 8200B uses melted solid-ink sticks instead of toner. The solid ink sticks are melted during the print process, and the liquid ink is used to create an image on a drum. The paper is then rolled over the drum to transfer the image. The Xerox Phaser 8200 can print on standard paper and on overheads.

Dye Sublimation Printers

Definition:

A *dye sublimation printer* is a printer that uses a thermal process to transfer dye to paper to create images. The ink is on large rolls of film. Sheets of cyan, magenta, yellow, and black dye are heated to turn the dye into a gas. A heating element boils away a tiny dot of the ink that diffuses into a specially manufactured paper's surface where it mixes with other ink to form a colored area and forms a solid again. The temperature controls the amount of ink added to the paper, so variations in the temperature setting can control the quantity of each colored ink added to every location on the paper. The paper requires four different passes, getting all the yellow on the page first, then cyan, magenta, and finally black. Some dye sublimation printers print on photo paper, while others can print on a variety of surfaces, including transparencies, which can be used on overhead projectors. Dye sublimation printers are widely used in demanding graphic arts and photographic applications because they can create clearer, more realistic photo reproductions than other printers, and the photos don't fade as much over time. Dye sublimation printers are often used in scientific research centers because of their ability to create near-perfect, photo-realistic reproductions.

Example: Kodak Professional 8500 Digital Photo Printer

The Kodak Professional 8500 Digital Photo Printer uses dye embedded in a ribbon, which is stored inside a cartridge. When the ribbon is exposed to heat from the thermal head, the dye turns to gas and is absorbed by special photo paper. Once absorbed into the paper, the dye turns to a solid again, reproducing the image that was sent to the printer. The Kodak Professional 8500 Digital Photo Printer is used to print pictures because of its ability to create near-perfect photo reproductions.

Other Types of Printers

Thermo autochrome uses special paper that has cyan, magenta, and yellow layers. A printer uses a specific temperature to activate the colors on one layer at a time. Ultraviolet light fixes the color before the next layer is heated.

Thermal wax is very similar to dye-sublimation but uses plastic films covered with colored wax. A heater melts dots of the wax onto a special thermal paper. This technology is excellent for making transparencies.

Windows Print Process

The Windows XP print process consists of the following stages.

1. A user prints a document in an application.
2. The Graphics Device Interface (GDI) calls the printer driver.
3. The printer driver creates a job in printer language for the target printer. (This is called *rendering*.) This determines the job's data type. Some data types can be printed directly; others will require additional rendering later in the process.
4. The client side of the print spooler returns control of the computer system to the application.
5. The server side of the print spooler inserts the job into the printing stream.
6. The print router determines whether the job is for a local or remote printer.
   - If the job is for a local printer, the print router routes it to the local print provider.
   - If the job is for a remote printer:
     — The print router routes it to the correct remote print provider for the print server. (For example, a Windows print server and a Novell NetWare print server will have different print providers.)
     — The remote print provider passes the job over the network to the spooler service at the print server, and the process resumes at the print server with the server side of the print spooler.
7. The local print provider *spools* the print job or writes it from memory to disk. By default, print jobs spool to the C:***system_root**\System32\Spool\Printers folder. The local print provider also locates a print processor that can render the job's data type.

Lesson 10: Peripheral Devices

Lesson 10

8. The print processor, WinPrint, completes any rendering needed for the job's data type. WinPrint supports all the general data types. In rare cases, a specialized printer might install a specialized print processor.
9. The separator page processor inserts a separator page, if indicated.
10. The port monitor software for the printer's port handles the physical data communication between the computer and printer.
11. The printer produces the output.

Figure 10-32 graphically represents the Windows print process.

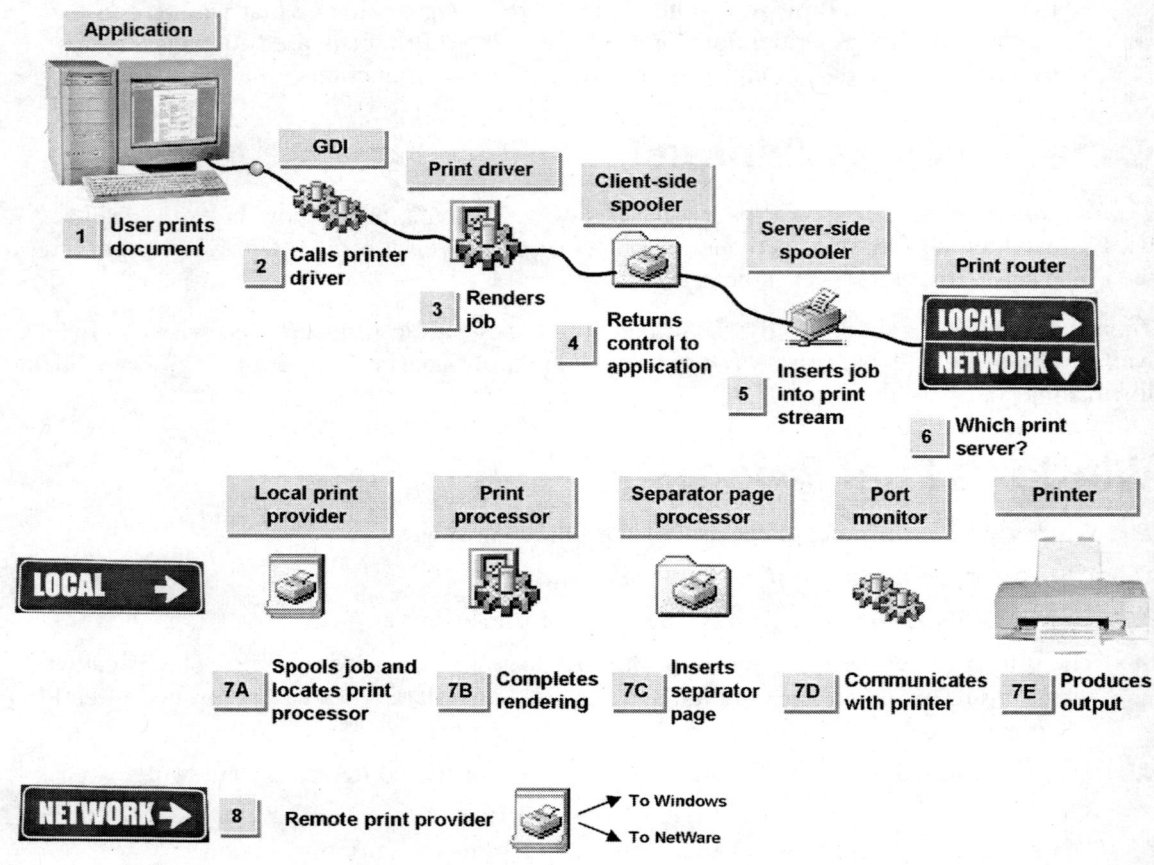

Figure 10-32: *The Windows print process.*

Common Printer Problems

Solving printer problems requires imagination and skill, as well as organization and logic. Table 10-12 a list of common printer problems.

Table 10-12: *Common Printer Problems*

Symptom	Possible Problem	Solution
Nothing will print from any application.	Physical printer problem including out of toner/ink or paper. Incorrect print driver. Printer is paused in Windows or in the network operating system.	Press the Test button on the printer. Check the printer driver; open the properties of the printer object in the Printers And Faxes window and check the driver name on the Advanced page. Click New Driver to change the driver. Right-click the printer in the Printers And Faxes window and uncheck Pause Printing.
Printer doesn't print the way the user expects it to.	Incorrect driver. Wrong page setup selections made in the application or in printer properties.	Check or change the printer driver. Check the page setup options in the applications or the properties of the printer.
User can't access network printer.	User lost network connection or network printer is down.	Reattach to the network and check the status of the printer.
Printer prints part of a document then prints garbage for the rest of the document.	Printer is low on memory. Incorrect printer driver. Intermittent cable problem.	Check whether additional memory can be installed in the printer. Check for correct or updated printer driver. Replace the cable.

Common Dot-matrix Printer Problems

Dot-matrix printers are known to be rugged and dependable. Most repairs are limited to the print head, which may be hot after a long period of use. Table 10-13 lists some common dot-matrix printer problems.

Table 10-13: *Common Dot-matrix Printer Problems*

Symptom	Possible Problem	Solution
Horizontal lines appear in the print so parts of characters are missing.	A pin in the print head is stuck or bent.	Attempts to repair a print head can damage it beyond hope. Cleaning the print head with a lubricant like WD-40 or alcohol. Remove any visible grime. Open the print head and look for bent pins; it is difficult to straighten pins and springs without permanently damaging the print head, so normally you will buy a new print head.
Flecks and smudges on the paper.	The ribbon is not aligned correctly, not feeding correctly, or is over-inked.	Reposition the ribbon. Replace the ribbon cartridge; cartridges are not economical to repair. Clean and lubricate the gears that advance the print head.
Poor print quality.	The printer adjustment for paper thickness is set to an incorrect value. Poor quality paper.	Set the thickness to match the paper you are using. Use good-quality paper.

Lesson 10

Symptom	Possible Problem	Solution
Continuous-feed paper jams.	Tractor feed problems.	Clean paper from gears. Align tractor feed. Replace worn gears.

Common Inkjet Printer Problems

Most problems unique to an inkjet printer can be solved by cleaning the printer, replacing the print cartridge, and using good-quality paper. Occasionally you might need to replace the print head. When other problems occur, except for very high-end models, it may be more cost effective to replace rather than repair the printer.

Table 10-14 shows some of the solutions for common inkjet printer problems.

Table 10-14: *Common Inkjet Printer Problems*

Symptom	Possible Problem	Solution
Poor print quality.	Clogged nozzles, incorrect paper. Empty or defective cartridge.	Clean the interior of the printer; perform one or more print cartridge cleaning cycles; switch to a paper specifically designed for inkjet printers. Replace the cartridge.
No output; paper passes through printer but is blank.	Empty ink cartridges; clogged nozzles; tape sealing ink cartridge; incorrect cartridge or cartridge improperly seated.	Replace empty or incorrect ink cartridges. Clean the printer and print cartridge. Remove tape seal from ink cartridge. Align cartridge. Check manufacturer's Web site for other troubleshooting procedures.
Fuzzy output.	Clogged nozzles, low ink cartridge, faulty print head.	Perform several cleaning cycles. Replace ink cartridge or print head.

Common Laser Printer Problems

Laser printers contain chemicals, high voltages, and high-temperature areas that can hurt you. Make sure the printer is off and the parts are cool before you attempt to work on the machine. Some of the exposed wires are very thin and can be damaged easily, so treat the printer gently. Table 10-15 lists problems common to laser printers.

Table 10-15: *Common Laser Printer Problems*

Symptom	Possible Problem	Solution
Smeared output, or output rubs off the paper.	Fuser temperature is too low: if the fuser is not hot enough, the toner will not melt into the paper. Fuser roller uneven. Problem in paper path. Paper not smooth enough.	Follow the manufacturer's instructions to set fuser mode for the paper. Adjust the fuser roller. Clear the paper path. Use good-quality paper.
Low-quality image.	Poor-quality paper does not accept charge and transfer toner. Transfer corona dirty or faulty. Transfer corona power supply problem. Faulty primary corona or power supply do not charge print drum.	Use good-quality paper. Follow the manufacturer's instructions to clean transfer corona. Follow the manufacturer's instructions to troubleshoot other faulty components.
Repeating horizontal lines or white spaces.	Dirty fuser roller. Warped or worn fuser roller. Scratched print drum due to debris between wipe blade and drum.	Clean all fuser rollers. Compare the distance between the repetitions of the lines to the circumferences of the rollers, and consult manufacturer's documentation to find which may have the problem. Follow the manufacturer's instructions to adjust or replace rollers. Follow the manufacturer's instructions to replace scratched print drum.
Repeating vertical lines or white spaces.	Scratched print drum. Dirty primary corona or transfer corona produces uneven charge.	Follow the manufacturer's instructions to replace scratched print drum. Follow the manufacturer's instructions to clean corona wires.

Environmental Effects on Printing

Printers are usually quite robust peripherals and can take quite a beating. However, some of the environments where printers are used are not ideal for printing. If you must install a printer in an unfavorable environment, you should be aware of some of the factors that might cause printer problems.

- A clean environment prolongs the life and usability of most equipment, including printers. However, printers are often needed on the factory floor, in a pet grooming salon, and other places where dirt, dust, and debris are flying constantly. Keeping the printer in an enclosure can reduce the amount of debris getting into the printer in such a case.

- Relative humidity of 50 to 60 percent is good for computer equipment. High humidity can lead to moisture problems. Low humidity can lead to static problems. Either situation can cause sporadic print problems.

Lesson 10

How to Troubleshoot Printer Problems

Procedure Reference: Troubleshoot Printer Problems

To troubleshoot some of the most common printer problems:

1. When attempting to print, the job appears in the print queue, but after a few minutes the system notification error message This Document Failed To Print is displayed.
   - Verify that the printer is connected to the parallel port using an IEEE 1284 cable.
   - Verify that LPT1 is configured with the correct port protocol; if the printer is bidirectional, it will need an ECP or EPP port.
   - Perform a printer self test and verify that the printer passes this test.
   - If the printer is piggy-backed to the LPT port on another device such as a Zip drive, scanner, or other daisy-chained device, connect the printer directly to LPT1 and attempt to print again.
   - Move the printer and cable to another PC and attempt to print from Notepad or WordPad.
   - Replace the printer cable.
   - Open the print queue from the System Tray. Choose Help→Troubleshooter. Select My Document Doesn't Print At All and then click Next. Then work through the troubleshooter trying their suggestions until you can resolve the problem.

2. Printer does not successfully print a test page.
   - Check the ink or toner levels; check for a dry ribbon.
   - Try to reproduce the problem:
     a. From the Start menu, choose Printers And Faxes.
     b. Right-click the printer in question and choose Properties.
     c. Click Print Test Page.
   - If the page did not print, click Troubleshoot and follow the Troubleshooting Wizard to help you resolve the problem.
   - Check the documentation for your printer and print a test page directly from the physical printer using printer controls.
   - If the printer still does not print, refer to the printer documentation for how to resolve this problem on your printer model.

3. To fix a paper jam on a laser printer:
   - Check the printer documentation and follow the directions on how to remove paper from a paper jam for your printer model.
   - Check input and output trays for stuck paper.
   - Check the rest of the paper path for jammed paper or stray bits of paper. A small bit of paper in the wrong location can cause the sensors to believe there is a paper jam.
   - Remove the tray and verify that the plates at the bottom of the tray move freely. Reinsert the tray and try to print again.
   - Reset the printer and try printing again.

> ⚠ Be very careful when working inside a laser printer. The fuser assembly can get very hot (180 degrees Celsius).

4. Repeated streaks on the page printed on a laser printer can indicate any number of problems. The spacing of the streaks helps identify which component is causing the problem. Refer to the troubleshooting guide for your printer model to determine the exact cause of the problem.

5. Inkjet printers are prone to problems. These are most often consumer level devices and not designed for the rigors of printing demanded in most business environments. Some solutions to common problems include:
   - Perform one or more print cartridge cleaning cycles.
   - Clean the interior of the printer.
   - Replace the print cartridge.
   - Use good-quality paper.
   - Replace the print head.

6. To correct most dot-matrix printer problems:
   - Replace dried out or used-up ribbons.
   - Adjust placement of the print head.
   - Replace a worn or damaged print head.
   - Clean or align tractor feed gears; replace worn gears

7. If you use a piggy-backed parallel port device with the printer plugged in to the device, and you have problems printing to the printer, you should check the documentation for the device on troubleshooting methods. You might find that the best solution is installing a second parallel port in the system or replacing the printer with one that uses USB or some other connection method.

8. USB printers can be plugged in to any USB port on the system. However, if a USB printer is using a USB port on an unpowered device such as a keyboard or unpowered hub, the printer might have sporadic problems because the port is so far away from the computer power supply. You might see the error message The Hub Does Not Have Enough Power Available To Operate The *Device Driver Name*. Would You Like Assistance In Solving This Problem? If You Click No, The Device May Not Function Properly. To resolve this problem, plug the printer into a USB port directly on the system or use a powered hub.

Procedure Reference: Configure the Parallel Port

To configure a parallel port with the correct print protocol:

1. Access the system BIOS.
2. Enable the parallel port protocol you want to use: EPP or ECP for bidirectional printers, or SPP for standard printers.
3. Save the BIOS settings. The system will then restart with the new settings.

Lesson 10

ACTIVITY 10-5

Troubleshooting Printer Problems

Scenario:

The following is a list of the printer trouble tickets that have been assigned to you today.

- Ticket: 215001

    Location: Main building, 21L39

    User: Greg Berndt

    User prints a document from WordPad. Shortly after that he gets the message This Document Failed To Print. He is using an inkjet printer connected to the parallel port.

- Ticket: 215002

    Location: Main building, 32J45

    User: Estelle Royston

    Printer does not successfully print a test page using the buttons on the printer.

- Ticket: 215003

    Location: Main building, 13E41

    User: Mark Dawson

    Paper jam on laser printer.

- Ticket: 215004

    Location: Training center, main office

    User: Tomas Ridley

    Laser printer output has repeated streaks on the pages it produces. This is an HP LaserJet 5si printer.

- Ticket: 215005

    Location: Training center, room 1

    User: Toni Mancuso

    Inkjet printers in the room have various problems including:
    - Poor print quality.
    - No output.
    - Fuzzy output.

- Ticket: 215006

    Location: Main building, 12B13

    User: Sheila Wright

    The dot matrix printer used for printing multi-part forms was printing poorly, and now, in addition, there is a paper jam.

- Ticket: 215007

Lesson 10

Location: Elmwood Place, cube 29

User: Janice Wharton

The user has a parallel port Zip drive and a printer plugged in to the piggy-back parallel port on the drive. The printer is not printing.

What You Do	How You Do It
1. Resolve trouble ticket 215001.	a. Verify that the printer is turned on.
	b. Verify that the printer is online.
	c. Verify that the printer is connected with an IEEE 1284 cable to LPT1 on his system.
	d. Verify that LPT1 is configured for a bidirectional print protocol.
	e. Perform a printer self test using the controls on the printer as specified in the printer documentation and verify that the printer passes this test.
	f. If the printer is piggy-backed on another device such as a Zip drive, scanner, or other daisy-chained device to the LPT port, **connect the printer directly to LPT1 and attempt to print again.**
	g. If you still cannot print, **replace the printer cable.**
	h. If the print process is still producing this error message, **move the printer and cable to another PC and attempt to print from Notepad or Wordpad.**

Lesson 10: Peripheral Devices

Lesson 10

2. **Resolve trouble ticket 215002.**

    a. From the Start menu, choose Printers And Faxes.

    b. Right-click the printer and choose Properties.

    c. Click Print Test Page.

    d. If the page did not print, **click Troubleshoot.**

    e. Follow the Troubleshooting Wizard to help you resolve the problem.

    f. Check documentation for the printer and print a test page directly from the physical printer using printer controls.

    g. If the printer test does not print, **refer to the printer's documentation for how to resolve this problem on your printer model.**

3. **Resolve trouble ticket 215003.**

    a. Check the printer's documentation and follow the directions on how to remove paper from a paper jam for your printer.

    b. Check input and output trays for stuck paper.

    c. Check the rest of the paper path for jammed paper or stray bits of paper.

    d. Remove the tray and verify that the plates at the bottom of the tray move freely.

    e. Reinsert the tray and try to print again.

    f. Reset the printer and try printing again.

4. Access the HP Web site at *www.hp.com* and locate possible reasons for the repeated pattern on the output described in trouble ticket 215004. Identify which component is the potential cause of the streaking.

LESSON 10

5. List some of the things you should check and try to do when resolving trouble ticket 215005.

6. Resolve trouble ticket 215006.

    a. Open the tractor feeds and carefully remove the paper from the paper path.

    b. Remove any bits of paper that are loose in the printer from the paper path.

    c. With the printer off, align the paper and carefully guide it through the paper path, and align the holes with the tractor feed. Close the tractor feed over the edges of the paper feed holes.

    d. Determine if the poor print quality is due to needing a new ribbon, bent or damaged pins on the print head, the print head being too far from the platen, sheet fed is selected instead of pin feed, or another reason.

    e. Make adjustments or replace the component as needed to resolve the problem.

7. Access the Iomega Web site at *www.iomega.com* and locate the document that describes how to resolve the problem described in trouble ticket 215007. After reviewing the steps, what are the two solutions they suggest?

Lesson 10: Peripheral Devices

Lesson 10

Topic D

Other Input/Output Devices

In addition to the input/output devices we looked at in the previous topics, other input/output devices are available and commonly in use today, such as scanners, digital cameras, still/video cameras, DVD players, microphones, speakers, and so on. These devices allow you to complete tasks such as transferring pictures, music, and video to your computer, as well as play back this data so that you can see and hear it. In this topic, you will learn how to connect and troubleshoot other commonly used peripheral devices.

Scanners

A *scanner* captures graphic images and printed text and then converts them to digital form for editing and manipulation in a PC. The scanner reflects light off an image or object and converts it into 0s and 1s, a computer-readable format. The image is recorded pixel by pixel; generally, the higher the resolution, the better quality of the resulting image. A high-end scanner will use high-quality glass optics that are color-corrected and coated for minimum diffusion. Lower-end models will typically skimp in this area, using plastic components to reduce costs. Some devices have automatic document feeders, to save the user from manually putting each sheet of paper into the scanner.

Flatbed scanners, shown in Figure 10-33, are the most versatile and popular format. They are capable of capturing color pictures, documents, pages from books and magazines, and—with the right attachments—transparent photographic film. They have a flat surface to hold material, which can be flat or three-dimensional, such as a book or other object. The image sensor moves across the material to scan it. Scanning areas vary by model.

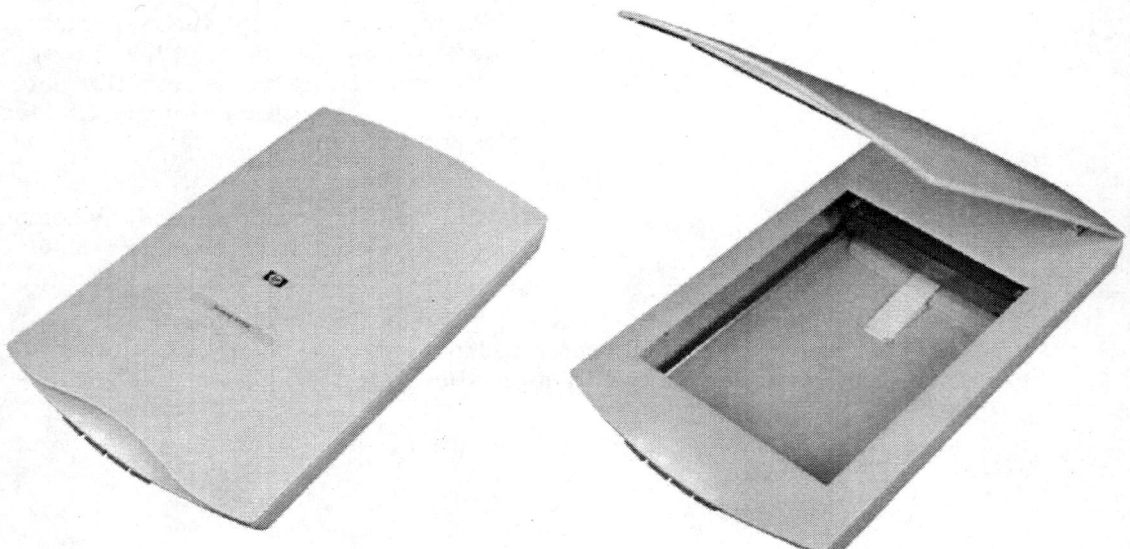

Figure 10-33: *A flatbed scanner.*

Other scanners are smaller than the flatbed; they take up less desk space and may have special functions:

- Hand-held scanners are inexpensive, manually operated, and have a limited scanning width.

- Sheet-fed scanners are for reflective material, such as documents, which are fed past the image sensor.
- Film scanners are used for negatives and slides; they usually have holders to help load the film.
- Photo scanners scan printed photographs and may also be equipped to handle negatives and slides.

Interface with the computer may be accomplished by:

- Parallel port, which is easy to use but slow; a connector can hook the scanner directly to the printer.
- SCSI port, which transfers data more quickly than the parallel; this is important for scans of high resolution.
- USB port, which is very flexible and easy to use, thanks to its Plug and Play capability; it is slower than SCSI.

Digital Cameras

Digital cameras are increasingly popular as their quality improves, prices drop, and consumers become more computer and Web savvy. Unlike film cameras, the image is captured digitally and stored as a file on a floppy disk, removable memory card, or optical disc. Some printers accept digital files on memory cards directly. An example of a digital camera is shown in Figure 10-34.

Figure 10-34: *A digital camera.*

Downloading to the hard drive is accomplished by:

- Floppy-disk drive; adapters hold small memory cards.
- Serial cable, which is time-consuming and requires a power source.
- Parallel cable, which is faster than a serial connection.
- Infrared, which does not use cables but is slow and requires a power source.

Lesson 10

- SCSI cable, which uses a high-speed bus cable system.
- USB or FireWire cable, which is much faster than serial or parallel cable.
- External drive, which requires installation and software. This method is also significantly faster than a serial connection.
- Card readers.
- PC Card; adapters hold small memory cards.

The digital file may then be resized, touched-up, recolored and labeled with image-editing software. Output options include:

- Viewing on the monitor.
- Printing on special photographic paper.
- Printing on special transfer sheets for application to fabric.
- Posting on the Web.
- Attaching to email.
- Importing into documents.

Touch Screens

Definition:

A touch screen input device is a monitor device that enables users to enter input by touching areas on the screen. All touch screens enable you to enter information by pressing the monitor surface rather than needing to use a keyboard or mouse for entering input. Touch screens are composed of:

- Touch sensors. The sensors can be a panel that lays over a standard monitor or can be built into a special touch screen monitor where the user actually touches the glass on the monitor.
- Controller. If using an overlay panel, the controller connects to the panel and then to a PC port. Many use a COM or USB port, although there are special instances where the controller connects to a drive or other device or port. For touch screens with built-in touch sensors, the controller is built into the monitor. In this case, the monitor contains two cables—one to the monitor port and one to the COM or USB port (or other port).
- Device driver or specialized software. This enables the operating system to receive and interpret information from the touch screen device.

Touch screens vary in the following ways:

- How the screens gather input. This might include technologies such as:
  - Infrared
  - Capacitive touch
  - Resistive touch
  - Surface acoustic wave
- Whether it is finger touch or stylus touch. Some touch screen surfaces must be touched with a bare finger in order to work. Others can be touched with gloved hands or a pointer or stylus of some type.

Example:

The example shown in Figure 10-35 shows a touch screen input device. It is implemented as a screen overlay and connects to the computer through the USB port. Users interact with it using their fingers to touch active areas on the Web page.

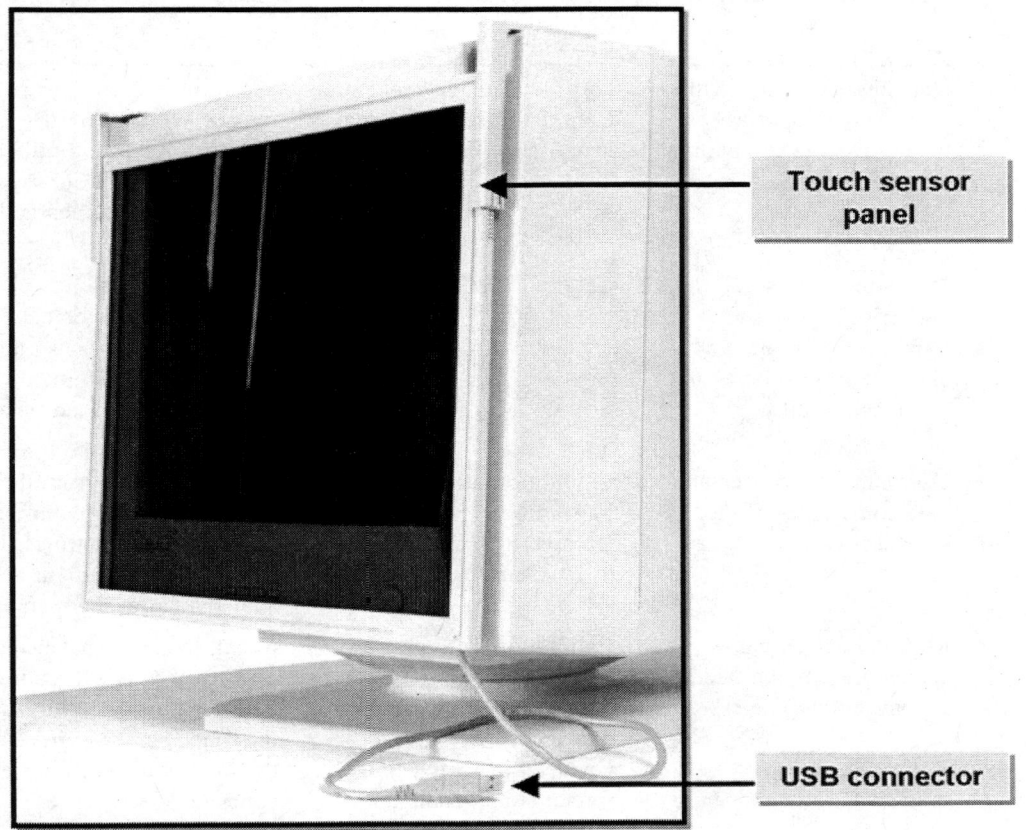

Figure 10-35: *A touch screen input device.*

How Touch Screen Devices Work

The following list describes the process a touch screen device uses to retrieve user input and send it to the computer for processing.

1. A user touches the touch sensor panel with their finger, a stylus, or other device.
2. The touch creates a change in the electrical flow through the screen.
3. The system evaluates the change in electrical flow to determine where the touch occurred.
4. The touch screen controller sends the touch sensor data to the computer as input data.
5. The driver for the touch screen device enables the computer to interpret the data that was sent. Usually the data is interpreted as mouse interactions.

Before this process can occur, the touch screen hardware and drivers need to be installed, and the device needs to be calibrated with the calibration software utility that came with the device. This sets the dimensions of the screen and the relative distance between points. There will be on screen instructions for where to touch the screen.

Lesson 10

Common Touch Screen Device Problems

Table 10-16 lists some of the most common symptoms of touch screen device problems and the possible problems that cause those symptoms.

Table 10-16: *Common Touch Screen Device Problems*

Symptom	Possible Problem	Solution
Handheld computer with touch screen interface is having trouble responding to screen input.	Dirty or damaged screen. Calibration settings were lost.	Clean the screen. If necessary, replace screen. Run the calibration utility to set screen dimension information. Be sure batteries are charged to retain settings.
Insertion point is not appearing where user touches. It appears well above that location or not on screen at all.	Calibration settings have been lost.	Set the effective area of the screen, then run the calibration utility. You might also need to set the dpi settings to match between the touch screen and what the program is expecting.
User cannot select or activate some areas of the screen.	Calibration utility needs to be re-run. Hardware connections need to be checked.	Run the utilities from the manufacturer to check calibration and other hardware settings. Hardware testing software might also be available from the manufacturer.
Results of touching the screen are not consistent or are inaccurately interpreted.	Calibration settings were lost. Screen surface is dirty or damaged. Connections between touch screen components are loose or damaged. Circuitry within a component of the touch screen system is damaged and needs replacement.	Check the hardware using the manufacturer's calibration and hardware testing utilities. Clean the touch screen surface. Verify that all connections are properly connected.

Speakers

While some users hook their computer up to a stereo system, others use smaller desktop speakers. Because speakers contain large electromagnets, specially shielded speaker cabinets are used for sound systems that will be placed near monitors. The better the speakers, the better the sound, until you reach a quality that is limited by the sound card and the source.

Microphones

Microphones change sound energy into electrical energy that sound cards turn into digital information. Computers can store, manipulate, and play back this digital information. Microphones are useless without functioning sound cards.

Activity 10-6

Identifying Other Input/Output Devices

Activity Time:

10 minutes

Scenario:

In this activity, you will be selecting the input/output device that meets the need presented in each situation.

1. A user is getting ready to do a presentation for a group of customers over the Web. The Web-based presentation software allows the audience to ask questions of the presenter. What input/output devices will the presenter need?

    a) Scanner

    b) Digital camera

    c) Touch screen

    d) Speakers

    e) Microphone

2. A user needs to email several paper-based documents to a customer. What input/output device would they use to transfer the paper-based documents to electronic format on their computer?

    a) Scanner

    b) Digital camera

    c) Touch screen

    d) Speakers

    e) Microphone

3. A customer has a kiosk where his patrons can use a keyboard and a mouse to search for auto parts that his store carries. He complains that he has had to replace the keyboard and mouse numerous times due to customer negligence. Is there another input solution, you would recommend?

Lesson 10: Peripheral Devices

4. A user needs to take and store photos of expensive equipment for insurance purposes. What input/output devices should they use to take the photos and transfer them to their PC?

   a) Scanner

   b) Digital camera

   c) Touch screen

   d) Speakers

   e) Microphone

Lesson 10 Follow-up

In this lesson, you identified the different peripheral devices that can be connected to the computer to input or output data. These peripheral devices allow the user to interact with the computer's operating system by sending data to the computer and viewing the results of their work. You also learned how to troubleshoot these devices—a computer and its internal system components is not much good to a user if they cannot get data in or out of the computer.

1. What input/output peripheral devices does your company have and support?

2. As an A+ technician, which input/output devices do you expect to see more of in a business setting? In a repair center catering to home users?

LESSON 11
Portable Computing

Lesson Time
3 hour(s)

Lesson Objectives:

In this lesson, you will install, configure, and work with various portable computing devices. You will:

- Identify components of a portable computing device.
- Dock a notebook computer.
- Install and remove drives from notebooks.
- Install or remove PC Cards.
- Install or remove a Mini-PCI card.
- Install or add memory to a portable computing device.
- Replace a system board in a portable computer.
- Connect PDAs to a computer.

Lesson 11

Introduction

Up to this point, you have been working on desktop systems; however, not all users are content with being tied to a specific location. They need systems they can take from place to place. In this lesson, you will be supporting portable computing devices.

In most companies, a hardware technician will need to work with more types of devices than just desktop systems. As today's workforce becomes more mobile, portable systems become more common, so, in any company, there are often a variety of portable computing devices you will also be asked to support. Many of the skills you acquired in supporting desktop systems also apply to portable systems, but there are some specialized skills you'll need as well. This lesson will give you those skills.

The following CompTIA A+ Core Hardware (2003) Examination objectives are covered in this lesson:

- Topic A:
  - 1.2 Identify basic procedures for adding and removing field-replaceable modules for desktop systems. Given a replacement scenario choose the appropriate sequences. Content includes: desktop components—AC adapter.
  - 1.3 Identify basic procedures for adding and removing field-replaceable modules for portable systems. Given a replacement scenario, choose the appropriate sequence. Content includes: power supply—AC adapter, DC adapter, and battery; and LCD panel.
  - 1.10 Determine the issues that must be considered when upgrading a PC. In a given scenario, determine when and how to upgrade system components. Components include: laptop power sources—lithium ion, NiMH, and fuel cell.
  - 2.1 Recognize common problems associated with each module and their symptoms, and identify steps to isolate and troubleshoot the problems. Given a problem situation, interpret the symptoms and infer the most likely cause. Content includes: portable systems—batteries.
- Topic B:
  - 1.3 Identify basic procedures for adding and removing field-replaceable modules for portable systems. Given a replacement scenario, choose the appropriate sequence. Content includes: docking station/port replicator.
  - 2.1 Recognize common problems associated with each module and their symptoms, and identify steps to isolate and troubleshoot the problems. Given a problem situation, interpret the symptoms and infer the most likely cause. Content includes: docking station/port replicator.
- Topic C:
  - 1.3 Identify basic procedures for adding and removing field-replaceable modules for portable systems. Given a replacement scenario, choose the appropriate sequence. Content includes: storage devices—CD/CDRW, DVD/DVDRW, and removable storage; and PCMCIA/MiniPCI adapters—storage.
- Topic D:
  - 1.3 Identify basic procedures for adding and removing field-replaceable modules for portable systems. Given a replacement scenario, choose the appropriate sequence. Content includes: PCMCIA/MiniPCI adapters—network adapter card, modem, SCSI, IEEE 1394/Firewire, and USB; and wireless—adapter/controller and antennae.

- 1.10 Determine the issues that must be considered when upgrading a PC. In a given scenario, determine when and how to upgrade system components. Components include: PCMCIA type I, II, III cards.
- 2.1 Recognize common problems associated with each module and their symptoms, and identify steps to isolate and troubleshoot the problems. Given a problem situation, interpret the symptoms and infer the most likely cause. Content includes: portable systems—PCMCIA.

- Topic F:
- 1.3 Identify basic procedures for adding and removing field-replaceable modules for portable systems. Given a replacement scenario, choose the appropriate sequence. Content includes: memory; and PCMCIA/MiniPCI adapters—storage.
- 2.1 Recognize common problems associated with each module and their symptoms, and identify steps to isolate and troubleshoot the problems. Given a problem situation, interpret the symptoms and infer the most likely cause. Content includes: portable unique storage.

- Topic G:
- 1.3 Identify basic procedures for adding and removing field-replaceable modules for portable systems. Given a replacement scenario, choose the appropriate sequence. Content includes: FDD; HDD; input devices—keyboard and mouse/pointing devices; and PCMCIA/MiniPCI adapters—network adapter card, modem, SCSI, IEEE 1394/Firewire, and USB.

- Topic H:
- 1.8 Identify proper procedures for installing and configuring common peripheral devices. Choose the appropriate installation or configuration sequence in given scenarios. Content includes the following: PDAs.

TOPIC A

Portable Computing Devices

In many respects, portable computing devices are similar to the desktop computer systems you've been working on up to this point in the course. To provide support for portable computing devices, you need to understand how these devices are similar to desktop systems and how they differ. In this topic, you will learn about the components that make up a portable computing device.

Portable Computing Device

Definition:

A portable computing device is a computer that can easily be moved from one location to another. Some of the features all portable computing devices share include:
- The devices are small and lightweight.
- They have their own internal power source, which is typically a rechargeable battery pack, but could be standard consumer batteries.
- They connect to other devices or systems.

- While in the portable state, they can function without being connected to other devices or systems.

The following list includes the ways that portable computing devices vary:

- The portable computing device can be a complete system (with all of the functions of a desktop computer) or it can have limited functionality (like a computer peripheral).
- How the batteries are recharged varies. Some systems recharge off of the AC power while the device is plugged in; other devices require that you remove the battery pack and place it in a recharger.
- The length of time the device can run from battery power varies.
- When connected to other systems or devices, its function can vary. It can be a network node, a peripheral, or even an input or output device to the computer.
- It can either use the same operating system as desktop systems; or it can require its own operating system; or it can operate using commands written to chips in the device.
- Most devices can be expanded in functionality by adding cards to the device. The cards and types of functionality you can add varies.
- Most devices use some sort of storage medium. This varies from removable drives to flash memory cards. The size, format, and connection type varies for each of these storage devices.
- The power cords are not usually interchangeable between brands or even models of notebook computers.

Example: Notebook Computer

Figure 11-1 shows an example of one type of portable computer, a notebook computer. This notebook computer model weighs only 3.5 pounds. Its battery power lasts about 1.5 hours per charge and takes about 8 hours to fully recharge. It includes integrated peripherals, but it can also use external peripherals. It includes standard desktop hardware interfaces. It uses a Windows desktop operating system. It can be connected to a network or used as a standalone system. Functionality can be expanded by adding adapter cards to the system.

Lesson 11

Figure 11-1: *A notebook computer as an example of a portable computing device.*

Example: Desktop Replacement

The largest of the portables, it generally weighs over 6.5 pounds and usually has the most features, including large screen, large hard drive, CD-ROM drive, multimedia capabilities, modem, and printer. It is expensive; however, it can serve as both a desktop and a portable without many compromises. In some instances, these types of portables are referred to as laptops.

Example: Sub-notebook

It weighs less than 5 pounds; the ultra-light weighs in at less than 3 pounds. To keep weight down, it has a minimum of features including a small display and small keyboard. Manufacturers are attempting to increase its functionality while maintaining its convenient size. Battery life tends to be good. The sub-notebook is built primarily for inputting text and retrieving data from a remote computer.

Example: PDA

A Personal Digital Assistant (PDA) is another type of portable computer. It can be used as a standalone device or as a peripheral to a notebook or desktop system. Figure 11-2 shows an example of a PDA. This PDA is powered by rechargeable batteries. It uses its own operating system, the Palm OS. To recharge it, it is connected to the computer through a standard peripheral port. This connection goes to the USB port and to the electrical outlet. This PDA has a slot to add additional functionality that was not built into the device. This PDA has software installed so the user can view and edit desktop documents. The input for this device is a stylus rather than a keyboard. Input can also be obtained through its connection with the host computer.

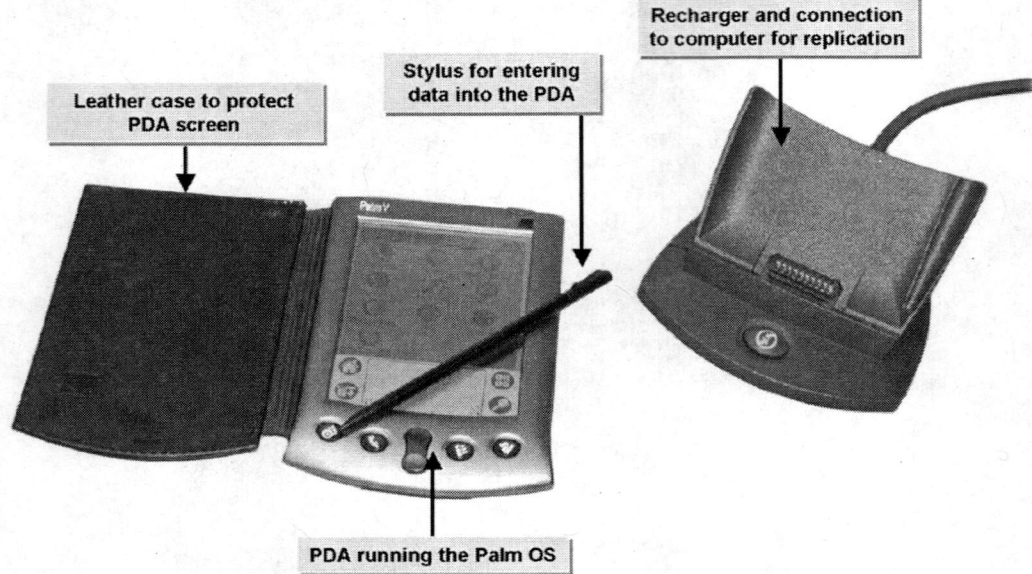

Figure 11-2: *A PDA as an example of a portable computing device.*

Notebook Computer

Definition:

A notebook computer is a complete computer system that is small, lightweight, and portable. All notebooks:

- Use a CPU designed especially for use in a portable computer.
- Use standard operating systems, such as Microsoft Windows.
- Have hard drives that can be easily removed.
- Have battery packs that can be easily removed.
- Can run on battery or AC power.
- Use memory designed especially for portable computers.
- Use integrated peripherals for the monitor, keyboard, and pointing device.
- Use PC Cards for expansion cards. PC Cards connect to the Card bus.
- Use SODIMM or proprietary memory.
- Have a monitor that is hinged at the bottom and swings down to form the cover for the laptop. It latches to the body of the computer to secure it for transport.
- Can connect to other devices.

Notebook computers vary by the following factors:

- Size of the notebook. Some larger ones are referred to as laptops because they fit on your lap. They typically have more features. Some smaller ones are referred to as sub-notebooks and typically have fewer features.
- Display size, quality, and technology.

Lesson 11

- Keyboard size, number of keys, and options.
- Pointing device used.
- Power supply type.
- Battery type used.
- Length of battery support time.
- How long it takes to recharge the battery.
- Power cord connection.
- Docking solutions.
- Connections for external peripherals.
- The power button can be located inside or outside of the closed case. It is more often located inside so that it isn't accidentally turned on when it is in the user's briefcase or being transported in some other bag.
- Bays or connections for additional drives such as floppy drives, and CD-ROM, CD-RW, or DVD drives.
- Since notebooks are easily stolen, there is usually a security cable slot.
- Alternate power source. Some notebooks can run through a DC power adapter that plugs into a cigarette lighter-type outlet in cars and some airplanes.

Example: A Notebook Computer

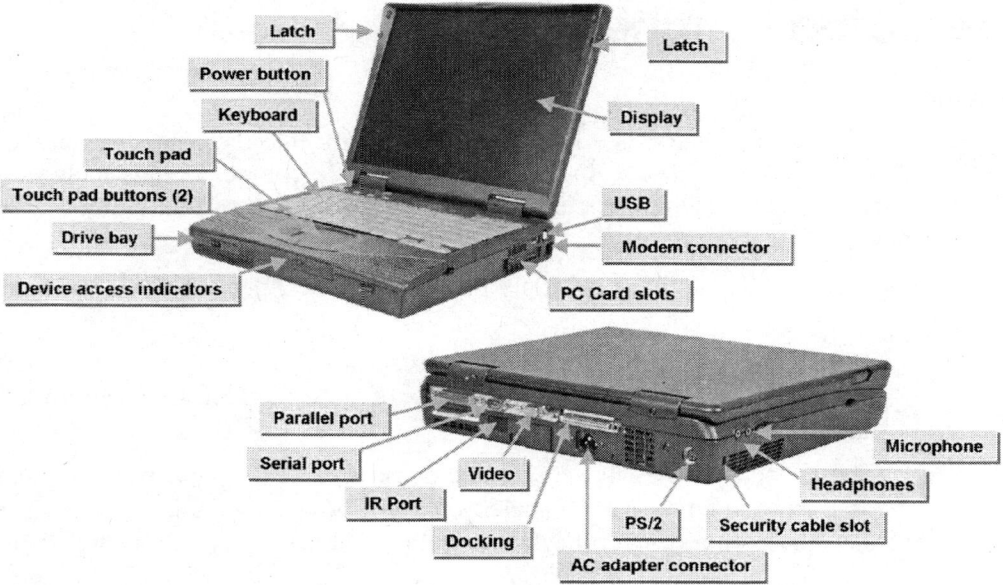

Figure 11-3: *A notebook computer.*

Security Slot and Cable

Most notebooks contain a security slot. A security cable with a plate that fits inside the slot can be secured around a stationary object such as a chair or table. Turning the key rotates the plate so that it cannot be slipped back out of the slot without breaking the computer case. This is shown in Figure 11-4.

Lesson 11: Portable Computing   471

Lesson 11

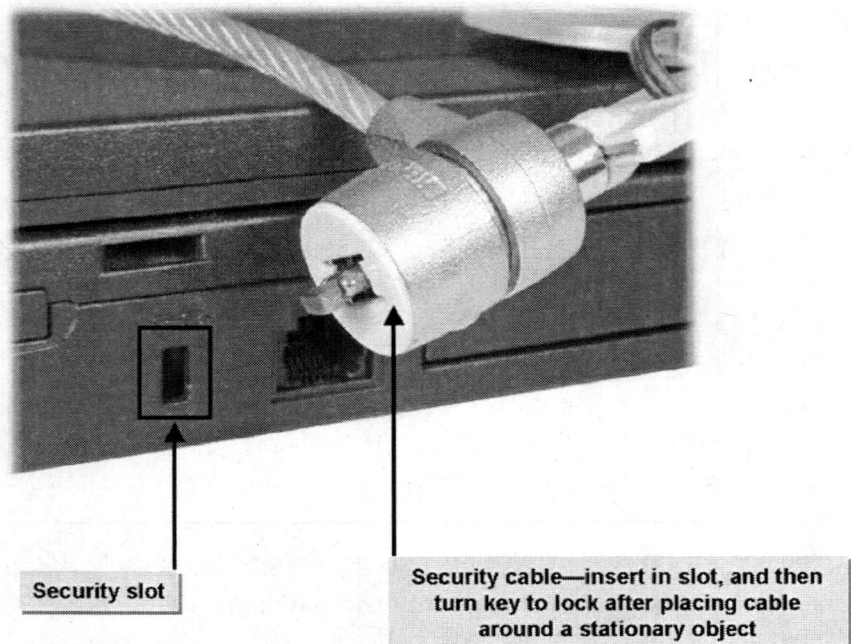

Figure 11-4: *A security slot and cable.*

Integrated Peripherals

Definition:

An integrated peripheral is a peripheral that is built into the computer and contained within the computer's case. In desktop and portable computers, this includes internal drives. In portable computers, this also includes the keyboard, pointing device, and monitor.

Integrated peripherals have a variety of characteristics, depending on the type of device.

- The monitor varies by size, resolution, and technology used to create the image. Notebook computers use LCD displays because they are flat, take up less room, and use less power.
- The keyboard varies in the size and number of keys. Some keys that are separate on a desktop keyboard are shared on a notebook keyboard. Keys might be smaller than those on a desktop keyboard and are almost always closer together.
- The pointing device varies in type and location.

Example: Integrated Monitor

Figure 11-5 shows an example of a notebook with an integrated monitor. This notebook uses an active matrix LCD monitor.

Lesson 11

Figure 11-5: *An integrated monitor.*

Example: Integrated Keyboard

Figure 11-6 shows an example of a notebook with an integrated keyboard. This keyboard uses the Fn key to access the functions that are shared with some of the alphabetical keys. These include the number pad keys, brightness and contrast for the integrated monitor, Home, and End, among others.

Lesson 11

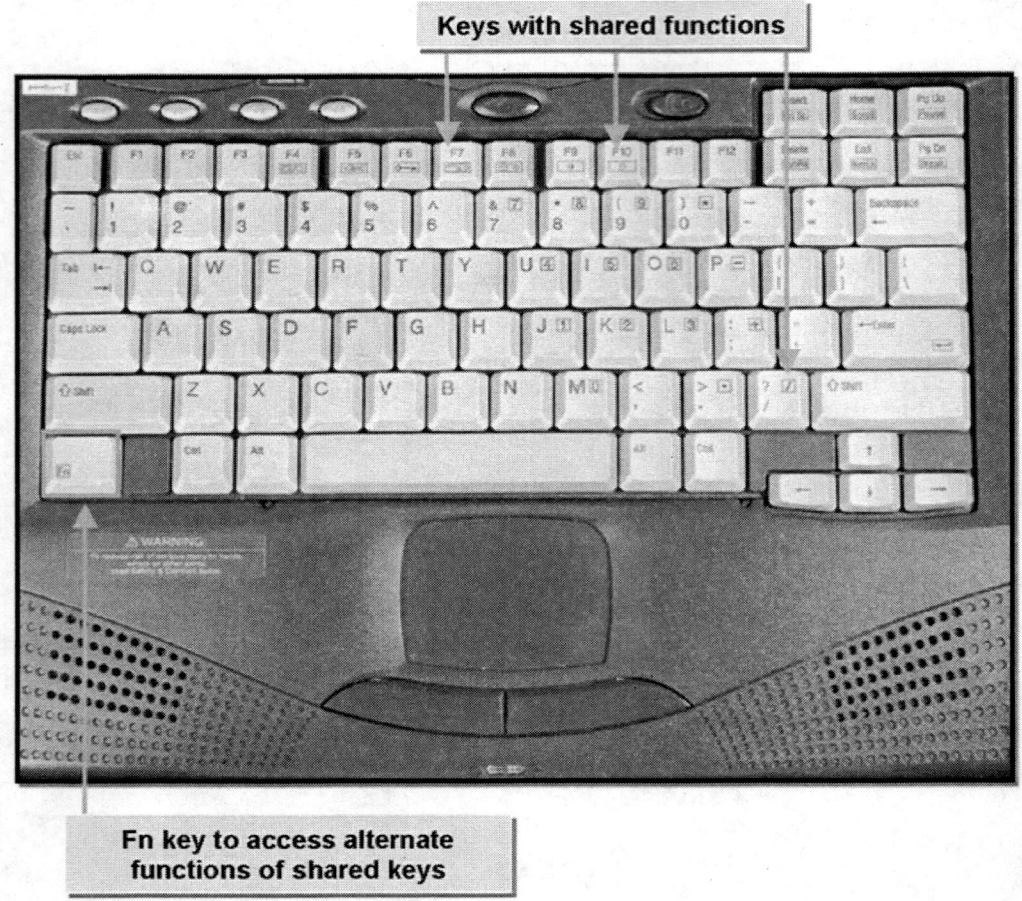

Figure 11-6: *An integrated keyboard.*

Example: Integrated Pointing Device

Figure 11-7 shows an example of a notebook with an integrated pointing device. This notebook computer uses a touch pad pointing device with separate mouse buttons. You can also tap the pad to simulate pressing mouse buttons.

Lesson 11

Figure 11-7: *An integrated pointing device.*

Types of LCD Screens

There are two types of LCD screens:

— Active Matrix—This is also known as Thin-Film Transistor or TFT. It uses one transistor for each pixel. It requires more power than a passive matrix monitor, but provides a better quality image with a wider viewing angle and faster screen updates.

— Passive Matrix—Uses two groups of transistors combined with a wire matrix to produce images. Images are lower quality than CRT or active matrix, usually limited to 256 colors. Screen updates are slow as they are drawn line by line.

Commonly Used Pointing Devices

Commonly used pointing devices include:

— Trackball—A trackball like those used on a desktop is integrated into the notebook case.

— Trackpoint—Also known as a pointing stick. A small eraser-shaped device in the center of the keyboard that works like a very short joystick.

— Trackpad—Also known as a touchpad or glide pad. An electromagnetically sensitive pad that tracks movement of a finger to move the mouse pointer. Mouse clicks can be simulated by tapping the pad. There are usually buttons for mouse clicks as well. This is less precise than the other integrated pointing options.

Portable Device Power Sources

Portable devices can use either AC power sources (alternating current from an electrical outlet) or DC power sources (direct current from a battery). While the portable device is in its portable state, it uses batteries. When the device is used as a desktop computer or peripheral, it can use either batteries or AC power from a power cord plugged into an electrical outlet.

Lesson 11: Portable Computing

AC power connectors vary from notebook to notebook. Desktop systems all use the same basic power cord, but often not even multiple notebooks from the same manufacturer use the same power cord. Figure 11-8 shows two different power cord connections. When the notebook is not being used as a portable device, it is usually plugged in using the AC power cord that matches the computer. The battery is also recharged through this connection.

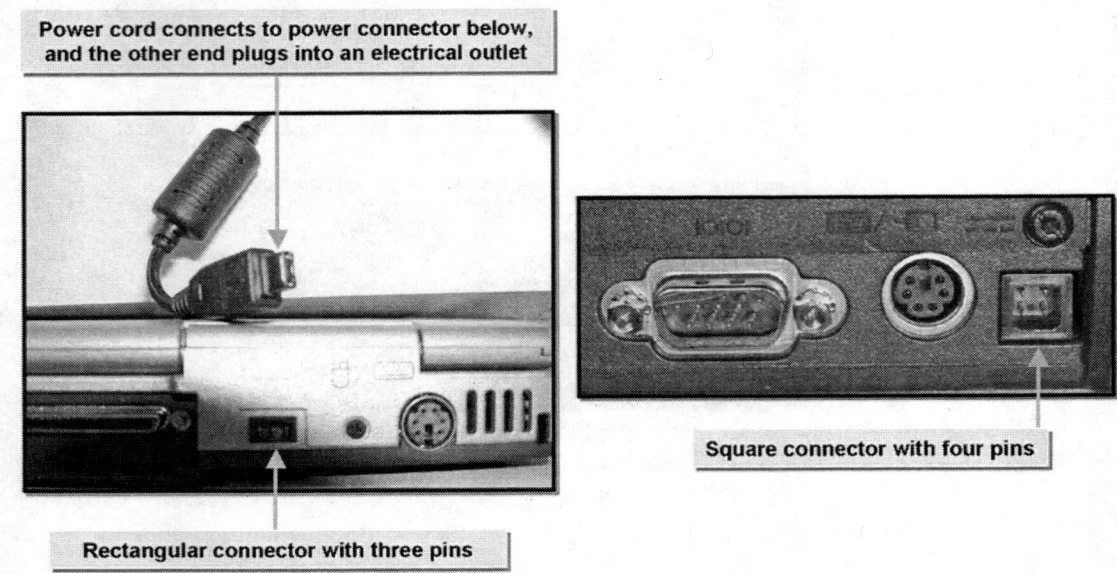

Figure 11-8: *AC power connections.*

Types of Batteries

The batteries in the battery pack might be:

- Nickel Cadmium (*NiCad*).
    — The battery type used in the original portable computers.
    — Heaviest and least expensive.
    — Short life of three to four hours.
    — Recharge can take up to 12 hours.
    — Can be recharged approximately 700 to 1,000 times.
    — Remembers how full it was when last recharged and doesn't go past that point the next time it is charged. This is referred to as the memory effect.
- Nickel Metal-Hydride (*NiMH*).
    — Environmentally friendly because it doesn't contain heavy metals that can be toxic.
    — Uses nickel and metal hydride plates with potassium hydroxide as the electrolyte.
    — Uses a liquid electrolyte, which must be contained in protective steel cans to prevent leakage.
    — Doesn't hold charges as well as NiCad when not in use, but provides up to 50 percent more power than NiCad for the same weight.
    — Doesn't suffer from memory effect.
    — More expensive than NiCad.
    — Can be recharged approximately 400 to 500 times.

- *Li-Ion.*
  - Lithium based. A lightweight metal.
  - Provides light, long-life battery.
  - Holds a charge well.
  - Can't be overcharged.
  - Holds twice as much power as NiCad.
  - Weighs about half as much as NiCad.
  - Provides higher power than NiCad.
  - More expensive than NiCad.
  - Can be recharged approximately 400 to 500 times.
  - Uses a liquid electrolyte, which must be contained in protective steel cans to prevent leakage.
- *Lithium Polymer.*
  - Similar to Li-Ion in power.
  - Uses a jelly-like material as an electrolyte instead of liquid. This enables power cells to be manufactured in various shapes and sizes for custom requirements.
- *Zinc Air.*
  - Provides more charge per pound than NiCad or NiMH.
  - Doesn't suffer from the memory effect.
  - Uses a carbon membrane that absorbs oxygen, a zinc plate, and potassium hydroxide as the electrolyte.
- *Fuel Cell.* Fuel cell batteries are currently under development for use in portable computers. Fuel cell technology combines hydrogen and oxygen to generate an electric current. Fuel cell batteries resemble other battery types in that their DC electrical output is due to an electrochemical process. However, unlike other battery types, fuel cells operate off a continuous stream of air as a source of oxygen, and a source of hydrogen fuel. This means that fuel cell batteries have much longer service lifetimes than other battery types.

Figure 11-9 shows three different batteries from notebook systems. The batteries shown in the figure are all different shapes. They were designed to fit as best as possible around other components in each of the systems they were designed for. Two of them are Li-Ion batteries and one is an NiMH battery. Any battery you use in a portable device must be compatible with the device and the device's operating system. Rechargeable batteries are used in most portable computing devices. Batteries usually last between one and six hours per charge. They are usually packaged in a battery pack.

Figure 11-9: *Batteries for portable computer systems.*

DC Controllers

The processor can be problematic, as it draws a considerable amount of power, which drains the battery and produces a noticeable amount of heat. To help with this problem, DC controllers are used in portable computers. A DC controller enables stepping down a higher input voltage to a lower output voltage. As an example, Linear Technologies' LTC1771 DC/DC controller enables stepping down an input voltage of 2.8 V to an output voltage of 1.23 V, and an input voltage of 20 V to an output voltage of 18 V. Output voltages are programmable. Using DC controllers, power can be conserved, which is essential for battery-powered devices, such as portable computers.

Advanced Power Management

Advanced Power Management (APM) is an Application Programming Interface (API) from Intel and Microsoft for battery-powered computers. It provides several power-saving options, including shutting off the display or hard drive, suspending to RAM, suspending to disk, and slowing the processor.

- *Suspend to RAM.* Also known as Sleep Mode or Instant On. The system writes data to memory and shuts everything down while keeping the data alive with a minimum amount of power from the battery. The system is immediately accessible by using certain keystrokes. This method uses a small amount of power, so data could be lost if the battery dies.
- *Suspend to disk.* Also known as Hibernate. The system writes data to disk and shuts off completely; no power is used, so no data can be lost. The system, while not needing to be rebooted, turns on more slowly than suspending to RAM.
- *Slowing the processor.* The system is on but not involved in heavy-duty calculations. The processor slows down to a point where it can still handle the user's needs, but does not waste energy trying to process data at an unnecessarily high rate.

How to Power a Portable Device

Procedure Reference: Power a Portable Device

To connect a portable device to a power source:

⚠ Using the incorrect power cord can destroy a portable device.

1. If you're going to run the device on battery power, insert the appropriate battery type if the device doesn't already have a rechargeable battery included.
2. If the device has a rechargeable battery and the battery needs to be recharged, plug the device into its cradle or docking station (if there is one) or plug the device directly into an electrical outlet using the supplied power cord (if applicable).
3. If the device needs to be connected directly to an electrical outlet, plug the device into the outlet using the supplied power cord.

Processors

Some of the processors you will encounter in portable computers include:

- *Intel Mobile Pentium (with voltage reduction)*. This 32-bit mobile processor has 3.3 million transistors, and is designed based on Intel's advanced, low-voltage BiCMOS silicone technology. It features SL Enhanced Power Management, including System Management Mode (SMM), and clock control. This processor is packaged in a TCP package. You will find this processor in older Pentium portable computers.
- *Intel Mobile Pentium MMX*. Also known as the Tillamook, this processor is often found in mobile units. Although being surpassed by the Pentium II and newer processors designed for mobile computing, it is still used, especially in ultra-lights, where limited heat production is an important consideration. The Intel Mobile Pentium with MMX is socket-compatible with the Intel Mobile Pentium if it's packaged in a TCP package. The Intel Mobile Pentium MMX process is shown in Figure 11-10.
- *Intel Mobile Celeron*. Several Intel Mobile Celeron processor types exist, with a wide range of features and specifications. For instance, clock speeds range from 266 MHz to 1.20 GHz. The earliest Intel Mobile Celerons were offered in PGA and BGA packaging, and featured an integrated math coprocessor, support for MMX technology, and *Quick Start* and *Deep Sleep* modes for low power dissipation. Later Intel Mobile Celeron processors are available in regular, low-voltage, and ultra-low-voltage configurations, and they feature an integrated math coprocessor, support for MMX, and Streaming SIMD extensions. Packaging ranges from Micro-BGA2 and Micro-PGA2 to Micro-FCBGA and Micro-FCPGA. They also support Quick Start and Deep Sleep modes for low power dissipation.
- *Intel Mobile Pentium II*. The Intel Mobile Pentium II is packed in either a BGA package or a Mini-cartridge package. It supports MMX, and uses Quick Start and Deep Sleep modes for low power dissipation. It also features an integrated math coprocessor and Dual Independent Bus (DIB) architecture.
- *Intel Mobile Pentium III*. Like the Mobile Celeron, the Intel Mobile Pentium III is available in a wide variety of configurations, including low-voltage and ultra-low-voltage. The Intel Mobile Pentium III uses a technology called *SpeedStep*, which offers two performance modes: a Maximized Performance Mode, and a Battery Optimized Mode. When in Maximized Performance Mode, the processor runs at its designated speed using an inter-

nal voltage of 1.6 V. When in Battery Optimized Mode, the processor runs at a reduced speed and an internal voltage of 1.35 V. For example, the 850 MHz processor runs at 700 MHz in Battery Optimized Mode. This chip is packaged in BGA2 and Micro-PGA2 packaging. It supports MMX technology and Streaming SIMD extensions. Finally, it uses Quick Start and Deep Sleep modes for low power dissipation, and features an integrated math coprocessor.

- *Intel Mobile Pentium III-M.* The Intel Mobile Pentium III-M processor line improves upon the Intel Mobile Pentium III line by incorporating Enhanced SpeedStep technology and Deeper Sleep mode, as well as the other features of the Mobile Pentium III. It is available in regular, low-voltage, and ultra-low-voltage chips, and is packaged in the Micro-FCPGA and Micro-FCBGA styles.

- *Intel Mobile Pentium 4-M.* The Intel Mobile Pentium 4-M series of processors is the latest offering from Intel. Designed to support high-performance processing operations, it is available in Micro-FCPGA packaging and includes Enhanced SpeedStep technology and Deeper Sleep, as well as the NetBurst micro-architecture that was introduced with the standard Pentium 4 processor.

AMD also makes several processors for portable computers such as the Athlon Mobile and Duron Mobile. However, the Intel processors are still the most common processor in portable computers. Additional information on the AMD processors can be found on AMD's Web site at **www.amd.com**, under Product Information.

Figure 11-10: *Intel Mobile Pentium MMX processor.*

Table 11-1 lists some specifications of common mobile processors. As you review the Cache column, remember that *on-die* indicates that the memory is integrated into the processor chip. For mobile processors, even L2 cache is included on the CPU chip.

Table 11-1: *Common Mobile Processor Specifications*

Processor	Clock Speeds	Internal Voltage	Cache	CPU Packaging
Intel Mobile Pentium	75 to 150 MHz	2.9 V	Two on-die 8 KB L1.	TCP
Intel Mobile Pentium MMX	133 to 300 MHz	2.45 V	Two on-die 16 KB L1.	TCP

Processor	Clock Speeds	Internal Voltage	Cache	CPU Packaging
Intel Mobile Celeron	266 to 466 MHz	1.6 V to 1.9 V	Two on-die 16 KB L1. One on-die 128 KB L2.	BGA
	500 to 850 MHz	1.6 V	Two on-die 16 KB L1. One on-die 128 KB L2.	BGA2 or PGA2
	1.06 to 1.20 GHz	1.45 V	Two on-die 16 KB L1. One on-die 256 KB L2.	BGA2 or PGA2
Intel Mobile Celeron (low-voltage)	500 MHz	1.35 V	Two on-die 16 KB L1. One on-die 128 KB L2.	BGA2
	600 MHz	1.35 V	Two on-die 16 KB L1. One on-die 256 KB L2.	BGA
	733 MHz	1.15 V	Two on-die 16 KB L1. One on-die 256 KB L2.	Micro-FCPGA or Micro-FCBGA
Intel Mobile Celeron (ultra-low-voltage)	500 to 600 MHz	1.1 V	Two on-die 16 KB L1. One on-die 128 KB L2.	BGA
	650 MHz	1.1 V	Two on-die 16 KB L1. One on-die 256 KB L2.	BGA
Intel Mobile Pentium II	233 to 300 MHz	1.6 V to 1.7 V	Two on-die 16 KB L1. One on-die 512 KB L2.	Mini-cartridge
	266 to 400 MHz	1.5 V to 1.6 V	Two on-die 16 KB L1. One on-die 256 KB L2.	BGA or Mini-cartridge
Intel Mobile Pentium III	400 to 500 MHz	1.35 V or 1.6 V	Two on-die 16 KB L1. One on-die 256 KB L2.	BGA or Micro-PGA
Intel Mobile Pentium III with SpeedStep	600 to 700 MHz	1.6 V	Two on-die 16 KB L1. One on-die 256 KB L2.	BGA2 or Micro-PGA
	750 MHz to 1 GHz	1.35 V	Two on-die 16 KB L1. One on-die 256 KB L2.	BGA2 or Micro-PGA
Intel Mobile Pentium III with SpeedStep (low-voltage)	600 to 750 MHz	1.1 V	Two on-die 16 KB L1. One on-die 256 KB L2.	BGA2
Intel Mobile Pentium III with SpeedStep (ultra-low-voltage)	500/300 to 700/300 MHz	1.1 V/less than 1 V	Two on-die 16 KB L1. One on-die 256 KB L2.	BGA
	750/350 MHz	1.1 V/less than 0.95 V	Two on-die 16 KB L1. One on-die 512 KB L2.	BGA
Intel Mobile Pentium III-M	866 to 933 MHz	1.15 V/1.05 V	Two on-die 16 KB L1. One on-die 512 KB L2.	Micro-FCPGA or Micro-FCBGA
	1.0 to 1.2 GHz	1.4 V/1.15 V	Two on-die 16 KB L1. One on-die 512 KB L2.	Micro-FCPGA or Micro-FCBGA
Intel Mobile Pentium III-M (low-voltage)	850/500 to 933/533 MHz	1.15 V/1.05 V	Two on-die 16 KB L1. One on-die 512 KB L2.	BGA, Micro-FCPGA, or Micro-FCBGA

Lesson 11: Portable Computing

Processor	Clock Speeds	Internal Voltage	Cache	CPU Packaging
Intel Mobile Pentium III-M (ultra-low-voltage)	800/400 MHz	1.15 V/1.05 V	Two on-die 16 KB L1. One on-die 512 KB L2.	Micro-FCPGA or Micro-FCBGA
Intel Mobile Pentium 4-M	1.4 to 1.8 GHz	1.3 V/1.2 V	Two on-die (8 KB and 12 KB) L1. One on-die 512 KB L2.	Micro-FCPGA

Generally, processors in portable computers are not upgradeable by the user. Most of them are soldered onto the system board, making them shock-proof but resistant to adaptation.

Processors produce heat, and systems can get hot. Manufacturers attempt to make systems that don't become too hot to touch, although they may avoid fans, which are a power drain. Older portables may contain variations on desktop processors, which can rapidly drain batteries and overheat. If the system becomes too hot to touch, the overheating may be caused by a desktop processor.

Processor Packaging

Due to the limited space in portable systems, different CPU packaging is used for processors for portable systems. All of the packaging types address the need for lightweight, small-footprint processors. Examples of mobile CPU packaging include Tape Carrier Package (TCP), Ball Grid Array (BGA) and BGA2 (BGA and BGA2 packaging uses solder balls rather than the metal leads found in PGA packaging), Micro PGA and Micro PGA2, and Mini-cartridges. Newer mobile processors from Intel might also be packaged in Micro versions of the Flip Chip PGA (FCPGA) and Flip Chip BGA (FCBGA) packaging technology.

Figure 11-11: *Three examples of BGA packaging.*

Sockets and slots used in portable computers include the BGA socket, Micro PGA socket, Mini-cartridge Connector, Mobile Module Connector 1 (MMC-1), and Mobile Module Connector 2 (MMC-2).

ACTIVITY 11-1

Comparing Portable and Desktop Computers

Activity Time:

10 minutes

Scenario:

In this activity, you will describe how portable computers differ from desktop computer systems.

1. Describe how a portable computer system differs from a desktop computer system in display technology.

2. Describe how a portable computer system differs from a desktop computer system in power source.

3. Describe how the processors designed for portable computer systems differ from those in desktop systems.

4. Select the components that are external peripheral components on a desktop system, but are integrated in portable computer systems.

    a) Monitor

    b) Keyboard

    c) Printer

    d) Pointing device

Lesson 11: Portable Computing

Lesson 11

Topic B

Docking Solutions

Many portable computer users also have a workstation or office where they regularly work. By using a docking solution, they can use monitors and keyboards that are larger than those integrated into their portable systems. These larger, external devices are kept at their regular workstations, many times providing a more ergonomically correct posture for the user than is possible when using the portable system. In this topic, you will learn about the docking solutions that are available for use with portable computers.

Docking Device

Definition:

Docking solutions are desktop devices that connect portable computers to standard desktop peripherals without the need to connect and disconnect the peripherals themselves when the user switches from stationary to mobile use. All docking solutions:

- Enable you to use full size peripherals such as mouse, keyboard, monitor, and printer, which are connected to the docking solution.
- Are proprietary; there are no standards, so you need to purchase the docking solution from the notebook manufacturer that is specific to your model notebook.
- Contain hardware interface ports.

Docking solutions vary in that they might:

- Use the same power cord that is used to plug in the notebook directly to an electrical outlet, or they might use a different power cord.
- Contain slots for desktop expansion cards.
- Contain bays for additional drives.
- Contain additional ports not found on the notebook computer.

Example: A Port Replicator

Figure 11-12 shows a port replicator. This port replicator includes standard desktop ports for full size peripherals, such as a mouse and keyboard, plus a proprietary connector for an external drive. This notebook does not have drive bays for removable media devices such as floppy drives or CD-ROM/DVD drives, so it connects them through a cable as an external device. The connector for the laptop to connect to the port replicator is located on the bottom of the notebook computer.

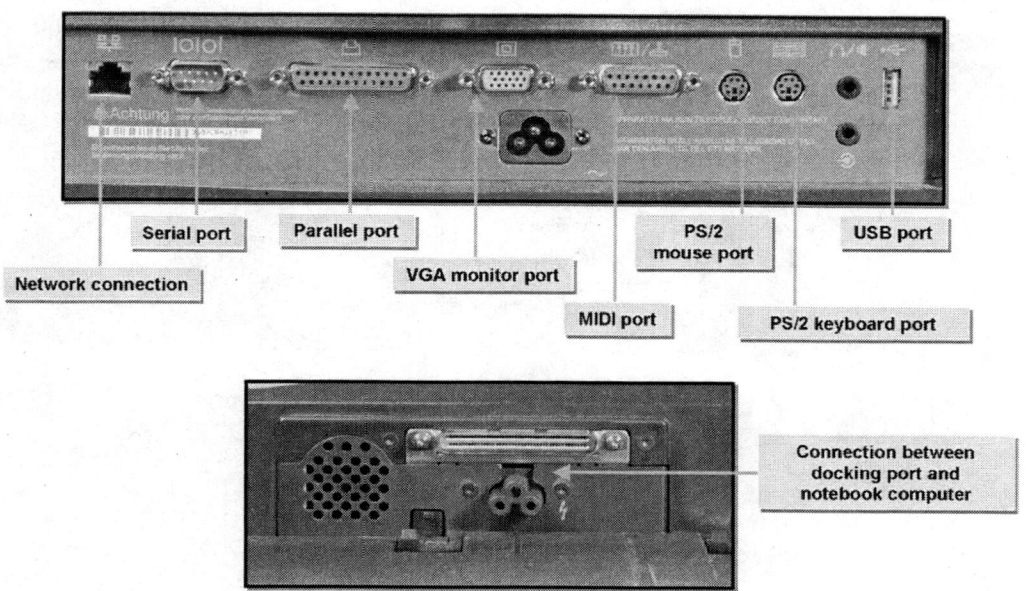

Figure 11-12: *A port replicator.*

Example: A Docking Station

A docking station is also known as a multiport. It is commonly used when a notebook computer replaces a desktop computer. The notebook is connected to docking station through a docking port located on the back or bottom of the notebook. Docking stations typically contain duplicates of the standard desktop ports that are also found on the notebook. In addition, there are often slots for desktop PCI or ISA expansion cards, drive bays for additional mass storage devices, and possibly additional ports and connectors. Figure 11-13 shows an example of a docking station.

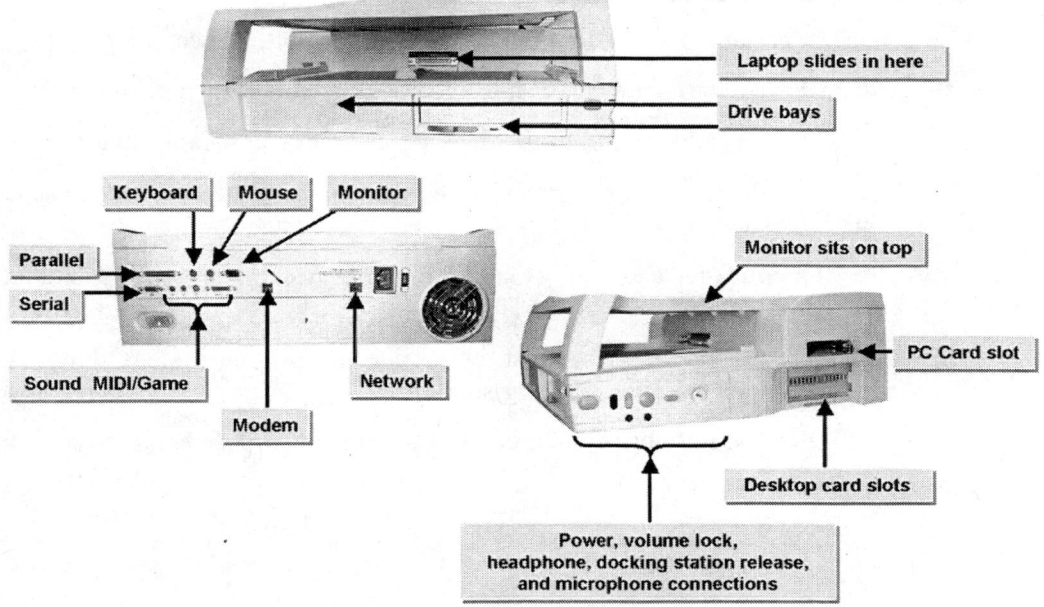

Figure 11-13: *A docking station.*

Lesson 11

Non-Example: Direct Connections

Connecting external peripheral devices directly to the ports on the notebook computer is not an example of a docking solution. This is because each time you want to switch between stationary and mobile use, you would need to disconnect or reconnect each of the peripheral devices from the computer. Figure 11-14 shows an example of the ports on a notebook computer.

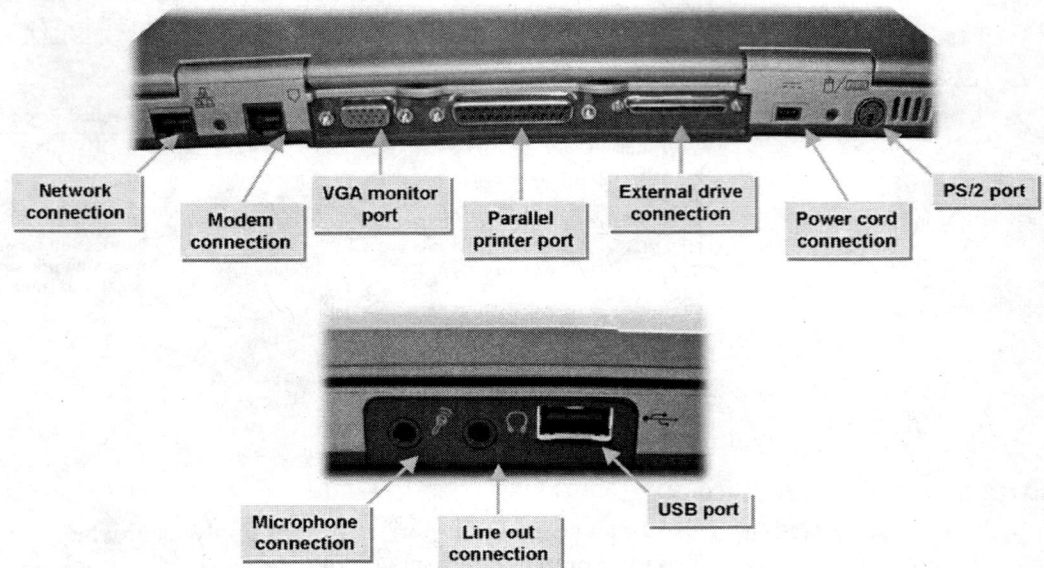

Figure 11-14: *Connecting peripherals directly to a notebook computer.*

How to Dock a Portable Computer

Procedure Reference: Dock Portable Systems

To connect a portable system to a docking station or port replicator:

1. Connect the external peripherals to the docking station or port replicator.

2. Connect the power supply to the docking station or port replicator.

3. Following the instructions shown in the manual for your system, connect the portable computer to the docking solution you are using.

4. Boot the computer and verify that the portable system can use the external peripherals while docked.

5. Following the instructions shown in the manual for your system, remove the portable computer from the docking solution.

6. Verify that the portable system can use its integrated peripherals while undocked.

ACTIVITY 11-2

Docking Portable Systems

Setup:

To complete this activity, you will need a portable computer and compatible port replicator or docking station.

Scenario:

Many members of the Marketing department have portable systems. They have all requested a docking solution for their system so that they don't have to plug and unplug the external peripherals when they switch between working at desks in the office and working on the road or at home. The systems are from a variety of vendors. Some of the users have received port replicators and some have received docking stations. They need your assistance in connecting the external peripherals to the docking solution and in how to insert and remove their portable system from the docking solution.

What You Do	How You Do It
1. Connect peripherals to the docking solution.	a. Connect the monitor to the monitor port on the docking solution.
	b. Connect the keyboard to the keyboard port on the docking solution.
	c. Connect the mouse to the mouse port on the docking solution.
	d. Connect the printer to the appropriate port for your printer on the docking solution.
	e. Connect the power source from the docking solution to the electrical outlet.

Lesson 11: Portable Computing

2.	Verify that the portable can use the peripherals while docked.	a. Insert the computer into the docking solution.
		b. **Turn on the power.** This might be the power switch on the portable system or it might be a power switch on the docking solution.
		c. Turn on the power to the monitor and to any other external peripherals that require powering on.
		d. Test that the external keyboard, mouse, monitor, and printer work properly.
3.	Verify that the portable can use its integrated peripherals while undocked.	a. Turn off the power to all peripherals and to the portable system.
		b. Undock the system.
		c. Power on the portable and verify that the integrated keyboard, mouse, and monitor work correctly.

TOPIC C
Portable Computing Device Drives

Desktop systems usually have lots of drive bays with room for one or more hard drives; one or more CD-ROM, CD-R, CD-RW, DVD, and/or DVD-R drives; one or more floppy drives; and one or more removable cartridge drives. Notebooks try to be as small as possible, and the first thing to go is often space for additional drives besides the hard drive. Knowing how to connect additional drives to portable computers will be important when your notebook users find that they need additional storage.

Portable Computer Drives

Definition:

Portable computer drives are drives that are specially designed to fit in portable computers. Drives are proprietary to their manufacturer and sometimes even to the computer model. All notebook computers have an internal hard drive. They might or might not include internal bays for other drives such as floppy, CD-ROM, or DVD drives. Some notebooks connect additional drives through a docking station, bay station, or via cable connections. Most notebook hard drives use 2.5-inch platters, as compared to the 3.5-inch platters used on desktop hard drives. The height and length of hard drives varies. Notebook hard drives tend to run at slower speeds than desktop hard drives.

Some internal hard drives are difficult to remove since you need to dismantle the computer. Others have a slide lock to unlock them from the case, so that you can slide the drive out. If it's too difficult to remove the internal drive from the notebook you are working on, then you might consider using alternate hard drive solutions such as USB or FireWire hard drives that can be connected externally.

Some notebook computers have room for a hard drive, floppy drive, and an optical drive all to be installed simultaneously. More often, though, especially as notebooks have gotten smaller, floppy and optical drives need to share a drive bay. You must switch the drives as needed, with either one or the other being available at a time.

Example:

Figure 11-15 shows an example of a notebook with the floppy drive being removed so that the CD-ROM drive can be inserted. The computer in this example contains an internal hard drive. It has one additional drive bay in which you can insert either the proprietary floppy drive or CD-ROM drive.

Figure 11-15: *Exchanging drives in a notebook computer.*

Lesson 11

How to Install or Remove Portable Computing Device Drives

Procedure Reference: Exchange Portable Computer Drives

To exchange which drive is installed:

1. Display a list of all of the removable devices that need to be stopped before removing or ejecting the device from the system.
   - Click the Safely Remove Hardware icon in the System Tray to show a list of devices;
   - Or, double-click the Safely Remove Hardware icon to open the Safely Remove Hardware dialog box.

2. Click the description of the device you want to remove. This will begin with the word Stop and be followed by a description of the drive or other device.

3. When the services for the device have been stopped, a Safe To Remove Hardware information box is displayed. Click OK to acknowledge the message.

4. If the Safely Remove Hardware dialog box is open, close it.

5. Different systems have various methods of releasing the drive from the bay. Refer to the documentation and any symbols on the system case for information on how to release the drive from the bay. Often it is a slide button that you need to pull down while sliding the drive out of the bay. On other systems, you might need to press a catch or disconnect a cable.

6. Slide the drive out of the bay and place it in a safe storage container where it won't be damaged by ESD or other environmental contaminants.

7. Slide the other drive into the drive bay. When it has been properly installed, a Removable Device icon will appear in the System Tray again. On some systems, you need to reboot before the replacement drive is available.

8. Verify that the drive was correctly installed by accessing the drive through Windows Explorer or some other application.

ACTIVITY 11-3

Exchanging Portable Computer Drives

Setup:

To complete this activity, you will need a portable computer system that has a single drive bay with a floppy drive in it and a compatible CD/DVD drive.

 If the system you are using does not have drive bays for the floppy drive and CD or DVD drives, they are either in a docking solution or are attached using a cable. You will need to adapt this activity to match your system if this is the case.

Scenario:

Sally Mendez recently received a new portable computer. Her system has only one drive bay to use for the floppy drive and CD/DVD drive. The floppy drive is currently in the drive bay and she needs to use the CD/DVD drive. She is not sure how to remove the drive from her system.

Lesson 11

What You Do	How You Do It
1. Remove the floppy drive from the drive bay or cable connector.	a. In the System Tray, **double-click the Safely Remove Hardware icon** to display a list of the devices that can be stopped.
	b. **Select the drive you want to remove.**
	c. **Click Stop** *drive description* (where *drive description* identifies the floppy drive you want to remove).
	d. In the Stop A Hardware Device information box, **click OK.**
	e. **Close the Safely Remove Hardware dialog box.**
	f. Referring to the documentation and any symbols on the system case, **locate the floppy drive and its release mechanism.**
	g. If the documentation specifies to, **shut down the system before continuing.**
	h. **Press the release mechanism for the floppy drive** to release it from the system.
	i. **Slide the floppy drive out of the drive bay or disconnect it from the cable.**
2. Insert the CD/DVD drive in the bay or connect it to the cable.	a. **Slide the CD/DVD drive into the drive bay or connect it to the cable.**
	b. If you had to shut down the system, **restart the system and log on.**
	c. **Verify that the Safely Remove Hardware icon appears in the System Tray.**
	d. **Access the CD/DVD drive** to verify that it was correctly installed.

Topic D
PC Cards

PC Cards are to notebooks as standard expansion cards are to full-size computers. From memory to modems, PC Cards provide many ways to expand the capabilities of portable systems. So, as a support technician, it's just as important for you to know how to install PC Cards on portables as it is to install expansion cards in desktop systems.

PC Card

Definition:

PC Cards are credit card-sized expansion cards that are used in portable computers rather than the full-sized ISA or PCI expansion cards used in desktop systems. The PC Card standard was developed by the *Personal Computer Memory Card International Association (PCMCIA)*. Some people refer to PC Cards as PCMCIA cards. PC Cards have a female 68-pin connector that plugs into a 68-pin male connector inside a slot in the side of the computer. They are 54 mm wide by 85.6 mm long.

 If users have more PC Cards than card slots, they will need to share the slots by exchanging the cards as needed.

PC Cards vary in thickness based on the type. PC Card types are shown in Table 11-2.

Table 11-2: *PC Card Types*

Type	Thickness	Used Primarily For
I	3.3 mm	Memory.
II	5.0 mm	Memory, modems, network adapters, wireless network adapters, USB, FireWire, and SCSI connectors. Might have pop-out connectors for network cables or phone line connections.
III	10.5 mm	Miniature hard drives.

Most PC Cards use *CardBus*. It enables PC Cards and hosts to use 32-bit bus mastering and to operate at speeds of up to 33 MHz. *Bus mastering* enables the PC Card to communicate directly with other cards without going through the CPU.

Some PC Cards use *Zoomed Video (ZV)*. This is a connection between the PC Card and the computer that enables the card to write video data directly to the video controller, bypassing the system bus.

Some cards use *eXecute In Place (XIP)*. This enables operating system and application code stored on the PC Card to run directly from the PC Card. This eliminates the need to use system RAM to execute the code.

Lesson 11

Example: A Type II PC Card

Figure 11-16 shows a Type II card that is 5 mm thick. This is a network adapter that uses the CardBus standard. It is being inserted into a Type II slot in the computer.

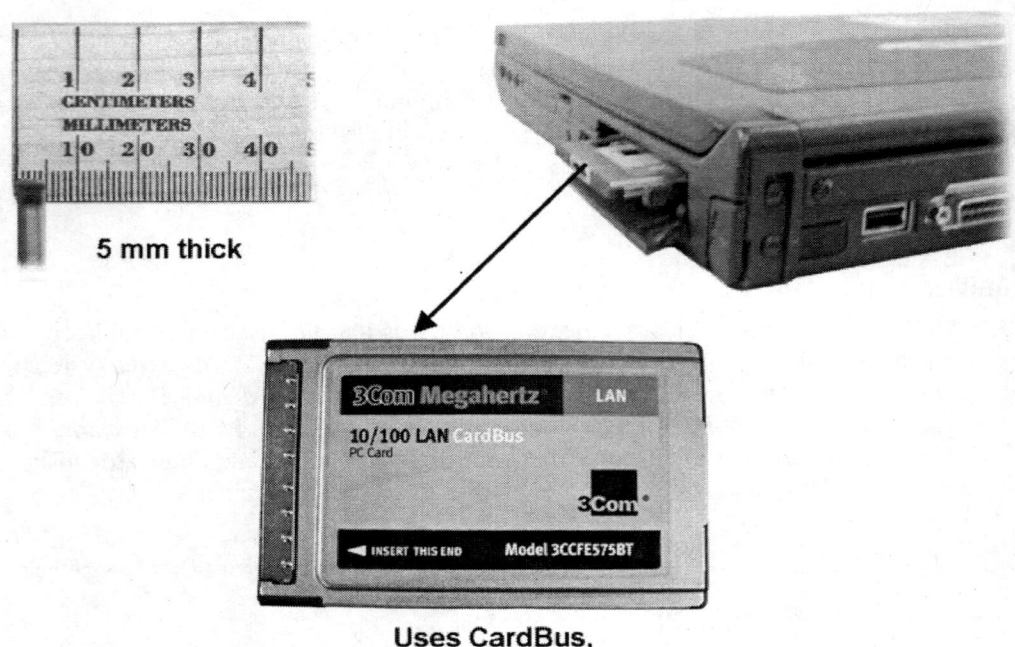

Figure 11-16: *A Type II PC Card.*

Card and Socket Services

All PC Cards use Card and Socket Services. These are layers of software loaded into memory. These two layers of software detect and support a PC Card when it is inserted into the portable computer. They are also responsible for managing the hot-swapping of PC Cards.

- *Socket Services* interacts with the system BIOS. When a PC Card is inserted or removed, Socket Services communicates that information to the system bus.
- *Card Services* is a software layer above Socket Services that communicates with the operating system to let it know when a card is inserted or removed. It automatically assigns system resources when the card is inserted.
- *Card Information Structure (CIS)* passes card information to the computer, including features and electrical characteristics, so that the computer can configure the card for use automatically.

PC Card Uses

PC Cards are used in a variety of ways to expand the capabilities of notebook computers. Table 11-3 describes some of the ways PC Cards are used.

Table 11-3: PC Card Uses

PC Card Use	Description
Modem	Adds modem capabilities to notebooks that don't have built-in modems. May have a retractable piece in which to plug the phone cord. Alternatively, you may need to use an adapter, called a *dongle*, to plug in the phone cord. One end of the dongle has a connector that plugs into the PC Card and the other end of the adapter has a connector to plug in the phone cord.
Network adapter (NIC)	Adds networking capabilities to notebooks that don't have built-in NICs. Like the modem card, it may have a retractable piece in which to plug a network cable or it may require you to use a network dongle.
Wireless network adapter	Provides wireless networking for notebooks that don't have built-in wireless capability. Often includes a built-in antenna for wireless communication.
SCSI adapter	Allows users to connect SCSI devices, such as a printer or external hard drive, to the notebook if it doesn't have a built-in SCSI adapter.
USB	Allows users to connect USB devices, such as external memory devices or printers, to the notebook if it doesn't have a built-in SCSI adapter.
IEEE 1394/FireWire	Provides a connection for devices such as external hard drives.

How to Install or Remove PC Cards

Procedure Reference: Install a PC Card

To install a PC Card:

1. Slide the PC Card into the PC Card slot until it is fully inserted. Make sure the PC Card is right side up. There is usually a label on the top with an arrow and/or the word Insert indicating which way to install it. You can bend the pins if you attempt to install it upside down.

2. If prompted, install any required drivers for the PC Card.

3. Verify that the system recognizes the PC Card. You can look for an icon in the System Tray, or you can use Device Manager to verify that the device is working properly. PC Cards must be compatible with the device and the device's operating system.

4. Connect any external devices or cables to the card. For example, PC Card network adapters might require a short adapter cable, called a dongle, between the PC Card's connector and the standard network cable.

Lesson 11

Activity 11-4

Installing PC Cards

Setup:
To complete this activity, you will need a portable computer systems with an empty PC Card slot and a compatible PC Card to insert.

Scenario:
Several users received new portable systems. These came with various expansion cards. You need to install the PC Cards so that the users can use them.

What You Do	How You Do It
1. Install the PC Card.	a. Locate the PC Card slot on your portable system.
	b. Slide the PC Card into the slot until it is fully inserted.
	c. If prompted, install any required drivers for the PC Card.
2. Verify that the PC Card was recognized by the system.	a. Determine if an icon for the PC Card appeared in the System Tray. Most cards will add an icon Unplug Or Eject Hardware.
	b. Open Device Manager.
	c. Select the hardware you just installed. You will need to expand the category under which the device is located to select it.
	d. Right-click the device and choose Properties.
	e. Verify that Device Status indicates that This Device Is Working Properly.
	f. Click OK.

Procedure Reference: Exchange PC Cards

To exchange PC Cards:

1. Install and test the first PC Card.

2. Use the Safely Remove Hardware icon to stop the device you want to remove.
3. Disconnect any devices or cables connected to the card to be removed.
4. Push the PC Card slot release lever once to pop it out.
5. Push the PC Card slot release lever again to release the PC Card from the slot.
6. Slide the card out of the slot.
7. Insert the replacement card into the slot.
8. If necessary, install drivers for the replacement card.
9. Verify that the system recognizes the card.
10. Connect external devices or cables to the replacement card.

ACTIVITY 11-5

Exchanging PC Cards

Setup:
To complete this activity, you will need a portable computer system with a PC Card slot that has a PC Card already installed and an additional, compatible PC Card to swap with the installed card.

Scenario:
Toby Macintosh has recently received a laptop system. He needs to connect it to the network while he is at work and to the phone line when he is at home. The system has only one PC Card slot. It came with both a network card and a modem card. He would like your help in learning how to insert and remove the cards and to test them to verify that they work properly.

What You Do	How You Do It
1. **Install the network card in the portable computer system.**	a. **Locate an empty PC Card slot.**
	b. Holding the card with the connectors facing the slot and the label with the Insert indicator on top, **slide the card into the slot.**
	c. **Verify that the Safely Remove Hardware icon appears in the System Tray** to indicate that the card was fully inserted and recognized.
	d. If prompted, **install network card drivers.**

Lesson 11

2.	Test the network card to verify that it was properly installed and that the computer can connect to the network.	a.	If necessary, connect the dongle to the network card.
		b.	Connect a network cable to the network card.
		c.	Access a network or Internet location.
3.	Remove the network card from the portable computer system.	a.	In the System Tray, click the Removable Device icon.
		b.	Choose the option to stop the network card device.
		c.	Disconnect the network cable from the card.
		d.	Push the PC Card slot release lever once to pop it out.
		e.	Push the PC Card slot release lever again to release the card from the slot.
		f.	Slide the card out of the slot.
4.	Install the modem card in the portable computer system.	a.	Insert the modem card in the PC Card slot.
		b.	If prompted, install drivers for the modem card.
5.	Test the modem to verify that it can connect over the phone line to the network.	a.	Connect the phone line to the modem.
		b.	Open Device Manager.
		c.	On the Modem Properties Diagnostics page, click the Query Modem button.

Topic E

Mini-PCI Cards

There is another, newer type of expansion card, the Mini-PCI card, that you might also need to support. While it isn't often that you need to install or remove a Mini-PCI card, there are three likely situations when you might have to:

- When an existing Mini-PCI card starts to malfunction or stops working altogether.
- When you need to upgrade an existing Mini-PCI card.
- When you want to add a wireless Mini-PCI card to a notebook.

When one of these situations arises, to ensure that the user has the resources necessary to complete his job, you're going to need to know how to identify a Mini-PCI card and install or remove one if necessary. In this topic, you'll learn how to install and remove Mini-PCI cards.

Mini-PCI Card

Definition:

A Mini-PCI card is an extremely small expansion card that is used to increase the functionality of a portable computer. Mini-PCI cards are internal expansion cards, not external like PC Cards, and are installed by the computer manufacturer. Mini-PCI cards are most often used to increase communications abilities by providing network adapters or modems. Mini-PCI cards are much smaller than other expansion cards, often measuring just a few centimeters in length. There are three types of Mini-PCI cards. They are listed in Table 11-4.

Table 11-4: *Types of Mini-PCI Cards*

Type	Description
I	Can be installed anywhere in the computer chassis, and uses internal cables to connect it to modem (RJ-11) and network (RJ-45) connectors on the computer's chassis. Connected to the motherboard using a mini 100-pin stacking connector with a 4 mm minimum stacking height.
II	Has built-in modem and network connectors, and therefore must be located against the computer's chassis. Connected to the motherboard using a mini 100-pin stacking connector with a 4 mm minimum stacking height.
III	Uses a SODIMM connector to slide into a slot onto the motherboard. Uses internal cables to connect it to modem and network connectors on the computer's chassis.

Example: Mini-PCI Card

Figure 11-17 shows a Mini-PCI card. This Mini-PCI card is much smaller than a normal PCI expansion card.

Figure 11-17: *A Mini-PCI card.*

How to Install or Remove Mini-PCI Cards

Procedure Reference: Install a Mini-PCI Card

To install a Mini-PCI card:

1. Shut down the system, close the cover, and unplug the power cord. If necessary, remove the computer from the docking station or disconnect any peripheral devices.
2. Ground yourself and dissipate any static electricity you might be carrying.
3. Turn over the laptop and follow the manufacturer's instructions to locate the Mini-PCI bay cover. If there is no Mini-PCI bay, follow the manufacturer's instructions to access the location where you can install the Mini-PCI card.
4. Remove the screw that secures the Mini-PCI bay cover.
5. Remove the Mini-PCI bay cover.
6. If necessary, connect the card to any cables.
7. Secure the card inside the bay using supplied screws or clamps.
8. Replace the cover on the bay and fasten it with the screw.
9. Plug in the computer or replace it in the docking station. Turn on the power.
10. Verify that the new Mini-PCI card has been recognized. If necessary, install any updated drivers.

Procedure Reference: Remove or Replace a Mini-PCI Card

To remove or replace a Mini-PCI card:

1. Shut down the system, close the cover, and unplug the power cord. If necessary, remove the computer from the docking station or disconnect any peripheral devices.
2. Ground yourself and dissipate any static electricity you might be carrying.

3. Turn over the laptop and follow the manufacturer's instructions to locate the Mini-PCI bay cover. If there is no Mini-PCI bay, follow the manufacturer's instructions to locate the existing Mini-PCI card.

4. Remove the screw that secures the Mini-PCI bay cover.

5. Remove the Mini-PCI bay cover.

6. Remove any screws or clamps holding the Mini-PCI card in place.

7. If necessary, remove any cables connecting the Mini-PCI card to a modem or network connector.

8. If replacing the existing card, connect the new card to the cables.

9. Secure the new card using the screws or clamps you removed from the old card.

10. Replace the cover on the bay and fasten it with the screw.

11. Plug in the computer or replace it in the docking station. Turn on the power.

12. Verify that the new Mini-PCI card has been recognized. If necessary, install any updated drivers.

ACTIVITY 11-6

Installing a Mini-PCI Card

Setup:
To complete this activity, you will need a portable computer with a Mini-PCI bay and an extra Mini-PCI card.

Scenario:
You've been asked to add a new wireless Mini-PCI card in a user's notebook computer. You know that this type of notebook has a dedicated Mini-PCI bay.

Lesson 11

What You Do	How You Do It
1. Install the wireless Mini-PCI card.	a. Shut down the system, close the cover, and unplug the power cord. b. If necessary, remove the computer from the docking station or disconnect any peripheral devices. c. Ground yourself and dissipate any static electricity you might be carrying. d. Turn over the laptop and follow the manufacturer's instructions to locate the Mini-PCI bay cover. e. Remove the screw that secures the Mini-PCI bay cover. f. Remove the Mini-PCI bay cover. g. Secure the card inside the bay using the supplied screws or clamps. h. Replace the cover on the bay and fasten it with the screw.
2. Verify that the card is installed properly.	a. Plug in the computer or replace it in the docking station. b. Turn on the power. c. Verify that the new Mini-PCI card has been recognized. If necessary, install any updated drivers.

Topic F
Portable Computing Device Memory

Users will often require additional memory over what was installed when the system was purchased. Just as you were able to install additional memory on a desktop system, you can install additional memory on a portable system. Knowing how to determine the kind of memory required for a specific portable system and how to install it will help you install it more quickly and efficiently. In this topic, you will install memory into a portable computing device.

Portable Device Memory Options

Portable devices use memory that was specifically designed for those devices. Since it is not produced in as high quantities as desktop memory, it tends to be much more expensive. Also, there is less standardization. Some notebooks take proprietary memory that must be purchased from the manufacturer of the notebook system. Some notebooks use Small Outline DIMM (SODIMM) modules, which are about half the size of standard desktop DIMMs, or MicroDIMMs, which are even smaller than SODIMMs. Other portable computing devices and some notebooks use flash memory modules rather than regular RAM. Be sure to check the documentation for your device so that you purchase the correct type of memory to use. Figure 11-18 shows examples of memory for notebook computers.

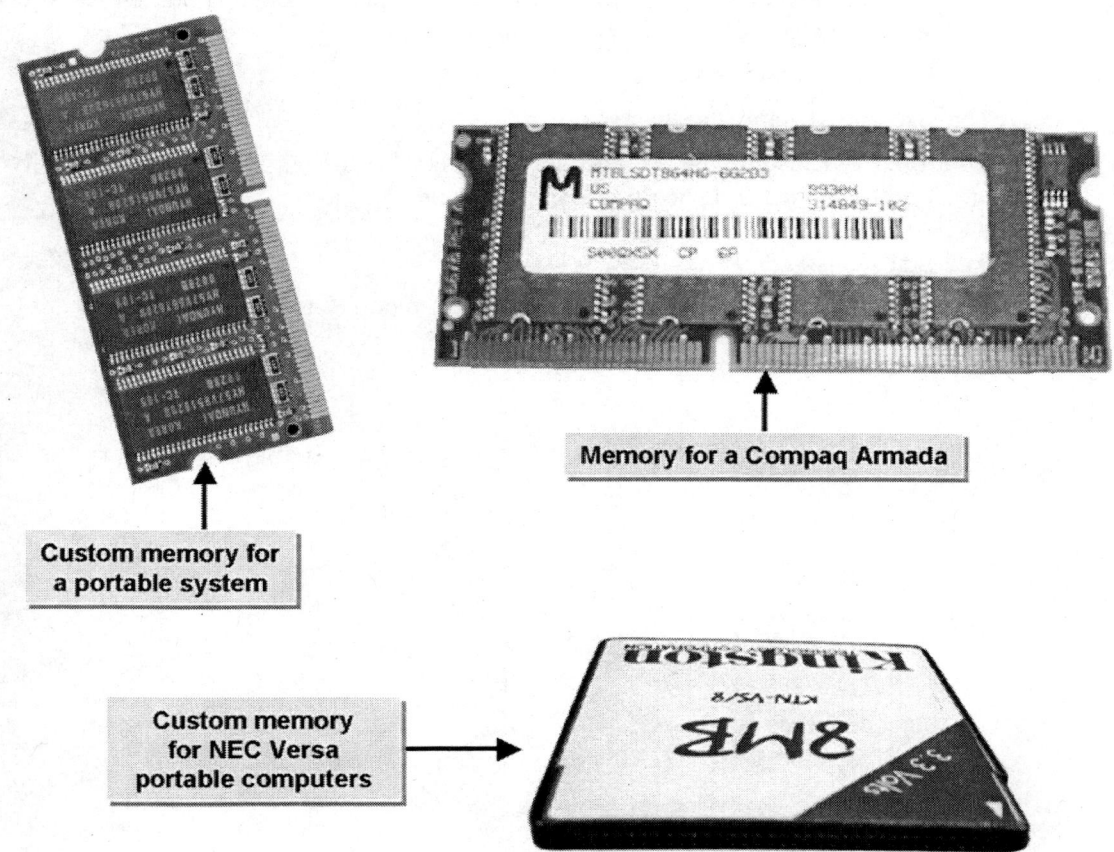

Figure 11-18: *Memory for notebook computers.*

Lesson 11

Flash Memory

Definition:

Flash memory is a removable solid-state mass storage device that resides on a small card. All flash memory:

- Uses EEPROM.
- Functions more like a removable disk than typical RAM or ROM.
- Is considered a solid-state device, because there are no moving parts.
- Can be written to and erased in blocks. This makes it fast since it is writing several bits at a time rather than one at a time.
- Is small and lightweight.
- Can be read directly from the device by connecting it to the computer with a cable or other wireless method.
- Can be read using a separate card reader or adapter. The adapters enable the flash memory card to be read through a USB port, PC Card slot, or through a floppy drive.

Flash memory varies by:

- Type. There are several different flash memory cards. They are not interchangeable or compatible with each other.
- The devices it can be used in. Some types of flash memory can be used in many devices and some can be used in limited devices. See the documentation for your device on which type of flash memory card it uses.
- Durability. Some are more fragile than others.
- The size and shape of the memory card.
- Controller type. Some use a controller built into the memory card and others rely on a controller in the device into which they are inserted.

Example: CompactFlash

Figure 11-19 shows an example of a CompactFlash memory card. CompactFlash memory cards contain a built-in controller.

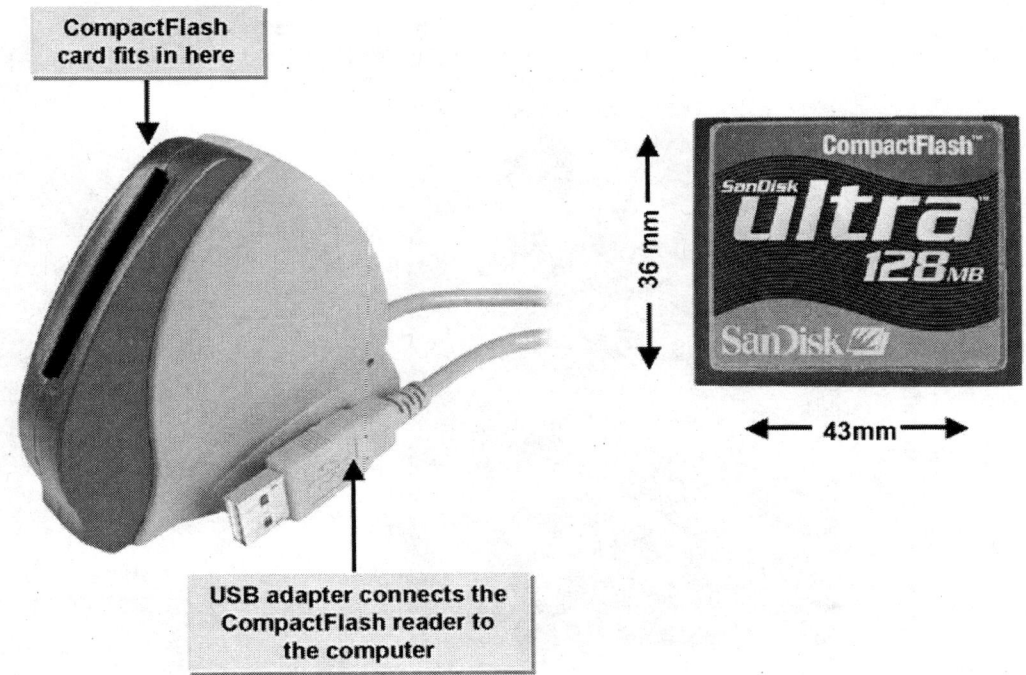

Figure 11-19: *A CompactFlash memory card.*

Example: SmartMedia

SmartMedia is a flash memory card that uses a memory chip and no built-in controller. It uses the controller in the device. Older SmartMedia cards ran at 5 V, but newer cards run at 3.3 V. You can tell the difference by the location of the notch. With the contact side of the card facing up, a notch on the left side indicates a 5 V card and a notch on the right indicates a 3.3 V card. Be sure to use the correct volt card for your device.

The SmartMedia card is 45 mm long, 37 mm wide, and 0.76 mm thick. It comes in 2, 4, 8, 16, 32, 64, and 128 MB capacities.

Lesson 11

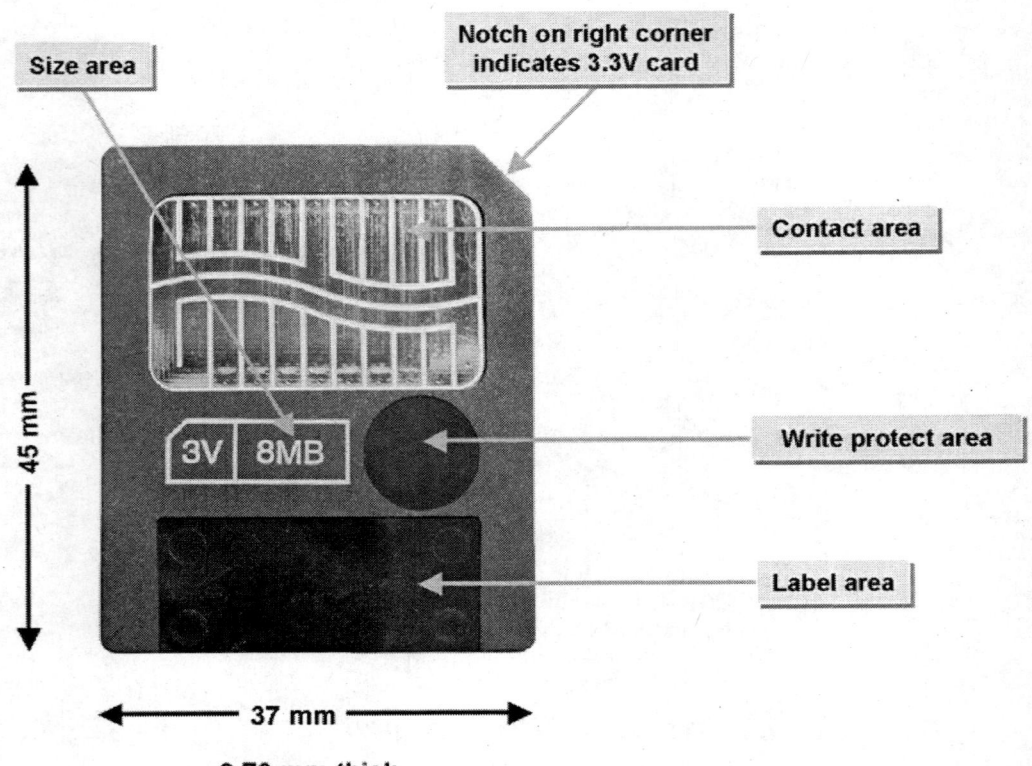

Figure 11-20: *A SmartMedia memory card.*

Types of Flash Memory Cards

compares the features of flash memory cards and how they vary.

Table 11-5: *Flash Memory Card Descriptions*

Name	Physical Size	Capacity	Description
CompactFlash	43 mm long x 36 mm wide. Type I is 3.3 mm thick and Type II is 5 mm thick.	8 MB to 1 GB	Composed of memory chips and a controller. Has a 50-pin contact. More information can be found at **www.compactflash.org/info/cfinfo.htm**.
SmartMedia	45 mm long x 37 mm wide x 0.76 mm thick. Weighs 1.8 grams.	2, 4, 8, 16, 32, 64, or 128 MB	Contains only a memory chip and no controller. Controller is in the device that the card is inserted into. Older cards ran at 5 V and have the notch on the left. Newer cards run at 3.3 V and have the notch on the right.
xD-Picture Card (xD)	20 mm long x 25 mm wide x 1.7 mm thick. Weighs 2 grams.	16 MB to 256 MB with plans for up to 8 GB	Contains only a memory chip and no controller. Controller is in the device that the card is inserted into. Half the size of SmartMedia cards. More information can be found at **www.dpreview.com/news/0207/02073002fujifilmxd.asp**.

Name	Physical Size	Capacity	Description
Memory Stick (MS)	50 mm long x 21.5 mm wide x 2.8 mm thick. Weighs 4 grams.	4, 8, 16, 32, 64, and 128 MB	Used extensively in Sony products. Memory Stick Pro is one-half the size of a MS card and is 1 GB.
Secure Digital (SD) and MultiMedia Card (MMC)	32 mm long x 24 mm wide x 2.1 mm thick.	4 to 512 MB	Composed of memory chip(s), controller module, and copper balls between chips. SD and MMC are the same physically, but technically they are different. Some systems can use only SD. A new variety, SD-I/O with built-in Bluetooth technology, is used for wireless transfer of data. There are also SD Audio and SD Memory Cards.

How to Install or Add Portable Computing Device Memory

Procedure Reference: Install Memory in Portable Computing Devices

To install the memory:

1. In a laptop or notebook portable computer:
   a. Shut down the system and unplug the power cord. You should never install memory while the system is powered on.
   b. Locate the memory cover and remove it. This could be on the bottom, on the side of the system, or under the keyboard. Refer to the documentation for how to access the memory.
   c. If you're going to remove the memory, remove the memory module.
   d. If you're going to add memory, verify that the memory is appropriate for the system. There are many types of memory, often proprietary to a specific system or manufacturer.
   e. Insert the memory module according to the directions in the system or memory documentation.
   f. If no memory slots are available, remove a smaller memory module following the directions in the system or memory documentation, then install the larger memory module.
   g. Replace the cover to the memory slots.
   h. Start the computer and verify that the additional memory was recognized.
2. In an MP3 player, a PDA, or a digital camera:
   a. Turn off the device.
   b. Locate the memory slot. This is often under a cover which needs to be opened to access the slot (in most digital cameras and MP3 players). Other times, it might just connect externally to the device (such as is the case for some PDA devices).
   c. Remove existing memory, if necessary.

d. Insert the memory according to the directions in the documentation. There is often a picture indicating the orientation of the device in relationship to the slot.

e. Turn on the device.

f. Verify that the memory was recognized.

ACTIVITY 11-7

Adding Memory to Portable Computing Devices

Setup:
To complete this activity, you need a portable computing device with an empty memory slot and a compatible memory chip.

Scenario:
You have just received the memory modules that were ordered for several portable computing devices. You need to deploy them to the devices for users.

What You Do	How You Do It
1. Install memory in a portable computer.	a. Shut down and unplug the portable computer.
	b. Locate and remove the memory cover on the case.
	c. Verify that the memory module you are about to install matches the specifications for the memory slot.
	d. Following the directions in the documentation, install the memory module.
	e. Replace and secure the cover to the memory.
	f. Restart the computer.
	g. Verify that the additional memory was recognized.

2. Install a memory module in an MP3 player, a PDA, or a digital camera.

   a. Turn off the device.

   b. Locate the expansion slot for the memory card.

   c. If necessary, **remove the existing memory card.**

   d. Verify that the memory card matches the specifications for adding memory to the device.

   e. Insert the memory card into the slot.

   f. Turn on the device.

   g. Verify that the memory was recognized.

TOPIC G

Replace Internal Components

So far the components you have replaced on a portable computer have been external or accessed through a special bay. However, like desktop systems, there are internal computers that could malfunction and need to be replaced. In this topic, you will learn how to replace internal components of a portable computer system.

Internal Components

Like a desktop system, the system board of a portable computer contains many internal components that are soldered to the board and other internal components that are connected to the system board. Components that are connected to the system board may be replaced independently of the system board. Components that are soldered to the system board cannot be replaced separately—a whole new system board must be installed to correct a problem with a soldered component.

Internal components that are typically soldered to the system board include:

- Processor
- Parallel port
- Serial port
- PS/2 port
- USB port
- Firewire port
- External monitor port

Lesson 11: Portable Computing

Lesson 11

509

Lesson 11

- AC adapter connection
- Infrared port

Internal components that are typically connected to the system board and can be replaced separately include:

- Hard disk
- Fan
- PCMCIA bay
- Battery
- Keyboard
- Pointing device

Items that can be on either a separate circuitry board connected to the system board or directly soldered to the main system board include:

- Modem
- Sound connectors for speakers, headphones, and microphone

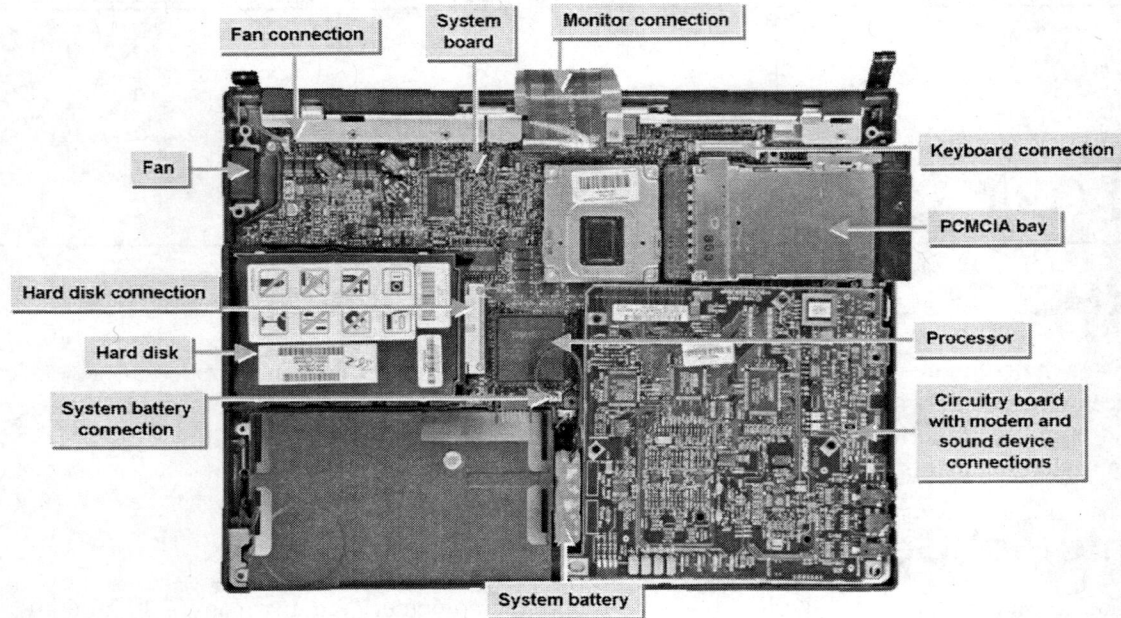

Figure 11-21: *The internal components of a Compaq notebook computer.*

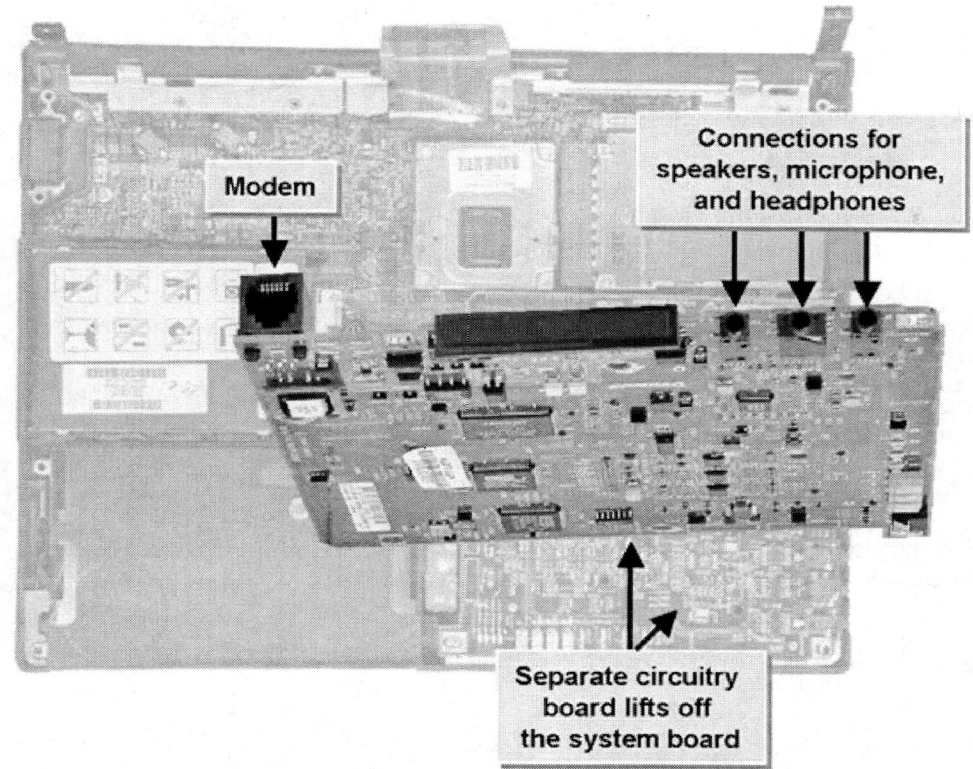

Figure 11-22: *Separate circuitry board for modem and sound devices.*

How to Replace a Hard Disk

Procedure Reference: Replace a Hard Disk through a Bay

Just like with desktop systems, an internal hard disk in a portable computer can fail or run out of space and need to be replaced. Some hard disks can be replaced through a special bay without opening the computer case. To replace a hard disk through a bay:

1. Shut down the system, close the cover, and unplug the power cord. If necessary, remove the computer from the docking station or disconnect any peripheral devices.
2. Ground yourself and dissipate any static electricity you might be carrying.
3. Turn over the laptop and remove the battery.
4. Each type of portable computer will have its own hard disk locking mechanism. This might be a screw, a latch, or other security device. Unlock the mechanism that secures your hard disk.
5. Gently pull the hard disk from its connection and carefully slide the hard disk out of its bay. You may need to release additional latches or clips that keep the hard disk in place.
6. Insert the new hard disk into the slot making sure it is fully connected and any latches or clips are secure.
7. Replace the hard disk locking mechanism.
8. Plug in the computer or return it to the docking station. Turn on the power.

Lesson 11

9. Verify that the new hard disk is recognized.
10. Install any firmware that came with hard disk. Partition and format the hard disk for use.

Procedure Reference: Replace an Internal Hard Disk

To replace an internal hard disk on a portable computer:

1. Shut down the system, close the cover, and unplug the power cord. If necessary, remove the computer from the docking station or disconnect any peripheral devices.
2. Ground yourself and dissipate any static electricity you might be carrying.
3. Turn over the laptop and remove the battery.
4. Remove the screws on the bottom and spine (back) of the computer. You may also have to remove screws from the monitor hinges. The screw locations in a Compaq laptop are shown in Figure 11-23.
5. Carefully remove the bottom from the top. You may need to press some tabs to get the plastic case to release.

   ⚠ Be careful not to separate the pieces forcefully—there will be connections to the keyboard and monitor that you don't want to damage or break.

6. Remove the screws that secure the metal cover over the system board. See Figure 11-24 for an example.
7. Find the hard disk.
8. Remove any screws or clamps holding the hard disk card in place. In some laptops, it will be held in place with screws. In other cases, clamps.
9. Gently pull the hard disk from its connection.
10. Insert the new hard disk into the slot making sure to connect it fully.
11. Secure the new hard disk using the clamps or the screws you removed from the old disk.
12. Replace the metal cover over the system board and fasten it with the screws you removed.
13. Carefully replace the bottom on the top.
14. Secure the bottom to the top by replacing all the screws you removed from the bottom, spine, and monitor hinges.
15. Plug in the computer or return it to the docking station. Turn on the power.
16. Verify that the new hard disk is recognized.
17. Install any firmware that came with hard disk. Partition and format the hard disk for use.

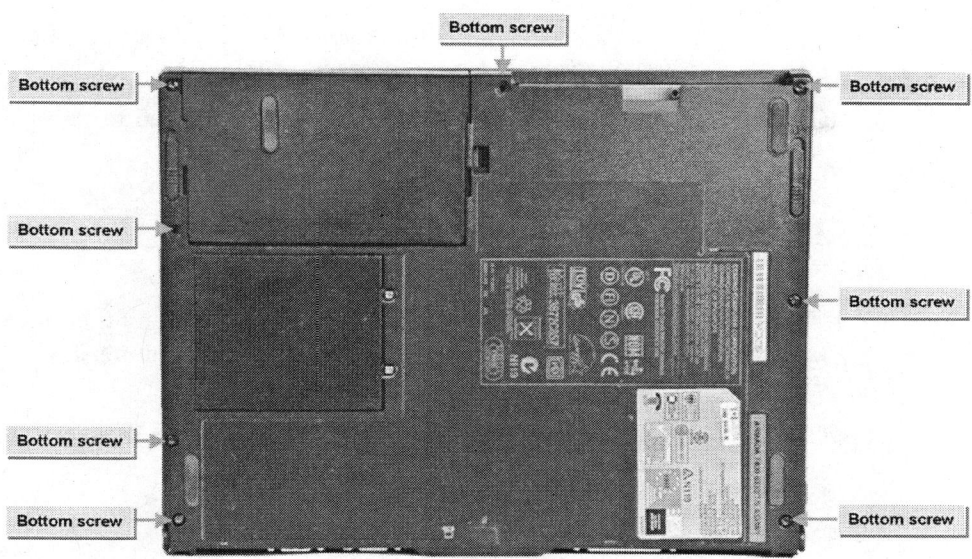

Figure 11-23: *Removing the screws to separate the bottom from the top.*

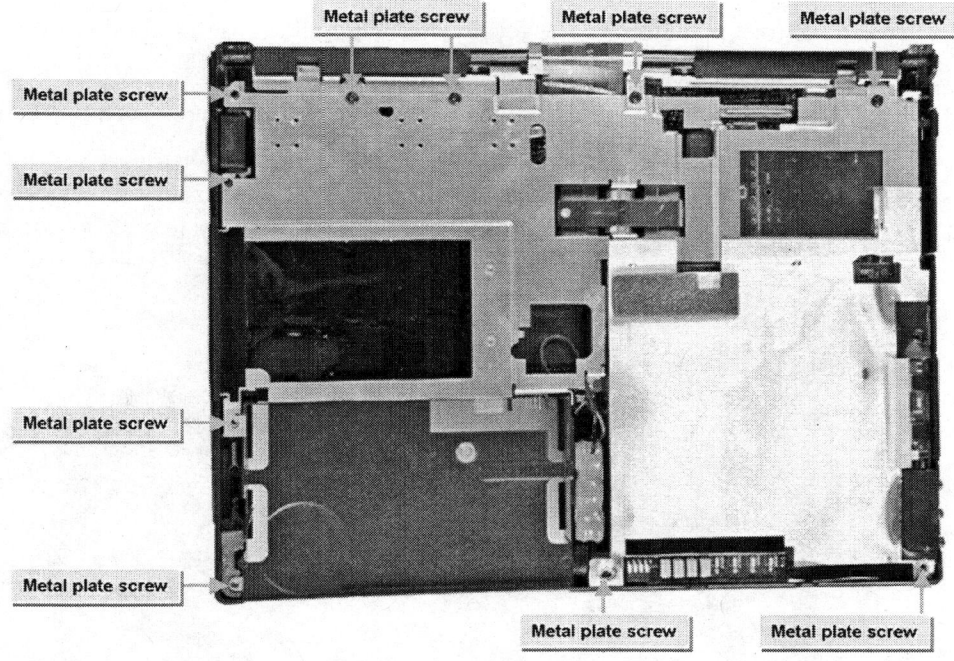

Figure 11-24: *Metal cover over the system board.*

How to Replace a Pointing Device

Procedure Reference: Replace an Internal Pointing Device

To replace the pointing device in a portable computer.

1. Shut down the system, close the cover, and unplug the power cord. If necessary, remove the computer from the docking station or disconnect any peripheral devices.
2. Ground yourself and dissipate any static electricity you might be carrying.

Lesson 11

3. Turn over the laptop and remove the battery.

4. Remove the screws on the bottom and spine (back) of the computer. You may also have to remove screws from the monitor hinges.

5. Carefully remove the bottom from the top. You may need to press some tabs to get the plastic case to release.

   ⚠ Be careful not to separate the pieces forcefully—there will be connections to the keyboard and monitor that you don't want to damage or break.

6. If your particular laptop allows the replacement of the pointing device separate from the keyboard, remove the screws that hold the pointing device in place. See Figure 11-25 for an example on a Compaq laptop.

7. Carefully disconnect the pointing device connector from the circuitry board.

8. Remove the pointing device and insert the new one.

9. Replace the screws that hold the pointing device in place.

10. Connect the new pointing device connector to the circuitry board.

11. Carefully replace the bottom on the top.

12. Secure the bottom to the top by replacing all the screws you removed from the bottom, spine, and monitor hinges.

13. Plug in the computer or return it to the docking station. Turn on the power.

14. Verify that the new pointing device is functional. The drivers for the pointing device should already be installed on the computer from the device you just replaced. If it is a different pointing device, you may need to install the drivers for the device.

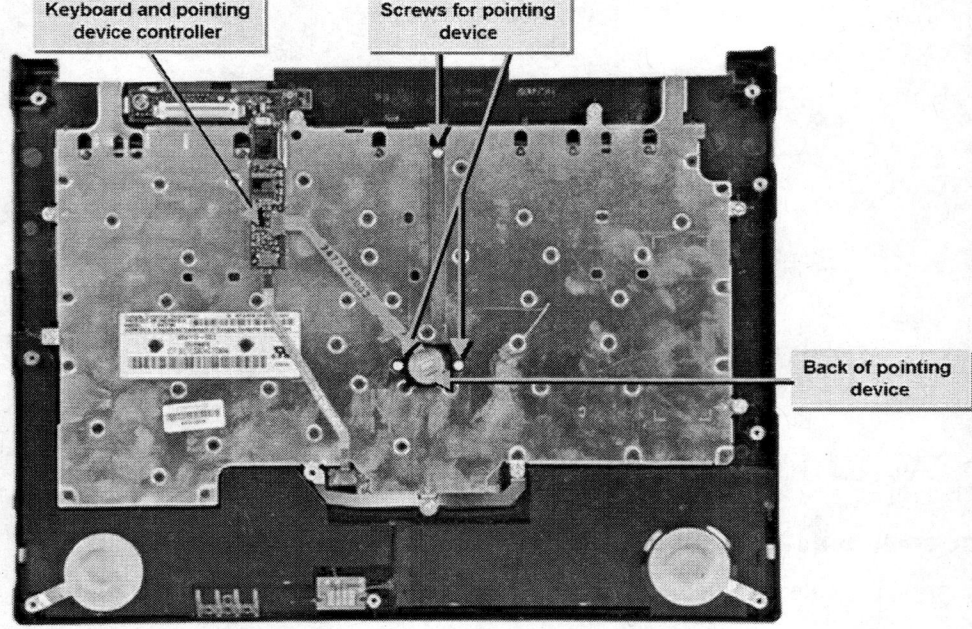

Figure 11-25: *Screws holding pointing device in a Compaq laptop.*

Lesson 11

How to Replace a Keyboard

Procedure Reference: Replace a Keyboard

To replace a keyboard:

1. Shut down the system, close the cover, and unplug the power cord. If necessary, remove the computer from the docking station or disconnect any peripheral devices.

2. Ground yourself and dissipate any static electricity you might be carrying.

3. Turn over the laptop and remove the battery.

4. Remove the screws on the bottom and spine (back) of the computer. You may also have to remove screws from the monitor hinges.

5. Carefully remove the bottom from the top. You may need to press some tabs to get the plastic case to release.

   ⚠ Be careful not to separate the pieces forcefully—there will be connections to the keyboard and monitor that you don't want to damage or break.

6. If the pointing device can be replaced separately from the keyboard, remove the pointing device and set it aside.

7. Remove the screws that secure the keyboard. See Figure 11-26 for an example on a Compaq laptop.

8. Gently remove the keyboard. You may need to release tabs on the circuitry board that controls the keyboard and pointing device to get it to release from the plastic case.

   📌 The circuitry board that controls the keyboard will typically be soldered to the metal plate that holds the keyboard and is replaced with the keyboard.

9. Insert the new keyboard and replace the screws that held the keyboard in place.

10. If necessary, snap the circuitry board for the keyboard and pointing device back into its tabs.

11. If necessary, reconnect the pointing device you set aside.

12. Carefully replace the bottom on the top.

13. Secure the bottom to the top by replacing all screws you removed from the bottom, spine, and monitor hinges.

14. Plug in the computer or return it to the docking station. Turn on the power.

15. Verify that the keyboard and the pointing device are functional.

Lesson 11

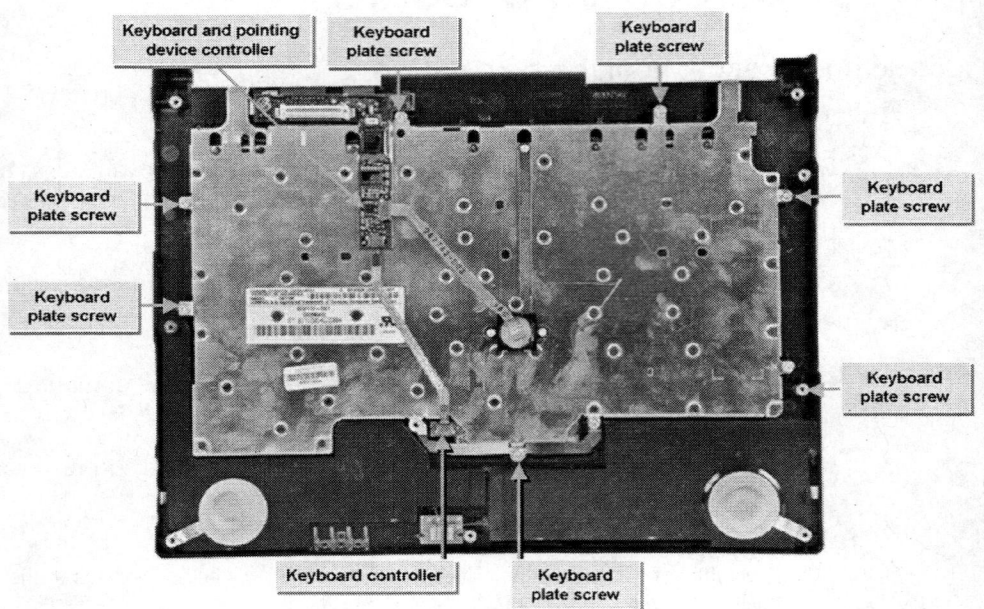

Figure 11-26: *Screws holding the keyboard in a Compaq laptop.*

How to Replace a System Board

Procedure Reference: Replace a System Board

To replace the system board in a portable computer:

1. Shut down the system, close the cover, and unplug the power cord. If necessary, remove the computer from the docking station or disconnect any peripheral devices.

2. Ground yourself and dissipate any static electricity you might be carrying.

3. Turn over the laptop and remove the battery.

4. If you have a hard disk that is connected through a bay, remove the hard disk and set it aside.

5. Remove the screws on the bottom and spine (back) of the computer. You may also have to remove screws from the monitor hinges.

6. Carefully remove the bottom from the top. You may need to press some tabs to get the plastic case to release.

   ⚠ Be careful not to separate the pieces forcefully—there will be connections to the keyboard and monitor that you don't want to damage or break.

7. If necessary, remove the screws that secure the metal cover over the system board.

8. Remove the metal cover.

9. In some laptops, a separate circuitry board will have the microphone, headphone, and speaker connections as well as the modem. If this is the case, you can replace these components separate from the system board by replacing just this board.

    If this circuitry board is separate, disconnect it from the main system board and set it aside.

10. If you have an internal hard disk, remove the hard disk and set it aside.
11. Remove the screws that hold the PCMCIA bay to the system board.
12. Undo any clamps holding the PCMCIA bay in place.
13. Disconnect the PCMCIA bay from the system board and set it aside.
14. Disconnect the system battery and the laptop battery connection from the system board.
15. Disconnect the fan connection from the system board.
16. Disconnect the monitor connection from the system board.
17. Remove the screws that hold the system board in place.
18. Remove the old system board and replace it with the new one.
19. Replace the screws that hold the system board in place.
20. Reconnect the monitor, fan, system battery, laptop battery connection.
21. Reinsert and reconnect the PCMCIA bay onto the system board.
22. Reinsert and reconnect the hard disk.
23. If necessary, reinsert and reconnect the modem/sound circuitry board.
24. Replace the metal cover over the system board and fasten it with the screws you removed.
25. Carefully replace the bottom on the top.
26. Secure the bottom to the top by replacing all the screws you removed from the bottom, spine, and monitor hinges.
27. Plug in the computer or return it to the docking station. Turn on the power.
28. Verify that the new system board is recognized.
29. Install any firmware that came with the system board.
30. Verify all devices in the portable computer are functional.

Procedure Reference: Replace Components Connected to the System Board

Any components that are plugged in (not soldered) to the system board can be replaced. To replace a component connected to a system board in a portable computer:

1. Shut down the system, close the cover, and unplug the power cord. If necessary, remove the computer from the docking station or disconnect any peripheral devices.
2. Ground yourself and dissipate any static electricity you might be carrying.
3. Turn over the laptop and remove the battery.

Lesson 11

4. Remove the screws on the bottom and spine (back) of the computer. You may also have to remove screws from the monitor hinges.

5. Carefully remove the bottom from the top. You may need to press some tabs to get the plastic case to release.

   ⚠ Be careful not to separate the pieces forcefully—there will be connections to the keyboard and monitor that you don't want to damage or break.

6. If necessary, remove the screws that secure the metal cover over the system board.

7. Remove the metal cover.

8. Disconnect the component you wish to replace from the system board.

9. Remove the component you wish to replace.

10. Insert and connect the new component onto the system board.

11. Replace the metal cover over the system board and fasten it with the screws you removed.

12. Carefully replace the bottom on the top.

13. Secure the bottom to the top by replacing all the screws you removed from the bottom, spine, and monitor hinges.

14. Plug in the computer or return it to the docking station. Turn on the power.

15. Verify that the new device is recognized.

16. Install any new software that came with the device.

DISCOVERY ACTIVITY 11-8

Discussing the Replacement of Internal System Components in a Portable Computer

Activity Time:
5 minutes

Scenario:
In this activity, you will discuss the internal replacement of internal system components in a portable computer.

Lesson 11

1. **Identify which components are typically soldered to the system board and cannot be replaced without replacing the entire system board.**

    a) Fan

    b) Processor

    c) USB port

    d) PCMCIA bay

    e) AC adapter connection

2. **Identify which components are typically connected to the system board and can be replaced independently of the system board.**

    a) Hard disk

    b) Infrared port

    c) External monitor port

    d) Fan

    e) Keyboard

Topic H

Personal Digital Assistants

The portable computing devices you have worked with so far are all still full-fledged computers. There is another class of limited-function computing devices, called Personal Digital Assistants (PDAs), that can interact with standard computer systems. PDAs are popular because they give users the convenience of taking electronic information from their computer with them in their shirt pocket or purse—but only if the PDA will connect correctly to the computer. In this topic, you will connect PDAs to computers.

PDA

Definition:

A *Personal Digital Assistant (PDA)* is a portable computing device that can be held in one hand. All PDAs:

- Use an operating system.
- Have applications.
- Can be used as organizers.
- Can be connected to a computer.
- Can be used as a peripheral to the computer as well as a standalone device.
- Synchronize information between the computer and the PDA.

PDAs vary by:

- Input method. These include:
  - A stylus to write on the screen. You might need to train the PDA to recognize your handwriting, but more often, you need to learn its handwriting characters.
  - An integrated keyboard. This might be a physical keyboard with very tiny keys or a graphical keyboard you type on using the stylus.
  - An add-on keyboard that plugs into the PDA.
- The screen can be color or black and white.
- The operating system the PDA uses. Some of the common operating systems include the following:
  - PalmOS
  - Windows CE
  - Symbian OS (Sometimes called EPOC)
  - FLEXOS
  - OS/9
  - JavaOS
- The applications installed, and whether you can add applications. Applications need to be compatible with the PDA operating system installed on your PDA. Some of the applications include the following:
  - Calculator
  - Document viewers
  - Document editors
  - Games
  - Calendar
  - Address book
  - Expense report tracking
  - To Do list
  - Notepad
- How it connects to a computer. It might connect through the serial port or the USB port. The PDA might need to be connected to a cradle to make the connection or it might connect directly to a cable.
- What other devices it can connect to. Some PDAs can connect to other PDAs, cell phones, or digital cameras. This might be a hard-wired physical connection or it might be through an IR port.
- Some PDAs enable you to increase their functionality by connecting other devices to them. Others increase functionality through the use of flash memory cards being added to the PDA.
- Some PDAs incorporate mobile communication features to enable you to access email or Web services from the PDA while travelling.
- The battery type. Most PDAs use rechargeable batteries that are recharged when you connect the PDA to the computer, but some, especially older PDAs, use standard AA or AAA batteries.

- The amount of memory installed. This determines how much information the PDA can hold. On some PDAs, you can add more memory, but others cannot be upgraded.
- Buttons and other physical features, including:
  - Power button function and location.
  - Contrast, brightness, and backlight controls.
  - Application buttons. On some PDAs, you can assign specific applications to physical buttons on the PDA to make them easily accessible if you use them often.
- The software on the computer used to synchronize data between the computer and the PDA.

> PDAs are part of a larger category of personal computing devices called *palmtops*. Other palmtops include warehouse inventory wands, electronic meter readers, global positioning satellite units, and Game Boy devices.

Example: A Palm V PDA

Figure 11-27 shows an example of a PDA. This PDA uses the Palm OS. Features of this example PDA include:

- It has a black and white screen.
- It has 2 MB of memory.
- It includes application buttons across the bottom of the PDA to access applications directly rather than selecting them through the icons on the screen. You can select any application through the icons on the screen from the main menu.
- It uses the Graffiti writing software as the primary input mode. You can also display a keyboard on screen and use the stylus to tap the keys. You can also connect an external keyboard designed specifically for the Palm.
- It connects to the computer through the serial port. You can also purchase an adapter to enable it to be connected to the USB port.
- It contains an Li-Ion battery. You place the Palm in the cradle to recharge its internal battery. The initial charge takes about three hours. Recharge a few minutes each day to maintain full battery power. Under normal use, you can usually go up to a month without recharging.
- It has an IR port. Through it you can connect to other Palm devices or a computer with an IR port.
- The cradle or the IR port are used to synchronize it with the files on your computer. Palm Desktop software is installed on the computer. Through it, you can keep a calendar up to date on the computer as well as the PDA. It is also the method for adding new applications and transferring data files between the two devices.
- Accessories are added through the serial connector on the lower edge of the PDA. Accessories include:
  - A portable keyboard.
  - A modem. The modem looks much like the cradle and is the same size as the PDA. The phone line connects to the top edge of the modem.

— A Global System for Mobile Communications (GSM) kit. This works with the modem to enable you to use specific GSM-enabled cell phones to make dial-up connections.

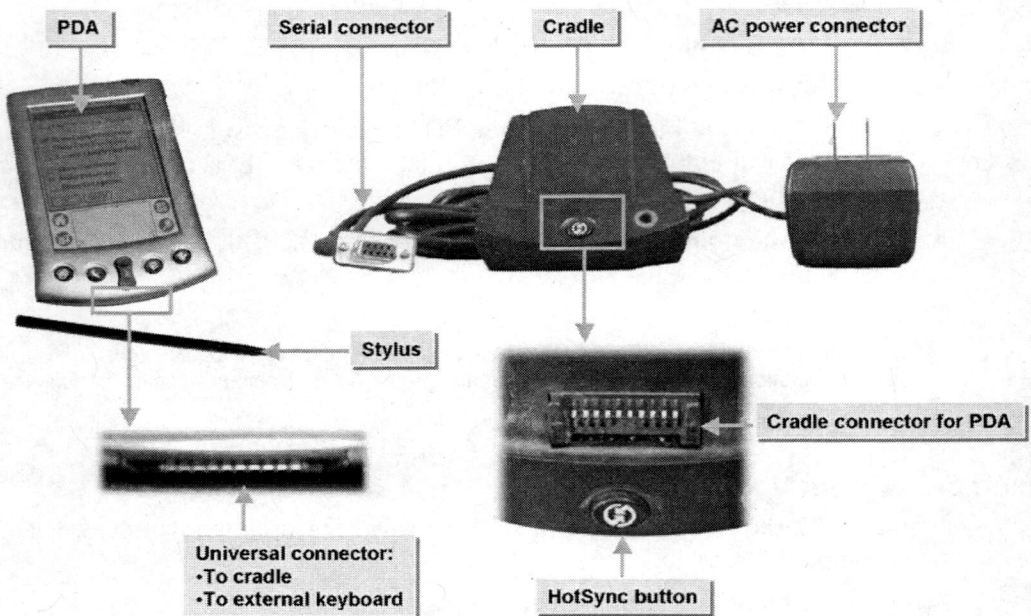

Figure 11-27: *A Palm V PDA.*

Example: Palm m130

Figure 11-28 shows another Palm with different features than the previous example. This PDA has most of the same features as the Palm V. It varies from the previous example in the following ways:

- It contains 8 MB of memory.

- It has a color display.

- It uses an SD/MMC/SDIO slot to add functionality. This includes additional memory (16 or 32 MB), backs up contents of the PDA to a separate card for safekeeping, eBooks (electronic books on a card), games, reference books and resources, and Bluetooth connection for wireless connection to Bluetooth-enabled devices such as other PDAs, cell phones, and printers.

- Its cradle uses a USB connection.

Lesson 11

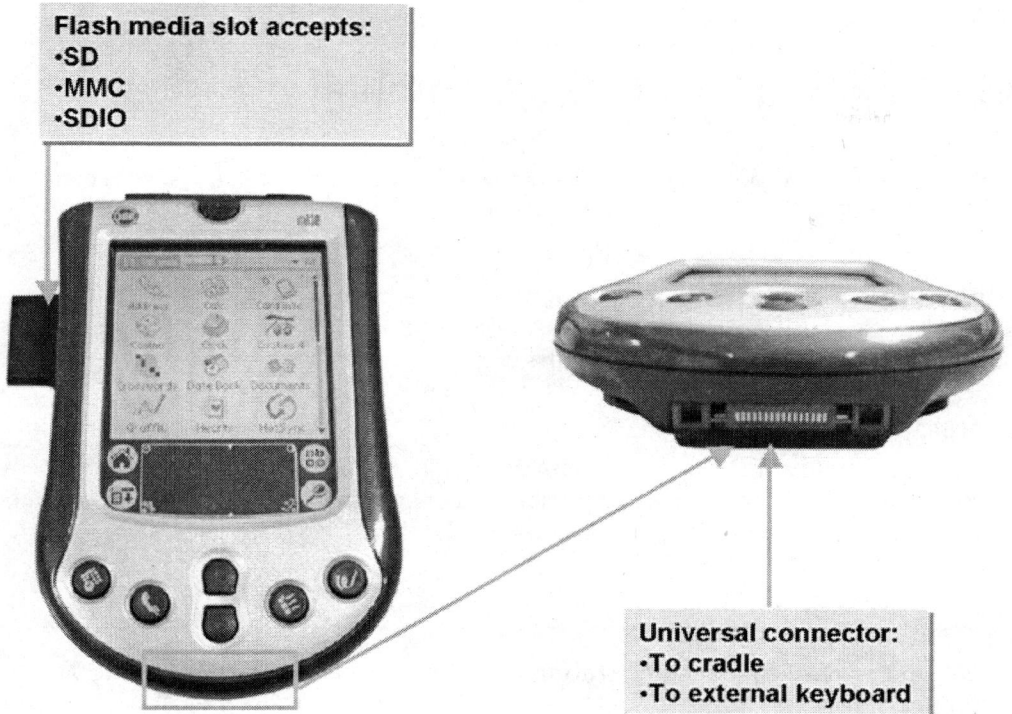

Figure 11-28: *A Palm m130.*

How to Connect Personal Digital Assistants

Procedure Reference: Connect a PDA to a Computer

To connect a PDA to a computer:

1. Connect the cable from the cradle or docking station to the appropriate port on the computer. Refer to the PDA documentation and determine which port the PDA should be connected to. Some companies refer to the stand that is used to connect the PDA to the computer and to recharge the PDA as a cradle and others refer to it as a docking station.

2. Connect the PDA to the cradle or docking station as described in the PDA documentation. There is a connector on the device that fits in the PDA to establish the connection.

3. If necessary, install software on the computer to recognize the PDA. The software is required to synchronize data between the PDA and the computer.

4. Verify the PDA can sychronize with the computer.

Lesson 11

ACTIVITY 11-9

Connecting a PDA to the Computer

This activity was developed using Palm PDAs. If you have another brand of PDA, check the documentation if the steps are not appropriate for your device.

Setup:

To complete this activity, you need a PDA device, its cables and connectors, as well as the software to install the PDA utilities on the computer.

Scenario:

Users recently received Palm PDAs. Some users have notebook computers and others have desktop computers. They all need to be able to connect their PDAs to their computers, in order to synchronize the calendar and update their To Do lists.

What You Do	How You Do It
1. Set up the cradle or docking station for the PDA.	a. If necessary, **connect the AC cable to the cradle or docking station connector.**
	b. **Connect the cradle or docking station to the computer port that matches the connector on the cable.**
	c. **Connect the PDA to the cradle or docking station.**
2. Install the PDA software on the computer.	a. **Insert the PDA software CD-ROM in the CD-ROM drive.**
	b. **Follow the on-screen instructions to install the software.**

Lesson 11 Follow-up

In this lesson, you learned how to support a variety of portable computing devices. You connected external peripherals to a portable system. Then you added and/or removed PC Cards, Mini-PCI cards, and memory in the system. You also replaced many of the internal components of the system. Finally, you connected a PDA to a computer. You'll need all these skills as you support users in the mobile workforce of today.

1. **Do you support more desktop or mobile systems? Why are there more of one than the other in your company?**

2. What types of portable computing devices are you responsible for supporting?

Notes

LESSON 12
Networking

Lesson Time
4 hour(s), 30 minutes

Lesson Objectives:

In this lesson, you will describe the basic components of a network.

You will:

- Describe the physical components needed to connect a computer to a network.
- Describe how computers communicate on a network.
- Describe the different network architectures.
- Describe different Internet connections.
- Describe different classifications of network devices.
- Correct network connection problems.

LESSON 12

Introduction

Why do you, the hardware support technician care about networks? Isn't that something for the network administrators? Not necessarily so. Networks enable users to share information and resources with other users both internal to their network and external via the Internet. As an A+ technician, you'll be required to install the hardware and software on individual PCs to allow them to communicate on various networks. In this lesson, you will learn how networks—the building blocks for the Internet—are classified based on geographical boundaries and the characteristics of different network topologies. In this lesson, you will learn about the hardware devices and network operating system software commonly found on networks, as well as how those networks function.

The following CompTIA A+ Core Hardware (2003) Examination objectives are covered in this lesson:

- Topic A:
  - 1.5 Identify the names, purposes, and performance characteristics, of standardized/common peripheral ports, associated cabling, and their connectors. Recognize ports, cabling, and connectors, by sights. Content includes the following: connector types—serial (RJ45).
  - 1.9 Identify procedures to optimize PC operations in specific scenarios. Predict the effects of specific procedures under given scenarios. Topics include: NICs.
  - 6.1 Identify the common types of network cables, their characteristics and connectors. Cable types include: coaxial—RG6, RG8, RG58, and RG59; plenum/PVC; UTP—Cat3, Cat5/e, and Cat6; STP; Fiber—single-mode and multi-mode. Connector types include: BNC; RJ-45; AUI; ST/SC; and IDC/UDC.
  - 6.2 Identify basic networking concepts including how a network works. Concepts include: installing and configuring network cards; full-duplex, half-duplex; cabling—twisted pair, coaxial, fiber optic, and RS-232; and networking models—peer-to-peer and client/server.

- Topic B:
  - 1.2 Identify basic procedures for adding and removing field-replaceable modules for desktop systems. Given a replacement scenario choose the appropriate sequences. Content includes: desktop components: adapters—network interface card (NIC).
  - 1.4 Identify typical IRQs, DMAs, and I/O addresses, and procedures for altering these settings when installing and configuring devices. Choose the appropriate installation or configuration steps in a given scenario. Content includes the following: NICs.
  - 6.2 Identify basic networking concepts including how a network works. Concepts include: addressing; status indicators; protocols—TCP/IP, IPX/SPX (NWLINK), AppleTalk, and NETBEUI/NETBIOS.

- Topic D:
  - 1.8 Identify proper procedures for installing and configuring common peripheral devices. Choose the appropriate installation or configuration sequence in given scenarios. Content includes the following: modems and transceivers—cable, DSL, and ISDN; wireless access points.
  - 6.2 Identify basic networking concepts including how a network works. Concepts include: bandwidth; infrared; and wireless.
  - 6.3 Identify common technologies available for establishing Internet connectivity and their characteristics. Technologies include: LAN, DSL, Cable, ISDN, dial-up; satellite, and wireless. Characteristics include: definition, speed, and connections.

Lesson 12

- Topic F:
  - 2.1 Recognize common problems associated with each module and their symptoms, and identify steps to isolate and troubleshoot the problems. Given a problem situation, interpret the symptoms and infer the most likely cause. Content includes: adapters—network interface card.

Topic A

Network Concepts

Today most business systems are networked. In more and more homes, users want to connect multiple systems in home networks and connect to the Internet through broadband. All computer networks, no matter how large or small, share certain physical characteristics. In this topic, you will identify and classify those characteristics and recognize these common attributes in a variety of different network scenarios.

Network

Definition:

A *network* is a collection of hardware and software that enables computers in a group to communicate with each other. It enables users to share resources. The hardware needed to network computers includes the components found in the Table 12-1.

Table 12-1: *Computer Network Hardware*

Component	Definition
Server	Any computer that makes resources available to other computers on the network.
Client	Any computer that uses the resources of a server.
Media	The physical means of communication between network computers. This is often a special cable, infrared transmission, or radio signals.
Network adapter	An adapter card installed in each of the computers on the network to enable the computers to send and receive data over the network medium. Each network adapter card has a unique Media Access Control (MAC) address burned into the card by the manufacturer.

The media and network adapter vary based on the physical network. They must be compatible with each other and with the computer. The server and client can each be dedicated machines or a single computer can perform some client and some server functions. The network adapter can have an interface to a specific type of cable or other media, or it might have interfaces to connect to several network media.

Lesson 12

The software needed to network computers includes server and client software. The network adapter requires drivers. *Network protocols* configure how the network computers communicate. All of the software and hardware working together provides users with network access. Some operating systems require separate client software and others have built-in client commands used to access network resources. The Windows XP operating system software can act as both the client and the server software. Each of the required components varies based on the equipment used and the needs of the users.

> Another term you might encounter when talking about networks is node. This refers to any of the devices that can be accessed on the network.

Example: Components of a Basic Network

The most basic network is composed of two computers, two network adapter cards, and a cable between them. This is shown in Figure 12-1.

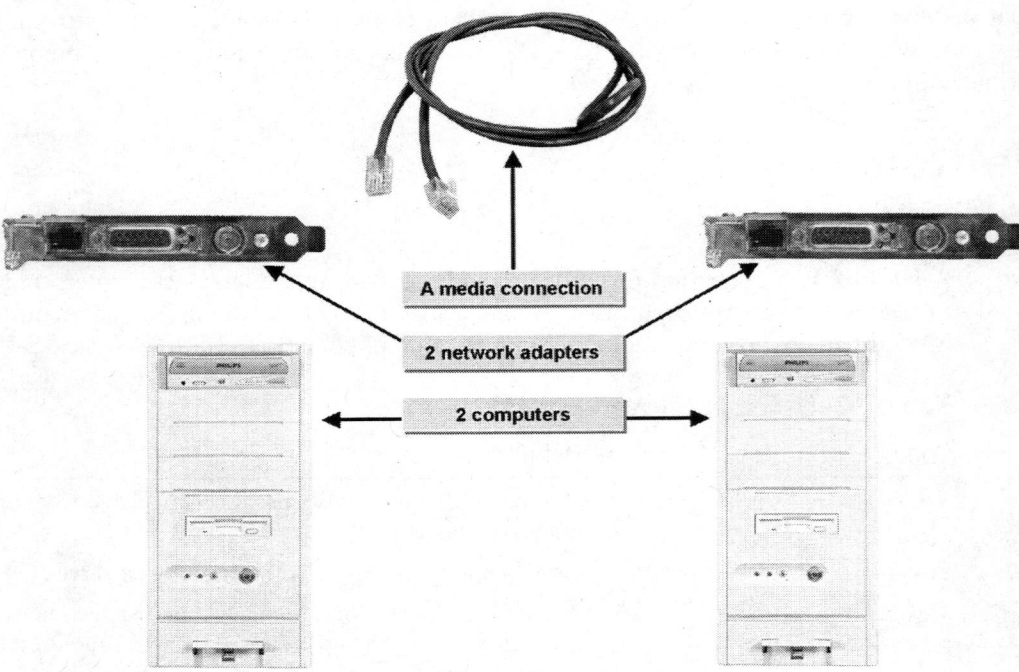

Figure 12-1: *Components of a basic network.*

OSI Model

The International Standards Organization (ISO) developed the Open Systems Interconnection (OSI) model to help provide standardization between different networking manufacturer's products. This model describes networking communications as consisting of seven layers that work together to provide network services.

> For additional information on the OSI model, refer to Appendix B.

Lesson 12

Network Interface Card

Network adapters provide services at the Data Link layer of the network (OSI Layer 2) and connect directly to the cable carrying the electronic signal throughout the network (OSI Layer 1). The most common adapters will connect a computer to an Ethernet or Token Ring network. Sometimes the adapter is built into the system board circuits, and sometimes it is a separate printed circuit board that is inserted into a slot on the system board. There are network adapters that can connect a computer to the network through the parallel port, and portable computers have a special PC Card that connects them to a network. A transmission medium, such as twisted-pair, coax cable, or fiber-optic cable, interconnects all the adapters in the network. A network adapter is commonly called a NIC, or network interface card. Most NICs are designed for a particular network and medium.

Typical Ethernet Network Interface Cards

A typical Ethernet NIC fits into either an ISA or PCI slot on the computer's system board. It can send and receive data at 10 Mbps and/or 100 Mbps. The media through which it will connect to the network may be twisted-pair and/or coaxial cable and/or fiber-optic cable. More expensive cards have more built-in flexibility and can communicate at both speeds over a variety of media. A typical Ethernet NIC with RJ-45, AUI, and BNC connectors is shown in Figure 12-2.

Figure 12-2: *NIC with RJ-45, AUI, and BNC connectors.*

Lesson 12

NICs have an internal, integrated *transceiver* built into the board that lets it send and receive data over the network cable. The cards also have software to support the Medium Access Control (MAC) data-link protocol built into firmware on the card. Every card has a permanent, unique Ethernet address burned into a PROM on the card. The electronics on the card determine what media the card will connect to. A wireless interface card has no jack or sockets to plug cables into because it transmits data using radio waves. A receiver must be installed as a connection to a standard Ethernet configuration for the computer to be on the network. Wireless cards go into slots on the system board and have an antenna built-in. Maximum distances range from 30 feet to 200 feet, depending on the environment.

Other Ethernet Adapters

As shown in Figure 12-3, Ethernet adapters can communicate with the computer through the USB port and the parallel port. PCMCIA cards the size of credit cards allow portable computers to join an Ethernet network.

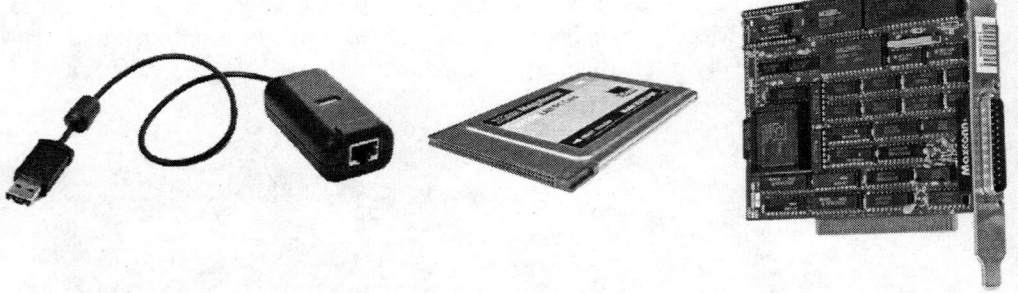

Figure 12-3: *USB adapter, PC Card, and parallel port network adapter.*

Network Cables and Connectors

Network cables and connectors are the media that are used to establish bounded media connections between clients and servers or Internet resources. Bounded media is any cable and connector system that is not a wireless connection method.

Network cables and connectors vary by:

- The gauge of the wires used in the cable.
- The number of wires used in the cable.
- The relationship of the wires to each other and the rest of the cable construction.
- Whether shielding is used in the cable to prevent or limit interference.
- The connectors used on the cable.
- The maximum length a cable segment can be.
- The cost of the cable.

Lesson 12

Twisted Pair Cables

Definition:

Twisted pair cable is a network cable that can be used to connect computers into a network. It consists of one or more pairs of independently insulated 22- to 26-gauge wires twisted around one another. One wire carries the signal while the other wire is grounded and absorbs signal interference. In LAN cables, several sets of twisted-pair wires are wrapped in one protective outer layer. Twisted-pair is the least expensive type of LAN cable, and it has a maximum cable length of 100 meters. The twisted pair cables end with an RJ-45 connector.

There are two types of twisted pair cabling:

- *UTP (unshielded twisted-pair)* cable has four sets of two unshielded wires twisted around each other. Because shielding is omitted, the price is low, but electrical interference can cause a problem.

- *STP (shielded twisted-pair)* cable is a twisted-pair cable that is wrapped in a metal sheath to provide extra protection from external interfering signals. This is commonly used in Token Ring networks. STP uses specialized connectors, including the IBM Data Connector (IDC) and the Universal Data Connector (UDC).

Example: UTP Cable

Unshielded twisted-pair cable is what is most commonly used in LANs and home networks.

Figure 12-4 shows the wires inside a UTP cable. Notice that each pair of wires is twisted around each other. One is a solid color wire and the other has a stripe of that same color. The connector has not yet been installed on this cable. It will have an RJ-45 connector crimped onto it before it is ready for use.

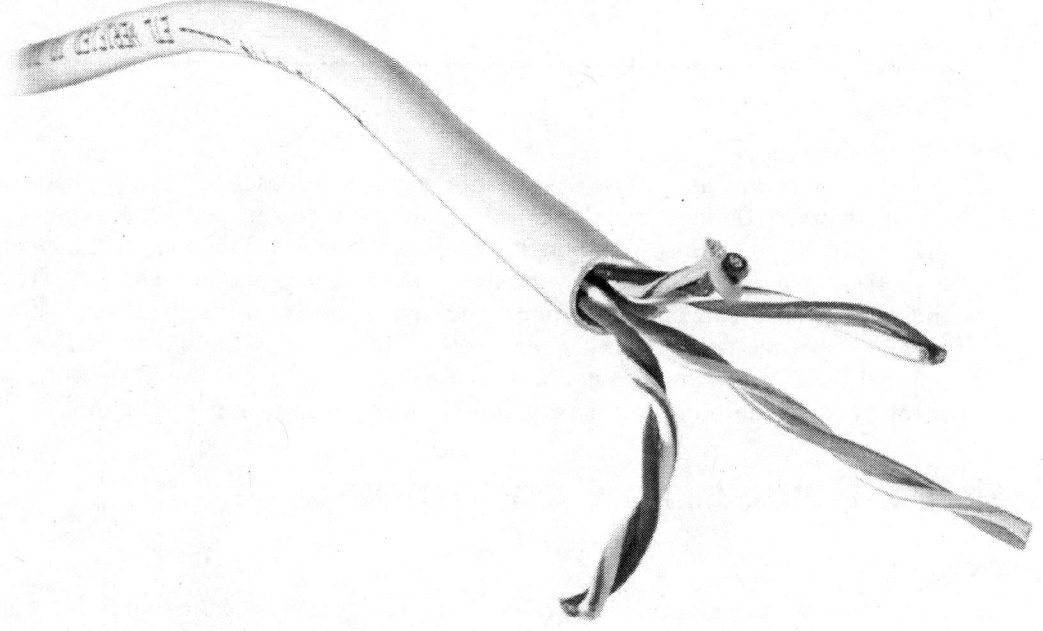

Figure 12-4: *UTP cable.*

Lesson 12: Networking

Lesson 12

Categories of Twisted Pair Cabling

As standards for twisted-pair cabling developed, they were given category numbers. Cable categories with lower numbers have a lower data transmission rate, while cable categories with a higher number support a higher transmission rate. Cat5 (Category 5) is the most recent standard for high-quality, reliable cable. Table 12-2 briefly describes the different cable categories.

Table 12-2: *Cable Categories*

Category	Usage	Speed	Description
1	Voice only	Not applicable	Traditional telephone cable.
2	Voice and data	Up to 4 Mbps	Usually includes four twisted-pair wires.
3	Voice and data	Up to 10 Mbps (10BaseT)	Usually includes four twisted-pair wires, at three twists per foot.
4	Voice and data	Up to 16 Mbps	Usually includes four twisted-pair wires.
5	Voice and data	Up to 100 Mbps (100BaseT)	Usually includes four twisted-pair copper wires.
5e	Voice and data	Up to 1 Gbps (1000BaseT)	Usually includes four twisted-pair copper wires.
6	Voice and data	Up to 1.2 Gbps (possible theoretical speeds of up to 2.5 Gbps)	Usually includes four twisted-pair copper wires.
7	Voice and data	Projected up to 4 to 10 Gbps	Under development, but expected to include four shielded twisted-pair copper wires.

10Base Terminology

A designation such as 10BaseT is a shorthand way to describe several characteristics of a network. "10" indicates the approximate transmission speed (10 megabits per second, or 10 Mbps). "Base" is short for baseband, which means that the channel carries a single signal. (Broadband networks carry multiple signals on a channel.) The "T" indicates twisted-pair cable. If you see a number instead of the "T," as in 10Base2, this indicates that the network uses coaxial cable. In this case, the number tells you the approximate maximum segment length of each cable. In a 10Base2 network, each segment of cable can be no more than approximately 200 meters in length.

Twisted Pair Cable Connectors

Definition:

Twisted pair cables end with an 8-wire modular connector called an RJ-45 connector. An example of an RJ-45 connector is shown in Figure 12-8. When connecting the RJ-45 connector to the twisted pair cable, the correct colored wire must go to its corresponding pin in the connector. When connecting an RJ-45 connector to a twisted pair cable, the eight individual wires are always thought of as four pairs and are connected to the RJ-45 connector according to pair. The four pairs are described in Table 12-3.

No matter which cabling standard you follow, the pairs are always colored the same. Pair 1 is always blue. The Telecommunications Industry Association (TIA) has two current networking standards for matching wires to pins: 568A and 568B. You can choose 568A or 568B as the standard for your network, but don't mix them. In both standards, you will find that the solid color wires and the striped wires always alternate. Pin 1 is always a striped wire. Pair 1, Blue, is always in the middle on pins 4 & 5.

Table 12-3: *Twisted Pair Cable Pairs*

Pair	Color	Wires
1	Blue	Blue and blue with white stripes.
2	Orange	Orange and orange with white stripes.
3	Green	Green and green with white stripes.
4	Brown	Brown and brown with white stripes.

TIA Standard 568A

The TIA standard 568A is the preferred method for terminating twisted pair cable. This method matches the one that Northern Telecom used for terminating ISDN cable.

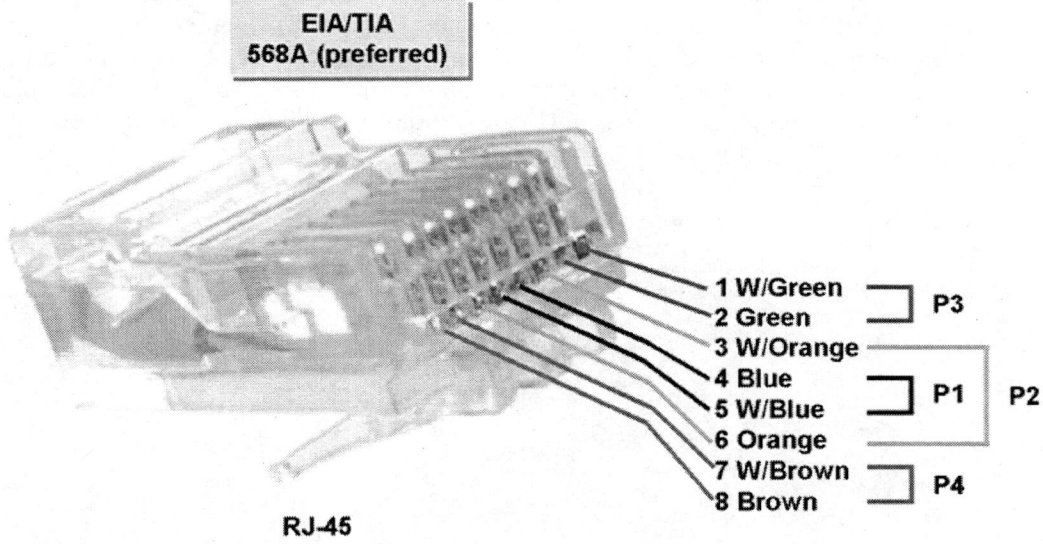

Figure 12-5: *Pin and wire orientation for TIA standard 568A.*

TIA Standard 568B

TIA standard 568B is copied from the AT&T standard for terminating their cable—258A. The 258A worked just as well as the newer TIA's standard 568A, so the TIA committee decided to include AT&T's 258A standard as their 568B standard. The 258A and 568B standards are exactly the same.

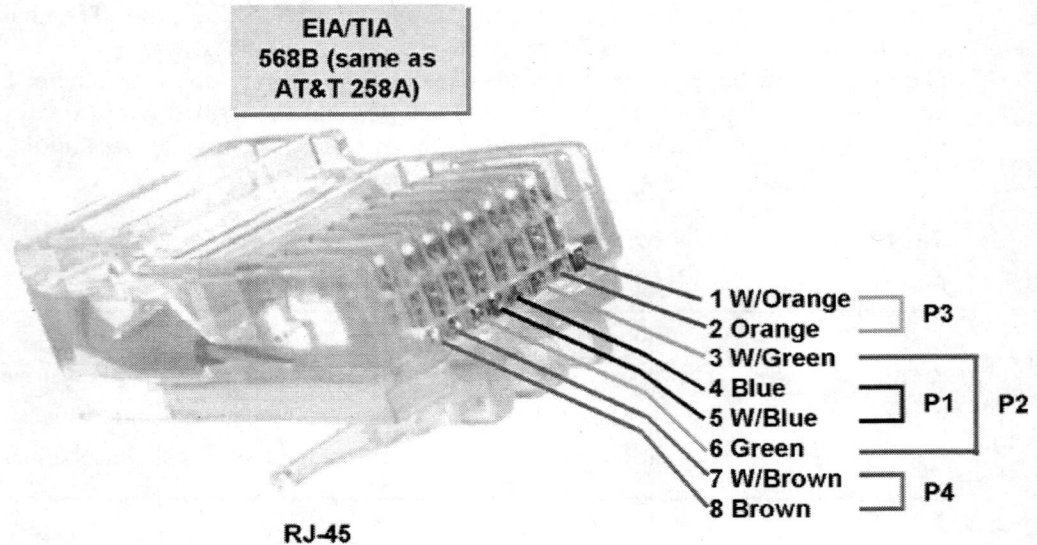

Figure 12-6: *Pin and wire orientation for TIA standard 568B.*

USOC Standard

USOC is an older connection standard that is used for voice and analog voice cabling only. In the USOC standard, pair 1 (P1) and pair 2 (P2)—which use pins 4/5 and 3/6—match P1 and P2 in 568A and P1 and P3 in 568B. These pairs can carry voice and analog voice. But because pins 1/2 aren't a pair (they aren't the same color or twisted together), an Ethernet NIC cannot transmit digital voice or data on them.

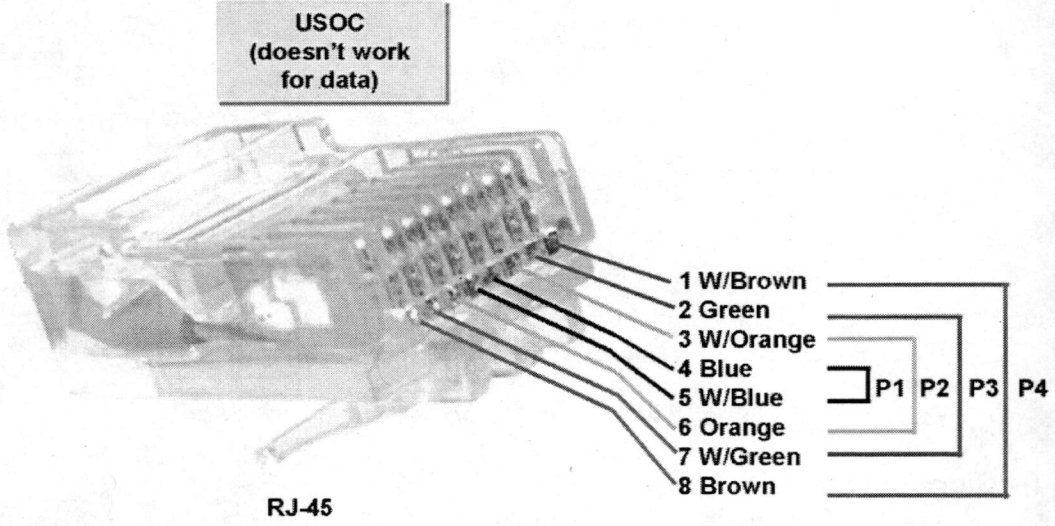

Figure 12-7: *USOC standard for voice cabling.*

Example: An RJ-45 Connector

An example of an RJ-45 connector is shown in Figure 12-8.

Lesson 12

Figure 12-8: *An RJ-45 connector on a twisted pair cable.*

Coaxial Cables

Definition:

Coaxial cable, or coax, is a network cable that consists of a single conductor that is surrounded by insulation and a conductive shield, with a heavy protective covering over the shield. The name coaxial means that the conductor, insulator, shield, and coating all share the same central axis. The shield is usually a braided wire that is connected to an electrical ground and prevents the cable from picking up or emitting electrical noise. Coax cable is more expensive than standard phone wires, but it can carry much more data and is more resistant to interference. Cable TV companies now use the same coax cable that brings cable stations into a home to bring in a high-speed Internet connection.

Example:

Figure 12-9 shows a coaxial RG58 cable with a solid core.

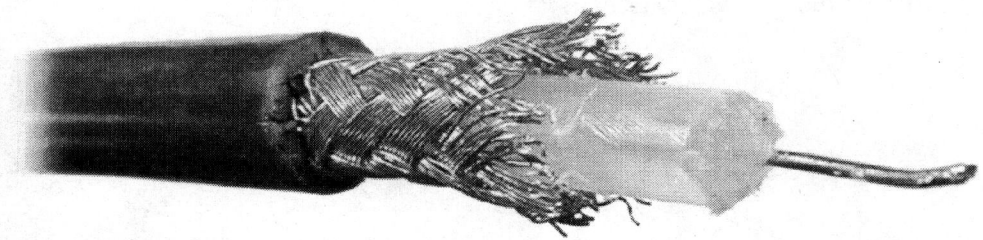

Figure 12-9: *Coaxial cable.*

Coaxial Cable Grades

There are several grades of coaxial cables. These are referred to as Radio Guide or RG. Table 12-4 describes some of the common grades you might encounter.

Table 12-4: *Common Radio Guide Grades*

Radio Grade	Description
RG6	Used for surveillance cameras and other video devices.

Lesson 12: Networking

Lesson 12

Radio Grade	Description
RG8	52 ohm cable used for thicknet (10Base5) Ethernet networks.
RG58	50 ohm cable used for thinnet (10Base2) Ethernet networks. RG58/U uses a stranded copper wire core. RG58A/U uses a solid copper core wire.
RG59	75 ohm cable used for cable television (CATV).
RG62	93 ohm cable used for ARCNET networks.

Coaxial Cable Connectors

Definition:

Coaxial cable connectors are connectors that are designed specifically for connecting coaxial cables to computers and other network devices to create a network. The connectors need to be able to reach through the plastic sheathing, the shielding, and any other layers to reach the core in order to make the connection to the network. The type of connector varies based on which type of coaxial cable is in use. The connector connects to the cable in various ways, depending on which connector is needed. All coax cable used for networking requires *termination* at each end to prevent signal bounce (digital signals at the end of the cable bouncing back onto the cable and causing distortion or interference.)

Example: BNC Connectors

BNC connectors (British Naval Connector or Bayonet Nut Connector) are used to join coaxial cables like RG58 A/U into a network. This connector is also used for cable TV and cable modem connections. Each cable end has a male BNC connector with a center pin connected to the center cable conductor and a metal tube connected to the outer cable shield. A rotating ring outside the tube locks the cable to any female connector. T-connectors are female devices for connecting two cables to a network interface card (NIC), and a barrel connector joins two cables. You can also use a T-connector to join two cables, but you must put a terminator device on the open leg of the T. Figure 12-10 shows BNC connectors used connecting coaxial cables.

Figure 12-10: *BNC connectors.*

Example: AUI Connectors

RG8 cables connect using Attachment Unit Interface connectors (AUI). This is a 15-pin female connector. The network card shown in Figure 12-11 shows an AUI connection (along with twisted pair and BNC connections).

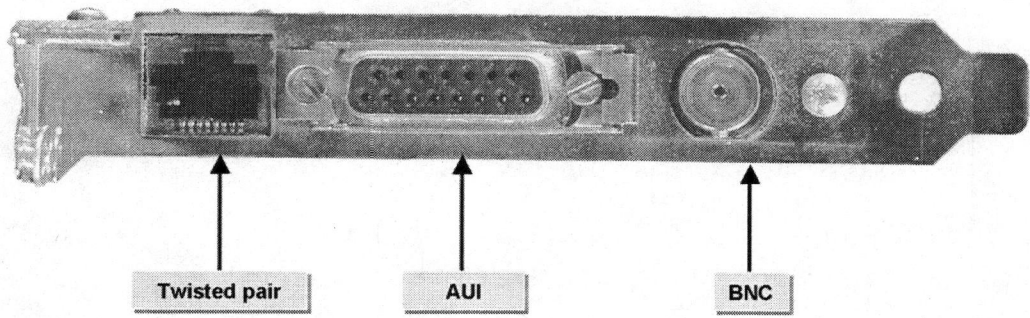

Figure 12-11: *Twisted pair, AUI, and BNC network connections.*

Fiber Optic Cables

Fiber optic cable uses glass to transmit network signals in the form of light waves. Fiber optic cable is expensive and hard to install, but it also provides very high transmission speeds and high signal quality. For this reason, fiber optic cable is not often used to connect individual computers to a network, but generally is used as a network backbone cable. The *backbone* is the portion of the network that links all of the other segments of the network together.

Fiber optic cable consists of:

- A core of glass, ranging from 50 micrometers (μm) to 1,000 m in diameter, which carries the light.
- Cladding, which surrounds the core, bends the light, and confines it to the core.
- A substrate layer of glass (in some fiber cables), which surrounds the cladding, does not carry light, and adds to the diameter and strength of the fiber.
- A primary buffer coating, which surrounds all the other layers and provides the first layer of mechanical protection.
- A secondary buffer coating, which surrounds and protects the primary buffer coating as well as the underlying fiber.

Fiber optic cables can be single-mode, with a narrow strand of glass that allows light to travel in only one path through the core. Fiber optic cables can also be multi-mode, in which the glass core is larger in diameter and allows multiple paths through the cable.

Lesson 12

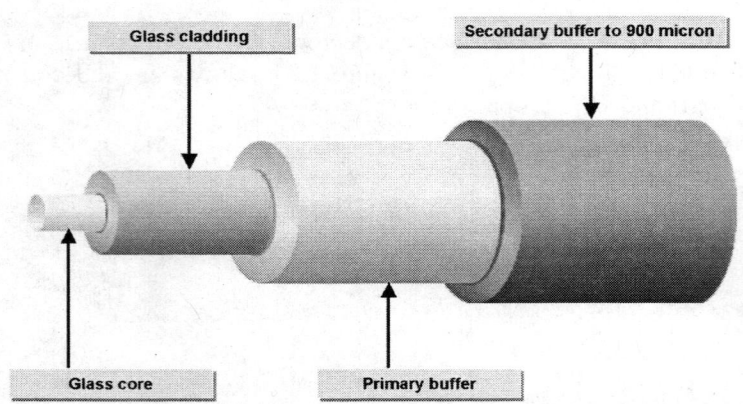

Figure 12-12: *A representation of a single fiber optic strand.*

Fiber Optic Cable Connectors

Fiber optic cable connectors must be able to direct and collect light. There are many different types of connectors. Some are used for single-mode fiber optic cables, others can be used for multi-mode cables. Table 12-5 describes the different types of fiber optic cable connectors.

Table 12-5: *Fiber Optic Cable Connectors*

Type	Description	Graphic
ST connector	A slotted bayonet type and spring loaded connector similar to a BNC connector. An ST connector can be used for both multi-mode and single-mode fiber optic cables. It has the ability to be inserted into and removed from a fiber optic cable quickly and easily. There are two versions: ST and ST-II. They are push-in and twist types. Currently, the ST connector is the most widely used connector for fiber optic cable.	
SC connector	A push/pull type connector with a locking tab. The SC connector is used primarily for single-mode fiber optic cables. However, some manufacturers will clip two connectors together to provide a duplex version of the connector. SC connectors are typically low cost, simple, and durable.	

Type	Description	Graphic
FC connector	A slotted screw-on type connector featuring a position locatable notch and a threaded receptacle. FC connectors are used for single-mode fiber optic cable. They provide precise positioning of the single-mode fiber optic cable with respect to the transmitter's optical source emitter and the receiver's optical detector. Once an FC connector is installed, it maintains its position with absolute accuracy.	
SMA connector	A screw-on type connector with a threaded cap and housing. The SMA connector is the predecessor of the ST connector and its use has declined significantly as it has been replaced by ST and SC connectors.	
FDDI connector	The FDDI connector is a push/pull type, two-channel snap-fit connector used for multi-mode fiber optic cable. Also called a MIC connector.	

Lesson 12: Networking

Type	Description	Graphic
Mini-BNC connector	A bayonet style connector using the traditional BNC connection method.	
Biconic connector	The biconic connector is a screw-on type connector with a tapered sleeve that is fixed to the fiber optic cable. The cap fits over the ferrule, rest against guided rings and screws onto the threaded sleeve to secure the connection. When the connector is inserted into its receptacle, the tapered end of the connector locates the fiber optic cable into the proper position. The biconic connector is one of the earliest connector types and is, for the most part, no longer in use.	
MT-RJ connector	A new RJ-style housing fiber connector with two fiber capability for both single- and multi-modes. The latch-type design is similar to the RJ connector on a Cat5 patch cable, and is half the size of the SC connector, taking up no more room than an RJ-45 jack.	

PVC and Plenum Cables

Many cables contain polyvinyl chloride (PVC), a plastic used to make the insulation in cables. PVC is flexible, making cable made with it easy to install. However, when PVC burns, it creates poisonous gases. National and local fire codes regulate where PVC cables can exist in a building. Specifically, you cannot run PVC cable in a *plenum,* which is an air-handling space that is part of a building's heating/cooling system, and is often used as a convenient place to run cables. Figure 12-13 shows examples of where PVC and plenum cables should be used.

Because poisonous gases and flames can spread quickly throughout the building via the plenum, a special cable must be used. *Plenum cable*, which gets its name from the plenum space, has special materials in the insulation layers that make it fire resistant. When plenum cable burns, it produces a minimal amount of smoke and chemical fumes.

Lesson 12

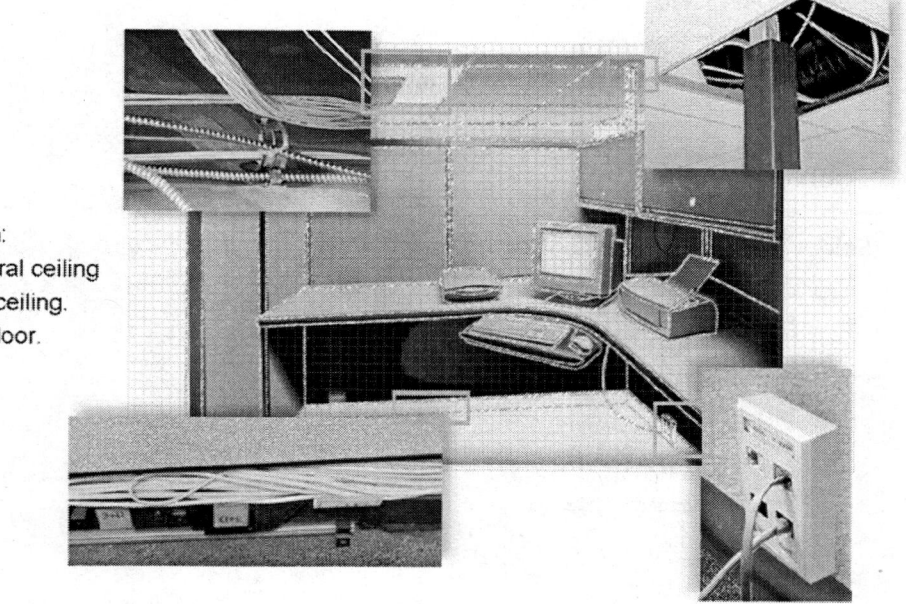

Plenum cable is run:
- ❏ Between structural ceiling and suspended ceiling.
- ❏ Under a raised floor.

Figure 12-13: *Examples of locations for plenum cables.*

Activity 12-1

Identifying Cable Connector Types

Activity Time:
5 minutes

Scenario:
In this activity, you will identify the cable type that each connector is used to terminate.

1. Select the connectors that can be used with fiber optic cabling.

    a) RJ-45 connector

    b) MT-RJ connector

    c) BNC connector

    d) Mini-BNC connector

    e) FDDI connector

Lesson 12: Networking 543

Lesson 12

2. **Select the connectors that can be used with coaxial cabling.**

    a) FDDI connector

    b) Mini-BNC connector

    c) BNC connector

    d) Biconic connector

    e) AUI connector

3. **Select the connectors that can be used with twisted pair cabling.**

    a) MT-RJ connector

    b) RJ-45 connector

    c) ST connector

    d) SC connector

    e) FDDI connector

Physical Network Architectures

Definition:

A *physical network architecture* is the model that determines how networked computers are connected and how they can communicate. The architecture is a general, comprehensive specification that encompasses all aspects of the network, from cables to protocols. It specifies the physical layout or *physical topology* the network uses.

Example: Star Topology

A *star topology* for a LAN is designed so that all nodes are connected individually to a central computer, multiport repeater, concentrator, or hub. Signals travel from the nodes to the central computer, which then sends the signals to other nodes on the network. You may add and remove nodes from a star topology network easily, and if a computer fails, it will not affect the rest of the network. However, if the hub or central computer fails, the entire network fails. More cabling is required because a separate cable must run from each node to the hub or central computer. An example of a star topology is shown in Figure 12-14.

Lesson 12

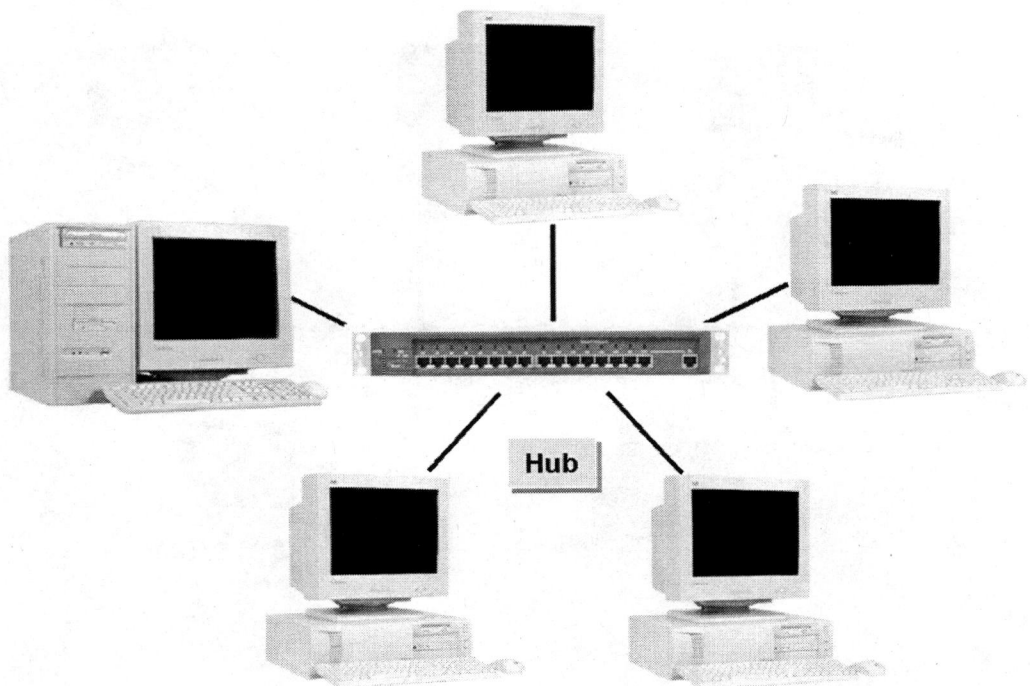

Figure 12-14: *A star topology.*

Example: Bus Topology

A *bus topology* for a LAN is designed so that a single main bus cable, sometimes called a backbone, transmits data to all nodes on the network. Every node on a bus network has a direct connection to the main bus cable. In many bus networks, the bus is a series of wire segments. Each segment runs from the network interface card on one computer to the network interface card on the next computer down the line. At each end of the bus, the cable must have a terminator attached to it to prevent the signal from bouncing—being reflected back to the rest of the network—which can cause network failure. The terminator absorbs the signal and acts as the second connection for the computers connected at the ends of the bus. A break or faulty piece of cable anywhere on the segment prevents all of the computers on the segment from being able to communicate. An example of a bus topology is shown in Figure 12-15.

Lesson 12: Networking

Lesson 12

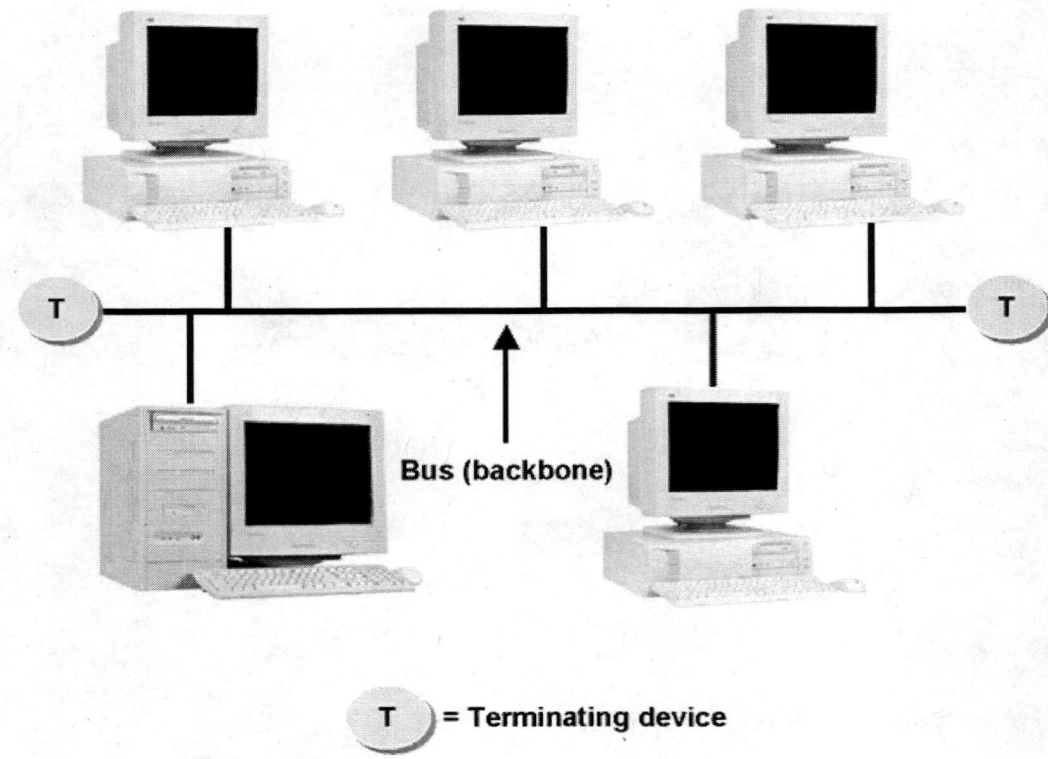

Figure 12-15: *A bus topology.*

Example: Ring Topology

A *ring topology* for a LAN is designed so that all the nodes are connected in a continuous loop with no end points and no terminators. Workstations relay signals around the loop in a round-robin fashion. This topology is used by a Token Ring network, where a packet called a *token* is passed from station to station. Only the machine holding the token can transmit data over the network, so no other machine can send signals that might interfere or conflict with the signal from the machine with the token. If a node on the ring goes down, all other stations on the ring are affected, making it difficult to troubleshoot network problems. Newer technology includes a device called a Multistation Access Unit (MAU) that looks like a hub but acts like a ring. Special circuitry inside the MAU enables it to bypass a node that's having problems. When MAUs are implemented, the entire network won't be affected by one node's problems, and troubleshooting can be easier because only one computer is affected. An example of a ring topology is shown in Figure 12-16

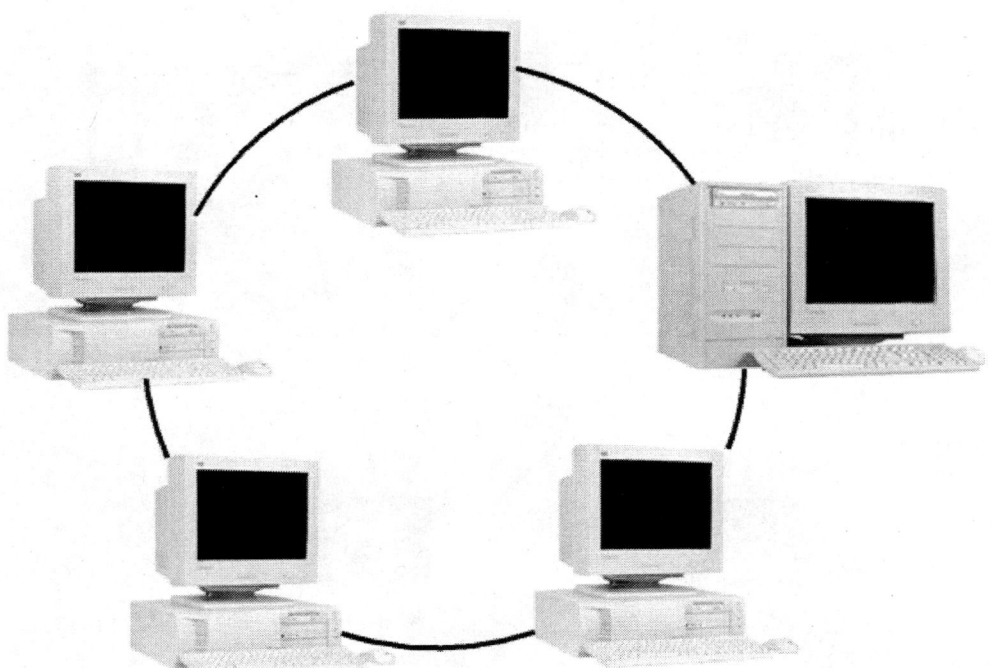

Figure 12-16: *A ring topology.*

Example: Mesh Topology

A full *mesh topology* occurs when every node on the network has a separate wire connecting it to every other node on the network. It provides each device with a point-to-point connection to every other device in the network. A full mesh topology is redundant because if any one node of connection fails, all remaining nodes can continue communicating. Full mesh is expensive to set up and modify. Adding a new node to a full mesh topology of five computers requires installing an additional five cables, one to each existing computer in the mesh. A partial mesh topology has only some of the nodes fully connected, while other nodes are connected to just one of the nodes on the full mesh portion of the network. An example of a mesh topology is shown in Figure 12-17.

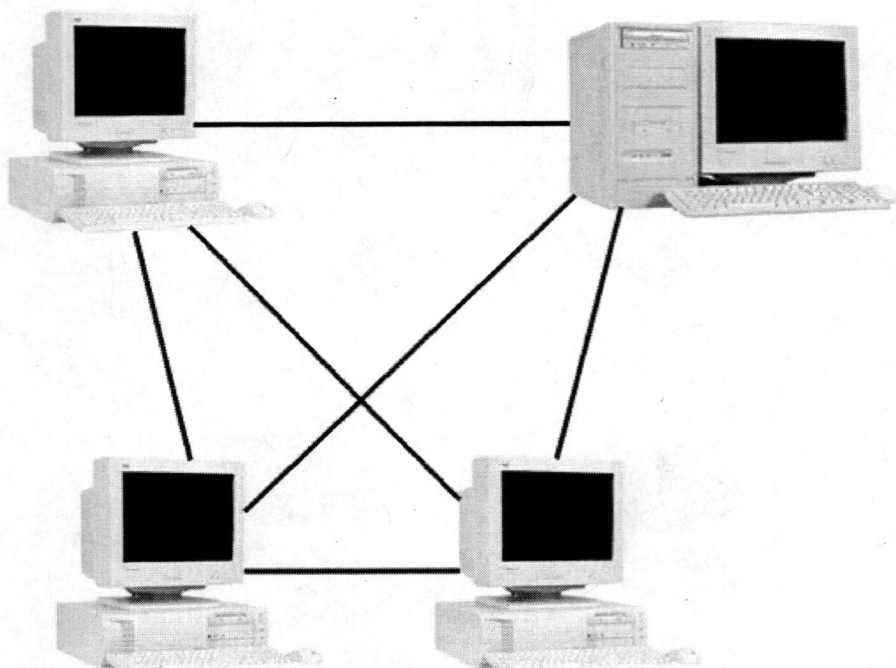

Figure 12-17: *A mesh topology.*

Example: Hybrid Topology

A *hybrid topology* for a LAN is designed by combining two or more different topologies. The advantage of hybrid topologies is that you can incorporate the features of different technologies. Implementing hybrid topologies is less costly and less complicated than implementing mesh topologies, but more expensive and more complicated than implementing star, bus, and ring topologies. An example of a hybrid topology is shown in Figure 12-18.

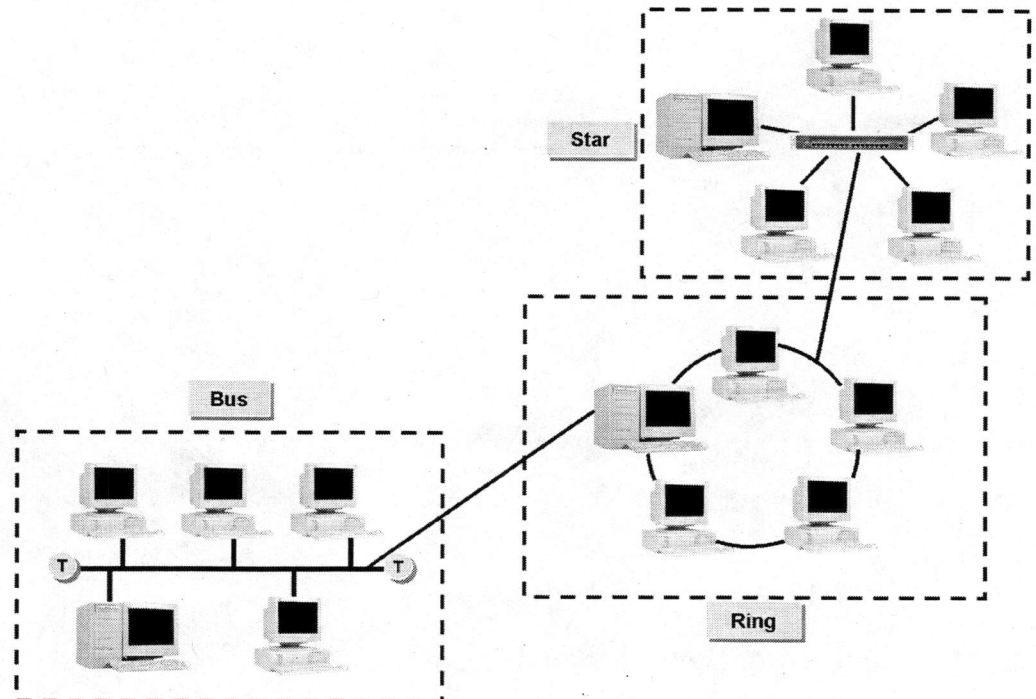

Figure 12-18: *A hybrid topology.*

Logical Network Architectures

Definition:

A *logical network architecture* is the model that describes the degree of centralized control built into the network. The architecture specifies which computers can provide resources, such as files, printers, or applications, to other computers on the network.

Example: Peer-to-Peer Network Architecture

In a *peer-to-peer network*, any computer can act as both a server and a client. Any computer can share resources with another, and any computer can use the resources of another if given access rights to the resource. This architecture is best suited for less than 10 computers. It is commonly used for small offices, home offices, or departmental workgroup needs. A peer-to-peer network is depicted in Figure 12-19. Peer-to-peer networks can use almost any network media and network topology.

Lesson 12

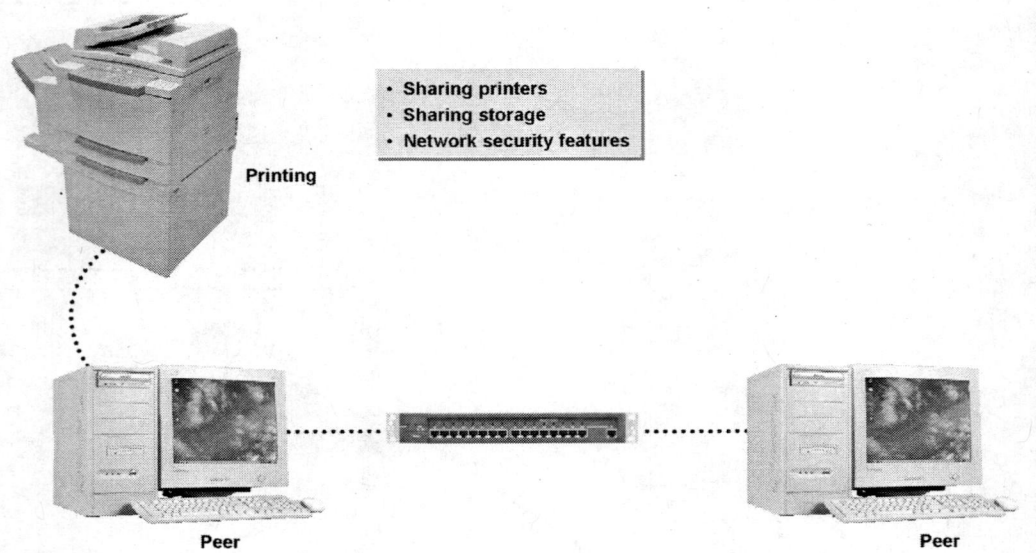

Figure 12-19: *A peer-to-peer network.*

Example: Client-server Network Architecture

In a *client-server network*, at least one centralized server manages shared resources and security for the other network users and computers. Generally, the network servers are not used as clients; they are dedicated to their network services and are usually physically secured by being locked in a server room to prevent casual access. A client-server network is depicted in Figure 12-20.

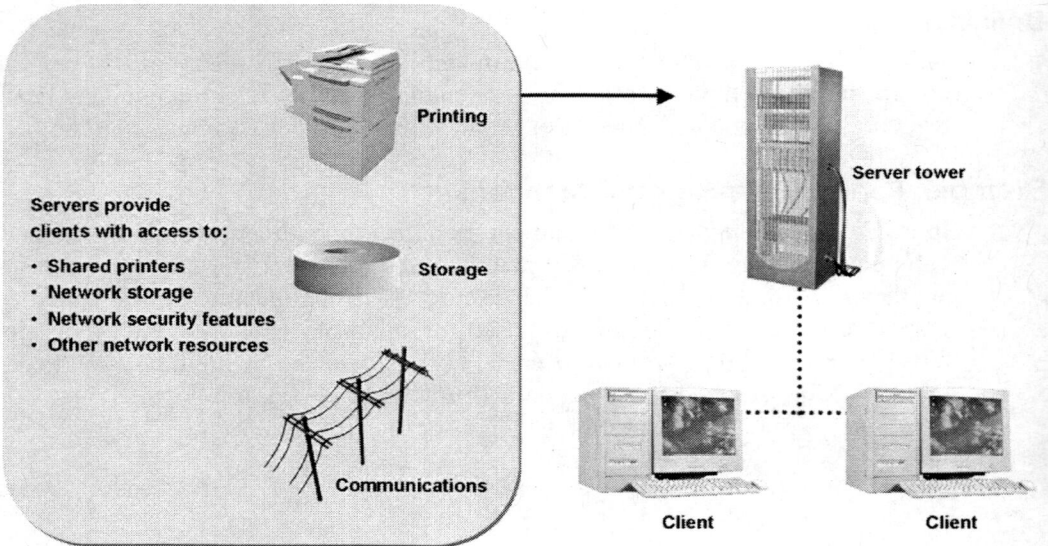

Figure 12-20: *A client-server network.*

Lesson 12

Example: Hybrid Networks

As the name implies, hybrid—or combination—networks combine both client-server and peer-to-peer network elements. As a matter of fact, most large networks today are likely to have some peer resource-sharing existing alongside the centralized system. These networks can be very flexible. However, they are also potentially difficult to administer and monitor. An example of a hybrid network is shown in Figure 12-21.

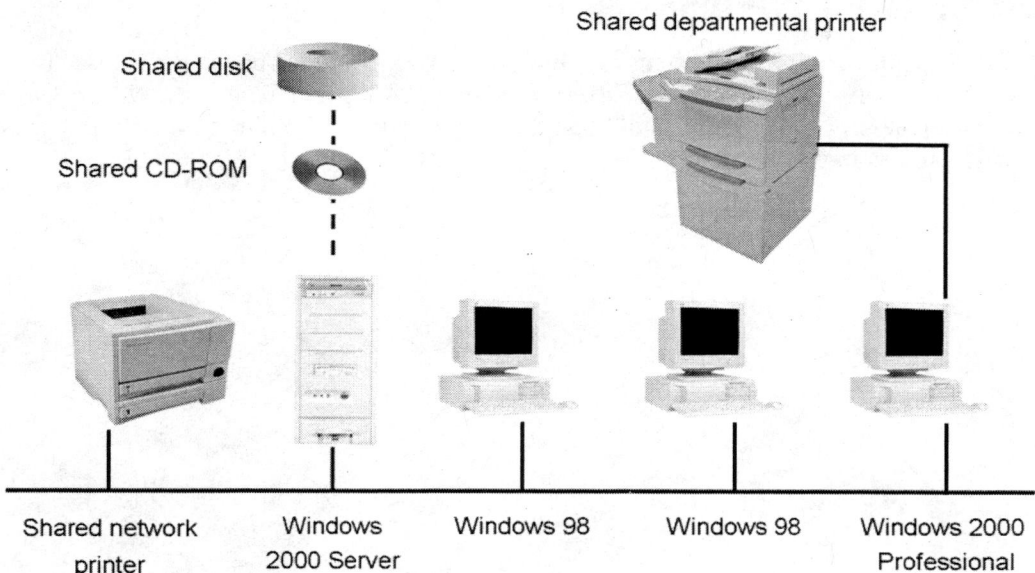

Figure 12-21: *A hybrid network.*

Example: Hierarchical Networks

Less common in today's PC computing landscape are the completely centralized networks known as *hierarchical networks*. In this scheme, all the resources and processing power exist on a large, powerful, central computer. This can be a powerful network server running an operating system like Windows 2000 or UNIX, or a dedicated mainframe (mainframes usually run specialized, proprietary operating systems provided by the computer manufacturer). Users work at dumb terminals that have no processing power of their own. The terminals only permit the user to perform a specified set of tasks. They are not independent clients and can't function at all if they're detached from the network. An example of a hierachical network is shown in Figure 12-22

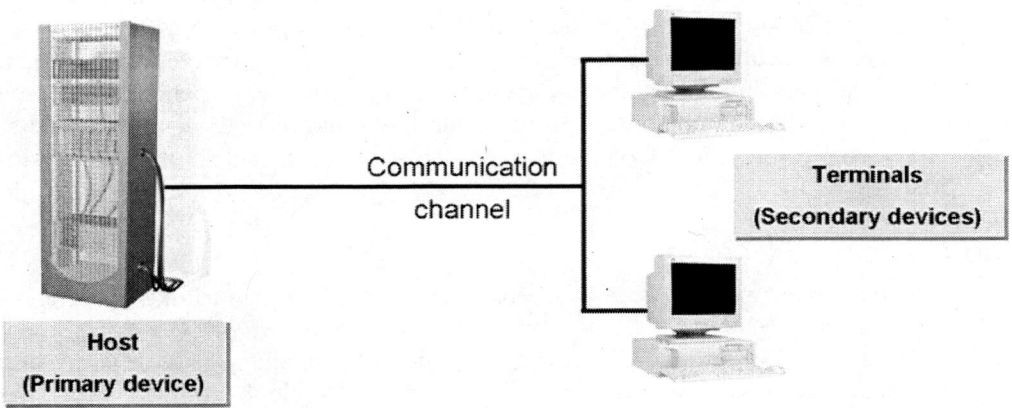

Figure 12-22: *A hierarchical network.*

Lesson 12: Networking

A bank's network of Automated Teller Machines (ATMs) is a hierarchical network you are familiar with. ATM terminals have very limited, pre-programmed functionality which doesn't permit any general work. All the information entered at the ATM is processed at a central server to ensure that only authorized persons can use the ATM and that all the transactions are posted promptly and accurately.

LANs and WANs

Network scope refers to the extent to which a network provides coverage. There are two major divisions of network scope—*Local Area Networks (LANs)* and *Wide Area Networks (WANs)*. Two computers in neighboring buildings that communicate through a satellite link would be on a WAN, for example.

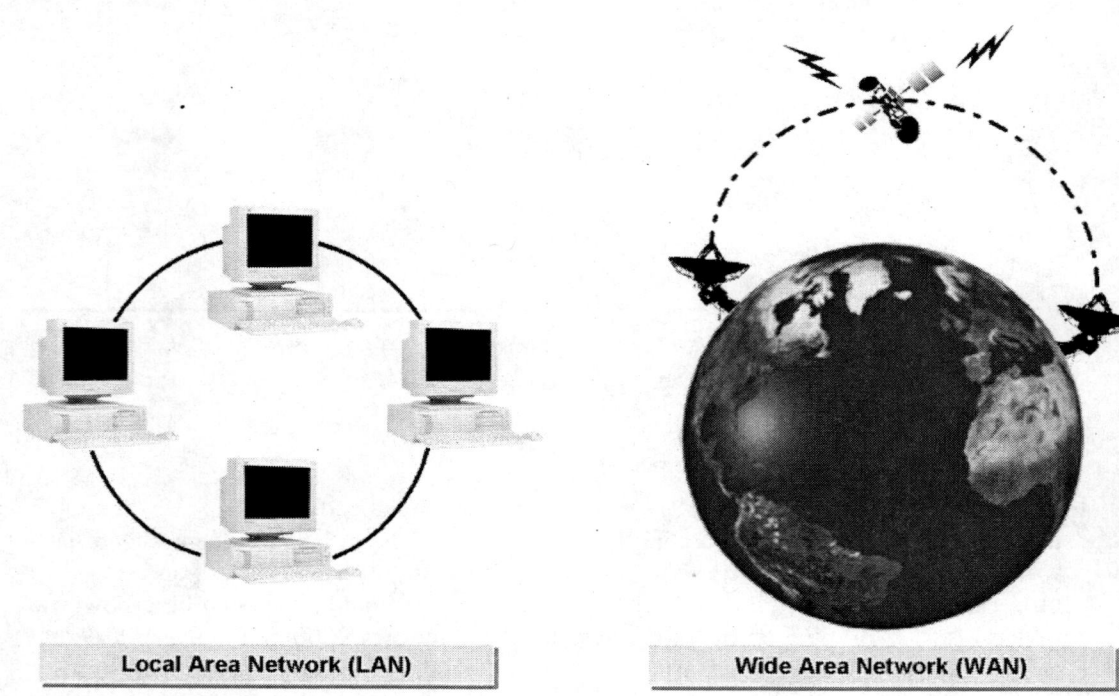

Figure 12-23: *Network scope.*

Local Area Network

A *Local Area Network (LAN)* consists of any number of computers that are linked directly together and are housed in a clearly defined geographic area, such as in a single building or single campus. A LAN can only be as large as the physical limitations of the cabling you use, which varies depending upon the cabling type. Usually the computers linked together in a LAN are workstations or personal computers that can access data on computers on the same LAN and use devices like printers that are connected to the LAN. Computer users can send email and set up chat sessions over the LAN.

Wide Area Network

A *Wide Area Network (WAN)* can span large geographic areas like countries and continents. WANs often contain two or more LANs. In a WAN, at least some of the connections rely on long-distance communications media such as satellite links, long-distance fiber-optic cable, or specialized high-speed telephone lines. These media are expensive; companies normally share the links or lease capacity from a public carrier such as a telecommunications company. But WAN technologies are essential to link all the computers in a multi-site or multi-national enterprise in a reliable way. WANs can be enormous; the Internet is the ultimate WAN.

Specialized Network Scopes

There are other, more specialized scopes used to describe networks. Here are some of the ones you might encounter:

- A *Metropolitan Area Network (MAN)* is a mini-WAN or a giant LAN that's typically confined to a single municipality. A company might use a private MAN to link several different office buildings together within the same city. Computers on a MAN are linked using high-speed media like fiber optics or dedicated digital lines.

- A *Storage Area Network (SAN)* is a specialized LAN that links several network servers that are dedicated to storing large amounts of data in a centralized, secure repository. The servers in the SAN manage large banks of hard disks or tape drives and are connected to each other by reliable, high-speed media. SANs are useful to firms that need extremely large data storage capacity, high reliability, and fast retrieval.

- A *Value-Added Network (VAN)* is a public network utility that provides both network access and additional proprietary services that are available only to its users. For example, America Online (AOL) is a VAN. It provides its subscribers with standard network services such as Internet access and email, and also offers additional features such as private AOL chat rooms, message boards, and news summaries.

- An *Enterprise-Wide Network (EWN)* is any private network that connects all of an organization's computers, no matter what operating system they run or where they're located. The EWN will probably incorporate several different LANs and WANs.

Lesson 12

ACTIVITY 12-2

Discussing Network Architectures

Activity Time:

20 minutes

Scenario:

In this activity, you will discuss the different physical and logical network architectures.

1. Describe the extent to which the bus topology offers fault tolerance—the ability to ignore or overcome problems.

2. Describe the extent to which the star topology offers fault tolerance—the ability to ignore or overcome problems.

3. Describe the extent to which the ring topology offers fault tolerance—the ability to ignore or overcome problems.

4. Describe the extent to which the mesh topology offers fault tolerance—the ability to ignore or overcome problems.

5. Contrast the ease of administration between a peer-to-peer network and a client-server network.

6. Contrast the scalability of a peer-to-peer network versus a client-server network.

7. Contrast the number of potential users of a peer-to-peer network versus a client-server network.

8. Contrast how the resources of a peer-to-peer network are managed versus a client-server network.

9. Contrast how security is managed in a peer-to-peer network versus a client-server network.

10. What are the main differences between a hybrid network and a hierarchical network?

TOPIC B

Network Communications

In order for computers to communicate on a network, there are several components that must be in place—an operating system that recognizes and allows for network communication, a network protocol common to all computers on the network so they are "speaking the same language" when they attempt to communicate with one another, and a network interface card that physically connects the computer to the network. In this topic, you'll learn how computers communicate on a network and what you need to do to ensure that an individual computer can communicate on the network.

Server and Network Operating Systems

A *Network Operating System (NOS)* refers to the software that manages all the resources accessible over the network. One piece of the network operating system resides in each client machine and another resides in each server. There are several different network operating systems that today's networks are built on:

- Microsoft's Windows Server 2003 and its predecessors, Windows 2000 Server and Windows NT Server, are completely self-contained network operating systems that may also be used to run just a single client machine.
- Novell's NetWare is also a self-contained system that functions only as a NOS. NetWare cannot function as a desktop operating system.
- The UNIX family of operating systems, including Linux, are completely self-contained network operating systems that may also be used to run just a single client machine.
- LAN Server is not independent and must be combined with IBM OS/2 to function.

Lesson 12

- LANtastic is not independent and requires DOS to function.
- Apple Computer's OSX Server works with OSX and the MacOS system to network Macintosh computers.

📌 NetWare is the only operating system in this list that can't also be used as a desktop operating system. However, NetWare does require DOS on the boot drive.

In addition to providing basic network services, some network servers can serve specialized functions, too. Some of these dedicated functions include:

- Print server, which is dedicated to managing network printers and print jobs.
- Communications server, which manages access to modems or other types of communication links.
- Database server, which stores large databases and runs database applications.
- Applications server, a generalized term for any server that runs an application for access across a network.
- Mail server, which provides access to email services, as well as storing and forwarding email messages.
- Internet or Web server, which provides a wide variety of information to the public Internet or to private intranets (private, internal Internet-type networks).

Workstation and Client Operating Systems

An *Operating System (OS)* refers to the software on a node, usually a personal computer, that lets it run applications, control peripherals, and communicate with other computers. There are several different operating systems that today's personal computers use:

- Windows was originally a Graphical User Interface (GUI) developed by Microsoft that allowed users to send commands to the Microsoft Disk Operating System (MS-DOS), controlling their machines by mouse clicks rather than text instructions. Later versions of Windows became independent operating systems. As Windows became more powerful, networking capabilities were built into the basic system. Client operating systems include Windows for Workgroups 3.1x, Windows 9x, Windows NT Workstation, Windows 2000 Professional, and Windows XP.
- The Apple Macintosh Operating System is designed specifically for Macintosh computers. The hardware differences between Macintosh and IBM-compatible PCs are significant. Software that runs under the MacOS will not function in Windows. Software programs now allow Macs and PCs to imitate each other so both machines can run both PC and Mac software. The MacOS is popular because of its innovative use of graphics and its user-friendly controls.
- UNIX is an operating system developed by Bell Labs in the early 1970s. Because UNIX was written in the programming language C, it could be run on any computer that could run C programs. UNIX was low in cost, flexible, portable, and powerful, so it was used in workstations. Early PCs did not have the power to make use of UNIX. Linux—an implementation of UNIX developed initially by Linus Torvald—is free, runs on many platforms, and is a popular alternative to the Windows' operating system. Because UNIX is run on many of the servers connected to the Internet, Internet users and administrators need to be familiar with the restrictions and requirements that UNIX/Linux places on filenames and notation.

📌 Many operating systems have built-in networking capability.

Operating systems can be grouped by their capability to do more than one thing at a time—for example:
- Multi-user, which supports two or more users running programs at the same time.
- Multiprocessing, which supports running a program on more than one CPU.
- Multitasking, which supports more than one program running concurrently.
- Multithreading, which supports different parts of a single program running concurrently.

ACTIVITY 12-3

Identifying Operating System Applicability

Activity Time:

15 minutes

Scenario:

In this activity, you will identify how different operating systems can be used.

1. _____ is most suitable as a client OS, but it needs to be installed in addition to at least one NOS for that NOS to operate correctly.

2. For Macintosh computers, what are the most prevalent client and network operating systems?

3. Which operating systems are equally suited to use as a client OS and a NOS?

4. True or False? Windows XP is primarily a network operating system.
   __ True
   __ False

5. Of the following NOSs, which cannot also be used as a client OS?
   a) Windows 2000 Server
   b) NetWare
   c) Linux
   d) Windows NT Server
   e) Windows Server 2003

Lesson 12

Network Protocols

Definition:

Network protocols configure how the network computers communicate. A network *protocol* is responsible for formatting the data packets that are sent between computers on a network. In order for two computers to communicate over a network, they must have a network protocol in common.

Windows 9x, Windows NT, Windows Me, and Windows 2000 support the TCP/IP, NWLink IPX/SPX, and NetBEUI network protocols. Windows XP and Windows 2003 supports the TCP/IP and NWLink IPX/SPX network protocols. You can install NetBEUI on a Windows XP or Windows 2003 computer, but it is not a supported network protocol in either operating system. Macintosh networks use the TCP/IP and AppleTalk protocols. The TCP/IP protocol is the recommended protocol for Macintosh OS versions 9.0 or later.

Example: TCP/IP

Transmission Control Protocol/Internet Protocol (TCP/IP) is a non-proprietary, routable network protocol suite that enables computers to communicate over a network, including the Internet. The TCP/IP protocol is the foundation for the Internet. When you install TCP/IP, you must configure the IP address and subnet mask.

You might also need to configure these TCP/IP properties:

- The *default gateway* address. This is the IP address of a *router* on the network. The computer uses the router to access computers on remote networks. Without a default gateway address, IP communications would be limited to the local network.

- Preferred and alternate DNS server addresses. Computers use DNS servers to enable users to access network or Internet resources by name (such as **www.redcross.org**) instead of by IP address.

- One or more Windows Internet Naming System (WINS) server addresses. Computers use the WINS server address to access Microsoft Windows network resources by name.

Lesson 12

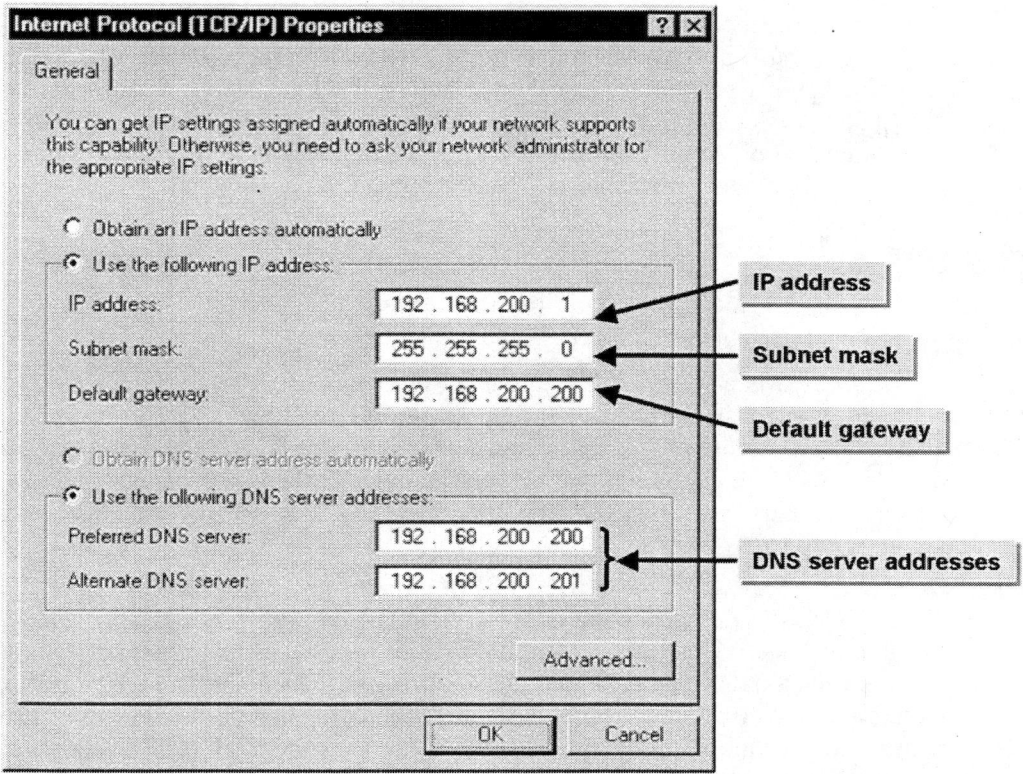

Figure 12-24: *TCP/IP configuration properties.*

Example: IPX/SPX

IPX/SPX was originally developed for Novell NetWare-based networks. Novell NetWare can work on different kinds of LANs, including Ethernet and Token Ring LANs.

- *Internetwork Packet Exchange (IPX)* routes datagrams from one node to another, and does not guarantee delivery of the complete message. The IPX packets contain the network addresses of the sending and destination nodes, so the packets can be routed from one network to another.

- *Sequenced Packet Exchange (SPX)* guarantees that the packets sent out by IPX can be accurately assembled into the entire message by the destination node. SPX is responsible for error recovery if packets are lost on the network.

Example: NetBEUI

NetBIOS Enhanced User Interface (NetBEUI) was developed by IBM. It is a non-routable, lightweight protocol that is easy to set up. Because NetBEUI relies on broadcast messages to locate and communicate with other nodes, it creates a lot of network traffic that can wreak havoc on routed networks, and IBM stopped using it. Microsoft subsequently adopted it, so now NetBEUI is supported by all but the newest versions of Windows—Windows 2003 and Windows XP.

Example: AppleTalk

AppleTalk is a Local Area Network protocol developed by Apple Computer, Inc. in 1985 and is built into all Macintosh computers and Apple LaserWriters. AppleTalk supports Apple's proprietary LocalTalk cabling scheme, as well as Ethernet and IBM Token Ring. With the proper additional hardware, PCs, UNIX, and VAX computers can connect to an AppleTalk network. Current implementations include LocalTalk, a 235 Kbps (kilobyte per second) LAN, and EtherTalk, a 10 Mbps LAN.

IP Addresses

Definition:

An *IP address* is a series of four numbers that you assign to a computer on a TCP/IP network. These four numbers will look something like this: 192.168.200.200. The IP address must consist of four numbers, separated by periods. Each number can be from 0 to 255, with the exception that the first number in the series cannot be 0. In addition, all four numbers cannot be 0 (0.0.0.0) or 255 (255.255.255.255).

Analogy:

An IP address is like a mailing address. Some of the numbers in the IP address identify the *network segment* on which a computer resides, just as a person's mailing address uses a street name to identify the street on which she lives. The rest of the numbers in the IP address uniquely identify the computer on the network, just as the house number uniquely identifies a specific house on a street. So, just as your mailing address consists of both a street name and a house number, so does an IP address consist of both numbers to identify the network segment and numbers to identify the individual computer.

Example: IP Address

In Figure 12-25, you see an example of an IP address with the network and computer portions of the address labeled. In this example, you can think of the street number as 192.168.200 and the house number as 200.

Figure 12-25: *An IP address.*

Address Classes

As an administrator, you use the four bytes that make up an IP address to identify both the network and host address of each computer. To make it easy for you to identify the network and host portions of an IP address, the Internet Assigned Numbers Authority (IANA) divided the available IP network addresses into classes. These classes determine how many of the four bytes you use to represent the network address and how many you use to represent each host. The IANA further restricted the value of the first byte so that it's possible for you to determine the class of an IP address simply by its first byte. For example, a Class A network address uses only the first byte to identify the network, and the remaining three bytes identify hosts. In addition, the value of the first byte must be between 1 and 126. Although the IANA defined classes A through E, you can assign addresses only within classes A, B, and C to hosts. Table 12-6 describes the available classes of IP addresses, their formats, default subnet masks, and what they're used for.

Table 12-6: *IP Address Classes*

Address Type	Format	Address Range	Used For
Class A	net.host.host.host	1.#.#.# to 126.#.#.#	Network and host addressing
Class B	net.net.host.host	128.0.#.# to 191.255.#.#	Network and host addressing
Class C	net.net.net.host	192.0.0.# to 223.255.255.#	Network and host addressing
Class D	net.net.net.host	224.0.0.# to 239.255.255.#	Multicasting
Class E	net.net.net.host	240.0.0.# to 240.255.255.#	Experimental purposes

Your IP address is considered classful if it conforms to the format and address ranges you see in Table 12-6. In other words, your IP address is based on the traditional byte boundaries for IP address classes. For example, a Class A IP address of 124.100.0.1 with a subnet mask of 255.0.0.0 is a classful address.

Subnet Masking

Definition:

A *subnet mask* is a series of four numbers that the computer uses to determine how many of the four numbers in the IP address are being used to specify the computer's network address. A subnet mask typically looks like this: 255.255.0.0. The first number of the subnet mask must be 255; the remaining three numbers can be any of the following numbers:

- 255
- 254
- 252
- 248
- 240
- 224
- 192

- 128
- 0

Where you see a number other than zero in the subnet mask, you can determine that the number in the same position in the IP address is part of the computer's network address. For example, if the computer's IP address is 192.168.200.200 and the subnet mask is 255.255.255.0, the numbers in the subnet mask tell you that the first three numbers in the IP address are being used to identify the network on which the computer resides. Likewise, where you see a zero in the subnet mask, this tells you that the number in the same position in the IP address is being used to identify the computer itself.

Example:

In Figure 12-26, you see an example of a subnet mask. The subnet mask is 255.255.255.0, which means that the first three numbers in the computer's IP address are being used to identify the network on which the computer resides.

```
IP Address  = 192.168.200.200
SubnetMask  = 255.255.255.0
```

The network address is 192.168.200

Figure 12-26: *A subnet mask.*

Default Subnet Masks

Your computer uses a subnet mask to identify the network and host portions of an IP address. The subnet mask's sole purpose is to "mask" the host portion of an IP address so that your computer can identify the network portion of the address. In essence, by using the subnet mask to identify the network portion of your address, the subnet mask makes TCP/IP routable. Your computer uses this network address information to make routing decisions. For example, your computer uses the subnet mask to determine if a host with which you want to communicate is on the same subnet as your computer (local), or on a different subnet from your computer (remote). If the destination host is remote, your computer must forward the data to a router in order to reach the destination host. The router will then forward the data on to its destination. You'll find that each class of IP address has a default subnet mask, as defined in Table 12-7.

Table 12-7: *Default Subnet Masks*

Address Type	Format	Default Subnet Mask
Class A	net.host.host.host	255.0.0.0
Class B	net.net.host.host	255.255.0.0
Class C	net.net.net.host	255.255.255.0

 Because each byte in the subnet mask is made up of 8 bits, you'll often see subnet masks indicated by a /## designation instead of its decimal equivalent. The ## represent the number of bits that make up the subnet mask. For example, it's easier (and shorter) to use the notation "145.10.1.1/16" to specify the IP address and subnet mask of a host than it is to specify "145.10.1.1 with a subnet mask of 255.255.0.0."

Lesson 12

Public and Private IP Addressing

One of your first decisions when designing your network's IP addressing strategy is to choose between public and private addressing, If you have computers on the network that aren't directly connected to the Internet, you can use either a private or a public IP addressing scheme. Let's take a look at the advantages and disadvantages of each strategy.

Private Addressing

The term private IP address refers to the blocks of network addresses reserved by the IANA for addressing those computers not on the Internet. Because the Internet's routers will not forward to these addresses, using a private network address can add to the security of your network. You should use a private IP addressing strategy if:

- Your company doesn't have many computers that need to be accessible from the Internet.
- Your company doesn't have enough available public IP addresses for all of your network hosts.

Table 12-8 describes the private IP address ranges reserved by the IANA.

Table 12-8: *IANA Reserved Public IP Address Ranges*

Address Class	Starting Address	Ending Address
Class A	10.0.0.0	10.255.255.254
Class B	172.16.0.0	172.31.255.254
Class C	192.168.0.0	192.168.255.254

⚠️ If you use a private network address, but still want access to the Internet, you must use a Network Address Translation (NAT) device such as Microsoft Proxy Server to enable your hosts to communicate with the Internet. When you use private IP addressing, only the IP address of the NAT device is accessible via the Internet.

Some of the advantages to using a private IP addressing strategy include:

- *Lower cost:* Using private IP addresses enables you to avoid having to lease public IP addresses from your Internet Service Provider. (You'll still need one public IP address for your NAT device if you want to connect to the Internet.)
- *Scalability:* It is much easier for you to assign IP addresses within a private network address as your network grows than to obtain additional public IP addresses.
- *Security:* Your internal network is more secure when you use private IP addresses. This is because the Internet's routers do not route to the reserved private IP addresses. Thus, computers on the Internet will not be able to access your internal network via the Internet.

Public Addressing

If you have several computers that you want to make accessible via the Internet, you might consider implementing a public addressing strategy. With public addressing, each host on your network must have a public, unique IP address. You'll typically obtain public IP addresses from an Internet Service Provider, and you'll need to implement a firewall in order to protect your internal network. You can also obtain public IP addresses from the IANA. You should use public addressing if:

- Your company has many computers that you want to be accessible from the Internet.

Lesson 12

- You have enough available IP addresses for all of your network hosts.

The biggest advantage to using a public addressing scheme is that you can make any or all of your network hosts accessible from the Internet. Keep in mind that it's critical that you plan for growth if you use a public address. If you run out of IP addresses, you won't be able to connect any additional hosts to your network until you obtain additional IP addresses. Also, the number of additional addresses you need might require that you change your addressing scheme on all computers.

Subnetting

Subnetting enables you to subdivide your IP network address (such as a Class B address) by borrowing part of your network's host addresses to identify subnet addresses.

 Subnetting was proposed in RFC 950. You can read specific RFCs by going to **www.rfc-editor.org**. This Web site includes a search engine by which you can search for RFCs by number or by keywords.

In order for your routers to route properly within your internal network, you must assign unique network addresses to each of your network segments. In the past, this meant that if your network was connected to the Internet, you had to obtain a separate public IP network address for each segment. To avoid having to obtain a separate public IP address from the IANA for each of your network segments, you can use subnetting to subdivide a single public IP address. This means that you'll need to obtain only one public IP address even if your network consists of multiple subnets.

For example, let's say that you've been assigned the Class C network address of 206.124.217.0—but your network consists of six subnets, each with a maximum of 25 hosts. You'll need to borrow bits from the host portion of the address in order to uniquely identify the subnets on your network. Once you borrow these bits, you'll then need a subnet mask that enables all of your hosts to see not only the network portion of the IP address, but also the bits you've borrowed to identify subnets. In this scenario, you'll need to use a custom subnet mask such as 255.255.255.224. This mask enables you to have up to eight subnets within your Class C address. You're using a custom subnet mask when you use a mask that contains more bits than the default mask for your address class. Keep in mind that you'll typically use subnetting when you're implementing a public IP addressing scheme. If you're using private addressing and your network consists of multiple segments, you can simply choose a different network address for each segment.

To subnet your IP network address, you'll need to complete the following tasks:

1. Identify the subnet mask you'll need to use to support the number of subnets that make up your network.
2. Determine the subnet addresses you can assign based on this mask.
3. Calculate the host addresses you can use on each subnet.

Let's walk through the subnetting process by starting with how to design a custom subnet mask.

Designing a Custom Subnet Mask

You design a custom subnet mask by determining how many bits you need to borrow from the host portion of the IP address to uniquely identify your subnets. Let's start by assuming that you've been given the public IP network address of 145.10.0.0. This is a Class B network address, so the default subnet mask is 255.255.0.0. You'll need to borrow bits from the third byte of your IP address in order to identify your subnets. You can determine how many bits you'll need to borrow to identify your subnets by taking 2 and raising it by the number of bits you can borrow. For example, a one-bit subnet mask (2^1) enables you to have 2 subnets. A two-bit subnet mask (2^2) enables you to have 4 subnets, and so on. You can use Table 12-9 as a guide for determining how many bits you should borrow to support the number of subnets within your network.

Table 12-9: *Custom Subnet Masking*

Number of Bits Borrowed	Number of Subnets Supported	Mask in Binary Form	Mask in Decimal Form
1	$2^1=2$	10000000	128
2	$2^2=4$	11000000	192
3	$2^3=8$	11100000	224
4	$2^4=16$	11110000	240
5	$2^5=32$	11111000	248
6	$2^6=64$	11111100	252
7	$2^7=128$	11111110	254
8	$2^8=256$	11111111	255

Using our Class B network address example, let's say that you will have a total of 8 subnets. As you can see from the table, we'll need to use a 3-bit subnet mask to accommodate 8 subnets. This means that instead of using the subnet mask of 255.255.0.0, we should use 255.255.240.0 instead. This subnet mask enables us to uniquely identify our subnets within our public IP address.

Once you've determined your subnet mask, you can then calculate the number of hosts you can have per subnet by calculating the value of 2 raised to the number of bits not used for the network and subnet address, and then subtracting 2 from this number. (You must subtract 2 because a host address of all 0s or all 1s is invalid.) Continuing with our Class B network address example, if we use a subnet mask of 255.255.240.0, this means that we're borrowing 3 bits from the third byte to identify subnets. As a result, we can use only the remaining 5 bits of the third byte, plus all of the fourth byte to identify hosts. Using our formula, this means that we can have a total $2^{13}-2$ host addresses per subnet, or 8,190.

Defining Subnet Addresses

When you've determined what the appropriate subnet mask is for your network, your next step is to define the subnet addresses you can use within this mask. You derive subnet addresses by varying the values in the bits that you borrow from the host portion of the address. The easiest way to determine your subnet addresses is to identify the subnet increment. The subnet increment is always the decimal value of the lowest-order bit in the subnet mask. For example, if we use a subnet mask of 255.255.240.0, we can determine the subnet increment by examining the binary value of 240. It's 11110000, and to determine our subnet increment, we convert the lowest order bit with a value of 1 to its equivalent value in decimal. In our example, this means that our subnet increment is 16. Thus, valid subnet addresses on the network 145.10.0.0, with a subnet mask of 255.255.240.0, are:

- 145.10.0.0
- 145.10.16.0
- 145.10.32.0

- 145.10.48.0
- and so on, up to 145.10.240.0

Defining Host Addresses

Now that you've identified your subnet addresses, your last step when subnetting a public IP network address is to identify the host addresses you can define on each subnet. Keep in mind that the first valid host address on any given subnet will be 1. So continuing with our Class B example, the first valid host address for the first subnet (145.10.0.0) is 145.10.0.1. Likewise, the last valid host address for a given subnet will be the last possible value before the next subnet address. In our example, we've said that our subnet increment is 16, and that our valid subnet addresses are 0, 16, 32, and so on. This means that on the 145.10.0.0 subnet, the last host address is 145.10.15.254. (We can't use 145.10.15.255 because this represents a host address of all 1s for the 145.10.0.0 subnet—and this address is reserved for subnet broadcasts.) Table 12-10 describes the range of host addresses for each of the subnets in our 145.10.0.0 example.

Table 12-10: *Subnetted IP Addresses Example*

Subnet	Starting Host Address	Ending Host Address
145.10.0.0	145.10.0.1	145.10.15.254
145.10.16.0	145.10.16.1	145.10.31.254
145.10.32.0	145.10.32.1	145.10.47.254
145.10.48.0	145.10.48.1	145.10.63.254
145.10.240.0	145.10.240.1	145.10.255.254

OPTIONAL ACTIVITY 12-4

Discussing and Designing Custom Subnet Masks

Activity Time:

30 minutes

Scenario:

In this activity, you will discuss and design custom subnet masking.

1. **How does the use of custom subnet masks counteract the problem of the Internet running out of available IP addresses?**

2. Your company has been assigned the public IP address of 137.72.0.0. You estimate that you will eventually have a total of 30 subnets. What subnet mask should you use to support this number of subnets?

3. How would you display this subnet mask by using the /## notation?

4. Given this subnet mask, how many total subnets can you define on your network? What are the subnet addresses you can assign?

5. How many hosts can you have on each subnet? What are the host addresses you can assign on the first subnet for your network?

Auto-IP Configuration

To configure the TCP/IP settings on a computer, you can enter the addresses manually. However, this method can be time-consuming and is also prone to error. Most networks rely on services that assign IP address information automatically.

Windows 2000, Windows Me, Windows 2003, and Windows XP support two methods for automatically assigning IP addresses to computers: by using a *Dynamic Host Configuration Protocol (DHCP)* server or by using *Automatic Private IP Addressing*. Windows NT and Windows 9x do not support APIPA, so you must have a DHCP server or assign addresses manually. Table 12-11 describes each of the automatic configuration methods.

Table 12-11: *Automatic TCP/IP Configuration Methods*

Method	Description
DHCP Server	A server that a network administrator configures with a pool of IP addresses (along with other IP addressing information such as the subnet mask, default gateway, and so on) to assign to clients.

Lesson 12

Method	Description
APIPA (Automatic Private IP Addressing)	A service that automatically configures a computer with an IP address on the 169.254.0.0 network. For example, this service might configure a computer with the IP address of 169.254.217.5. APIPA addresses are not routable, so computers with APIPA addresses cannot communicate outside the local network. So, APIPA is a good choice for automatic configuration in a small business or home network, but not for a large company.

Name Servers

On a TCP/IP-based network and even the Internet, you connect to computers by using their names, not their IP addresses. For example, you probably can connect to a computer on your network by using a short, descriptive name such as LocalServer; on the Internet, you connect to computers by using *host names* such as **www.redcross.org**. In order for your computer to find and connect to the computer with that name, however, your computer must know the other computer's IP address. There are two ways computers find the IP addresses for specific computer names: *Domain Name System (DNS)* and *Windows Internet Naming System (WINS)* servers. These servers contain databases that consist of computer names and their associated IP addresses.

How to Install a Network Adapter

Procedure Reference: Install a Network Adapter

To install a network card:

1. Install the network card into the system.
2. If prompted, install drivers for the network card.
3. Connect the network cable from the wall or the hub to the network card.
4. Test the network card.

You can open an Internet browser and access a Web site, or you can use the ping command to test connectivity to a host.

 A working network adapter will have two status indicator lights. One light will be on steadily, showing that the card is connected to the network. The other light will flash to indicate network activity.

Network Commands

Several command-line tools are available in Windows for testing and troubleshooting network connections. Some of the commands that you might find useful are shown in Table 12-12.

Table 12-12: *Commands for Testing and Troubleshooting Network Connections*

Command	Syntax Examples	Description
ipconfig	`ipconfig /all`	Displays statistics about your network connection including IP address, subnet mask, and default gateway.
ping	`ping host`	A command that can be used to check connectivity between two IP-based devices.

ACTIVITY 12-5

Installing a Network Card

Setup:
There is a server set up with DHCP to automatically issue IP addresses to each student. Drivers for the network card are provided.

Scenario:
The computers that were deployed for the marketing department need to be connected to the network. Some systems might already have a network card installed and need a second network card to connect to a separate test network.

What You Do	How You Do It
1. Install the network card.	a. Disconnect the power to the computer.
	b. Turn off the computer.
	c. Open the computer case.
	d. Determine the edge connector type of the network card.
	e. Insert the network card in the slot that matches the edge connector of the network card.
	f. Close the computer case.
	g. Connect the network cable from the network access point to the network card.

Lesson 12: Networking

Lesson 12

2. **Test the network card.**
   a. **Reconnect the power to the computer.**
   b. **Turn on the computer.**
   c. **If prompted, install network card drivers.**
   d. **Choose Start→Run, and then type** *cmd* **and press Enter** to open a Command Prompt window.
   e. **Type** *ipconfig* **to display the current settings for your network connection.**

      If no network number has been assigned or if the network number is 169.254.0.1, type *ipconfig /release* and press Enter.

      Type *ipconfig /renew* and press Enter to obtain a new IP address.
   f. **Type** *ping www.irs.gov* **and press Enter** to verify that you can communicate with another system.
   g. **Type** *exit* **to close the command window.**

Network Architecture Standards

The Institute of Electrical and Electronic Engineers (IEEE) is an international professional association for electrical and electronics engineers that sets standards for telecommunications and computing applications. The International Organization for Standardization (ISO) has accepted the IEEE 802 series of Local Area Network (LAN) standards under ISO 8802. Manufacturers who follow these standards help make network communication reliable between different makes and models of computing devices. The IEEE 802 standards are included in Table 12-13.

 The term 802 came from the committee convening Feb (the second month—2) of 1980 (80).

Table 12-13: *IEEE 802 Standards*

Standard	System
IEEE 802.1	High-level Interface—standards related to network management.
IEEE 802.2	Logical Link Control—general standard for the Data Link layer in the OSI reference model. The IEEE divides this layer into two sublayers—the Data Link Control (DLC) layer and the Media Access Control (MAC) layer.

Standard	System
IEEE 802.3	Carrier Sense Multiple Access with Collision Detect (CSMA/CD)—defines the MAC layer for bus networks that use CSMA/CD. This is the basis of the Ethernet standard.
IEEE 802.4	Token Bus—defines the MAC layer for bus networks that use a token-passing mechanism (Token Bus networks).
IEEE 802.5	Token Ring—defines the MAC layer for Token Ring networks.
IEEE 802.6	Metropolitan Area Networks (MANs).
IEEE 802.7	Broadband LANs.
IEEE 802.8	Fiber-optic LANs.
IEEE 802.9	Integrated Data and Voice Networks.
IEEE 802.10	Security.
IEEE 802.11	Wireless LANs.
IEEE 802.12	Demand Priority Access—100VG-AnyLAN.
IEEE 802.13	Not used.
IEEE 802.14	Cable TV—broadband MANs.
IEEE 802.15	Wireless Personal Area Networks (PANs).
IEEE 802.16	Broadband Wireless Access.
IEEE 802.17	Resilient Packet Ring.
IEEE 802.18	Radio-based LANs and MANs.
IEEE 802.19	Virtual LANs (VLANs).

Topic C

Network Architecture

The theory and standards described in the previous topic are applied in four different network architectures that are used to link PCs. In this topic, you'll learn about the Ethernet, Token Ring, ARCNet, and AppleTalk network architectures.

Ethernet

Ethernet is a LAN protocol—developed by Xerox Corporation in cooperation with DEC and Intel in 1976—that uses a bus or star topology. The IEEE 802.3 standard is based on the original Ethernet specifications. The standard was first published in 1985, with the formal title of "IEEE 802.3 Carrier Sense Multiple Access with Collision Detection (CSMA/CD) Access Method and Physical Layer Specifications." The IEEE standard has since been adopted by the ISO, which makes it a worldwide networking standard. All Ethernet equipment since 1985 is built according to IEEE 802.3.

 Ethernet networks use full duplex communications.

Lesson 12

Ethernet is by far the most popular LAN technology in use today, ensuring a large market for competitively priced Ethernet equipment. Ethernet is easy to use, reliable, and an open technology that anyone can incorporate in their hardware and software. The vast majority of computer vendors today equip their products with 10/100 Mbps (million bits per second) Ethernet attachments. This makes it possible to network all manner of computers with an Ethernet LAN. There are currently several Ethernet standards in use:

- *10Base5* is the original cabling standard for Ethernet that uses coaxial cables. The name derives from the fact that the maximum data-transfer speed is 10 Mbps, it uses baseband transmission, and the maximum length of cables is 500 meters. 10Base5 is also called thick Ethernet, Thickwire, and Thicknet.

- *10Base2* standard (also called Thinnet) uses 50 ohm coaxial cable (RG-58 A/U) with maximum lengths of 185 meters. This cable is thinner and more flexible than that used for the 10Base5 standard. The RG-58 A/U cable is both less expensive and easier to place. Cables in the 10Base2 system connect with BNC connectors. The Network Interface Card (NIC) in a computer requires a T-connector where you can attach two cables to adjacent computers. Any unused connection must have a 50 ohm terminator. The 10Base2 system operates at 10 Mbps.

- *10BaseT* standard (also called twisted-pair Ethernet) uses a twisted-pair cable with maximum lengths of 100 meters. The cable is thinner and more flexible than the coaxial cable used for the 10Base2 or 10Base5 standards. Cables in the 10BaseT system connect with RJ-45 connectors. A star topology is common with 12 or more computers connected directly to a hub or concentrator. The 10BaseT system operates at 10 Mbps.

- *Fast Ethernet (100BaseT)* supports data-transfer rates of 100 Mbps. There are several different cabling schemes that can be used with 100BaseT, including 100BaseT (two pairs of high-quality twisted-pair wires), 100BaseT4 (four pairs of normal-quality twisted-pair wires), and 100BaseFL (fiber-optic cables). Officially, the 100BaseT standard is IEEE 802.3u.

- *Gigabit Ethernet* supports data rates of 1 gigabit (1,000 megabits) per second. The first gigabit Ethernet standard (802.3z) was ratified by the IEEE 802.3 Committee in 1998.

How Ethernet Works

A real-life Ethernet network system consists of three basic elements:

1. The physical medium used to carry Ethernet signals between computers.
2. A set of media access control rules embedded in each Ethernet interface that allow multiple computers to fairly arbitrate access to the shared Ethernet channel.
3. An Ethernet transmission consists of a standardized set of bits used to carry data over the system.

Every computer on an Ethernet network has embedded in its circuits a Media Access Control (MAC) mechanism that uses a system called *Carrier Sense Multiple Access with Collision Detection (CSMA/CD)* to ensure that all computers on the network can have an equal chance to transmit data over the wires.

In this system, a station listens to data traffic on the channel. When there is no traffic, the computer is free to transmit a frame or packet of data. If two computers start to transmit data at the same time, the Collision Detection portion of CSMA/CD stops both transmissions and assigns a random delay to each computer after which time it can check to see if it can send. Figure 12-27 shows an Ethernet collision occurring.

Figure 12-27: *An Ethernet collision.*

Every Ethernet network interface card has a unique, 48-bit address assigned to it by the manufacturer of the card. The IEEE determines the first 24 bits of the address by assigning a different Organizationally Unique Identifier (OUI) to every company that makes Ethernet cards. The company then uses another 24 bits to assign a different number to every card it manufactures. The 48-bit address is called the Media Access Control (MAC) address and is different for every Ethernet card in the world. Ethernet relies exclusively on the MAC address to identify the receiving and sending nodes.

Token Ring

Token Ring is a type of computer network in which all computers are connected in a continuous loop (ring topology). All computers on a Token Ring network send messages over the same cable, so some system had to be developed to keep two computers from using the cable at the same time. A token is a special bit pattern that is sent around the loop from computer to computer. Only one token exists on any Token Ring network. Before a computer can send a frame, it must wait until it can catch the token. It captures the token, which keeps all other computers from attempting to send frames. The computer with the token then sends a frame around the loop until the destination computer grabs the frames. The computer then releases the token so another node on the network can send its frame. This network protocol was developed by IBM, and the IEEE wrote standards for it in IEEE 802.5. Transmission speeds for Token Ring can be 4 Mbps, 16 Mbps, or 100 Mbps (High Speed Token Ring, IEEE 802.5t). Implementations of 1 GB Token Ring are also available (IEEE 802.5v).

All stations on a Token Ring network must transmit at the same speed; otherwise, the ring won't work at all. That means that if you want to upgrade a ring from, for example, 4 Mbps to 16 Mbps, you will have to replace all of the network cards in the entire network. Some Token Ring cards have dip switches to set the speed. If your ring doesn't work at all, you might suspect an incorrect dip switch setting on a NIC.

Token Ring networks use Multi Station Access Units (MSAUs), also referred to as MAUs, to connect network stations. An MSAU is similar to a hub, with eight port-to-connect stations, and a Ring In and a Ring Out port to daisy-chain MSAUs. If regular ports on an MSAU fail, the network is not affected. However, if a Ring In or Ring Out port fails, stations connected to that MSAU won't be able to communicate. Figure 12-28 shows the communication on a token ring network.

Lesson 12

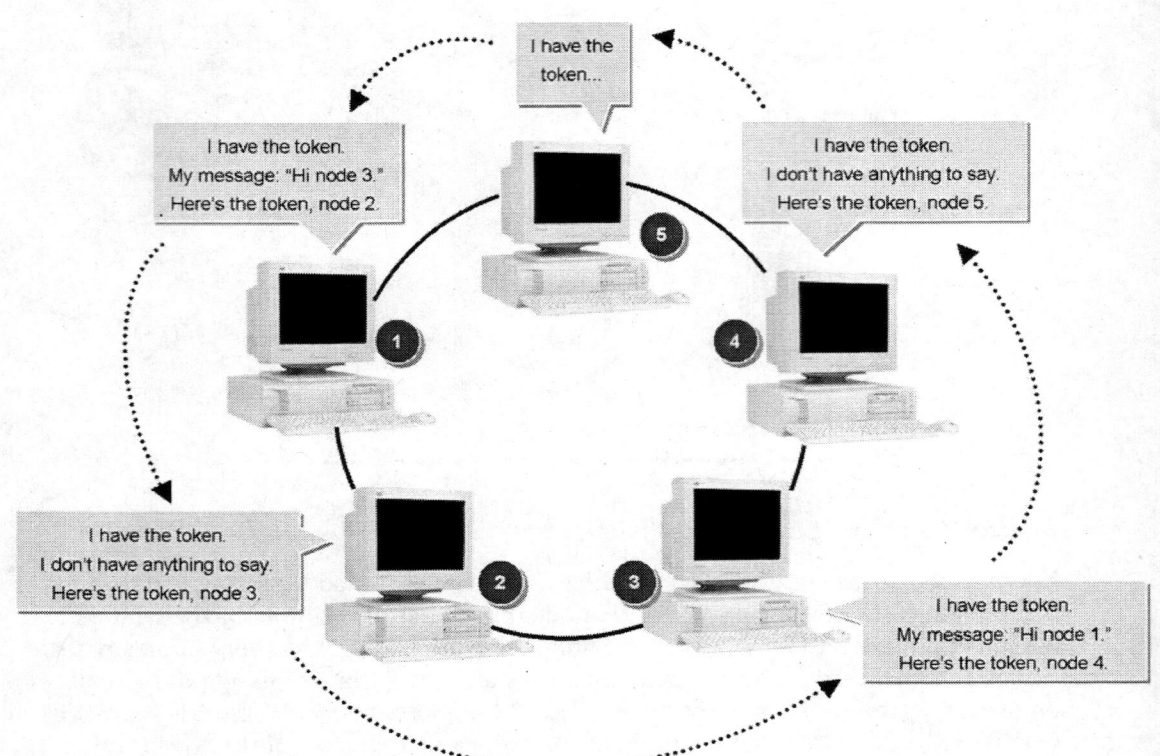

Figure 12-28: *A Token Ring network.*

ARCNet

Attached Resource Computer Network (ARCNet) is a network developed by the DataPoint Corporation in 1968 and is one of the oldest, simplest, and least expensive LAN technologies. ARCNet can connect up to 255 nodes in a star topology using twisted-pair or coax cable and originally could transmit data at a rate of 2.5 Mbps. Like a Token Ring network, ARCNet passes a token to control access to the network. Until the late 1980s, ARCNet had about as large a market share as Ethernet among small businesses, but its popularity has decreased since then. ARCNet Plus has a data-transfer rate of 20 Mbps.

AppleTalk

AppleTalk is a Local Area Network protocol developed by Apple Computer, Inc. in 1985 and is built into all Macintosh computers and Apple LaserWriters. AppleTalk supports Apple's proprietary LocalTalk cabling scheme, as well as Ethernet and IBM Token Ring. With the proper additional hardware, PCs, UNIX, and VAX computers can connect to an AppleTalk network. Current implementations include LocalTalk, a 235 KBps (kilobyte per second) LAN, and EtherTalk, a 10 Mbps LAN.

Topic D

Internet Connections

In just about every business and more and more homes, users want to connect to the Internet. The wealth of knowledge and information sharing available to them through the Internet is astounding. In this topic, you will learn about the different options available to establish a connection to the Internet to both send and receive information.

Internet Connections

Definition:

An *Internet connection* is a connection that enables a client computer to access the Internet, a global, public network that provides access to information, applications, and services on computers throughout the world. All Internet connections:

- Use the TCP/IP network protocol.
- Require a unique IP address for each node.
- Require an Internet Service Provider (ISP) to connect to the Internet.

Internet connections might:

- Be established using different connection methods. These include:
  — Local Area Network (LAN)
  — Digital Subscriber Link (DSL)
  — Cable
  — Integrated Services Digital Network (ISDN)
  — Dial-up
  — Satellite
  — Wireless
- Require different hardware based on which connection method is being used.
- Transfer files at different speeds. This also varies between files being uploaded and downloaded in some connection methods.
- Support different numbers of computers on single ISP connection. For example, in a home network with several computers but only one Internet connection, additional networking hardware or software can be used so that all the computers can share the connection to the ISP.

Example:

In Figure 12-29, the user is connecting to the Internet through a cable connection to their ISP. The ISP they are using provides Web hosting, mail, and Internet access services, as well as the physical connection to the Internet.

Lesson 12

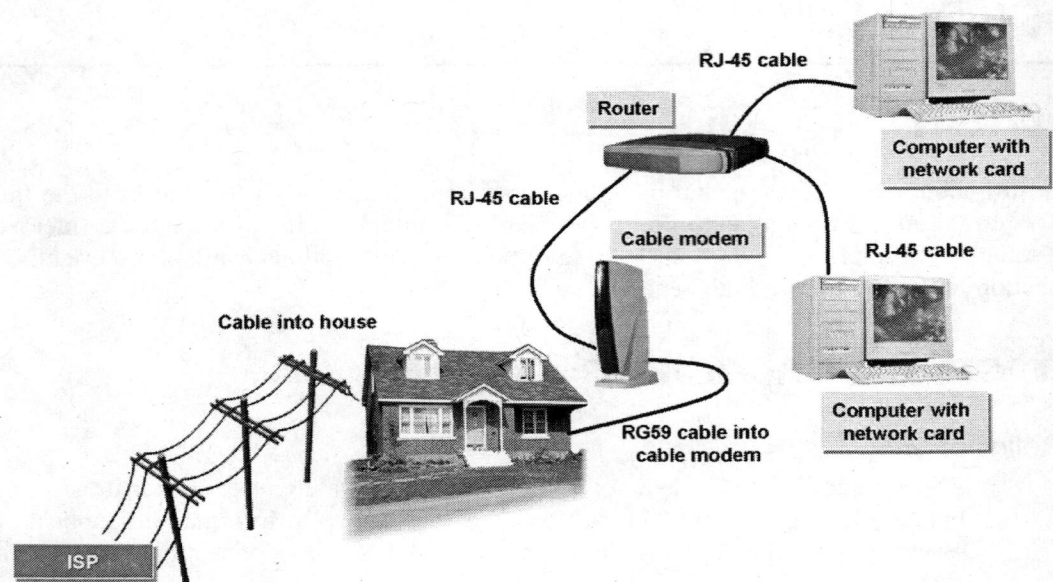

Figure 12-29: *A cable-based Internet connection.*

LAN Internet Connection

Definition:

A LAN Internet connection is an Internet connection that utilizes network hardware (server, media, and other necessary hardware), a router, and the TCP/IP protocol to establish a connection between a client and the Internet. LAN Internet connections are always on and available for use (unless the router goes down) and are relatively fast.

LAN Internet connections vary by:

- The network media used on the LAN.
- The servers on the LAN.
- The speed of the connection between the LAN and the Internet. Connections might be:
    - Dedicated 56 K digital connections. These older connections are being phased out, but in some areas they are still in use.
    - T1, T2, T3, or T4 connections. These are the four standard digital voice systems developed by AT&T. T1 is composed of 24 multiplexed voice channels for a *bandwidth* of 1.54 Mbps, T2 uses 96 channels for 6.312 Mbps, T3 uses 672 channels for 44.736 Mbps, and T4 uses 4,032 channels for 274.1 Mbps. These lines are leased from a telecommunications company. You can also subscribe to a portion of a T line; this is referred to as fractional T service.
    - Microwave satellite based. Uses a stationary satellite dish, usually placed on top of a building or other high area, that communicates with a satellite in outer space in a *geosynchronous* orbit with the planet.

Lesson 12

Example:

Figure 12-30 shows an example of a LAN-based Internet connection. This example includes a T3 line for the Internet backbone. Big Co uses a T1 line to connect from its company Internet hardware to the Internet backbone. Employees also connect at their second location through a dedicated 56 K digital connection. Both of these locations are using the LAN to establish employees' connections from their desktop to the Internet.

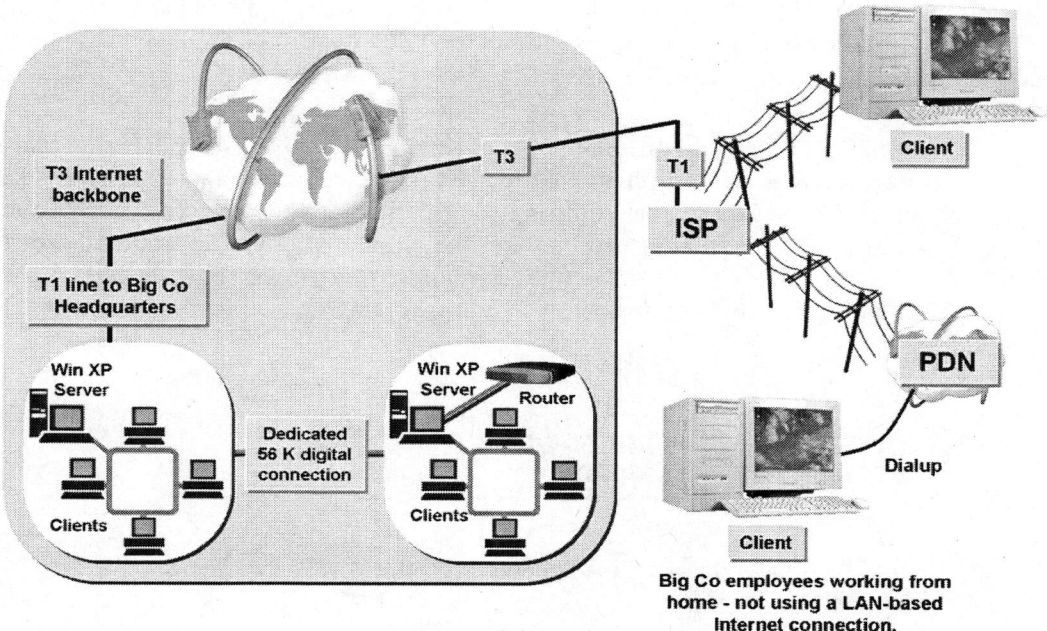

Figure 12-30: *Big Co's Internet connections.*

Non-Example:

Employees can also dial in or connect to the Internet from home through their dial-up or cable connections, but they would not be using the LAN connection in that case. Figure 12-30 also shows the employees' connections outside the LAN to the Internet.

DSL Internet Connection

Definition:

Digital Subscriber Line (DSL) is an Internet connection method that uses standard copper phone wires and a transceiver. It carries voice and data traffic simultaneously over standard phone lines. The data portion remains connected all of the time. To use DSL, the customer must be within 5.5 km of the phone company central office where the DSL equipment is located, unless a router or fiber optic cable is used to extend the distance.

DSL connection components include:
- Splitter. A splitter may or may not be required at the customer location. The splitter is what enables the line to carry voice and data simultaneously. Several splitterless technologies have evolved. In splitterless technologies, the splitting is performed at the phone company central office. Splitterless is also known as G.Lite, DSL Lite, and Universal ADSL.
- Data Rate. The closer the customer is to the phone company central office, the faster the data rate. Also, a heavier gauge wire improves data rates.

Lesson 12: Networking

Lesson 12

- Modulation Technologies. These vary based on the type of DSL in use. Discrete Multitone Modulation (DMT) is most commonly used. It divides the frequency range of the phone line into 256 different 4.3125 kHz channels. Other modulation techniques are Carrierless Amplitude Modulation (CAP) and Multiple Virtual Line (MVL) techniques.
- Upstream and downstream speeds. Some DSL connections are up to twice as fast at receiving information as they are at sending information. Other connections vary, but by a smaller degree. When the speeds vary like this, it is referred to as asymmetric since the speeds are not symmetrical to each other.

Example:

Figure 12-31 shows a DSL Internet connection. This is a DSL connection that uses splitters in front of each phone that is used for voice communications. The location is within 5.5 km of the phone company central office, so the customer is able to use DSL. A DSL modem is placed between the phone outlet on the wall and the computer. Even though it is called a modem, it is really a transceiver since the signal is digital from end to end and needs no conversion from analog to digital and back.

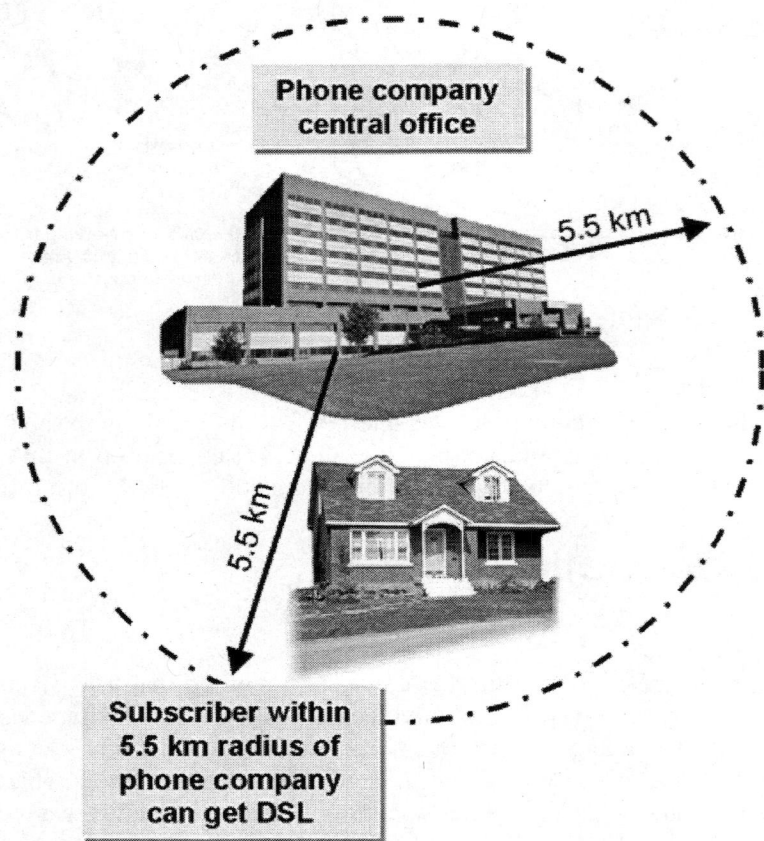

Figure 12-31: *DSL Internet connections.*

Cable Internet Connections

An Internet connection through a *cable modem* takes advantage of the cable television line running through most neighborhoods. A splitter is installed on the cable line running into the house to split the TV channel traffic from the data traffic. A cable modem connects via an RG-59 coaxial cable from the splitter to the cable modem on one side. An RJ-45 cable connects from the cable modem to the network card in the computer to complete the connections.

For more information about how cable Internet connections work, refer to **www.cabledatacomnews.com/cmic/cmic2.html**.

ISDN Internet Connection

Integrated Services Digital Network (ISDN) connections were popular in some major metropolitan areas, but they have largely been replaced by cable and DSL connections. ISDN uses a single wire or fiber optic line to carry voice, data, and video signals. It uses existing phone company switches and wiring, which are upgraded to make a 64 Kbps end-to-end digital channel. Japan and North America use one standard; Europe uses another.

Basic Rate Interface (BRI) is most commonly used in residential ISDN connections. It is composed of two bearer (B) channels at 64 Kbps (used for voice and data) and one delta (D) channel at 16 Kbps (used for controlling the B channels and signal transmission). The total bandwidth is up to 144 Kbps. The two B channels can be bonded together at the phone company central office to provide 128 Kbps bandwidth. Frequently, six channels are bonded for a 384 Kbps bandwidth.

Primary Rate Interface (PRI) is most commonly used between a Private Branch Exchange (PBX) at the customer's site and the phone company central office. It is composed of 23 B channels at 64 Kbps and one D channel at 64 Kbps. The total bandwidth is up to 1,536 Kbps. In both BRI and PRI, the D channel is used to reassign channels for voice, fax, and data as required.

In Europe, the BRI is the same as above, but the PRI is composed of 30 B channels and one D channel. The total bandwidth is up to 1,984 Kbps. A Network Terminal Interface (NTI) device is needed to connect your data or telephone equipment to the ISDN line. It provides connection terminal equipment (TE) and terminal adapter (TA) equipment to the phone company local loop. This is a coding and decoding device. It takes the place of a modem in an analog situation.

The TA replaces a modem. It is used to adapt ISDN BRI channels to RS-232 and V.35 standards. It can be a standalone device or an interface card that is installed in the computer, router, or PBX. You might also need other ISDN interfaces and ISDN LAN topology bridges.

Dial-up Internet Connection

A dial-up connection to the Internet is usually the least expensive method available. It uses an analog modem connected to a serial port on your computer and connects to the analog phone line. When the modem is in use, you generally cannot use that phone line for voice communications. It is limited to 56 Kbps.

Satellite Internet Connection

Definition:

A satellite Internet connection is a connection to the Internet that uses satellite technology to establish and maintain the connection. All satellite connections require a satellite dish at your location as well as a service contract with a company that provides access to a satellite in geosynchronous orbit. A satellite connection requires a satellite dish antenna, which is placed outside, facing a southerly direction (for the United States). It also requires a satellite modem or transceiver and standard cable to connect between the modem and the PC's network card or USB port.

Sending data, also known as uplink or upstream data, is slower than receiving data. It is usually in the 50 to 150 Kbps range. Receiving data is also referred to as downlink or downstream data. Downstream data is usually received in the 150 to 1,200 Kbps range. Speed can be affected by server limitations, the amount of traffic the satellite is handling, and file sizes. Heavy rain or snow can cause a poor signal. Solar interference in early spring and early fall when the sun and satellites align with each other briefly each day can also interfere with transmission.

There is a certain degree of delay when using satellite transmissions. You have to wait while data is being transferred between your computer and the satellite. You also have an additional wait as the satellite provider receives your transmission at their network operations center (NOC) and then sends the request on to the Web site you are trying to access. This delay is referred to as *latency*.

Satellite connections can be one-way or two-way. One-way satellite connections receive data via satellite but send data through a standard phone line. Two-way satellite connections receive and send data through the satellite connection and do not require a phone line. The FCC requires that two-way satellite systems be installed by a trained professional because they are transmitter devices. One-way systems can be installed by anyone.

Example:

Figure 12-32 shows a two-way satellite Internet connection. The connection uses a small dish on the user's roof to both send and receive transmissions. The satellite provider's network operation center receives the requests and passes them on to the requested Web site servers.

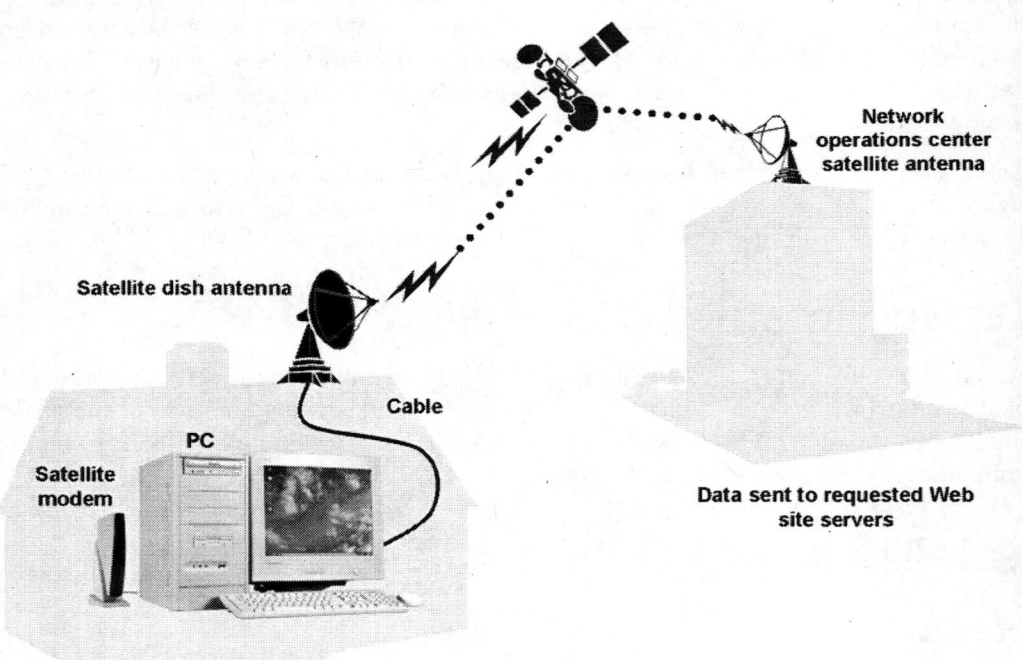

Figure 12-32: *A satellite Internet connection.*

Wireless Internet Connection

A wireless Internet connection uses an antenna on a tower that broadcasts Internet signals. It is set up by a wireless ISP, or WISP. To access the signal, customers need to be within the range of the antenna—usually between 3 and 35 miles in circumference.

Customers place an antenna on their roof and connect a special wireless transceiver or modem to their PC to access the signal. Data rates of between 1.5 and 128 Mbps are available based on what the WISP has to offer. Obstructions between the two antennas degrade the signal strength and quality.

Wireless Access Points

A *wireless access point* provides a connection point for multiple computers with wireless network cards to connect to a network. A wireless access point does not in and of itself access the Internet, however, if the wireless access point has a broadband Internet service connection, such as a cable or DSL connection, it can allow multiple users to share that single Internet connection.

Wireless access points have become common in airports, Internet cafés, some restaurants, and business conferences, forming what are called *Wi-Fi networks*. In public venues, users typically pay a flat fee for unlimited Internet access through the wireless access point while they are at the site. They are popular with business travelers who need a method of accessing email and their company's network while traveling.

This technology has also spawned the proliferation of neighborhood area networks, freenets, parasitic or piranha grids, and broadband bootlegging by individual users who pay for a single ISP connection, connect it to a wireless access point and then allow neighbors and friends to use the connection. A number of Internet service providers now require that subscribers sign agreements that limit the use of the service by third parties.

In addition to the wireless Internet access provided intentionally by businesses and community groups, many corporations are using wireless access points for their own corporate networks. However, many of these businesses are giving nearby Internet users a free ride at the cost of their own security. Wireless network hackers and security analysts drive through neighborhoods and industrial areas *war driving*—looking for wireless access points that allow them to connect without security validation. The war driving term is adapted from *war dialing*, which is the brute force method of locating insecure dial-up computer connections by random dialing of phone numbers by a computer program.

One emerging protocol, 802.1x, is designed to address these security problems by establishing methods for user authentication on wireless networks. Microsoft implemented the 802.1x protocol in its Windows XP operating system. Using 802.1x certificates to validate the identity of authorized users, Windows XP allows users to access various Wi-Fi networks and travel securely and seamlessly between one wireless network to the next.

Lesson 12

Activity 12-6

Discussing Internet Connections

Activity Time:

15 minutes

Scenario:

In this activity, you will discuss the different types of Internet Connections.

1. Janet lives in a rural area that doesn't have cable access. Her home is about 30 miles from the town where the phone company's central office is located. The nearest wireless ISP is two towns over about 50 miles away. What options for an Internet connection are available to Janet?

    a) DSL
    b) Cable
    c) Wireless
    d) Dial-up
    e) Satellite

2. From the Internet connections you determined were available to Janet, if she is on a tight budget and uses her computer for personal, not business use, which Internet connection would you recommend?

3. John lives in a large, metropolitan area and has subscribed to an ISDN Internet service. Unfortunately, his ISDN provider is going out of business and there isn't another ISDN provider in his area.

   John lives three miles from his phone company's central office, so he can get DSL. He also is currently a subscriber to digital cable TV. There are many companies who offer inexpensive dial-up Internet connection services.

   What Internet connection would you recommend for John? Why?

TOPIC E

Networking Devices

Many devices can connect computers to networks, and networks to other networks. Choosing the correct device is critical to having data move through the entire network correctly. In this topic, you will learn the different classification that help organize these devices.

Networking Device

Computer networking devices, also called network equipment, are mechanical devices that direct and in some cases alter data as it passes through the device in a computer network. Some examples of computer networking devices are hubs, bridges, routers, gateways, Channel Service Unit/Digital Service Unit, firewalls, and all-in-one stations.

Lesson 12

Hubs

A *hub* is an electronic device that connects several computers or networks together. In a network using the star topology, a hub is the center device that all the nodes connect to. The hub must have enough ports to accommodate all the nodes in the star. An example of a hub is shown in Figure 12-33.

Figure 12-33: *A hub.*

Different types of hubs can provide different functions.

- A *passive hub* simply forwards network messages. It can be the center of a star network. A passive hub does not process, modify, or regenerate signals in any way.

- An *active hub*, or *repeater*, regenerates and amplifies the data bits in order to maintain a strong signal that might otherwise deteriorate over a long distance. Adding an active hub allows computers on the network to be physically farther apart. Active hubs are also called *multiport repeaters*. All the signals that come into an active hub are regenerated and sent out to all the nodes on the network. An example of a repeater is shown in Figure 12-34.

- An *intelligent hub* is a central connecting device in a network that provides intelligent functions, as well as forwarding signals. An intelligent hub can provide bridging, routing, and switching, and even more complex functions such as network management and LAN emulation. The functions of an intelligent hub can also be performed by the group of specialized devices described in the following sections.

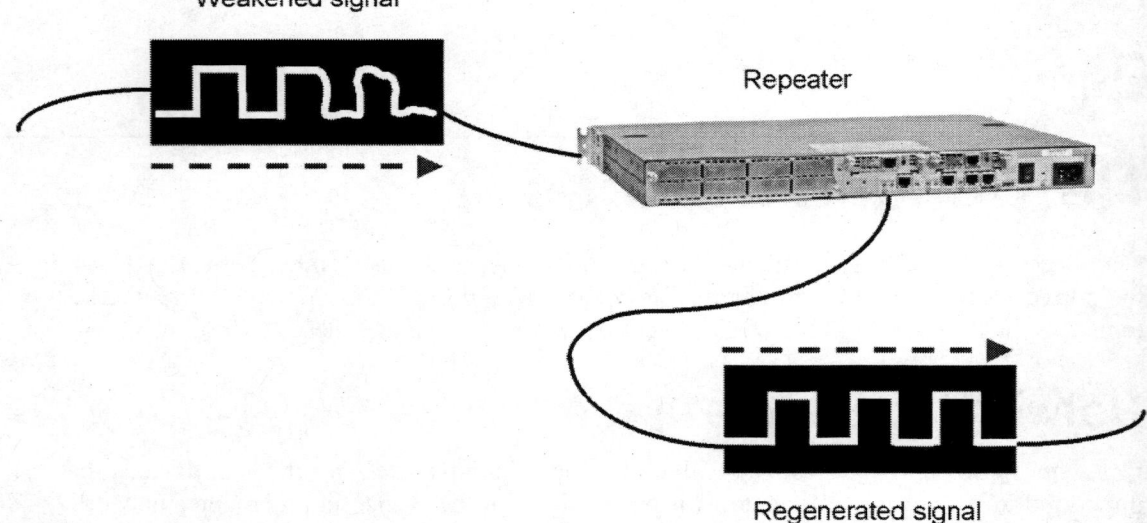

Figure 12-34: *A repeater.*

Lesson 12

Bridges

A *bridge* controls the flow of information between LAN segments or networks, even if they are different types of networks using different communication protocols. A bridge allows a message to cross from one network to another if it is addressed to the other side. Local messages are not sent across to the second network, which makes the traffic flow more efficiently. Bridges build and maintain address tables of the nodes on the network to speed up the flow of data.

Bridges with more than two ports (multiport bridges) perform a switching function. LAN switches are really multiport bridges that can switch at full wire speed.

An example of a bridge is shown in Figure 12-35. If the bridge receives a data unit from Segment 1, it examines the destination node address for that data unit. If the data unit is destined for a node on Segment 1, the bridge ignores the data unit; the data unit has already found its way to the correct network segment. If the data unit is destined for a node on another segment, then the bridge forwards the data unit to the next segment.

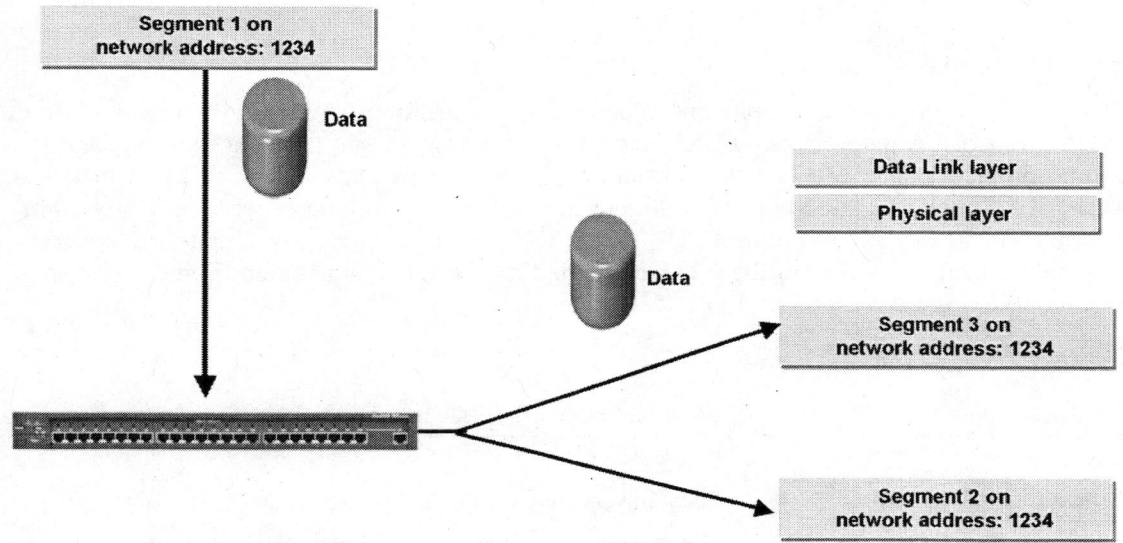

Figure 12-35: *Bridges can filter inter-segment traffic.*

In this scheme, traffic local to a particular segment is confined only to that segment; however, internetwork traffic is allowed to pass through the bridge. You can use bridges when you need to restrict traffic across network segments.

Routers

A *router* determines the best path for a data packet to be sent from one network to another. A router first stores the electronic message, reads the network destination address stored in the message, examines all possible paths to the destination address, chooses a path based on current traffic and number of other routers, and finally sends the message along that path. A router can also be used to balance traffic and filter traffic for security and management purposes. Specially designed routers can handle several different protocols. Software on a server can make it function like a router, if the server contains more than one NIC.

Lesson 12

A router functions much like a bridge, however, there are important differences aside from whether you transmit data between segments or networks. A router is more intelligent than a bridge. It requires more time to determine a datapath, so its processing speed (the time it takes to forward data blocks, or packets) is typically slower than a bridge's. However, a bridge can't determine the most efficient datapath like a router can. The decision to use one or the other should be based on network needs and environment.

Brouters

A *brouter* is a communication device that functions as both a bridge and a router, depending on which function is needed. A brouter functions like a router, relaying data transmissions between networks. When it encounters a data unit that uses a protocol with which it is unfamiliar, it works like a bridge and forwards the data to the next segment by using a physical address. Because of this ability, you can use a brouter for networks on which there is mixed-protocol traffic and for networks that use protocols that do not support routing, such as NetBEUI.

Gateways

A *gateway* is a protocol converter that supports communication between networks that use different protocols. A gateway completely converts a message in one protocol to a message in a second protocol that is used on the destination network. A gateway allows different makes and models of computers on completely different networks to communicate with each other. For example, a gateway might connect PCs on a LAN to a mainframe. A mail gateway converts messages containing email to the protocol needed by the receiving station. Some common gateway types are described in Table 12-14.

Table 12-14: *Common Gateway Types*

Gateway Type	Connects Networks that Use Different
Protocol	Protocols
Format	Encoding schemes (for example, ASCII and EBCDIC)
Address	File systems and directory structures

Channel Service Unit/Digital Service Unit

Because the installation and upkeep of large quantities of transmission media can become very costly, you might choose to use a public or private service organization for your transmission media needs. By using one of these organizations, you can connect to their media and save yourself the installation and maintenance of your own. Sometimes public service organizations require their customers to use *Channel Service Units/Digital Service Units (CSU/DSU)* in the interest of safety. The units are designed to shield network users from electric voltages, as well as electrical interference. They also ready data for transmission by adhering to any network rules.

Both units are parts of a Data Communications Equipment (DCE) device and are collectively referred to as a CSU/DSU. A CSU/DSU operates like a modem, however, it is a digital-to-digital device rather than digital-to-analog. It readies digital signals and guarantees that they have sufficient strength and the proper format to be transmitted over digital WAN links. Typically, a CSU/DSU connects to a router or remote bridge.

Lesson 12

Firewalls

Firewalls control access between networks—both inbound traffic (entering your network) and outbound traffic (leaving your network). Firewalls can be used to prevent unauthorized access between intranets and the Internet or an extranet (an intranet external to your intranet). You can also configure firewalls to prevent access to other intranets within your company (for example, keeping marketing users out of the R&D intranet).

Controlling inbound access protects servers and resources on your intranet from access by unauthorized Internet users. Controlling outbound access can be used to limit your users' access to Internet resources (for example, allowing access only to work-related sites).

Firewalls contain packet-filtering routers, circuit gateways, application gateways, or a combination of these components. A combination is most effective because each component provides access control at different levels.

All-in-one Devices

Many companies combine the software and hardware capabilities of several network connection devices into one physical box. This reduces both the cost and the complexity of the network connections.

An example of a multi-function network appliance is the Intel InBusiness Small Office Network. It connects PCs and provides shared access to files, printers, and the Internet. This device includes an 8-port hub, 13 GB of storage space, POP3 client email, optional mirroring, built-in modem, two network adapter cards, firewall software, and embedded operating system, all in one box.

 Because new products appear daily, the Internet is the best source of current information on network connection devices.

Activity 12-7

Identifying the Purpose of Common Connection Devices

Activity Time:
5 minutes

Scenario:
In this activity, you will identify the purpose of common connection devices.

Lesson 12: Networking   **587**

Lesson 12

1. **Match the connection device with its functional description.**

   ___ Repeater   a. Connects several computers together at a central point.

   ___ Hub   b. Routes one protocol while bridging another.

   ___ Bridge   c. Determines the best path for sending data.

   ___ Router   d. Divides network into segments to increase performance.

   ___ Brouter   e. Connects dissimilar networks.

   ___ Gateway   f. Extends the maximum length of a network by amplifying signals.

TOPIC F

Troubleshoot Networks

In many companies, it is the responsibility of the hardware technician to determine if the network card and cable are working properly before the network administrator starts troubleshooting the network software and systems. The fact is that both the home and business users that you might support rely every day on their network connections for access to all types of information. So, in many cases, it will be your responsibility to correct local network connection problems. In this topic, you'll learn how to troubleshoot basic network problems that can occur at the client computers.

Common Network Problems

Users rely on being able to access files, Web sites, server applications, and networked hardware to do their jobs. When their connection to any of those networked resources is disrupted, they need to have it restored as soon as possible. Table 12-15 lists some of the common network problems and their possible causes.

Table 12-15: *Common Network Problems*

Problem	Possible Cause
User cannot connect to the network.	TCP/IP settings are incorrect. Ethernet frame type is incorrect. Network settings are incorrectly set.
User had a connection to the network, but during their work session, lost their connection.	Network hardware or software experienced a problem. Workstation network connection hardware is damaged. Cable became disconnected from workstation.
User is connected to the network, but cannot access desired resources.	User does not have access rights to the desired resource. Resource is experiencing a technical problem.

The Help And Support Center

The Windows XP Help And Support Center utility provides a unified way to access the local Help system as well as to get assistance from online sources. It also includes guided troubleshooting wizards to help you locate a problem. Through this utility you can view Help, perform diagnostics, use troubleshooters, ask for help from another user, post questions in online support groups, and more.

How to Troubleshoot NICs

Procedure Reference: Troubleshoot Network Interface Cards

Many of the problems associated with network interface cards can be traced back to a resource conflict or hardware failure. To identify problems associated with NICs:

1. If a user can start the computer but cannot connect to the network, verify that:
    - The computer has a NIC installed in it.
    - The right type of cable is plugged into the NIC and to an applicable connection device.
    - The correct network protocols are installed and are properly configured.
    - The NIC's link light is lit.
    - The user has followed the proper network logon procedures. If there is any question about this, restart the computer and try logging on again.
    - The network is functioning properly. Usually, if the network itself is the problem, you'll be getting many more than just one request for assistance.

2. If trying the quick fixes doesn't solve the problem:
    - Check for resource conflicts, especially if a new peripheral has been recently added to the computer. You can use either a diagnostic utility disk for the specific NIC type or Windows Device Manager. Both of these tools can help you find IRQ, DMA, and I/O address conflicts.
    - Verify that the correct device drivers are being loaded for the NIC and the network, particularly if the NIC's link light isn't on. Reinstall or update drivers as necessary.
    - Open the computer case and verify that the NIC is completely seated in the expansion slot. Like RAM chips and processors, expansion cards are susceptible to chip creep.
    - Use a loopback device to check communication. This gadget mimics a network and tells you if the NIC's firmware is functioning as expected.
    - Replace the suspect NIC with one that you know works properly. If possible, use the same brand and type as the original. If that's impossible, make sure that you have the appropriate installation disk available so that you can properly configure the new card.

How to Troubleshoot Networks

Procedure Reference: Troubleshoot Network Connections

To troubleshoot some of the common network connection problems:

1. Troubleshoot the network connection settings.

Lesson 12

- At another system, at a command prompt, run `ping` to verify that the network is up and to help isolate the problem. If multiple systems cannot connect, you will need to escalate the problem to the network administrator.
- At a command prompt, run `ipconfig` to display the basic TCP/IP configuration information for each network connection on the system. Use the `/all` switch to show complete information.
- From Control Panel, open Network And Internet Connections and display the properties of each connection object to verify the TCP/IP configuration. If the configuration is incorrect for your network, update it.

> Other operating systems use different commands rather than ipconfig. For example, Windows 95/98 use winipcfg and Linux uses ifconfig.

2. Troubleshoot the local system network connection hardware and cables.
   - The cable should be firmly connected to the network card and the wall, hub, router, or other connection to the network.
   - Verify that the correct cable is being used. Some cables look alike.
     — The TV cable and the Ethernet thin cable look similar, but the wire is different and the connectors might be different. A TV cable on a network connection might work sporadically or not at all.
     — A twisted pair cable comes in various categories. Most networks use Category 5 cable. Category 3 cable looks the same except that the casing says Cat 3 rather than Cat 5.
   - Run the diagnostics test for the network card. This is usually software that comes with the network card and is specific to that network card.
   - If necessary, replace the network cable.
   - If necessary, replace the network card.

3. Verify that the system can connect to the network. You should be able to log in and access resources. For example, if the network connection enables you to access the Internet, you can try the `ping` command to connect to a remote IP address or an Internet site. Be aware, however, that not all Internet sites are configured to respond to the `ping` command.

ACTIVITY 12-8

Troubleshooting a Network Connection

 It is possible that you will not need to perform all of the steps in this activity, or you might not be able to perform some steps. It will depend on the problem that the system is experiencing.

Scenario:

Alex Francis cannot connect to the local network or the Internet today. He is located at the Elmwood Place facility in cube 21. He needs to be able to access the ieee.org Web site to do some research. The network administrator has ruled out general network and server errors because all of the other users in the vicinity of his cube have been able to connect to the network.

Lesson 12

What You Do	How You Do It
1. Troubleshoot the network connection settings.	a. On the system experiencing problems, open a command prompt and enter *ping www.google.com* to verify that the system cannot connect to the Internet.

```
C:\>ping www.google.com
Unknown host www.google.com.
```

b. On a second system, open a command prompt and ping the IP address of the **system experiencing problems** to determine if you can reach the system over the local network.

c. On the second system, enter *ping www.google.com* to determine if the Internet access problem is limited to the first system.

```
C:\>ping www.google.com
Pinging www.google.com [216.239.33.99] with 32 bytes of data:
Reply from 216.239.33.99: bytes=32 time=101ms TTL=42
Reply from 216.239.33.99: bytes=32 time=90ms TTL=42
Reply from 216.239.33.99: bytes=32 time=90ms TTL=42
Reply from 216.239.33.99: bytes=32 time=90ms TTL=42

Ping statistics for 216.239.33.99:
    Packets: Sent = 4, Received = 4, Lost = 0 (0% loss),
Approximate round trip times in milli-seconds:
    Minimum = 90ms, Maximum = 101ms, Average = 92ms
```

d. On the system experiencing problems, open a command prompt window and enter *ipconfig* to verify that the network connection settings are correct.

e. If the network configuration settings are incorrect, **use the properties of the Local Area Connection object in Network And Internet Connections to correct the settings.**

f. **On the system you are troubleshooting,** enter *ping www.ieee.org* at a command prompt to see if the problem has been resolved.

2. **Troubleshoot the local system's network connection hardware and cabling.**

   a. Check that the network cable is firmly attached to the network card and to the network port.

   b. Verify that the correct cable is being used to connect to the network.

   c. If available, run the diagnostics test for the network card from the software for that particular network card.

   d. If necessary, **replace the network cable.**

   e. If necessary, **replace the network card.**

   f. At a command prompt, **enter** *ping www.ieee.org* to see if the problem has been resolved.

3. **Use the Help And Support Center to troubleshoot the network connection.**

   a. From the Start menu, choose Help And Support.

   b. Under Pick A Help Topic, **click Fixing A Problem.**

   c. **Click Networking Problems.**

   d. **Click Diagnose Network Configuration And Run Automated Networking Tests.**

   e. **Click Scan Your System.**

   ```
   Modems and Network Adapters
   ☐ Modems
   ⊞ Network Adapters    [00000011] MAC Bridge Miniport         PASSED
   ⊞ Network Clients
   ```

   f. **Expand Network Adapters and review the results.**

4. **Did the Network Diagnostics scan point to any problems?**

Lesson 12: Networking

Lesson 12

5. Correct any problems indicated by the diagnostic scan.	a. Correct the network configuration.
	b. Correct any hardware problems. Replace the network card if necessary.
	c. At a command prompt, enter *ping www.ieee.org* to see if the problem has been resolved.
6. Verify that the user can access the IEEE Web site.	a. From the Start menu, choose Internet to run Internet Explorer.
	b. In the Address bar, type *www.ieee.org*

Lesson 12 Follow-up

In this lesson, you learned how networks are classified based on geographical boundaries and the characteristics of different network topologies. You learned how different hardware of devices and network software enable communication on a network. plus identified the characteristics of Internet bandwidth technologies that are available for both home and business use. Finally, you learned how to troubleshoot common problems that can occur to prevent a PC from communicating on the network.

1. As an A+ technician at your company, what type of network architectures will you be supporting?

2. Will you be enabling Internet access on PCs? If so, through what connection method?

Lesson 13
Performing Preventative Maintenance

Lesson Time
2 hour(s)

Lesson Objectives:

In this lesson, you will perform preventative maintenance procedures.

You will:

- Maintain hard disks.
- Perform printer maintenance.
- Configure and test a UPS.
- Clean peripheral components.
- Clean the inside of the computer.
- Decide when to upgrade system hardware.
- Identify how to properly dispose of hazardous materials.

Lesson 13

Introduction

You have learned how to install, configure, and fix component problems with your PC. You can keep those components in good working condition by performing preventative maintenance. In this lesson, you will learn how to perform preventative maintenance procedures on the components of your PC.

One of the best ways to prevent problems with computer systems is to perform preventative maintenance on a regular schedule. It's similar to taking your car in for regular service—the mechanic can find and replace a worn belt before it breaks and leaves you stranded on the side of the road. In the same way, by performing periodic PC maintenance, you can help prevent system downtime cutting into the productivity of your users.

The following CompTIA A+ Core Hardware (2003) Examination objectives are covered in this lesson:

- Topic A:
  — 3.1 Identify the various types of preventative maintenance measures, products and procedures and when and how to use them. Content includes the following: hard disk maintenance—defragging, scan disk, and CHKDSK.

- Topic B:
  — 5.2 Recognize common printer problems and techniques used to resolve them. Content includes the following: preventative maintenance.

- Topic C:
  — 1.8 Identify proper procedures for installing and configuring common peripheral devices. Choose the appropriate installation or configuration sequence in given scenarios. Content includes the following: UPS and supressors.

- Topic D:
  — 3.1 Identify the various types of preventative maintenance measures, products and procedures and when and how to use them. Content includes the following: liquid cleaning compounds; connections; and cleaning monitors.

- Topic E:
  — 3.1 Identify the various types of preventative maintenance measures, products and procedures and when and how to use them. Content includes the following: liquid cleaning compounds; and non-static vacuums—chassis, power supplies, fans.

- Topic F:
  — 1.10 Determine the issues that must be considered when upgrading a PC. In a given scenario, determine when and how to upgrade system components. Components include: drivers for legacy devices; bus types and characteristics; cache in relationship to motherboards; memory, capacity, and characteristics; processor speed and compatibility; hard drive capacity and characteristics; system/firmware limitations; and power supply output capacity.
  — 4.3 Identify the most popular types of motherboards, their components, and their architecture (bus structures). Content includes the following: basic compatibility guidelines.

- Topic G:
  — 3.3 Identify environmental protection measures and procedures, and when/how to use them. Content includes the following: special disposal procedures that comply with environmental guidelines; batteries; CRTs; chemical solvents and cans; and MSDS (material safety data sheet).

— 5.2 Recognize common printer problems and techniques used to resolve them. Content includes the following: consumables and environment.

TOPIC A
Maintain the Hard Disk

An improperly maintained hard disk can cause a host of problems, including slow performance and system crashes. Maintaining the disks properly prevents disk problems that can lead to lost data, unhappy users, and lots of support calls. Simple regular maintenance procedures will not only avert these problems, but also keep your hard disks running at an optimum performance level. In this topic, you'll learn how to perform hard disk maintenance.

Fragmentation

The Windows operating systems do not write a file to disk as a single large block. Instead, they break up the file into smaller pieces. When Windows writes these smaller pieces to the disk, it tries to write them close together so that the disk can retrieve the file quickly whenever a user opens it. As a disk fills up and files are added and removed, it becomes harder for Windows to find enough contiguous space to write all the pieces of a file. As a result, Windows ends up writing the file wherever it can find free space on a disk. The end result is that files can become fragmented, meaning their pieces can be spread out all over the disk. The greater the amount of *fragmentation*, the more work the operating system must perform to retrieve and write files. You can counteract fragmentation by defragmenting a computer's hard disk. In Windows 9x, Windows 2000, Windows Me, Windows Server 2003, and Windows XP products, you defragment a computer's hard disk using the Disk Defragmenter tool.

Hard Disk Maintenance Tools

There are several software tools included with the Windows operating system products that you can use to manage and maintain hard disks. Table 13-1 describes the common hard disk maintenance tools included with the Windows family of operating systems.

Table 13-1: *Hard Disk Maintenance Tools*

Tools	Operating System	Description
Chkdsk.exe	Windows 9x, Windows NT 4.0, Windows 2000, and Windows XP	A command-line tool that enables you to check the hard disk for bad sectors or errors in the file system and then attempt to repair any errors found. Bad sectors or errors in the file system can cause data loss and intermittent system crashes.
Check Disk	Windows 2000 and Windows XP	A graphical Windows version of the Chkdsk.exe tool.
Disk Defragmenter	Windows 9x, Windows 2000, and Windows XP	Defragments the hard disk by locating fragmented files and moving the pieces of each file or folder to one location on the volume, so each file then occupies a single, contiguous space on the disk. Seriously fragmented files (more than 5-10 percent fragmentation) can slow down a hard drive.

Lesson 13

Tools	Operating System	Description
Scan Disk (Scandisk.exe)	Windows 9x	Automatically corrects damaged files and helps you regain unused disk space. Checks your hard disk for physical errors. If the error occurs in a data storage area, it will relocate the data and mark off the damaged area so that no further data is stored there. Checks files and folders for invalid file names, dates, or times. Detects "lost file fragments." You may either have them automatically deleted or converted to files for viewing.

How to Maintain the Hard Disk

Procedure Reference: Check for Hard Disk Errors Using the Command Line in Windows 9x, Windows NT 4.0, Windows 2000, and Windows XP

To check a hard disk for errors in Windows 9x, Windows NT Workstation 4.0, Windows 2000, and Windows XP:

1. Open a Command Prompt window.

2. At the command prompt, enter `chkdsk volume:`, where `volume:` is the volume you want to scan.

   When entering a drive, you must use the colon. Entering just `chkdsk` will display statistics for the current drive. You may also use any of the `chkdisk` switches. See Table 13-2.

3. If you choose to fix errors using the /f switch, enter the appropriate choice to schedule Chkdsk to run at the next system restart.

4. If necessary, restart the computer.

5. If any errors are found, that information will be displayed. Read the resulting report.

Chkdsk Switches

Table 13-2 lists and describes switches for the `chkdsk` command.

Table 13-2: *Chkdsk Switches*

Switch	Description
filename	On a FAT volume, specifies the file you want to check for fragmentation.
/f	Specifies that you want to fix errors.
/v	On FAT and FAT32 volumes, will output the file name and path for every file on the disk.
/r	Used with /f, recovers readable information from bad sectors.
/l:size	On NTFS volumes, lets you set the size of the log file in KB.

Switch	Description
/x	Used with /f, this switch forces a volume to dismount before it's checked.
/i	On NTFS volumes, reduces scan time by scaling back the check of index entries.
/c	On NTFS volumes, reduces scan time by scaling back the check of folders.

Procedure Reference: Check for Hard Disk Errors in Windows 2000 & Windows XP

To check for hard disk errors in Windows 2000 and Windows XP:

1. Open My Computer or Windows Explorer.
2. Right-click the drive you want to check and choose Properties.
3. Select the Tools tab.
4. In the Error-Checking section, click Check Now.
5. In the Check Disk dialog box, you can choose whether to automatically fix errors and whether to try to recover bad sectors. Click Start.
6. Read the resulting report.

Procedure Reference: Defragment a Hard Disk in Windows 9x

To defragment a drive in Windows 9x:

1. Choose Start→Programs→Accessories→System Tools→Disk Defragmenter.
2. In the Select Drive dialog box, select the drive you want to defragment.
3. If desired, customize the defragmentation settings.
   - In Windows 95, click the Advanced button if you want to change the settings of the defragmentation utility from the default. Click OK.
   - In Windows 98, click the Settings button if you want to change the settings of the defragmentation utility from the default. Click OK.
4. Click OK.
5. Select the level of defragmentation detail you want to see.
   - If you want to see the details of the defragmentation process on your hard disk, click Show Details.
   - Click Hide Details to show only the summary information.
6. Click Yes to close Disk Defragmenter when the defragmentation process is complete.

Procedure Reference: Defragment a Hard Disk in Windows 2000 and Windows XP

To defragment a hard disk in Windows 2000 and Windows XP:

1. Log on as a local administrator.
2. From the Start menu, choose Programs→Accessories→System Tools→Disk Defragmenter.

3. In the top pane of the Disk Defragmenter window, select the disk you want to defragment.

4. If you want to analyze the fragmentation state of the disk before defragmenting, click Analyze.

5. After the analysis, you will see a message box with a recommendation as to whether you should defragment or not. This recommendation is made based on a Disk Defragmenter algorithm, rather than a specific fragmentation level, but it is common practice to defragment disks that are more than five percent fragmented.

   Click View Report to see details of the fragmentation state of the disk.

6. To begin the defragmentation, in the Analysis Report dialog box, or in the Disk Defragmenter window itself, click Defragment in the analysis message box. Disk Defragmenter will reanalyze the disk and begin the defragmentation. You can view the progress in the progress bar.

   Defragmentation of a large, highly fragmented, and very full disk can take several hours.

7. When the defragmentation is complete, you can click View Report to see detailed information about the defragmentation.

Procedure Reference: Run ScanDisk in Windows 98

To run ScanDisk in Windows 98:

1. Choose Start→Programs→Accessories→System Tools→ScanDisk.

2. Select the drive you want to check for errors.

3. Choose the type of test you want to perform.
   - Standard will check files and folders for errors.
   - Thorough performs a Standard test and also scans the disk surface for errors.

4. If you want ScanDisk to automatically fix errors it finds, select Automatically Fix Errors.

5. Click Start.

6. Read the resulting report and click Close when you're done.

ACTIVITY 13-1

Defragmenting a Hard Disk

Scenario:
One of your clients is complaining that his hard disk in his Windows XP computer is very slow. He says that he can hear the hard disk "crunching away" whenever he attempts to save a file to the hard disk. He's asked you to do what you can to resolve the problem.

What You Do	How You Do It
1. Run Chkdsk on the hard disk to scan for file-system errors.	a. Choose Start→Run, and enter *cmd* to open a Command Prompt window. b. Enter *chkdsk c:* c. To close the command prompt window, enter *exit*
2. Did you find any errors on your drive?	
3. Analyze the fragmentation on the hard disk.	a. On the Start menu, **choose All Programs→Accessories→System Tools→ Disk Defragmenter.** b. In the Volume list, **select the C drive.** c. **Click Analyze.** d. In the Disk Defragmenter message box, **click View Report.** e. In the Volume Information area, **scroll to the Volume Fragmentation statistics.** You can determine the overall fragmentation percentage here. f. In the Most Fragmented Files list, **click the Fragments column heading** to sort by this column. The larger files have the greatest amount of fragmentation. g. **Click Close.**
4. Based on the analysis you see in the report, should you defragment this disk?	

Lesson 13: Performing Preventative Maintenance

Lesson 13

5. **Defragment the disk.**

   a. **Click Defragment.** The information displayed in Disk Defragmenter and the status bar changes as the defragmentation progresses.

   📌 If you don't want to take the time for defragmentation to complete, click Stop.

   b. **Close Disk Defragmenter.**

Topic B

Perform Printer Maintenance

Printers are a very common peripheral device in both home and business computing environments. Once you set up a printer, you need to keep it working well. One way to do that is to have a maintenance schedule and clean your printers regularly. Jammed paper, streaky printouts, and low toner are some of the printer service calls you will receive. To avoid these types of calls and keep your printers in good working condition, be proactive in performing regular printer maintenance. In this topic, you will learn how to perform printer maintenance.

Cleaning Compounds and Materials

Cleaning materials for computers range from standard household cleaning supplies to supplies specifically designed for computers and electronics. Table 13-3 lists the cleaning supplies that you can use to clean computers and electronics.

Table 13-3: *Computer Cleaning Supplies*

Cleaning Supply	Description
Monitor cleaning wipes	Alcohol-based, lint-free, pre-moistened wipes for cleaning monitor screens. These should be used only on CRT or TV monitors and not on plastic-coated LCD screens.
Keyboard cleaning wipes	Pre-moistened wipes for cleaning keyboards.
Lint-free cloths	If you choose not to use pre-moistened wipes, you can use rubbing alcohol applied to a lint-free cloth to wipe down screens and keyboards. They can also be used to clean other peripherals.
Rubbing alcohol	Used with cotton swaps or lint-free cloths, this is a useful solution for cleaning many peripherals.
Mild household cleaner	Keeping the exterior of peripherals clean helps prevent dirt and debris from getting inside the equipment. (Never spray directly on the equipment. Avoid using ammonia-based cleaners around laser printers; the ammonia may react chemically with the toner.)

Cleaning Supply	Description
Cotton swabs	Tightly wound cotton swabs are useful in getting cleaning solution into tight places. They are also useful when used dry to get dust and debris out from between keys and around buttons or other tight areas.
Window cleaner	Standard household window cleaner can be used if sprayed on a lint-free cloth first. Be sure to use it only on glass screens and not on plastic-based screens.
Toothpicks	Toothpicks come in handy in getting dirt out from around keys, buttons, and other tight spaces. They are also useful for removing the gunk that builds up on the rollers in a mouse. Another use for toothpicks is for when you are trying to retrieve jumpers that have fallen onto the motherboard.
Artist's paint brush	A small paint brush can be used to remove dust from between keys on a keyboard. If the brush has long bristles, they can reach under the keys where other cleaning objects would not be able to reach.
Compressed air canister	A canister with a nozzle that can be aimed at components to blow dust out. This is often used when removing dust from the interior of a computer. Be sure to blow the dust away from the power supply and drives. It can also be used to blow dust out of the power supply fan area, from keyboards, and from the ventilation holes on other peripherals.
Computer or electronics vacuum	A computer or electronics vacuum is a non-static vacuum that can be used on the chassis, the power supply, fans, and in printers. Regular vacuum cleaners can create static, which will damage computer equipment. It should have a filter and bag fine enough to contain toner particles so that you can use it to clean up toner spills from laser printers or photocopiers. These vacuums can often be used to blow as well as suck, so they can replace the need for compressed air canisters for blowing dust out of machines. Sucking the dust up is usually better, though, since blowing the dust can cause it to get onto or into other components. Sucking it up into a vacuum cleaner bag gets it out of the system without the chance of it getting into something else.
Toner cloth	A special cloth that you stretch that picks up toner particles that are either in the printer or around the printer. Be careful if using it inside the printer so that the cloth doesn't get caught on any components, leaving fibers behind.
Mask	A mask that fits over your mouth and nose should be worn when using a compressed air canister or working around toner spills. This will keep the particles out of your body.
Latex gloves	You should wear latex gloves when cleaning up a toner spill.

Lesson 13

How to Perform Printer Maintenance

Procedure Reference: Maintain Dot-matrix Printers

To maintain a dot-matrix printer:

1. Print a test page to verify that the ribbon prints satisfactorily.
2. If necessary, replace the printer ribbon based on the results of the previous step.
3. If the test print shows indications of printhead wear or damage, make arrangements to repair or replace the printhead or printer.
4. Verify that there is enough paper for a day's printing. If necessary, have extra paper available for users to install.
5. Using compressed air or a printer vacuum, remove the dust and paper bits from the inside of the printer. You can also use toothpicks, artist's paint brushes, or cotton swabs to assist in removing debris from the printer.
6. Use tweezers to remove any paper caught in the paper feed mechanism. Rolling a manila folder through the paper path also works to remove bits of paper caught in the paper path.
7. Use mild household cleaner to wipe down the exterior of the printer case.

Procedure Reference: Maintain Inkjet Printers

To maintain an inkjet printer:

1. Print a test page to verify that the printer prints satisfactorily.
2. If necessary, replace the ink cartridges based on the results of the previous step.
3. If the test print shows indications of printhead wear or damage, make arrangements to repair or replace the printhead or printer.
4. Verify that there is enough paper for a day's printing. If necessary, have extra paper available for a user to add.
5. Using compressed air or a printer vacuum, remove the dust and paper bits from the inside of the printer. You can also use toothpicks, artist's paint brushes, or cotton swabs to assist in removing debris from the printer.
6. Use tweezers to remove any paper caught in the paper feed mechanism.
7. Use mild household cleaner to wipe down the exterior of the printer case.
8. Place an inkjet cleaning sheet in the paper tray. Using the form feed button(s), send the paper through the paper path. This assists you in cleaning the paper path from excess ink and other debris.

Procedure Reference: Maintain a Laser Printer

To maintain a laser printer:

1. Print a test page to verify that the printer prints satisfactorily.
2. If necessary, replace the toner, drum, or other printer components based on the results of the previous step. The components that need replacing will vary depending on the printer. Refer to printer documentation for which component might cause poor print quality as seen on the test printout. Documentation will also show you how to replace the worn component.

3. Verify that there is enough paper for a day's printing. If necessary, have extra paper available for a user to install.

4. Using compressed air or a printer vacuum, remove the dust and paper bits from the inside of the printer. You can also use toothpicks, artist's paint brushes, or cotton swabs to assist in removing debris from the printer.

   ⚠ Only use specially designed laser printer vacuums so you don't reverse the polarity of the electrons on the drum.

   Don't use compressed air if there is a toner spill. This will just spread the toner around, making it harder to clean up and possibly getting it into other parts of the printer.

5. Verify that the fan is working properly and is not clogged. Without the fan, the printer can overheat.

6. Clean the corona wires and check the fuser wand and ozone filter each time you replace the toner.

7. The rollers can be cleaned with alcohol. They get dirty over time and can leave marks on the paper if they are not cleaned.

8. Use tweezers to remove any paper caught in the paper feed mechanism.

9. Use mild household cleaner to wipe down the exterior of the printer case.

10. Place a laser printer cleaning sheet in the paper tray and use the form feed button(s) to send it through the paper path.

Procedure Reference: Maintain a Solid Ink Printer

To maintain a solid ink printer:

1. Print a test page to verify that the printer prints satisfactorily.

2. If necessary, replace the ink sticks based on the results of the previous step. Follow the manufacturer's instructions to replace the solid ink supply.

3. If the test print shows indications of printhead wear or damage, make arrangements to repair or replace the printhead or printer.

4. Verify that there is enough paper for a day's printing. If necessary, have extra paper available for a user to install.

5. Using compressed air or a printer vacuum, remove the dust and paper bits from the inside of the printer. You can also use toothpicks, artist's paint brushes, or cotton swabs to assist in removing debris from the printer.

6. Use tweezers to remove any paper caught in the paper feed mechanism.

7. Use mild household cleaner to wipe down the exterior of the printer case.

Procedure Reference: Maintain a Dye Sublimation Printer

To maintain a dye sublimation printer:

1. Print a test page to verify that the printer prints satisfactorily.

2. If necessary, replace the dye sheets based on the results of the previous step. Follow the manufacturer's instructions to replace the dye sheets.

3. Verify that there is enough paper for the expected workload. If necessary, have extra paper available for a user to install.

Lesson 13

4. Using compressed air or a printer vacuum, remove the dust and paper bits from the inside of the printer.

5. Use mild household cleaner to wipe down the exterior of the printer case.

Printer Safety

While maintaining printers, there are some important safety tips to keep in mind:

- Be careful not to touch some of the internal elements inside inkjet and laser printers. These elements can be very hot and can cause burns.
- Use caution when disposing of used printer supplies; some items are combustible.
- Treat any fire in a printer as an electrical fire; do not try to extinguish it with water or foam.
- Excessive exposure to toner can cause respiratory or skin irritation.
- Plug printers only into appropriately grounded outlets.

ACTIVITY 13-2

Maintaining Printers

Setup:

To complete this activity, you will need:

- A compressed air canister.
- A printer vacuum.
- Tweezers.
- A lens cloth.
- A mild household cleaning solution.
- A lint-free cloth.
- Toothpicks.
- An artist's paint brush.
- Cotton swabs.
- Printer cleaning sheets to run through the paper path.
- Replacement parts, ribbons, ink cartridges, toner cartridges, and cleaning supplies that correspond to the manufacturer of the printer you are going to perform maintenance on.

Scenario:

Your company developed a schedule for maintaining printers. The following table documents what procedures need to be completed for each type of printer and how often it needs to be performed. It is the end of the quarter.

Lesson 13

Frequency	Tasks to be Performed
Daily	Check consumables such as ink, ribbons, and paper. Print a test page to verify that the print quality is acceptable.
Monthly	Surface dust and debris removal.
Quarterly	Cleaning of the entire printer.

What You Do	How You Do It
1. If your printer is a dot-matrix printer, perform the appropriate preventative maintenance for a dot-matrix printer.	a. **Print a test page** to verify that the ribbon prints satisfactorily.
	b. Based on the results of the previous step, if necessary, **replace the printer ribbon**.
	c. **Verify that there is enough paper for a day's printing.** If necessary, have extra paper available for users to install.
	d. **Use the compressed air canister and/or vacuum to remove dust and paper bits from the inside of the printer.**
	e. **Use tweezers to remove any paper caught in the paper feed mechanism.**
	f. **Use a mild household cleaner to wipe down the exterior of the printer case.**

Lesson 13: Performing Preventative Maintenance

Lesson 13

2. If your printer is an inkjet printer, **perform the appropriate preventative maintenance for an inkjet printer.**

    a. **Print a test page** to verify that the printer prints satisfactorily.

    b. Based on the results of the previous step, if necessary, **replace ink cartridges.**

    c. **Verify that there is enough paper for a day's printing.** If necessary, have extra paper available for users to install.

    d. **Use the compressed air canister and/or vacuum to remove dust and paper bits from the inside of the printer.**

    e. **Use tweezers to remove any paper caught in the paper feed mechanism.**

    f. **Use a mild household cleaner to wipe down the exterior of the printer case.**

    g. **Place an inkjet cleaning sheet in the paper tray and use the form feed button(s) to send it through the paper path.**

Lesson 13

3. If your printer is a laser printer, **perform the appropriate preventative maintenance for a laser printer.**

   a. **Print a test page** to verify that the printer prints satisfactorily.

   b. Based on the results of the previous step, if necessary, **replace the toner cartridge.**

   Follow the directions to replace any other components that need to be replaced, and reset any counters as needed.

   c. **Verify that there is enough paper for a day's printing.** If necessary, have extra paper available for users to install.

   d. **Use the compressed air canister and/or vacuum to remove dust and paper bits from the inside of the printer.**

   e. **Use tweezers to remove any paper caught in the paper feed mechanism.**

   f. **Use a mild household cleaner to wipe down the exterior of the printer case.**

   g. **Place a laser printer cleaning sheet in the paper tray and use the form feed button(s) to send it through the paper path.**

4. When performing preventative maintenance on a laser printer, why is it important to use a specially designed laser printer vacuum?

5. Which preventative maintenance steps apply to all printer types?

   a) Print a test page to verify that the printer prints satisfactorily.

   b) Verify that there is enough paper for a day's printing.

   c) Clean the rollers with alcohol.

   d) Use mild household cleaner to wipe down the exterior of the printer case.

   e) Verify that the fan is working properly and is not clogged.

6. **True or False? Printer fires should be extinguished with foam.**
   ___ True
   ___ False

Lesson 13

Topic C

Use a UPS

So far you have set up PCs assuming that there will be electrical power available for users to be able to boot without errors and for the computer to function properly. In some locations, this assumption is frequently challenged by brief (and not so brief) power outages. In this topic, you will learn how you to configure and test an Uninterruptible Power Supply (UPS) that can provide power to your equipment when the power goes out.

UPS

Definition:

An *Uninterruptible Power Supply (UPS)* is a battery-operated device that is intended to save computer components from damage due to power problems such as power failures, spikes, and sags. Computer systems require a steady supply of electricity. Interrupts in that power can cause your systems to fail. All UPSs:

- Use battery power to supply power to the devices connected to the UPS.
- Can be configured through the operating system as to what happens when there is a power failure.
- Keep the computer powered up long enough for you to perform an orderly shutdown of the operating system.
- Have a method for testing that the UPS works properly.

UPSs vary in that:

- They can be online or standby.
  - An online UPS powers your equipment from their batteries at all times.
  - A standby UPS powers your equipment only when the wall outlet power fails completely.
- Some can keep connected components powered longer than others.
- Some have more software configuration options.
- Most connect to a hardware interface on the computer such as the USB or serial port. This enables the UPS and the computer to work together in monitoring the available power and shutting down the computer.
- Some are rated on their switching time. This is the time it takes to switch from wall voltage to the battery during a power anomaly.
- They can use different software interfaces to configure UPS settings.
  - A UPS installed on COM1 or COM2 can normally be configured using the Power Options tool in the Windows Control Panel.
  - A UPS installed on a USB port or some other port is normally configured using the software that came with the UPS. The documentation that came with the UPS will provide configuration instructions.

Example: Online UPS

An *online UPS* supplies power to your systems from its batteries at all times. Figure 13-1 shows an example of an online UPS. Power from the normal electrical system is used to constantly charge the batteries. Online UPSs usually supply cleaner battery power than standby UPSs. The batteries usually don't last as long as standby UPS batteries.

Online UPSs generally filter power to reduce or remove power spikes. Since online UPSs supply power from the battery at all times, they can prevent power sags.

Example: Standby UPS

A *Standby UPS* (SUPS) uses a battery to supply power when a power problem occurs. At times of normal power operation, power is supplied from the normal electrical system. This method places minimal burden on the batteries and power inverters in the UPS, leading to longer UPS life. These UPSs are rated on their switching time since their batteries are in use only when the regular power is unavailable.

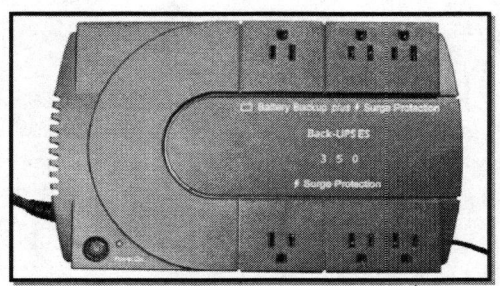

Figure 13-1: *A standby UPS.*

Non-Example: Surge Suppressor

A surge suppressor is not a UPS. While it is meant to help protect components from power spikes, it does not protect components from power failures or sags, nor does it provide a steady supply of electricity. It also doesn't provide power to components in the case of a power failure.

Determining UPS Size Needs

To determine the size of UPS you need, you can use one of the following techniques:

- Perform a manual calculation.
    1. Multiply the volts by amps for each device you will connect to the UPS.
    2. Add together the results of each device in step 1.
    3. Purchase this size UPS.
- Use the tool found on most UPS manufacturers' Web sites to determine the size you need. By filling out a form about the equipment you will be plugging into the UPS, the tool will recommend the manufacturer's UPSs that meet your needs.

Lesson 13

How to Use a UPS

Procedure Reference: Configure and Test a UPS in Windows

To configure and test a UPS by using the Power Options tool in Windows:

1. Set up the UPS.
   a. If necessary, connect the battery in the UPS.
   b. Plug the UPS directly into the wall. Do not plug the UPS into a surge suppressor or power strip.
   c. Plug the computer components you want to be powered through the UPS into the UPS.
2. Configure the steps that will be taken when a power failure occurs.
   a. Open Control Panel.
   b. Click Performance And Maintenance.
   c. Click Power Options.
   d. Display the appropriate page of the dialog box to configure the settings.
      - If the UPS tab appears, click it to display the UPS page.
      - If other power-specific tabs appear instead of the UPS tab, such as Alarms or Power Meter, select the appropriate tab to configure each of the UPS settings.
   e. If there is a UPS page, in the Details section of the UPS page, click Select and select the manufacturer and model of the UPS.
   f. If there is a UPS page, click Configure.
   g. Configure the UPS settings.
      - Configure alarm settings to indicate how you want to be notified of a power failure and how often.
      - If desired, configure the UPS to run a program before shutting down the computer.
      - Configure whether the UPS should put the computer in standby mode or shut the computer down completely.
   h. Click OK as needed to apply your changes and close the Power Options Properties dialog box.
3. Test the UPS. You can:
   - Unplug the UPS from the wall and verify that the components remain powered. If you configured it to run a specific program, shut down the computer, or put it in to hibernation, you can leave it unplugged until this occurs if you want to test that feature as well. When you are done testing, plug the UPS back into the wall.
   - Most models have a Test button. Press the Test button to verify that the UPS can power the components plugged into the UPS.

Other Configuration Methods

If the UPS settings are not available through the Power Options dialog box, you will need to use the software that came with the UPS to configure it. See your UPS documentation for information and procedures.

ACTIVITY 13-3

Using a UPS

Setup:
To complete this activity, you will need a UPS.

Scenario:
There are periodic power outages at your customer's site due to old power lines and high winds. They have had several corrupted files due to power loss. They have purchased a UPS and have contracted with you to install and test it for them.

What You Do	How You Do It
1. Set up the UPS to power a computer system.	a. If necessary, **connect the battery in the UPS**.
	b. **Plug the UPS into the power outlet.**
	c. **Shut down each of the components that will be powered through the UPS.**
	d. **Unplug the components from the wall or surge protector, and then plug them into the UPS.**
	e. If your UPS is equipped with a cable to connect to a peripheral port on your computer, **connect the UPS to the USB or COM port.**

Lesson 13

2. **Configure what happens when the UPS encounters a power failure.**

   a. From the Start menu, **choose Control Panel→Power Options.**

   b. If available, **click the UPS tab.**

   If no UPS tab is displayed, **click the tab related to UPS configuration.**

   c. If necessary, **configure the UPS port, manufacturer, and model.**

   d. Following the directions that came with your UPS, or using the UPS tab in the Power Options Properties dialog box, **configure the computer to sound an alarm as soon as there is a power failure and to repeat it every minute.**

   e. **Configure the settings to perform a shutdown when the critical alarm threshold is reached.**

3. **Test the UPS.**

   a. **Turn on the components** to make sure they can be powered through the UPS.

   b. When all of the components plugged into the UPS have come up to the functional state, **unplug the UPS from the power outlet** to simulate a power outage. All equipment should remain on with no blips in power.

   c. **Plug the UPS back into the wall outlet.**

   d. If your UPS is equipped with a Test button, **press the Test button.**

Topic D

Clean Peripheral Components

Keyboards, mice, and monitors are always getting dirty—fingerprints on monitors, crumbs in keyboards, and gunk in mice all contribute to this problem. If you want peripherals to stay clean, you would have to leave them in their boxes. Unfortunately, your users won't get any work done that way! By routinely cleaning your peripheral devices, you can help prevent these components from functioning poorly or failing completely. In this topic, you will identify the materials used to clean these peripherals and perform basic peripheral cleaning procedures.

How to Clean Peripheral Components

Procedure Reference: Clean Peripherals

To clean peripherals:

1. Clean the keyboard using compressed air, an artist's paint brush or business card, toothpicks, and rubbing alcohol.

2. Before cleaning the mouse, shut down the system and unplug the mouse.

3. Clean the mouse by removing the ball and cleaning the rollers with rubbing alcohol, toothpicks, and the mouse interior with compressed air.

4. Turn on the power and test the mouse.

5. Before cleaning the CRT monitor, shut down the system, turn off the monitor, and unplug the monitor cable and power cord.

6. Clean the CRT monitor by spraying glass cleaner on a lint-free cloth, and then wiping the glass. Clean the vents using a small vacuum.

7. Turn on the power and test the monitor.

8. Before cleaning a PDA, turn it off.

9. Clean PDAs using a lint-free cloth to wipe the screen and lint-free cloth dampened with rubbing alcohol to wipe down the entire PDA.

10. Turn on the PDA and test it.

11. Before cleaning a scanner, turn it off.

12. Clean scanners by spraying glass cleaner on a lint-free cloth, and then wiping the glass. Wipe the exterior with a lint-free cloth dampened with household cleaner.

13. Turn on the scanner and test it.

14. Clean contacts and connections with a lint-free cloth or an artist's paint brush.

Lesson 13

Activity 13-4

Cleaning Peripherals

Setup:

To complete this activity, you will need a cleaning kit consisting of:

- Monitor cleaning wipes
- Keyboard cleaning wipes
- Lint-free cloths
- Rubbing alcohol
- A mild household cleaner
- Cotton swabs (tightly wound)
- Lens cloth
- Window cleaner
- Toothpicks
- Artist's paint brush
- Compressed air canisters
- Computer vacuum

Scenario:

In an effort to cut down on the number of peripheral problems that have been occurring, your company has decided to perform preventative maintenance on peripherals each month. As one of the junior members of the support team, you have been assigned the task of cleaning the department's keyboards, mice, and monitors at the beginning of each month. If users have PDAs or scanners, you are also to clean those peripherals.

 Your instructor will provide you with a peripheral device or multiple peripheral devices to clean.

Lesson 13

What You Do	How You Do It
1. If you have a keyboard, **clean the keyboard.**	a. Shut down the system and unplug the keyboard.
	b. **Turn the keyboard upside down and gently shake it** to remove debris from under the keys.
	c. **Spray compressed air under the keys** to dislodge particles of dust and dirt.
	d. **Drag a small paint brush or a business card between the keys to remove any particles left behind.**
	e. **Wipe each key with keyboard wipes or a soft cloth with rubbing alcohol applied to it.**
	f. **Reconnect the keyboard and restart the system.**
	g. **Verify that all of the keys work.**

Lesson 13

2. If you have a mouse, **clean the mouse.**

   a. **Shut down the system and unplug the mouse.**

   b. **Turn the mouse upside down and rotate the cover** to unlatch it. Rotate the cover in the direction indicated on your mouse.

   c. **Place your hand over the cover and ball, and then turn the mouse right side up and the cover and ball should drop out into your hand.** If they don't drop out, gently shake the mouse. If they still don't drop out, make sure that the cover has been turned far enough to unlatch it.

   d. Using a toothpick or your fingernail, **scrape off the line of dirt on each roller.** There should be three rollers and the dirt is usually in the center of each roller.

   e. **Spray compressed air into the mouse** to remove any remaining debris, including the debris you scraped off the rollers.

   f. **Wipe the ball, inside, outside, and the cord of the mouse with mouse cleaning wipes or a soft cloth dampened with rubbing alcohol.**

   g. **Place the ball back inside the mouse.**

   h. **Place the cover over the mouse and rotate it until it locks in place.**

   i. **Reattach the mouse and restart the system.**

   j. **Verify that all of the mouse functions work.**

Lesson 13

3. If you have a monitor, **clean the monitor.**

   ⚠ If you have an LCD monitor, do not use window cleaner on it. Instead, you should use a lint-free cloth to wipe the screen. If more cleaning power is needed, dampen the cloth with rubbing alcohol and wipe the screen.

   a. **Shut down the system, turn off the monitor, and unplug the monitor cable and power cord.**

   b. **Spray glass cleaner on a lint-free cloth.** Alternatively, you can use specially prepared wet monitor wipes and drying wipes.

   c. **Wipe the monitor screen using the cloth.**

   d. **Vacuum the exterior or wipe with a cloth dampened with a mild household cleaner** to remove dust and debris from the case.

   e. **Reconnect the monitor to the system and plug it back in.**

   f. **Restart the system and verify that the monitor works.**

4. If you have a PDA, **clean the PDA.**

   a. **Turn off the PDA.**

   b. **Dampen a lint-free cloth with rubbing alcohol and wipe the PDA screen.**

   c. **Dampen a lint-free cloth with a mild household cleaner and wipe down the rest of the PDA.**

   d. **Turn on the PDA and verify that it works properly.**

Lesson 13

5. If you have a scanner, **clean the scanner.**

   a. Turn off the scanner, disconnect it from the system, and unplug it from the power outlet.

   b. Dampen a lint-free cloth with rubbing alcohol and wipe the scanner glass.

   c. Dampen a lint-free cloth with a mild household cleaner and wipe down the rest of the scanner.

   d. Reconnect the scanner to the system and plug it back in.

   e. Verify that the scanner works properly.

Topic E

Clean Internal System Components

It is not enough to clean just peripherals and the outside of computer cases. Lint, dust, hair, and other contaminants are likely to find their way inside users' systems over time. Keeping foreign bodies out of systems is easier in a clean office environment than it is in a home with several pets or out on a factory floor, but all systems eventually accumulate some internal debris. The openings in the case and around the fan seem to draw particulate matter into the system as if they were iron filings being drawn to a magnet. By taking the time to remove this material from a system, you can help prolong the system life and reduce the number of trouble calls you get. In this topic, you will learn how to clean internal system components.

How to Clean Internal System Components

Procedure Reference: Clean the Internal System Components

To clean internal system components:

1. Clean the case with a damp lint-free cloth.

2. Remove the case cover.

3. Clean the system board using a compressed air canister and computer vacuum.
   - Try to hold the case at an angle with the back corner.
   - Blow the air so the dust is blown away from the drives and power supply.
   - If it is extremely dusty, you might want to wear a mask over your mouth and nose since the dust particles will fly up when you spray the compressed air.

4. Clean the CD-ROM drive using a CD-ROM cleaning kit and following the directions it comes with.

5. Clean the floppy drive using a floppy drive cleaning kit and following the directions it comes with.

6. Clean removable media drives using the cleaning kit that is compatible with the drive and following the directions it comes with.

> ⚠ Iomega Zip and Jaz drives should not be cleaned. This will damage the drives. Imation SuperDrives can be cleaned. If a removable drive is cleanable, the manufacturer will sell an approved cleaning kit.

ACTIVITY 13-5

Cleaning Internal System Components

Setup:
To complete this activity, you will need a cleaning kit consisting of:
- Monitor cleaning wipes
- Keyboard cleaning wipes
- Lint-free cloths
- Rubbing alcohol
- A mild household cleaner
- Cotton swabs (tightly wound)
- Lens cloth
- Window cleaner
- Toothpicks
- Artist's paint brush
- Compressed air canisters
- Computer vacuum
- CD-ROM cleaning kit
- Floppy drive cleaning kit
- Manufacturer-approved removable drive cleaning kit

Scenario:
To help prevent system problems, a yearly preventative maintenance plan has been put in place to clean the internal system components. This includes the system board, drives, and any adapter cards.

Lesson 13

What You Do	How You Do It
1. If you have a complete PC to clean, **clean the case.**	a. Shut down the system, and then unplug the peripherals and the power cord.
	b. Remove the cover from the system.
	c. **Wipe the case with a water-dampened, lint-free cloth.** If the case requires additional cleaning power, use a mild household cleaner on the cloth instead of water.
2. If you have a system board, **clean the system board.**	a. Position the system so that you can hold the compressed air canister upright.
	b. Spray the compressed air so that you blow the dust and debris off the system board and out of the case.
	c. If you have a computer-safe vacuum, **vacuum any remaining particles from inside the system, being careful not to suck up any jumpers or other components.**
	d. Reattach the case cover.
	e. Reconnect the external devices and power cord.
3. If you have a CD-ROM drive, **clean the CD-ROM drive.** ⚠ Refer to the instructions that come with your cleaning kit and use those steps if they are different from those listed here.	a. Power on the system.
	b. Insert the CD-ROM cleaner disk in the drive.
	c. Access the CD-ROM drive.
	d. Remove the CD-ROM cleaner disk from the drive.
	e. Test the drive by reading a CD-ROM.

4. Clean the floppy disk drive.

    a. Insert the floppy disk cleaner disk in the drive.

    b. Access the floppy disk drive.

    c. Remove the floppy cleaner disk from the drive.

    d. Test the floppy disk drive by writing to and reading from a floppy disk.

5. Clean the removable media drive.

    a. Insert the compatible cleaning product in the drive.

    b. Follow the manufacturer's directions to clean the drive.

    c. Remove the product from the drive.

    d. Test the drive by reading from and writing to compatible media in the drive.

TOPIC F
Decide When to Upgrade

Even if you perform routine maintenance on systems and keep them in good repair, eventually there will come a time when you have to decide if a component or system has reached the end of its useful life. Upgrading computer hardware can be a costly undertaking. While the price of some hardware components might be lower now than in the past, a company-wide upgrade could mean considerable expense in both the cost of materials and the man-hours needed to actually perform the upgrade. As a result, sometimes companies will need real convincing that a hardware upgrade is absolutely necessary. A thorough understanding of upgrade requirements is important to help you make an informed decision. In this topic, you'll learn how to make the right decision.

Indications you Need to Upgrade

There are many occasions that will indicate when you might need to upgrade system components. Table 13-4 includes some indications that you might need to upgrade your system hardware.

Lesson 13

🖈 You might find that upgrading one component will require the upgrade of another component.

Table 13-4: *When You Might Need to Upgrade*

Component	You Might Need to Upgrade When
Memory	You want to upgrade the operating system or install high-end software that requires more RAM; or when users report that system response time is slow and you can demonstrate a resultant increase in productivity to justify the cost.
Processor	You want to upgrade the operating system or install high-end software that requires a faster processor; or when users report that system response time is slow and you can double the speed of the machine, and you can demonstrate increased productivity to justify the cost. (Look for a CPU with a cache, which will be faster than a cache on the motherboard.)
System BIOS (firmware)	You want to install a new hardware component, such as a hard drive or processor, that may not be supported by the current system BIOS; the manufacturer has released a bug fix or security patch; or the newer BIOS supports a necessary feature, such as USB devices, that the current BIOS doesn't support.
Power supply	The power supply isn't adequate for the system components that rely on it.
System boards (motherboards)	You need to install a device or hardware component, such as a processor, that the current motherboard doesn't support, or you need to install a device, such as a network card, but all the motherboard's slots are in use.
Network adapter card	The current network card doesn't support the current or planned network configuration; or if the vendor removes support for a legacy device, because you won't be able to obtain updated drivers or drivers for new operating systems.
Hard drive	The hard drive is running out of free space when all unnecessary files are deleted, especially important if free space falls below 200 MB.
Video cards	The video card doesn't support the kind of graphics your applications output, or if your video card doesn't support a new monitor.
PCMCIA cards (Type I, II, or III)	The slots on a new notebook don't support your current cards.
Bus	The motherboard is incompatible, or a necessary system component is not supported.
Device Drivers	Fix bugs or enhance the performance of your computer. Newer operating systems may not support older legacy devices—the device drivers may cause your system to behave unpredictably.

Decide When to Upgrade

Deciding when to upgrade a system's hardware can be a complex task. You will need to balance the requirements of the business against the cost of the upgrade and against the benefits of the upgrade to users. But if you make the correct decision, you will have a system that supports all the necessary hardware components, operating systems, and applications that a user needs to be productive.

Guidelines

To make the decision to upgrade:

1. Determine the components that you need to upgrade.
   - Determine if the memory is sufficient for the current operating system, applications, and other system resources, or for the operating system, applications, and other system resources you plan to upgrade to.
   - Determine if the processor is adequate for the current operating system, applications, and other system resources, or for the operating system, applications, and other system resources you plan to upgrade to.
   - Determine if the system BIOS supports current hardware or hardware you plan to install; if the current system BIOS contains the necessary security configurations; or if there are any bugs in the current system BIOS that are hindering performance.
   - Determine if the power supply is adequate for the installed internal system components or for additional internal system components you're going to install.
   - Determine if the motherboard will support a device you need to add.
   - Determine if the network card supports the current or planned network configuration.
   - Determine if there is sufficient hard disk space to support current or planned applications.
   - Determine if the video card supports graphics generated by current applications or those you plan to install, or if the video card adequately supports the current monitor or one you plan to add.
   - Determine if the PCMCIA cards are supported by the slots in the current or planned notebook computers.
   - Determine if the bus is compatible with the current motherboard and system components or those you plan to install.
   - Determine if device drivers for your system's devices are available for your operating system.
2. Determine the total cost of upgrading all components, and compare this to the cost of a system replacement. A complete system replacement might be disruptive to users, but it is possible that the overall cost might be less, and you can be confident that all the components in the new system will be compatible with each other.
3. Determine the business requirements for the upgrade. Is the upgrade necessary to meet business goals? For example, will the current systems support the company's software applications? What is the value of the upgrade to users in terms of job satisfaction and productivity increases.
4. Determine the budget you have available.
5. Perform a cost/benefit analysis.
   - If the value of the upgrade or replacement exceeds the cost and you have the budget available, you should upgrade.
   - If you determine that the upgrade is necessary and you do not have the budget, you will need to be prepared to present your analysis to company management to support a request for additional equipment funds.

Lesson 13

- If the cost of the upgrade outweighs the benefit, you should not upgrade. The company will have to consider other options to meet user needs, such as providing additional network storage to supplement users' local hard disks.

Example: New Operating System

You have a Windows 98 system with a Pentium 133 processor, 32 MB of RAM, and a 2 GB hard disk that has 250 MB of free hard disk space. Your company's business plan is to upgrade all systems from Windows 98 to Windows XP. To determine if the current hardware will support the new operating system, you look at the minimum configuration requirements for Windows XP. You determine that you will need to upgrade the processor, the RAM, and the hard disk to support the new operating system.

DISCOVERY ACTIVITY 13-6

Determining Whether to Upgrade

Scenario:

You're an A+ technician who supports users and systems in a publishing company. You've been given a list of computers and their configuration, and you've been asked to determine if you need to upgrade any of their hardware components.

 You can use the Microsoft Web site at www.microsoft.com to look up operating system requirements.

1. Computer A is a Pentium II computer running Windows NT 4.0. The system has a video card that does not support 3D graphics or the new 21-inch monitor its user has acquired. The user needs the monitor to create and modify the graphics for one of your company's top publications. A new video card will cost $200. Should you upgrade the video card?

    a) Yes

    b) No

    c) Maybe

2. Computer B has a Pentium II processor, 64 MB of RAM, and is running Windows 98. The user needs to install several new programs to create and manage large files used in the layout of several publications. You will also need to upgrade this computer to Windows XP within the next six months as part of the upgrade within that user's department. Should you upgrade or replace the system?

    a) Upgrade

    b) Replace

3. Computer B also has a 20 GB hard disk that has 8 GB of free space. Should you upgrade the hard disk too?

    a) Yes

    b) No

    c) Maybe

4. Computer C is a Pentium III computer with 256 MB of RAM and a 30 GB hard disk with 10 GB of free space. The user is an administrative assistant who uses the computer for email and word processing. She complains that the computer isn't as fast as the computer she has at home. Upon further investigation you find that at most she has only three programs open at one time. A new processor will cost $450 and more memory will cost $175. Should you upgrade the processor and the memory?

    a) Yes

    b) No

    c) Maybe

5. If you're planning to upgrade from Windows 98 to Windows 2000, which component(s) might you need to consider upgrading?

    a) Hard disk

    b) Processor

    c) Sound card

    d) System BIOS

    e) Network card

Topic G

Dispose of Computer Equipment

When you upgrade a component or system, you then have to dispose of the item you replaced. Many computer components, such as monitors and batteries, contain hazardous materials. When you dispose of these materials, you need to make sure that your company complies with applicable environmental-safety laws. You also protect yourself and your co-workers from toxic exposure when you follow the guidelines established for dealing with hazardous materials. This topic will enable you to identify the hazardous materials contained in obsolete system components and how to recycle, reuse, or dispose of old equipment.

Material Safety Data Sheets

Material Safety Data Sheets (*MSDS*) are technical bulletins designed to give users and emergency personnel information about the proper procedures for the storage and handling of a hazardous substance. Companies are required by the Occupational Safety & Health Administration (OSHA) to make MSDS information available to employees who might be exposed to hazardous materials.

Manufacturers of a product create the MSDS. They ship it with the first shipment of a product to a new customer. They also need to ship an MSDS any time there is an update to it. MSDSs cover information such as the following:

- Physical data
- Toxicity
- Health effects
- First aid
- Reactivity
- Storage
- Safe handling and use precautions
- Disposal
- Protective equipment
- Spill/leak procedures

Hazardous Materials

Definition:

Hazardous materials are any materials that must be handled in a special way in order to prevent injury to people or damage to the environment. All hazardous materials must:

- Be handled to prevent injury to people.
- Be handled properly to prevent environmental damage.
- Be handled according to OSHA requirements.
- Be disposed of properly.
- Have an MSDS available.

Hazardous materials vary in the following ways:

- They might be chemicals, chemical solvents, cans, or other containers that hold chemicals.
- They might be computer components that contain hazardous elements such as the following:
    — Lead
    — Mercury
    — Cadmium
    — Phosphorous
    — Barium
- How exposure to the material should be treated.
- How they are disposed of.
- How they are to be handled and stored.
- Any local, regional, state, or government requirements for handling and disposing of hazardous materials.

Example: Liquid Cleaning Materials

The household cleaning materials you use to clean equipment must be handled to prevent injury to people and to prevent environmental damage. Some contain caustic chemicals and solvents that could cause respiratory distress or skin irritation. Figure 13-2 shows an example of the precautions you need to take when handling glass cleaner.

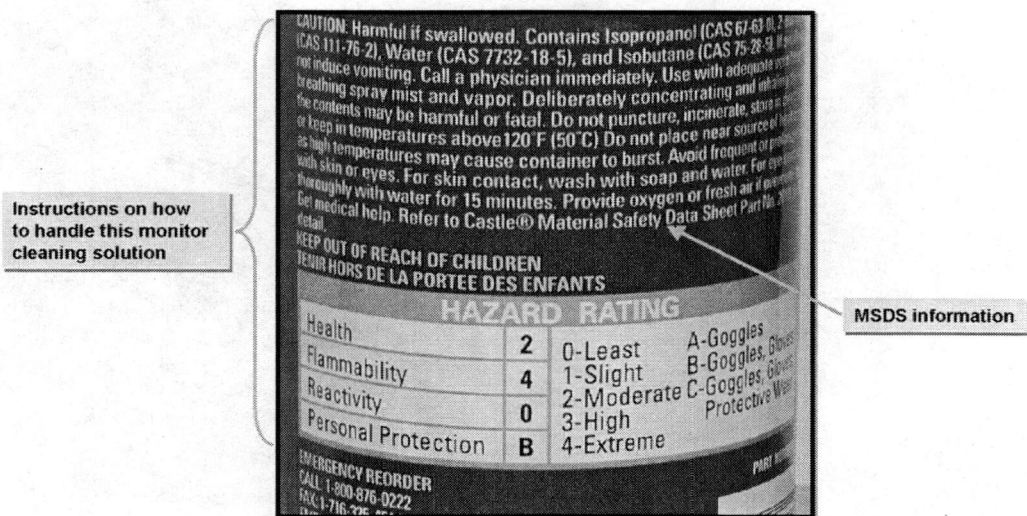

Figure 13-2: *Glass cleaner.*

Example: Laser Printer Toner

Laser printer toner is made of fine particles of iron and plastic approximately 7 to 10 microns in size that can cause problems when exposed to heat. Also, the residual chemicals can do severe damage to the environment. Handling procedures for toner cartridges are usually printed on the cartridge, as well as detailed in documentation that comes with the cartridge. Figure 13-3 shows an example of the printed handling instructions.

Lesson 13

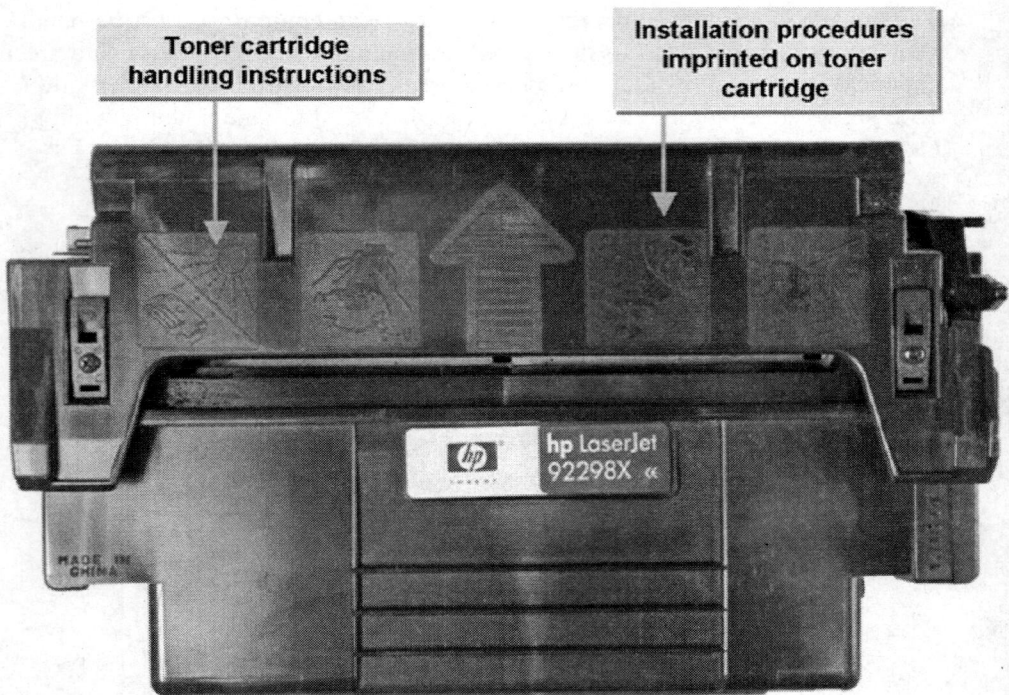

Figure 13-3: *A laser printer toner cartridge.*

Example: Metals

Most computer equipment contains soldered joints, which use lead, as well as other metal such as copper, gold, and silver. The lead is toxic. The other metals can be recycled and reused.

Monitors contain mercury, cadmium, phosphorous, and barium. These are safely enclosed in a vacuum-sealed case when the monitor is in everyday use. If you were to send it to a landfill, though, the glass and plastic housing would be crushed, exposing the dirt to these dangerous elements.

Example: Ozone

Laser printers produce ozone gas, usually when the corona wires produce an electrical discharge during printing. Depending on the levels, ozone can be a mild to severe irritant. Regulatory agencies have established limits regarding the amount of ozone that employees are exposed to. Be sure to replace the ozone filter as recommended by the manufacturer and follow proper procedures to dispose of the used filter.

Example: Batteries

Batteries are used to maintain the data in CMOS chips and to supply power to remote controls, portable devices, and notebook computers. These batteries might contain any one of a number of dangerous chemicals, including:

- Lithium
- Lead
- Nickel metal hydride

- Nickel cadmium

How to Dispose of Computer Equipment

Procedure Reference: Dispose of Hazardous Materials

To dispose of computer equipment:

1. Determine if any equipment needs to be treated as hazardous materials by referring to the MSDS for the product.

2. Dispose of household cleaners properly.
   - Read labels and follow instructions for disposing of them and the containers they were stored in.
   - Check whether the container can be recycled.

3. Dispose of batteries according to the type of battery and the recommended method of disposal or recycling.
   - Used batteries should not be tossed in the trash, but disposed of by following proper procedures.
   - Alkaline batteries can usually be disposed of in the regular trash, but check with your municipality to determine if they have a recycling program in place for those batteries.
   - Batteries containing heavy metals must be disposed of by following hazardous materials guidelines.

4. When disposing of toner and toner cartridges, use the following procedures:
   a. Toner spills should be cleaned up using a special printer or electronics vacuum that has a fine filter and bag to contain the material. Using a regular vacuum can melt the toner if it gets on the vacuum motor. Use a dry paper towel, toner spill cloths, or cool water to clean toner from skin or clothing.
   b. Toner cartridges should be refilled or recycled. Empty toner cartridges should not be disposed of in regular trash. Your company should have an established set of guidelines for how to dispose of used toner cartridges.

5. Find a computer recycler who can take your old equipment.

   Many municipalities sponsor hazardous materials recycling drop-offs at certain times of the year for their residents.

Lesson 13

DISCOVERY ACTIVITY 13-7

Disposing of Computer Equipment

Scenario:
The warehouse department has several older pieces of equipment that have reached the end of their useful life. You have deployed new equipment to the department and now need to dispose of the old equipment. The company has also accumulated several broken pieces of equipment that need to be discarded. You are responsible for properly disposing of the equipment. Your manager asks you the following questions to find out how you will be disposing of the equipment.

1. Why do CRTs need to be recycled rather than disposed of through normal waste management procedures?

2. Various types of batteries have been accumulated for disposal. These are from digital cameras, PDAs, laptops, and wireless devices among other sources. Indicate the proper disposal method for each battery type.

   | Alkaline |
   | Lithium |
   | Sealed lead batteries |
   | Nickel metal hydride |
   | Nickel cadmium |

3. Which printer consumables need to be handled in a special manner and be recycled?

4. What is an MSDS and where can you obtain one?

Lesson 13 Follow-up

In this lesson, you learned about the importance of performing preventative maintenance. You learned how to perform preventative maintenance on printers, UPSs, interior components, exterior components, as well as how to dispose of equipment that has reached the end of its useful life. Proper preventative maintenance can detect and prevent severe system problems before they occur.

1. **How often does your company perform periodic maintenance on computer equipment? Would you recommend that the company stay with this policy, perform maintenance more frequently, or less frequently?**

2. **How does your company handle disposing of old or broken equipment? Would you recommend that the company stay with this policy or change it? Does it meet environmental guidelines?**

FOLLOW-UP

Follow-up

In this course, you have installed, removed, upgraded, maintained, and corrected problems with computer hardware. You now have not only the skills to perform all the key job tasks of a qualified computer service technician, but also the knowledge you will need if you choose to pursue the CompTIA A+ certification.

1. **Will you be installing more internal or more external hardware?**

2. **What will be the most challenging issues to troubleshoot?**

3. **Do you feel you can transfer what you learned in this course using Windows XP to other operating systems?**

What's Next?

A+ Certification: Core Hardware Third Edition - A CompTIA Certification prepares you for the A+ Core Hardware certification exam. If you haven't done so already, you should take the *A+ Certification: Operating Systems Third Edition - A CompTIA Certification* course.

Appendix A
Customer Satisfaction

Topic A
Importance of Customer Satisfaction

You are a representative of your profession, as well as your company. The way you conduct yourself professionally directly influences the satisfaction of your customer, which in turn influences the productivity of your company.

Professional Manner

What is your mission statement? Think about the professional you want to be. What do you expect of yourself? What traits do you expect of a service provider? A good rule to follow when providing support to your customers is to treat them the way you would want to be treated under similar circumstances.

The personal traits shown in the following table are helpful for a person who is providing customer service.

Trait	How You Demonstrate It
Acceptance	Be non-judgmental about your customer's level of computer competence, choice of hardware, personal traits, and environmental conditions.
Competence	Instill confidence and credibility in your customers by demonstrating your skills and, when necessary, stating the limits of your knowledge.
Courtesy	Be polite and friendly on the phone and in person; address your customer as "sir" or "ma'am"; use titles such as Dr., Mr., or Ms. with last names; ask permission before entering your customer's personal space.
Dependability	Be there when you say you will; keep your promises or let the customer know of any changes; work efficiently and accurately; be prepared with the right equipment; don't make promises you can't keep.

Appendix A

Trait	How You Demonstrate It
Flexibility	Work around the customer's time and space demands; think on your feet; apply what you have previously learned; try alternate solutions; ask for help when you need it.
Honesty	Tell the truth about needed repairs, costs, and time estimates; be honest about your level of expertise and make professional referrals when appropriate; promptly admit your errors.
Patience	Be patient with angry customers, computer-illiterate customers, baffling equipment, unavoidable delays, and frustrating policies and procedures.
Punctuality	Be on time; call if you will be detained; make follow-up calls as promised.

The following table provides examples of these helpful personal traits demonstrated in different situations.

Situation	Less-effective Response	More-effective Response	Trait Demonstrated
You meet the customer for the first time.	"Where's the printer?"	"Hi, I'm ___ from ___. Nice to meet you, Ms. ___."	Courtesy
You brought the wrong cartridge because the customer told you the incorrect model number.	"Don't you even know what kind of printer you have? Now I'll have to waste time..."	"We have a little problem here. I need to go back to the shop for a different part."	Patience
You need to go back and get the right cartridge.	"I don't know when I'll be back to finish the job."	"I can probably have this done by noon. I need to call my next customer and let them know when I'll be there."	Dependability, Punctuality
You replace the cartridge, but printer still doesn't work.	"Sorry. You need a new printer."	"First, let's run a self-test to see if the printer is okay."	Flexibility
The printer is functioning smoothly.	"Call the office if you have any problems."	"Could I take a minute to show you what I did? Maybe we can prevent this from happening in the future."	Competence

Professional Appearance

Your work environment may be in a repair shop, at a help desk, or on-site at the customer's business. Whatever the situation, you will want to present a neat, clean, business-like appearance. On-site work may take you into many settings, from muffler repair shops to executive offices. You may be asked to remove your shoes or put on a hard hat. Be aware of the corporate culture and respond accordingly.

Be sure to keep your work area at the customer site neat. Don't pile materials on your customer's books and files. Clean up after yourself; a customer who doesn't know a multimeter from a mizzenmast may chase after you with the anti-static bag you left behind. When on-site, ask where to dispose of materials; find out where the recycling bin is for printer test-run paper.

Professional Behavior

The following list describes some aspects of professional behavior that you should exhibit when providing support to your customers:

- *Accountability.* Do not misrepresent your credentials, competence, or training. Take responsibility for your actions, and admit your mistakes. In questions of conflict of interest between your company and the customer, refer to your supervisor or follow your company's procedure. Be aware of your company's policy for accepting gifts or samples, and socializing with customers.

- *Confidentiality.* Many fields—including medicine, social work, and special education—are regulated by state laws concerning the confidentiality of their consumers. All companies have personal information about their employees. Many corporations have sensitive information about the development of their products or services. Treat any information you learn about your customer's business as confidential. Know your company's policies concerning confidential information and follow them.

- *Ethical conduct.* You have an obligation to take responsibility for ethical conduct within your delivery of service. The issues involved are complex and ever-changing in the computer industry. An unethical practice may become so routine that it is falsely assumed to be acceptable behavior. Learn your company's policies and adhere to them.

- *Pirating.* Software copyright infringement, or pirating, relates to the legal issues surrounding the distribution and use of software. The Federal Copyright Act of 1976 protects the rights of the holder of a copyright. Typically a backup copy of software is allowed and a site license allows for multiple use at one facility. You are responsible for upholding the law by complying with the license agreements that both your company and your customer hold. Learn your company's policies and adhere to them. Pirating carries penalties and risks including:
    - Fines
    - Imprisonment
    - Corrupted files
    - Virus-infected disks
    - Lack of technical support
    - Lack of upgrades

- *Setting priorities.* You will often need to set priorities and make judgment calls. You will recommend whether your customer should repair or replace equipment. You will rank the urgency of your customers' needs. Base your decisions on common courtesy, fundamental fairness, and keeping promises. Be familiar with your company's policies and follow them.

Customer Needs

Is the customer always right? No, the customer may be flat-out wrong at times; however, the customer is the bread-and-butter of your business. Rudeness is never an option. Challenge yourself to find the positive in every situation. Ask yourself: "What is my job here? What are my obligations to the customer? What are my obligations to my employer?"

APPENDIX A

Respect

Because the customer is responsible for providing business to you as a service technician, the customer deserves your respect. The customer will have varying levels of computer experience, from novice to expert. He or she may be emotionally charged by the equipment problem, and you may become the target of anger or frustration.

You and the customer bring your own individual differences in values, beliefs, age, gender, personality, and communication styles. Whatever the circumstances, be sure to look beyond the immediate differences. Keep your focus on: "This is a person who needs my help. How can I provide it?" Treat all customers as you would like to be treated.

Response to Urgency

Your customers call because they need help, and they usually need it yesterday. Their sense of urgency is about deadlines and production; they may display frustration and anger. Remember, it's not about you; it's about their need to get back online as quickly as possible.

Your best response is to be supportive using the communication and problem-solving techniques described in this topic. Be patient and honest; let the customer know that you are working for a timely solution to the problem.

Customer Satisfaction

Your goal is to achieve and maintain customer satisfaction by providing good service at a reasonable cost and in a timely fashion. The satisfied customer is the one who continues to do business with your company. The dissatisfied customer will take his or her business elsewhere.

Studies show that a customer who complains may be more valuable than the one who says nothing and silently moves on. The complaining customer may continue to do business with you, providing useful feedback for your company. A sincere apology may be in order, as well as investigating the complaint.

Table A-1 describes scenarios and responses that appropriately identify customer needs.

Table A-1: *Identifying Customer Needs*

Customer Says	Your Response	Need
"I've got a fleet of trucks out there waiting for manifests!"	"I estimate you'll be back in business in an hour. If not, I'll let you know ASAP."	Urgency
"They should have sent a *man* out to fix this."	"Let's see what we can do to get you back online."	Respect
"The last guy I talked to didn't know what he was doing, and it cost me two hundred bucks!"	"I'd be willing to follow up on that if you want to give me the details."	Satisfaction
"I didn't know what to do, so I kept pushing buttons. Sorry... I don't know much about computers."	"Let's back up a bit and try to figure out the original problem."	Respect
"My term paper is due at 5:00 tomorrow!"	"Let's try a few things over the phone. It may save you having to bring your computer into the shop."	Urgency

Customer Says	Your Response	Need
"How do I know it's not going to break down again, as soon as you leave?"	"Let's take a minute to go through the procedure. Would it help if we wrote down the steps?"	Satisfaction

Better Business

What does combining your technical skills with good customer relations translate to for your customers? Customer satisfaction. What do satisfied customers translate to for your company? Increased business opportunities through repeat and possibly expanded contacts.

During 2002, the national Better Business Bureau system handled over 620,000 written consumer complaints. Poor customer service translates into plunging profits, falling productivity, and missed opportunities, to the tune of billions of dollars. As you increase customer satisfaction, you may see the benefits of improved productivity, which can include more income, higher profit margins, and greater employment opportunities.

Repeat Business

Repeat business is the backbone of your company. You will want to be part of developing and maintaining customer accounts, regardless of size. Your company may have incentives for the repair technician or for the customer. Remember, the customer has power—to do business with you, or to take that business elsewhere. The customer also has the power to spread the word about the service provided by your company, satisfactory or otherwise.

Ease for Technician

One benefit of repeat business is that it gives you a sense of ease, because you are familiar with the territory. You can work more efficiently because you have already established a business relationship. You don't have to start over every time. When you are on-site, you may already know:

- Where to park.
- How to get a visitor pass.
- The company's dress code.
- The physical layout of the plant.
- The people involved.
- The level of technical support you can expect.
- The equipment you are dealing with.

Working on the help desk requires you to visualize what the customer is describing. Your work will go more smoothly if you have previously dealt with this customer; you will be familiar with the equipment and have access to records.

Communication Skills

Let's look at the communication skills that are important for a person providing customer support to help you interact successfully with your customers.

Appendix A: Customer Satisfaction

Appendix A

Non-verbal Clues

Body language communicates more than actual words. Studies show that up to 70 percent of a message is conveyed through actions. Even when you are talking on the phone, non-verbal characteristics—such as tone of voice—will add meaning to your message and help you interpret your customer's concerns.

Eye Contact

You and your customer will make, maintain, and break eye contact as you talk with each other. When attention is directed to the problem at hand, eye contact may be minimal. You will want to avoid staring directly at your customer—a form of invading personal space—or letting your gaze wander, which indicates disinterest, or even worse, inappropriate interest.

Gestures and Facial Expression

Gestures—such as nodding, pointing, or measuring the air—help expand the spoken message. Broad, friendly gestures indicate being open to the conversation, while sharp or jabbing gestures usually mean anger.

The variety, intensity, and meaning of facial expressions are almost endless. You and your customer read each other's faces to gain insight into the spoken words. Your expression must match the content of your words; if there is a mismatch, your customer will believe the message in your face rather than what you say.

Non-verbal Encouragement

Encourage your customer to continue with "Mm-hmm" and a slight nod of your head. You convey that you are listening and want to know more.

Passive Listening

Your message is: "I'm listening. Tell me more." You are alert, attentive, and accepting, but do not participate actively in the conversation. Your silence may help your customer to collect his or her thoughts, especially if upset or angry. Listen for factual data and be alert for feelings and attitudes, which are conveyed non-verbally. It may be difficult to keep from jumping in with a question or a "Yes, but...". Resist the temptation by writing down your thoughts to refer to later.

Positioning and Posture

Respect your customer's personal space. Depending on the circumstances, you may be from 1.5 to 4 feet away from your customer. If the customer backs up, you're too close. You may be working in close quarters; ask permission before you move into your customer's personal space—for example, sitting in the office chair.

Messages are conveyed by body position. Slouching indicates "I'm bored with this conversation." Holding one's arms across the chest says "I'm closed to what you are saying." Watch your body's signals, as well as those of your customer.

Timing

You can set the pace of a conversation. A pause may be more valuable than an immediate answer, as it allows you time to formulate your response. If a situation escalates and your customer becomes agitated, you may ask him or her to slow down so that you can get all the information. When a customer is having difficulty ending a call to the help desk, you may gently step up the pace to indicate your need to move on.

Tone of Voice

The tone of voice indicates many internal moods: excitement, boredom, sarcasm, fear, or uncertainty. A rise in your voice at the end of a sentence makes it sound like a question, implying lack of assurance instead of competence. Listen to your customer's tone. Volume—loudness or softness—colors the spoken message. If your customer's agitation escalates, try lowering your volume to re-establish a sense of calm.

Touch

A firm handshake is appreciated and may be expected in some business dealings. Other forms of touching are generally unnecessary, inappropriate, and risky.

Active Listening

When your customer is describing the problem, listen actively to elicit as much information as you can. These techniques may feel awkward at first, so try them out in a situation outside your job. With practice, you will use active listening skills more easily and creatively.

Questioning

Ask questions to gain information, clarify what you have heard and direct the conversation. Open-ended questions can elicit a lot of information. Close-ended questions limit the amount of information by giving a choice of answers. Yes-no questions further limit information exchange and can be used when you need to get to the point. Examples of each of these question styles are:

- Open-ended: "What happened after you pressed Ctrl+Alt+Delete?"
- Close-ended: "What kind of a printer do you have, laser or inkjet?"
- Yes-no: "Are you on a network?"

What if the answer to your open-ended question is "I don't know" or "I'm not sure"? Go down the list—using close-ended and then yes-no—until you reach the customer's level of expertise.

Examples of less helpful question styles:

- Confusing multiple questions: "What did you do next? Did you try...? What happened?"
- Accusations: "What did you do *that* for?"

Empathizing

Let your customer know that you perceive and support what he or she is feeling. Try to be specific in naming the emotion and link it to the customer, using "you," not "I." Examples of helpful empathetic responses include:

- "This delay is frustrating for you."
- "You're afraid you'll lose business while your computer is down."
- "You must be worried about the cost."

Examples of less helpful empathetic responses include:

- "I know how you're feeling."
- "I can identify..."

Appendix A: Customer Satisfaction

Appendix A

Paraphrasing

Restate what the customer says in your own words to make sure that you interpreted correctly, to bring order to the customer's thoughts, and to relay that their message is important. Use statements, not questions, and don't add or change anything. Examples of starters for paraphrasing include:

- "You're saying that..."
- "It sounds like..."
- "I'm hearing you say..."

Summarizing

Outline the main points of your conversation to summarize what has been said. You can begin by summarizing your understanding of the problem and then checking for clarification. During the conversation, you can re-establish the focus by listing the important facts. Bring closure by summing up the work performed. If a follow-up plan is needed, restate the responsibilities and timeline. Helpful starters for summarizing include:

- "Let's see what we have so far."
- "Why don't we back up a minute and go through that again?"
- "Let's go over our plan."

Table A-2 describes some examples of active listening skills.

Table A-2: *Active Listening Skills*

You Say	Skill Demonstrated
"Is your computer back up and running?"	Yes-no question
"Did the power go off before you saved, during the save, or after you saved your data?"	Close-ended question
"You must really be nervous right now."	Empathy
"You're saying that the computer was in the process of writing to the disk when the power went off. Is that accurate?"	Paraphrase
"What happens when you try to open the presentation?"	Open-ended question
"Before I come over, let's make sure of our game plan. You won't do anything more on the computer, and I'll bring some recovery software that may rescue your presentation."	Summarization

Conflict Resolution

You aim for customer satisfaction, and many times your interactions will go smoothly. You may be greeted with: "We sure are glad to see you!" When a customer specifically requests you—as in, "We usually work with Sharon"—then you know you are doing something, or many things, right. Unfortunately, not all your interactions will be ideal. Your customer may be under stress for a number of reasons:

- Limited productivity.
- Missed deadlines.
- Unforeseen delays.
- Unexpected repair costs.

Appendix A

Your customer may direct anger and frustration to you. Remember, don't take the attack personally, and don't counter-attack. As a service provider, your job is to relieve some of the stress. Conflict resolution techniques can help you make a difference in customer satisfaction.

Agreeing with Perception

You can agree with the customer's perception of a situation without necessarily agreeing with what is said. As the customer realizes that you are not going to argue, he or she may see a safe place to begin to solve the problem. Helpful phrases to agree with perception include:

- "I can understand why you would think that."
- "I see what you're getting at."
- "It sounds like a big responsibility."

Less helpful phrases include:

- "But..."
- "That's not correct."
- "That's not what I said!"

Reflecting Feelings

You can acknowledge what the customer is feeling without accepting the display of emotion. Check the customer's non-verbal messages, including tone of voice and facial expression. Be accurate and specific in naming the feeling. The feeling belongs to the customer; don't apologize for it or try to take it away. Helpful responses to reflect feelings include:

- "I'm sensing your frustration."
- "I can understand your anger."
- "You sound unsure."

Less helpful responses include:

- "I'm sorry you're angry."
- "Calm down."

Forming an Alliance

Your customer needs to know that you are an ally, not an enemy. When the customer knows that you share their concerns, the problem-solving process can move forward. Give a sense of unity by using "we," instead of "you" or "I." Helpful phrases to form an alliance include:

- "Where are we heading with this?"
- "Would it help us if...?"
- "These are our options."

Less helpful phrases include:

- "I think you should..."
- "That's your choice."

Appendix A: Customer Satisfaction

APPENDIX A

Finding a Solution

Together you and your customer can work out a specific plan for working through the problem. Brainstorm some ideas. Be careful about giving advice or solutions too early or too often in the process. Your job is to facilitate the decision-making. The decision itself ultimately rests with the customer. Be sure to follow through with any commitments you make. Helpful phrases to assist your customer in finding a solution include:

- "What has worked before?"
- "What resources are available right now?"
- "Does this sound like something we could try?"

Less helpful phrases:

- "I'll leave it up to you."
- "Call me if you have any problems."

Table A-3 compares less helpful responses and their more helpful equivalents when working to resolve conflicts with customers.

Table A-3: *Resolving Conflicts*

Less-helpful Response	More-helpful Response	Reason
"Yeah, but..."	"I can understand what you're saying."	Agree with perception
"I've only got one pair of hands!"	"It sounds like you're under a tight deadline."	Agree with perception
"I'm sorry you feel that way."	"You sound really frustrated."	Respect feelings
"There's nothing to get excited about."	"I hear your urgency."	Respect feelings
"If I were you..."	"Let's see if this works."	Form alliance
"It's your money you're throwing away."	"Why don't we...?"	Form alliance
"I guarantee my way will work."	"Does this sound like a reasonable possibility?"	Find solution
"Trust me, it'll never fly."	"Let's go over our plan of action."	Find solution

Service Calls

Whether you provide technical support over the phone or in person, a satisfied customer is your goal. Service calls follow the same basic format. The environment will dictate differences in the way you handle certain aspects of the job.

The Initial Call

If your company has an establish procedure for taking customer calls, follow those guidelines in filling out necessary forms, and be familiar with your company's customer service policies. Remember, you may be the customer's first contact with your company. Be sure you present yourself professionally.

APPENDIX A

Simple troubleshooting over the phone will help determine the next step—using the help desk, bringing the computer into the shop, or an on-site visit. Each setting brings its own set of challenges.

The Help Desk

Your communication skills will be of prime importance on the Help Desk as you guide your customer through the troubleshooting process. You are, in effect, teaching the customer to be your eyes, ears, and hands. You will find it helpful to make diagrams and take notes as you go along. Table A-4 describes helpful non-verbal cues that can be used on a Help Desk.

Table A-4: *Non-verbal Cues on a Help Desk*

Situation	Communication Skill	Non-verbal Cues
The customer begins to describe problem.	Passive listening	Allow information to flow without interruption; you should take notes.
The customer hesitates.	Non-verbal encouragement	Use a gentle "Mm-hmm" or "Uh-huh" to let the customer know you are listening.
The customer begins to talk faster.	Timing	Listen for agitation; prepare to use your active listening skills.
The customer's voice rises in pitch.	Tone of voice	Listen for anger or frustration; prepare to use your active listening skills.

Table A-5 describes active listening skills that can be used on a Help Desk.

Table A-5: *Active Listening on a Help Desk*

Situation	Communication Skill	Active Listening
The customer has difficulty describing problem.	Questions	Use open-ended, close-ended, and yes-no questions as you determine the customer's level of expertise.
The customer expresses anger or impatience.	Empathy	Name the emotion to let the customer know that you are an ally.
The customer describes problem in own words.	Paraphrase	Repeat what you have heard to check for accuracy.
The customer rambles on.	Summarize	Bring focus to the call by outlining the main points.

The Repair Shop

When customers come to you, they are on your territory. You are able to speak face-to-face with them and walk through the problem together. However, a dissatisfied customer's actions and words can influence other patrons in the shop. Your conflict resolution skills will be useful in de-escalating a situation and helping your customer achieve satisfaction.

APPENDIX A

Consider the following scenario: A customer brings his printer into the shop for the second time in a week. He is angry that he has had to take time off from work again and that his invoices won't go out at the end of the month. He demands immediate action, including a credit for the first repair. Your conflict resolution techniques can defuse the incident. Table A-6 lists conflict resolution skills and describes appropriate responses in this scenario.

Table A-6: *Conflict Resolution Skills and Responses*

Customer's Remarks	Conflict Resolution Skill	Your Response
"You guys don't know anything!"	Agreeing with perception	"I can understand why you think that."
"This is the second time this week I've had to drop everything and come in here!"	Reflecting feeling	"This is frustrating for you."
"How am I supposed to get my invoices out?"	Forming an alliance	"We are going to take care of this right now. Let's talk to my supervisor together."
"So, I'm supposed to pay for this twice?"	Finding a solution	"For my part, I will talk to Accounting and get back to you by tomorrow."

The On-site Service Call

Like the repair shop, during the on-site visit, you will interact with the customer as well as the equipment. Moreover, the on-site visit takes you to the customer's turf. As the balance of power shifts slightly, you will need to be even more aware of the personal traits valued in a service technician. Table A-7 lists personal traits and possible actions to demonstrate those traits during an on-site visit.

Table A-7: *Personal Traits for the On-site Service Call*

Situation	Personal Trait	Your Action
The customer needs to use the office where you are working.	Flexibility	Service other workstations if possible; determine how long the office will be unavailable and adjust your schedule accordingly.
The equipment presents a problem that is new to you.	Honesty	Admit to the customer that you would rather take the time to research and get help than make a costly mistake based on guesswork.
After several repairs, the customer continues to yank on mouse cord.	Patience	Show the customer the damage in a non-threatening way; suggest a more ergonomic rearrangement of workstation.
A service call is taking longer than you anticipated.	Punctuality	Discuss the time over-run with your current customer; call your next customer to explain the situation and make alternate arrangements.
The customer's first language is not English.	Flexibility	Ask if someone is available to help interpret; use gestures, diagrams, and demonstrations to communicate.

Appendix A

Customer Interaction

As you provide technical support, be aware of your interactions with the customer. You are not expected to be chatty; however, the customer may be your best source of information about the technical problem.

Establishing Rapport

It will be well worth your time to establish a friendly alliance with your customer. Take time to:

1. Greet the customer.
2. Introduce yourself.
3. Use the customer's title and last name, unless asked to use first names.
4. Make a general remark, such as commenting on the weather.
5. Fill out initial forms.
6. Suggest a cooperative solution, such as "Let's see what we can do to get you up and running."

Responding to Customer's Technical Level

As you communicate with the customer, listen and watch for his or her technical level. Adjust your questions and use of technical jargon to match your customer's expertise and understanding.

The customer may lack training and be fearful of appearing foolish. His or her non-verbal cues, such as lack of eye contact, may reveal a discomfort level. Make an effort to find an area of strength and comment on that. Helpful phrases to respond to a customer's technical level include:

- "It might help if we..."
- "Let's take this one step at a time."
- "Is the green light on?"

Your customer, on the other hand, may be a know-it-all who tries to take charge or play games to trip you up. Remember the personal trait of acceptance, and treat this as a learning experience. Your actions can include:

- Recognizing the customer's knowledge by using technical jargon.
- Sincerely complimenting the customer's expertise; the customer may feel less need to impress you if you acknowledge his or her skills.
- Asking questions and learning what you can; the customer may have helpful suggestions.
- Letting the customer know that you are working together.

Isolating the Source of the Problem

Use an organized, common-sense approach to isolate the source of a problem and find the solution. Because it is in the customer's best interest to solve the problem as quickly and efficiently as possible, you should enlist his or her help. Be sure to adjust your questions and use of technical jargon to match the customer's level.

Appendix A: Customer Satisfaction

APPENDIX A

Warning: If the customer becomes defensive, change your questions to focus on the equipment, rather than the person. For example, change "What have you done to try to solve the problem?" to "What attempt has been made to solve the problem?" Table A-8 lists some questions you can use to enlist the customer's help to isolate the source the problem.

Table A-8: *Questions to Isolate the Source of the Problem*

Question	Information You are Seeking
What is the nature of the problem?	Many reported problems are based on false expectations of the user, rather than malfunctions of equipment or software. For example, audio files cannot be heard if there is no sound card.
Has the equipment ever worked correctly?	If the equipment has functioned properly in the past, chances are good you can make it work again. If it has never worked correctly, there may be a flaw or incompatibility that you need to isolate.
When did you first notice the problem?	Pinning down the time the problem appeared will help you isolate the cause. Concentrate on any changes that occurred between the time it last operated correctly and the time the problem was noticed.
Have you ever had this problem before?	If the problem has happened before, determine the cause of the previous occurrence, find the solution used then, and try it again.
What attempt has been made to try to solve the problem?	Often attempts to fix a problem introduce an unrelated set of changes that can mask the cause of the original problem. You might need to undo any previous attempts to fix the problem before you can isolate its cause.
Did you install or remove any software or hardware just before you noticed the problem?	Installing and removing hardware and software are major sources of problems. Installing new items can introduce conflicts, and removing old items can also destroy files needed by current items.
Did you change the physical setup before you noticed the problem?	Moving the computer very carefully from one office to another may cause connections to fail if the computer is on a different branch of the network. Cables and cards can work loose during a move, and sometimes wires are reconnected incorrectly.
What software are you using?	Software is constantly being upgraded, so knowing the exact version of all software is crucial.

Teaching the Customer

As part of providing quality customer service, you are obligated to consider the economic health of your customer's organization. Problem prevention is less costly, in human and economic terms, than problem repetition. You have the opportunity to demonstrate excellence in support when you take the time to teach your customer about the equipment you are servicing. When you offer to give information:

- Make sure the customer has the time and interest.
- Be concise, clear, and organized.
- Pace your explanation to match the customer's rate of understanding.
- Adjust your use of technical jargon to match the customer's vocabulary.
- Check for understanding by asking questions.
- Be aware of any resistance to receiving help or making changes.

- Include a rationale so the customer understands the reasoning.
- Summarize the essential points.
- Suggest that the customer write the procedure down.
- Walk the customer through the procedure.
- Ask for feedback.

Table A-9 provides some examples of questions that can move the focus away from the customer and toward the equipment.

Table A-9: *Comparison of Questions Focusing on Customers vs. Equipment*

Focus on Customer	Focus on Equipment
"When did you first notice the problem?"	"When did the problem first occur?"
"Have you ever had this problem before?"	"Has the problem ever occurred before?"
"What have you done to try to solve the problem?"	"What attempt has been made to solve the problem?"
"Did you install or remove any software or hardware just before you noticed the problem?"	"Was any software or hardware installed just before the problem appeared?"
"Did you change the physical setup before you noticed the problem?"	"Was there any physical change to the setup before the problem appeared?"
"What software are you using?"	"What software is being used?"

Finishing the Service Call

When you have completed the technical aspects of the service call, wrap up business as efficiently as possible. You and your customer are both busy people.

Forms

Complete all forms accurately and promptly. Get necessary signatures, and route your documentation according to your company's procedures. Record-keeping can help you keep track of the kinds of problems you encounter and the solutions used. This may prove to be an invaluable reference for you in the future.

Making Referrals

Unfortunately, not every problem is remedied immediately. When a problem is beyond the scope of your expertise, refer to a co-worker or to the next level of support. Be sure to let the customer know that you are directing the problem to a person with more experience and resources. Inform your customer of the procedure and when to expect a call from the support person.

Ending

In wrapping up your service call, summarize the important points with your customer. Review any plans you have made for future service or follow up. At an on-site visit, be sure to clean your work area. Thank the customer for doing business with your company.

APPENDIX A

Follow-up

Be sure to track any referrals you made to other technicians. Be accountable for your follow-up plan; keep your customer informed of any changes or delays.

Table A-10 summarizes the tasks to be completed when finishing a service call.

Table A-10: *Tasks to Finish a Service Call*

Area	Task #1	Task #2	Task #3
Forms	Complete accurately and promptly.	Get signature.	Route documentation.
Making Referrals	Refer to co-worker or next level of support.	Tell customer you are referring.	Inform customer of procedure, when to expect call.
Ending	Summarize important points and review plans.	Clean up.	Say "thank you."
Follow-up	Track referrals.	Be accountable for follow-up plan.	Keep customer informed of changes or delays.

APPENDIX B
The OSI Model

Introduction to the OSI Model

When computer networks were first implemented, manufacturers designed and created networking hardware, such as NICs, according to whatever standards they devised. This was acceptable if you were willing to standardize your network on one manufacturer's products, but problems arose when people used different products from different manufacturers. As this issue became more prevalent, the International Standards Organization (ISO) stepped in and developed the *Open System Interconnection (OSI) model*—a model that describes network communications as consisting of seven layers that work together to provide network services. The OSI model provides a standard, organized way to look at network communications.

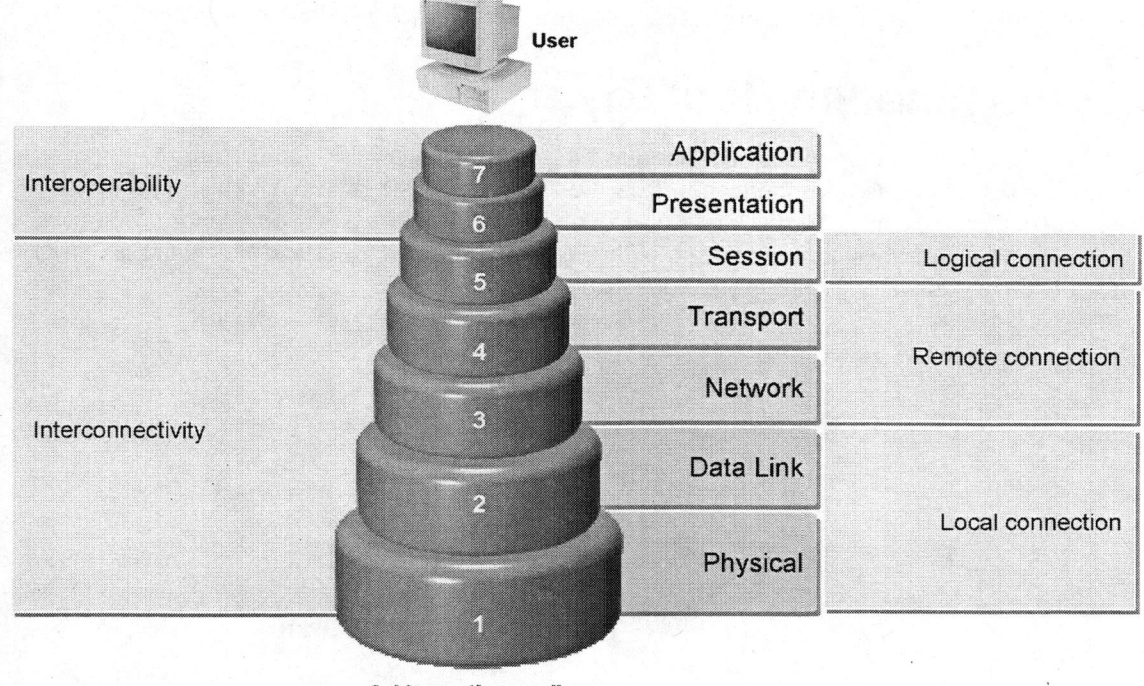

Figure B-1: *The OSI model.*

Appendix B

Originally, the International Organization for Standardization (ISO), which developed the model, hoped that different computer makers around the world would incorporate the details included in the model so all systems from all vendors would be able to communicate with each other. The seven layers had seven sets of standards which tried to isolate problems to certain layers. People working on some aspect of network design could assume that the layers above and below their area of development followed the OSI standards, and would make sure their work followed OSI standards so it would have worldwide compatibility. Table B-1 summarizes the seven layers in the OSI model.

Table B-1: *Summary of OSI Model Layers*

Layer	Name	Function
7	Application	Responsible for program-to-program communication.
6	Presentation	Manages data representation, such as data format, data compression, protocol conversion, and encryption.
5	Session	Responsible for establishing and maintaining communications channels.
4	Transport	Responsible for end-to-end integrity of data transmission.
3	Network	Routes data from one node to another.
2	Data Link	Responsible for physically passing data from one node to another.
1	Physical	Manages putting data onto the network media and taking the data off.

Control is passed from one layer to the next. Communication begins with the Application layer on one end (for example, a user opening an application and typing a request). The communication is passed through each of the seven layers down to the Physical layer (which is the actual transmission of bits). On the receiving end, control passes back up the hierarchy.

Layer 1: The Physical Layer

The *Physical layer* is responsible for passing bits onto and receiving them from the connecting medium. This layer has no understanding of the meaning of the bits, but treats them as voltages, currents, or flashes of light passing through copper, radio waves, fiber optic, or some other medium. The Physical layer deals with the functional electrical and mechanical characteristics of the signals and signaling methods.

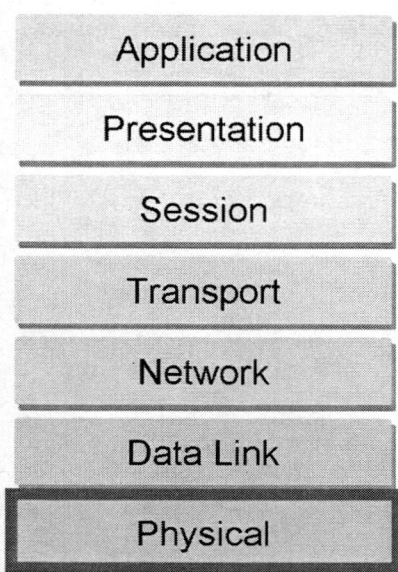

- Provides electrical and mechanical interfaces for a network.
- Specifies type of medium used to connect network devices.
- Specifies how signals are transmitted on network.

Figure B-2: *The Physical layer.*

The standards developed for this layer, and the devices that function on this layer, have to solve problems such as:

- How do you transmit strings of 0s and 1s at faster speeds over longer distances?
- How do you transmit a long series of just 0s that can be detected at the other end?

Layer 2: The Data Link Layer

The *Data Link layer* is responsible for node-to-node validity and integrity of the transmission. The Data Link layer detects and may correct errors in data packets caused by problems in the Physical layer. The Physical layer is responsible for sending signals through a medium as reliably as possible. The Data Link layer examines the signals and determines if the transmitted data is accurate.

APPENDIX B

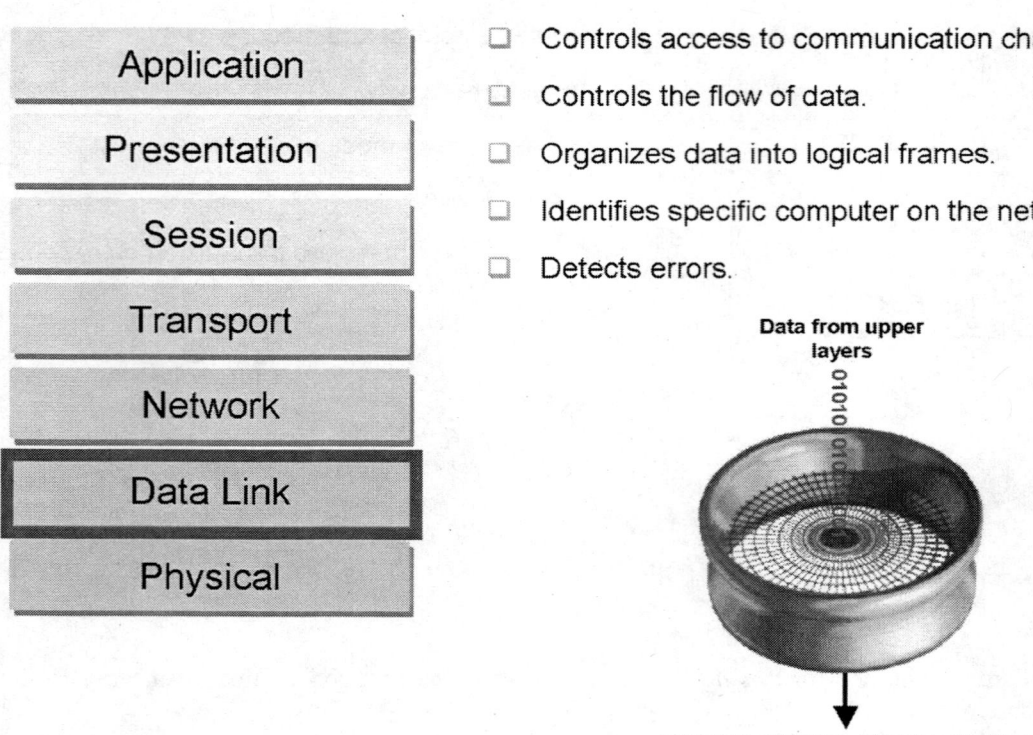

Figure B-3: *The Data Link layer.*

The standards developed for this layer, and the devices that function on this layer, have to solve problems such as:

- How do you frame a long string of bits so it is clear where each message begins and ends?
- How do you detect an error in a corrupted message, or confirm that the data is accurate?
- How do you tell the sender to retransmit the corrupted message so the error can be corrected?
- How do you control the flow of messages to prevent overwhelming the physical capabilities of the receiving computer?

The Data Link layer is composed of two sublayers: Logical Link Control (LLC) and Media Access Control (MAC). These sublayers were defined by the IEEE as part of the original IEEE 802 standards. *Logical Link Control (LLC)* is the Ethernet portion of the Data Link layer that connects the network software in Layer 3 to the *Media Access Control (MAC)* sublayer, which then connects to the bottom Physical layer of the OSI model. The LLC provides a common interface to the MAC layers, which specify the access method used.

Layer 3: The Network Layer

The *Network layer* establishes the route between the sending and receiving stations. The Network layer, the Data Link layer, and the Physical layer are all technology-dependent and have to work together. The Network layer establishes the communication path between two nodes on the network; the Data Link layer ensures the data sent through that path is accurate; and the Physical layer places the proper electrical signals on the media that make up the path.

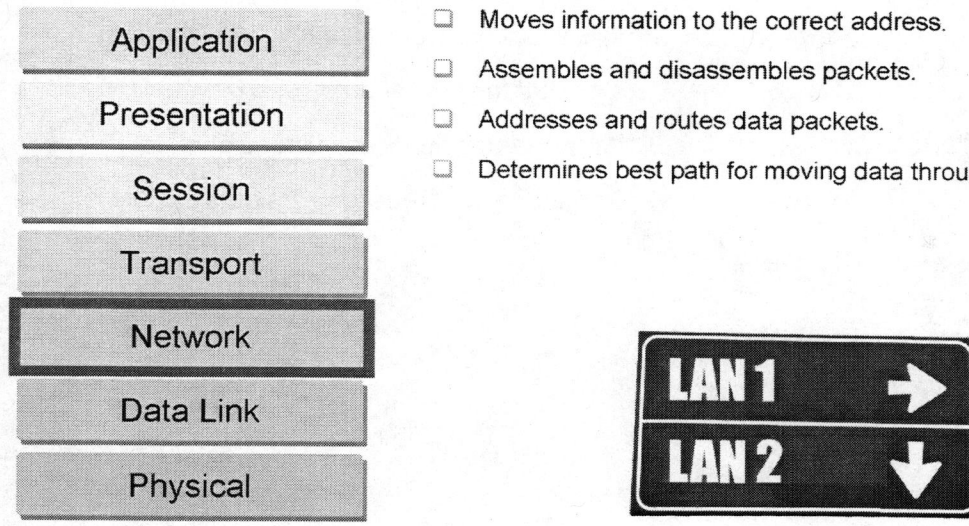

Figure B-4: *The Network layer.*

- Moves information to the correct address.
- Assembles and disassembles packets.
- Addresses and routes data packets.
- Determines best path for moving data through the network.

The OSI standards and hardware at the Network layer try to solve problems such as:

- How can a link in the network carry several messages at the same time, keep the messages separate, and deliver them to the proper end node on the network?
- How can a node address a message so it goes to the intended end node, and how can the sending node determine the best path to use to send a message to another node on another network?

Layer 4: The Transport Layer

The *Transport layer* is responsible for overall end-to-end validity and integrity of the transmission. The Transport layer works with the three layers below it to make sure the final file or message is complete and accurate. For example, the Physical layer puts bits on the wire, the Data Link layer makes sure the data packets a node receives are accurate, the Network layer sets up the path of communication between the sending and receiving node, and the Transport layer examines all the packets and makes sure that they can be reassembled into the complete, exact message that was sent. The Transport layer is network technology-independent and deals with the quality of the service provided by the bottom three layers, not the actual operation of the layers.

Appendix B

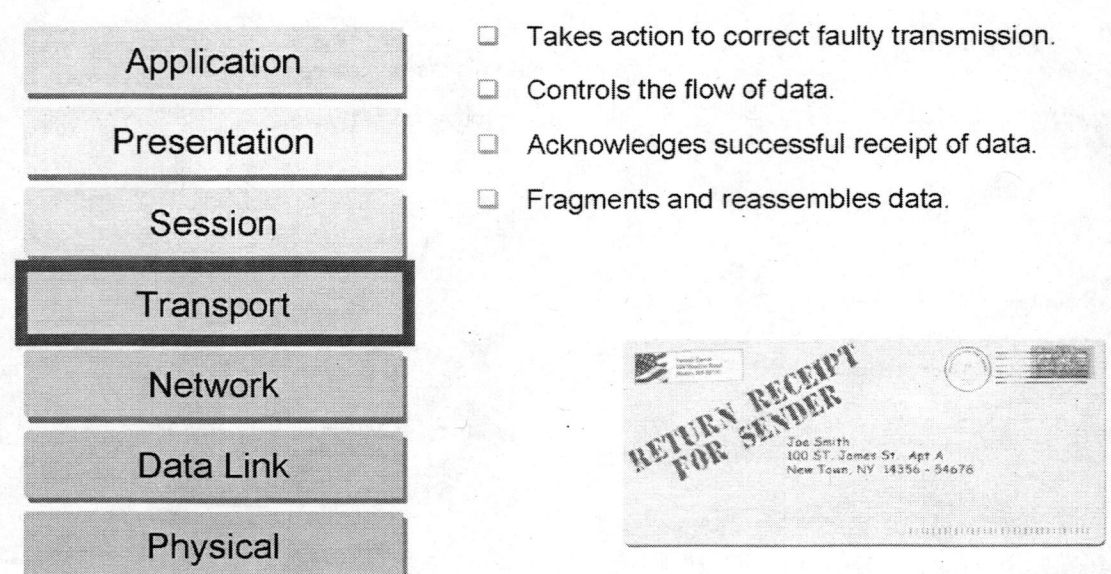

Figure B-5: *The Transport layer.*

An error on the Network layer can instruct the Data Link layer to send a packet of data to the wrong address. The packet arrives and is exactly what was sent, thanks to the Data Link layer, but it is in the wrong place. The Transport layer has to resolve this problem. The chances of sending data over a network and never getting an error are very small. The more time and money spent on equipment and error checking, the smaller the chance of an undetected error slipping through the system. The Transport layer is a practical compromise between the quest for perfection and the cost of perfection.

Layer 5: The Session Layer

The *Session layer* creates, maintains, and terminates communication sessions in an orderly manner. It also marks significant parts of the transmitted data with check points to allow for fast recovery in the event of a connection failure.

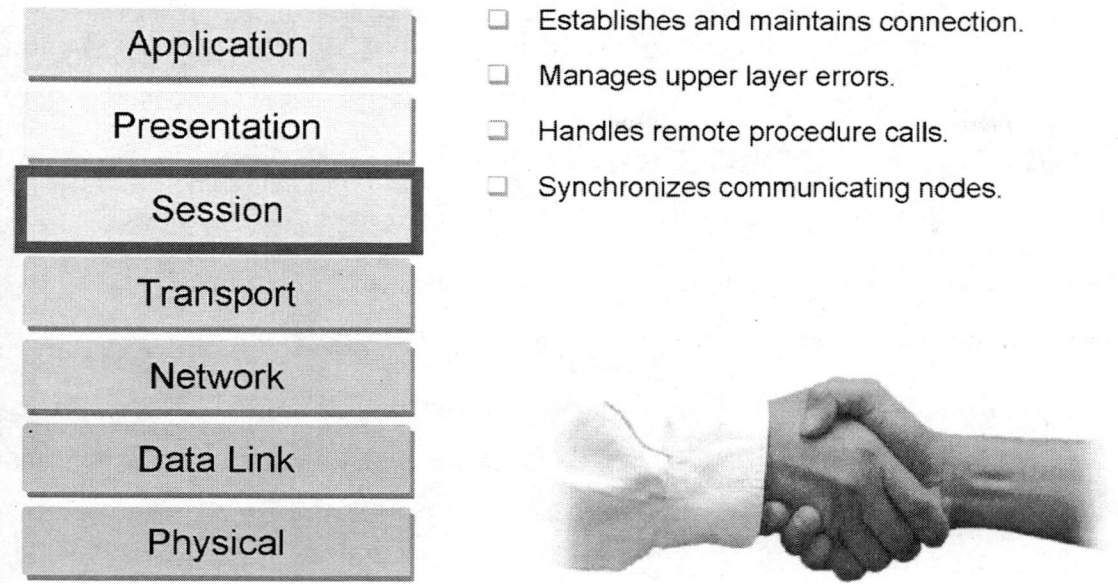

Figure B-6: *The Session layer.*

The Session layer provides guidelines for operating in Two-Way Alternate (TWA) mode, when two nodes take turns sending messages to each other, and in Two-Way Simultaneous (TWS) mode, when both nodes can send and receive at the same time. This layer also provides guidelines for setting check points so that if a transmission is interrupted, it can resume from an intermediate point, rather than starting from the beginning again.

Layer 6: The Presentation Layer

The *Presentation layer* negotiates and manages the way data is represented and encoded when data is transmitted between two nodes. This layer is responsible for file compression and encryption. This layer determines the best encoding system for data, taking into consideration the bandwidth, speed of the computers, and security requirements.

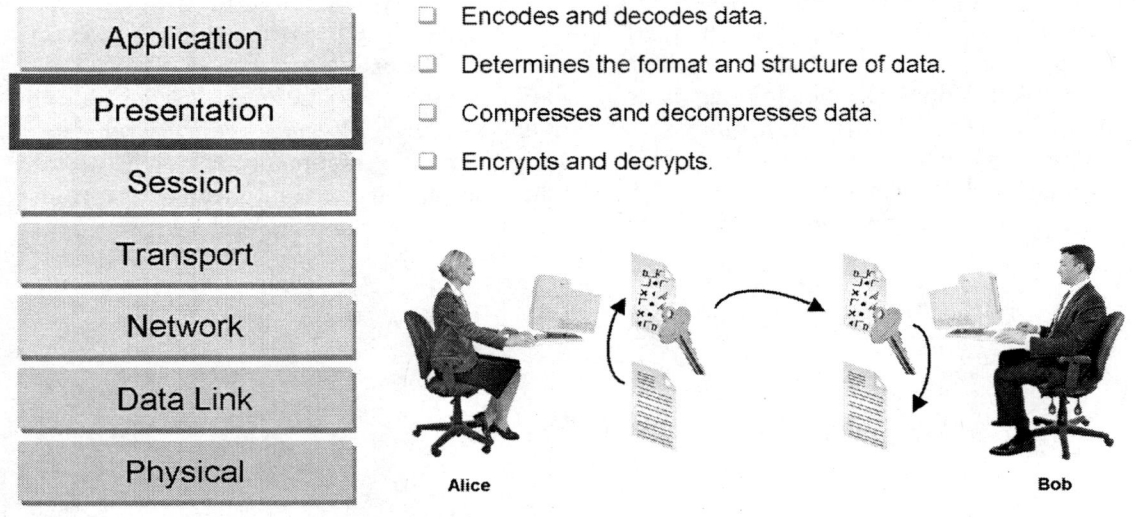

Figure B-7: *The Presentation layer.*

The time spent to compress a file might speed up the overall time needed to transfer a file sent over a slow connection, while the compression process might take up more time than is saved when the file is sent over a high-speed connection. The Presentation layer also makes sure that the receiving computer can understand the encoding of the message.

Layer 7: The Application Layer

The *Application layer* defines the language and syntax that programs use to open, close, read, write, request, and transfer files. It determines how programs communicate with other programs, like an email client program with an email server program.

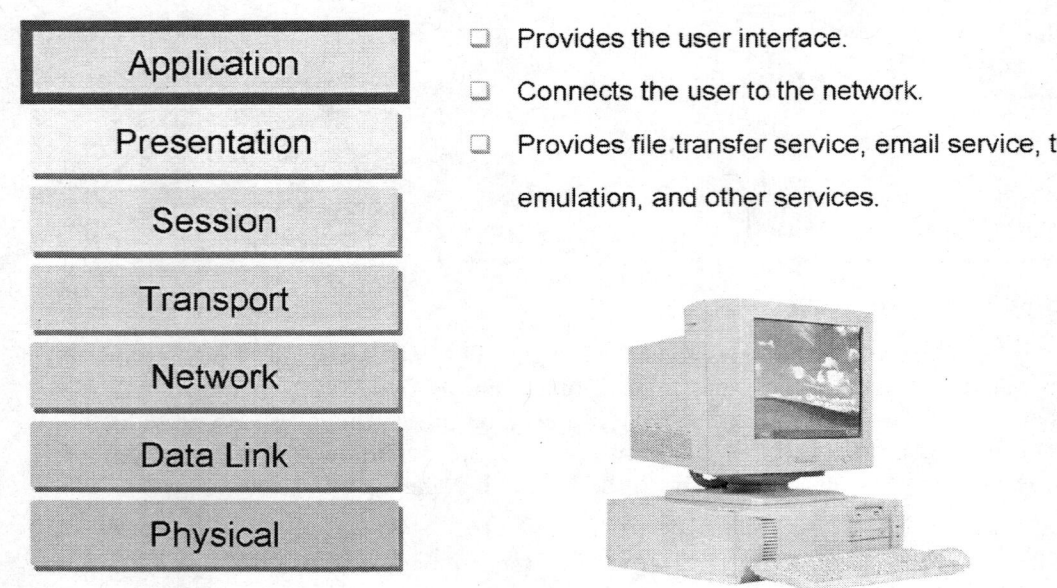

- Provides the user interface.
- Connects the user to the network.
- Provides file transfer service, email service, terminal emulation, and other services.

Figure B-8: *The Application layer.*

A Network in Action

As mentioned previously, the protocols in the OSI model layers communicate with each other to complete tasks. It is similar to sending a letter to a friend. The communications involved in that transaction extend well beyond you and your friend. For example, when you place the stamped and addressed letter in your mailbox, you communicate to the postal carrier that you want the letter taken to the post office for sorting and eventual delivery to your friend. The postal carrier's placement of the letter in a bin at the post office communicates to the postal clerk that the letter needs to be sorted. Several other transactions need to occur before your letter reaches its destination.

Appendix B

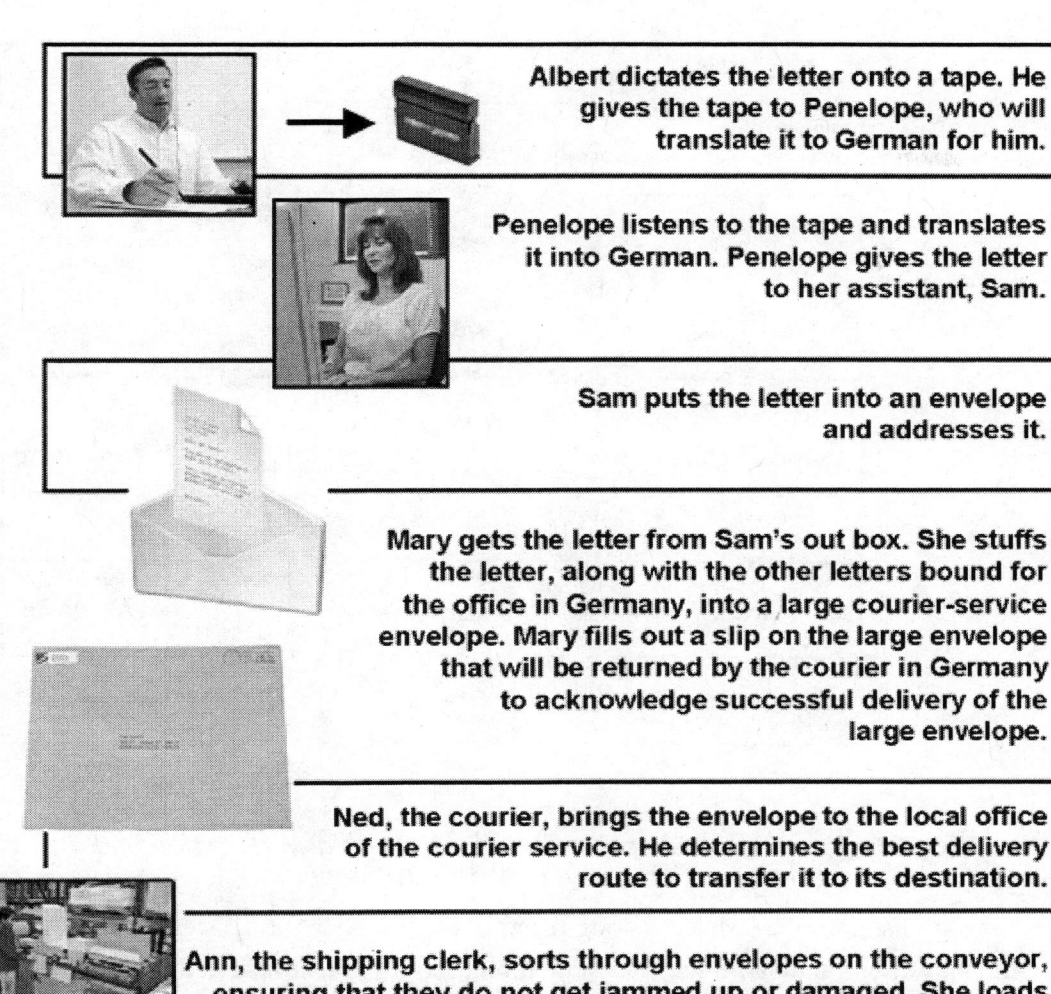

Figure B-9: *A network in action.*

Figure B-10 depicts a simple exchange in which a network node requests a file from a file server. Network components are shown in relation to the OSI reference model. As shown here, it is not unusual for some components to span more than one layer of the OSI model to accomplish the communication task at hand.

Appendix B

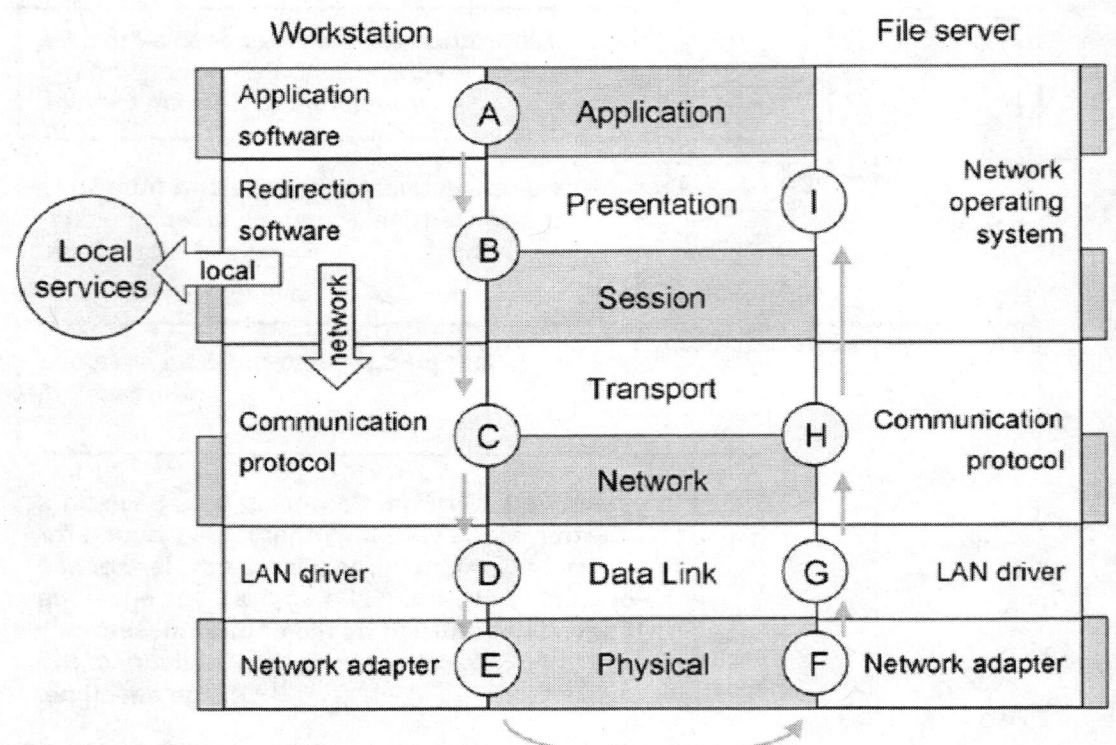

Figure B-10: *Components in a simple exchange between a workstation and a file server, shown in relationship to the layers of the OSI model.*

The following list describes what is taking place in Figure B-10:

A. An application running on the workstation requests a file that is stored on the network.

B. Redirection software on the workstation determines that the request is for network services. It directs the request to the communication protocol for transmission on the network.

C. The communication protocol determines the best route through the network and passes the request to the LAN driver, along with instructions that the message should be delivered to the file server.

D. The LAN driver copies the request into frames (bundles that can be moved across the network) and sends the frames to the network adapter for transmission.

E. The workstation's network interface board transmits the frames across the network.

F. The file server's network interface board receives the frames and passes them to its LAN driver.

G. The file server's LAN driver takes the message out of the frames and sends a confirmation to the workstation that it has received the frames.

H. The communication protocol verifies that the message was received intact, and it passes the message to the network operating system.

I. The network operating system receives the request and acts on it. The network operating system will use the layers of the network to transfer the requested file from a network hard disk to the workstation.

Appendix B

The Benefits of the OSI Model

By separating the tasks necessary for network access into a number of distinct layers, the OSI model enables the upper layers to work independently of the lower layers. For users, this translates (at least theoretically) to network transparency. Due to layering, your application should work as well over an Ethernet network as over a Token Ring or ARCNet network. Other than speed differences, the networks should work identically because the OSI model enables the components (the implementations of a layer or layers) to work independently. Again, in theory, on a workstation to switch from an Ethernet to a Token Ring network, you should have to switch only the network interface card (which takes care of the Physical and some of the Data Link functions) and some of the drivers (to take care of the remainder of the Data Link layer). The rest of the layers, and the drivers that implement them, should be able to remain in place without modification.

The ISO's publications describe the specifics of each layer in great detail. Even so, variations exist between network implementations that purportedly follow the OSI model. Only your testing can ensure that OSI-compliant systems are truly compatible for your environment. However, on their own, the ISO's detailed specifications go a long way toward ensuring compatibility.

Notes

APPENDIX C
A+™ Core Hardware Exam Objectives

CompTIA A+ Core Hardware Exam Objectives	Lesson	Topic
Domain 1: Installation, Configuration, and Upgrading		
Objective 1.1: Identify the names, purposes, and characteristics of system modules.		
Motherboard	1 4	B D
Firmware	1	C
Power Supply	4	A
Processor/CPU	1 4	B C
Memory	1 4	B E
Storage Devices	1	B
Drive Controllers	7	A
Display Devices	10	B
Adapter Cards	1	B
Ports	6	A
Cases	4	D
Riser Cards	4	D
Objective 1.2: Identify basic procedures for adding and removing field-replaceable modules for desktop systems. Given a replacement scenario, choose the appropriate sequences.		
Desktop components:		
Motherboard	4	D
Storage Devices	8	B
• Drive Controllers	7	A
• FDD	9	A
• HDD	8	B

Appendix C

CompTIA A+ Core Hardware Exam Objectives	Lesson	Topic
• CD/CDRW	9	B
• DVD/DVDRW	9	B
• Tape Drive	9	D
• Removable Storage	9	A, B, C, D
Power Supply	4	A
• AC Adapter	11	A
• AT/ATX	4	A
Cooling Systems		
• Fans	4	C
• Heat sinks	4	C
• Liquid cooling	4	C
Processor/CPU	4	C
Memory	4	E
Display device	10	B
Input devices		
• Keyboard	10	A
• Mouse/pointer devices	10	A
• Touch screen	10	D
Adapters		
• Network Interface Card (NIC)	12	A
• Sound card	7	C
• Video card	7	B
• Modem	7	D
• SCSI	7	A
• IEEE 1394/FireWire	6	E
• USB	6	D
• Wireless	6	F

Objective 1.3: Identify basic procedures for adding and removing field-replaceable modules for portable systems. Given a replacement scenario, choose the appropriate sequences.

Portable components:		
Storage Devices		
• FDD	11	G
• HDD	11	G
• CD/CD-RW	11	C
• DVD/DVD-RW	11	C
• Removable Storage	11	C

Appendix C

CompTIA A+ Core Hardware Exam Objectives	Lesson	Topic
Power supplies		
• AC Adapter	11	A
• DC adapter	11	A
• Battery	11	A
Memory	11	F
Input devices		
• Keyboard	11	G
• Mouse/pointer devices	11	G
• Touch screen	10	D
PCMCIA/Mini PCI Adapters		
• Network Interface Card (NIC)	11	D, G
• Modem	11	D, G
• SCSI	11	D, G
• IEEE 1394/Firewire	11	D, G
• USB	11	D, G
• Storage (memory and hard drive)	11	C, F
Docking station / port replicators	11	B
LCD panel	11	A
Wireless		
• Adapter / controller	11	D
• Antennae	11	D
Objective 1.4: Identify typical IRQs, DMAs, and I/O addresses, and procedures for altering these settings when installing and configuring devices. Choose the appropriate installation or configuration steps in a given scenario.		
Legacy devices (e.g. ISA sound card)	5	C
Specialized devices (e.g. CAD/CAM)	5	A
Internal modems	7	D
Floppy drive controllers	5	A
Hard drive controllers	7	A
Multimedia devices	7	C
NICs	12	A
I/O ports		
• Serial	6	A
• Parallel	6	B
• USB ports	6	D
• IEEE 1394/FireWire	6	E
• Infrared	6	F

Appendix C: A+™ Core Hardware Exam Objectives

APPENDIX C

CompTIA A+ Core Hardware Exam Objectives	Lesson	Topic
Objective 1.5: Identify the names, purposes, and performance characteristics of standardized/common peripheral ports, associated cabling, and their connectors. Recognize ports, cabling, and connectors by sight.		
Port types		
• Serial	6	A
• Parallel	6	B
• USB ports	6	D
• IEEE 1394/FireWire	6	E
• Infrared	6	F
Cable types		
• Serial (straight through vs. null modem)	6	A
• Parallel	6	B
• USB	6	D
Connector types		
• Serial:		
—DB-9	6	A
—DB-25	6	A
—RJ-11	12	A
—RJ-45	12	A
• Parallel:		
—DB-25	6	B
—Centronics (mini, 36)	6	B
• PS2/Mini-DIN	6	C
• USB	6	D
• IEE 1394 / FireWire	6	E
Objective 1.6: Identify proper procedures for installing and configuring common IDE devices. Choose the appropriate installation or configuration sequences in given scenarios. Recognize the associated cables.		
IDE Interface Types		
• EIDE	7	A
• ATA/ATAPI	7	A
• Serial ATA	7	A
• PIO	7	A
RAID (0, 1, and 5)	8	E
Master/Slave/Cable Select	8	B
Devices per channel	8	B
Primary/Secondary	8	B
Cable orientation/requirements	8	B

APPENDIX C

CompTIA A+ Core Hardware Exam Objectives	Lesson	Topic
Objective 1.7: Identify proper procedures for installing and configuring common SCSI devices. Choose the appropriate installation or configuration sequences in given scenarios. Recognize the associated cables.		
SCSI Interface Types		
• Narrow	8	C
• Fast	8	C
• Wide	8	C
• Ultra-wide	8	C
• LVD	8	C
• HVD	8	C
Internal versus external	8	C
SCSI IDs		
• Jumper block/DIP switch settings (binary equivalents)	8	C
• Resolving ID conflicts	8	D
RAID (0, 1, and 5)	8	E
Cabling		
• Length	8	C
• Type	8	C
• Termination requirements (active, passive, auto)	8	C
Objective 1.8: Identify proper procedures for installing and configuring common peripheral devices. Choose the appropriate installation or configuration sequences in given scenarios.		
Modems and transceivers		
• Dial-Up	7	D
• Cable	12	D
• DSL	12	D
• ISDN	12	D
External storage	8	C
Digital cameras	10	D
PDAs	11	H
Wireless Access Points	12	D
Infrared devices	6	F
Printers	10	C
UPS and Suppressors	13	C
Monitors	10	B
Objective 1.9: Identify procedures to optimize PC operations in specific situations. Predict the effects of specific procedures under given scenarios.		
Cooling systems		
• Liquid	4	C

Appendix C: A+™ Core Hardware Exam Objectives

APPENDIX C

CompTIA A+ Core Hardware Exam Objectives	Lesson	Topic
• Air	4	C
• Heat sink	4	C
• Thermal compound	4	C
Disk subsystem enhancements		
• Hard drives	8	A
• Controller cards (e.g. RAID, ATA-100, etc.)	7 8	A E
• Cables	8	C
NICs	12	A
Specialized video cards	7	B
Memory	4	E
Additional processors	4	C
Objective 1.10: Determine the issues that must be considered when upgrading a PC. In a given scenario, determine when and how to upgrade system components.		
Drivers for legacy devices	13	F
Bus types and characteristics	13	F
Cache in relationship to motherboards	13	F
Memory capacity and characteristics	13	F
Processor speed and compatibility	13	F
Hard drive capacity and characteristics	13	F
System/firmware limitations	13	F
Power supply output capacity	13	F
Components:		
Motherboards	4	D
Memory	4	E
Hard drives	8	A
CPU	4	C
BIOS	4	B
Adapter cards	7	A
Laptop power sources		
• Lithium ion	11	A
• NiMH	11	A
• Fuel cell	11	A
PCMCIA Type I, II, and III cards	11	D
Domain 2: Diagnosing and Troubleshooting		
Objective 2.1: Recognize common problems associated with each module and their symptoms, and identify steps to isolate and troubleshoot the problems. Given a problem situation, interpret the symptoms and infer the most likely cause.		
I/O ports and cables		
• Serial	6	A

Appendix C

CompTIA A+ Core Hardware Exam Objectives	Lesson	Topic
• Parallel	6	B
• USB ports	6	D
• IEEE 1394/FireWire	6	E
• Infrared	6	F
• SCSI	8	D
Motherboards		
• CMOS/BIOS settings	4	B
• POST audible/visual error codes	4	B
Peripherals	10	A
Computer case		
• Power supply	4	A
• Slot covers	4	D
• Front cover alignment	4	D
Storage devices and cables		
• FDD	9	A
• HDD	8	D
• CD/CD-RW	9	B
• DVD/DVD-RW	9	B
• Tape drive	9	D
• Removable storage	9	D
Cooling systems		
• Fans	4	C
• Heat sinks	4	C
• Liquid cooling	4	C
• Temperature sensors	4	C
Processor/CPU	4	C
Memory	4	E
Display device	10	B
Input devices		
• Keyboard	10	A
• Mouse/pointer devices	10	A
• Touch screen	10	D
Adapters		
• Network Interface Card (NIC)	12	F
• Sound card	5	H
• Video card	5	H

Appendix C: A+™ Core Hardware Exam Objectives

APPENDIX C

CompTIA A+ Core Hardware Exam Objectives	Lesson	Topic
• Modem	7	D
• SCSI	8	D
• IEEE 1394/FireWire	6	E
• USB	6	D
Portable systems		
• PCMCIA	11	D
• Batteries	11	A
• Docking stations/Port replicators	11	B
• Portable unique storage	11	F
Objective 2.2: Identify basic troubleshooting procedures and tools, and how to elicit problem symptoms from customers. Justify asking particular questions in a given scenario.		
Troubleshooting/Isolation/Problem determination procedures	2	C
Determining whether a hardware or software problem	2	C
Gathering information from user		
• Customer environment	2	C
• Symptoms/error codes	2	C
• Situation when the problem occurred	2	C
Domain 3: Preventive Maintenance		
Objective 3.1: Identify the various types of preventive maintenance measures, products, and procedures and when and how to use them.		
Liquid cleaning compounds	13 13	D E
Connections	13	D
Non-static vacuums (chassis, power supplies, fans)	13	E
Cleaning monitors	13	D
Cleaning removable media devices	13	E
Ventilation, dust and moisture control on the PC hardware interior	13	E
Hard disk maintenance (defragging, scan disk, CHKDSK)	13	A
Verifying UPS (Uninterruptible Power Supply) and suppressors	13	C
Objective 3.2: Identify various safety measures and procedures, and when/how to use them.		
ESD precautions and procedures		
• What ESD can do, how it may be apparent or hidden	3	B
• Common ESD protection devices	2	A
• Situations that could present a danger or hazard	3	A

Appendix C

CompTIA A+ Core Hardware Exam Objectives	Lesson	Topic
Potential hazards and proper safety procedures relating to:		
• High-voltage equipment	3	A
• Power supply	4	A
• CRTs	10	B
Objective 3.3: Identify environmental protection measures and procedures, and when/how to use them.		
Special disposal procedures that comply with environmental guidelines	13	G
• Batteries	13	G
• CRTs	13	G
• Chemical solvents and cans	13	G
• MSDS (Material Safety Data Sheet)	13	G
Domain 4: Motherboard/Processors/Memory		
Objective 4.1: Distinguish between the popular CPU chips in terms of their basic characteristics.		
Popular CPU chips (Pentium class compatible)	4	C
Voltage	4	C
Speeds (actual vs. advertised)	4	C
Cache level I, II, III	4	C, E
Sockets/slots	4	C
VRM(s)	4	D
Objective 4.2: Identify the types of RAM (Random Access Memory), form factors, and operational characteristics. Determine banking and speed requirements under given scenarios.		
Content may include the following:		
Types		
• EDO RAM (Extended Data Output RAM)	4	E
• DRAM (Dynamic Random Access Memory)	4	E
• SRAM (Static RAM)	4	E
• VRAM (Video RAM)	4	E
• SDRAM (Synchronous Dynamic RAM)	4	E
• DDR (Double Data Rate)	4	E
• RAMBUS	4	E
Form factors (including pin count)	4	E
• SIMM (Single In-line Memory Module)	4	E
• DIMM (Dual In-line Memory Module)	4	E
• SoDIMM (Small outline DIMM)	4	E
• MicroDIMM	4	E
• RIMM (Rambus Inline Memory Module)	4	E

Appendix C: A+™ Core Hardware Exam Objectives

Appendix C

CompTIA A+ Core Hardware Exam Objectives	Lesson	Topic
Operational characteristics	4	E
• Memory chips (8-bit, 16-bit, and 32-bit)	4	E
• Parity chips versus non-parity chips	4	E
• ECC vs. non-ECC	4	E
• Single-sided vs. double-sided	4	E
Objective 4.3: Identify the most popular types of motherboards, their components, and their architecture (bus structures).		
Types of motherboards		
• AT	4	D
• ATX	4	D
Components		
• Communications ports	4	D
• Serial	4	D
• USB	4	D
• Parallel	4	D
• IEEE 1394/FireWire	4	D
• Infrared	4	D
Memory		
• SIMM	4	C
• DIMM	4	C
• RIMM	4	C
• SoDIMM	4	C
• MicroDIMM	4	C
Processor sockets		
• Slot 1	4	C
• Slot 2	4	C
• Slot A	4	C
• Socket A	4	C
• Socket 7	4	C
• Socket 8	4	C
• Socket 423	4	C
• Socket 478	4	C
• Socket 370	4	C
External cache memory (Level 2)	4	E
Bus Architecture	5	A
ISA	5	C

Appendix C

CompTIA A+ Core Hardware Exam Objectives	Lesson	Topic
PCI	5	F
• PCI 32-bit	5	F
• PCI 64-bit	5	F
AGP	5	G
• 2X	5	G
• 4X	5	G
• 8X (Pro)	5	G
USB (Universal Serial Bus)	6	D
AMR (audio modem riser) slots	4	D
CNR (communication network riser) slots	4	D
Basic compatibility guidelines	13	F
IDE (ATA, ATAPI, ULTRA-DMA, EIDE)	7	A
SCSI (Narrow, Wide, Fast, Ultra, HVD, LVD (Low Voltage Differential)	8	C
Chipsets	4	D

Objective 4.4: Identify the purpose of CMOS (Complementary Metal-Oxide Semiconductor) memory, what it contains, and how and when to change its parameters. Given a scenario involving CMOS, choose the appropriate course of action.

CMOS Settings:		
Default settings	4	B
CPU settings	4	B
Printer parallel port—Uni, bi-directional, disable/enable/ ECP, EPP	4	B
Com/serial port—memory address, interrupt request, disable	4	B
Floppy drive—enable/disable drive or boot, speed, density	4	B
Hard drive—size and drive type	4	B
Memory—speed, parity, non-parity	4	B
Boot sequence	4	B
Date/Time	4	B
Passwords	4	B
Plug & Play BIOS	4	B
Disabling on-board devices	4	B
Disabling virus protection	4	B
Power management	4	B
Infrared	4	B

Domain 5: Printers

Objective 5.1: Identify printer technologies, interfaces, and options/upgrades.

Technologies:		
Laser	10	C

Appendix C: A+™ Core Hardware Exam Objectives

Appendix C

CompTIA A+ Core Hardware Exam Objectives	Lesson	Topic
Ink dispersion (inkjet)	10	C
Dot matrix	10	C
Solid ink	10	C
Thermal	10	C
Dye sublimation	10	C
Interfaces:		
Parallel	10	C
Network	10	C
SCSI	10	C
USB	10	C
Infrared	10	C
Serial	10	C
IEEE 1394/FireWire	10	C
Wireless	10	C
Options/Upgrades include:		
Memory	10	C
Hard drives	10	C
NICs	10	C
Trays and feeders	10	C
Finishers (e.g. stapling, etc)	10	C
Scanners/fax/copier	10	D
Objective 5.2: Recognize common printer problems and techniques used to resolve them.		
Printer drivers	1 10	C C
Firmware updates	1 10	C C
Paper feed and output	10	C
Calibrations	10	C
Printing test pages	10	C
Errors (printed or displayed)	10	C
Memory	10	C
Configuration	10	C
Network connections	10	C
Connections	10	C
Paper jam	10	C
Print quality	10	C
Safety precautions	10	C
Preventive maintenance	13	B
Consumables	10 13	C G
Environment	10 13	C G

Appendix C

CompTIA A+ Core Hardware Exam Objectives	Lesson	Topic
Domain 6: Basic Networking		
Objective 6.1: Identify the common types of network cables, their characteristics and connectors.		
Coaxial		
• RG6	12	A
• RG8	12	A
• RG58	12	A
• RG59	12	A
Plenum/PVC	12	A
UTP		
• CAT3	12	A
• CAT 5/e	12	A
• CAT6	12	A
STP	12	A
Fiber		
• Single-mode	12	A
• Multi-mode	12	A
Connector types include:		
BNC	12	A
RJ-45	12	A
AUI	12	A
ST/SC	12	A
IDC/UDC	12	A
Objective 6.2: Identify basic networking concepts including how a network works.		
Installing and configuring network cards	12	A
Addressing	12	B
Bandwidth	12	D
Status indicators	12	B
Protocols		
• TCP/IP	12	B
• IPX/SPX (NWLink)	12	B
• AppleTalk	12	B
• NetBEUI/NetBIOS	12	B
Full-duplex, half-duplex	12	A
Cabling—Twisted Pair, Coaxial, Fiber Optic, RS-232	12	A
Networking models		
• Peer-to-peer	12	A
• Client/server	12	A

Appendix C: A+™ Core Hardware Exam Objectives

APPENDIX C

CompTIA A+ Core Hardware Exam Objectives	Lesson	Topic
Infrared	12	D
Wireless	12	D
Objective 6.3: Identify common technologies available for establishing Internet connectivity and their characteristics.		
Technologies:		
LAN	12	D
DSL	12	D
Cable	12	D
ISDN	12	D
Dial-up	12	D
Satellite	12	D
Wireless	12	D
Characteristics include:		
Definition	12	D
Speed	12	D
Connections	12	D

Appendix D

A+™ Certification Core Hardware Online Tutorial Components

Online Components	Courseware Lesson	Courseware Topic
Introduction to Computers:		
A Brief History of Computers	1	A
Desktop Computer System Component and Their Functions	1	B
Software and Firmware	1	C
Numbering Systems	1	D
Setting Up a Personal Computer		
Install Video Output Devices	7	A
Install PS/2 Devices	6	C
Install Parallel Devices	6	B
Install Serial Devices	6	A
Install Game and Sound Devices	7	C
Install USB Devices	6	D
Install FireWire Devices	6	E
Connect Wireless Devices	6	F
Installing of Removing Internal Hardware		
Establish an ESD-free Work Area	3	B
Install or Remove Adapter Cards	12	B
	7	A, B, C, D
Install a Network Adapter and Cable	12	A, B
Install or Remove IDE Drives	8	B
Install or Remove Internal SCSI Drives	8	C
Install External SCSI Drives	8	C

Appendix D

Online Components	Courseware Lesson	Courseware Topic
RAID	8	E
Upgrading System Components		
Add Memory	4	E
Upgrade the CPU	4	C
Add a CPU	4	C
Upgrade the System BIOS	4	B
Upgrade the Power Supply	4	A
Upgrade the System Board	4	D
Decide When to Upgrade	13	F
Supporting Portable Computing Devices		
Connect External Peripherals to a Portable Computer	11	B
Install or Remove Portable Computing Device Drives	11	C
Install or Remove PCMCIA Cards	11	D
Install or Remove Mini-PCI Cards	11	E
Install or Add Memory to a Portable Computing Device	11	F
Connect PDAs to Computers	11	H
Performing Preventative Maintenance		
Hard Disk Maintenance	13	A
Perform Printer Maintenance	13	B
Use a USB	13	C
Clean Peripheral Components	13	D
Clean Internal System Components	13	E
Dispose of Computer Equipment	13	G
Troubleshooting Device Problems		
Diagnose System Problems	2	C
Correct Monitor Problems	10	B
Correct Input Device Problems	10	A
Correct Adapter Card and PC Card Problems	5	H
	11	D
Correct Hard Drive Problems	7	D
Correct Internal Removable Media Device Problems	9	D
Correct CD or DVD Problems	9	B
Correct Printer Problems	10	C
Troubleshooting System Problems		
Correct Network Connection Problems	12	F
Correct Modem Problems	7	D
Correct Power Problems	4	A
Correct Boot Problems	4	B
Correct Memory Problems	4	E
Correct System Board Problems	4	C

APPENDIX D

Online Components	Courseware Lesson	Courseware Topic
Correct Portable System Problems	11	G

Notes

Lesson Labs

Due to classroom setup constraints, some labs cannot be keyed in sequence immediately following their associated lesson. Your instructor will tell you whether your labs can be practiced immediately following the lesson or whether they require separate setup from the main lesson content.

Lesson 1 Lab 1

Examining Computer Basics

Activity Time:

15 minutes

Objective:

Scenario:

As part of your application for a job supporting Windows 2000 and Windows XP computers, you've been asked to answer some questions. Provide appropriate answers to the following questions.

---

1. Arrange the following mechanical computers in the order they were invented.

    Difference Engine

    Arithmometer

    Abacus

    Pascaline Machine

    Stepped Reckoner

Lesson Labs

2. **Arrange the following technologies in the order they were invented.**

   UNIVAC

   Mark I

   Integrated circuits

   8008 microprocessor

   ENIAC

   Transistors

3. **Match the technology with its description.**

   ___ Chipset   a. The collection of wires that connect an interface card and the microprocessor, and the rules that describe how data should be transferred through the connection.

   ___ CMOS RAM   b. Special memory that stores information about the computer setup that the computer refers to each time it starts.

   ___ Hard disk   c. A fixed unit inside a computer that magnetically stores data on rigid circular platters.

   ___ CD-R   d. A CD on which you can write information.

   ___ Bus   e. The set of chips on the system board that support the CPU and other basic functions.

4. **Match the decimal number with its binary or hexadecimal equivalent.**

   ___ 5   a. 7A120
   ___ 500   b. 1100001101010000
   ___ 5000   c. 1388
   ___ 50,000   d. 101
   ___ 500,000   e. 1F4

LESSON 2 LAB 1

Discussing Tools of the Trade

Activity Time:

15 minutes

Objective:

You will identify tools and methodologies that can be used to troubleshoot personal computer problems.

Scenario:

In this activity, you will identify tools that can be used to install and remove PC components, as well as discuss the different troubleshooting methodologies you can employ as an A+ technician.

Lesson Labs

1.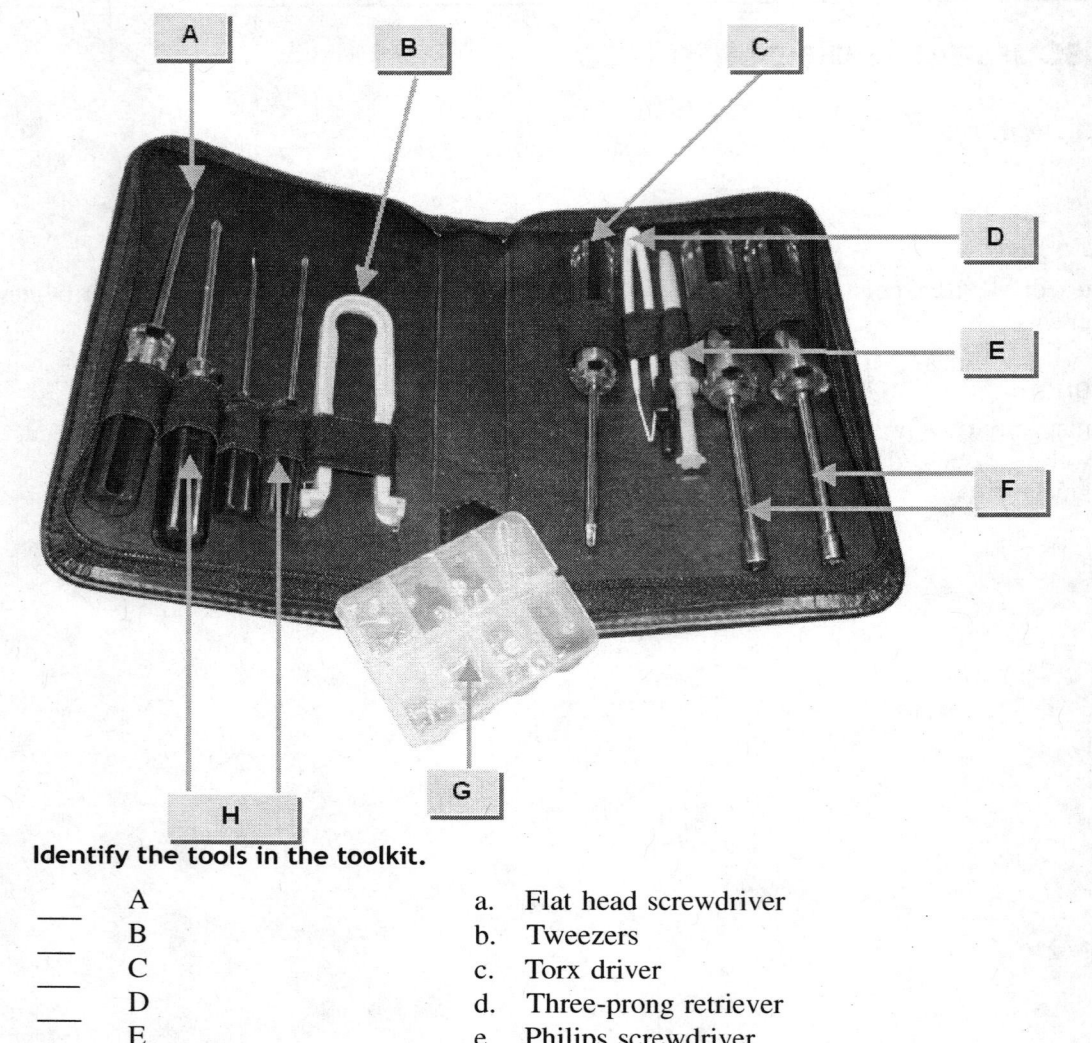

    Identify the tools in the toolkit.

    ___ A   a. Flat head screwdriver
    ___ B   b. Tweezers
    ___ C   c. Torx driver
    ___ D   d. Three-prong retriever
    ___ E   e. Philips screwdriver
    ___ F   f. Chip extractor
    ___ G   g. Storage container
    ___ H   h. Nut driver

2. **Which files need to be copied to a Windows 2000 boot disk?**

    a) Io.sys

    b) Msdos.sys

    c) Boot.ini

    d) Ntdetect.com

    e) System.ini

3. **Which files are optional on an MS-DOS boot disk?**

    a) Io.sys

    b) Edit.com

    c) Autexec.bat

    d) Format.com

    e) Command.com

4. **In the Help desk example, match the help desk technician task with the correct stage in the Collect, Isolate, and Correct troubleshooting model.**

    ___ The help desk technician asks the user questions to gather information about why the user's monitor is not working and finds out that the user just moved to a new office.   a. The collect stage.

    ___ The help desk technician asks the user to verify the monitor is plugged into a working outlet, the monitor power light is lit, and the monitor connector is firmly attached to the monitor connector in the back of the PC without any bent pins.   b. The isolate state.

    ___ The help desk technician determines a lose monitor cable connection from the move is the most likely culprit of the problem.   c. The correct stage.

Lesson 3 Lab 1

Investigating Safety

Activity Time:

10 minutes

Scenario:

You're at a customer's site servicing various computers and peripherals. They have asked you for advice on safe computing practices.

1. **Name at least three factors that you should consider when setting up an ergonomic work station.**

2. **True or False? You enter the computer room to find a server in the equipment rack is on fire. You should use a Class A rated fire extinguisher to put out this kind of fire.**
   ___ True
   ___ False

3. **Select the three hazardous situations you are likely to encounter while servicing PCs.**
   a) Electrocution
   b) Poor air quality
   c) Toxic chemicals
   d) Lasers

4. **True or False? Computer components can be harmed by static electricity, but you are very unlikely to be hurt by it.**
   ___ True
   ___ False

LESSON 4 LAB 1

LESSON LABS

Troubleshooting Power Problems

Activity Time:
20 minutes

Scenario:
The following list of trouble tickets are power problems that have been assigned for you to resolve.

- Trouble ticket: 125001

    Location: Main building, 51B24

    User: Darlene Burley

    When the user turns on the PC, it doesn't always come on and sometimes it just shuts itself down abruptly, with no warning. When she turns on the system again, there is no fan noise. She is using a legacy database application and the data is being corrupted during the improper shutdowns.

- Trouble ticket: 125002

    Location: Main building, 21K37

    User: Earle Washburn

    The user turns on the power switch, but the system does not come on. He does not hear the fan, there is no power light on, and he hears no beeps or other sounds coming from the system. His system is plugged into a surge protector.

- Trouble ticket: 125003

    Location: Elmwood Place, cube 20

    User: Sylvania Rawleigh

    One of the other hardware technicians has been trying to troubleshoot a power problem. The system will not come on when the user turns on the power switch. He determined that the user has an ATX system board and power supply. You have been assigned to take over this trouble ticket.

1. **What should you do to resolve trouble ticket 125001?**

2. **Resolve trouble ticket 125002.**

3. Resolve trouble ticket 125003.

 When you have finished, you can refer to the Troubleshooting Power Problems Lab Results.txt file to check your work.

LESSON 4 LAB 2

Troubleshooting Boot Problems

Activity Time:

20 minutes

Scenario:

The following are the trouble tickets to which you have been assigned. All of the users are experiencing some type of problem when trying to boot their systems.

- Trouble ticket: 175001

  Location: Main building, 12C42

  User: Eric Spender

  The system is slow to boot. On responding to the user's trouble ticket, you find that the system contains an Intel D815EEA motherboard.

- Trouble ticket: 175002

  Location: Elmwood Place, cube 12

  User: Samantha Condello

  The user hears beeps when starting the system. She hears four beeps followed by another four beeps followed by one beep.

- Trouble ticket: 175003

  Location: Main building, 22G44

  User: Patti Lu

  One long beep followed by three short beeps sound when the user attempts to start the system. This system has AMI BIOS.

- Trouble ticket: 175004

  Location: Main building

  User: Garold Martin

  When the user tries to boot, the message Non-system Disk Or Disk Error is displayed.

- Trouble ticket: 175005

  Location: Main building, 51A12

User: Joellen Folts

The user inherited this system from a previous employee. The previous employee set a power-on password for the system and nobody knows what it is.

1. **What are some potential causes and solutions to the problem described in trouble ticket 175001?**

2. **Search using a Web search engine such as Google for the beep code pattern indicated in trouble ticket 175002. Which BIOS manufacturer uses this beep code pattern and what are some potential causes and solutions to the problem described in trouble ticket 175002?**

3. **What are some potential causes and solutions to the problem described in trouble ticket 175003?**

4. **What are some potential causes and solutions to the problem described in trouble ticket 175004?**

5. **What are some potential causes and solutions to the problem described in trouble ticket 175005?**

When you have finished, you can refer to the Troubleshooting Boot Problems Lab Results.txt file to check your work.

Lesson Labs

LESSON 4 LAB 3

Adding and Removing a Second Processor

Activity Time:

20 minutes

Setup:

The hands-on steps in this activity can be completed only if you have a dual-processor system board, two matching processors, and a termination board.

Scenario:

One of your users is a software developer. She has a system with dual processor capability. She needs to test the application she is writing to see how much the second processor affects the processing speed.

1. If you are running a dual-processor system with only one processor, which socket does the processor go in?

2. If you are running a dual-processor system with only one processor, what do you need to do to the empty socket?

3. What needs to be similar about both processors? How is it best to make sure of this?

4. Remove the second processor.

5. Verify that the single processor is functioning properly.

6. Install the second processor.

7. Verify that both processors are functioning properly.

> When you have finished, you can refer to the Adding and Removing a Second Processor Lab Results.txt file to check your work.

LESSON 4 LAB 4

Troubleshooting Memory Problems

Activity Time:
20 minutes

Scenario:
The following are the trouble tickets to which you have been assigned. All of the users are experiencing some type of problem related to the memory installed in their systems.

- Trouble ticket: 401001

    Location: Main building, 12B52

    User: Roger Wheaton

    The user is experiencing corrupted data in his database application. The hard drive has been checked and no problems were found with it. The application was reinstalled and the database was reindexed and all data problems have been corrected. No other users are experiencing this problem when they enter data. He has been successfully entering data until just recently.

- Trouble ticket: 401002

    Location: Elmwood Place, cube 6

    User: Rory Waldon

    The user is complaining of application crashes. He is fine if he is only running his email and word processing programs. If he also opens his graphics program at the same time, then the applications are crashing.

- Trouble ticket: 401003

    Location: Main building, 22G42

    User: Hazel Beech

    Additional memory was installed in her system and now it won't boot.

1. After troubleshooting trouble ticket 401001, you believe it is memory related. Why might the memory experience problems all of a sudden?

LESSON LABS

2. You are attempting to resolve trouble ticket 401002. Why is the user only experiencing the problem when additional applications are opened? What can you do to determine the cause?

3. Resolve trouble ticket 401003.

> When you have finished, you can refer to the Troubleshooting Memory Problems Lab Results.txt file to check your work.

LESSON 5 LAB 1

Troubleshooting PC Adapter Card Problems

Activity Time:
30 minutes

Scenario:
The call center has received several trouble calls that have been assigned to you. All of the tickets on your list are related to internal PC adapter card problems. You need to resolve the problems and get the users back to work. The following is a list of the trouble tickets you are responding to:

- Ticket 399001:

    Location: Main building, 33J27

    User: Aminah Sinclair

    The user is still having problems with his video system. All monitor problems were reviewed and none of these resolved the problem. Therefore, it points toward a problem with the video card.

- Ticket 399002:

    Location: Main building, 31L19

    User: Randi Keene

    A second parallel-port adapter ISA card was added to the system by the user. Now, she cannot connect to the network and the new card is not working.

- Ticket 399003:

    Location: Elmwood Place, cube 14

    User: Conroy Ives

LESSON LABS

Last night a lightning storm struck. Most equipment was fine, but this user is having problems with getting on the network. All other users in the area are connecting without problems.

- Ticket 399004:

    Location: Training center, room 8

    User: Kai Beyer

    The user reports that the speakers connected to his sound card produce a hum all the time.

- Ticket 399005:

    Location: Main building, 11A12

    User: Ardon Blandon

    The user reports no sound coming from the speakers connected to his sound card.

1. **Respond to trouble ticket 399001.**

2. **Respond to trouble ticket 399002.**

3. **Respond to trouble ticket 399003.**

4. **Respond to trouble ticket 399004.**

5. **Respond to trouble ticket 399005.**

 When you have finished, you can refer to the Troubleshooting PC Adapter Card Problems Lab Results.txt file to check your work.

LESSON 6 LAB 1

Setting Up PCs for a New Home Office

Activity Time:

2 hour(s)

Objective:

To assemble a typical set of components and peripherals to create a new, working desktop personal computer system.

Setup:

To perform this lab, you will need:

- One Pentium 4 desktop computer with a Windows operating system pre-installed, containing:
  — Two PS/2 ports (keyboard and mouse)
  — One parallel port
  — One serial port
  — Two USB ports
  — One FireWire port
- One wireless keyboard and mouse set.
- One PS/2-style keyboard and mouse set.
- One SVGA CRT-style monitor.
- Two PDAs with serial, infrared, and USB connection options and a cradle.
- One laser printer with parallel port and infrared connection options.
- One color inkjet printer with parallel port and USB connection options.
- One scanner with a USB connection.
- One digital camera with a USB connection.
- One USB hub.
- One digital video camera with an iLink/FireWire interface cable.
- Four USB cables.
- One parallel printer cable.
- Any other cables included with the various devices.
- Any equipment manufacturer's manuals included with the various devices.

LESSON LABS

- Access to the Windows installation media and to any other device drivers needed for the various devices.

Scenario:

You work for the R. A. Kash Computer Sales and Support company. A customer is setting up a new home business with her husband. They purchased equipment for a new desktop computer that you will be setting up at their home office.

R. A. Kash has the opportunity to become this customer's single source vendor for all hardware purchases and support requirements. You have been assigned to this account and need to set up all of the equipment so that the customer can begin using it tomorrow morning.

1. **Remove the system from the box, and then connect the included PS/2-style keyboard and mouse to the system.**

2. **Remove the monitor from the box and connect it to the monitor port.**

3. **Connect the laser printer to the system using the parallel printer cable.**

4. **Connect the PDA cradle to the serial port.**

5. **Connect the USB hub to the system.**

6. **Connect the color inkjet printer, the scanner, and the digital camera to the USB hub using USB cables.**

7. **Connect the digital video camera using the FireWire/iLink port.**

8. **Power on the system and install any drivers you are prompted for.**

9. **Test each device to verify that it works.**

10. **Connect the second PDA through an infrared connection, installing required drivers as needed.**

11. **Power down and remove the PS/2-style keyboard and mouse from the system in preparation for replacing them with the wireless units.**

12. **Connect the wireless keyboard and mouse to the desktop system, and then verify that they work correctly.**

13. **Print to the laser and ink jet printers through the appropriate connections.**

   When you have finished the lab, you can refer to the Setting Up PCs for a New Home Office Lab Results.txt file to check your work.

Lesson Labs

Lesson 7 Lab 1

Troubleshooting Modem Problems

Activity Time:

20 minutes

Setup:
You have access to an analog telephone and analog telephone line in order to test the modem connection. You have already installed and tested a modem in your system. You also have a dial-up account and phone number of a dial-up service to which you can connect.

Scenario:
The company has only recently started allowing employees to dial in to the network while on the road or working from home. The help center has been inundated with modem-related trouble tickets. The following is the list of tickets you have been assigned to handle.

- Trouble ticket: 415001

  Location: Elmwood Place, cube 26

  User: Amy Schweib

  User receives the message There Was No Dial Tone.

- Trouble ticket: 415002

  Location: Elmwood Place, cube 4

  User: Augusta Lindsay

  User sees the error message Modem Not Responding There Was A Hardware Failure In The Modem when she attempts to dial in.

- Trouble ticket: 415003

  Location: Elmwood Place, cube 9

  User: Caitlyn Thorp

  After attempting to connect, user sees the error message Dial-Up Networking Could Not Negotiate A Compatible Set Of Network Protocols, and the connection is dropped.

- Trouble ticket: 415004

  Location: Elmwood Place, cube 3

  User: Carm Traphagan

  After the modem dials, the user gets a message that the server is busy. She tried at various times of day and night and cannot believe it is always busy even during the middle of the night.

- Trouble ticket: 415005

  Location: Elmwood Place, cube 35

  User: Samuel Bolivier

Lesson Labs

The user's new modem does not respond when the user attempts to use dial-up networking.

- Trouble ticket: 415006

  Location: Elmwood Place, cube 2

  User: Maggie Palmateer

  The user receives the message The Remote Computer Did Not Respond even though it seems like it connected. She can hear the modem making the chhh sound.

1. **Resolve trouble ticket 415001.**

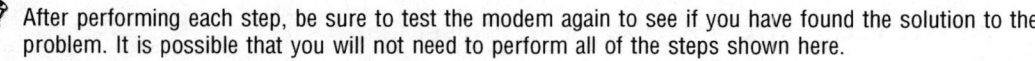
After performing each step, be sure to test the modem again to see if you have found the solution to the problem. It is possible that you will not need to perform all of the steps shown here.

2. **Resolve trouble ticket 415002.**

3. **Resolve trouble ticket 415003.**

4. **Resolve trouble ticket 415004.**

5. **Resolve trouble ticket 415005.**

6. **Resolve trouble ticket 415006.**

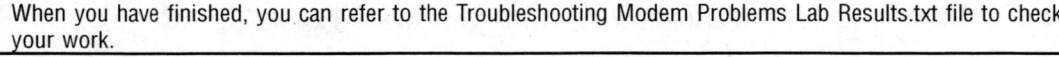
When you have finished, you can refer to the Troubleshooting Modem Problems Lab Results.txt file to check your work.

Lesson Labs

LESSON 8 LAB 1

Installing Storage Components

Activity Time:

1 hour(s)

Setup:

To perform this lab, you will need:

- 1 Pentium 4 desktop computer with:
  - A Windows operating system installed
  - 1 expansion slot available to install the additional adapter card
  - 2 empty drive bays to install the additional drives
- 1 IDE internal hard drive drive
- 1 PCI SCSI host bus adapter card, with driver disk (if the drivers are not supplied with Windows)
- 1 SCSI hard drive

Scenario:

You work for the R. A. Kash Computer Sales and Support company. The customer for whom you set up a new home business has purchased several new internal system devices for the desktop computer at their home office. The customer has contracted with your company to have you install the new devices.

1. **Establish an ESD-free work area in which to work on the systems.**

2. **Install the IDE drive in the system.**

3. **Install the SCSI host bus adapter in the system.**

4. **Install the SCSI internal drive in the system.**

    When you've finished the lab, you can refer to the Installing Storage Components Lab Results.txt file to check your work.

LESSON 9 LAB 1

Troubleshooting Removable Storage Systems

Activity Time:

1 hour(s)

Objective:

In this lab, you will troubleshoot removable storage systems.

Scenario:

You've been assigned several trouble tickets to resolve regarding malfunctioning removable storage systems.

- Ticket: 235005

    Location: Elmwood Place, cube 16A

    User: Wendy Jones

    User can't read any floppy disks on her drive, even if other users can read the disks on their systems. Also, other users can't read floppy disks she creates on her system.

- Ticket: 232003

    Location: Main building, 22C25

    User: Phillip Ward

    The user's system was recently upgraded to Windows XP. He can no longer access the CD-ROM drive on the system.

- Ticket: 234005

    Location: Main building, 41A41

    User: Kyria Shaver

    User has an older Zip drive attached through the Parallel port on a new system. The user is unable to access files on the Zip drive.

1. **Resolve trouble ticket 235005.**

2. **Resolve trouble ticket 232003.**

3. **Resolve trouble ticket 234005.**

 When you have finished the lab, you can refer to the Removable Storage Solution.txt file in the Lesson Lab Solution Files folder to check your work.

Lesson 10 Lab 1

Troubleshooting Input/output Devices

Activity Time:
1 hour(s)

Objective:
In this activity, you will troubleshoot input/output peripheral devices.

Setup:
To complete this lab, you will need a PDA device.

Scenario:
You've been assigned several trouble tickets to resolve regarding malfunctioning input/output peripheral devices.

- Ticket 299006:

    Location: Main building, 32B14

    User: Trudi Steele

    User's Palm touch screen is not responding when she touches it with her finger. Stylus input works sometimes.

- Ticket 296004:

    Location: Training center, room 4

    User: Tom Fisher

    The monitor comes on, and he works on the system for awhile. Then, he turns to do paperwork. When he turns back to work on the PC, the monitor is blank.

- Ticket: 215008

    Location: Main building, 13A36

    User: Terri Maximillion

    User has a USB inkjet printer. The user is connecting it through the USB port on their keyboard. She received the message The Hub Does Not Have Enough Power Available To Operate The Device Driver Name. Would You Like Assistance In Solving This Problem? If You Click No, The Device May Not Function Properly.

1. **Resolve trouble ticket 299006.**

2. **Resolve trouble ticket 296004.**

3. How could you resolve the problem described in trouble ticket 215008?

 When you have finished the lab, you can refer to the Input-Output Solution.txt file in the Lesson Lab Solution Files directory to check your work.

LESSON 11 LAB 1

Supporting Portable Computing Devices

Activity Time:
30 minutes

Objective:
To configure a typical portable computer system, including docking station and peripheral devices.

Setup:
To perform this lab, you will need:
- A portable computer with a Windows operating system installed.
- A compatible docking station.
- Standard desktop peripheral components, including monitor, keyboard, and mouse.
- A PDA device and software.
- A digital camera.
- An MP3 player.

Scenario:
You work for R. A. Kash Computer Sales and Support company. One of the customers you support is expanding their business. Everyone in the company spends a lot of time traveling, so they have purchased PDAs for all employees. The new employees will be traveling several days each month, so they will be set up with notebook computers and a matching docking solution so that they can use a full size monitor, keyboard, and mouse when they are at the home office. One of the users has a digital camera and needs to upload the pictures to the home office each day while traveling. She also has an MP3 player she would like to use while flying.

1. Set up the notebook computer.

2. Set up the docking solution connecting all of the desktop components the user will use through it while the notebook is docked.

LESSON LABS

3. Set up the PDA.

4. Install the PDA software on the computer.

5. Connect the digital camera to the notebook or insert the flash media in the PDA.

6. Connect the MP3 player to the computer.

 When you have finished the lab, you can refer to the Supporting Portable Computing Devices Lab Results.txt file in the Lesson Lab Solution Files folder to check your work.

LESSON 12 LAB 1

Connecting a PC to a Network

Activity Time:
30 minutes

Objective:
In this lab, you will be connecting a PC to a network.

Setup:
For this activity, you will need a personal computer that does not have a NIC installed, a NIC that is compatible with your PC, and appropriate cables and connectors.

Scenario:
A home user has brought their PC in to you so that it can be outfitted with a network card. They will be using the network card to connect to a cable modem for Internet access. Their ISP will be providing a valid IP address and other TCP/IP configuration values for them through a DHCP server.

1. **Install the network interface card in the PC.**

2. **Verify the NIC is functioning correctly and you can communicate with other PCs on your subnet.**

3. **If the NIC is not functioning correctly or you cannot communicate with other PCs on your subnet, troubleshoot and resolve the problem.**

4. **Verify the computer can communicate with servers on the Internet.**

5. If you cannot communicate with servers on the Internet, **troubleshoot and resolve the problem.**

 When you have finished the lab, you can refer to the Networking PC Solution.txt file in the Lesson Lab Solution Files folder to check your work.

LESSON 13 LAB 1

Performing Preventative Maintenance

Activity Time:
1 hour(s), 30 minutes

Objective:
To perform preventative maintenance on standard computer systems and peripherals, and to perform correct disposal procedures for obsolete computer equipment.

Setup:
To perform this lab, you will need:
- A desktop computer with a CRT monitor and a Windows operating system installed.
- A laptop computer with an LCD screen and a Windows operating system installed.
- A dot-matrix, inkjet, or laser printer.
- Assorted peripheral equipment: for example, a scanner and a PDA.
- A UPS.
- Assorted obsolete equipment and batteries.

Scenario:
The R. A. Kash Computer Sales and Support company has begun offering a preventative maintenance contract to its customers. Several customers have signed up to take advantage of this service. Today, you have been assigned the project of going to a customer's site and performing the preventative maintenance on all of his equipment. The customer also has some old equipment and batteries that need to be disposed of.

1. **Perform printer maintenance on the printer.**

2. **Install and configure the UPS.**

3. **Clean all peripherals.**

Lesson Labs

4. **Clean the interior of the desktop system.**

5. **Mark each of the pieces of obsolete equipment with the appropriate disposal method: computer recycler or regular garbage collection.**

 When you have finished the lab, you can refer to the Performing Preventative Maintenance Lab Results.txt file to check your work.

SOLUTIONS

Lesson 1

Activity 1-1

1. Match the inventor on the left with his contribution on the right.

    _d_ John Napier   a. Processed census data using punched cards.

    _e_ Blaise Pascal   b. Designed a mechanical calculator that could add, subtract, multiply, and divide.

    _b_ Gottfried von Leibniz   c. Designed the Difference Engine and the Analytical Engine.

    _a_ Herman Hollerith   d. Developed a series of rods that let users do multiplication by adding numbers.

    _c_ Charles Babbage   e. Developed the first digital calculating machine that could add and subtract.

2. Arrange the following devices in the order in which they were invented.

    _3_ Pascaline Machine

    _4_ Stepped Reckoner

    _6_ Babbage's Difference Engine

    _1_ Abacus

    _2_ Napier's Bones

    _5_ Punch cards

3. Match each technology with its description.

    _c_ Vacuum tubes   a. Replaced vacuum tubes to make electronic computers faster, smaller, and more efficient.

    _a_ Transistors   b. Allowed multiple transistors to exist on the same base material and connected transistors without using wires.

    _b_ Integrated circuits   c. Eliminated the need to manually wire a machine and set switches for each different program that was to be executed.

    _d_ Microprocessors   d. Allowed an entire computing device to reside on a single chip whose function could be controlled by programmed instructions.

SOLUTIONS

4. Arrange the following technologies in the order they were invented.

   _2_ UNIVAC

   _6_ Apple Macintosh

   _1_ EDSAC

   _5_ IBM PC

   _4_ Altair 8800

   _3_ Integrated circuits

Activity 1-2

1. Match the system component to its description.

_a_	System board	a.	Main circuit board of the computer.
_e_	Processor	b.	The actual chips that keep track of computer data.
_b_	Memory	c.	Means of connecting devices to the system board so that they can communicate with the microprocessor.
_c_	Interfaces	d.	The collection of wires that connect an interface card and the microprocessor, and the rules that describe how data should be transferred through the connection.
_d_	Bus	e.	The real brains of the computer where most of the calculations take place.

Activity 1-3

1. What role does application software play in the function of a desktop computer?

   Application software enables users to complete specific kinds of tasks—for example, writing a memo, developing a budget, or maintaining a mailing list.

2. What role does operating system software play in the function of a desktop computer?

   Operating systems perform basic tasks, such as recognizing input from the keyboard, sending output to the display screen, keeping track of files and directories on the disk, and controlling peripheral devices, such as disk drives and printers.

3. What role does driver software play in the function of a desktop computer?

   Driver software enables the operating system and application software to communicate with the hardware; for example, a printer driver enables you to print your word-processing document.

Activity 1-4

1. The decimal value for the exponential notation $7*10^0$ is _7_.

2. The decimal value for the exponential notation $4*10^1+3*10^0$ is _43_.

3. The decimal value for the exponential notation $4*10^2+6*10^1+5*10^0$ is _465_.

4. The decimal value for the exponential notation $8*10^3+6*10^2+7*10^1+2*10^0$ is _8,672_.

Activity 1-5

1. The decimal value of the binary number 1 is _1_.
2. The decimal value of the binary number 10 is _2_.
3. The decimal value of the binary number 101 is _5_.
4. The decimal value of the binary number 1101 is _13_.
5. The binary value of the decimal number 72 is _1001000_.
6. The binary value of the decimal number 283 is _100011011_.
7. The binary value of the decimal number 4,096 is _1000000000000_.

Activity 1-6

1. The hexadecimal equivalent of the decimal number 8 is _8_.
2. The hexadecimal equivalent of the decimal number 57 is _39_.
3. The hexadecimal equivalent of the decimal number 166 is _A6_.
4. The hexadecimal equivalent of the decimal number 3,416 is _D58_.

Activity 1-7

1. You try to save a 1.4 MB file on a disk with 1,400 KB of free space, but the computer states you don't have enough room. What is going on?

    *1.4 MB is really 1.4*1,024 KB or 1,433 KB. Your file is 33 KB larger than the disk can handle.*

2. The value of 4,095 (Base 10) in binary is _111111111111_.

3. The value of 4,095 (Base 10) in hexadecimal is _FFF_.

4. How many different values can you store in a binary number that is 16 bits long? What is the maximum value you can store?

    Sixteen bits can range from 0000 0000 0000 0000 to 1111 1111 1111 1111 or from 0 (Base 10) to 65,535 (Base 10) for a total of 65,536 different values.

Solutions

Lesson 1 Follow-up

Lesson 1 Lab 1

1. Arrange the following mechanical computers in the order they were invented.

    _5_ Difference Engine

    _4_ Arithmometer

    _1_ Abacus

    _2_ Pascaline Machine

    _3_ Stepped Reckoner

2. Arrange the following technologies in the order they were invented.

    _3_ UNIVAC

    _1_ Mark I

    _5_ Integrated circuits

    _6_ 8008 microprocessor

    _2_ ENIAC

    _4_ Transistors

3. Match the technology with its description.

    _e_ Chipset   a. The collection of wires that connect an interface card and the microprocessor, and the rules that describe how data should be transferred through the connection.

    _b_ CMOS RAM   b. Special memory that stores information about the computer setup that the computer refers to each time it starts.

    _c_ Hard disk   c. A fixed unit inside a computer that magnetically stores data on rigid circular platters.

    _d_ CD-R   d. A CD on which you can write information.

    _a_ Bus   e. The set of chips on the system board that support the CPU and other basic functions.

4. Match the decimal number with its binary or hexadecimal equivalent.

_d_	5	a.	7A120
_e_	500	b.	1100001101010000
_c_	5000	c.	1388
_b_	50,000	d.	101
_a_	500,000	e.	1F4

Lesson 2

Activity 2-1

1. You've been asked to repair a system board in a customer's PC. Which set of tools would be best suited for the task?

    a) Phillips screwdriver (#0); torx driver (size T15); tweezers; and a three-prong retriever.

    ✓ b) 30w ceramic solder iron; miniature pliers; wire cutters; and a solder iron stand with sponge.

    c) Wire strippers; precision wire cutters; digital multimeter; and cable crimper with dies.

    d) Chip extractor; chip inserter; rachet; and allen wrench.

    e) Anti-static cleaning wipes; anti-static wrist band; flashlight; and cotton swabs.

2. You've been asked to correct a network cabling problem at a customer site. Which set of tools would be best suited for the task?

    a) Phillips screwdriver (#0); torx driver (size T15); tweezers; and a three-prong retriever.

    b) 30w ceramic solder iron; miniature pliers; wire cutters; and a solder iron stand with sponge.

    ✓ c) Wire strippers; precision wire cutters; digital multimeter; and cable crimper with dies.

    d) Chip extractor; chip inserter; rachet; and allen wrench.

    e) Anti-static cleaning wipes; anti-static wrist band; flashlight; and cotton swabs.

3. You suspect that contaminants from the environment have prevented the fan on a PC from working optimally. Which set of tools would be best suited to fix the problem?

    a) Phillips screwdriver (#0); torx driver (size T15); tweezers; and a three-prong retriever.

    b) 30w ceramic solder iron; miniature pliers; wire cutters; and a solder iron stand with sponge.

    c) Wire strippers; precision wire cutters; digital multimeter; and cable crimper with dies.

    d) Chip extractor; chip inserter; rachet; and allen wrench.

    ✓ e) Anti-static cleaning wipes; anti-static wrist band; flashlight; and cotton swabs.

Activity 2-3

1. What do the troubleshooting models discussed in this section have in common?

    They all provide a systematic approach to solving problems, and they all include steps for collecting information about the problem, isolating the cause of the problem, and implementing a solution to the problem.

SOLUTIONS

2. **When troubleshooting a device problem on a Windows-based computer, what common troubleshooting tips are helpful to try first?**

   1. Check the device's physical connection.

   2. Check the adapter card to which the device is connected.

   3. Check Device Manager for indications on whether the OS sees a problem with the device.

   4. Use the Help And Support Center utility to help troubleshoot common problems with a particular device.

3. **When you receive notice that a user is having trouble with their computer, which is the best first step?**

   a) Determine how many users are having similar troubles.

   b) Isolate the cause of the problem.

   c) Ask the user leading questions to gather information.

   ✓ d) Check for simple solutions.

4. **According to the three troubleshooting methodologies, when is a problem considered solved?**

   a) When the device is working correctly.

   b) When the problem has been documented.

   ✓ c) When the user is satisfied that the problem is solved.

   d) When standards are developed to prevent future occurrences of the problem.

Lesson 2 Follow-up

Lesson 2 Lab 1

1. Identify the tools in the toolkit.

_a_	A	a.	Flat head screwdriver
_f_	B	b.	Tweezers
_c_	C	c.	Torx driver
_b_	D	d.	Three-prong retriever
_d_	E	e.	Philips screwdriver
_h_	F	f.	Chip extractor
_g_	G	g.	Storage container
_e_	H	h.	Nut driver

2. **Which files need to be copied to a Windows 2000 boot disk?**

   a) Io.sys

   b) Msdos.sys

   ✓ c) Boot.ini

   ✓ d) Ntdetect.com

   e) System.ini

Solutions

3. Which files are optional on an MS-DOS boot disk?

    a) Io.sys

    ✓ b) Edit.com

    c) Autexec.bat

    ✓ d) Format.com

    e) Command.com

4. In the Help desk example, match the help desk technician task with the correct stage in the Collect, Isolate, and Correct troubleshooting model.

    _a_   The help desk technician asks the user questions to gather information about why the user's monitor is not working and finds out that the user just moved to a new office.   a. The collect stage.

    _b_   The help desk technician asks the user to verify the monitor is plugged into a working outlet, the monitor power light is lit, and the monitor connector is firmly attached to the monitor connector in the back of the PC without any bent pins.   b. The isolate state.

    _c_   The help desk technician determines a lose monitor cable connection from the move is the most likely culprit of the problem.   c. The correct stage.

Lesson 3

Activity 3-2

1. **What recommendations would you make to reduce the ESD damage that has been occurring?**

    Keep the vinyl- and plastic-covered documents away from the work area. If possible, use online documentation. If the technicians need printouts, use a cloth-covered notebook and anti-static page protectors, or heavy-duty pages that don't need protection.

    If technicians wear their nylon jackets to work, they should be sure to use an anti-static spray after removing their jackets to help discharge the static build-up these garments create.

    Since there should not be coffee mugs in the work area, whether covered or not, this should not be a problem. They should be using these in a separate area. If there is still static build-up, they can use anti-static sprays again.

SOLUTIONS

2. **List the objects that need to be purchased to establish an ESD-free work area at the new branch office.**

   For each technician's work area, items might include:
   - *A dedicated ground connection, not a point in the electrical system.*
   - *Grounded anti-static workbench mat.*
   - *Grounded floor mat.*
   - *Grounded wrist or floor straps.*
   - *Anti-static spray.*
   - *Anti-static containers and storage bags for parts.*

Activity 3-3

1. Match the computer components with the potential hazards they pose.

_f_	Enclosure	a.	Chemical; metals used in manufacturing can cause environmental damage if improperly discarded.
_d_	Power supply	b.	Electrical; stored charges might not dissipate for long periods of time. Chemical; contains caustic electrolytes.
_a_	Battery	c.	Laser; emissions from an embedded laser can burn eyes, skin, and other objects.
_b_	Capacitor	d.	Electrical; retains high voltage even when power is off if unit is still plugged in to an outlet.
_g_	Monitor	e.	Chemical; toner can burn or melt when heated and is reactive with ammonia-based cleaners. Laser; emissions from an embedded laser can burn eyes, skin, and other objects.
_e_	Printer	f.	Electrical; sharp edges can cut through insulation on wires and cables. Physical; sharp edges can cut skin.
_c_	DVD drive	g.	Electrical; remains electrocution hazard even after unplugging unit. Physical; glass can shatter and cut skin.

2. **Electrical injuries include electrocution, shock, and collateral injury. Can you be injured if you are not part of the electrical ground current?**

   Yes, you can receive a thermal burn from the head of an electric arc or electric equipment. Your clothes can catch on, or your skin can be burned.

3. **Consider this scenario: A novice technician arrives at a user's workspace to troubleshoot a sound card. The user assures the technician that the power to the PC is off. As the technician begins working, he finds that the anti-static wrist strap gets in the way, so he removes it. Once the PC cover is off, the technician pulls the sound card out of the expansion slot and places it on a nearby metal filing cabinet, replacing it with a network card that he knows works properly. Finding that the network card doesn't**

work when installed in that expansion slot, the technician determines that there is a resource conflict, corrects the conflict, and replaces the network card with the user's original sound card. After testing the sound card, the technician and user agree that the problem is resolved. As the user helps the technician clean up by spraying window cleaner on the monitor screen, she mentions a funny ozone smell coming from her laser printer. The technician assures the user that an occasional whiff of ozone is normal, and ends the service call. What would you do differently?

Responses should include the following safe practices: Never assume anything; verify for yourself that the power is off and power cables unplugged before starting the troubleshooting process. No matter how uncomfortable it seems, wear the anti-static wrist strap and connect it to ground unless you are working on power supplies or monitors. Always store electronic parts that you intend to reuse in anti-static bags or on a dissipative mat. Caution the user that she should always apply cleaning products to the cloth instead of directly on the monitor glass, and that she should verify that the monitor is off and unplugged before cleaning it. Check the area surrounding the laser printer to ensure that the printer is properly ventilated—if the airflow seems adequate, the ozone filter in the printer might need to be replaced.

Activity 3-4

1. Match each ergonomic factor with the appropriate description.

_b_	Chair	a.	Keyboard lower than monitor, room for legs under desk, phone not squeezed with shoulder, standing computer station.
_e_	Posture	b.	Adjustable seat height, correct height, backrest, footrest, padded armrests.
_d_	Keyboard and mouse placement	c.	Short, frequent breaks, move around before feeling fatigued, relaxation exercises, adjust furniture.
_f_	Monitor placement	d.	Adjustable keyboard height, keyboard on foam pad, elbows at sides, forearms parallel to the floor, wrists straight, mouse at same height as keyboard, mouse close to keyboard.
_a_	Work environment	e.	Feet on floor, knees at right angles, upper body straight, arms straight at sides, wrists straight, head forward with slight downward tilt.
_c_	Project design	f.	Adjustable monitor height, monitor 1.5 to 2 feet from eyes, directly in front of user, copy stand, glare controlled.

2. Consider this scenario: You are called in to repair a network connection. You notice that the customer's monitor sits on a two-drawer filing cabinet to the right of the desk, the keyboard is on the desk, and paperwork is flat on the desk to the left of the keyboard. In addition, the customer uses an 8-point font and sits in a cafeteria chair. The only light is an overhead incandescent fixture behind your customer. What ergonomic changes could you suggest?

   If possible, move monitor directly in front of customer; raise monitor above keyboard height; move paperwork close to monitor and at eye level; enlarge font size; use rolling chair with adjustable height; and install task lighting closer to work area without causing glare on screen.

SOLUTIONS

Activity 3-5

1. List three ways to prevent fires in computer equipment.

    Answers might include: Turn off the monitor, keep liquids away from the equipment, make sure equipment is properly grounded, and make sure the facilities meet local fire codes.

2. Match the extinguishing agent with the type of fire it is best suited to extinguish.

_b_	Water	a.	Electronics fires.
_a_	Carbon dioxide	b.	Wood, paper, or cloth fires.
_c_	Dry chemical, standard type	c.	Flaming liquids.

3. You encounter a small fire at your office, some papers are on fire. You decide to use the extinguisher that is nearby. Remembering the mnemonic P.A.S.S., what are the steps you take to use the extinguisher?

    P = Pull the pin from the handle. A = Aim the nozzle at the base of the fire. S = Squeeze the handle. S = Sweep the base of the fire from side to side.

4. List five considerations in making a fight-or-flight decision in the event of a fire.

    Answers might include: Is the building already evacuated? Has the fire department been called? Is the exit clear? Is a class C extinguisher available? Is the fire small and contained? Is someone else available to back me up? Can I eliminate the source of ignition?

5. Consider this scenario: You go on a call to repair a printer. The customer has just put out a small fire in the monitor with a fire extinguisher. The customer assures you that the fire is out and urges you to start work on the printer. What should you do?

    Suggest that the customer call the fire department to make sure the fire is out and that it is safe to stay in the building. Tell the customer that you would need to use the monitor to check the printer, but it is not safe to restart the equipment; that is a job for an expert.

Lesson 3 Follow-up

Lesson 3 Lab 1

1. Name at least three factors that you should consider when setting up an ergonomic work station.

    Answers might include: Chair height, monitor placement, keyboard and mouse placement.

2. True or False? You enter the computer room to find a server in the equipment rack is on fire. You should use a Class A rated fire extinguisher to put out this kind of fire.

    ___ True
    _✓_ False

3. Select the three hazardous situations you are likely to encounter while servicing PCs.
   - ✓ a) Electrocution
   - b) Poor air quality
   - ✓ c) Toxic chemicals
   - ✓ d) Lasers

4. True or False? Computer components can be harmed by static electricity, but you are very unlikely to be hurt by it.
   - ✓ True
   - ___ False

Lesson 4

Activity 4-5

2. Determine the packaging type for your processor.

   Answers will vary.

3. Does your processor use a heat sink, fan, or other cooling method?

   Answers will vary.

4. What type of processor is in your system?

   Answers will vary.

Activity 4-7

2. What form factor motherboard is in this system?

   Answers will vary.

3. Does this system use a daughter board?

   Answers will vary.

4. Can you determine the clock speed for this motherboard, or the range it supports, by looking at the motherboard itself?

   Answers will vary.

Activity 4-9

1. Match the type of RAM with its description.

SOLUTIONS

_b_	VRAM	a.	A replacement for SDRAM.
_a_	DDR SDRAM	b.	A special type of DRAM used on video cards that can be written to and read from at the same time. It also requires less refreshing than normal DRAM.
_d_	SRAM	c.	A special type of video memory, which can be simultaneously read from and written to in blocks.
_e_	DRAM	d.	Used for cache memory. It does not need to be refreshed to retain information. It can use synchronous, asynchronous, burst, or pipeline burst technologies.
_c_	WRAM	e.	Used on SIMMs and DIMMs. It needs to be refreshed every few milliseconds. Uses assigned memory addresses.

2. True or False? RAM will not run any faster than the motherboard's bus speed.

   ✓ True

   ___ False

3. True or False? A nanosecond is one-trillionth of a second.

   ___ True

   ✓ False

4. In a system that contains RAM modules that run at 6 ns and 10 ns, what speed will the RAM run at?

   a) 4 ns

   ✓ b) 10 ns

   c) 6 ns

   d) 16 ns

5. On a typical system with RAM that runs at a speed of 10 ns, you could add RAM that runs at which speed?

   a) 6 ns

   b) 10 ns

   c) 12 ns

   ✓ d) All of the above

6. Match the cache with its description.

Solutions

_c_	L1	a.	Memory on the motherboard between the processor and RAM when there's a built-in L2 cache on the processor.
_b_	L2	b.	A type of high-speed RAM that is placed between the processor and conventional RAM to improve computing speed.
_a_	L3	c.	A type of high-speed RAM that is added directly to a processor to improve computing speed.

7. The number of SIMMs or DIMMs needed to create a bank is the width of the CPUs data bus divided by the width of the _SIMM or DIMM_ .

8. On a system with a CPU with a 64-bit data bus, how many SIMMs would you need to create a bank?

    a) 2

    b) 4

    ✓ c) 8

    d) 16

9. On a system with a CPU with a 32-bit data bus, how many SIMMs would you need to create a bank?

    a) 2

    ✓ b) 4

    c) 8

    d) 16

Activity 4-10

2. **How much memory is currently installed?**

    Answers will vary based on the RAM physically installed in the system. It can be found on the General page of the System Properties dialog box.

Lesson 4 Follow-up

Lesson 4 Lab 1

1. **What should you do to resolve trouble ticket 125001?**

    Unplug the system and remove the system cover. Using compressed air, blow out any dust around the fan spindle. Verify that there is no obvious reason the fan is not spinning. If these do not fix the problem, replace the power supply. Leaving the problem alone would allow heat to build up to dangerous levels, causing serious damage to the system.

SOLUTIONS

Lesson 4 Lab 2

1. **What are some potential causes and solutions to the problem described in trouble ticket 175001?**

   Refer to the Intel Web site at **www.intel.com/support/motherboards/desktop/slowboot.htm** *for information on resolving this problem.*

   They suggest that you check that IDE jumpers are correctly configured, that the boot order lists the hard drive as the first boot device, to disable some unused functions, and to verify that your BIOS uses the Intel Rapid BIOS boot selection.

2. **Search using a Web search engine such as Google for the beep code pattern indicated in trouble ticket 175002. Which BIOS manufacturer uses this beep code pattern and what are some potential causes and solutions to the problem described in trouble ticket 175002?**

   Searching in Google for the criteria `bios beep codes 4-4-1` *shows that this is an older Phoenix BIOS pattern. It indicates that the serial port is being tested or that there is a problem with the serial port.*

3. **What are some potential causes and solutions to the problem described in trouble ticket 175003?**

   Search using a search engine such as Google for `AMI beep codes, 1 long, 3 short` *to obtain a list of AMI beep codes. This pattern indicates a problem with the memory. Try reseating the memory modules or replacing them to attempt to resolve the problem.*

4. **What are some potential causes and solutions to the problem described in trouble ticket 175004?**

   Verify that the user did not leave a data or program disk in the floppy drive. This is the most common reason for this error message. If that is not the problem, troubleshoot the hard drive boot problem.

5. **What are some potential causes and solutions to the problem described in trouble ticket 175005?**

   You can usually recover from this by removing the CMOS battery for a period of time.

Lesson 4 Lab 3

1. **If you are running a dual-processor system with only one processor, which socket does the processor go in?**

   It must be placed in the primary processor socket.

2. **If you are running a dual-processor system with only one processor, what do you need to do to the empty socket?**

   A terminator board or processor needs to be placed in the second socket if you remove the second processor.

3. **What needs to be similar about both processors? How is it best to make sure of this?**

   They need to be identical. It is best to purchase the system with both processors at the same time.

Lesson 4 Lab 4

1. After troubleshooting trouble ticket 401001, you believe it is memory related. Why might the memory experience problems all of a sudden?

    The user might have been attacked by a virus, the system might have experienced a loss of power, or there might have been a power surge. All of these problems can affect the memory in a system.

2. You are attempting to resolve trouble ticket 401002. Why is the user only experiencing the problem when additional applications are opened? What can you do to determine the cause?

    The problem is most likely caused by memory errors in higher memory than is normally used. If you move the memory modules around in the system, putting the potentially bad memory module in the first memory bank, the problem will probably exhibit itself when you open the first application.

Lesson 6

Activity 6-2

5. The manager would like the printer on the far side of the office so that it is out of his way. You measure the distance the cable would need to reach (down the desk leg, across the floor next to the file cabinet, and then around the edge of the room to the far corner) and find that the cable would need to be 25 feet long. Explain to the manager whether moving the printer to this location is possible. Also, explain any issues or problems that might arise from the longer cable.

    The IEEE 1284 specification allows for cables up to 33 feet long, so there should be no problem with going 25 feet. Longer cable runs can result in loss in performance.

Lesson 8

Activity 8-7

1. List at least two POST messages that would indicate a problem with the hard drive. What does the message mean? How would you fix it?

    - *POST code 17xx—Indicates that the hard drive or controller was not found. Check that both devices are connected and functional.*
    - *No Boot Device Available—Indicates that the BIOS could not find an installed operating system on the hard drive or a bootable floppy disk. Verify that the operating system was installed. If it was, try to boot from floppy disk and access the hard drive, then check the boot partition for errors.*
    - *Configuration or CMOS error—Indicates that the information reported by CMOS is different than the hard drive found by the POST. Check CMOS settings. If the settings won't stick, check the battery on the system board.*

SOLUTIONS

- *Hard Drive Not Found or Fixed Disk Error—Indicates that the hard drive was not found during the POST. Check all connections for hard drives and hard drive controller. Hard drive or controller might be dead.*
- *Reboot And Select Proper Boot Device Or Insert Boot Media In Selected Boot Device—Indicates that the BIOS found no bootable device in the system. It could also indicate that a removable media drive does not contain media if no hard disk was found and it found a removable media drive (such as a floppy disk drive, Zip drive, SuperDrive, or the like).*

Activity 8-8

1. One of the things you need to check when a newly installed drive isn't recognized is the CMOS settings for the drive. What in particular do you need to check in CMOS for this problem?

   You need to verify that CMOS lists the correct device settings for the hard drive. This includes the correct type, whether LBA is enabled, and the CHS settings.

2. Another thing you should check when you encounter this problem is that the drive was installed correctly. What exactly would you be checking?

   Verify that the power cable is connected to the drive, that the power cable voltages are correct, and that the data cable is connected correctly to the drive and to the controller or host bus adapter. For an IDE drive, verify that it is set to master, cable select, or slave as appropriate to its place in the drive chain. For a SCSI drive, verify that the termination and SCSI ID are set properly for its place in the SCSI chain.

3. The drive was properly installed but you can't access it by its drive letter. What should your next step be?

   Use DOS or Windows disk utilities to verify that the drive has been properly partitioned and formatted.

Activity 8-9

1. List some of the steps you might take to resolve trouble ticket 112001.
   - *Determine if the user actually has a D drive.*
   - *Attempt to copy a file from the D drive to C.*
   - *Attempt to copy a file from the C drive to D.*
   - *Open My Computer, right-click the D drive and choose Properties. On the Tools pane, click Check Now. Click Start.*
   - *In the Local Disk (D:) Properties window, display the Hardware pane. Select the drive corresponding to drive D and click Troubleshoot. Follow the Troubleshooting Wizard to help resolve your problem.*
   - *If none of these fixed the problem, back up the data and try reformatting the drive.*
   - *If the previous step does not fix the problem, replace the drive.*

   The Can't Access This Drive message indicates that you are trying to read a disk that is not readable. It also is displayed if there is no disk in the drive (for removable disk drives).

2. **What steps might you take to attempt to resolve trouble ticket 112002? What is the most likely cause of the problem?**

   You could try running the Windows XP Error-checking option on the Tools pane of the Local Disk Properties dialog box. You could also try an older version of SCANDISK from floppy disk to try to identify and repair the errors it encounters. Definitely back up the data if you can get to any of it. You can try using other software utilities to recover the data or take the drive to a data recovery facility. You will probably need to replace the hard drive.

   The most likely cause of this problem is a bad hard drive. Some of the sectors of the hard disk are damaged.

3. **What steps might you take to attempt to resolve trouble ticket 112003? What is the most likely cause of the problem?**

   Even though this sounds like a different problem, you would attempt to resolve it the same way you did trouble ticket 112002. You should also check the system for viruses because the result of some infections looks like this problem.

   If it is not caused by a virus, the most likely cause of this problem is a bad hard drive.

Activity 8-10

1. **A 30 GB hard drive was installed, but the system reports that the drive is about 500 MB. What can be done to resolve this problem?**

   The system contains an old BIOS that doesn't recognize large drives. Update the BIOS so that the entire drive can be recognized. Some drive manufacturers also supply a driver that can be installed to enable the old BIOS and the new large drive to work together.

2. **The system is running Windows 98 SE. After installing and partitioning a 70 GB drive with FDISK, FDISK reports that the drive is less than 64 GB. Why is this happening? How can you resolve the problem?**

   This is a known problem with FDISK on Windows 95/98/98 SE. You can resolve the problem by downloading a fix from the Microsoft Web site at **http://support.microsoft.com/default.aspx?scid=KB;EN-US;Q263044&.**

3. **A user is questioning the difference between the sizes in GB and bytes. Why is there such a big difference? The disk reports in some places as 9.33 GB and in other as 10,025,000,960 bytes. Why isn't it 10GB?**

   When people talk, they usually round 1024 bytes to 1000 since it is easier to work with round numbers. By the time you get up to billions of bytes, those extra 24 bytes really add up.

Activity 8-11

1. **Your customer can afford to install only one additional disk to the system, yet they want the benefits of RAID technology. Which RAID level should they implement?**

   RAID Level 0.

2. **Your customer needs to improve fault tolerance and performance, and they also need to hot swap failed drives. Which RAID level should they implement?**

   RAID Level 5.

SOLUTIONS

3. If the customer would like to protect the boot partition and can afford duplicate disks and duplicate controller cards, they should implement <u>RAID Level 1, also known as disk duplexing</u>.

Lesson 9

Activity 9-2

1. Identify some issues you should check in resolving trouble ticket 235001.

   Some issues include:
   - *Check that the disk is readable.*
   - *Try reinserting the disk in the drive.*
   - *Verify that the floppy disk functions properly: the shuttle window opens and shuts easily, there is no foreign matter on the mylar disk surface, and the mylar disk spins easily within the plastic casing.*
   - *Check for viruses on the floppy disk.*
   - *Check the floppy disk for bad sectors.*
   - *Check whether or not other floppy disks can be read in the drive.*
   - *If you received a floppy disk containing data from another user, verify that it wasn't formatted as a Macintosh or Linux disk.*
   - *Try to read it on another system.*

2. List the issues to check in resolving trouble ticket 235002.
   - *Check that the disk is not write-protected; if it is, move the switch to unprotect the floppy disk.*
   - *Verify that the floppy disk has been properly formatted.*
   - *Verify that the floppy drive is working properly.*
   - *Clean the drive read/write heads.*

3. What might cause the user to receive the error message shown in trouble ticket 235003?

   The operating system cannot locate the floppy disk drive. You should check the CMOS settings to make sure the system knows there is a floppy drive, then clean the drive, check the alignment of the drive, and check all connections to the drive.

4. What would you recommend to the user to resolve trouble ticket 235004?

   It is likely that the disk was formatted under a different operating system such as Macintosh or Linux. If that is the case, then the original owner of the disk will need to give the user the information on a medium that the Windows XP system can read.

Activity 9-4

3. Regarding trouble ticket 232003, explain to the user what the reason for their problem is and what needs to be done to correct it.

   When the new drive was added, it became D and the CD-ROM drive became E. You can use Windows Explorer to assign drive letter D explicitly to the CD-ROM drive, or you can modify the configuration files for the applications in question to locate the CD-ROM on drive E.

4. What would you suggest that the user try in resolving trouble ticket 232004?

   Answers might include:
   - *Make sure the user is writing the data at the speed for which the media is rated.*
   - *Make sure the user is not trying to write more than the CD can hold.*
   - *Check for software error messages that may indicate what the problem might be.*
   - *Check whether the operating system or the hardware is causing the problem by unplugging the data cable from the drive before inserting the disc. If there is a pause before the disc is ejected or if the drive light blinks steadily, it might be because the media is defective (or not good enough for your drive to use). Try a different brand of discs.*
   - *If the hardware appears to be fine, the operating system might be causing a problem. You can try disabling auto insert for all CD devices.*
   - *Level the drive. Some drives, in particularly older drives, will only work properly if they are level. Turn the system upright if it is on its side.*
   - *See if it will write after the system has been turned off for awhile. Some systems overheat and have trouble writing when the drive gets too hot.*

5. After checking over the hardware for the DVD drive on the system, you find no problems. What else might the problem be in trouble ticket 232005?

   To play DVD movies on your computer using your DVD-ROM drive, you need to install third-party software. The DVD hardware in this system does not appear to contain a hardware decoder, so the software decoder is required in order to play the movies.

Activity 9-5

1. Cartridge drives are available in which connection types?

   ✓ a) IDE
   ✓ b) SCSI
   ✓ c) USB
   ✓ d) FireWire
      e) Serial

2. True or False? The disk in a cartridge drive is referred to as a cookie.

   ✓ True
   __ False

SOLUTIONS

3. The hub in a cartridge disk drive enables the disk to spin at roughly 3,000 RPMs. True or False? This is faster than both floppy and hard disks spin.

    ___ True

    _✓_ False

4. Which cartridge disks are no longer manufactured and considered legacy devices?

    a) Syquest drives

    b) Zip drives

    ✓ c) Jaz drives

    ✓ d) SuperDisk drives

Activity 9-6

1. How many tape sets are required when using the Grandfather rotation method?

    One set each for Monday through Thursday (four), one set for each Friday of the month (five, because some months could contain five Fridays), and one month end set (for the last day of the month), for a total of 10.

2. How many tape sets are required when using the Tower of Hanoi rotation method?

    a) One

    b) Three

    ✓ c) Five

    d) Seven

3. Match the backup type with its description.

_b_	Full	a.	New files and files created or modified since the last full or incremental backup are backed up and the archive bit is cleared.
_a_	Incremental	b.	All information is backed up.
_c_	Differential	c.	All files created or modified since the last full backup are backed up and the archive bit isn't cleared.

4. List some of the backup media choices available today.

    Magnetic tape (including reel-to-reel, DAT, DLT, and QIC), optical drives, recordable CDs, and additional drives and cartridges (such as Iomega Zip disks).

Activity 9-7

1. What options are listed when you right-click the Iomega removable disk drive in My Computer?

    The standard Windows Explorer options for a drive are listed.

Lesson 10

Activity 10-5

4. Access the HP Web site at *www.hp.com* and locate possible reasons for the repeated pattern on the output described in trouble ticket 215004. Identify which component is the potential cause of the streaking.

    The business support document number bpl 11858 lists possible causes based on the distance at which the streaks repeat. You might need to replace the toner cartridge, replace a roller, or clean the rollers.

5. List some of the things you should check and try to do when resolving trouble ticket 215005.

    If the print quality is poor, perform one or more cleaning cycles. Clean the printer to make sure there are no lint or other debris dragging across the wet ink. Change to a paper specifically designed for inkjet printers.

    Replace empty ink cartridges. Perform one or more cleaning cycles. Check the documentation or Web site for the printer to see if there are any sequences to perform to get output when there is nothing printing.

    Make sure the user pulled the tape off before installing the ink cartridge. Verify that the cartridge is seated correctly in the printer. Verify that the correct cartridge was installed. Make sure the printer is not paused.

    Perform several cleaning cycles. Try a fresh ink cartridge. If the print head is separate, you might need to replace the print head. Perform an alignment after installing new cartridges as per the documentation for the printer.

7. Access the Iomega Web site at *www.iomega.com* and locate the document that describes how to resolve the problem described in trouble ticket 215007. After reviewing the steps, what are the two solutions they suggest?

    Document 11146 describes a generic solution for this problem. If the steps listed resolve the problem, the problem was with the bidirectional settings for the printer. If the steps listed did not resolve the problem, you should install a second parallel port and use one for the Iomega drive and one for the printer.

Activity 10-6

1. A user is getting ready to do a presentation for a group of customers over the Web. The Web-based presentation software allows the audience to ask questions of the presenter. What input/output devices will the presenter need?

    a) Scanner

    b) Digital camera

    c) Touch screen

    ✓ d) Speakers

    ✓ e) Microphone

SOLUTIONS

2. A user needs to email several paper-based documents to a customer. What input/output device would they use to transfer the paper-based documents to electronic format on their computer?

    ✓ a) Scanner

    b) Digital camera

    c) Touch screen

    d) Speakers

    e) Microphone

3. A customer has a kiosk where his patrons can use a keyboard and a mouse to search for auto parts that his store carries. He complains that he has had to replace the keyboard and mouse numerous times due to customer negligence. Is there another input solution, you would recommend?

    Yes, a touch screen input solution would eliminate the need for a keyboard and mouse.

4. A user needs to take and store photos of expensive equipment for insurance purposes. What input/output devices should they use to take the photos and transfer them to their PC?

    a) Scanner

    ✓ b) Digital camera

    c) Touch screen

    d) Speakers

    e) Microphone

Lesson 10 Follow-up

Lesson 10 Lab 1

3. How could you resolve the problem described in trouble ticket 215008?

    Move the printer to a USB port on the system so that it is closer to a power source. If necessary, use a powered hub to connect the printer to the USB port directly on the system.

Lesson 11

Activity 11-1

1. **Describe how a portable computer system differs from a desktop computer system in display technology.**

   Portable computers use LCD technology because the monitors are flat, take up less room, and use less power. The typical desktop system still uses a CRT monitor as it is less expensive—although as the price of LCD technology for external monitors comes down in price, they are being used more often.

2. **Describe how a portable computer system differs from a desktop computer system in power source.**

   Portable computer systems are run by rechargeable batteries so that they can be used away from a typical work area. However, portable systems can be plugged into a AC adapter to use for a longer time than the battery power allows. Desktop systems are run exclusively by AC power sources.

3. **Describe how the processors designed for portable computer systems differ from those in desktop systems.**

   The processors for portable systems offer low-voltage usage optimized for battery-use and many offer power savings modes. In addition, the packaging types for the processors in portable systems provide for a lightweight, small-footprint.

4. **Select the components that are external peripheral components on a desktop system, but are integrated in portable computer systems.**

   ✓ a) Monitor
   ✓ b) Keyboard
      c) Printer
   ✓ d) Pointing device

Activity 11-8

1. **Identify which components are typically soldered to the system board and cannot be replaced without replacing the entire system board.**

      a) Fan
   ✓ b) Processor
   ✓ c) USB port
      d) PCMCIA bay
   ✓ e) AC adapter connection

SOLUTIONS

2. Identify which components are typically connected to the system board and can be replaced independently of the system board.

    ✓ a) Hard disk

    b) Infrared port

    c) External monitor port

    ✓ d) Fan

    e) Keyboard

Lesson 12

Activity 12-1

1. Select the connectors that can be used with fiber optic cabling.

    a) RJ-45 connector

    ✓ b) MT-RJ connector

    c) BNC connector

    ✓ d) Mini-BNC connector

    ✓ e) FDDI connector

2. Select the connectors that can be used with coaxial cabling.

    a) FDDI connector

    b) Mini-BNC connector

    ✓ c) BNC connector

    d) Biconic connector

    ✓ e) AUI connector

3. Select the connectors that can be used with twisted pair cabling.

    a) MT-RJ connector

    ✓ b) RJ-45 connector

    c) ST connector

    d) SC connector

    e) FDDI connector

Activity 12-2

1. Describe the extent to which the bus topology offers fault tolerance—the ability to ignore or overcome problems.

    No fault tolerance, a single break in the cable can bring the whole network down.

2. **Describe the extent to which the star topology offers fault tolerance—the ability to ignore or overcome problems.**

   Limited fault tolerance, a defective hub can bring down all the workstations connected to that hub.

3. **Describe the extent to which the ring topology offers fault tolerance—the ability to ignore or overcome problems.**

   Very fault tolerant, removing a node from the ring does not affect the remaining nodes on the ring.

4. **Describe the extent to which the mesh topology offers fault tolerance—the ability to ignore or overcome problems.**

   Extremely fault tolerant, every node has a path to every other node.

5. **Contrast the ease of administration between a peer-to-peer network and a client-server network.**

   Peer-to-peer: Administration becomes more difficult as the number of nodes increases.

   Client-server: Because administration is performed centrally, you can support hundreds of nodes efficiently.

6. **Contrast the scalability of a peer-to-peer network versus a client-server network.**

   Peer-to-peer: Limited growth potential.

   Client-server: Can be expanded as needs dictate.

7. **Contrast the number of potential users of a peer-to-peer network versus a client-server network.**

   Peer-to-peer: Recommended for 10 users or fewer.

   Client-server: Recommended for hundreds or even thousands of users.

8. **Contrast how the resources of a peer-to-peer network are managed versus a client-server network.**

   Peer-to-peer: Each node manages its own resources.

   Client-server: All resources are managed centrally.

9. **Contrast how security is managed in a peer-to-peer network versus a client-server network.**

   Peer-to-peer: Each node is responsible for its own security.

   Client-server: Security is centralized at the server.

10. **What are the main differences between a hybrid network and a hierarchical network?**

    A hybrid network can contain elements usually found in other network types, such as peer-to-peer and client-server. A hierarchical network contains large, centralized computers—such as mainframes—to store information and provide processing power, and dedicated, limited-capacity clients to request and receive information from the central computers.

SOLUTIONS

Activity 12-3

1. <u>MS-DOS</u> is most suitable as a client OS, but it needs to be installed in addition to at least one NOS for that NOS to operate correctly.

2. For Macintosh computers, what are the most prevalent client and network operating systems?

    MacOS and MacOSX Server.

3. Which operating systems are equally suited to use as a client OS and a NOS?

    UNIX and Linux.

4. True or False? Windows XP is primarily a network operating system.

    ___ True

    ✓ False

5. Of the following NOSs, which cannot also be used as a client OS?

    a) Windows 2000 Server

    ✓ b) NetWare

    c) Linux

    d) Windows NT Server

    e) Windows Server 2003

Activity 12-4

1. How does the use of custom subnet masks counteract the problem of the Internet running out of available IP addresses?

    Subnetting helps avoid the depletion of IP addresses because it enables a company to subdivide their single assigned network address for use with multiple subnets. Without support for subnetting, a company would need to obtain multiple network addresses from the IANA if they had multiple network segments. And if the company didn't use all of the host addresses for each network address, those host addresses would simply be wasted.

2. Your company has been assigned the public IP address of 137.72.0.0. You estimate that you will eventually have a total of 30 subnets. What subnet mask should you use to support this number of subnets?

    You'll need to borrow 5 bits from the host portion of the address in order to support 30 subnets. In binary, the third byte of your subnet mask will be 11111000, which is 248 in decimal. This means that you should use a subnet mask of 255.255.248.0 for your network.

3. How would you display this subnet mask by using the /## notation?

    This subnet mask uses a total of 21 bits: 8 bits from each of the first and second bytes, plus the 5 bits your borrowing from the third byte to identify your subnets.

4. Given this subnet mask, how many total subnets can you define on your network? What are the subnet addresses you can assign?

    You can define a total of 2^5 subnets, which means you can have up to 32 subnets on your network. Your subnet increment is 8, so the subnet addresses you can assign are: 137.72.0.0, 137.72.8.0, 137.72.16.0, 137.72.24.0, 137.72.32.0, and so on, up to 137.72.248.0.

SOLUTIONS

5. How many hosts can you have on each subnet? What are the host addresses you can assign on the first subnet for your network?

   You can have a total of 2^11-2 (2,046) hosts on each subnet. Your first subnet is 137.72.0.0. You can assign host addresses on this subnet from 137.72.0.1 to 137.72.7.254.

Activity 12-6

1. Janet lives in a rural area that doesn't have cable access. Her home is about 30 miles from the town where the phone company's central office is located. The nearest wireless ISP is two towns over about 50 miles away. What options for an Internet connection are available to Janet?

   a) DSL
   b) Cable
   c) Wireless
   ✓ d) Dial-up
   ✓ e) Satellite

2. From the Internet connections you determined were available to Janet, if she is on a tight budget and uses her computer for personal, not business use, which Internet connection would you recommend?

   Dial-up is significantly cheaper than satellite.

3. John lives in a large, metropolitan area and has subscribed to an ISDN Internet service. Unfortunately, his ISDN provider is going out of business and there isn't another ISDN provider in his area.

   John lives three miles from his phone company's central office, so he can get DSL. He also is currently a subscriber to digital cable TV. There are many companies who offer inexpensive dial-up Internet connection services.

   What Internet connection would you recommend for John? Why?

   John is accustomed to a bandwidth of up to 144 Kbps. Dial-up service is limited to 56 Kbps. Although it is inexpensive, John probably would not be happy with the significant drop in transfer speeds.

   DSL and cable Internet connections provide comparable services. John would probably be happy with either of these options.

   He should consider pricing a factor. Many companies offer discounts as you add additional services with them. For example, adding DSL to his existing phone service or cable Internet service to his existing digital cable TV service. He should also look at the customer support available for both options. Some questions to consider in making his decision:

   * Will the company do a full installation and verify the connection is working or is he responsible for installing and configuring all the equipment needed?

   * If there is a problem with the equipment or service, what are the hours of phone tech support?

   * Is there a fee to have a technician come out and diagnose problems?

SOLUTIONS

Activity 12-7

1. Match the connection device with its functional description.

   _f_ Repeater   a. Connects several computers together at a central point.

   _a_ Hub   b. Routes one protocol while bridging another.

   _d_ Bridge   c. Determines the best path for sending data.

   _c_ Router   d. Divides network into segments to increase performance.

   _b_ Brouter   e. Connects dissimilar networks.

   _e_ Gateway   f. Extends the maximum length of a network by amplifying signals.

Activity 12-8

4. Did the Network Diagnostics scan point to any problems?

   Answers will vary based on the nature of the problem. In most cases, the actions in the previous steps should have corrected the problem. If the network card still does not pass the test, this points to a hardware problem with the network card.

Lesson 13

Activity 13-1

2. Did you find any errors on your drive?

   Answers will vary, but generally there shouldn't be any errors on the drive.

4. Based on the analysis you see in the report, should you defragment this disk?

   Answers will vary depending on the student computers.

Activity 13-2

4. When performing preventative maintenance on a laser printer, why is it important to use a specially designed laser printer vacuum?

   So that you don't reverse the polarity of the electrons on the drum.

5. Which preventative maintenance steps apply to all printer types?

   ✓ a) Print a test page to verify that the printer prints satisfactorily.

   ✓ b) Verify that there is enough paper for a day's printing.

       c) Clean the rollers with alcohol.

   ✓ d) Use mild household cleaner to wipe down the exterior of the printer case.

       e) Verify that the fan is working properly and is not clogged.

6. True or False? Printer fires should be extinquished with foam.

    ___ True

    _✓_ False

Activity 13-6

1. Computer A is a Pentium II computer running Windows NT 4.0. The system has a video card that does not support 3D graphics or the new 21-inch monitor its user has acquired. The user needs the monitor to create and modify the graphics for one of your company's top publications. A new video card will cost $200. Should you upgrade the video card?

    ✓ a) Yes

    b) No

    c) Maybe

2. Computer B has a Pentium II processor, 64 MB of RAM, and is running Windows 98. The user needs to install several new programs to create and manage large files used in the layout of several publications. You will also need to upgrade this computer to Windows XP within the next six months as part of the upgrade within that user's department. Should you upgrade or replace the system?

    ✓ a) Upgrade

    b) Replace

3. Computer B also has a 20 GB hard disk that has 8 GB of free space. Should you upgrade the hard disk too?

    a) Yes

    ✓ b) No

    c) Maybe

4. Computer C is a Pentium III computer with 256 MB of RAM and a 30 GB hard disk with 10 GB of free space. The user is an administrative assistant who uses the computer for email and word processing. She complains that the computer isn't as fast as the computer she has at home. Upon further investigation you find that at most she has only three programs open at one time. A new processor will cost $450 and more memory will cost $175. Should you upgrade the processor and the memory?

    a) Yes

    ✓ b) No

    c) Maybe

5. If you're planning to upgrade from Windows 98 to Windows 2000, which component(s) might you need to consider upgrading?

    ✓ a) Hard disk

    ✓ b) Processor

    c) Sound card

    d) System BIOS

    e) Network card

SOLUTIONS

SOLUTIONS

Activity 13-7

1. **Why do CRTs need to be recycled rather than disposed of through normal waste management procedures?**

   CRT monitors contain hazardous materials including traces of lead, phosphorous, cadmium, barium, and mercury. These are safe during use because they are sealed, but in a landfill, the CRT would be crushed, allowing the hazardous materials to become airborne or to leach into soil and water. Also, the plastic and glass can be recycled.

2. **Various types of batteries have been accumulated for disposal. These are from digital cameras, PDAs, laptops, and wireless devices among other sources. Indicate the proper disposal method for each battery type.**

Alkaline	*Regular waste management procedures.*
Lithium	*Should be recycled.*
Sealed lead batteries	*Must be recycled.*
Nickel metal hydride	*Regular waste management procedures.*
Nickel cadmium	*Must be recycled.*

3. **Which printer consumables need to be handled in a special manner and be recycled?**

   Laser toner cartridges.

4. **What is an MSDS and where can you obtain one?**

   Material Safety Data Sheets are available from the manufacturer of products containing hazardous (or potentially hazardous) materials. The MSDS contains information about how to handle and dispose of the product, as well as other safety information about the product.

Glossary

10Base2
Ethernet standard that uses 50 ohm coaxial cable (RG-58 A/U). Also called Thinnet. Transfer speed is 10 Mbps. Uses BNC connectors.

10Base5
Ethernet standard that uses coaxial cable and supports transfer speeds of 10 Mbps. Also called thick Ethernet, Thickwire, or Thicknet.

10BaseT
Ethernet standard that uses twisted-pair cable. Also called twisted-pair Ethernet. Operates at 10 Mbps. Uses RJ-45 connectors.

8008
Introduced by Intel in 1972, the 8008 was the first microprocessor to be supported by a high-level language compiler.

abacus
An early calculating instrument that uses sliding beads in columns that are divided in two by a center bar.

AC
(Alternating Current) Electrical current that flows in two directions at variable voltages.

ACPI
(Advanced Configuration and Power Interface) A power-management specification that enables the operating system to manage the power supplied to system devices.

active hub
A connecting unit that regenerates the data bits in order to maintain a strong signal. Also referred to as a multiport repeater.

adapter
A device that allows one system to connect to and work with another. An adapter is often a simple circuit that converts one set of signals to another; however, the term often refers to devices which are more accurately called controllers. For example, display adapters (video cards), network adapters (NICs), and SCSI host adapters perform extensive processing, but they are still called adapters.

adapter card
Add-on boards or cards that provide special functions for customizing or extending a computer's capability.

AGP
(Accelerated Graphics Port) A bus architecture based on PCI and designed specifically to speed up 3D graphics.

ALU
(Arithmetic and Logic Unit) The CPU component that performs math and boolean operations.

amp
An abbreviation for ampere, the unit of measurement of current.

Analytical Engine
Charles Babbage's vision of a mechanical calculator that would follow programmed instructions to perform any mathematical operations. The engine could store results for use later, and look up values in tables and call on standard subroutines.

Glossary

ANSI
(American National Standards Institute) A standards body that produced a well-known number code for English language characters and symbols, known as ANSI code. Pronounced AN-see.

APIPA
(Automatic Private IP Addressing) The private IP address range from 169.254.0.1 to 169.254.255.254 used by Microsoft to provide temporary IP connectivity between Windows computers that are part of a single network segment and are not connected to the Internet.

APM
(Advanced Power Management) A power-management specification that enables the system BIOS to manage system power use.

AppleTalk
Apple Computer's network protocol. Network protocol that supports Apple's proprietary LocalTalk cabling scheme, as well as Ethernet and IBM Token Ring.

Application layer
A layer of the OSI model that provides the starting point of the communication session. Also referred to as Layer 7 of the OSI model.

application software
High-level programs that are written to run on specific operating systems and that provide specific functionality such as word processing, graphics creation, or database management.

ARCNet
Connects up to 255 nodes in a star topology at a transmission rate of 2.5 Mbps.

ASCII
(American Standard Code for Information Interchange) A standards body that produced one of the best-known number codes for English language characters and symbols, known as ASCII code. Pronounced ASK-ee.

aspect ratio
The ratio of the width of a display to its height.

asynchronous
A bit synchronization transmission technique that uses start and stop bits.

AT commands
The modem command set developed by the Hayes company for use on its modems and now used on most modems.

ATA
(Advanced Technology Attachment) The official ANSI term for IDE drives.

ATAPI
(AT Attachment Packet Interface) An extension to EIDE that enables support for CD-ROM, CD-R, CD-RW, DVD-ROM, DVD-R, and tape drives.

AUI
(Attachment Unit Interface) Connects to an external transceiver that then connects to a half-inch thick coaxial cable. Used with 10Base5 (Thicknet).

backbone
The portion of the network that links all of the other segments of the network together.

backside bus
A bus connecting the CPU to L2 cache. It runs faster than the frontside bus. It connects the two chips at the same clock rate as the CPU itself, as opposed to the frontside bus, which runs at only a fraction of the CPU clock speed.

bandwidth
The amount of data that a given network channel can potentially transmit.

bank
Multiple rows of DRAM in a single system that can be accessed simultaneously.

Base Memory address
The memory address of any memory that might be on the adapter card.

Berg connector
A small flat power supply connector, typically used for connecting power to floppy drives, Zip drives, or SuperDisk drives. There are usually only one or two of these connectors in a system.

binary number system
A numbering system based on two discrete states.

GLOSSARY

BIOS
(Basic Input Output System) Low-level software that acts as the interface between the hardware and the operating system in a computer.

bit
A single binary digit having a value of 0 or 1.

BNC connector
(British Naval Connector or Bayonet Nut Connector) Used to join coaxial cables like RG58 A/U into a network. Also used for cable TV and cable modem connections.

boolean
An expression where the results are either true or false. The expression uses AND, OR, and NOT functions to compare values.

boot disk
A floppy disk that you can use to boot a computer when the operating system installed on the hard disk will not boot.

bridge
An electronic device that controls the flow of information between LAN segments or networks, even if they are different types of networks using different communication protocols.

brightness
The level of white in a display image.

brouter
A communication device that functions as both a bridge and a router, depending on which function is needed.

bus
The collection of wires that connect an interface card and the microprocessor, and the rules that describe how data should be transferred through the connection. Examples include ISA, EISA, and PCI.

bus master
Takes control of the bus away from the CPU to transfer data directly to RAM or other devices.

bus topology
A physical topology where a single main cable called the bus or backbone carries all network data. Nodes connect directly to the bus.

byte
A group of 8 bits.

cable select
A method for designating IDE devices as master or slave by using connectors on a special data cable, rather than jumpers on the devices themselves.

Card Services
Assigns resources of PC Cards and detects when a card is inserted or removed.

CardBus
A bus mastering technology used on PC Cards.

Cat5
(Category 5) A type of cabling that consists of four twisted pairs of copper wire terminated by RJ-45 connectors. Can be used for Token Ring, 1000BaseT, 100BaseT, and 10BaseT networking.

CGA
(Color Graphics Adapter) An IBM video display standard that provided low-resolution text and graphics.

chipset
The set of chips on the system board that support the CPU and other basic functions.

CHS
(Cylinders, Heads, Sectors addressing) Used to manually configure hard drives smaller than 504 MB.

CIS
(Card Information Structure) A PC Card feature that passes information about the PC Card to the computer so that the card can be automatically configured for use.

client
A computer on a network that makes use of the resources managed by a server.

Glossary

client-server network
A network where one or more computers act primarily as providers of network resources (servers), and one or more computers act primarily as consumers of network resources (clients).

clock speed
The frequency at which the system board and CPU operate.

CMOS
(Complementary Metal Oxide Semiconductor) The most widely used type of integrated circuit for digital processors and memories. Virtually everything is configured through CMOS today. Pronounced "see-moss."

CMOS RAM
(Complementary Metal Oxide Semiconductor) A special type of memory that stores information about the computer's setup.

coaxial cable
A high-capacity cable used in communications and video, commonly called coax. It contains an insulated solid or stranded wire surrounded by a solid or braided metallic shield, wrapped in a plastic cover.

collateral injuries
Injury caused by involuntary muscle movement.

color depth
The number of bits used to store the color of a pixel.

computer networking device
A mechanical device that directs data in a computer network.

conductor
Any material that easily transmits the flow of electricity.

contrast
The difference in intensity between adjacent colors or shades of gray in an image.

Control Unit
The CPU component that performs the fetch, decode, execute, and store functions.

conventional memory
In a PC, the first 640 K of memory.

corona
An assembly within a laser printer that contains a wire (the corona wire), which is responsible for charging the paper.

CPU
(Central Processing Unit) The main chip on the system board, the CPU performs software instructions and mathematical and logical equations.

CPU cache
A type of high-speed RAM that is added directly into a processor to improve computing speed. Often referred to as onboard cache. primary cache, or L1 (Level 1) cache. Compare with L2 cache and RAM.

CPU package
The physical construction or form factor of a CPU.

CRT
(Cathode Ray Tube) Displays images using phosphorous dots with a scanned electron beam.

CSMA/CD
(Carrier Sense Multiple Access with Collision Detection) A system that enables dealing with packet collisions in an Ethernet network. Computers transmit when the channel is free. If two computers transmit at the same time, a collision occurs and is detected (by the Collision Detection mechanism). Both computers stop transmitting and retransmit at a random point in the future

CSU/DSU
(Channel Service Unit/Data Service Unit) Combines the functions of CSU and DSU in one device. The CSU terminates a digital circuit. The DSU terminates a data circuit to the Data Terminal Equipment and converts customer transmission data into a bipolar format.

current
The flow of electrons past a given point in a circuit.

Glossary

cylinder
The aggregate of all tracks that reside in the same location on every disk surface. On multiple-platter disks, the cylinder is the sum total of every track with the same track number on every surface. On a floppy disk, a cylinder comprises the top and corresponding bottom track.

DAT
(Digital Audio Tape) A backup tape format that offers higher storage capacity at a lower cost than QIC technology. Capacity is from 1 GB to 4 GB and up.

data bus
The connection between the CPU, memory, and peripheral devices.

Data Link layer
A layer of the OSI model that manages node-to-node validity and integrity of the transmission. Also referred to as Layer 2 of the OSI model.

datapath
The width (in bits) of the bus, or the number of channels in the bus.

daughter board
Any circuit board that is added to the motherboard and accesses the memory and CPU directly.

DC
(Direct Current) Electrical current that flows in only one direction and at a constant voltage.

DDR SDRAM
(Double Data Rate SDRAM) SDRAM that transfers data twice per clock cycle.

decimal number system
A numbering system based on 10 discrete states.

Deep Sleep
Drastically reduced power mode entered into after certain conditions (such as prolonged inactivity) have been met.

default gateway
An IP address used to identify a TCP/IP-based router that provides access to a remote network. When you configure a computer's default gateway, the computer forwards any communications for remote networks to the IP address of the default gateway.

degauss
Remove magnetism from a device.

device conflict
A conflict between devices that have been assigned the same resources.

device driver
Software that enables the operating system and a peripheral device to communicate with each other.

DHCP
(Dynamic Host Configuration Protocol) A protocol that enables a Windows NT or Windows 2000 server to dynamically assign IP addresses to clients.

digital cameras
captures an image digitally and stores the image as a file on a floppy disk or removable memory card.

DIMM
(Dual In-line Memory Module) A group of memory chips that transfer information 64 bits at a time.

diode
An electronic component that acts like a one-way valve. Diodes are often used to change Alternating Current (AC) to Direct Current (DC), as temperature or light sensors, and as light emitters.

DIP switch
Switches on a card used to configure hardware settings. These are usually rocker switches (like light switches) to turn on or off.

direct glare
Results when a light source is exposed directly to the eye.

Glossary

display adapter
A PC expansion board that converts the images created in the computer to the electronic signals required by the monitor.

dissipative material
A conductive material with high resistance that dissipates a charge slowly.

DLT
(Digital Linear Tape) A backup tape technology developed by DEC. Current storage capacity is up to 50 GB.

DMA
(Direct Memory Access) Specialized circuitry or a dedicated microprocessor that transfers data from adapters to memory without using the CPU.

DNS
(Domain Name System) A static, distributed, hierarchical database system used to map computer (host) names to IP addresses.

dongle
An adapter that plugs into a PC Card and has a connector on the other end for plugging in a phone cord or network cable.

dot pitch
The distance between the same color dots on a video screen.

dot-matrix printer
A printer that forms images out of dots on paper. Dot patterns are created by a set of pins that strike an inked ribbon.

DRAM
(Dynamic RAM) A type of RAM that needs to be refreshed.

drive
A computer component that stores data for the long term. Data on the drive is retained even if the power is turned off.

drive controller
The circuitry that enables the drive and the CPU to communicate with each other.

drive interface
The collection of electrical and logical connections between a hard drive and a PC.

DSL
(Digital Subscriber Line) A network connection method that uses standard phone wires and a specialized transceiver to transmit digital network data over the same line as standard voice communications.

dual-voltage
Design that enables use of a higher external voltage (also called I/O voltage), and a lower internal (also called core) voltage for processors. This design is also called split-rail.

dye sublimation printer
A type of printer that uses a thermal process to transfer dye to paper to create images.

ECC
(Error Correction Code) A type of memory that corrects errors on the fly.

ECHS
(Extended CHS) Enables use of hard drives of up to 8.4 GB.

ECP
(Extended Capability Port) Newer-generation parallel port standard that provides roughly 10 times faster throughput than the Centronics standard. Used by newer-generation printers and scanners.

EDO RAM
(Extended Data Output RAM) A type of DRAM that enables a memory address to hold data for multiple reads.

EDSAC
(Electronic Delay Storage Automatic Computer) A well-engineered machine built by Maurice Wilkes and colleagues at the University of Cambridge Mathematics Lab in 1949 and was a productive tool for mathematicians.

EDVAC
(Electronic Discrete Variable Automatic Computer) The first computer to use stored programs.

EGA
(Enhanced Graphics Adapter) An early IBM video display standard that provided medium-resolution text and graphics.

GLOSSARY

EISA bus
(Extended Industry Standard Architecture bus) A PC bus standard that extends the 16-bit ISA bus (AT bus) to 32 bits and provides bus mastering.

electrical energy
The total amount of electrical power delivered in a given time period.

electrical power
The energy delivered by a flow of electrons in one second.

electricity
The flow of electrons through a material or through a vacuum.

electron
Negatively charged sub-atomic particles that carry energy with them when they move from one place to another.

EMI
(ElectroMagnetic Interference) Interference caused when a magnetic field builds up around one electrical circuit and affects the transmission on an adjacent electrical circuit.

ENIAC
(Electronic Numerical Integrator And Computer) Developed for the U.S. Army by J. Presper Eckert and John Mauchly at the University of Pennsylvania in Philadelphia. ENIAC was programmed by plugging in cords and setting thousands of switches to direct how 18,000 vacuum tubes would perform 5,000 calculations per second.

EP drum
(Electrostatic Photographic drum) The component in a laser printer that carries the electrical charge to attract toner and then to transfer the toner to the paper.

EPP
(Enhanced Parallel Port) Newer-generation parallel port standard that offers roughly 10 times faster throughput than the Centronics standard. Used mostly by non-printer peripherals such as CD-ROM drives and network adapters.

ergonomics
The study of people in their working environments.

ESCD
(Extended System Configuration Data) A special extension of CMOS memory designed to hold information about specific hardware devices, including legacy and Plug and Play devices.

ESD
(ElectroStatic Discharge) Sparks (electrons) that jump from an electrically charged object to an approaching conductive object.

ESDI
(Enhanced Small Device Interface) A drive interface similar to the ST-506 interface that provides increased performance over the ST-506. Pronounced "ez-dee."

Ethernet
The most widely used LAN access method, which is defined by the IEEE 802.3 standard.

EWN
(Enterprise-Wide Network) A computer network that links all the computers in an organization.

exception interrupt
An interrupt used by the processor to handle errors.

Fast Ethernet
Ethernet standard that supports transfer rates of 100 Mbps. Also called 100BaseT. Uses two pairs of twisted-pair wire. Other implementations include 100BaseT4 (uses four pairs of twisted-pair wires), and 100BaseFL (uses fiber-optic cables).

fastIrDA
Infrared standard that uses a transfer speed of 4 Mbps.

fiber optic cable
Cable that uses glass to transmit network signals in the form of light waves.

firewall
A method for keeping a network secure.

Glossary

FireWire
A high-speed serial bus developed by Apple and Texas Instruments that allows for the connection of up to 63 devices.

firmware
Software stored in memory chips that retains data whether or not power to the computer is on.

flash memory cards
A removable solid-state mass storage device that resides on a small card.

Flash ROM
Memory that stores data similarly to EEPROM, but uses a super-voltage charge to erase a block of data. Can be erased and rewritten only a few times.

font
A size and style of typeface.

footcandle
A unit of measure of the intensity of light falling on a surface.

form factor
The size and shape of a given component. Often used in terms of motherboard and drive characteristics.

formatting
A system function that prepares a mass storage medium to hold data.

FPM RAM
(Fast Page Mode RAM) Used in older 32-pin SIMMs.

fragmentation
The degree to which the pieces that make up files are spread across the hard disk.

Fuel Cell
A battery technology that combines hydrogen and oxygen to generate an electric current.

fusing assembly
A component in a laser printer that uses two rollers to heat toner particles, melting them into the paper.

gateway
A computer that performs protocol conversion between different types of networks or applications.

GB
(Gigabyte) A means of measuring file or disk size, equivalent to 1,024 MB.

geosynchronous
Maintaining an orbit with a fixed relationship to Earth.

gig
A measure of hard drive storage capacity that equals 1 billion bytes.

Gigabit Ethernet
Ethernet standard that supports transfer rates of 1 gigabit per second.

gigahertz
A million cycles per second.

ground
Any conducting body with a potential of zero; usually, the earth itself or something connected to the earth.

GUI
(Graphical User Interface) A means of communicating with an operating system by using a mouse or other device to work with pictorial screen elements, instead of typing text commands at the keyboard.

hardware interrupt
An interrupt caused by some action of a hardware device, such as a keystroke or mouse movement.

hazardous materials
Any materials that must be handled in a special way in order to prevent injury to people or damage to the environment.

HBA
(Host Bus Adapter) A dedicated adapter that manages data transfer between multiple devices on a channel, such as multiple SCSI devices on a SCSI chain.

head crash
When read/write heads bang against the surface of the disk.

GLOSSARY

heat sink
A device attached to a processor that addresses the problem of overheating processors. Cool air is blown by a fan onto the device's main elements, keeping the air around the processor cool.

Hercules Graphics
A monochrome display adapter capable of producing both high-resolution monochrome graphics and text.

hexadecimal number system
A numbering system based on 16 discrete states.

hierarchical network
A network where one or more central computers, such as a mainframe, provides all processing power and resources to all other network nodes.

high-level formatting
An operating system function that builds file systems on drives and partitions.

host name
A descriptive name for a computer on a TCP/IP network.

hotswap
To change out a device without needing to power down the PC during installation or removal of the device.

hub
A central connecting device in a network that joins communication lines together in a star configuration.

HVD
(High Voltage Differential Signaling) A SCSI device that uses two wires, one for data and one for the inverse of data. These devices use high voltage and can't be used on a single-ended SCSI chain.

hybrid topology
A physical topology where two or more of the basic physical topologies, such as bus, ring, star, and mesh, are combined.

I/O address
A range of memory, usually in the lowest portions of memory (conventional memory), that is used for communications between the processor and the adapter. Each adapter must have its own unique, non-overlapping I/O address space.

IDE
(Integrated Drive Electronics) A drive interface that provides inexpensive, high-speed data transfer between the IDE drive and the other components of the computer.

IEEE
(Institute of Electrical and Electronic Engineers) Pronounced "I-triple-E." An organization of scientists, engineers, and students of electronics and related fields whose technical and standards committees develop, publish, and revise computing and telecommunications standards.

inductance
A circuit or device in which a change in the current generates an electromotive force.

infrared
Technology that uses a beam of light to transmit data, rather than cables, using line-of-sight technology.

inkjet printer
A printer that forms images by spraying ink on the paper.

instruction set
The collection of commands used by a CPU to perform calculations and other computing operations.

insulator
Any material that does not easily transmit the flow of electricity.

integrated circuit
An electronic component consisting of several transistors and resistors, connected together on a semiconductor chip.

intelligent hub
A connecting device that forwards signals and provides other functionality such as routing and bridging.

Glossary

interface card
A means of connecting devices to the system board so that they can communicate with the microprocessor.

internal bus
The bus within the CPU itself.

Internet connection
A network connection that enables a computer to access the Internet.

interrupt
A signal sent over an IRQ that informs the processor that the device needs its attention.

Interrupt 13h (INT13h) extensions
Interrupt 13h extensions is an updated set of BIOS commands that enable support for hard drives exceeding 8.4 GB.

IP address
Four numbers that uniquely identify a computer on the network. This address is typically shown in the format 192.168.200.200. A portion of the IP address is used to identify the network on which the computer resides (similar to the street name in a mailing address); the remaining portion of the IP address is used to identify the computer itself (similar to the house number portion of a mailing address).

IPX
(Internetwork Packet Exchange) A NetWare communications protocol used to route messages from one node to another.

IRQ
(Interrupt Request line) A hardware line connected to a controller chip and assigned to a device. When the device needs to request the attention of the computer processor, it sends a signal over the IRQ line.

ISA bus
(Industry Standard Architecture bus) An expansion bus commonly used in PCs.

ISDN
(Integrated Services Digital Network) A method for carrying voice, data, and video signals using existing phone lines that has largely been superseded by DSL.

jumper
Pins and connectors used to configure hardware settings. You physically connect or disconnect a circuit by adding or removing a jumper block, which is a small rectangular connector, from a pair of pins attached to the system board or add-on card.

KB
(Kilobyte) A means of measuring file or disk size, equivalent to 1,024 bytes.

keyboard
A set of typewriter-like keys that enable you to enter data into the computer.

L1 cache
See primary cache.

L2 cache
See secondary cache.

L3 cache
Memory on the motherboard between the processor and RAM when there's a built-in L2 cache on the processor.

LAN
(Local Area Network) A network confined to a local physical area, such as a single building or floor.

Large LBA
An LBA translation mode that extends hard-disk capacities beyond 137 GB.

laser printer
A type of printer that produces images on paper by using a laser beam and an electrophotographic drum. Produces high-quality output.

latency
The time between when a message is sent and received by the other party.

LBA
(Logical Block Addressing) Used to support increased capacity of IDE drives to over 504 MB, up to 8.4 GB. Some BIOS versions enable you to choose whether to use LBA mode.

GLOSSARY

LCD
(Liquid Crystal Display) A monitor constructed of a liquid crystal solution between two sheets of polarized material.

Li-Ion
Portable computer lithium battery with a long life.

Lithium Polymer
Portable computer battery using a jelly-like material.

LLC
(Logical Link Control) The Ethernet portion of the Data Link layer that connects the network software in Layer 3 to the Media Access Control (MAC) sublayer.

load
Power consumption of a device. A load is calculated with inductance, capacitance, and other electrical characteristics.

logical network architecture
The model that describes the degree of centralized control built into the network.

low-level formatting
The process of writing track and sector markings on a disk.

LVD
(Low Voltage Differential signaling) A SCSI device that uses two wires, one for data and one for the inverse of data. These devices use a low voltage and can be used on a single-ended SCSI chain.

MAC
(Media Access Control) The portion of the Data Link layer in the OSI model that specifies the access method used to connect to the Physical layer at the bottom of the OSI model.

magnetic core memory
Memory that stores binary data (0 or 1) in the orientation of magnetic charges in ferrite cores about one-sixteenth-inch in diameter.

MAN
(Metropolitan Area Network) A computer network confined to a single municipality that uses high-speed media like fiber optics or dedicated digital lines.

Mark I
A programmable, electromechanical calculator that combined 78 adding machines to perform three calculations per second. It was designed by Howard Aiken, built by IBM, and installed at Harvard in 1944.

math coprocessor
A mathematical circuit that performs high-speed floating point operations. It is generally built into the CPU chip. In older PCs, such as the 386SX and 486SX, the math coprocessor was an optional and separate chip.

MB
(Megabyte) A means of measuring file or disk size, equivalent to 1,024 KB.

MDA
(Monochrome Display Adapter) The first IBM PC monochrome video display standard for text only.

media
In a network, the transmission media that links computers together in a network. Usually a cable, but could be a wireless medium. In drives, the storage object on which data is stored.

meg
A measure of hard drive storage capacity that equals 1 million bytes.

megahertz
A thousand cycles per second.

memory
Internal storage areas of the computer.

memory bank
The collection of memory expansion slots in a computer.

memory package
A circuit board that holds the memory chips that are plugged into the memory expansion slots on the motherboard.

Glossary

mesh topology
A physical topology where each node has a direct connection to all other nodes on the network, providing dedicated, permanent, point-to-point communication paths.

Micro Channel Architecture bus
A proprietary 32-bit bus from IBM that was used in PS/2, RS/6000, and certain ES/9370 models.

microprocessor
A complete central processing unit on a single chip, the microprocessor controls the operation of all the other computer components.

MIDI
(Musical Instrument Digital Interface) An interface that allows you to connect and control electronic musical devices such as electric keyboards (pianos), synthesizers, drum kits, and guitars.

MNP
(Microcom Networking Protocol) Five modem standards offering different levels of error correction and detection.

modem
A device that adapts a computer to an analog telephone line by converting digital pulses to audio frequencies and vice versa. The name is short for MOdulate/DEModulate, which is what modems do to adapt the signals.

Molex connector
The standard peripheral connector for powering internal IDE and SCSI drives. Molex connectors are larger than Berg connector. There are usually four or more of these connectors in a system.

monitor
A display screen used to present output from a computer.

motherboard
The main circuit board in a personal computer. Also referred to as a system board.

MSDS
(Material Safety Data Sheets) Technical bulletins designed to give users and emergency personnel information about the proper procedures of storage and handling of a hazardous substance.

multimeter
Electronic test equipment that can perform multiple tasks, usually including measurement of voltage, current, and resistance.

multiport repeater
A connecting unit that regenerates the data bits in order to maintain a strong signal. Also referred to as an active hub.

Napier's Bones
A set of rectangular rods with numbers etched on them that let users do multiplication by adding the numbers on properly positioned rods. Precursor of the slide rule.

NetBEUI
(NetBios Enhanced User Interface) The default networking protocol for the Windows desktop operating system.

network
A collection of hardware and software that enables computers in a group to communicate with each other.

network adapter
A printed circuit board that plugs into both the clients and servers and controls the exchange of data between them. Also referred to as network boards, network cards, and Network Interface Cards (NICs).

Network layer
A layer of the OSI model that provides internetworking for the communication sessions. Also referred to as Layer 3 of the OSI model.

network protocol
A special electronic language that enables network computers to communicate.

network scope
The effective coverage area of a network, such as local area network or wide area network.

GLOSSARY

network segment
A group of computers that share the same network IP address.

nibble
A group of 4 bits. An 8-bit byte is written as 2 nibbles to make it easier to read.

NiCad
Portable computer battery made of nickel and cadmium with a three to four hour life.

NiMH
Environmentally friendly battery for portable computers.

node
Any of the devices that can be accessed on the network. This includes devices such as servers, clients, and printers.

NOS
(Network Operating System) Computer software that manages all the resources accessible over the network.

ohm
The unit of measurement of resistance.

on-die
Integrated directly into a semiconductor chip.

online UPS
A UPS that supplies power from a battery at all times. The battery is charged from the regular electrical supply.

operands
The values being compared in a logical or mathematical operation.

OS
(Operating System) A type of system software that provides the basic interface between the user and the computer components.

OSI model
(Open System Interconnection model) A model that describes network communications as consisting of seven layers that work together to provide network services.

overclocking
Configuring your system board to run at a speed greater than your CPU is rated to handle. Doing so can cause the CPU to overheat, produce random results, or be damaged or destroyed.

palmtop
A larger category of personal computing devices that contains PDAs..

parity
An error-checking method for electronic communications.

park
Read/write heads move over an unused section of the disk when the computer is powered off.

partition
An isolated section of a disk that functions like a separate physical drive.

Pascaline machine
A calculating machine that could add and subtract, developed in 1642 by Blaise Pascal.

passive hub
Connecting units that add nothing to the data passing through them.

PC
(Personal Computers) Stand-alone, single-user desktop, or smaller, computers that can function independently. PC used to refer to any personal computer, but now refers to personal computers that follow the original design by IBM, use Intel or compatible chips, and usually have some version of Windows as an operating system. PCs are sometimes called IBM compatibles.

PC Card
The credit-card-sized devices that are used in portable computers instead of desktop-sized expansion cards.

PCI bus
(Peripheral Component Interconnect bus) A peripheral bus commonly used in PCs that provides a high-speed data path between the CPU and peripheral devices.

GLOSSARY

PCMCIA
(Personal Computer Memory Card International Association) An association of organizations that establishes standards for PC Cards.

PDA
(Personal Digital Assistant) A very small computer that can be held in one hand. Often used to keep an electronic calendar and address book, get email, send faxes, and take notes on the go.

peer-to-peer network
A network where all computers connected to the network can act as a provider (server) or consumer (client) of network resources.

peripheral
Any computing device that is connected to the CPU and main memory.

PGA
(Pin Grid Array) A type of CPU packaging design on which pins are distributed evenly in parallel rows on the entire bottom of a square chip.

Physical layer
A layer of the OSI model that provides rules for the transmission of bits over the network medium. Also referred to as Layer 1 of the OSI model.

physical network architecture
The resource access model that determines how network computers can be connected and how they can communicate.

physical topology
The layout of networked computers in physical relationship to each other.

pinouts
Specifications for the signal carried on each pin and connection for a port.

pixel
The smallest discrete element on a video display.

plenum
An air-handling space that is part of the heating and cooling system in a building and is often a convenient place to run cables.

plenum cable
Cable made of special materials in the insulation layers that make it fire resistant. When it burns, it produces a minimal amount of smoke and chemical fumes.

PnP
(Plug and Play) A method in which the operating system automatically configures adapter settings.

pointing device
A device that sends electronic signals to the computer to control the movements of a pointer drawn on screen in the Graphical User Interface (GUI).

port
A hardware connection interface on a computer system that enables devices to be connected to the system.

potential difference
A measurement of the difference in electrical potential energy between two different objects. Also called voltage.

power supply
An internal system component that converts AC power from an electrical outlet to DC power needed by system components.

Presentation layer
A layer of the OSI model that provides conversion of codes and formats for the communication session. Also referred to as Layer 6 of the OSI model.

primary cache
A type of high-speed RAM that is added directly to a processor to improve computing speed. Often referred to as onboard cache, CPU cache, or L1 (Level 1) cache. Compare with L2 cache and RAM.

processor
Another way to refer to the microprocessor, or CPU.

proprietary
A design that is unique to a specific manufacturer. The design has not been shared so there are no competing product lines making a component, so you are forced to purchase it directly from the manufacturer.

GLOSSARY

protected mode
In PCs, starting with the 286, an operational state that allows the computer to address all of its memory. It also prevents an errant program from entering into the memory boundary of another. In a 386 and higher machine, it provides access to 32-bit instructions and sophisticated memory management modes.

protocol
An electronic communications standard. See network protocol.

PS/2
From the IBM Personal System/2, PS/2 is the name for the standard connector used for most PC keyboards and mice.

PS/2 interface
A round 6-pin port used to connect keyboards and mice to PCs.

QIC
(Quarter-Inch Cartridge) The oldest, most standardized backup tape technology, available for most computer platforms.

Quick Start
Power-saving mode supported by many Intel Mobile processors.

RAID
(Redundant Array of Inexpensive Disks) An arrangement of multiple disk drives and a sophisticated controller that provides higher performance or reliability, or both, than a single disk drive.

RAM
(Random Access Memory) The system's primary working memory. It is a temporary storage location for dynamic information, such as the contents of a program currently running on the computer.

RAM chip
An integrated circuit that acts as the computer's primary temporary storage place for data. RAM stands for Random Access Memory.

RAMDAC
(Random Access Memory Digital-Analog Converter) Component on the video card that reads the bytes of video data in the card's memory and converts the digital data in memory to continuous analog signals that tell the monitor what to display.

RDRAM
(Rambus Dynamic RAM) A new memory architecture by Rambus, Inc. that supports speeds up to 800 MHz.

real mode
An operational state in Intel CPU chips (starting with the 286) in which the computer functions like the first Intel CPU chip (8086/8088), which is limited to accessing 1 MB of memory. DOS applications run in real mode, unless they have been enhanced with a DOS extender that allows them to use more memory.

reflective glare
Created by a monitor screen's mirror-like surface.

refresh rate
The number of times per second a monitor is scanned to illuminate all the pixels.

register
A high speed memory location within a CPU. The CPU stores data and commands in registers as it operates on those pieces of information.

rendering
Converting a print job sent by an application into printer language.

repeater
A communications device that amplifies or regenerates the data signal in order to extend the transmission distance. Also referred to as active hubs.

resistance
The opposition to the flow of electric current through a material.

resistor
An electronic component that resists the flow of electric current in an electronic circuit.

Glossary

resolution
The maximum number of pixels a monitor can display.

RIMM
(Rambus Inline Memory Module) A memory module for RDRAM. Supports from 1 to 16 direct RDRAM devices in a Rambus channel. Used primarily as main memory on a system board.

ring topology
A physical topology where all nodes are connected in a continuous loop, and nodes relay information around the loop in a round-robin manner.

riser card
A board that's plugged into the motherboard; it "rises" above the motherboard and is used to connect modems, audio cards, and network cards to the system.

RJ-45 connector
An 8-wire modular connector for twisted pair cables.

ROM
(Read-Only Memory) A special type of memory that is permanent. It stores programs necessary to boot the computer and to diagnose problems.

router
A network device that provides access to resources outside the local network segment.

RSI
(Repetitive Strain Injury) Damage to muscles, tendons, or nerves caused by overuse or misuse.

SAM
(Sequential Access Memory) Used for memory areas where data can be stored in sequential order, such as memory buffers.

SAN
(Storage Area Network) A computer network consisting of large-capacity storage devices.

scanner
A device that can convert printed images into a computer readable format.

SCSI
(Small Computer System Interface) A drive controller that provides high-performance data transfer between the SCSI device and the other components of the computer. Pronounced scuzzy.

SDRAM
(Synchronous DRAM) Memory that has a clock that is coordinated with the system clock to synchronize the memory chip's input and output signals.

SECC
(Single Edge Contact Cartridge) Type of CPU packaging that refers to a design where the processor is located on a circuit board that is inserted into a slot on the system board.

secondary cache
A type of high-speed RAM that is placed between the processor and conventional RAM to improve computing speed. Often referred to as L2 (Level 2) cache. Compare with CPU cache and RAM.

sector
The smallest unit of storage read or written on a disk.

sector interleave
The mapping of logical sectors to physical sectors on a disk.

semiconductor
A solid-state substance that can be electrically altered to act as either a conductor or an insulator.

server
A computer on a network that manages resources for other computers on the network.

Session layer
A layer of the OSI model that initiates and manages the communication session. Also referred to as Layer 5 of the OSI model.

SIMM
(Single In-line Memory Module) A group of memory chips that transfer information 32 bits at a time.

GLOSSARY

single-ended device
SCSI device that uses a single wire for each bit of data.

slowIrDA
Infrared standard that uses a transfer speed of 9.6 Kbps.

Socket Services
Device driver software for a PC Card.

SODIMM
(Small Outline Dual Inline Memory Module) A memory module standard used in some notebook and iMac systems.

software
A series of electronic instructions that tell a computer to complete a specific task.

software interrupt
An interrupt caused by an instruction in a software program.

soldered
A means of securing electronic components to a circuit board by using a combination of lead, tin, and silver (solder) and a tool called a soldering iron.

solid ink printer
A type of printer that uses ink from melted solid-ink sticks.

sound card
An internal card used to convert digital signals to sound waves. Includes several external ports for connecting electronic musical instruments, game controllers, speakers, and microphones. Usually also includes internal connections for playback of audio CDs.

SpeedStep
Technology that enables two different performance modes, Maximized Performance Mode and Battery Optimized Mode. In Maximized Performance Mode, the processor runs at its highest speed and normal internal voltage. In Battery Optimized Mode, the processor runs at a reduced speed and a reduced internal voltage.

SPGA
(Staggered Pin Grid Array) This CPU packaging design staggers pins so that more pins will fit on the same amount of surface.

spooling
Writing a print job as a file to disk so that it can be sent to the printer.

SPX
(Sequenced Packet Exchange) The NetWare communications protocol used to control the transport of messages across a network.

SRAM
(Static RAM) A type of RAM that doesn't need to be refreshed.

ST-506
A legacy drive interface still in use today. Also referred to as the ST-412 interface.

Standby UPS
SUPSs are UPSs that supply power from a battery when power problems are detected. Also referred to as a Standby Power Supply (SPS).

star topology
A LAN physical topology where all nodes individually connect to a central computer or other device such as a multiport repeater, concentrator, or hub.

static electricity
The build up of a stationary electrical charge on an object.

Stepped Reckoner
A mechanical calculator developed by Gottfried von Leibniz that improved Pascal's design to include multiplication and division.

STP
(Shielded Twisted-Pair) Twisted-pair cable that is wrapped in a metal sheath. This reduces the possibility of problems caused by electrical interference.

Glossary

subnet mask
Four numbers used to distinguish the network portion of the IP address from that of the computer portion. For example, if a computer's IP address is 192.168.200.200 and the subnet mask is 255.255.255.0, this means that the network portion of the address is 192.168.200, and the computer portion is the remaining byte (200).

synchronous
Transmission of a bit stream of data where the transmitter and receiver are synchronized.

system board
The main circuit board in a personal computer. Also referred to as a motherboard.

system bus
The primary communication pathway between a microprocessor and other parts of the chipset. Often referred to as the frontside or local bus, the system bus enables data transfer between the CPU, BIOS, and RAM.

system software
Low-level programs that provide the most basic functionality, such as operating systems.

tape drive
Internal or external, read/write drives that store data magnetically on a removable tape.

TCP/IP
(Transmission Control Protocol/Internet Protocol) A suite of related protocols that enables computers to communicate across a network and over the Internet.

termination
The process of properly ending a chain of ESDI or SCSI disk drives by installing a terminating resistor.

thermal compound
Used to attach a heat sink to a CPU. Manufactured to provide maximum heat transfer from the CPU to the heat sink.

throughput
The amount of data that can be processed from input through to output within a given time period.

token
A device used in ring networks to ensure that only one node transmits data at any one time. If a node doesn't hold the token, it can't transmit data until it does hold the token.

Token Ring
A computer network connected in a loop configuration so that only the computer holding the token can communicate.

toner
An electrically charged dry ink substance used in laser printers.

track
A storage channel on a disk or tape. On disks, tracks are concentric circles (hard and floppy disks) or spirals (CDs and video discs). On tapes, they are parallel lines.

transceiver
Device built into NICs that enables sending and receiving data over the network cable.

transistor
A device containing semiconductor material that can amplify a signal or open and close a circuit. In computers, transistors function as an electronic switch.

Transport layer
A layer of the OSI model that provides end-to-end management of the communication session. Also referred to as Layer 4 of the OSI model.

triboelectric generation
Using friction to create a static charge.

TSR
(Terminate and Stay Resident) A program that always stays in memory.

TTL monitor
A monitor that uses Transistor-Transistor Logic signals, which are the same type of signals used in the computer.

Ultra DMA
A newer faster drive technology for data transfers on IDE drives. Also called Ultra ATA and Fast ATA-2. Provides for transfer speeds of up to 100 MBps.

GLOSSARY

UMB
(Upper Memory Block) An unused block in the upper memory area (640 KB to 1 MB).

UNIVAC
The Universal Automatic Computer was completed in 1951 by Eckert and Mauchly for the U.S. Bureau of the Census. It was the first commercial computer in the United States and could handle both numerical and alphabetical information.

UPS
(Uninterruptible Power Supply) A battery-operated device that is intended to save computer components from damage due to power problems such as power failures, spikes, and sags.

USB
(Universal Serial Bus) A hardware interface for connecting up to 127 USB peripherals.

UTP
(Unshielded Twisted-Pair) Twisted-pair cable that has two unshielded wires twisted around each other. This type of cabling is inexpensive, but electrical interference can be a problem.

vacuum tube
A sealed glass or metal container that controls a flow of electrons through a vacuum.

VAN
(Value-Added Network) A computer network that provides services above and beyond the transmission of data.

VGA
(Video Graphics Array) The minimum standard for PC video display, which originated with IBM's PS/2 models in 1987.

video output device
A computer peripheral that enables users to view information on a computer system.

virtual machine
The ability of a CPU to perform as multiple 8086 CPUs. Under direction of a control program, each virtual machine runs as a stand-alone 8086 running its own operating system and applications; thus, DOS, UNIX, and other operating systems can be running simultaneously. All virtual machines are multitasked together.

VL-Bus
VESA Local-Bus is a peripheral bus from VESA that was primarily used in 486s and provides a high-speed datapath between the CPU and peripherals.

VLSI
(Very Large-Scale Integration) The process of placing thousands of electronic components on a single chip.

volt
The unit of measurement of voltage.

voltage
A measurement of the difference in electrical potential energy between two different objects. Also called potential difference.

VRAM
(Video RAM) These chips have two access paths to a single memory address to improve performance. One path is used for reads, the other for writes.

VRM
(Voltage Regulator Module) A module on the system board that regulates the voltage that's passed to the CPU.

WAN
(Wide Area Network) A network that spans large geographical areas.

watt
The unit of measurement of electrical power.

Wi-Fi networks
A wireless network.

WINS
(Windows Internet Naming System) A Windows network service used to enable clients to obtain the IP address for a given computer name.

GLOSSARY

wireless access point
Provides a connection point for multiple computers with wireless network cards to connect to a network.

WRAM
(Windows RAM) Developed by Samsung Electronics, this type of RAM is optimized for display adapters.

XIP
(Execute In Place) A PC Card feature that enables operating system and application code stored on the PC Card to run directly from the PC Card rather than executing in RAM.

ZIF socket
(Zero Insertion Force socket) A type of processor socket that uses a lever to tighten or loosen the pin connections between the processor chip and the socket.

Zinc Air
Portable computer battery that uses a carbon membrane that absorbs oxygen.

zoned-bit recording
A method of creating sectors on a hard disk so that there are more sectors on the outer tracks than on inner tracks.

ZV
(Zoomed Video) A connection between a PC Card and the host system that allows the card to write video data directly to the VGA controller.

INDEX

10Base2, 571
10Base5, 571
10BaseT, 534, 571
2X, 200
32-bit bus, 196
4X, 200
64-bit bus, 196
8 mm, 376
8008, 5
8X (Pro), 200

A

abacus, 2
AC, 63
  portable device power sources, 475
  power, 111
Accelerated Graphics Port
  See: AGP
ACPI, 111
active hubs, 584
adapter cards, 16
  problems, 203
  troubleshooting, 203
adapters, 177, 494
Add Printer Wizard, 226
Advanced Configuration and Power Interface
  See: ACPI
Advanced Power Management
  See: APM
Advanced Technology Attachment
  See: ATA
AGP, 199
  versions, 200
alternating current
  See: AC
ALU, 126
American National Standards Institute
  See: ANSI

American Standard Code for Information Interchange
  See: ASCII
amps, 63
AMR, 147
Analytical Engine, 2
ANSI, 398
APIPA, 567
APM, 111, 478
AppleTalk, 560, 574
application software, 20
ARCNet, 574
Arithmetic and Logic Unit
  See: ALU
ASCII, 398
aspect ratio, 416
AT Attachment Packet Interface
  See: ATAPI
AT commands, 282
ATA, 255
  standards, 258
ATAPI, 255, 359
Attached Resource Computer Network
  See: ARCNet
Attachment Unit Interface
  See: AUIs
Audio/Modem Riser
  See: AMR
AUIs, 531, 532
  connectors, 539
Automatic Private IP Addressing
  See: APIPA

B

Babbage's Difference Engine, 2
backbone, 539
backside bus, 163
backups, 374
  methods, 377

INDEX

rotation method, 377
storage, 381
tape drives, 374
bandwidth, 576
banks, 163
Base Memory addresses, 180
Basic Input Output System
 See: BIOS
basic toolkit, 36
batteries, 476
 disposing of, 630
 fuel cell, 476
 Li-Ion, 476
 Lithium Polymer, 476
 NiCad, 476
 NiMH, 476
 Zinc Air, 476
Berg connectors, 105
binary number system, 26
BIOS, 116
 accessing, 118
 configuring, 119
 PnP, 185
 settings, 117
 upgrading, 123
bis, 280
bits, 32
BNC connectors, 538
boolean, 127
boot disks, 41
 AntiVirus, 42
 creating for Windows 2000/XP/NT, 45
 creating for Windows 98, 42
 creating for Windows XP, 43
boot process, 120
 troubleshooting, 125
boot sequence
 CMOS setting, 117
bridges, 585
brightness, 418
brouters, 586
bus, 16, 146, 177
 architecture, 195
 upgrading, 623
bus master, 493
bus topology, 545
bytes, 32

C

cable modems, 578
cable select, 302, 304
cables
 for networks, 532
 null-modem, 216
 parallel, 223, 225
 SCSI cable length, 313
 serial, 213, 215
 twisted-pair, 533
 USB, 235, 236
cache
 upgrading, 623
cache level
 of CPUs, 133
CAD/CAM, 184
Card and Socket Services, 494
Card Information Structure
 See: CIS
Card Services, 494
CardBus, 493
Carrier Sense Multiple Access with Collision Detection
 See: CSMA/CD
cartridge disk drives, 370
 how cartridge drives work, 371
Cat3, 534
Cat6, 534
Cathode Ray Tube
 See: CRT
CD-R, 17
CD-ROM, 17
 using, 361
CD-RW, 17
Central Processing Unit
 See: CPU
Centronics, 224
CGA, 269
Channel Service Unit/Data Service Unit
 See: CSU/DSU
chipsets, 11, 146
CHS, 256
circuit board toolkit, 39
CIS, 494
client-server networks, 550
clients, 529
clock speed, 147
 of CPUs, 131
CMOS, 116, 192

INDEX

default settings, 116
error codes, 123
CMOS RAM, 15
CNR, 147
coaxial cables, 537
  connectors, 538
  grades, 537
collateral injuries, 78
Collect, Isolate, and Correct troubleshooting model, 55
color depth, 417
Color Graphics Adapter
  See: CGA
Communication and Networking Riser
  See: CNR
communication ports, 152, 153
Complementary Metal Oxide Semiconductor
  See: CMOS
Complementary Metal Oxide Semiconductor RAM
  See: CMOS RAM
CompTIA Network+ troubleshooting model, 50
computer cases, 151
  front cover alignment, 151
  power supplies, 102
  slot covers, 151
computer networking devices, 583
computers
  cleaning, 602
  desktop, 6
  disposal, 627
  electronic, 4
  handleld, 6
    Also See: PDA
  history, 2
  mechanical, 2
  minitower, 6
  personal
    See: PCs
  portable, 6
  tablet, 6
conductors, 66
connectors, 213
  AUI, 539
  BNC, 538
  IDC, 533
  RJ-45, 536
  SC, 540
  ST, 540

UDC, 533
contrast, 418
Control Unit, 126
controller card, 266
controllers, 332, 478
conventional memory, 130
cooling systems
  air, 108
  fans, 139
  heat sinks, 139
  liquid cooling, 140
  temperature sensors, 140
  thermal compounds, 139
corona, 443
CPU, 13, 126
  adding a processor, 145
  cache, 128, 133, 163
  cooling systems, 139
  factors affecting performance, 129
  internal characteristics, 132
  multiprocessor support, 133
  packages, 137
  popular processors, 131
  removing a processor, 145
  servicing, 142
  sockets, 126
  slots
  speeds, 134
CRT, 410, 414
  problems, 430
  safety, 424, 430
CSMA/CD, 572
CSU/DSU, 586
current, 63
  measuring, 66
cylinders, 296
Cylinders, Heads, Sectors addressing
  See: CHS

D

DAT, 375
data buses, 163
datapaths, 146
date/time CMOS setting, 117
daughter board, 146
DB-25, 213
DB-9, 213
DC, 63
  controllers, 478

INDEX

DDR SDRAM, 161
decimal number system, 24
Deep Sleep, 479
default gateways, 558
degaussing, 416
desktop computers, 6
   Also See: computers
  components
    See: external components
    See: internal components
  functions, 9
device conflicts, 177
device drivers, 21, 22, 232
  upgrading, 623
Device Manager, 22
DHCP, 567
dial-up modems, 283, 579
digital cameras, 459
Digital Linear Tape
  See: DLT
Digital Subscriber Line
  See: DSL
DIMM, 15, 167
DIN connectors, 396
diodes, 4
DIP switches, 155
direct current
  See: DC
direct glare, 88
Direct Memory Access
  See: DMA
display adapters, 267
display devices, 410
  adjusting, 425
  installing, 424
  troubleshooting, 432
dissipative material, 71
DLT, 376
DMA, 181
  assignments, 181
DNS, 568
docking stations, 484, 485
Domain Name System
  See: DNS
dongle, 494
dot pitch, 415
dot-matrix printers, 436
  problems, 449
DRAM, 15, 161, 163

drive bays, 302
drive controllers, 255, 260
  installing, 265
drive failure
  recovering, 342
drive power connectors, 105
  Berg connectors, 105
  Molex connectors, 105
drives, 293, 349
  backups, 374
  bays, 302
  cartridge disk, 370
  cylinders, 296
  floppy disk, 349
  formatting, 305
  hard, 294
  head crash, 295
  high-level formatting, 305
  Jaz, 373
  low-level formatting, 305
  optical disc, 358
  park, 295
  partitions, 305
  portable, 488
  sector interleave, 298
  sectors, 296
  SuperDisk, 373
  SyQuest, 372
  tape, 374
  tracks, 296
  Ultra DMA, 305
  write protection, 351
  Zip, 372
  zoned-bit recording, 296
DSL, 577
Dual In-line Memory Modules
  See: DIMM
dual-voltage, 126
dye sublimation printers, 446
Dynamic Host Configuration Protocol
  See: DHCP
Dynamic RAM
  See: DRAM

E

ECC, 168
ECHS, 256
ECP, 224
EDO, 161

INDEX

EDO RAM, 161
EDSAC, 4
EDVAC, 4
EEPROM, 161
EGA, 269
EIDE, 262
EISA buses, 192
electrical energy, 63
electrical power, 63
electricity, 62
  measuring, 64
electromagnetic interference
  See: EMI
electrons, 62
electrostatic discharge
  See: ESD
Electrostatic Photographic drum
  See: EP drum
EMI, 73
Enhanced Graphics Adapter
  See: EGA
Enhanced Parallel Port
  See: EPP
Enhanced Small Device Interface
  See: ESDI
ENIAC, 4
EP drum, 443
EPP, 224
EPROM, 160
ergonomics, 84
  chairs, 86
  keyboard and mouse placement, 87
  monitor placement, 88
  posture, 86
  project design, 90
  vision, 90
  work environment, 89
error codes
  CMOS, 123
  POST, audio, 121
  POST, visual, 122
Error Correction Code
  See: ECC
ESCD, 116
ESD, 72
  creating a safe work area, 74
  preventing, 73
ESD toolkit, 38
ESDI, 259, 262

Ethernet, 571
  10Base2, 571
  10Base5, 571
  10BaseT, 571
  Fast Ethernet, 571
  Gigabit Ethernet, 571
EWNs, 553
exception interrupts, 178
eXecute In Place
  See: XIP
Extended Capability Port
  See: ECP
Extended CHS
  See: ECHS
Extended System Configuration Data
  See: ESCD
external cache memory
  See: L2 cache
external components, 9
  keyboard, 10
  monitor, 10
  mouse, 10
  printer, 10
  speaker, 10
extinguishing agents, 94

F

Fast Ethernet, 571
fast IrDA, 247
fast SCSI, 314
fiber optic cables, 539
  connectors, 540
fire emergency procedures, 94
fire extinguishers, 93
fire safety, 93
  emergency procedures, 94
  extinguishing agents, 94
  fire extinguishers, 93
firewalls, 587
FireWire, 241
  See: connectors
  chips, 243
  connecting, 244
firmware, 23
flash memory, 504
  types, 506
Flash ROM, 161
floppy disks, 17
floppy drives, 349

INDEX

CMOS setting, 117
controllers, 178, 181
how floppy drives work, 350
installing, 351
replacing, 352
troubleshooting, 354
font, 417
footcandle, 89
form factors, 102, 137, 146, 148
formatting, 305
high-level, 305
low-level, 305
FPM, 161
FPM RAM, 161
fragmentation, 597
friction feed printers, 439
front cover alignment, 151
fuel cell batteries, 476
fusing assemblies, 443

G

gateways, 586
GB, 32
geosynchronous, 576
Gigabit Ethernet, 571
gigabytes, 32
  Also See: GB
gigahertz, 147
gigs, 33
grounds, 65
GUI, 20

H

handheld computers, 6
  Also See: computers
hard disks, 17
fragmentation, 597
replacing, 511, 512
hard drives, 293, 294
CMOS settings, 117
data access problems, 328
formatting, 306
maintaining, 323
problems, 321
slow drives, 323
troubleshooting, 324
upgrading, 623
hardware
for networks, 529

hardware interrupts, 178
hazardous materials, 628, 631
HBA, 260
head crash, 295
heat sinks, 139
Hercules Graphics, 269
Hercules Graphics Card
  See: HGC
hexadecimal number system, 29
HGC, 269
hierarchical networks, 551
High Voltage Differential Signaling
  See: HVD
high-level formatting, 305
host bus adapters
  See: HBA
host names, 568
hotswap, 241
hubs, 584
active, 584
intelligent, 584
passive, 584
HVD, 313
hybrid networks, 551
hybrid topology, 548

I

I/O addresses, 179
I/O ports
FireWire, 241
IEEE, 241
infrared, 246
parallel, 223
serial, 212
USB, 235
IBM Data Connector
  See: IDC
IDC, 533
IDE, 255, 262
installing IDE drives, 306
removing IDE drives, 306
troubleshooting, 322
IEEE, 153, 224
inductance, 299
Infrared, 153, 246
ink dispersion printers
  See: inkjet printers
inkjet printers, 440
how they work, 442

INDEX

interfaces, 440
problems, 450
input devices, 394, 458
   keyboards, 394, 395, 397, 399
   mouse, 400, 402, 404, 406
   touch screens, 460, 461, 462
   troubleshooting, 406
Institute of Electrical and Electronic Engineers
   See: IEEE
instruction sets, 141
insulators, 66
integrated circuits, 5
Integrated Drive Electronics
   See: IDE
integrated peripherals, 472
   keyboards, 473
   monitors, 472
   pointing devices, 474
Integrated Services Digital Network
   See: ISDN
intelligent hubs, 584
interface cards, 16
interface types, 259
   EIDE, 262
   ESDI, 262
   IDE, 262
   SCSI-I, 262
   SCSI-II, 262
   SCSI-III, 262
   ST-506, 262
   Ultra DMA, 262
interfaces, 16
   parallel, 16
   serial, 16
interlaced monitors, 415
internal bus, 128
internal components, 9, 509
   CPU, 10
   motherboard, 10
   power supply, 10
   RAM, 10
   ROM BIOS, 10
internal modems, 279
Internet connections, 575
   cable modem, 578
   dial-up, 579
   DSL, 577
   ISDN, 579
   LAN, 576

   satellite, 579
   wireless, 581
Internetwork Packet Exchange
   See: IPX
Interrupt 13h (INT13h) extensions, 257
Interrupt Request line
   See: IRQ
interrupts, 178
   exception, 178
   hardware, 178
   software, 178
IP addresses, 560
   classes, 561
IPX, 559
IRQ, 178
IRQ assignments, 178
ISA, 178
ISA buses, 189
ISDN, 579

J

Jaz disk drives, 373
jumpers, 155

K

KB, 32
keyboards, 394
   alternative, 395
   DIN connectors, 396
   how they work, 397
   problems, 399
   replacing, 515
   troubleshooting, 406
kilobytes, 32
   Also See: KB

L

L1 cache, 163
L2 cache, 163
L3 cache, 163
LAN connectivity disks, 50
LANs, 552
laptop power sources, 476
Large LBA, 257
laser printers, 443
   corona, 443
   EP drum, 443
   fusing assembly, 443
   how they work, 445
   interfaces, 444

INDEX

paper jam, 452
problems, 450
toner, 443
lasers, 81
latency, 579
LBA, 256
LCD, 410
LCD screens, 475
   Active Matrix, 475
   Passive Matrix, 475
legacy devices, 184, 185
   ISA cards, 183
Li-Ion batteries, 476
line printers, 223
liquid cleaning compounds, 629
Liquid Crystal Display
   See: LCD
Lithium Polymer batteries, 476
load, 196
Logical Block Addressing
   See: LBA
logical network architecture, 549
Low Voltage Differential Signaling
   See: LVD
low-level formatting, 305
LVD, 313

M

magnetic core memory, 5
MANs, 553
Mark I, 4
master drive, 302
Material Safety Data Sheets
   See: MSDS
Math coprocessors, 127
MB, 32
MDA, 268
media, 529
megabytes, 32
   Also See: MB
megahertz, 147
megs, 33
memory, 15, 158
   CMOS setting, 117
   DIMM, 167
   flash, 504
   installing in portable devices, 507
   MicroDIMM, 167
   RIMM, 167
   SIMM, 166
   SODIMM, 167
   troubleshooting, 173
   upgrading, 623
memory banks, 166
memory chips, 142, 161
memory packages, 166
memory problems, 173
mesh topology, 547
Micro Channel Architecture bus, 194
Microcom Networking Protocol
   See: MNP
MicroDIMM, 167
microphones, 462
microprocessors, 5
MIDI, 277
Mini-PCI cards, 499
   installing, 500
   replacing, 500
minitower computers, 6
   Also See: computers
mirrored volume, 338
   mirroring an existing volume, 340
MNP, 281
modems, 279
   asynchronous, 280
   bis, 280
   configuring, 283
   installing, 283
   problems, 286
   synchronous, 280
   terbo, 280
Molex connectors, 105
monitors, 267
   direct glare, 88
   display characteristics, 417
   power management, 424
   problems, 430
   reflective glare, 88
   safety, 430
   settings, 422
   specifications, 418
Monochrome Display Adapter
   See: MDA
motherboard, 11
   components, 152
   configuring, 154
   problems, 157
   repair vs. replace, 154

INDEX

replacing, 516
troubleshooting, 158
upgrading, 154, 623
mouse, 400
  problems, 404
  types, 401
MSDS, 80, 627
multi-mode cable, 539
multimeter, 64
multiport repeaters, 584
Musical Instrument Digital Interface
  See: MIDI

N

name servers, 568
Napier's Bones, 2
narrow SCSI, 314
NetBEUI, 559
NetBIOS Enhanced User Interface
  See: NetBEUI
network adapters, 529, 531
network architecture, 570
network cables, 532
network connections
  troubleshooting, 589
Network Operating System
  See: NOS
network protocols, 529, 558
network scope, 552
network segments, 560
network toolkit, 39
networks, 529
  AppleTalk, 574
  ARCNet, 574
  hardware, 529
  Token Ring, 573
  troubleshooting, 588
nibbles, 32
NiCad batteries, 476
NICs, 531
  tranceivers, 531
  troubleshooting, 589
NiMH batteries, 476
nodes, 529
NOS, 555
notebook computers, 468
Novell troubleshooting model, 53
null-modem cables, 216
numbering systems

binary number system, 26
decimal number system, 24
hexadecimal number system, 29

O

ohms, 64
on-board devices
  disabling with CMOS, 117
online UPSs, 611
Open Systems Interconnection model
  See: OSI model
operands, 127
Operating System
  See: OS
optical disc drives, 358
  how optical drives work, 359
  issues, 360
  problems, 363
  replacing, 362
  troubleshooting, 364
OS, 20, 556
  boot disks, 41
OSI model, 530
overclocking, 147

P

palmtops, 519
paper feed problems, 448
Parallel, 153
parallel devices
  connecting, 226
parallel interfaces, 223
Parallel ports
  CMOS settings, 117
parity, 168, 217
park, 295
partitions, 305
Pascaline machine, 2
passive hubs, 584
passwords
  CMOS setting, 117
PC bus
  removing, 188
PC buses, 186
PC Cards, 493
  exchanging, 496
  installing, 495
  types, 493
PCI bus, 196

Index

PCMCIA, 493
PCs, 6
  chemical hazards, 80
  electrical hazards, 78
  hazards of servicing, 77
PDA, 6, 469, 519
  connecting to a computer, 523
  features, 521
  palmtops, 519
peer-to-peer networks, 549
peripherals, 393
  integrated, 472
  keyboards, 394
  mouse, 400
  pointing devices, 400
Personal Computer Memory Card International Association
  See: PCMCIA
Personal Digital Assistant
  See: PDA
Personals Computers
  See: PCs
PGA, 138
physical network architecture, 544
physical topology, 544
Pin Grid Array
  See: PGA
pinouts, 231
PIO Mode, 257
pixels, 417
plenum cables, 542
Plug & Play BIOS
  CMOS setting, 117
Plug and Play, 184
  Also See: PnP
PnP, 184
  BIOS, 185
  OS, 185
pointing devices, 400
  how they work, 402
  replacing, 513
  troubleshooting, 406
port replicator, 484
portable computers, 6
  Also See: computers
portable computing devices, 467
  docking, 486
  exchanging, 490
  installing memory, 507

  memory, 503
  physically securing, 471
  power sources, 475
  powering, 479
  processors, 479
ports, 210
  genders, 211
POST, 121
  audio error codes, 121
  visual error codes, 122
potential difference, 62
power management
  CMOS setting, 117
power supplies, 102
  AT, 148
  ATX, 104, 149
  calculating power needs, 106
  common problems, 113
  fans, 111
  pinouts, 104
  protecting, 114
  replacing, 110
  safety, 107, 108
  servicing, 108
  system board connectors, 103
  testing, 107
  troubleshooting, 115
  upgrading, 623
  wire color conventions, 103
Power-On Self Test
  See: POST
primary cache, 163
primary drive, 302
print drivers, 22
printer interfaces
  AppleTalk, 440
  IEEE, 440
  Infrared, 440
  Parallel, 440
  SCSI, 440
  Serial, 440
  USB, 440
  Wireless, 440
printers
  calibration problems, 448
  configuration, 448
  consumables, 448
  dot-matrix, 436
  dye sublimation, 446

INDEX

environmental considerations, 451
errors, 452
friction feed, 439
inkjet, 440
laser, 443
maintenance, 448
memory problems, 448
network connection, 448
print quality, 448
problems, 448
rendering, 447
safety, 448
solid ink, 446
spooling, 447
test pages not printing, 452
thermal wax, 447
thermo autochrome, 447
tractor feed, 438
private addressing, 563
processor
   See: CPU
processor sockets
  Slot 1, 136
  Slot 2, 136
  Slot A, 136
  Slot M, 136
  Socket 370, 135
  Socket 423, 135
  Socket 478, 135
  Socket 7, 135
  Socket 8, 135
  Socket A, 135
processors, 13
  for portable computing devices, 479
  specifications for portable devices, 480
  upgrading, 623
Programmed Input/Output Mode
   See: PIO Mode
PROM, 160
proprietary, 167
protected mode, 130
protection devices
  ESD, 38
protocols, 558
PS/2, 230
PS/2 interfaces, 230
public addressing, 563
PVC cables, 542

Q
QIC, 375
Quarter-Inch Cartridge
   See: QIC
Quick Start, 479

R
RAID, 332
  level 0, 332
  level 1, 333
  level 5, 334
RAID 5
  creating a RAID-5 volume, 343
RAM, 158
  adding, 169
RAM chips, 5
RAM speed, 162
RAMBUS, 161
RAMDAC, 414
Random Access Memory
   See: RAM
Random Access Memory Digital-Analog Converter
   See: RAMDAC
RDRAM, 161
Read-Only Memory
   See: ROM
real mode, 130
Redundant Array of Independent Disks
   See: RAID
reflective glare, 88
refresh rate, 417
register, 127, 163
removable storage, 349
  problems, 382
  troubleshooting, 382
rendering, 447
repeaters, 584
Repetitive Strain Injury
   See: RSI
resistance, 64
  measuring, 66
resistors, 5
resolution, 417
RG58, 537
RG59, 537
RG6, 537
RG8, 537
RIMM, 167

INDEX

ring topology, 546
riser cards, 147
RJ-11 jacks, 281
RJ-45 connector, 534, 536
ROM, 15, 159
ROM BIOS
  updating, 123
routers, 558, 585
RSI, 84
  contributing factors, 84

S

SAM, 158
SANs, 553
satellite, 579
  latency, 579
scanners, 458
SCSI, 255, 262
  binary jumper settings, 312
  cable length, 313
  connecting external device, 317
  interface types, 313, 314, 315
  internal vs. external, 310, 315
  termination, 313
SCSI addressing, 311
SCSI drives, 310
  installing, 317
  troubleshooting, 322
SCSI signaling, 313
SDRAM, 161
SECC, 138
secondary cache, 128, 163
secondary drive, 302
sector interleave, 298
sectors, 296
semiconductors, 64
Sequenced Packet Exchange
  See: SPX
Sequential Access Memory
  See: SAM
Serial, 152
serial devices
  installing, 219
serial interfaces, 212
serial ports
  cables, 213
  communication, 212
  configuring, 219
  pinouts, 215

settings, 217
Serial/COM ports
  CMOS settings, 117
servers, 529
shielded twisted-pair
  See: STP
SIMM, 15, 166
Single Edge Contact Cartridge
  See: SECC
Single In-line Memory Module
  See: SIMM
single-ended devices, 313
single-mode cable, 539
slave drive, 302
slot covers, 151
slots, 126, 136
  types, 136
slow IrDA, 247
Small Computer System Interface
  See: SCSI
SmartMedia, 505
Socket Services, 494
sockets, 126
  types, 135
  ZIF, 137
SODIMM, 167
software, 20
software interrupts, 178
software utilities, 41
  boot disk, 41
soldered, 11
solid ink printers, 446
sound cards, 273
sound devices, 274
speakers, 462
SpeedStep, 479
SPGA, 138
spooling, 447
SPX, 559
SRAM, 15, 161
ST-506, 259, 262
Staggered Pin Grid Array
  See: SPGA
Standby UPSs, 611
star topology, 544
startup disks, 44
static electricity, 71
Stepped Reckoner, 2
storage devices, 15, 17

Index

CD-R, 17
CD-ROM, 17
CD-RW, 17
floppy disk, 17
hard disk, 17
STP, 533
striped volume, 335
subnet masks, 561
subnetting, 564
SuperDisk drives, 373
surge protectors, 114
SVGA, 271
SyQuest disk drives, 372
system boards, 146, 11
   Also See: motherboard
   ATX, 149
   Baby AT, 148
   components, 151
   full-size AT, 148
   LPX, 149
   NLX, 150
system bus, 128
system components
   replacing, 517
system firmware
   upgrading, 623
system software, 20

T

tablet computers, 6
   Also See: computers
tape drives, 374
   how tape drives work, 376
TCP/IP, 558
temperature sensors, 140
terbo, 280
Terminate and Stay Resident
   See: TSR
termination, 259, 538
thermal compounds, 139
thermal wax printers, 447
thermo autochrome printers, 447
throughput, 224
Token Ring, 573
tokens, 546
toner, 443
toolkits
   basic, 36
   circuit board, 39

   ESD, 38
   network, 39
touch screens, 460
   operation, 461
   troubleshooting, 462
tracks, 296
tractor feed printers, 438
transceiver, 532
transistors, 5
Transmission Control Protocol/Internet Protocol
   See: TCP/IP
triboelectric generation, 71
troubleshooting
   Collect, Isolate, and Correct model, 55
   CompTIA Network+ model, 50
   Novell model, 53
   tips, 58
TSR, 180
TTL monitors, 268
twisted-pair cables, 533
   Cat5, 534
   connectors, 534
   STP, 533
   UTP, 533

U

UDC, 533
Ultra DMA, 255, 262
Ultra DMA drives, 305
ultra-wide SCSI, 314
UMB, 180
Uninterruptible Power Supplies
   See: UPSs
UNIVAC, 4
Universal Data Connector
   See: UDC
Universal Serial Bus
   See: USB
unshielded twisted-pair
   See: UTP
upgrading, 623
   deciding when, 624
Upper Memory Block
   See: UMB
UPSs, 610
   online, 611
   Standby, 611
USB, 152, 235
   cables and connectors, 236

INDEX

classes, 235
common problems, 240
power, 238
standards, 237
USB devices
  connecting, 238
UTP, 533
  categories, 534
UVGA, 271

V

vacuum tubes, 4
VANs, 553
Very Large-Scale Integration
  See: VLSI
VESA Local-Bus
  See: VL-Bus
VGA, 270
video adapters, 267
video cards, 201, 267
video display devices
  touchscreen monitors, 413
  video projectors, 413
Video Graphics Array
  See: VGA
video output devices, 410
  CRT, 410
  LCD, 410
  personal display devices, 412
virtual machines, 130
virus protection
  AntiVirus boot disks, 42
  disabling with CMOS, 117
VL-Bus, 199
VLSI, 187
voltage, 62
  measuring, 65
  of CPUs, 132
Voltage Regulator Module
  See: VRM
volts, 62
VRAM, 161
VRM, 146

W

WANs, 552
watts, 63
Wi-Fi networks, 581
wide SCSI, 314

Windows Internet Naming System
  See: WINS
WINS, 568
wireless, 246
  connections, 246
wireless Internet connections, 581
  Wi-Fi networks, 581
  wireless access point, 581
WRAM, 161

X

XIP, 493

Z

ZIF sockets, 137
Zinc Air batteries, 476
Zip disk drives, 372
zoned-bit recording, 296
Zoomed Video
  See: ZV
ZV, 493